The Handbook of Child and Adolescent Psychotherapy

Second edition

D1500703

This updated edition of *The Handbook of Child and Adolescent Psychotherapy: Psychoanalytic Approaches* reflects the many changes in the profession. It includes:

- additional chapters on neuroscience, work with 'looked after children' and with foster parents, working in schools
- enlarged chapters on research, attachment theory, work with parents, and developments in child and adolescent psychotherapy around the world
- chapters on areas of specialist interest including violence, sexual abuse and abusing, trauma, parent–infant psychotherapy, autism, victims of political violence, delinquency, gender dysphoria.

The handbook remains accessible and jargon-free. It will be a valuable resource for all who work in allied professions where the emotional well-being of children is of concern – health, education, social services – as well as trainee psychotherapists and experienced practitioners.

Monica Lanyado is a training supervisor at the British Association of Psychotherapists (BAP). She is co-editor with Ann Horne of the first edition of *The Handbook of Child and Adolescent Psychotherapy*, *A Question of Technique* and *Through Assessment to Consultation* and author of *The Presence of the Therapist*.

Ann Horne trained in the Independent tradition at the BAP. She has discovered that retirement (after 10 years latterly at the Portman Clinic, London) can become very crowded and makes occasional sorties from behind the keyboard to speak and teach in the UK and abroad.

The Handbook of Child and Adolescent Psychotherapy

Psychoanalytic Approaches

Second edition

Edited by Monica Lanyado and Ann Horne

Routledge
Taylor & Francis Group

LONDON AND NEW YORK

First edition published 1999 by Routledge
27 Church Road, Hove, East Sussex BN3 2FA

This edition published 2009 by Routledge
27 Church Road, Hove, East Sussex BN3 2FA
Simultaneously published in the USA and Canada
by Routledge
270 Madison Avenue, New York, NY 10016

*Routledge is an imprint of the Taylor & Francis Group, an Informa
business*

Typeset in Garamond by Garfield Morgan, Swansea, West Glamorgan
Printed and bound in Great Britain by TJ International Ltd, Padstow,
Cornwall
Paperback cover design by Lisa Dynan

This publication has been produced with paper manufactured to strict
environmental standards and with pulp derived from sustainable
forests.

British Library Cataloguing in Publication Data
A catalogue record for this book is available from the British Library

Library of Congress Cataloging-in-Publication Data
The handbook of child and adolescent psychotherapy :
psychoanalytic approaches / edited by Monica Lanyado and Ann
Horne.
        p. cm.
    Includes bibliographical references and index.
    ISBN 978-0-415-46368-3 (hardback) – ISBN 978-0-415-46369-0
(pbk.) 1. Psychodynamic psychotherapy for children. 2.
Psychodynamic psychotherapy for teenagers. 3. Child analysis. 4.
Adolescent analysis. I. Lanyado, Monica, 1949- II. Horne, Ann, 1944-
    RJ505.P92H36 2009
    618.92'8914–dc22

                                                2008048533

ISBN: 978-0-415-46368-3 (hbk)
ISBN: 978-0-415-46369-0 (pbk)

Contents

Contributors

Katie Argent trained as a child and adolescent psychotherapist at the Tavistock Clinic. She works in the Child and Family Department at the Tavistock Clinic, manages the Tavistock Outreach in Primary Schools project and co-convenes the Tavistock Groups Workshop.

Gabrielle Crockatt qualified as a child and adolescent psychotherapist from the Tavistock Clinic in 1972. Since then has worked as a child and adolescent psychotherapist in a variety of settings, both hospital and community. She has a particular interest in service development, with a view to ensuring that services are accessible to those most in need. She is currently Consultant Child and Adolescent Psychotherapist at Parkside Clinic in North Kensington, London and Lead Clinical Advisor on CAMHS for Kensington and Chelsea, London where she has helped to establish services including the Family Resource Project (a Tier 2 CAMHS), 'A Place to Talk' (a walk-in counselling service for young people), the Parental Mental Health Service (jointly with NSPCC), and an Arabic Families Service.

Denis Flynn initially studied and did research in philosophy. After a few years in social work, he has worked as a child psychotherapist in the Families Unit at the Cassel Hospital for twelve years, latterly as Head Child Psychotherapist, with abused children and the rehabilitation of families in a therapeutic community context. For a further ten years he was Consultant Psychotherapist and Head of the Inpatient Adolescent Unit, treating suicidal, self-harming and borderline adolescents, aged 16–23. He is a psychoanalyst and child analyst, teaching at the Institute of Psychoanalysis, London and working in private practice. He has published papers and two books: *The Internal and External Worlds of Children and Adolescents: collaborative therapeutic care* (2003, Karnac, London, ed. with Lesley Day), *Severe Emotional Disturbance in Children and Adolescents: psychotherapy in applied contexts* (2004, Brunner Routledge, Hove and New York).

Barbara Gaffney trained as a child psychotherapist with the British Association of Child Psychotherapists having previously worked with deprived and abused children at the Mulberry Bush Residential School. She worked at the Gender Identity Development Clinic, St George's Hospital, South London (which subsequently moved to the Tavistock and Portman NHS Trust) from 1992 to 1997. She currently works at the William Harvey Clinic, South West London and St George's Mental Health NHS Trust.

Iris Gibbs trained as a child and adolescent psychotherapist with the British Association of Psychotherapists. She has worked for a private fostering organisation for the last thirteen years as a therapist and is also involved in their teaching programmes and the supervision of other therapists. She worked for five years in the Parent and Infant project at the Anna Freud Centre and is in private practice. She has written chapters for .two recent publications: *The Practice of Parent–Infant Psychotherapy* (2005) and *A Question of Technique* (2006). She has a particular interest in race and cultural issues.

Viviane Green is Head of Clinical Training at the Anna Freud Centre, a child and adolescent psychoanalytic psychotherapist and adult psychotherapist. She is a full member of London Centre for Psychotherapy and Senior Honorary Lecturer at University College London. She is widely published and is editor of *Emotional Development in Psychoanalysis, Attachment Theory and Neuroscience*, published by Routledge.

Juliet Hopkins trained as a child and adolescent psychotherapist at the Tavistock Clinic and worked on the staff of the Child Guidance Training Centre and the Tavistock Clinic until her recent retirement from the National Health Service. She has continued to teach at the Tavistock where she is an honorary consultant child psychotherapist. Juliet also trained as an adult psychotherapist at the British Association of Psychotherapists and works in private practice. She has published widely on a variety of themes concerned with child psychotherapy, attachment theory, infant development and parent–infant psychotherapy.

Ann Horne is a member of the British Association of Psychotherapists (where she trained), the Scottish Institute of Human Relations and an Honorary member of ČSPAP, the Czech Society for Psychoanalytic Psychotherapy. She served terms of office at the BAP as head of training and later of post-graduate development. A previous joint editor of the *Journal of Child Psychotherapy*, she is co-editor with Monica Lanyado of *The Handbook of Child and Adolescent Psychotherapy* (1999) and *A Question of Technique* (2006). Now retired from the Portman Clinic, London, she talks, writes and teaches.

Margaret Hunter-Smallbone is author of *Psychotherapy with Young People in Care* (2001) and has contributed chapters and articles to several publications, including *The Handbook of Child and Adolescent Psychotherapy* (1999). She is a Consultant Child Psychotherapist for CAMHS in Hertfordshire, having worked for South London and Maudsley Trust for fifteen years, where she established a dedicated mental health team for looked after children. Margaret was trained at the Tavistock Clinic and began her professional life as a psychotherapist in a Local Authority children's home. She has retained a connection with looked after children ever since and currently contributes to a specialist fostering service, Integrated Services Programme, in Chesham and Enfield.

Leslie Ironside is a child and adolescent psychotherapist. He trained at the Tavistock Clinic and has a specialist interest in working in the area of fostering and adoption. He was a Consultant in the Health Service for many years and now works full time in private practice. He is also Director of the Centre for Emotional Development.

Monica Lanyado trained at the Tavistock Clinic and was the founding course organiser of the Child and Adolescent Psychotherapy Training in Edinburgh. She is a training supervisor at the British Association of Psychotherapists and is joint Series Editor, with Ann Horne, of the Independent Psychoanalytic Approaches with Children and Adolescents (IPACA) Series. She was joint Series Editor of the EFPP Book Series. Her publications include *The Presence of the Therapist: Treating Childhood Trauma* (2004) and, co-edited with Ann Horne, *The Handbook of Child and Adolescent Psychotherapy: Psychoanalytic Approaches* (1999), *A Question of Technique* (2006) and *Through Assessment to Consultation* (2009).

Meira Likierman is a consultant child and adolescent psychotherapist working in the Child and Family Department at the Tavistock Clinic. She lectures widely, nationally and internationally, and has published many papers. Her book *Melanie Klein: her Work in Context* was published in 2001 by Continuum.

Claudia McLoughlin qualified as a child psychotherapist from the Tavistock Clinic in 2002. Since then she has worked in the Islington CAMHS Service based in the Northern Health Centre, London. Alongside her clinic-based work, two years ago she became the Deputy Coordinator of the Outreach Islington CAMHS in Education Service, a multi-disciplinary service working in the Borough's nine secondary schools and three pupil referral units. Having been a teacher herself in the past, she has a particular interest in the positive potential of work discussion groups for staff teams in schools and PRUs, and in finding effective ways of working therapeutically with conduct disordered children.

Sheila Melzak is a consultant child and adolescent psychotherapist who has worked for many years with traumatised and abused children and adolescents in various therapeutic and psychotherapeutic contexts and in recent times with children and young people who are asylum seekers and refugees. She has a particular interest in thinking about therapeutic and psychotherapeutic processes and in the links between children's needs and rights and current and future child-centred legislation and policy. She works currently as head of the Medical Foundation for the Care of Victims of Torture Child and Adolescent Team.

Nick Midgley is a child and adolescent psychotherapist who has taken a particular interest in making links between research and clinical practice. He is Head of Programme for Adolescents and Young Adults at the Anna Freud Centre, London and an Honorary Lecturer at the Centre for Psychoanalytic Studies, University of Essex. His publications include (with Eilis Kennedy) *Process and Outcome Research in Child, Adolescent and Parent-Infant Psychotherapy: a Thematic Review* (NHS London, 2007) and (as co-editor) *Child Psychotherapy and Research: New Approaches, Emerging Findings* (Routledge, 2009).

Roberta Mondadori trained at the Tavistock Clinic and worked as a consultant child and adolescent psychotherapist in an NHS service for adolescents at risk. She teaches a number of Tavistock courses in England and in Italy. She is a tutor for the Postgraduate Diploma MA course in Working with People with Eating Disorders (Tavistock Clinic and University of East London) in London and in Bologna. She contributed to *Exploring Eating Disorders in Adolescence* edited by G. Williams *et al.* (Karnac, 2004).

Graham Music is a consultant child and adolescent psychotherapist working in the NHS and an adult psychotherapist in private practice. He works at the Tavistock Clinic where his clinical interests are in the field of fostering and adoption, early years and in developing community-based therapeutic work, particularly in school settings. He teaches on the Child Psychotherapy Training and various other courses at the Tavistock Centre, and elsewhere in England and abroad, and is a member of the Editorial Board of the *Journal of Child Psychotherapy*.

Caryn Onions trained as a child and adolescent psychotherapist at the British Association of Psychotherapists. She is Head of the Psychotherapy Department at the Mulberry Bush School near Oxford, a non-maintained residential school for children with severe emotional disturbance, and a clinician at OXPIP (the Oxford Parent–Infant Project). She has a special interest in work with parents and infants, groupwork, and teaches and supervises in the field of parent–infant psychotherapy.

Marianne Parsons is a consultant child and adolescent psychotherapist at the Portman Clinic, London and is Course Director of the Portman Clinic Diploma in Forensic Psychotherapeutic Studies. She was a member of the Portman Clinic Study Group on Violence under the leadership of Dr Mervin Glasser. She is a Member of the Institute of Psychoanalysis, as both a child and adult psychoanalyst, and a Senior Member of the Child and Adolescent Section of the British Association of Psychotherapists. She is a former Head of Clinical Training at the Anna Freud Centre, where she did her child training. She is in private practice, is the author of a number of journal papers and book chapters, and teaches widely in this country and abroad, including acting as visiting lecturer for psychoanalytic trainings in Finland, Florida and Berlin.

Gail Phillips trained at the BAP and works as a child and adolescent psychotherapist at the PIMHS (Parent-Infant Mental Health Service) in North East London and at the CAMHS in Barnet. She also works as a school counsellor. She has worked with the Portage Service in Hackney, and has a particular interest in autism and work with parents and infants.

Paulina Reyes recently retired from her posts as Consultant Child and Adolescent Psychotherapist at the Gender Identity Development Service at the Tavistock and Portman NHS Trust and at Kingston Child and Adolescent Mental Health Service. She has worked for many years with children and young people with gender identity difficulties and their families. She has taught, written and presented papers on this subject. She also has an interest in and written about extreme trauma in victims of political exile. She is currently in private practice.

Maria Rhode is Professor of Child and Adolescent Psychotherapy at the Tavistock Clinic/University of East London, where she co-convenes the Autism Workshop. She has co-edited *Psychotic States in Children* (Duckworth, 1997), *The Many Faces of Asperger's Syndrome* (Karnac, 2004), and *Invisible Boundaries: Autism and Psychosis in Children and Adolescents* (Karnac, 2006). She works in private practice with children and adults, and lectures widely in Britain and abroad.

Margaret Rustin is Consultant Child Psychotherapist at the Tavistock Clinic, London, and Head of Child Psychotherapy. She is also a child analyst and Honorary Affiliate of the Institute of Psychoanalysis. She has co-authored with Michael Rustin *Narratives of Love and Loss* (Verso, 1987) and *Mirror To Nature* (Karnac, 2002), and co-edited *Closely Observed Infants* (Duckworth, 1989), *Psychotic States in Children* (Duckworth, 1997) and *Assessment in Child Psychotherapy* (Duckworth, 2000), and published many journal papers and book chapters.

Lydia Tischler trained at the Anna Freud Clinic (formerly Hampstead Child Therapy training) and was Head of the Child Psychotherapy department at the Cassel Hospital, London, for twenty-three years. She has been Chair of the Training Council of the Association of Child Psychotherapists, Chair of the Child and Adolescent Training at the British Association of Psychotherapists and is convenor of the sub-committee for Central and Eastern European Networks for the European Federation of Psychoanalytic Psychotherapy in the Public Sector. She was the co-founder of the Child and Adolescent Psychotherapy Training in the Czech Republic and participated in setting up trainings in Estonia and St Petersburg.

Elizabeth Urban is a highly specialist child psychotherapist and a pro-fessional member of the Society of Analytical Psychology, where she undertook the child and adult analytic trainings. From 2000 to 2006 she was co-organiser of the Child Analytic Training. She works in private practice with adults, and in the London Borough of Brent CAMHS, where she specialises in infant mental health. She leads a community service for parents and under-two's, and works therapeutically with mothers and babies in an in-patient mother–baby unit, where she is also is a member of a parenting assessment team. She holds a long-standing interest in Fordham's model and developmental and neurological research, and teaches and publishes in this combined area.

Peter Wilson trained as a child psychotherapist at the Anna Freud Centre. He worked in Child Guidance clinics in South London and was Senior Clinical Tutor at the Institute of Psychiatry and Maudsley Hospital Children's Department. He became Director of the Brandon Centre in 1984 and was Consultant Psychotherapist to the Peper Harow Thera-peutic Community. He later was co-founder and Director of Young-Minds, the national children's mental health charity. He retired in 2004 and became the Clinical Adviser of The Place2Be, a charity providing emotional and therapeutic support in primary schools.

John Woods is a member of the Association of Child Psychotherapists, the British Association of Psychotherapists, and the Institute of Group Analysis. Currently he is a consultant psychotherapist at the Portman Clinic. He is the author of *Boys Who Have Abused, psychoanalytic psychotherapy with victims/perpetrators of sexual abuse* (Jessica Kingsley Publishers), *The End of Abuse; a playreading in three parts*, and a play about psychotherapy, *'Compromise'*, both published by Open Gate Press.

Acknowledgements

The first edition of *The Handbook* was received with an enthusiasm that has more than rewarded us for the work involved. So we were delighted, if somewhat daunted, when our publisher suggested – 'suggested' is something of a euphemism as the 'suggestions' demonstrated a remarkable persistence over a year or two's duration – that in view of continued good sales around the world, plus translation into Italian and Czech, we update the handbook with a second edition. We were assured that it need not involve too much work but in the event the number of new contributions is far greater than chapters that have remained largely unchanged.

We thank Routledge and our editor the suggestive Joanne Forshaw for the stimulus she gave us, and also vow to be extremely cautious next time we are told that 'not too much work will be involved'. So much has changed in the profession in the last ten years that this became inevitable – but it has also been very gratifying to track development and change in this way.

Our thanks to the contributors who patiently worked on their chapters until we arrived at what is once more a very readable and accessible volume. In addition gratitude must be expressed to Domenico Di Ceglie and the Gender team at the Tavistock; to a large number of colleagues abroad who responded to Lydia Tischler's call for an update on the international scene; and to Rachel Brake, Natalie Barnes, Tammy Fransman and Cain Snipp.

Monica Lanyado and Ann Horne

1 Introduction

Ann Horne and Monica Lanyado

The second edition of this handbook continues the tradition established in the first of offering an overview and explication of the profession of Child and Adolescent Psychoanalytic Psychotherapy. It is not, in any common sense, actually a handbook – there is no intent to train the reader who will not, in turn, emerge as a child psychotherapist from the reading. Rather, we would hope to broaden knowledge about the profession and the range of work with children and young people that this adaptation of psychoanalysis encourages; we would wish in addition to explore what a psychoanalytic understanding – in terms of theory, research and the implications for practice – offers in work with distressed and 'stuck' children and young people today.

It is thus designed for several types of reader. For those who are already training or working as child psychotherapists the value may well lie mainly in the chapters on work of specialist interest, although many of the other contributions will offer creative ideas and sparks to further thinking. For those contemplating a career in child psychotherapy – perhaps undertaking pre-clinical Masters courses – this is the volume that hopefully helps your friends and family understand what you want to be about. For the reader in allied professions, we offer an overview of the profession, its context and settings, and hope to clarify some of the assumptions about and insights of the psychoanalytic approach. Most chapters are therefore deliberately written to be accessible to a general audience and the authors have responded to that brief. Those seeking greater depth may find the suggestions for further reading helpful.

Our hope would be that the more generalised introduction will make accessible some of the excitement and potential in recent thinking about practice and research, and that the general reader will also find much in the more specialised chapters to enhance practice in other professions as well as to facilitate understanding of why and how the child psychotherapist is working in a specific field.

We have also included writers from a variety of theoretical backgrounds: Contemporary Freudian, Independent, Jungian and Kleinian. In general, these are experienced writers with proven interest and expertise in specific areas. This multi-authored approach should give the reader a sense of the diversity within the profession, and of a vibrant profession able to discuss, differ and develop, while sharing clear underlying principles.

Structure

The book is structured in four main parts but each chapter stands in its own right. The first part introduces the theoretical foundations of the work. While the first two chapters reprise the themes of the first edition, they have been updated – and the chapter on attachment theory has been rewritten and expanded to incorporate current knowledge and research. Neuroscience represents an important addition to the theoretical base and we welcome the clarity of Graham Music's contribution. Finally, in the ten years since the first edition appeared, research has moved on considerably: we are most grateful to Nick Midgley for an erudite and measured exposition of the field. Throughout, authors have used straightforward language to introduce important ideas and concepts. These introductory chapters also provide plentiful references for those readers who wish to have more detailed knowledge.

The theoretical section is followed by three chapters about the child and adolescent psychotherapist in context – the cultural and racial context today; the most usual setting for the UK therapist working in the public sector (the multi-professional team); and as good an international overview of child psychotherapy as we could manage from colleagues abroad, encouraged by Lydia Tischler who was in 2005 celebrated for her work as co-ordinator of Central and Eastern European Networks for the European Federation for Psychoanalytic Psychotherapy in the Public Sector (EFPP). We are, of course, delighted that the first edition has already been translated into Czech and Italian; and that this second edition will appear in Japanese.

The third part of the book describes the diversity of treatment models offered by child and adolescent psychotherapists, beginning with the therapeutic setting and process. The tradition of intensive psychoanalysis (of four- or five-times weekly frequency) with which the profession began retains its rightful place; the principles, however, have become applied and developed in once-weekly work, probably the norm for most individual treatments. It is important that Part III then goes on to demonstrate the extent of work undertaken by the profession as many would assume individual psychotherapy to comprise the bulk of the child psychotherapist's day. Not so. Brief interventions are explored, as is consultative work which applies psychoanalytic principles to enable colleagues in a variety of settings to make sense not only of the young people with whom they work but also of their own responses and feelings. Expanded chapters appear on work with parents and parent–infant psychotherapy. Both have generated a great increase in interest and engage child psychotherapists in most work settings. We are fortunate to have a child psychotherapist, also a group analyst, co-write the chapter on group work and have added a new chapter on working in educational settings, another growth area. The chapters on in-patient work and therapy and consultation in residential care remain as before.

The final section of the book describes areas of special clinical interest: autism, trauma, work with looked after children and foster carers, delinquency, violence, sexual abuse and sexually abusive behaviour, gender dysphoria, eating disorders, work with young people exposed to political violence. These chapters provide a mixture of an overview of ways of working with these specific problems as well as giving access to the theoretical thinking behind the interventions. They are rich in case illustrations and provide an intimate and impressive view of how far the profession has come in adapting classical psychoanalytic practice, originally developed for the treatment needs of mainly neurotic patients, to the more complex nature of a child and adolescent psychotherapist's work today. Six chapters are new – or almost totally revised; four have been reviewed and updated.

A note on history

A full history of developments in psychoanalytic work with children and young people, leading to the establishment of training schools, is contained in the Introduction to the first edition of this handbook, to which the curious reader is directed.

Although the lasting impetus to the establishment of the profession of Child and Adolescent Psychotherapy comes from the theoretical interest and practice of both Anna Freud and Melanie Klein (Daws 1987), other influences helped found the structure for psychoanalytic work with children and young people. In Vienna, Hermine Hug-Hellmuth (or Hug von Hugenstein) combined her experience as a teacher with her growing interest in psychoanalysis, publishing her first monograph in 1912 and a paper on child analysis in 1921 (MacLean and Rappen 1991). Geissman and Geissman conclude: 'Her work, buried for sixty years, is being unearthed at last: and that work was the invention of child psychoanalysis' (Geissman and Geissman 1998: 71).

In the 1920s the child guidance movement, begun in the USA, reached the UK. The first specially trained psychodynamic workers with children in the child guidance multi-professional teams were the psychiatric social workers (PSWs). Following the establishment of the first child guidance clinics in the UK (by Emanuel Miller and Noel Burke in London and the Notre Dame Clinic in Glasgow) the 'Mayflower ladies' – the first PSWs – went out to the USA to be trained by colleagues there. This interest in gaining particular expertise in work with children and young people grew amongst the early professions in the new clinics – psychologists, psychiatrists (originally specialists in Psychological Medicine) and social workers. Although there was a stimulating ethos of interest in applying psychoanalytic and child development understanding to children, many clinics remained voluntary, reliant until the advent of the National Health Service in 1948 upon jumble sales and donations to keep going. This picture of committed enthusiasm by professionals, yet a backcloth of it being difficult for society to take seriously child mental health issues, remains with us.

At University College, London, the 1920s saw the first courses in child development and observation, run for social workers and teachers. It was during this period of early enthusiasm that Dr Margaret Lowenfeld established in 1928 the Children's Clinic for the Treatment and Study of Nervous and Delicate Children:

> Here Lowenfeld's wartime experience and research observations had already led her into the belief that, in addition to environmental con-siderations, there were processes inherent in children themselves which would enable them to find more adaptive solutions. For Lowenfeld the key to these possibilities was play.
>
> (Urwin and Hood-Williams 1988: 42–3)

This developed in 1931 into a one-year training course and, in 1935, into a three-year 'training in psychopathology and psychotherapy with children and leading to a diploma' (ibid.: 89). The first child psychotherapy training was thus established at Lowenfeld's Institute of Child Psychology.

Melanie Klein's move to England in 1926 greatly influenced the British psychoanalytic world not only through her theoretical exploration of the internal world of the infant and the very early mother–infant relationship but through her practice of child psychoanalysis and her belief in the availability of very young children to psychoanalysis through the analytic play technique that she developed (Klein 1955). Klein's influence led the Psychoanalytic Society to develop its own criteria for training in child analysis, beginning with the supervised analysis of two adult patients, and followed by supervised work with a pre-latency, a latency and an ado-lescent, all while the candidate was in full analysis.

Notable at this time was the work in applied psychoanalysis undertaken in Vienna by Anna Freud, Sigmund Freud's daughter, and colleagues: the establishment of the Jackson Day Nursery (forerunner of the Hampstead War Nurseries) and the use of systematic, detailed observation of children; two child guidance clinics in Vienna for children and for adolescents; work with Aichhorn on juvenile delinquency; the establishment of a school, run by Eva Rosenfeld, to give disturbed children an appropriate learning environment; lectures for teachers and the development of a growing relationship between teaching and psychoanalysis.

The final scene in the pre-war setting for post-war developments in child psychotherapy, therefore, was that of the Freud family's arrival in London in 1938. Daws gives a singular insight: 'It is characteristic of Anna Freud's directness and the practicality of her interest in children that her luggage included 10 little stretcher beds – a foreshadow of the War Nursery she later helped create' (Daws 1987).

Anna Freud and Melanie Klein, as psychoanalysts, provided a rare combination of the close observation of children with psychoanalytic theory. Despite important theoretical differences, harshly disputed in the Psychoanalytic Society's 'Controversial Discussions' (King and Steiner 1991), these two principles remained central in the development of that application of psychoanalysis which was child psychotherapy.

Multiple influences arose from the experiences of the Second World War: evacuation of children which, for the first time, probably alerted the middle classes to the conditions of the poor and especially of the inner-city child; loss of parents in war; the work of John Bowlby on maternal deprivation and on separation, foreshadowing his thesis on attachment (Bowlby 1969); an Army Medical Corps, influenced by leadership from the Tavistock Clinic, taking seriously issues of war neurosis, mental health and trauma; and the influence of the child guidance movement on the establishment of the National Association for Mental Health. Together with the climate of change heralded by the Beveridge Report and the advent of the Welfare State, it seemed an atmosphere in which development could be nurtured.

In 1947 Anna Freud established at the Hampstead Clinic (now the Anna Freud Centre) a child psychoanalytic training based on her approach and accepting lay and analyst candidates. The following year the Tavistock, where John Bowlby was Director of the Children's Department, instituted a psychotherapy training under the joint auspices of Bowlby and Esther Bick (who developed the Infant-Observation model that was to become a central part of all analytic trainings (Bick 1964)). Doris Wills has described the processes leading up to the establishment of the Association of Child Psychotherapists (Wills 1954, 1978) – initially the Provisional Association of Child Psychotherapists (non-medical) – and the essential involvement and support of John Bowlby, Ethel Dukes (a colleague of Lowenfeld), Margaret Lowenfeld, Kenneth Soddy and Donald Winnicott who helped draft standards and engaged in successful negotiation. In 1949 the Association of Child Psychotherapists (ACP) was born.

Although many graduates of the ICP (Institute of Child Psychology) had Jungian analyses, it was not until the late 1950s that the first moves towards a Jungian child training began at the Society of Analytical Psychology (SAP) in London, under the guidance of Michael Fordham. Davidson (1996) gives a personal insight into this process, which culminated in the arrival of the first trainees in 1974, and: 'In 1979 the training was finally granted accreditation and our members were entitled to membership of the ACP' (Davidson 1996: 45).

The contribution of Michael Fordham to work with children is, for a profession where theoretical differences can sometimes assume large dimensions, both an immense and an integrative one. Astor writes:

His innovative researches into childhood gave a genetic basis to Jung's ideas about the importance of the self as both an organizing centre and the thing being organized within the personality. He connected it both to Jung's work on the self in the second half of life and to emotional development as described by psychoanalysts (the depressive position), while making clear what was distinctive about his 'Jungian model'.

(Astor 1996)

In the 1980s and 1990s three further training schools were established and gained accreditation from the ACP. The London-based British Association of Psychotherapists, established in 1951 and training psychoanalytic psychotherapists and Jungian analysts in work with adults, set up a child and adolescent training in 1982. The theoretical emphasis is that of the Independent Group in psychoanalysis (Kohon 1986), an object-relations-based training. The Scottish Institute of Human Relations runs a training in Edinburgh and Glasgow, although trainees come from all over Scotland and the north of England. The Birmingham Trust for Psychoanalytic Psychotherapy training marked a further welcome development in the establishment of training courses beyond the London nucleus, and in the new century, the arrival of the Northern School, Yorkshire based, provided a most welcome northerly extension of training and provision of child psychotherapy.

All schools run introductory courses in observational studies at Masters level for a range of participants from a wide variety of professional backgrounds; and many are involved in trainings abroad. The clinical doctorate is becoming established as the baseline qualification for the clinician and all training schools are linked to university departments for research and accreditation. Moreover, there has been an explosion of Psychoanalytic Studies – university level courses at undergraduate and post-graduate level – indicative of increased interest amongst the general public and often with child psychotherapists on the academic staff.

The role of the ACP today, in setting standards for the profession, in accrediting and reviewing trainings, in appointing assessors for interviews for Child Psychotherapy posts, in acting on behalf of the Department of Health in assessing the qualifications, for work in the UK, of EU nationals, has expanded greatly since the inception in 1949 of the Provisional Association of Child Psychotherapists (non-medical). In addition, its committees have been greatly involved in educating service commissioners and funders as to the reality of the role and impact of psychotherapists within the public sector. Robust participation in forums responding to governmental initiatives – ways of working, training escalators, protocols and standards for CAMHS work – takes up a great deal of time and has necessarily made many members into political as well as clinical animals. Some of the current pressures of work in a changing NHS are outlined by Gabrielle Crockatt in Chapter 7.

The demise of the ICP as a training school in 1978 followed the closure for economic reasons of its clinic, and the decision of the ICP in 1948 not to become part of the then fledgling NHS must have played a role in this. (One recalls John Bowlby's prescience in insisting that the Tavistock training be from its inception within the new National Health Service.) Other UK schools are similarly vulnerable: recently two London trainings have suffered – the SAP and the Anna Freud Centre, although the latter has recently announced that its future focus will be on purely analytic rather than psychotherapy training. It is also part of the ACP's brief to balance and promote claims for access to NHS monies (where there be any) by schools not in the NHS network, a role that is essential if diversity of theoretical perspective is to be sustained.

Training

The content of present-day training has built on the base of the original trainings but there now is a growing and wider body of theory and research information, tremendous expansion in child development, attachment and neuroscience theory, greater variety in individual children helped, and a broader experience of different ways of working within the multi-professional team and beyond the clinic.

The core of training remains fourfold:

- personal psychoanalysis (preferably four- to five-times weekly)
- psychoanalytic theory, research and practice
- training in Child Development and Parent–Infant Observation
- clinical work under supervision.

All trainees are required to be in four- or five-times weekly personal psychoanalysis, although this may exceptionally be three-times weekly where there are access/geographical pressures. The ACP regulates strictly the qualifications required of those who become training analysts. 'This is an essential and central requirement of training' (ACP 1998). Such a requirement is not, simplistically, to give an experience of analysis and 'being a patient': it is vital that the child psychotherapist explores his or her own unconscious motivations, defences and anxieties and is as 'grounded' as possible before engaging with the inner world of children. The trainee is in analysis throughout training and most continue after qualification. Such requirement was first agreed at the Budapest Congress of the International Psychoanalytical Association in 1918 (King and Steiner 1991: 14).

For trainees who enter training without adult mental health experience, a supervised placement is required. Trainees should be aware of adult psychopathology, of the roots of that in childhood, and of the particular predicament of the child with a mentally ill parent.

All trainees have undertaken a Parent–Infant Observation, usually during the pre-clinical Masters course. A newborn infant and carer are visited for an hour a week for a two-year period. The trainee records these observations, bringing the recordings to a weekly seminar group (no more than five members, to allow frequent discussion and presentation) where an experienced seminar leader enables the group exploration of the material. A pass in the final written paper is essential. The importance of this cannot be stressed too highly: it marks the development of skills in close, detailed observation that will be necessary professionally, and begins the integration of child development theory and psychoanalytic theory into a framework combining what is observed, what one knows and what one thinks. Bick, who established the approach, describes the development of this part of training (Bick 1964) and it is now a feature of all child psychoanalytic trainings in this country. For a fuller view, the reader is directed to Miller *et al.* (1989) and Sternberg (2005). In addition, the sustained observation of young children is also a requirement.

Throughout training, trainees attend both theoretical and clinical seminars. Areas to be covered include:

- human growth and development (including non-psychoanalytic perspectives and particularly including developmental psychology and attachment theory)
- developmental disturbance and psychopathology
- psychodynamic theories (each school will differ in emphasis, according to its theoretical stance, but 'this should be set in the context of other theories' (ACP 1998))
- psychotherapeutic techniques
- the range of treatment techniques is taught and trainees are encouraged to explore other approaches
- research methodology and practice.

In their clinical settings, trainees must see at least three intensive (*at least* three-times weekly) cases under weekly supervision by an approved supervisor. These are an under-five-year-old, a latency (primary school age) child and an adolescent, and the group must include both boys and girls. At least one must be in therapy for not less than two years and the others for a minimum of one year. Additionally, at least six children and young people must be seen once or twice weekly on a long-term basis for which the trainee is offered regular supervision. These should include a range of presenting clinical problems, levels of disturbance, ages and both sexes. Instead of a non-intensive case a trainee may substitute running a children's group, treat a mother and young child on a long-term basis, participate in longer-term family therapy or undertake some time-limited treatments.

Trainees also undertake weekly work with the parent(s)/carer of a child in therapy with another psychotherapist: this is not adult psychotherapy but aims to hold the child in mind and address the parents as carers of the child. An assessed report is written on this work. Assessments are also undertaken, both with the trainee as colleague contributing to a multi-professional diagnostic and assessment process and with the aim of making appropriate recommendations to the team, parents or outside agencies. Joint working as a member of the multi-disciplinary team is of course a prerequisite in the training. In their work settings, trainees are expected to learn the structure and management of the NHS (especially as it operates in that workplace), current legislation and child protection procedures, and to keep appropriate records and write appropriate reports. These structures are taught by the training schools but local systems differ.

Towards the end of their training, trainees will explore aspects of brief and time-limited work, family work, group work and parent–infant counselling. 'Trainees need to have knowledge of the variety of settings across health, education, social service and forensic provision within which children and young people are at higher risk of mental ill health. These include paediatric wards, child development centres, residential children's homes, special schools and off site educational units and young offender units. Training Schools and work placements should liaise together to ensure that such knowledge is provided' (ACP 2007). Consultation to other institutions and other professionals working with children and young people is also required experience. Such applications of psychoanalytic understanding are essential.

Such an intensive training requires four years to complete. It is also expensive, the main cost being the personal psychoanalysis. A major achievement since the appearance of the first edition of this volume has been the establishment in many clinics of trainee posts where training fees are paid and a significant contribution is made towards the cost of analysis and the three intensive case supervisions. Although not every candidate can succeed in gaining such a post, their numbers have grown significantly. Some posts are directly linked to training schools jointly with clinics; others are open to competition from trainees of any school.

Post qualification expectations are also high. The ACP recommends further training in:

- the dynamics of groups and institutions
- teaching courses to other professionals and caregivers
- understanding other forms of treatment, e.g. cognitive and behavioural methods, family therapy, medication
- experience of consultation to other professionals
  (ACP 2007 paragraph 3.54).

The ACP has established a Code of Ethics. Concerns about the practice of any child psychotherapist are referred to the Ethics Committee of the ACP.

A note on confidentiality

At the very heart of any therapeutic contact is the need to protect the privacy of the client – adult or child. When working with an adult, the boundaries of privacy are usually fairly straightforward as contact between the therapist and other people in the patient's life is likely to be minimal. However, with children, there is often an equally important need for the therapist to be in regular contact with the key adults in the child's life – parents and foster parents in particular, but also teachers, social workers, residential workers and medical staff. In practice, issues of confidentiality are worked out within the guidelines of the Code of Ethics of the profession for each child who is seen, as appropriate. The complexity of therapeutic work with children means that a flexible balance has to be found between the child's need for confidentiality and the need to communicate helpfully with the child's parents, carers, family, and the multi-professional team.

The experience of a private and protected therapeutic space is so central to the child and adolescent psychotherapist's work that the question of how to write publicly without compromising this privacy raises many issues. As with any other profession that needs an ever-evolving theoretical and experiential base, we have to share our clinical experience with each other and outside the profession if we are not to become moribund. The problem is how best to achieve this without sacrificing our relationship with our patients.

Some case illustrations will have been disguised. It is always tricky to know how much one can do this before it begins to sound unconvincing. Some of the children and families discussed in this handbook will have been directly approached by their therapists asking for permission to write about their treatment; some therapists ask for permission to use disguised material for teaching or publication at the outset of treatment. This request is made in the spirit of advancing knowledge, training and practice, so that, should it be helpful to share what has been learned from a particular treatment, permission has been given.

The way in which the rich variety of clinical examples throughout this handbook brings the work alive is perhaps the best testimony to the value of grappling with such issues. As editors, we have found it a pleasure and a privilege to collate this overview of the profession of child and adolescent psychotherapy.

Concluding introductory thoughts

The following chapters will speak eloquently for themselves. We are grateful to the colleagues who took time to elaborate their work and its meaning. The wider benefit is best described below:

We do not need only specialist services. We need a framework for understanding extreme emotions – love, hate, jealousy, envy, destructiveness. This is something that psychoanalysis can provide. It also helps us understand how these emotions come to be violently evoked and enacted and how they can be modified and channelled more constructively. We believe that psychoanalysis can function as a shared framework of understanding between professionals from a variety of disciplines, even if they are not using it as a therapeutic tool.

(Trowell and Bower 1995: 4)

References

Association of Child Psychotherapists (ACP) (1998) *The Training of Child Psychotherapists: Outline for Training Courses*, London: ACP.

Association of Child Psychotherapists (ACP) (2007) *Quality Assurance Framework for the Training of Child Psychotherapists*, London: ACP.

Astor, J. (1996) 'A tribute to Michael Fordham', *Journal of Child Psychotherapy* 22(1): 5–25.

Bick, E. (1964) 'Notes on infant observation in psychoanalytic training', *International Journal of Psychoanalysis* 45: 558–66.

Bowlby, J. (1969) *Attachment and Loss: Vol. 1 Attachment*, London: Hogarth.

Davidson, D. (1996) 'The Jungian child analytic training: an historical perspective', *Journal of Child Psychotherapy* 22(1): 38–48.

Daws, D. (1987) 'Thirty years of Child Psychotherapy: the psychoanalytic approach to children's problems', Tavistock Clinic Paper, No. 48, London: Tavistock Clinic.

Geissman, C. and Geissman, P. (1998) *A History of Child Psychoanalysis*, London: Routledge.

Hug-Hellmuth, H. (1912) 'Analyse eines Traumes eines Fünfeinhalbjahrigen', *Zentralblatt für Psychoanalyse und Psychotherapie* 2(3): 122–7.

—— (1921) 'On the technique of child analysis', *International Journal of Psychoanalysis* 2: 287–305 (Abstract printed in the same journal (1920) 2: 361–2).

King, P. and Steiner, R. (eds) (1991) *The Freud–Klein Controversies 1941–45*, London: Routledge.

Klein, M. (1955) 'The psychoanalytic play technique: its history and significance', in *Envy and Gratitude and Other Works 1946–63: The Writings of Melanie Klein*, Vol. III, London: Hogarth, 1975.

Kohon, G. (1986) *The British School of Psychoanalysis: The Independent Tradition*, London: Free Association Books.

MacLean, G. and Rappen, U. (1991) *Hermine Hug-Hellmuth*, London: Routledge.

Miller, L., Rustin, M., Rustin, M. and Shuttleworth, J. (1989) *Closely Observed Infants*, London: Duckworth Press.

Sternberg, J. (2005) *Infant Observation at the Heart of Training*, London: Karnac.

Trowell, J. and Bower, M. (eds) (1995) *The Emotional Needs of Young Children and their Families: Using Psychoanalytic Ideas in the Community*, London: Routledge.

Urwin, C. and Hood-Williams, J. (eds) (1988) *Child Psychotherapy, War and the Normal Child: Selected Papers of Margaret Lowenfeld*, London: Free Association Books.

Wills, D. M. (1954) 'The Association for Child Psychotherapists (non-medical)', *Bulletin of the British Psychological Society*, May.

—— (1978) 'Fifty years of child guidance: a psychologist's view', *Journal of Child Psychotherapy* 4: 97–102.

Further reading

Astor, J. (1995) *Michael Fordham's Innovations in Analytical Psychology*, London: Routledge.

Freud, A. (1992) *The Harvard Lectures*, J. Sandler (ed.), London: Karnac.

Klein, M. (1955) 'The psychoanalytic play technique: its history and significance', in *Envy and Gratitude and Other Works 1946–63: The Writings of Melanie Klein*, Vol. III, London: Hogarth, 1975.

Ramsden, S. (ed.) (1991) *Psychotherapy: Pure and Applied*, Occasional Papers, No. 6, London: ACPP.

Part I

Theoretical foundations

Theoretical foundations

2 The roots of child and adolescent psychotherapy in psychoanalysis

Meira Likierman and Elizabeth Urban

This chapter provides a brief historical overview of psychoanalysis, the body of thought that underpins the practice of child psychotherapy and that equally informs a wide range of therapies that are practised today.

Psychoanalysis is a clinical and theoretical discipline that is only a century old and yet has accumulated a body of knowledge that is substantial and complex. Having started as a single theory, it has branched out into several substantial schools of thought around the world, each with its distinctive culture, training institutions, favoured techniques and theoretical contributions. Whilst traditionally these schools have competed for a monopoly on the 'truth' about mental life, many contemporary psychoanalysts are able to sustain a pluralist position whereby they accommodate a theoretical diversity in their clinical approach.

Psychoanalysis began with the efforts of Sigmund Freud shortly after he completed his medical training in Vienna in 1885. Before deciding on the area in which he should specialise, Freud obtained work experience in Paris under the tutoring of Jean Martin Charcot who was making groundbreaking discoveries in the treatment of hysteria.

Hysteria was a major public health concern throughout the nineteenth century, afflicting women with symptoms such as paralysis of the limbs or loss of vital functions such as sight or speech. The symptoms would strike suddenly and would typically baffle medical experts, which even led some to dismiss it as no more than a female excuse for opting out of responsibilities.

Charcot was among the progressive medical scientists who viewed the condition as a genuine neurological disorder and, while he assumed that it indicated a degeneration of the nervous system, he also hypothesised a possible traumatic trigger for it in the patient's life circumstance. In order to substantiate this, Charcot began to hypnotise hysterical patients, managing to demonstrate that in an altered state of mind some of their symptoms could vanish.

Freud was impressed by witnessing these experiments at first hand and, furthermore, had an immediate intuition of the implications of what he saw. If indeed ideas had agency and could affect the body to such a degree, then there was a whole region of human experience, which was as yet undiscovered, as were the scientific principles that governed it.

Freud returned to Vienna to set up his own practice for nervous disorders. He continued to hypnotise his patients, trying to use this as a means of uncovering the possible traumatic triggers of their condition. Hypnosis, however, proved too clumsy a method for eliciting the detailed information that Freud soon found he required. He gave it up for a new method of introspection that he taught his patients – free-association. He asked his patients to follow their natural train of thought using as guidance their spontaneous associations. They were to relinquish the normal self-critical standard of their speech and to narrate to him in full what their minds led them to, whether this seemed trivial, irrational, rude, embarrassing or otherwise.

His patients had some success with this method. Furthermore, the narratives that emerged from their attempts to disclose thoughts without self-censorship uncovered a hidden world of human mental activity. This was governed by secret desires and urges that often conflicted with the patient's self-approval. The method of free-association revealed that one's everyday mind, far from being occupied mainly with intellectual content, was close to the life of the body with its primitive pleasures and urges. Patients often felt at odds with their intimate bodily states and found the force of their raw sexuality obtrusive and threatening. The result was a distressing psychological conflict which patients tried to end by fending off unacceptable ideation.

Their unease led Freud to what he thought was his first clinical discovery, for he assumed that it pointed to the traumatic trigger of hysteria hypothesised by Charcot. Thus in his first theoretical model Freud suggested that the trauma at the root of hysteria was a sexual one and that his patients had all been the victims of childhood sexual abuse. The reason that his patients could not tell him this directly was that their minds had never been able to assimilate the traumatic event and store it as an ordinary memory. The patient 'forgot' or repressed the event without dealing with its forceful impact. Unbearable traumatic tension thus remained trapped within the patient, and this now found an outlet via neural pathways into the body – hence extreme physical symptoms.

It did not occur to Freud at this early stage that human subjective experience was, in itself, a worthwhile object of study. He regarded his work as essentially medical, hoping to demonstrate the organic processes at the root of nervous illness. He believed that neurological psychic energy, though still not fully understood, justified attempts at a scientific quantification and investigation.

However, psychoanalysis was to take a different turn from a purely neurophysiological direction, and this coincided with a change of mind in Freud about his 'seduction theory' that attributed all neurotic illness to childhood sexual abuse. This theoretical revision resulted from his new and hitherto most ambitious project of research. Freud decided to put his method of free-associations to a rigorous test via an analysis of his own mental life, specifically an area of it that seemed the most free of his conscious control – his dreams. Since he did not suffer from a major nervous disorder he was not expecting to discover a trauma in his own background, but what he did discover surprised him.

His dream material revealed to him the almost equally powerful impact of apparently ordinary life frustrations. Each night his dreams resurrected fragments of the previous day, which were connected with areas of failures, anxieties, disappointments and hurts. His frustrated professional ambitions, his envy of successful colleagues, his anxiety about promotion, his small jealousies of his wife and his pain when he thought she was slighting him, all surfaced again at night, but not as he had actually experienced them. Rather, his dreaming mind transformed the reality of his daily lacks, made good his frustrations and presented to him his wishes as fulfilled.

Freud was struck by how insistently his mind wished to compensate him for the frustrations of living. Further exploration led him to realise that ordinary daily disappointments had accrued a traumatic-like force because they were underpinned by hurts that had accumulated over an extended period, dating all the way to childhood. The sorrows and resentments of childhood lived on in his unconscious, infusing each new disappointment in his life and influencing his mental well-being.

In this new understanding, the helplessness of the human child with its unfulfilled needs itself seemed traumatic, and this led Freud to realise that the needs and wishes of the child were far more acute than had been suspected. The childhood memories that linked with his dreams revealed that, far from desiring a simple care regime, the child has powerful cravings for love and physical pleasure, as well as an intense primitive sexuality. Freud thus realised that it was not necessarily actual sexual abuse that had been at the root of his patients' disturbances. Nervous illness was not a sudden phenomenon with a single traumatic cause, but a condition that developed over time and was intimately bound up with the life history of the human individual. It seemed to Freud that the most delicate and formative area in this history was childhood, dominated as it was by the unruly forces of infantile sexuality.

It was thus that Freud reached one of his theoretical milestones, which was his theory of infantile sexuality. Along with this achievement, Freud's exploration of his dream life had a further crucial outcome, and this was an updated and newly understood version of the unconscious mind. Freud had made use of the term 'unconscious' from the very beginning of his psychological researches, but did so initially in a purely descriptive sense. In other words, he used the term as an all-purpose label for a range of mental states in which the individual was not aware of certain ideation. This now seemed too superficial to Freud. His dream life had just provided a 'royal road to the unconscious', suggesting to him that it was far more useful to view the unconscious as a separate mental system which was subject to its own, distinct patterns of logic, and which had a complex relationship with the very different system of consciousness.

Freud noted that the dreaming mind offered a first-hand knowledge of unconscious processes because its activity was not restricted to a mere gathering and reproducing of portions of reality from the preceding 'dream day'. Rather, the dreaming mind subjected such portions to alterations which followed typical patterns; unconscious activity either condensed disparate fragments of reality so as to create multiply determined symbols, or else it did the opposite, breaking apart what should have remained together, for example, by shifting the appropriate feeling stirred by an event to a trivial substitute. It is thus that an individual can dream of the death of a loved one without feeling appropriate grief, or that the person who appears to us in a dream is often a condensed creation which combines features drawn variously from family members, friends, colleagues, each selected because it contributes to the symbolic meaning of the dream.

Freud reasoned that such manipulations of the truth had a function, which was to enable the nightly processing of those of the day's thoughts which had been too unbearable to own during waking hours. The sleeping mind used stratagems to conceal the full impact of the meaning which it was addressing so as not to raise levels of anxiety and awaken the individual. The very intricacy of the mind's stratagems led Freud to realise that unconscious content causes anxiety precisely because, once repressed, it refuses to lie still and continues to press for discharge. Unconscious wishes continually press to reach the conscious mind, which alone commands the body's movements and thus the route to need-fulfilling action.

These insights led Freud to further realisations. Whilst awake, the mind was surely equally under a continual pressure from unconscious impulses. And even when this does not result in neurotic symptoms, repressed unconscious impulses keep returning to hound consciousness in various large and small ways. Freud was to explore how this happens in our everyday life, manifesting as slips of the tongue or built into the comic moment in jokes. These explorations highlighted for Freud the need to discover why the human mind needs to repress wishes to such an extent, and he found the answer in his conception of infantile sexuality.

Childhood sexuality was not a new idea in the late nineteenth century, but Freud's originality consisted in his ability to draw on pre-existing theories and integrate them in a unique way with his own findings. This culminated in a groundbreaking theory of psychosexual development that accounted both for normal development and for neurotic illness.

In this vision, childhood psychosexual development was posited as the biological underpinning of human mental development. Freud described the infant as bringing with it into the world elemental aspects of its sexuality which infuse every facet of its existence. Sensations, sights, smells, tastes and sounds all carry some sexual charge with a potential for excitation and arousal. Of particular intensity are sensations in the body orifices of mouth and anus where the internal membranes are sensitive, hence becoming focal sexual centres.

As the infant develops and its experiences cohere, the still immature components of its sexuality find a more intensified expression. Since the small child is not self-conscious or ashamed, it expresses its developing sexual trends uninhibitedly in its family circle, much like an adult afflicted with perversions. For example, in its normal daily routine the child derives sexual pleasure from activities that variously enable elements of voyeuristic, exhibitionistic, fetishistic, sadistic or masochistic excitement. Its oral and anal experiences mingle with these to create particular 'pre-genital' configurations of sexuality.

In this thinking Freud's interest shifted to an 'instinct theory' in which sexual instincts underpinned human urges and were the prime motivational energies in mental life. Freud felt that normal development requires a gradual subsuming of infantile sexuality with its 'perversions' in a normal reproductive adult sexuality, leaving only symbolic traces in the sexual activities of fore-pleasure. But if this process is disrupted for some reason, the child becomes fixated to a particular primitive sexual urge in a damaging way. This results in later pathology, with the individual taking the path either of perversion or else of neurosis, depending on whether the fixated sexual activity is retained in its explicit, primitive form, or whether it is repressed at the cost of developing symptoms.

Tying the theory of mental development to biological sexuality seemed promising, as it appeared to ground psychoanalysis in an established branch of science. However, one aspect of Freud's thinking on infantile sexuality intruded on this purely scientific aspiration, inserting the perplexing topic of human subjectivity into an otherwise watertight biological theory. This aspect was Freud's (now widely familiar) concept of the Oedipus complex. It was this concept that obliged Freud to recognise that biology, along with the mental life, which it underpins, does not take place in a vacuum. Human sexuality and its instincts are inseparable through their very aims from interactions with others, initially caregivers and eventually sexual partners. The social behaviours of seeking, and interacting with, love objects are inherent in psychosexual development.

Taking the male child as an example (but suggesting an analogous female experience), Freud delineated an intimate psychosexual bond with the mother from the time of conception. The mother not only carries the foetus in her body and feeds the newborn from her body, but also continues, through her physical proximity, to cater to basic infantile needs. She is thus the natural recipient of her infant's nascent sexuality. By the time the boy develops into a small child, his primitive component instincts give way to a new focus of pleasure, which is his penis. But the boy is not mature enough to understand the significance of this event. Since his mother has always looked after all his bodily and emotional needs, and apparently regards herself as responsible for satisfying these, he assumes that she will similarly continue to be responsible for satisfying his growing genital desires.

Normally the boy's open expression of desire meets with disapproval in the family. Not only are his attempts to induce his mother to witness or touch his genitalia rebuffed, but he is now cognitively mature enough to make sense of her disapproval. His growing awareness has bred in him self-consciousness, enabling him to experience shame, disgust and guilt for the first time in his life. As well as this, the boy is much more perceptive in registering obstacles to his desires. He realises that the genital pleasure refused to him by his mother is nonetheless awarded to his father. In referring to this stage in life Freud did not use the term 'complex' lightly. He realised that it raised emotional storms of desire, pain and rage that lead to extreme conflicts between love and hate in the boy. It thus amounts to the first life crisis or infantile neurosis.

Freud suggested that, as with earlier stages of infantile sexuality, the Oedipus complex needs to be outgrown. However, this event is a developmentally complex task. It is not enough for the boy to surrender his desires uncomprehendingly, as this only leaves him feeling defeated and 'castrated'. A genuine resolution requires a fundamental psychical change which expands the boy's mental horizons, enabling an altered and developmentally broadened perspective on his situation.

Freud visualised this psychical change in structural terms. The mind acquires a new and qualitatively distinct extension, and this happens when the child absorbs into itself aspects of parental authority. These are internalised to create an intra-psychic agency of a 'super-ego', enabling the boy to find a more mature perspective on the procreative sexual roles of his parents. The boy identifies with this newly understood family structure, internalises parental values and instates his father in his mind as a role model which points the way to his own future sexual aspirations.

In his last 'structural model' Freud put much more emphasis on mental life as the product of subjective human experience – that is, of the child's mode of interacting with its caregivers and family. However, Freud also wanted his structural model to absorb his lifelong scientific interest in instinctual energies that propel the human organism. He thus hypothesised a tripartite structural model which accommodated a 'super-ego' internalised from the external world, an 'id' which consists of raw instinctual activity, and an 'ego' – the mind's central organising agency which mediates between the id and the super-ego (instincts and the world), thus negotiating an optimal developmental route for a growing 'self'.

From Freud to ego psychology and object relations

Freud's final theory attempted to bring into dialogue two aspects of his own thinking – his scientific concern with the organic, biological energies that propel the individual from within, and his humanistic concern with subjective, narrative meaning that emerges from the individual's relationship with his human environment.

This synthesis was not straightforward, at least not in the sense of bequeathing to the psychoanalytic movement a single theory that could be agreed upon. Freud's followers found it easier to focus on partial aspects of his structural model, giving prominence either to its interpersonal aspect as exemplified in the relationship of ego and super-ego, or else to its biological-instinctual aspect as exemplified in the relationship of ego and id. One crucial result for psychoanalysis was a cleavage between an 'object relations' school favoured in Britain and an 'ego-psychology' school favoured in North America.

Two thinkers who were instrumental in influencing this division were the pioneers of child psychoanalysis, Anna Freud and Melanie Klein. It is important to stress that neither saw herself as dispensing with Freud's tripartite structural model. Their differences emerge from subtle but crucial shifts in emphasis onto different aspects of it.

Anna Freud

Anna Freud focused on the id–ego aspect of the model, exploring the effects of instinctual pressures on the ego's development. She realised that the ego is unlikely to fend off id impulses in simple, easily distinguishable ways. Rather, defences infuse the ego's entire mode of functioning and are integrated into its very life. Whilst the ego's healthy survival does indeed depend on its ability to master turbulent id functioning, if defences are too entrenched in the ego's habits, instinctual impulses are stifled rather than processed and mastered, hence continuing to overwhelm the individual with pathological manifestations.

Anna Freud's thinking led to emphasis on the ego's complex tasks in its move towards an adaptation to reality, and this theme was taken much further by an 'ego-psychology' school which included among its thinkers Ernest Kris, Edith Jacobson and Heinz Hartmann. A further dimension of Anna Freud's influence was evident in the work of Margaret Mahler, who demonstrated how the complex task of separating from the mother and loosening the most primitive psychical ties with her paved the way to ego autonomy and a coherent sense of self.

Melanie Klein

Unlike Anna Freud, Melanie Klein explored the interpersonal aspect of the structural model. She believed that it was not helpful to view the super-ego as a mere conceptual abstraction because its internalisation is experienced subjectively in a highly anthropomorphic manner. Contradicting Freud,

Klein suggested that the infant could relate to its mother from birth, even though it possesses only a rudimentary capacity to apprehend aspects of her nurturing. However, these are qualitatively distinguished as 'good' or 'bad' and internalised as archaic 'part-objects'. An archaic phantasy life thus emerges in the infant, infusing its perceptions of, and interactions with, caregivers. Growth and cognitive development enable the child to internalise increasingly understood, realistic objects which complete and refine its formerly internalised primitive ones.

Klein felt that the internal world created through these processes is the key to mental health, provided that it isn't populated with disturbing, persecuting objects but is, rather, a domain in which objects emit benevolence and continually infuse the personality with warmth and security.

Divergences between Anna Freud and Melanie Klein

Anna Freud and Melanie Klein proceeded from the same significant starting point, which was their study and treatment of children. And since this was a new field of enquiry, its principles needed to be established even as it was being used as a research tool. It was thus that they both became engaged in pioneering a psychoanalysis for children, and at the same time utilised this process to investigate and discover the nature of earliest mental life. Yet theirs was not a joint venture; quite the contrary, they did not perceive any complementarity in their respective findings and conclusions, and in fact engaged in a lifelong professional debate.

Melanie Klein's belief that the infant relates to others from the beginning of life required her to assert that an ego exists from birth. Although she felt that the infantile ego was not unified or coherent, she nonetheless assumed that it could carry out a few essential operations such as a limited registering of reality, an ability to welcome or fear its impact and also an ability to defend against this. Such thinking led her to conceive of an array of archaic defence mechanisms and, in a further controversial step, to link these to the kinds of defences employed in adult schizophrenic and manic-depressive disorders. This threw light on the infantile origin of adult mental illness, but it also portrayed early ego activity as strangely destructive to the very process of growth which it was supposed to promote.

Anna Freud felt that such thinking was negative and also that it attributed too much complexity to the early psyche. Like her father, she continued to believe that the infant is unlikely to arrive in the world with a psyche that is sufficiently formed to possess a clearly differentiated entity such as the ego. The infant's post-natal existence amounted to an undifferentiated, foetal-like state of 'primary narcissism', and he only emerged from this gradually and in response to environmental impingements. In this view, identity and mental structure were shaped during the process of early acculturation, and were thus constructs which did not exist outside of this process. Anna Freud suggested that in keeping with this, defence mechanisms develop later and express a broader and more diverse relational repertoire than that expressed by the limited archaic defences which Klein envisaged.

Anna Freud and Melanie Klein might have continued to develop their views separately and to have their thinking go by unchallenged were it not for circumstances which brought them into the same professional organisation. The war in Europe obliged them to settle in London and join the British Psychoanalytic Society, where it was difficult to find a mode of professional co-existence. This was to lead, in 1941, to a theoretical confrontation between the two of them which was popularly referred to as the 'controversial discussions', and which also drew the entire British Society into a debate on early mental life and the origins of the psyche. In spite of the discussions being careful and lengthy, no consensus was reached and members of the British Society were obliged to accommodate a greater diversity. This gave rise to three schools of thought, since to the classical Freudian group were now added a Kleinian and a further 'Independent' group. It was this last which provided the foundation for a distinct British object relations school, the members of which chose to draw on the thinking of both Anna Freud and Melanie Klein, and to add further original discoveries to this mixture.

Object relations theorists

Klein's theories gave rise to an 'object relations' school, which included among its thinkers Donald Winnicott, Michael Balint, Ronald Fairbairn and Wilfred Bion. However, while these thinkers agreed with Klein on the activities of the early ego, they also, unlike Klein, and with an awareness of Anna Freud's insights, emphasised the utter helplessness of this ego in the absence of external support from the mother. Winnicott noted that, viewed philosophically, the newborn's ego exists only in a potential sense, since it is activated and brought into being only in the context, and through the agency, of maternal handling.

In spite of areas of disagreement, the object relations group which Klein inspired were at one with her on a crucially significant issue. They underscored the fragility of the newborn psyche at moments of distress, and outlined a range of archaic defensive manoeuvres which it employs to break down and disperse portions of disturbing reality that impinge on it. Bion, for example, pointed out that repeated and excessive deflections of reality can damage an individual's capacity to absorb and process experiences and hence to mature mentally. Anna Freud and her followers were sceptical about the suggestion of a very early onset of defence mechanisms, but they did agree that defensive functioning begins in childhood and should be explored with the child where appropriate.

With this thinking Melanie Klein, Anna Freud, and the schools which they inspired, made a unique mark not only on psychoanalysis, but also on the broader canvas of twentieth-century thinking. Their legacy is evident in the degree of sensitivity which our culture, to this day, considers as appropriate for infants.

While Anna Freud and Melanie Klein exemplify some of the ways in which creative thinking extended and refined the foundation provided by Freud, it is important to remember that psychoanalysis had other important strands which enriched it and which therefore need to be taken into account.

Fordham and the influence of Jung

Another major contributor to child analysis was Michael Fordham. Although he drew upon Freud and Klein, his central concepts were derived from Carl Jung.

Jung was a young Swiss psychiatrist when his studies at the Burghölzli Hospital led him into an intense collaboration with Freud lasting six years. From the outset there were theoretical differences between them. Jung had held that the energy of libido was neutral, rather than exclusively sexual. Added to this, Jung thought that psychic contents included not only repressed sexual wishes, but also an innate psychic endowment, which he called 'archetypes'. Archetypes are organising structures, expressed in typical and universal themes across time and cultures, such as those found in rituals, myths and religions. He studied archetypal themes in the material of his patients, expanding his investigations by examining analogies between various cultures and religions throughout history.

When the split with Freud came in 1913, Jung was deeply affected. He gradually recovered and each morning sketched formalised circular patterns, or mandalas, which he found containing. He came to see this series of drawings as a reflection of psychic changes from day to day within the conscious and unconscious whole of himself; changing over time yet having continuity within an overall totality. He considered the mandala to be an archetypal symbol of the totality of the personality, which he conceptualised as the 'self'. For Jung the self had a centralising, organising and integrating function, thus making the self similar to Freud's notion of the ego. However, Jung's concept goes beyond this. For Jung the self is the organisational centre of the whole personality, of which the ego, the perceptual centre, is only a part; a secondary, although important, organiser.

Jung's ideas arose from experiences with adults, and it was Fordham, a London child psychiatrist, who was the first to extend Jungian thinking to childhood by integrating archetypal theory with clinical and observational experiences of children. Fordham entered child psychiatry a year after Klein published *The Psychoanalysis of Children* (1932), and just as he was coming to appreciate Jung's ideas. Fordham soon began to discern archetypal elements in children's clinical material. Recognising that unconscious phantasies were conceptually identical to primitive archetypal images, he readily linked Jung's theory of the psyche with Klein's description of the infant's inner world. Fordham borrowed Klein's technical handling of material, which enabled him to enter more fully into the psychic lives of children.

Through work with some very young children, Fordham noted that their circular scribbles (mandalas) accompanied episodes of ego growth. He sensed that a more fundamental organiser lay behind these developments, which drew his attention to Jung's concept of the self. Out of this Fordham postulated a primary self, conceived as a psychosomatic integrate evident from before birth. Hence, in contrast to Winnicott, Fordham concluded that the infant's first state is one of integration rather than unintegration.

Conceptually the primary self represents the psychosomatic whole of the organism and its potential. The potential unfolds through the complementary processes of deintegration and reintegration, lifelong processes that involve coming into relation with the environment and then assimilating these experiences. These processes are structured by the self, which organises them in distinctively human, archetypal ways, such as the universal, over-arching patterning and timing of the unfolding of infancy, Oedipal development and adolescence. The mental contents that are built up do not simply represent external experiences that are internalised. They also are influenced by the self, which organises reintegrated contents, for instance, into good and bad objects.

The purpose of Fordham's postulate was to account for the global organisation of the infant, conveying his view that even a very young infant, or, as later became clear, a foetus, is not in an overall sense disorganised, unintegrated or disintegrated, but functions as a whole. His model formulates a self that is not constructed by the infant, but is, rather, the starting point of development. This notion of the self is more comprehensive and extensive than that in psychoanalysis, which tends to refer to the sense of self. Despite this difference, Fordham's work brought archetypal theory much closer to the instinctual phenomena as understood by psychoanalysts, especially Klein and her followers. Fordham also turned to Klein for a more precise understanding of the primitive processes, like projective and introjective identification, which are elements of early de- and reintegration. For instance, autistic children have serious impairments to deintegration and those with 'no-entry defences' have impairments to reintegration.

What Anna Freud, Klein, Fordham, and the schools which they inspired, all had in common was a strong belief in the importance of the child's imaginative life as developed in the matrix of family relationships and as expressed symbolically through play. Understanding how play could be used clinically took time to develop. Freud had indirectly treated a five-year-old, 'Little Hans', through the boy's father, and Jung wrote a paper concerning observations of his daughter. Other early psychoanalytic practitioners had attempted some direct work with children, but it was Klein who worked out a technique that combined the rigorous technical tools in work with adults with the child's natural expression in play. This technical development proved an effective way of reaching the child's unconscious, and others, like Winnicott and Fordham, drew upon this. Thus play, as the crucial idiom of childhood, remains the medium through which child analytic therapy is conducted.

Conclusions

To conclude, divergences between the psychoanalytic schools described in this chapter have produced conflicts but have also been advantageous, as they have led to the development of psychoanalytic theory through the collective effort of gifted practitioners.

Further reading

Astor, J. (1995) *Michael Fordham's Innovations in Analytical Psychology*, London: Routledge.

Gay, P. (1988) *Freud: A Life for Our Time*, London: Dent.

Grosskurth, P. (1986) *Melanie Klein*, London: Hodder and Stoughton.

Hinshelwood, R. (1994) *Clinical Klein*, London: Free Association Books.

King, P. and Steiner, R. (eds) (1991) *The Freud–Klein Controversies 1941–1945*, London: Tavistock/Routledge.

Kohon, G. (ed.) (1988) *The British School of Psychoanalysis: The Independent Tradition*, London: Free Association Books.

Petot, J.-M. (1991) *Melanie Klein*, Vols I and II, Madison, CT: International Universities Press.

Sandler, J., Dare, G., Holder, A. and Dreher, A. U. (1997) *Freud's Models of the Mind: An Introduction*, London: Karnac.

Sidoli, M. and Davies, M. (1988) *Jungian Child Psychotherapy: Individuation in Childhood*, London: Karnac.

Wollheim, R. (1991) *Freud*, 2nd edn, London: Fontana Modern Masters.

Young-Bruehl, E. (1988) *Anna Freud*, London: Macmillan.

3 Normal emotional development

Ann Horne

Introduction and context

Child and adolescent psychotherapists are constantly aware of the developmental processes at work – or obscured and obstructed – in the children and young people whom they see. In simple terms, the normal capacity of the child to adapt to and embrace growth and change, both physically and emotionally, is an ally of the therapist. Given that our caseloads today, however, tend towards children who have experienced severe and often very early trauma, where the survival of any sense of self seems an amazing achievement, it has become even more vital that we retain as part of our repertoire a clear sense of the normal developmental tasks and processes which lead to 'good enough' emotional health and functioning.

Each psychotherapist, in considering emotional development, will tend to use the constructs and vocabulary of his or her own theoretical orientation. In practice, one integrates this with what is found to be clinically useful and valid. This chapter will inevitably present the author's view of key developments but attempt to incorporate major theoretical positions. A workable brief overview is the aim.

The reader should also keep in mind Stern's dictum that developmental progress does not take place at a smooth, even pace. Rather, the infant and child is subject to quantum leaps in physical, emotional and cognitive achievement (Stern 1985). One would add that it is also important for the therapist to keep in mind that, although each sign of progress represents a gain for the child, it also contains a loss: the infant who achieves walking has made a step (or several!) which leaves behind the perhaps comfortable dependency of the pre-mobile nursing state. The child's world, moreover, has suddenly become a very different place. It is not unusual for sleep problems to be associated with such developmental gains as mobility, as separation anxiety sets in (Daws 1989). Developmental achievement thus incorporates loss and the child can feel a regressive pull to earlier states at times of anxiety and uncertainty. Anna Freud gave probably the clearest early model of normal development from which pathological diversion could be assessed, with the emphasis on normality (Freud 1965).

Early infancy

The development of the infant's psychological sense of self paradoxically begins, for the psychotherapist, with the development of the 'body ego' or sense of physical boundariedness in the baby. The first defensive man-oeuvres – ways of protecting and enabling the growing 'self' (see Chapter 10) – are physical: crying, kicking, using the body and the musculature to cope with internal anxiety or external intrusion. An experience of the body as potent, to be enjoyed, therefore, is important for the developing baby, as is the mother/carer's capacity to meet, understand and enjoy the com-munication involved. Where the communication is one of distress, the infant needs the mother to make sense of this and respond in a way which both alleviates the distress and does not leave the baby with an over-whelming feeling of uncontainment and 'falling to pieces'. A colleague who observed Sikh friends with a new baby boy noted that part of his care involved his mother oiling his body and lovingly massaging his limbs and torso – an interaction clearly delighting both. While this example may be culture-specific, the need for the baby to feel that his body, and therefore his person, is wanted, understood and valued is an important one. The quality of touch in containing and confirming body boundaries can be seen in this vignette, as can the mother as *active* participant with her infant, calling forth and 'meeting' his capacities and ventures.

This sense of omnipotent functioning, of expecting and receiving a caring experience in line with one's needs, is described in different ways by various commentators: the caregiving mother of attachment theory, the 'dance' of the mother–infant dyad outlined by Daniel Stern (Stern 1977), and probably most famously the in-tune 'good-enough' mother of Winnicott's writings (Winnicott 1965). The critical experience for the infant is of being protected, kept safe, of maternal containment (Bion 1962). The corollary is to leave the infant with overwhelming anxieties that have to be coped with by pathological means: avoidance/denial/a recourse and retreat to the bodily self as the only available resource.

Freud termed the first stage of infant psychosexual development the 'oral stage': the infant uses the mouth to test objects, to gain pleasure, and a major focus of that pleasure is in the feeding relationship with the mother. Although the concept of infantile sexuality is one of Freud's most important legacies, it is important to keep in mind that this sexuality or 'proto-sexuality' of the infant is *not* the adult sexuality of equals. Thus total physical and emotional satisfaction can be engendered by a good experi-ence, such as a good feeding relationship where the infant's sensuality is met and encouraged by the touch and holding of the mother as the infant feeds. Winnicott describes the gradual move into reality made by the baby as the mother, in careful accordance with what the baby can manage, allows gentle frustration and 'an experience of disillusionment' (Winnicott 1953). Should the lessening availability of the mother occur at a pace with which the infant cannot cope, the immature sense of self is overwhelmed and a range of early defence mechanisms is called into play to deal with the primitive anxieties of annihilation, disintegration and abandonment. These, if they persist into childhood and adolescence, augur badly for peer relations and the capacity for independent functioning.

Although the focus of most commentators on the first months of childhood has been on the mother–child relationship, the work of attachment researchers has made us very aware of the infant's capacity and drive to engage and communicate with others in his environment. The role of fathers thus becomes important early on, not simply as the 'facilitating environment' described by Winnicott (1979), but also as an alternative to the intensity of the mother–infant dyad with its potential fears of merging and over-closeness. Wright (1997) has developed an elegant thesis about the father's place in the development of creativity: that the receptive, good-enough Winnicottian mother meets the infant's primary creativity and encourages it, while the father's role is to help the infant direct that creativity towards the outside world and to take advantage of what that world offers. The different nature of the father's relationship with his child is also outlined by Colarusso (1992), who finds that task-achievement, setting limits and looking outwards to being a socialised person in the world are part of the paternal function.

Toddlers

With mobility and further development of sensorimotor functions, the infant takes a major leap forward. In Chapter 24 the author describes the growing independence and assertiveness of the toddler. Ambivalence in the relationship with the mother who has to refuse his demands, the place of magical thinking ('I hate her therefore she has been made to go or been killed off by me'), and the growing capacity to integrate love and hate in the same person are features of this stage (Klein 1937). The child by two has a primary sense of gender and a sense of agency that is constantly exercised and tested. The anal stage of Freudian theory contains this sense of wilfulness, taking control for oneself, and the ability to enjoy saying 'No!' In the temper tantrum of the toddler can be seen a real sense of disbelief and acutely-felt insult to the omnipotent self that is now being challenged. The toddler begins to explore leaving mother, making sorties with her in sight, but returning to the secure base for reassurance and congratulations. This develops into the capacity to make the adults pursue the child, another significant sensation for the toddler. Games of escape and capture create high excitement but are not always tactfully located: the queue at the supermarket is an all too frequent venue. Language is developing and with it, the capacity to symbolise rather than to enact – to use words rather than the body of earliest childhood. Crucial progress lies in the affirmation of identity, now internalised, demonstrated in the appropriate use of 'I'. Play at this stage is still very much interactive with mother, but an ability to be 'alone in the presence of the object', engaged in his own fantasy, has developed (Winnicott 1958). Play with objects has not yet acquired symbolic content but seems to focus on tactile exploration of basic concepts – shape, sensation, hardness, softness – and on motor competencies of stacking and knocking over, pulling and pushing, as 'What can I do with this?' is investigated.

Finally, progress towards the use of 'transitional objects' (toys or materials like a comfort blanket, which can contain aspects of the mother–child relationship and so help in the tolerance of independence and absence) should be mentioned (Winnicott 1953). Such objects, often from very early infancy and treated with both attachment and contempt, provide a space that is transitional between infant-and-mother and infant-alone, an 'intermediate area of experience' (ibid.: 2). They can remain important to the child for many years.

The child's preoccupation with his anatomy is a feature of genital stage development: theories of difference between boys and girls emerge along with fears of castration in boys and reactions to male potency in girls. The sense of an internal space for babies in girls can be paralleled by an envy of this child-bearing capacity by boys. A more narcissistic, self-centred child appears, almost in preparation for the integrated identity that is consolidated after the Oedipal resolution.

Play

The ability to play is important for the growing child. Early creativity and curiosity depend greatly on the mother's attunement to her infant. Responsive playfulness and the potential to initiate play appear even before the infant is mobile, although mobility adds to the possibilities. The capacity for symbolisation is linked, psychoanalytically, to the perception of separateness from the mother and the need to bridge that gap. Although this differs from the inborn drive for engagement and communication seen by the attachment researchers, both approaches contain the inherent element of the need to attract and engage the primary person in the infant's life.

As the toddler grows, so does his ability to endow toys and play materials with genuinely symbolic meaning and his competence in using others in this play: the child who begins nursery may at first 'play alongside' others, but develop the ability to 'play with' as he advances. Earlier experiences of 'good-enough' attachments and separation of a non-overwhelming kind will obviously play a role in allowing the growing toddler the internal security that enables him to explore how he can interact with others safely and with curiosity (Furman 1992).

The purpose of play is diverse: a rehearsal for future life; dealing with anxiety and conflict; exploring the space between fantasy and reality; and cognitive and social experimentation. As one three-year-old reportedly said to Winnicott, 'Play is work, of course!' All toddlers at some time engage in play which copies the roles and tasks they have observed their parents undertake. This is not necessarily gender-specific and can be very fluid in the possibilities thus entertained. One may see precursors here to the use of day-dreaming in the adult, trying out possibilities and exploring dreams and hopes (Freud 1908; Rycroft 1974). Perhaps less obvious is the play which helps the child make sense of things which cause anxiety – the visit to the dentist repeated with a teddy bear as the patient or using dolls to re-enact a family quarrel or trauma. This ability to symbolise what has been feared and to place it outside, for perusal and hence to acquire control, is important for later adolescent and adult capacities to think, to gain mastery and not be overwhelmed, and helps in the process of not having to act out what might otherwise feel uncontainable. This is patently of importance in child psychotherapy where the child's capacity to symbolise anxiety through play is a route to unconscious conflicts (Klein 1955). When a child cannot play, it is the task of the therapist, through work on the immature ego and early attachments, to help the child's abilities develop safely.

Oedipal resolution and parental sexuality

In classical theory the importance of the Oedipal phase and its successful resolution cannot be overstressed. This involves the renouncing of the intense emotional relationship with the mother (most parents of boys will recall the stage where their child was certain that 'When I grow up I am going to marry Mummy'). Winnicott's description of the Oedipal child as 'all dressed up and nowhere to go' gives a succinct picture of infantile sexuality and passion (Winnicott 1964). For the boy, ambivalence in the relationship with the father, admired and feared as possessor of the mother and a potentially castrating rival for her, becomes gradually replaced by a developing closeness to an available father-figure, allowing identification with him and the outward-looking described earlier. For girls, the intensity of the maternal relationship is replaced with passion for the father who, equally unavailable as a sexual object, has to be renounced as partner. As the girl turns away from parental partners, identification with the mother becomes possible.

Most modern commentators would now view the significant parts of the Oedipal resolution as those centring on the realisation of parental sexuality and partnership, three-person relationships, and on the boundaries between adults and children, parents and offspring. For the child in a single-parent family, as for the child with two parents available, the *idea* of a parental relationship matters – that the parent living with the child does not decry adult partnership but can keep the possibility benignly in mind for the child. The child, therefore, turns from the parents and infantile amnesia sets in ('Did I used to do that? No I didn't!') and embarrassment at family myths and stories is common. The normally developing child will focus with relief on external peer relations and the continuing acquisition of skills and competencies as his cognitive development grows.

Hamilton (1993) in her eloquent reassessment of narcissism and the Oedipus complex offers an important and wider reinterpretation:

> The resolution of the Oedipus complex entails a renunciation; not only must the child give up the fantasy that he can have an exclusive relationship with the parent of the opposite sex, he must also accept that there is an objective order of things which he will never completely understand or control. In *some* cases this realisation is experienced as a castration or narcissistic blow. The blow is to the child's budding feelings of power and curiosity and to the satisfactions gained by learning.
>
> (Hamilton 1993: 273)

It is useful here to think a little further about the role of the parents immediately post-Oedipally. For the girl, identification with the mother and engaging in play as a rehearsal for her future as a woman is a feature. It is also vital, however, in the consolidation of her sense of femininity to have a sense of being valued as a girl by her father. For many of the girls who present with gender dysphoria, the emotional or physical absence of the father seems to play a part. The opposite process, with the mother, is important for boys. For parents it is vital that this affirmation of the opposite-sex child does not become sexualised and confusing.

At this point, one finds the presence of the capacity for guilt and shame: the child has an 'ego ideal', a sense of who he is and who he would like to be, based on internalisations of his parents and the 'self' they reflect back to him, and is aware when he falls short of achieving this internal ideal.

Psychoanalytic theoreticians differ as to the age at which such developments occur. Perhaps one could say that, while seeing development in absolute stages to be achieved by a particular age may not be helpful, to see a continuum of development on which the child takes up a changing position, according to nature, environment, growth and internalisation, is useful. Indeed 'most of the processes that start up in early infancy are never fully established, and continue to be strengthened by the growth that continues in later childhood, and indeed in adult life, even in old age' (Winnicott 1963).

The primary-school-aged child

With the move into school, other identifications not only become more available to the child but can also be useful in separating from and challenging the parents. 'But my teacher said . . .' is not unheard in families with latency children, as 'greater' external authority becomes internalised into what is initially a fairly rigid conscience or super-ego. 'Latency' (in psychosexual terms) or primary-school age is par excellence the time of rules, fairness and the acquisition of self-control, as the child struggles to leave behind the conflicts and embarrassing desires of the Oedipal stage and focuses on internalising mechanisms of competence and control. As the years go by, the severity of this conscience eases and an autonomous, non-persecuting super-ego should be established before the child has to deal with the changes and regressive pull of the pre-pubertal period.

This is the time of the 'family romance', the sense that one has been taken home by the wrong parents from the hospital or that there has been a dreadful mistake and really there are a princess and a pop star somewhere waiting sadly to find their real child. Such fantasies aid the necessary distancing of the child from the passion of earlier inter-familial feelings.

Children at this time tend mostly to play with their own sex. Clubs, groups and games with clear rules are important; new rules will be created but must be adhered to. A clear and rigid perception of right and wrong is at work. Nevertheless, there is also a delightful sense of subversion at this time – a glance at children's literature will show children defeating or being cleverer than the adults, and a gentle mocking of adult roles, hypocrisies and pretensions (Lurie 1991; Allen 1993). Indeed, few would now agree with the idea that sexuality has disappeared in a 'latency' phase. Although the intensity of parentally directed passion has lessened, children of this age are still developing theories about sex and explore these with peers, away from adult view. 'Doctors and nurses', with all its variations, is an early latency game, after all. Curiosity about the sexuality of others (outsiders, not family members who are simply embarrassing when they make children aware of sexuality and towards whom a certain prudishness can often be found) is ongoing and a rehearsal for adult wishes and possibilities. Identifications with heroes and idols are a feature of this age range – it is always interesting to note which pop stars appeal to pre-pubertal girls with a glossy but safely packaged sexuality and which become the heroes of the adolescent, when individuality of choice and discrimination are coming to the fore.

The rhythmic games of girls in the playground have long been seen as a sublimation of sexual feelings, enacted safely and physically. It is also possible to see the rough and tumble of boys' play, and the intrepid rush towards contact sports, as an affirming rehearsal for their adult sexuality as they establish a sense of boundary to their bodies in preparation for an adult penetrative role.

Puberty and adolescence

Adolescence begins with biology and ends with psychology. It is kick started by puberty and cruises slowly to a halt at adult identity, the point at which the petrol is getting low and we need to think about saving it for the long, straight road ahead.

(Van Heeswyk 1997)

This wry comment comes as the author notes the tendency of our profession to list developmental tasks as absolutes. For the child approaching puberty, comparison in any kind of straight-line physiological way with his peers may be the source more of anxiety than consolation. There is a gulf between the girl who reaches her menarche at nine and the one who desperately hopes that menstruation will start now that she is sixteen. Indeed, a rapidly changing body with its overture to adult sexual roles can be more difficult for the younger girl to encounter without the parallel experiences of her peers to support and confirm her feelings (Orford 1993). Similarly, the boy whose growth spurt comes later than his peers can find the idea of ever coping as an adult a terrifying and bizarre prospect. Shifts in the body self in pre-puberty (Tyson and Tyson 1990) can often be accompanied by regression in relationships with key adults: a swing back to the safety of previous experience in the face of the inevitability of adolescence.

Although puberty can often be presented as '*Sturm und Drang*', most young people make their way successfully through adolescence despite the projections of adult envy and adult fears that accompany every step. That said, there *are* important psychological negotiations to be made. 'Who will I be?' is the sub-text as the adolescent faces external, physiological and internal pressures about future role and identity.

Intimacy once more becomes an issue, but intimacy of *mind* as well as of the body. This can be perceived as finally taking over from the parents responsibility for and ownership of one's body at a time when the earliest sexual feelings of infancy are revived, but with the addition of a sexually functioning body: no longer 'all dressed up and nowhere to go' but potent. Adapting emotionally involves somehow making the parental intimacies less intense – a reworking of the oedipal experience. This occurs in the realm of ideas and opinions, too, where separation from parental assumptions and family values can feel shocking to suddenly disparaged parents. The silent adolescent is not a myth: keeping quiet keeps fantasy, thought and internal life private (the use of a personal diary is not uncommon), and helps with finding the optimal safe intimate distance as the adolescent seeks to accommodate change. The reluctance to care for the body – often a contentious issue in families in early puberty and perhaps an attempt to ignore the imperative of physiological and sexual changes – gives way to great attention and concern in later adolescence. Family pressures refocus on ownership of the bathroom. Acting via the body – discos, flirtation with drugs, alcohol and nicotine, sports, body piercing, sexual exploration – takes the teenager back to early mechanisms for dealing with what might feel unmanageable and rehearses possible futures. The capacity to tolerate this new, fluid body-self is crucial: adolescence is not surprisingly the risk time for eating disorders and suicide in those who find the move towards establishing an adult, sexual self too impossible a task.

The availability of peers and alternative adults takes on even greater priority in early and mid-adolescence than at earlier ages. This can be the time of the 'crush', of passionate feelings for same- and opposite-sex grown-ups and young people. Identifications are part of these, as is exploration and integration of aspects of others into a modified ideal, hoped-for self.

The use of the group in mid-adolescence provides a similar function to the relationship with a close, same-sex friend in early adolescence. The mirroring obtained from peers is important at this stage and is based on the early identity formation of infant years. The group, moreover, offers a variety of roles and the opportunity to share responsibility and irresponsibility, trying out different aspects of the self and perceiving these in others. The risk-taking that can be indulged in during adolescence has in it qualities of the omnipotence of the toddler stage, a heady disregard for danger that, it is assumed, will never ever strike personally. Failure in friendships and relationships with peers leaves the adolescent developmentally very handicapped in his resources for trying out himself in the world. Family pressure moves to 'Where were you?' or 'Where are you going?' and to the size of the telephone bill.

Mid-adolescence is also the time at which we place heavier educational burdens on the young, when intellectual challenge becomes serious and achievement or failure is seen in stark terms, incorporated into the fluidity which is the emerging identity. As with all aspects of adolescent development, there is a danger that this can polarise and the whole sense of self be felt to be bound up with progress in one single area. One can be left with a dramatic sense of 'all or nothing'; it is hard to keep open the transitional space so creative in early childhood (Hamilton 1993).

Theoretically, but not always in practice, by late adolescence 'stability of identity' (Tyson and Tyson 1990) has been achieved. No longer conflicted over parental relationships, the young person can find a disengaged intimacy with family, which allows rapprochement and appreciation. This occurs from a position of security as a separate, functioning young adult.

Approaching adulthood: conclusions

There is, in psychoanalytic theory, an assumption that one achieves adulthood by about twenty-five years of age. This entails a developed capacity for intimacy, responsibility and autonomy. Perhaps this is so. Perhaps, on the other hand, it is also important for us, in adulthood, to retain something of the fluidity of childhood and adolescence: the tolerance of states of not knowing, the curiosity to engage with the world, a sense of playfulness linked to the aptitude to be creative with ideas (Winnicott, after all, in 1971 described psychotherapy as 'done in the overlap of two play areas, that of the patient and that of the therapist') and the ability (however muddled the prospects might seem) to greet change as an indicator of further potential in our lives as social beings. In adulthood, we should not lose the developmental strengths of childhood.

References

Allen, N. (1993) *The Queen's Knickers*, London: Red Fox.

Bion, W. R. (1962) *Learning from Experience*, London: Heinemannn.

Colarusso, C. A. (1992) *Child and Adult Development: A Psychoanalytic Intro-duction for Clinicians*, New York/London: Plenum Press.

Daws, D. (1989) *Through the Night: Helping Parents and Sleepless Infants*, London: Free Association Books.

Freud, A. (1965) *Normality and Pathology in Childhood: Assessments of Develop-ment*, New York: International Universities Press.

Freud, S. (1908) 'Creative writers and day-dreaming', *SE* 9: 141–53, London: Hogarth Press.

Furman, E. (1992) *Toddlers and their Mothers*, Madison, CT: International Universities Press.

Hamilton, V. (1993) *Narcissus and Oedipus: The Children of Psychoanalysis*, 2nd edn, London: Karnac.

Klein, M. (1937) 'Love, guilt and reparation', in (1975) *Love, Guilt and Reparation and Other Works 1921–1945: The Writings of Melanie Klein*, Vol. I, London: Hogarth Press.

—— (1955) 'The psychoanalytic play technique: its history and significance', in M. Klein *et al.* (eds) *New Directions in Psychoanalysis*, London: Tavistock.

Lurie, A. (1991) *Not in Front of the Grown-ups: Subversive Children's Literature*, London: Sphere Books.

Orford, E. (1993) *Understanding your 11 Year Old*, Tavistock Clinic series, London: Rosendale Press.

Rycroft, C. (1974) 'Is Freudian symbolism a myth?', in P. Fuller (ed.) *Psychoanalysis and Beyond*, London: Hogarth Press, 1985.

Stern, D. (1977) 'Mis-steps in the dance', in *The First Relationship: Infant and Mother*, London: Fontana/Open Books.

—— (1985) *The Interpersonal World of the Human Infant*, New York: Basic Books.

Tyson, P. and Tyson, R. L. (1990) *Psychoanalytic Theories of Development: An Integration*, New Haven: Yale University Press.

van Heeswyk, P. (1997) *Analysing Adolescence*, London: Sheldon Press.

Winnicott, D. W. (1953) 'Transitional objects and transitional phenomena', in *Playing and Reality*, Harmondsworth: Penguin, 1971.

—— (1958) 'The capacity to be alone', in *The Maturational Processes and the Facilitating Environment*, London: Hogarth Press, 1979.

—— (1963) 'The development of the capacity for concern', in *The Maturational Processes and the Facilitating Environment*, London: Hogarth Press, 1979.

—— (1964) 'The child and sex', in *The Child, the Family and the Outside World*, Harmondsworth: Penguin.

—— (1965) *The Family and Individual Development*, London: Tavistock.

—— (1971) 'Playing: creative activity and the search for self', in *Playing and Reality*, London: Tavistock.

—— (1979) *The Maturational Processes and the Facilitating Environment*, London: Hogarth Press.

Wright, K. (1997) 'Stories of creation', paper given at Annual Conference of British Association of Psychotherapists, November 1997.

Further reading

Brazelton, T. B. and Cramer, B. G. (1991) *The Earliest Relationship: Parents, Infants and the Drama of Early Attachment*, London: Karnac.

Colarusso, C. A. (1992) *Child and Adult Development: A Psychoanalytic Introduction for Clinicians*, New York/London: Plenum Press.

Furman, E. (1992) *Toddlers and their Mothers*, Madison, CT: International Universities Press.

Hindle, D. and Vaciago Smith, M. (1999) *Lectures in Personality Development: A Psychoanalytic Perspective*, London: Routledge.

Solnit, A. J., Cohen, D. J. and Neubauer, P. B. (eds) (1993) *The Many Meanings of Play: A Psychoanalytic Perspective*, New Haven/London: Yale University Press.

Tyson, P. and Tyson, R. L. (1990) *Psychoanalytic Theories of Development: An Integration*, New Haven, CT: Yale University Press.

van Heeswyk, P. (1997) *Analysing Adolescence*, London: Sheldon Press.

Waddell, M. (1998) *Inside Lives: Psychoanalysis and the Growth of the Personality*, London: Duckworth.

Winnicott, D. W. (1964) *The Child, the Family and the Outside World*, Harmondsworth: Penguin Books.

4 Some contributions of attachment theory and research

Juliet Hopkins and Gail Phillips

Attachment theory developed from the pioneering work of John Bowlby (1907–1990), a British child psychiatrist and psychoanalyst. At a time when many psychoanalysts were focusing their attention on the role of internal factors, such as instinct and fantasy, in the development of psychopathology, Bowlby turned his attention to the role of external factors which he believed to be of more significance. He intended, following Freud, that psychoanalysis should be respected, not only as a method of psychotherapy, but as a reputable science, 'the science of unconscious mental processes' (Freud 1925: 70). Since scientific research begins with observation, Bowlby decided to study the responses of young children to separation and bereavement, for these could be accurately observed and were thought likely to be of pathogenic significance.

Bowlby's early observations of young children, separated from their parents in hospitals or institutions, revealed that they characteristically passed through three phases of response to their loss: protest, despair and detachment. Each of these phases could be seen to be linked to a particular psychoanalytic concept: separation anxiety (threat of loss), grief and mourning (acceptance of loss) and defence (protection from the pain of loss). To these central concepts, Bowlby added another: the nature of the child's tie to the parent (or main caregiver) which could be disrupted or lost. This tie he termed attachment. In the course of his study of attachment and loss Bowlby found it necessary to reformulate psychoanalytic theory in terms compatible with modern scientific thinking and with empirical findings. His aim was to develop hypotheses which could be tested by research. His trilogy *Attachment and Loss* (1969, 1973, 1980) combines ideas from ethology, systems theory and cognitive psychology.

This chapter aims to introduce the biological basis for attachment theory and to describe some of the findings from subsequent attachment research which are of value for child psychotherapists.

Evolution and the need for attachment

Bowlby approached the early mother–child relationship from the stand-point of a biologist concerned with the central biological theory of our time: evolution. Our hunter-gatherer ancestors inhabited an environment in which only the fittest survived to reproduce and our instinctive behaviour must have evolved to increase our chances of survival in these conditions. Bowlby avoids Freud's use of the term 'instinct' with its outmoded concept of some internal driving force, and prefers the term 'instinctive behaviour'. This, in accordance with modern ethology, is conceived as a pattern which is activated or terminated by particular internal or environmental conditions and can be observed.

Attachment behaviour is an excellent example of such instinctive behaviour. Bowlby conceives of it as being separate from the instinctive systems subserving feeding and sexual behaviour. Its aim is proximity or contact and its subjective goal is felt security. It is activated in infancy by the internal conditions of fatigue, hunger, pain, illness and cold and by external conditions indicating increased risk: darkness, loud noises, sudden movements, looming shapes and solitude. When it is activated the child seeks contact with one of his particular attachment figures whom he has learned to discriminate.

Babies are clearly pre-programmed at birth to learn the specific details of a few caregiving adults. They show their capacity to discriminate by their preference for their caregiver's qualities. Although clear preferences develop from birth, the full intensity of the baby's attachment behaviour is only manifest from the latter half of the first year.

Bowlby's evolutionary perspective offers us a simple explanation of the development of infants' fears. In the second half of the first year babies become increasingly afraid of strangers, heights, the dark and solitude. This development can be understood as a maturational concomitant of the baby's new capacity for independent locomotion, a capacity which clearly increases the risk of encountering danger. Natural selection has equipped infants with a behavioural repertoire which increases their tendency to seek proximity to their mother at times of increased risk. There is no need to postulate the irrational projection of hostility to explain infantile fears, although of course such fears can be increased by projection. Typically, the very timid, fearful baby is one who has learned to expect that his attachment figure will not be reliably available when he is distressed; this is certainly a realistic cause for both fear and anger.

Bowlby's initial research focused on the effects of physical separation of young children from their parents. Later attachment research has focused on the nature of the mother's availability when she is present – her sensitivity and responsiveness. Evidence shows that the toddler who knows his mother is physically and emotionally available when he needs her can use her as a secure base from which to venture to explore his environment. He can concentrate well and play independently because he feels safe. Further research has also shown a strong positive correlation between the security of children's attachments and their capacity to co-operate with adults, to concentrate on play, to persist at problem-solving and to be popular with peers.

The concept of security is not entirely new to psychoanalysis. In 1959 Sandler suggested the notion of safety as a feeling state quite distinct from sensual pleasure. He went on to describe how patients might thwart analytic work by regressing to childhood relationships associated with punishment or pain, because the security associated with these relationships made them more rewarding than the insecurity and isolation belonging to new ventures not associated with familiar parent figures. A 'negative therapeutic reaction' may be a return to a secure base.

Security of attachment: the observed infant

Since biologists have found each organism to be highly adapted to its environment, Bowlby always supposed the infant to be more influenced by real aspects of parenting than by internal fantasy. This assumption has been supported by Ainsworth's research (Ainsworth *et al.* 1971), which reveals that certain characteristics of a mother's parenting are more important for determining the infant's security of attachment at a year than any innate quality of the infant that has yet been assessed.

Ainsworth's 'Strange Situation test' has been widely used to provide an assessment of infant security. In this standardised test the infant is left briefly alone in a strange room and then reunited with his mother: his reactions on reunion are considered indicative of the nature of his security with his mother, since they reveal the expectations he has developed about her physical and emotional availability when he is afraid.

Secure attachment (Group B)

In general, patterns of behaviour on reunion with mother fall into two broad categories. The exact proportions of babies falling into each category vary with the sample (many nationalities have been assessed), but roughly speaking nearly two-thirds of babies are rated as securely attached. On reunion these babies immediately seek contact with their mother: on being picked up they are quickly comforted by her and they soon ask to be put down so that they can pursue their exploration of the toys provided. They may express some anger with mother, especially if she tries to interest them in the toys too soon, but their crossness is easily assuaged. These babies can be said to have developed basic trust.

Insecure attachment

The remaining third of babies are classified as anxiously attached. These babies have developed either of two major strategies: avoidance or resistance. Psychotherapists are clinically familiar with the distinction between these two solutions to insecurity: the self-sufficient avoidants who seek safety in independence and the clinging resistants who rely on physical proximity to feel safe, but never feel satisfied. The revelation of Ainsworth's research is that these defensive patterns of response to stress are clearly established by the first birthday.

Avoidant attachment (Group A)

The characteristic response of these babies on reunion in the Strange Situation is not to greet their mother, and, in some instances, not even to look at her. Any approaches tend to be abortive. If picked up they may lean away or squirm to get down. Frequently they divert their mother's attention to a toy or distant object. However, it is clearly perplexing that stressful events which normally heighten attachment behaviour apparently diminish it. Bowlby (1988: 132) interprets the avoidant response to indicate that 'already by the age of twelve months there are children who no longer express to mother one of their deepest emotions, nor their equally deep-seated desire for comfort and assurance that accompanies it'.

It is sometimes supposed that autistic children make avoidant attachments. However, research has shown that autistic children manifest the entire range of attachment patterns and that for children with less severe symptoms of autism there is no difference in the distribution of attachment patterns from that in the normal population.

Ambivalent or resistant attachment (Group C)

These babies are intensely upset by the separation and are highly ambivalent to the mother on her return. They want to be close to her but are angry with her and so are very difficult to soothe. They cling, resist being put down and are slow to return to play.

As Ainsworth has pointed out, the psychological significance of the three patterns of attachment behaviour which she described rests upon their association both with mother–infant interaction observed in the home, and with their predictable continuity over time.

Observations in the home

Observations in the home reveal that the reaction of babies in the Strange Situation is related to the nature of the mothering which they have received during their first year.

(a) Briefly, babies with a secure attachment have mothers who have proved sensitively responsive to their babies' signals and physically accessible. Their babies are observed to be happier and more co-operative than babies who manifest an insecure attachment.

Recent research (Cassidy *et al.* 2005) suggests that it is maternal responsiveness specifically to infant attachment behaviour that is crucial for security. Indeed, unusually high global sensitivity has been associated with insecurity.

(b) Babies with an avoidant response generally have mothers who are restricted in their range of emotional expression and who exhibit an aversion to close physical contact; these are babies whose bids for comforting have been consistently rebuffed. Their mothers hold and carry them less comfortably than other mothers do, tending to avoid close ventro-ventral contact. Their babies have been found to be no less cuddly at birth than other babies are, but by a year they neither cuddle nor cling but are carried like a sack of potatoes.

(c) Babies with an ambivalent attachment generally have mothers who enjoy physical contact, but who provide it erratically, often in response to their own needs rather than in response to their babies' needs. Their babies' anger towards them can be understood as an attempt both to express frustration at their inconsistent handling, and to force their mothers to provide the care and comfort of which they know they are capable.

Fathers

Another major finding has emerged from attachment research. Contrary to psychoanalytic expectation, the infant's relationship to his father (or other major caregiver) cannot be predicted from the nature of his relationship to his mother. It is independent of it and reflects the qualities which the father himself has brought to the relationship. This means, moreover, that the nature of the infant's security is not a function of his general temperament but depends on the history of interaction which he has had with each caregiver.

Internalisation

Bowlby (1973: 203) developed the idea of 'internal working models' to resolve some of the difficulties inherent in the psychoanalytic concept of 'internal objects' and to explain the tendency for a child's attachment patterns gradually to become a property of himself. Although the family context continues to influence the child, the perpetuation of his attachment patterns becomes increasingly a matter of self-regulation. As Bowlby (ibid.) describes, 'present cognitive and behavioural structures determine what is perceived and what ignored, how a new situation is construed, and what plan of action is likely to be constructed to deal with it. Current structures, moreover, determine what sorts of person and situation are sought after and what sorts are shunned. In this way an individual comes to influence the selection of his own environment.'

It is proposed that the infant constructs models of the world which enable him to interpret events, predict the future and plan action. Because working models of relationships develop in transaction, the child internalises both sides of the relationship, and the working models of the parent and of the self are complementary. For example, if a child has experienced reliably responsive caregiving he will construct a working model of the self as competent and lovable, but if he has experienced much rebuff he will construct a model of the self as unworthy of help and comfort.

For a relationship to proceed optimally each partner must have reliable working models of each other, which can be revised and updated in accord with communication between them. Here there is a striking difference between the directness of communication between the secure and insecure infants and their mothers. Secure couples show more eye contact, verbalisation, emotional expression and shared interaction with toys than do insecure pairs. This disparity is even more marked when the infants are distressed. The secure infants remain in direct communication with mothers and express their anger, fear and desire for her, while avoidant infants only engage in direct communication when they are content.

These differences persist. Main *et al.*'s longitudinal study (1986) found that at six years of age children with mothers who had shown a secure pattern of attachment five years earlier engaged in free-flowing conversation, including a wide range of topics, personal issues and expression of feelings. Six-year-old children who had had an avoidant pattern with mother at a year had limited conversations which avoided both personal issues and feelings.

Intergenerational transmission

After Ainsworth, the next major step in attachment research was taken when Main *et al.* (1986) established that there was a significant correlation between the nature of a child's attachment to a parent and that parent's state of mind with regard to attachment. This was achieved by means of the Adult Attachment Interview (AAI), which questions parents about their childhood experiences with their own parents, especially with regard to the occurrence of separations, loss, trauma and abuse and the availability of supportive, comforting and confiding experiences. The parents' responses are analysed according to their capacity to produce a coherent, relevant and collaborative text and the nature of their defensiveness. They reveal as much by the nature of their communication to the interviewer as they do by the content of their replies.

Parents of insecurely attached infants are alike in giving accounts which typically are characterised by unrecognised inconsistencies and contradictions, but their accounts also differ from each other's in predictable ways. Parents likely to have avoidant infants generally give brief accounts, partly because they minimise the importance of relationships and partly because they tend to have forgotten childhood experiences. They are likely to make generalised statements about having had happy childhoods, but to be unable to support this with evidence, which is either lacking or contradictory. They are termed Dismissive.

Parents likely to have resistant infants generally give a lengthy account of unhappy, entangled relationships with ample evidence that they have remained entangled with their own parents or with memories of them. They are termed Entangled.

In contrast to the parents of insecurely attached infants, the parents of securely attached infants generally give a fluent, consistent and coherent account of their childhoods in which they treat relationships with significance and recall events with appropriate affect. They are termed Free. The vast majority of these parents have had secure childhoods themselves, but among them are a number who recall childhoods of extreme unhappiness and rejection. They have thought and felt deeply about their experiences and have tried to understand them. Some of them have remained very angry with their parents while others have achieved forgiveness. The outcome of this research clearly supports the clinical finding that the repetition of adverse childhood relationships can be avoided when adults come to terms with their unhappy past.

Insecure disorganised/disoriented attachment (Group D)

Not all infants were found to fit neatly into Ainsworth's three groups. The discovery of the disorganised/disoriented (D) attachment group (Main and Solomon 1986) coincided with the first findings of the AAI. Whereas infants with insecure avoidant and ambivalent attachments have developed consistent strategies for dealing with stress on reunion, infants with D attachment have not. In the Strange Situation they reveal their inability to cope in a wide variety of disorganised or disoriented behaviour. For example, the infant may exhibit a simultaneous display of contradictory behaviour patterns, such as approaching with head averted, or may fall prone, freeze motionless or show tic-like stereotypies. Usually disorganised behaviours occur in conjunction with attempts to employ an organised attachment strategy, so infants may be classified A/D, C/D or even B/D.

Much research is needed on the complex antecedents of this very varied group, but it is generally agreed that their parents have been frightening or frightened or both. Infants' innate responses to fear (to flee, freeze or fight) conflict with the organised attachment strategies and disrupt them. When the course of a child's security is also a source of fear, the child is placed in a paradoxical position of irresolvable and self-perpetuating conflict that disorganises both cognition and behaviour.

Not surprisingly, a high proportion of D attachments is regularly found among maltreating samples, but an average of 15 per cent is found among normal populations. One of the striking findings from the AAI is that parents whose responses reveal that they are suffering from unresolved grief or trauma predictably have infants with a D attachment. It seems that at times they must convey their underlying fear in threatening, dissociative or fearful behaviour. In some cases the baby itself can be the trigger for the parent's alarm.

Longitudinal studies have shown that for the majority of infants the helplessness associated with disorganised behaviour is mastered through the development of controlling behaviour. This may be predominantly bossy or punitive or may be solicitous and caregiving. At age six years, children who were D with mother in infancy express catastrophic fantasies in their play or story telling or else are too inhibited to express their imagination at all. Some stories contain uncanny examples of actions without an agent, as though the children have had mysteriously inexplicable experiences with their parent. Some children reveal ideas of having a bad self. In adolescence there is increased liability to dissociative disorders.

The infant's contribution

What part do individual differences between babies play in the development of their security at a year? Infant temperament is not a significant factor in the development of security, as shown by the findings that security with mother and with father are independent of each other, and that either can change with changes in parental availability. Indeed the overall findings of attachment research are firmly weighted in favour of the overriding influence of parental care in determining infant security.

However, statistical generalisations can be misleading when it comes to the consideration of individual cases. The majority of attachment research has been carried out on samples of normal, healthy, full-term babies. Ainsworth herself has acknowledged that the effect of infant behaviour on the mother might be much greater among infants thought to be developmentally at risk.

As attachment research expands more is being learned about the infant's contribution. For example, the neonate's ability to orient towards a face has been found to be correlated with secure attachment at a year while babies whom neonatal nurses found difficult were more likely to develop insecure attachments.

Recently genetic research has revealed that infants are differentially susceptible to developing a D attachment in response to parental loss or trauma according to the presence of a certain gene. This confirms clinical intuition that some children are innately more vulnerable than others.

Changes in attachment pattern

Attempts to predict the course of child development from individual characteristics assessed during the first year have always failed, but the nature of the child's attachments both to mother and to father at the first birthday have emerged as factors with significant predictive power. This must be because the attachment pattern is an aspect of a relationship, not just of the child himself, so as long as the child continues within the same relationship, the stability of the attachment pattern is high.

However, changes in attachment patterns do occur and they are found to be a function of the availability of the parent concerned. For example, with regard to mothers, attachments are likely to become more secure if mother gets more support. Attachment to mother may become less secure when mother works long hours, gives birth to a sibling, is depressed or bereaved. Another potential source of insecurity is trauma of parent and/or child that destroys basic trust. As the child grows older his attachment pattern becomes increasingly a property of himself, and is less responsive to changes in parenting. Individual psychotherapy may then be needed to increase the security of an insecure child. Before this, therapeutic work with the insecure child and his parent(s) is likely to be the treatment of choice.

Attachment disorders

The term 'attachment disorder' is not synonymous with an insecure or disorganised attachment pattern, but is a medical term used to describe a condition, which requires treatment, and which meets diagnostic criteria (see ICD-10 and DSM-IV-TR). It describes disturbed relationship patterns, arising before the age of five, in children with a history which has left them without a consistently available primary caregiver, and where the difficulties cannot be attributed to other disorders. Classification can be as 'reactive' or 'inhibited' on the one hand, and 'disinhibited' on the other.

A child with inhibited attachment disorder shows contradictory behaviour socially, often replacing effective attachment behaviour with a mixture of extreme watchfulness, and ambivalent behaviours of a sort similar to those seen in children with Group D attachment. In such cases, it might be suggested that environmental deficit has led to a failure to activate appropriate attachment behaviour. In children with disinhibited attachment disorders, attachment behaviours are activated, but in a 'promiscuous' way, often directed towards relative strangers rather than a discriminated primary caregiver. For such children, the instinct to seek proximity, which so enhances chances of survival, has required that any available, though not necessarily appropriate, adult, be treated as a potential source of safety.

Adoption

Attachment-based interventions designed to help children with attachment disorders, or insecure attachment organisation, seek to address the deficit in the child's environment through the provision of responsive caregiving. This may be by way of work to enhance the sensitivity of an existing caregiver, or may, more radically, involve a change in caregiver, as in adoption. Research with adopted children has been helpful in looking at whether it is possible for more secure attachments to be formed after the developmentally appropriate age. Such children are likely to have histories of neglect, abuse and instability, and, therefore, to have established insecure patterns of attachment. Studies have included those of children brought up in extremely adverse settings, such as those from Romanian orphanages.

Broadly speaking, indications are that adopted children show an increase in attachment security in the relationship with their new, permanent caregivers. Improvements are particularly apparent in those placed in infancy, but have been seen in children adopted well into latency. Research has allowed an exploration of the roles of the child and the caregiver in the establishment of the new relationship.

Improvement in attachment status of the child is closely correlated with the attachment status of the permanent caregivers, as measured by the AAI (Dozier *et al.* 2001; Steele *et al.* 2003). The attachment status of caregivers needs to be seen alongside that of adopted children, looking at what each brings to the new relationship, and the interaction between them in attachment terms. The 2003 paper suggests that care needs to be taken in matching children and adopters with regard to attachment status, and that 'a secure, reflective adult' may *not* always be best placed as a carer to a particularly damaged child; they point out, for instance, that a high proportion of successful adopters of more damaged children are rated as insecure-dismissing, and suggest that such adopters are less likely to require the reciprocity of positive interactions which might be difficult for such children to provide.

A new, consistently available, sensitive caregiver provides the child with a figure to whom a secure attachment might be made. However, unless the internal models, or mental representations and expectations, of the child are able to change following adoption, a shift in attachment pattern is impossible. Such models are relied on by children in their attempts to predict the response of caregivers in a given situation. Children with expectations that their attachment needs will not be met commonly not only anticipate caregiving behaviour which will meet their established model, but unconsciously seek to provoke in the new caregiver behaviour which meets these expectations. Relinquishing established defences against frightening situations requires the child to trust, and to do so in the face of a wealth of experience which suggests to him that this is likely to lead to exposure to intolerable anxiety.

Jill Hodges, Miriam Steele and colleagues have looked at the impact of previous maltreatment on the ways in which the internal models of adopted children changed over the years following their adoption (Hodges *et al.* 2005). The children were assessed using a narrative tool, the Story Stem Assessment Profile (see Chapter 6). The profile uses a battery of carefully chosen story stems, each of which provides the child with the beginning of a story which he is invited to continue, using words and play. The way in which the child develops the story reflects the model he has developed of the relationship between child and adult in situations in which one might expect to see attachment behaviour activated or attachment defences mobilised. The authors found subtle changes in components of the children's attachment organisation over the two years following adoption, with clear differences between those adopted in infancy and those adopted with histories of maltreatment. While positive improvements in the children's internal working models of attachment relationships were found, particularly where there was a lower level of abuse in their histories, they also found that negative representations continued alongside and in competition with these, allowing the formation of multiple models.

The benefits and challenges of individual psychotherapy with looked after and adopted children are explored more fully in Chapter 21. Work with adoptive parents is helpful in aiding an understanding that the continuing, negative representations in the child's mind are not incompatible with the establishment of those that are more positive, and in helping parents to avoid provoking the responses on which the child has hitherto relied. Individual psychotherapy provides the child with an object, in the therapist, in relation to whom attachment difficulties and associated anxieties can be explored, and a more secure attachment tested. Moves towards the development of trust in the therapist facilitate the establishment of a positive attachment relationship with the adoptive parent (Hopkins 2000).

Reflective functioning or mentalisation

Fonagy *et al.* (1991) approached the analysis of the AAI from a new angle. They found that it was possible to predict a baby's security in the second year not only from the parent's security in pregnancy but also from the parent's capacity for reflective function, later termed mentalisation. These new terms refer to the capacity to understand and interpret behaviour in terms of mental states and intentions, both of oneself and others. Subsequently Fonagy and Target (2003) developed a model that explored the role of the caregiver in facilitating the child's development of mentalisation. The model also considers the psychopathology of this process. For example, the authors believe that mentalisation can only fully emerge in a secure attachment that enables the child to feel safe enough to explore the mind of the caregiver, while children who experience maltreatment may defensively inhibit the capacity to mentalise. There is much of significance for our profession in the model which is firmly rooted in attachment theory.

Attachment research continues to present us with new findings. Bowlby's development of Freud's 'science of unconscious mental processes' has provided the evidence base from which a new science of developmental psychopathology is growing.

References

Ainsworth, M. D. S., Bell, S. M. V. and Stayton, D. J. (1971) 'Individual differences in strange situation behaviour of one-year-olds', in H. R. Schaffer (ed.) *The Origins of Human Social Relationships*, London: Academic Press.

Bowlby, J. (1969/1982) *Attachment and Loss, Vol. 1: Attachment*, London: Hogarth.

—— (1973) *Attachment and Loss, Vol. 2: Separation*, London: Hogarth.

—— (1980) *Attachment and Loss, Vol. 3: Loss, Sadness and Depression*, London: Hogarth.

—— (1988) *A Secure Base. Clinical Applications of Attachment Theory*, London: Routledge.

Cassidy, J., Woodhouse, S., Cooper, G., Hoffman, K., Powell, B. and Rodenburg, M. (2005) 'Examination of the precursors of infant attachment security: implications for early intervention and intervention research', in L. Berlin, Y. Ziv, L. Amaya-Jackson and M. Greenburg (eds) *Enhancing Early Attachments: Theory, Research, Intervention and Policy*, New York: The Guilford Press.

Dozier, M., Stovall, K., Albus, K. and Bates, B. (2001) 'Attachment for infants in foster care: the role of care-giver state of mind', *Child Development* 72: 1467–77.

Freud, S. (1925) 'An autobiographical study'. *SE* 20.

Fonagy, P. and Target, M. (2003) *Psychoanalytic Theories. Perspectives from Developmental Pathology*, London and Philadelphia: Whurr Publishers.

Fonagy, P., Steele, H. and Steele, M. (1991) 'Maternal representations of attachment during pregnancy predict the organization of infant-mother attachment at one year of age', *Child Development* 62: 891–905.

Hodges, J., Steele, M., Hillman, S., Henderson, K. and Kaniuk, J. (2005) 'Change and continuity in mental representations of attachment after adoption', in D. Brodzinsky and J. Palacios (eds) *Psychological Issues in Adoption Research and Practice*, Westport, CT: Praeger.

Hopkins, J. (2000) 'Overcoming a child's resistance to late adoption: how one new attachment can facilitate another', *Journal of Child Psychotherapy* 26(3): 335–47.

Main, M. and Solomon, J. (1986) 'Discovery of an insecure disorganized/disoriented attachment pattern', in T. Brazelton and M. Yogman (eds) *Affective Development in Infancy*, Norwood, NJ: Ablex.

Main, M., Kaplan, N. and Cassidy, J. (1986) 'Security in infancy, childhood and adulthood: a move to the level of representation', in I. Bretherton and E. Waters (eds) *Growing Points of Attachment Theory and Research*, Monograph 50 of the Society for Research in Child Development, pp. 66–104.

Sandler, J. (1959) 'The background of safety', in *From Safety to Superego*, London: Karnac Books, 1987.

Steele, M., Hodges, J., Kaniuk, J., Hillman, S. and Henderson, K. (2003) 'Attachment representations and adoption: associations between maternal states of mind and emotion narratives in previously maltreated children', *Journal of Child Psychotherapy* 29(2): 187–205.

Further reading

The most recent comprehensive survey of research:

Prior, V. and Glaser, D. (2006) *Understanding Attachment and Attachment*

Disorders. Theory, Evidence and Practice, Child and Adolescent Mental Health Series, London and Philadelphia: Jessica Kingsley Publishers.

Attachment issues written for a psychoanalytic readership:
Journal of the American Psychoanalytic Association (2000) 48(4): 1055ff, 'Psychoanalysis, Development and the Life Cycle'.

5 Neuroscience and child psychotherapy

Graham Music

Introduction

There have been many developments in our understanding of children's psychological and emotional development in recent decades, but no field has altered more dramatically and presented more challenges that that of neuroscience. In this chapter I will outline some of the main developments, in an uncomplicated way, and consider just what impact this new research might have both on our understanding of children's psyches and on how we might actually work clinically with children and adolescents. Of course neuroscience is by no means new to psychoanalysis. Freud himself, with his neurological training, showed enormous prescience in predicting the kind of developments that would not actually occur for another century: 'we must recollect that all our provisional ideas in psychology, will presumably some day be based on an organic superstructure' (Freud 1914: 78).

Innovations such as the MRI scan have opened up to scientific examination vast areas of brain functioning heretofore hidden from view. In the past our knowledge was gleaned only by cruder means such as autopsies on dead brains: if the brains of a dead person with a particular disorder showed a particular organic feature then scientists assumed that the symptom was due to organic causes, with no idea that experiences might affect the brain. Although neuroscience might still be in its infancy, our understanding is becoming more sophisticated, and it is now possible to observe, through scans, brain activity corresponding to very specific emotional states such as excitement or fear.

I will try to keep to the least technical and most clinically pertinent features of the research, taking in some fascinating facts about the human brain and its evolutionary history, about how experience affects both the architecture of the brain and its hormonal system, about the impact of trauma and neglect on the brain, in passing touching on mirror neurons and on some questions about memory and how emotional learning and remembering takes root. The chapter will also pay some attention to differences between right and left brain functioning, and – without any of us needing to be neuroscientists – I hope to convey a sense of the role of a few of the key parts of the brain that seem central to emotional functioning. Thinking about such matters can prod us to consider carefully what we prioritise in the therapeutic process and also raises questions about whether we should be hopeful or pessimistic about the possibility of change and growth after the first few years of life.

The brain: some facts and evolutionary history

Our brains are highly complicated and able to make incredibly complex calculations about psychological matters via almost infinite links and complex structures, within fractions of seconds. The fundamental units of the brain are 'neurons', which are long entities with a central nucleus (containing genes), and long extensions called axons (Figure 5.1).

Neurons connect to each other via synapses, which enable the transmission of neurotransmitters, which can then fire neuronal activity further 'downstream'. The average neuron incredibly connects directly to 10,000 other neurons and the average brain has 100 billion neurons. Each neuron has one or more axons, which send messages to other neurons, and axons branch so that there are far more synapses than neurons. In fact Pinker (2002) refers to 100 trillion synapses in the human brain. Each neuron has a cell body and tens of thousands of tiny branches (dendrites) which do the receiving via electro-chemical messages. A piece of brain the size of a grain of sand contains 100,000 neurons, 2 million axons and a billion synapses (Siegel 1999).

Furthermore different parts of our complex brains have evolved at different stages in our evolutionary history and serve different functions. Although slightly simplified, MacLean's (1985) concept of the triune brain is a useful starting point. This theory states that human brains can be related to three main stages in our evolutionary history: the reptilian brain, the limbic system and the neocortex (Figure 5.2).

Many aspects of our brain functioning have changed little since the reptilian brain reached its most advanced stage some 250 million years ago in reptiles, although it first evolved in fish 500 million years ago. As well as controlling things like heart rate, breathing, temperature and balance, it contains structures such as the brain stem which controls ancient but vital survival instincts, the best known of course being 'fight, flight or freeze', physiological and psychological states we see all too often in traumatised children. Some 100 million years later, with mammals, the limbic system came into existence, maybe the region that psychotherapists particularly interact with as it is really the seat of our emotional life, and concerns how we make judgements, learn whether an experience is likely to be pleasurable or not, and how we form emotional memories. It also contains vital structures that I will return to later, such as the amygdala and the hippocampus. The 'new kid on the block' is the neocortex, a mere two or three

A NEURON

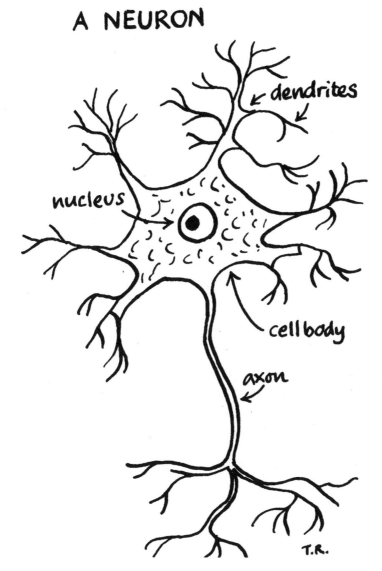

Figure 5.1

million years old, and its most complex form is seen in humans with our two cerebral hemispheres, responsible for human thought, language, imagination and consciousness.

It might be that the cerebral cortex undertakes, albeit loosely, many of the 'higher' functions that Freud believed resided in the ego, and which he saw as more highly evolved. An exercise I quite often undertake with myself when working with patients is to ask whether it is the reptilian or

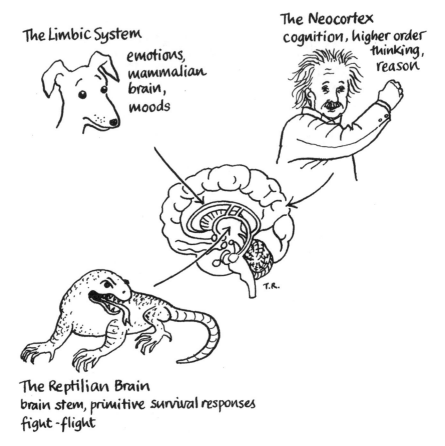

THE TRIUNE BRAIN
(after Maclean)

The Limbic System
emotions,
mammalian
brain,
moods

The Neocortex
cognition, higher order
thinking,
reason

T.R.

The Reptilian Brain
brain stem, primitive survival responses
fight-flight

Figure 5.2

mammalian brains or the cerebral cortex that is active at a particular moment. Basic instinctual responses emanate from the reptilian brain, responses such as hate, lust, aggression, and particularly the powerful defensive strategies of fight, flight or freeze. If one is confronted by massive anger or hatred in a child who at that moment has a highly active brain stem and is in 'fight' mode, it is folly to make an intellectually complex comment that only the cerebral cortex could make sense of, as those more complex parts of the brain are not active at such moments. Similarly, how often might we engage with intellectually advanced but emotionally fragile adolescents in territory they feel all too comfortable with, intellectual ideas, whilst the terrifying emotional issues lurking below the surface are sidestepped? Of course more and more we work with children whose emotional lives have been unformed, or as Alvarez (1992) has written 'unmantled', and we then need to be working at very basic levels with the limbic system, to build basic emotional understanding in a developmental way (Hurry 1998). The three parts of the brain are not separate units by any means, and complex relationships and pathways have developed between them over the millennia. Indeed, the neuroscientist Daniel Siegel (1999) has argued firmly that psychological health is marked by ever-increasing complexity and interdependence of aspects of brain functioning, and that many of the people who have developed psychological 'issues' of one form or another show a less complex and interwoven structure, with more chaos and more rigidity, and less organisation. This emphasis on complexity and linking parts of the brain might echo Bion's theories about linking (1967) and about the value of 'capacious' containing functions.

Experience dependency

The brain is basically like a muscle group, albeit an extraordinarily complex one, and the bits that are used are strengthened from the exercise, and others can wither from neglect. The human brain is born prematurely, having an overabundance of brain cells at the start but with very few connections between them. In the post-natal period there is a massive process of 'pruning', a process called 'use it or lose it', and cells that are not used simply die off. Schwartz and Begley (2002: 117), quoting a figure of 20 billion synapses pruned every day between childhood and early adolescence, say: 'like bus routes with no customers, they go out of business'. Once a connection is formed it remains wired, but unused neurons are 'pruned', although new pathways and wiring can still form later in life. New experience is filtered through already-formed pathways, just as water will naturally flow down already formed channels, hence the phrase 'cells that fire together wire together', coined by the neuroscientist Hebb (1949), and called Hebb's law. This is what is meant by humans having an 'experience dependent' brain and describes the process whereby particular pathways form at the expense of other potential pathways and become standard ways by which one experiences the world. Possibly similar to Bion's (1967) concept of linking, it is literally the case that physical (synaptic) links are formed in the brain as psychological links are made. Where neuroscience adds to, or even challenges Bion, is that, once formed, links are fairly solidly made; what we work with in many children may not simply be an attack on linking but a lack of links, of synaptic connections capable of joining two thoughts together.

This revisits the nature–nurture debate, which appears to have been given a whole new slant by recent research findings. Despite constant press reports about specific genes being discovered for particular disorders, research shows that in whatever ways one's genetic potential might vary, that potential also needs certain experiences to be triggered. There are, for example, two versions (long and short) of the 5HTT serotonin transporter gene. Several studies (e.g. Caspi *et al.* 2003) show that if one has particularly adverse experiences, such as abuse or neglect, one is very likely to develop aggressive behaviour if one has the short version of the gene, but if one has the long version the same adverse experiences do not seem to lead to violent behaviour. The short version also predisposes people to anxiety and depression (Caspi *et al.* 2002). Having a particular form of another gene, the MAO-A, has similarly been shown to predispose people to violence, again if the carrier has certain kinds of adverse experiences (Meyer-Lindenberg *et al.* 2006). Equally, it is proposed that the gene DRD4, when accompanied by certain experiences, is likely to lead to various kinds of novelty-seeking behaviours, making it more likely that the carrier might indulge in substance abuse and even possibly develop disorganised attachment patterns (Gervai *et al.* 2007). In these examples experience turns on genetic potentials, and one cannot elevate the influence of one over the other.

The human brain learns fast, according to experience, and is an extraordinarily powerful predictor of the future. If the presence of adults triggers either fear or dissociative processes, as it does in many children who have suffered early and ongoing trauma, these same fear responses will in all likelihood also be triggered by other more benign adults, such as kindly teachers or adoptive parents. The human brain, and particularly the infant brain, is hugely malleable, a capacity that Schore (2003) and others have described as 'neuroplasticity'. The period from the last trimester of pregnancy through to the second year of life is very crucial, although thankfully some plasticity remains throughout the lifespan, particularly during adolescence. Schore states the parent is the psychobiological regulator of the developing infant brain, and the mother's face can be the environment that stimulates particular neuronal circuitry, especially in the first few years. We are beginning to move from a model encompassing the single brain into one in which one brain activates another, an idea reminiscent of Winnicott's (1972) view that not only can one not conceive of a baby without also taking into account its primary carer, but also that a baby's self-understanding develops through seeing itself reflected in its mother's eyes.

Hormones and opiates

Experience affects not just the structure of the brain but also the whole hormonal system. The human brain produces many hormones and opiates, and the best known are the stress hormone, cortisol, and oxytocin, sometimes called the 'love hormone'. The mother's stress level during pregnancy affects the unborn child (Field 2004), and cortisol in pregnant mothers crosses the placenta and can adversely affect the developing foetus. Stress impacts on us via the HPA (hypothalamus-pituitary-adrenal) axis, a system that humans share with many organisms from way back in evolutionary history. With activation of the HPA axis comes the release of adrenaline into the bloodstream, faster heart rate and higher blood pressure, and readying the body for 'fight or flight'. Cortisol is nowadays easily measured on saliva samples and it is clear that when children are fearful, or when left without their closest attachment figures, their cortisol levels tend to become higher and their blood pressure and heart rates increase. Children who have been subjected to high levels of trauma or suffered consistent anxiety, such as many in our clinical caseloads, can have ongoing elevated cortisol rates. Cortisol has a number of pernicious effects, leading Sue Gerhardt (2004) to dub it 'corrosive cortisol', particularly in light of how it can attack cells in the hippocampus, the part of the brain that is central to memory, so being implicated in memory loss. Occasionally extreme trauma can have the opposite effect and result in extremely low cortisol levels – often seen in post-traumatic stress disorder victims such as Holocaust survivors (Yehuda *et al.* 2000). Either way, too much or too little cortisol or stress is not what the human body was designed for. Of course, quick surges of adrenaline and cortisol are essential and lifesaving when a predator suddenly pops into view. Generally after such shocks the body goes quickly back to a more normal state, with blood pressure and heart rates reducing again as we relax. However, if one has been subjected to constant assaults or cumulative trauma (Khan 1963) it is possible to become either hyper-aroused, sensing danger everywhere and barely ever calming down, or the opposite, a suppressed, closed down self-protective state that one sees in massive dissociation. As therapists we need to learn to be extremely sensitive to the nuances of such different psychological states.

Good or loving experiences lead to very different chemicals being released. The best known of these is probably oxytocin, a hormone that promotes warm and affiliative feelings, and also its close relation, vaso-pressin. Primates that 'pair bond', such as humans, have more oxytocin receptors than species that do not. Oxytocin levels increase when we are with someone we love, when breast-feeding, in sexual relations, when receiving a massage, and oxytocin also reduces the impact of stress, lessens pain and can boost the immune system. If we have higher oxytocin levels, research shows that we are more generous (Kosfeld *et al.* 2005), and if experimentally given oxytocin we also become more trusting and helpful (Zak 2007). With higher oxytocin levels we have less social fear (Meyer-Lindenberg *et al.* 2005), less activation of the parts of the brain concerned with fear and stress. Interestingly, preliminary evidence (Pollak 2005) suggests that late adopted Romanian orphans do not release oxytocin when cuddled or sitting on their mothers' laps in the same way that birth children do. This might explain how the capacity for affection, and its neuronal concomitants, might well atrophy with profound neglect, and it also might well be part of the explanation for why it can also be hard to warm to some neglected children. Such findings suggest that the role of the psycho-analytic child psychotherapist might also include the fostering of positive or more hopeful feelings as well as managing negative ones, something that has maybe historically been somewhat neglected in some traditions.

There are of course myriad other opiates and hormones, including dopamine and serotonin. Dopamine is central to the reward system, activated when we are positive, excited or eager for something, but it is also involved in addiction, such as to drugs and alcohol. Serotonin is similarly well known, and low levels of serotonin are seen in people who are less happy, more irritable and volatile, and particularly in violent males. We produce serotonin naturally when we feel good, something interestingly that antidepressants such as Prozac also do. Depressed mothers have low dopamine levels, but more worryingly so do their babies as young as a month old. Many current medical and recreational drugs target specific brain areas, and indeed many mimic the body's own opiates. Cocaine, for example, impacts on the dopamine system, and experiments have shown that if you put cocaine in a room full of rats, it is mainly the low-status ones that imbibe it (Wilkinson 2005). As Wilkinson and others (e.g. Marmot 2004) have shown by examining data across many societies, low social status gives rise to higher stress levels, weaker immune systems, and far poorer health and mental health outcomes, and also often increased use of opiates that induce positive feeling. The hormonal system is a complex one, and as psychotherapists we might unwittingly often find ourselves resonating with its impact in our countertransference responses to patients.

Aggression, violence and the negative

Neuroscientific, genetic and biological research challenges naive views that, given sufficient dosages of loving care, all will be well or the equally worrying, blame-filled idea that anything less than perfectly harmonious synchrony is a sign of bad parenting. Conflict is engrained in human nature: Trivers (1974) was the first evolutionary psychologist to point out the natural conflicts of interest between parents and children. Mothers and infants share only 50 per cent of their genes, and so do not always have the same goals. Haig (1993) has illustrated that it is in the interest of the foetus, not the mother, to transfer as many nutrients as possible across the placental wall. The foetus manipulates the mother by sending hormones into the mother's bloodstream that might, for example, raise maternal blood pressure, possibly giving rise to symptoms ranging in seriousness from swollen calves to more dangerous conditions such as pre-eclampsia, all in the service of increasing *its own* supply of nutrients. The not-so-innocent foetus cleverly controls supply lines of nutrients by remodelling the mother's very arteries, leading some to liken it to a cosmonaut taking charge of a spacecraft. Such research might find echoes in many of Melanie Klein's (1957) descriptions of primitive aggressive phantasies and aggressive urges in the infant.

Such evolutionary conflict is not just between foetus and mother. The foetus itself is the locus of innumerable conflicts, perhaps the best documented being that between the male and female genome. Haig (1993) developed the idea of genetic imprinting, whereby the same gene will express itself differently depending on which parent it comes from. In an experiment done with mice, the male and female instructions in a specific gene were alternately 'knocked out', leaving only one gender's genome 'in charge' of the foetus. Those foetuses where the female genome ruled over the male became smaller and cleverer babies, seemingly as the mother would have it, whereas those born by rule of the male genome were huge and brawny, not at all in the interests of the mothers. Pregnancy would seem at a molecular level to be a kind of silent and hidden battle, with conflict engrained in our very genes and cell structure. Evolutionary psychologists have similarly suggested that the kinds of phantasies Klein (1957) described of infants wanting to kill unborn babies in their mothers' tummies might in fact have deadly serious survival functions in a barren hunter-gatherer environment which could only sustain at most the life of one infant every three or four years.

Aggression and its origins and how we work with it has long been a source of debate within psychoanalytic thinking. Many psychoanalysts (e.g. Klein 1957) have argued that aggression is primary, innate and basic to human nature, whereas others (e.g. Fairbairn 1952; Guntrip 1992) have believed that aggression is secondary, and likely to be a defensive response to other feelings such as shame or hurt. However, as Solms and Turnbull (2002) point out, there are in fact two very different aggression systems wired into us. One form is the aggression of the lion on the hunt stalking its prey – the *cold aggression* system, to do with need, not anger or rage, linked with 'moving towards' one's needs (aggression literally means moving towards). This kind of aggression simply dissipates when we are sated. Quite a different system leads to the *reactive aggression* of the hurt/ angry person which derives from rage/shame/threat, and is linked to the amygdala and to fight/flight responses. This might well be the form of aggression we witness so often in many of our more deprived patients who easily see an attack where others would not, and whose aggression can be an extreme form of a much needed and developmentally helpful survival mechanism. We need to work differently with different forms of aggression and their concomitant brain states, and the apparently cold criminal adolescent requires a very different intervention from the hyper-reactive physically abused child or the spoilt narcissistic child.

Mirror neurons and Rizzolatti's monkeys

Psychotherapists have been increasingly aware of the need to adopt different therapeutic approaches with children who struggle to understand other minds, such as autistic children and those suffering massive early neglect.

The ability to empathise and understand other minds is more developed in children who are securely attached, or who have parents who are what Meins *et al.* (2002) have termed 'mind-minded', and have capacities that Fonagy and Allen (2006) describe by the term 'mentalisation'. We know that the human infant is primed from birth to be sensitive to and respond to other humans, particularly the mother. In the last ten years scientists have made a discovery that explains some of this, a discovery of which the neuroscientist Ramachandran (2000) wrote, 'I predict that mirror neurons will do for psychology what DNA did for biology.' The discovery was actually made by the Italian neuroscientists Rizzolatti and Gallese (Rizzolatti *et al.* 2001) who were experimenting with macaque monkeys, and found not only that a particular neuron will fire up when a monkey performs an action such as grasping, but that a monkey who was simply watching another monkey reach for a peanut also had a firing of that very same neuron. Indeed the 'eureka' moment occurred when one of the main scientists, Gallese, reached for a peanut himself and was shocked to note that the equipment similarly registered the same neuronal firing in the monkey at the moment that the monkey just *saw* him grasp his lunchtime snack.

There is a complex mirror neuron circuit in humans (Wolf *et al.* 2001). If I see you walk near a washing line as if you might walk into it, I might find myself ducking sympathetically – the corresponding neurons for that action are firing in my brain, too. Others have found close links between the neural mechanisms for imitation, language and empathy in humans (Iacoboni 2005). Such neurons fire at the sight of the grasping of an object, but not at the sight of the object, nor at a pantomime grasp, so the neurons respond to and simulate actual *intentions*, which is the way actions are learnt and then later replicated. Mirror neurons are similarly activated when we observe or imitate emotion, which in turn relates to how we learn to read and understand another's intentions, and thus to how we develop a sophisticated 'theory of other minds'.

Mirror neurons provide evidence of the human capacity to form powerful connections between people as they allow one person to understand from the inside what another person is doing or feeling. Interestingly, this activity seems to be dominant in the left hemisphere and mirror neurons are found in Broca's area in humans, a region central to language use, and it is believed that mirror neurons are involved in the expression of phonetic gestures and actions, possibly forming the basis of language development itself.

Current research suggests that deficits in the capacity for theory of mind and imitation in autism is linked to poorly functioning mirror neuron systems (Williams *et al.* 2001; Oberman *et al.* 2005), which would make sense of many of the struggles of our autistic patients. One wonders also about children such as those adopted from emotionally depriving care situations who seem to lack a developed capacity to be in touch with their own and other people's minds and emotions. Maybe their mirror neuron systems had no opportunity to develop, and certainly much of our work with these children can be trying to facilitate the development of such capacities. The neuronal circuit which houses mirror neurons confirms the central role of imitation in both learning and communication, and possibly also in developmental change in the therapeutic process too (Trevarthen *et al.* 1999).

Memories and emotional learning

Neuroscience and linked research has hugely increased our understanding of the different kinds of memories that we have, how we develop these and indeed the implications for clinical work. Much has changed since Freud's day and the belief that psychoanalytic cure necessitated the recovery of repressed memories. A simple starting point is to outline two different forms of memory. The first is often called declarative or explicit memory and is concerned with memories of facts and events that can be actually, consciously recalled and spoken about. Recalling a date or name would fall into this category, as would remembering a childhood event. The other kind of memory is procedural or implicit memory – although I am grossly simplifying here and these definitions can be more subtly defined (e.g. Solms and Turnbull 2002). Procedural memory is a kind of knowledge which describes non-conscious bodily-based memories such as 'how we do' things, and also describes the residues of certain traumas remembered at a somatic, non-conscious level. Procedural memories include skills such as riding a bike or playing an instrument, and also memories of how relationships are likely to go, based on previous experience. More often than not these are the kind of memories people take into new social contacts and relationships, and into the transference relationship in therapy, and are the result of prior learning. An abused child, for example, might have learnt to expect violence from adults and so might push away real caring gestures, based on an earlier, procedural memory of abusive adults.

Research has shown that by about six months of age children of depressed mothers act in a depressed way even with non-depressed, attuned adults (Pickens and Field 1993). The well-known 'still-face' experiments that Tronick (1989) and others undertook illustrate procedural expectations in young babies. When an interacting mother is suddenly asked to keep a still face, the babies become disturbed, self-soothe, try to seduce the mothers back and in many ways show that they already have expectations of relationships that are suddenly being challenged. Such preconceptions of relationships seem to become inscribed viscerally in our central nervous systems, and more primitive parts of our brains such as the basal ganglia are central in this. The child who expects violence may well be hyper-alert and jumpy, irrespective of who he is with; the brain circuits to do with violent reactivity might well be to the fore while those to do with self-regulation and processing emotional experience might be little used and not available. Similarly loving, attuned caregiving will in all likelihood give rise to a trusting view of other people, again all based on behavioural patterns and expectations laid down far outside consciousness.

Psychoanalytic psychotherapy has taken much of this on board already, with our emphasis on the 'here-and-now' transference relationship, the emphasis on working with the 'total situation' (Joseph 1985), and the idea that the therapist might be a new 'developmental object' (Hurry 1998) and so aid patients to learn new expectations of their objects, internal and external. We also work less with attempting to lift the veil of repression to reveal actual memories, and also less with cognitive based insights 'about' the patient, and more with procedural expectations about relationships as manifested in the transference. We struggle sometimes with the subtlety required to work with traumatic memories, which are often procedural and bodily based, and which it is not always helpful to talk about directly for a very long time. How one moves towards integrating such memories, often encapsulated and split off, into everyday understanding remains an ongoing debate.

Left and right hemispheres

No discussion of the brain would be complete without some mention of the left and right hemispheres, regions which, although linked and working together, tend to specialise in different functions. The left brain leads on language, instrumentality and logic while the right brain has particular strengths in intuitive and emotional processing, creativity and more 'holistic' skills. As a rule of thumb, the right brain receives signals from and controls the left side of the body, and the left brain links with the right side of the body. The left and right brain are linked by a part of the brain, really a bundle of nerves, called the 'corpus callosum'. When this was removed in some patients (Sperry *et al.* 1970) it was found that the two hemispheres seemed to work independently. For example, when a pencil was shown to such a patient's right hand and eye (controlled by their left hemisphere) the patient could name the pencil but could not describe what it was used for; similarly when shown to the left eye and hand, the patient knew what one did with the pencil but could not name it.

Schore (2003) stresses the importance of the early months and years of life, when huge developments are taking place in the right hemisphere, which can be viewed as the seat of emotional processing, along with other elements of the limbic system. The part of the brain which deals with logic and thinking, the left brain and parts of the cortex, which in evolutionary terms are relatively new, are in fact not much 'on-line' in the first couple of years when many vital neuronal pathways and synaptic connections are forming. Similarly the part of the brain that contextualises explicit or declarative memories, the hippocampus, is also not very developed in the first year or so of life. In other words, massive developments are taking place before the human mind is able consciously to remember actual events, and in particular many vital procedural memories and expectations are firmly entrenched well before very much conscious declarative functioning occurs. This might well suggest that much more of our work is or should be with these early developing psychological and emotional states, in which language and cognition play a lesser role (e.g. Lanyado 2004).

The other key difference between left and right brain functioning is that negative emotions tend to be processed more in the right brain, and positive ones in the left, so that, for example, when we watch an amusing film our brains are more likely to evidence left brain activity. Also, with more right brain activity our immune systems are less efficient, something that has been shown in experiments by exposing people to the flu virus, and noting that those with more right pre-frontal cortex activity were far more likely to succumb to the virus and had less anti-flu antibodies (Davidson *et al.* 2003). Stress has a bad effect on the immune system whilst happiness seems to enhance it. A fascinating retrospective study was done in Milwaukee of nuns (Danner *et al.* 2001) whose diaries, written on entering the order in the 1930s, were recently examined in detail, for example in terms of how many positive and negative words were used. Although the daily lives of all the nuns barely differed in terms of routine, diet, climate or how they spent their days, their relative longevity did differ vastly, and in direct proportion to how happy they had been over half a century before! Of the less positive ones, two-thirds had died before reaching 85 years, whereas 90 per cent of the happy ones were still going strong. These nuns would have had more left pre-frontal cortex activity and a boosted immune system. What the neuroscience research is showing is that there are very different systems in the brain for managing and processing negative as opposed to positive affect. Psychotherapy today needs to ensure that we are both working with managing the negative and helping patients to develop the capacity to sustain positive affect, ideas that have been around in child psychotherapy for quite some time (Freud, A. 1959; Alvarez 1992), if not always as common currency.

It may be that in much of our work with children, particularly the more disturbed, we are increasingly working with what might be loosely termed their right brains, including capacities for emotional regulation, or with procedural memories as manifested in the consulting room, or just in attuning to subtle emotional states. As a result there is probably less focus on 'left brain' more cognitive and interpretative work than in the past. However, as Siegel (1999) has argued clearly, it is the linking of left and right brain and the development of new pathways that is so vital, and we should not privilege one over the other. One central way of linking right and left brain functioning is via the development of narrative capacity, something we often see in children as they begin to play imaginatively and expressively in therapy. As Siegel has written, autobiographical memory appears to be dependent on parts of the cortex that undergo rapid growth and change in the first few years of life and are likely to mediate auto-biographical consciousness. These capacities are apparent in both securely attached children and in their parents, as shown by analysis of Adult Attachment Interviews. Rich tales, stories and narratives about their lives become prominent in more secure children by the third year of life, but such narrative capacity seems to be under-developed in avoidant children or their often 'dismissive' (in attachment terms) parents. What seems vital for psychological health is that therapeutic work develops not just left and right brain functioning but the links between the two. Story-telling led by the left brain alone can be rather wild when not harnessed by right brain emotional understanding, as evidenced in the remarkable but oddly out-of-touch stories seen in studies of those with right hemisphere brain damage (Ramachandran 1999). We hope to develop not just a capacity to tell a story, but to develop a narrative that is emotionally true, that we trust, and it appears that this is something that requires both left and right brain functioning and good links between the two.

Trauma, neglect, the amygdala and the hippocampus

Child psychotherapists have always argued that the early years are vital. Just as the rat pup that is licked by its mother will cope better with stress as it gets older, so the parent's good emotional and physical contact with the infant is an innoculatory factor in growing up. With loving contact all manner of helpful and calming chemicals, opiates and hormones are released in both mother and infant, and distinctive synaptic connections and neuronal pathways take shape. When early experience is of trauma or neglect then quite different chemicals are released, and different neuronal pathways form. Blood pressure is higher, the stress hormones cortisol and adrenaline are released, heart rates increase, and high stress levels can become the infant's natural way of being. A small almond-shaped part of the brain called the amygdala is vital in such processes; it is the organ that responds to fear, and is very ancient in evolutionary terms, being present in pre-mammalian creatures (Figure 5.3).

From our primordial history we are primed to be alert to danger and to respond in micro-seconds to any threat, and the amygdala is the central organ involved in this. The kind of startle response we all might have to a loud noise might be an example of the amygdala in action. Infants and children subjected to trauma appear to have an amygdala on constant hyper-alert. Perry *et al.* (1995) have taught us a lot about the impact of trauma on brain development, and he has written of how such children can barely relax at all, are often constantly 'on the move', and can be prone to being given a diagnosis of attention-deficit hyperactivity disorder. The sympathetic nervous systems of such people are highly aroused.

There is an opposite response of the nervous system to stress and trauma, an activation of the parasympathetic nervous system. When this is

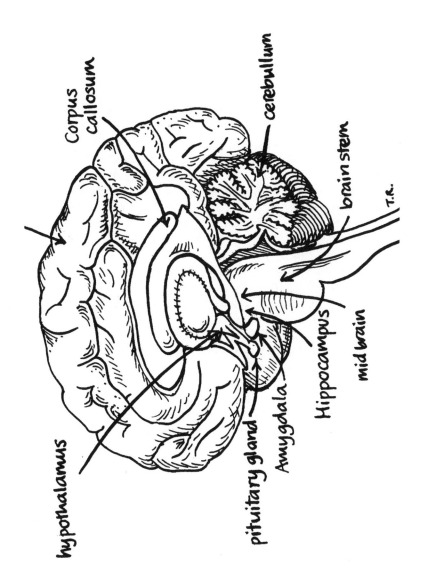

Corpus callosum

cerebullum

brain stem

T.R.

hypothalamus

pituitary gland

Amygdala

Hippocampus

mid brain

Figure 5.3

triggered the body closes down, rather like a creature playing dead in front of a predator. Blood pressure becomes low, as does the heart rate, and the mind goes into a kind of 'shut-down'. Such parasympathetic processes can then form the basis of the personality long after the original traumatic incidents are over. In fact the left side of the brain, the bit which specialises in logical thought, conscious memory and such, can often shut down when faced with trauma. At such times the survival mechanisms of the right brain take over. This is why many victims of trauma cannot consciously remember what happened to them. It is not that the memories were suppressed so much as that the part of the brain that would do the remembering had been shut down. This can also give rise to the phenomenon of dissociation, in which people can seem to be cut off from their own experiences, and might be another explanation for why many of the children from traumatising backgrounds often do not achieve well academically. They have learnt to cope either by being hyper-alert to danger, which impedes ordinary relaxed concentration, or they go into a shut-down, dissociative mode in which the thinking part of the brain becomes inactive. In trauma not only might the left brain shut down, but also the links between the left and right hemispheres are less strong. Indeed, trauma victims have been shown to have a smaller corpus callosum, that part of the brain that joins the left and right hemispheres, as well as having an enlarged amygdala, and there is also increasing evidence that the hippocampus can atrophy as a result of exposure to trauma, and that an excess of cortisol is directly implicated in this. There have been various reports of war veterans having diminished hippocampi (Greenfield 2002). As Siegel (1999) has stated, mental health might be characterised by increased complexity and interdependence of parts and right and left brains need each other, and a thick and active corpus callosum linking them is healthful, whereas an overactive amygdala or a corroded hippocampus or a diminished link between left and right brain is not. Maybe the role of much psychotherapy is in developing just these links, which is what happens for example in the consulting room when a patient realises with one's help that a noise outside, or a movement by the therapist, is not necessarily as dangerous or frightening as initially feared.

Severe neglect is different from trauma, but can lead to serious atrophy in certain parts of the brain, leading to massive developmental delay and serious deficits in the ability to empathise, to regulate emotions, and consequent deficits in the capacity to manage intimacy and ordinary social interaction. Studies of extreme cases of deprivation such as some terribly neglected children adopted from Romanian orphanages (e.g. Rutter *et al.* 1998), have shown the impact of such early deprivation not only on the behaviours of the children but on their actual brains as well. Indeed, their right hemispheres, brain areas which are primed for emotional understanding and expressiveness, seemed in the scans of the seriously neglected orphans to be almost like 'black holes', with shockingly little activity and life. Perry *et al.* (1995) have published research which shows that the actual circumference of the brain of severely abused children is often severely diminished compared to the norm, although brain growth and actual brain circumference will recover should they be adopted sufficiently early. Much research (e.g. Dozier 2001) seems to be converging to demonstrate that children who are fostered or adopted by sensitive carers very early, particularly in the first year to 18 months, have a far better prognosis than those adopted later. What also seems clear from work with such patients is that the level at which we work with them has had to change as a result of current knowledge. A lot of work with very deprived or neglected children needs to be in slowly building up emotional capacities (Hurry 1997), often in what Greenspan (1998) would call 'upregulating them' as well as in developing some capacities to understand other minds. With more traumatised children, much of what we are doing is 'downregulating' their sympathetic nervous systems, trying to break into their procedural expectations of the unsafeness of the world and to build more sense of trust and safety.

Hope or hopeless?

How hopeful or gloomy should such research leave us? We know that the behavioural patterns that are established early on can be very hard to shift, and that once an experience is burnt into the circuits of the amygdala it is there forever, but we also know that new circuits can also grow and form. Interestingly, this is also what story-stem research (Hodges *et al.* 2003) has shown, that after good adoptions the old stories and ways of being remain, but new expectations of parental behaviour and new views of the world can grow and become stronger. There are definite windows of opportunity during which certain aspects of brain growth can occur, and the brain can certainly change throughout the lifespan. It is also true that some opportunities can be lost forever if not taken in time. Language development is one well-known example, and it seems the same is also true for certain emotional capacities. The best-known windows of opportunity, when there is massive brain growth and change, are from pregnancy through the first few years of life, but also in adolescence when huge changes equally occur in the brain. Maybe it is not surprising that so much therapeutic effort and zeal is directed towards those age-groups.

Little research has been done on the effect of psychoanalytic psychotherapy, but some talking therapies have been shown to make a definite impact on the brains of patients (Mayberg 2006) and importantly it appears that such talking therapies affect a different part of the brain from drug treatments. Schwartz has written about how the mind, or a particular mental attitude, in fact changes brain states. From another angle Marci and colleagues (2007) found that patients whose treatment went best seemed to have attuned empathic therapists, and such empathy was measured via their skin conductivity as well as by other techniques. Treatment that went well showed high skin conduction concordance, much as more empathetic mothers show larger skin responses than those with lower empathy when watching five-month-olds.

Where the neuroscience research will take us in relation to psycho-therapy is uncertain, but we do know that psychological and neurological change is genuinely possible throughout the lifespan. This can happen through good parenting, as is seen in studies of successful adoption (Hodges *et al.* 2003) or fostering (Dozier *et al.* 2001), and therapy, it seems, can also contribute to this, even if it is sometimes the result of slow and painstaking work. Therapeutic work might be helpful in a number of very different ways. The neuroscientist Joseph le Doux (1998) states that therapy is 'another way of creating synaptic potentiation in brain pathways that control the amygdala'. The amygdala's emotional memories are indelibly burned into its circuits, but we can regulate their expression. The way we do this is by getting the cortex to control the amygdala' as shown in Figure 5.4.

The amygdala is the seat of our primitive fear responses and reacts in a fraction of a second to any perceived danger. Experiences will often be filtered straight to the amygdala via the thalamus. However, there is a slightly longer route whereby experience is filtered via the more cognitive bit of the brain, and so the 'direct route' can be mediated by benign new experiences. A loud noise, for example, might cause an initial startle in a war veteran who then allows himself to become aware that the noise was simply a carpenter hammering next door, and he then relaxes. Therapeutic work can enhance such processes, building up the capacity to interpret experience in new and less frightening ways. This is but one way in which change can take place, and other effects of therapeutic work are likely to include the laying down of new procedural memories; strengthened links between left and right hemispheres; enhanced reflective capacities; better understanding of other minds; greater ability to form a coherent narrative about oneself; improved capacity to regulate emotions, to tolerate depen-dency and difficult emotions without acting out and to sustain positive affect; and the capability of course to form and manage attachments better in general.

Although there is a lot more to discover, neuroscience research has hugely increased our understanding of the ways in which children develop, as well as opening up all manner of challenges to the ways in which we have traditionally worked. 'Learning from experience' (Bion 1962), which inevitably also means changes in the brain, has been shown to take place throughout the lifespan, and child psychotherapy has a central part to play in ensuring this happens. It is increasingly clear that psychotherapy cannot ignore neuroscience; hopefully psychotherapy and neuroscience can develop in partnership in the coming years.

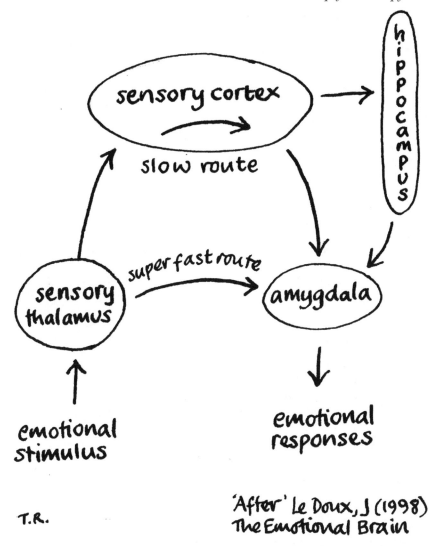

Figure 5.4

References

Alvarez, A. (1992) *Live Company: Psychoanalytic Psychotherapy with Autistic, Borderline, Deprived and Abused Children*, London: Tavistock/Routledge.

Bion, W. (1962) *Learning from Experience*, London: Karnac.

—— (1967) *Second Thoughts*, London: Karnac.

Caspi, A., McClay, J., Moffitt, T. E., Mill, J., Martin, J., Craig, I. W. *et al.* (2002) 'Role of genotype in the cycle of violence in maltreated children', *Science* 297: 851–4.

Caspi, A., Sugden, K., Moffitt, T. E., Taylor, A., Craig, I. W., Harrington, H. *et al.*

(2003) 'Influence of life stress on depression: moderation by a polymorphism in the 5-HTT gene', *Science* 301: 386–9.

Danner, D. D., Snowdon, D. A. and Friesen, W. V. (2001) 'Positive emotions in early life and longevity: findings from the Nun Study', *Journal of Personality and Social Psychology* 30: 804–13.

Davidson, R. J., Kabat-Zinn, J., Schumacher, J. *et al.* (2003) 'Alterations in brain and immune function produced by mindfulness meditation', *Psychosomatic Medicine* 65: 564–70.

Dozier, M., Stovall, K. C., Albus, K. E. and Bates, B. (2001) 'Attachment for infants in foster care: the role of caregiver state of mind', *Child Development* 72: 1467–77.

Fairbairn, R. (1952) *Psychoanalytical Studies of the Personality*, London: Routledge.

Field, T. (2004) 'Prenatal depression effects on the fetus and neonate', in J. Nadel and D. Muir (eds) *Emotional Development: Recent Research Advances*, Oxford: Oxford University Press.

Fonagy, P. and Allen, J. G. (2006) *Handbook of Mentalization-Based Treatment*, Chichester: John Wiley.

Freud, A. (1959) *The Psychoanalytical Treatment of Children*, London: Hogarth Press.

Freud, S. (1914) 'On Narcissism. An Introduction', *SE* XIV, London: Hogarth Press.

Gerhardt, S. (2004) *Why Love Matters. How Affection Shapes a Baby's Brain*, Hove: Brunner-Routledge.

Gervai, J., Novak, A., Lakatos, K., Toth, I., Danis, I., Ronai, Z., Nemoda, Z., Sasvari-Szekely, M., Bureau, J., Bronfman, F. and Lyons-Ruth, K. (2007) Infant genotype may moderate sensitivity to maternal affective communications: attachment disorganization, quality of care, and the DRD4 polymorphism', *Social Neuroscience* 2(3–4): 307–19.

Greenfield, S. (2002) *The Private Life of the Brain*, London: Penguin.

Greenspan, S. (1997) *Developmentally Based Psychotherapy*, Madison, CT: International Universities Press.

Guntrip, H. (1992) *Schizoid Phenomena, Object-Relations and the Self*, London: Karnac.

Haig, D. (1993) 'Genetic conflicts in human pregnancy', *The Quarterly Review of Biology* 68(4): 495–532.

Hebb, D. (1949) *The Organization of Behavior*, New York: Wiley.

Hodges, J., Steele, M., Hillman, S., Henderson, K. and Kaniuk, J. (2003) 'Changes in attachment representations over the first year of adoptive placement: narratives of maltreated children', *Clinical Child Psychology and Psychiatry* 8(3): 351–67.

Hurry, A. (ed.) (1998) *Psychoanalysis and Developmental Theory*, London: Karnac.

Joseph, B. (1985) 'Transference: the total situation', *International Journal of Psycho-Analysis* 66: 447–54.

Iacoboni, M. (2005) 'Understanding others: imitation, language, empathy', in S. Hurley and N. Chater (eds) *Perspectives on Imitation: From Cognitive Neuroscience to Social Science*, Cambridge, MA: MIT Press.

Khan, M. M. R. (1963) 'The concept of cumulative trauma', *Psychoanalytic Study of the Child* 18: 286–306.

Klein, M. (1957) *Envy and Gratitude*, London: Tavistock.

Kosfeld, M., Heinrichs, M. Zak, P. J., Fischbacher, U. and Fehr, E. (2005) 'Oxytocin increases trust in humans', *Nature* 435: 673–6.

Lanyado, M. (2004) *The Presence of the Therapist*, London: Routledge.

Le Doux, J. (1998) *The Emotional Brain*, New York: Phoenix.

MacLean, P. D. (1985) 'Evolutionary psychiatry and the triune brain', *Psychological Medicine* 15: 219–21.

Marci, C. D., Ham, J., Moran, E. K. and Orr, S. P. (2007) 'Physiologic concordance, empathy, and social-emotional process during psychotherapy', *Journal of Nervous and Mental Disease* 195: 103–11.

Marmot, M. (2004) *Status Syndrome – How Your Social Standing Directly Affects Your Health and Life Expectancy*, London: Bloomsbury.

Mayberg, H. S. (2006) 'Defining neurocircuits in depression', *Psychiatric Annals* 36: 259–66.

Meins, E., Fernyhough, C., Wainwright, R., Das Gupta, M., Fradley, E. and Tuckey, M. (2002) 'Maternal mind–mindedness and attachment security as predictors of theory of mind understanding', *Child Development* 73(6): 1715–26.

Meyer-Lindenberg, A., Hariri, A. R., Munoz, K. E., Mervis, C. B., Mattay, V. S., Morris, C. A. and Berman, K. F. (2005) 'Neural correlates of genetically abnormal social cognition in Williams syndrome', *Nature Neuroscience* 8: 991–3.

Meyer-Lindenberg, A., Buckholtz, J. W., Kolachana, B., Hariri, A. R., Pezawas, L., Blasi, G. *et al.* (2006) 'Neural mechanisms of genetic risk for impulsivity and violence in humans', *Proceedings of the National Academy of Sciences USA* 18: 6269–74.

Oberman, L. M., Hubbard, E. M., McCleery, J. P., Altschuler, E. L., Ramachandran, V. S. and Pineda, J. A. (2005) 'EEG evidence for mirror neuron dysfunction in autism spectral disorders', *Cognitive Brain Research* 24(2): 190–8.

Perry, B. D., Pollard, R., Blakely, T., Baker, W. and Vigilante, D. (1995) 'Childhood trauma, the neurobiology of adaptation and "use-dependent" development of the brain: how "states" become "traits"', *Infant Mental Health Journal* 16(4): 271–91.

Pickens, J. and Field, T. (1993) 'Attention getting vs. imitation effects on depressed mother–infant interactions', *Infant Mental Health Journal* 14(3): 171–81.

Pinker, S. (2002) *Blank Slate: The Modern Denial of Human Nature*, New York: Viking Press.

Pollak, S. (2005) 'Attachment Chemistry', 2 December *Science* 310.

Ramachandran, V. S. (1999) *Phantoms of the Brain*, London: Fourth Estate.

—— (2000) Mirror neurons and imitation learning as the driving force behind 'the great leap forward' in human evolution. Edge Foundation. http://www.edge.org/3rd_culture/ramachandran/ramachandran_p1.html (accessed 15 March 2008).

Rizzolatti, G., Fogassi, L. and Gallese, V. (2001) 'Neurophysiological mechanisms underlying the understanding and imitation of action', *Nature Reviews Neuroscience* 2: 661–70.

Rutter, M. and the English and Romanian Adoptees (ERA) Study Team (1998) 'Developmental catch-up and deficit, following adoption after severe global early privation', *Journal of Child Psychology and Psychiatry* 39(4): 465–76.

Schore, A. N. (2003) *Affect Regulation and the Repair of the Self*, New York: Norton.

Schwartz, J. and Begley, S. (2002) *The Mind and the Brain*, New York: Harper Collins.

Siegel, D. J. (1999) *The Developing Mind: Toward a Neurobiology of Interpersonal Experience*, New York: Guilford Press.

Solms, M. and Turnbull, O. (2002) *The Brain and the Inner World: an Introduction to the Neuroscience of Subjective Experience*, New York: Other Press.

Sperry, R. W., Vogel, P. J. and Bogen, J. E. (1970) 'Syndrome of hemisphere deconnection', in P. Bailey and R. E. Foil (eds) *Proceedings of the 2nd Pan-American Congress of Neurology*, Puerto Rico.

Trivers, R. (1974) 'Parent-offspring conflict', *American Zoologist* 14: 249.

Trevarthen, C., Kokkinaki, T. and Fiamenghi, G. (1999) 'What infants' imitations communicate', in J. Nadel and G. Butterworth (eds) *Imitation in Infancy*, Cambridge: Cambridge University Press.

Tronick, E. Z. (1989) 'Emotions and emotional communication in infants', *American Psychologist* 44: 112–19.

Wilkinson, R. G. (2005) *The Impact of Inequality: How to Make Sick Societies Healthier*, New York, NY: The New Press.

Williams, J. H. G., Whiten, A., Suddendorf, T. and Perrett, D. I. (2001) 'Imitation, mirror neurons and autism', *Neuroscience and Biobehavioural Review* 25: 287–95.

Winnicott, D. W. (1972) 'Basis for self in body', *International Journal of Child Psychotherapy* 1(1): 7–16.

Wolf, N. S., Gales, M. E., Shane, E. and Shane, M. (2001) 'The developmental trajectory from amodal perception to empathy and communication: the role of mirror neurons in this process', *Psychoanalytic Inquiry* 21(1): 94–112.

Yehuda, R., Bierer, L. M., Schmeidler, J., Aferiat, D. H., Breslau, I. and Dolan, S. (2000) 'Low cortisol and risk for PTSD in adult offspring of Holocaust survivors', *American Journal of Psychiatry* 157: 1252–9.

Zak, P. J., Stanton, A. A. and Ahmadi, S. (2007) 'Oxytocin increases generosity in humans', PLoS ONE 2(11): e1128. doi:10.1371/journal.pone.0001128 (accessed March 2008).

6 Research in child and adolescent psychotherapy: an overview

Nick Midgley

Introduction

In 1989, Mary Boston wrote a classic paper in the history of child psycho-therapy research. In it, she began by remarking that members of this profession 'are not noted for their enthusiasm for research'. She went on to explain that 'there had long been a split between the academic researcher and the clinician, each discipline pursuing its separate ways, with minimal interaction between the two, or worse, active disparagement of the other' (p. 15). On the side of the clinician, most research was seen as 'meaningless and superficial'; while on the side of the academic researcher, psycho-analytic concepts were seen as highly subjective and unsubstantiated, and clinicians were often seen as unwilling to expose their cherished ideals to scientific scrutiny. In what followed, Boston recognised some of the pressures on psychotherapy to engage with empirical research (especially around issues of outcome and accountability), and argued that the work of clinicians and academic researchers should be seen as 'complementing and cross-fertilising each other', rather than remaining apart.

Ten years later, when Jill Hodges came to write an overview of child psychotherapy research for the first edition of this handbook, she noted that research into the effectiveness of psychotherapy for children still lagged far behind that on adult treatments, and had often been of poor quality. Yet she also referred to a number of recent studies (including one by Mary Boston and her colleagues, on the outcome of psychotherapy for severely deprived children) that were 'beginning to make up the gap' (p. 106), and commented on the importance of further work in this area. Such work was vital, she argued, given the increasing emphasis within public sector services on providing 'evidence' of the usefulness and cost-effectiveness of various forms of treatment.

Despite some cautious progress at the time, Hodges still felt the need to ask why so little research has been done, and in trying to answer this question, identified three reasons: ethos; problems of operationalisation; and reasons to do with the position of psychoanalytic training and work in institutional structures (p. 119).

- In terms of *ethos*, the sense that most clinicians felt that their work cannot be properly evaluated in research terms, with a fear that 'the nuance of process and transference will be lost' (p. 119).

- In terms of *problems of operationalisation*, the gap between crude measures of behavioural change often used in research studies and the more sophisticated ways in which psychoanalytic therapists think about how children respond to psychoanalytic treatment.

- In terms of *institutional structures*, the fact that child psychotherapy training, unlike some other forms of psychological therapies, has not traditionally been based in academic departments, and so there is little development of a 'research skills base', or even an expectation that clinicians will also be pursuing research.

Less than ten years on, and significant developments have taken place in all of these domains. Links between child psychotherapy trainings and university departments are stronger than ever before, and the first generation of child psychotherapists emerging from their trainings with clinical doctorates are beginning to make an impact on the profession, armed with a whole range of measures and approaches which go beyond the mere behavioural to a more psychodynamically meaningful level. Professionally, the Association of Child Psychotherapists now has a very active 'research committee'; regular research reports are published in the profession's *Journal of Child Psychotherapy*; two reviews of child psychotherapy research have been commissioned by the NHS (Kennedy 2004; Kennedy and Midgley 2007); and two edited collections of papers devoted to this field have recently been published (Midgley *et al.* 2009; Tsiantis and Trowell 2009).

A lively debate has also developed about the meaning of 'research' itself in the field of psychoanalytic child psychotherapy. In the papers by Boston (1989) and Hodges (1999), while making some reference to other forms of activity, the meaning of 'research' was primarily taken to be 'outcome research', and most of the studies reviewed in those papers were studies examining the effectiveness of this form of treatment. While this was entirely understandable, especially in a political climate in which failure to provide such evidence was likely to have huge impact on the very survival and provision of psychoanalytic child psychotherapy within the public sector, some would argue that this is to accept too narrow a definition of 'research'. Michael Rustin has been one of the chief exponents of this view, arguing in a series of papers for a debate about how we think about the production of 'knowledge' in psychoanalysis, and what forms of activity can be considered appropriate to produce such knowledge (Rustin 2003).

Rustin's questions have been taken up by several commentators, who have begun a valuable debate about the most appropriate methodologies for research in the field of child psychotherapy (e.g. Fonagy 2003; Midgley 2006a; Desmarais 2007). Methods of investigation such as the practitioner's workshop or study group have been re-evaluated as possible models of research activity (Rustin 1984), with a recognition that to restrict research activity to the statistical analysis of empirical data is to sacrifice the rich diversity of research questions and methodologies appropriate to them. In the wider psychoanalytic community, there has been a rapid growth of interest in what has come to be termed 'conceptual research' (Dreher 2000); while methods such as infant observation, which have long been central elements in the *training* of child psychotherapists, are now being seen as potentially valuable forms of research (see Rhode 2004). There has also been a growing interest in incorporating methods of research from other fields, such as qualitative methodologies developed within the social sciences (Midgley 2004), with approaches such as 'grounded theory' being considered highly complementary to traditional methods of psychoanalytic research (Anderson 2006; Midgley 2006b). More 'real world' research, exploring questions such as the nature of child psychotherapy training (Sternberg 2005) or the process of referral and assessment for treatment (Kam and Midgley 2006; Urwin 2007) has also widened the scope and clinical relevance of the work now taking place.

The widening of the definition of research, and the incorporation of methodologies from other disciplines, does not mean that the traditional ways of creating knowledge and making new discoveries in the field of psychotherapy – especially the narrative case study based upon intensive clinical work with a particular patient – are redundant. As Margaret Rustin pointed out some time ago, 'in one sense an individual piece of psycho-therapeutic work is a research project – patient and therapist do not know what the outcome of their exploration together will be' (1984: 380), and the knowledge of the inner worlds of children evident in each of the chapters of this handbook is testament to the ongoing value of this approach. But in order to limit the scope of this chapter, such case studies are not reviewed here.

Yet even when restricting the definition of research in this way, the field of child psychotherapy research has now got to the point at which a review chapter, such as this one, is no longer able to make reference to all the studies that have been undertaken. For that reason, this chapter will review only two broad fields of research:

- first, research evaluating the question of whether psychoanalytic child psychotherapy works, and the possible ways in which it might work (i.e. outcome and process research); and
- second, empirical research that investigates the 'internal world' of particular groups of children.

While being selective, and neglecting certain areas – such as parent–infant psychotherapy research (see Sleed and Bland 2007) – almost com-pletely, it is hoped that this chapter will give a sense of where formal research in the field of child psychotherapy is now at; what the preliminary findings appear to be; and transmit some of the sense of energy and excitement which now attaches itself to the field of psychoanalytic child psychotherapy research.

Process and outcome research in child and adolescent psychotherapy[1]

For those outside the field of child psychotherapy – especially those concerned with commissioning or funding clinical services – perhaps the most important question that psychotherapy research is asked to address is the seemingly straightforward one, 'does the treatment work?' As the authors of a major review of outcome research in the field of child mental health generally recognise, this question (as well as the whole philosophy of 'evidence-based medicine' which it supports) is founded on an ideal, that 'decisions about care of individual patients involve the conscientious, explicit and judicious use of current best evidence' (Fonagy *et al.* 2002: 1). Yet these same authors also recognise that 'the real driving force behind evidence-based medicine is unlikely to be solely concern for the quality of care but rather economic considerations and the hope that health care organisations may be able to reduce escalating costs by focusing on the most cost-effective option' (ibid.: 1).

The development of the 'evidence-based practice' approach to mental health treatment is evident in documents such as 'What works for whom?' (Fonagy *et al.* 2002), and the various guidelines from the National Institute for Health and Clinical Excellence (NICE) offering advice for mental health professionals working with children and adolescents. The development of such guidelines is potentially of great value; after all, history teaches us that to rely solely on 'clinical expertise' to tell us what treatments are most effective is not necessarily a good idea (remember leeches?), and the ideal of evidence-based practice is that it guarantees the optimum use of limited resources; allows more fully-informed decision-making to take place; and therefore ultimately leads to greater understanding and better quality of care (Fonagy *et al.* 2002).

In practice, however, there are some serious problems with the 'evidence-based' approach, some of which are general, and others of which are quite specific to the study of complex psychological treatments such as psychoanalytic child psychotherapy. Many of the difficulties derive from the simple fact that 'evidence-based practice' has to make decisions about what kind of information counts as proof that a treatment really works, and what doesn't. This had led to the emergence of a 'hierarchy of evidence', in which different types of research are seen as providing better (or worse) evidence for the efficacy of any particular form of treatment. Single case studies written by the therapist, based on their own view of the treatment (which has been the most common form of communication in child psychotherapy traditionally) would be at the very bottom of this hierarchy, while at the top is evidence from the meta-analysis of randomised controlled trials (RCTs).[2]

It is not possible here to go into all the arguments about the strengths and limitations of an 'evidence-based' approach, which have been debated at great length in the literature (e.g. Boethius and Berggren 2000; Fonagy *et al.* 2002). While some of the criticisms are related to the *quality* of much outcome research, others see a fundamental flaw in the very *conception* of evidence-based practice. In brief, some of the primary areas of concern are as follows:

- The model used in most outcome studies is a medical one (patient is 'diagnosed', offered a 'dose' of one type of therapy or a 'placebo', and 'outcomes' are measured using standardised technologies), which some would argue is not appropriate for a complex psychological intervention such as child psychotherapy.
- Patients are often selected for research studies because they fit a particular diagnosis, and children with more complex problems are excluded from many studies. Yet child psychotherapists often work with some of the most complex cases in the clinical setting (Kennedy 2004) – the kinds of children who are mostly excluded from outcome studies, because they may have a range of difficulties (co-morbidity). Many studies therefore fail to reflect the clinical reality of the child psychotherapist's work.
- Findings from research settings (efficacy studies), carried out in artificial settings, are often very different from studies carried out in a naturalistic setting (effectiveness studies), such as a child and adolescent mental health clinic, therefore making the results of many studies of limited relevance to the clinical setting (Fonagy *et al.* 2002: 26–30).
- Often the need to control for as many variables as possible in order to make the research design of an outcome study methodologically sound (internal validity) is at the cost of making the research lack any meaningful connection to what goes on in the 'real world' (external or ecological validity).
- What it means for a therapy to be 'successful' is also by no means clear. Measures of outcome are often very global and focus on symptoms, but this may overlook subtler – but possibly more significant – forms of change, such as those in one's internal state of mind. Such change, which psychodynamic treatments tend to focus on, is far harder to measure using standardised tools.
- Outcome is often measured at the end of treatment, yet for change to be meaningful, it may be that longer-term follow-up is necessary. Some research suggests that psychoanalytic treatment may have a sleeper effect, which might not be detected without a sufficiently long follow-up period.

- The emphasis on *statistical significance* in most outcome studies means that the *clinical significance* of change may be neglected (e.g. a change may be small, but make a huge difference to a family; or be quantitatively large, yet mean little in terms of the quality of life) yet neither of these distinctions will be picked up by most research designs.
- By focusing on *average* rates of improvement, most outcome studies ignore specific findings (e.g. an especially disturbed child who was helped by a particular form of treatment) and often have very little to say about the mechanisms of change.
- There are ethical concerns about using a 'no treatment' group as a control group within a psychotherapy outcome study.
- The RCT, as the best example of a particular model of scientific research, also implies a particular construction of reality, in which the 'voice of science' (McLeod 2001: 167) is created in a way that excludes ambiguity, complexity, emotion or the social dimension of both therapy and the research process itself, not to mention the voice of the client or service user.
- The importance placed on random allocation of patients to different forms of treatment in RCTs is ethically questionable, because clients may be offered a form of treatment that they did not wish to have in the first place, or a form of treatment which the clinician, using their own clinical judgement, might not recommend for that particular individual.
- RCTs cost a huge amount of money to stage, so that vested interest groups, such as drug companies, are far more likely to be able to fund such research compared to small professions without financial clout. RCTs therefore tend to 'reinforce the status and economic power of existing elite groups' (McLeod 2001: 165). In addition, the smallness of samples usually available for treatments such as psychoanalytic child psychotherapy often makes it impossible to have the large number of participants required for most outcome research to be able to demonstrate a statistically significant difference between groups.
- Sometimes a lack of evidence is taken as equivalent to *evidence for lack of effectiveness*, especially when it comes to funding decisions about the provision of services.

Yet despite all these limitations, approaches such as the RCT still have enormous influence, because they are recognised as a rigorous, objective way of trying to compare the effectiveness of one form of treatment in comparison to others. As Fonagy *et al.* (2002) put it, articulating a view widely held in the mental health field, the 'logic of RCTs is unassailable; their superiority to observational methods is so self-evident that alternative strategies can be justified only in terms of the limitations of the RCTs' (p. 17). It may well be that child psychotherapists, like other similar modalities, may need to operate a dual strategy, both engaging with the evidence-based research culture as it exists, while simultaneously challenging some of its assumptions and working towards more meaningful ways of evaluating treatment.

Having indicated some of the debates in the field of 'evidence-based practice', and with due awareness of some of the limitations of such research, this chapter will now go on to summarise what has actually been found out about the outcome of child psychotherapy in the research carried out to date.

Does child psychotherapy work?

Shirk and Russell (1996), in their historical overview of outcome research, point out that early reviews of the outcome of child therapy generally (not just psychodynamic therapy) came in response to the critique of the effectiveness of psychotherapy by Hans Eysenck, who in 1952 published an infamous paper in which he argued that there was no evidence to suggest that psychotherapy (for adults) was any more effective that having no treatment at all. While many people criticised the methodology that Eysenck used to establish this view, others took it upon themselves to counter this argument by investigating more thoroughly the question of whether psychotherapy works.

Such activity gained further momentum in the 1970s, with the advent of the system of *meta-analysis*, which allows various different research studies to be brought together to produce a single, common metric, known as 'effect size', which describes the difference between those offered treatment and those in a 'control' group (e.g. on a waiting list or having no treatment). The findings of a whole range of meta-analyses of the outcome of *adult* psychotherapy found that patients who received treatment were about 0.74 of a standard deviation better off than those offered no treatment, with few differences between the various *types* of treatment. This indicates a significant level of improvement in relation to those not offered therapy. Equivalent meta-analyses of the psychotherapeutic treatment of children were carried out by Casey and Berman (1985) and Weisz *et al.* (1987), which found a similar overall effect size to the treatment of adults (0.71).

Yet behind the headlines the findings of these meta-analyses were frustratingly imprecise: there appeared to be little difference in outcome depending on the type of treatment, the length of treatment or even the type of problem treated, although the methodological quality of much of the research was so poor that it was hard to know whether this was a reflection of the way the research was carried out more than the treatment itself. Moreover, the types of treatment described in these research studies bore little resemblance to those used in clinical practice (only 3.6 per cent of the studies reviewed by Kazdin (2000) were of individual psychotherapy and only 1 per cent examined psychodynamic treatments) and the clinical relevance of many of the findings was arguably negligible.

Despite the limitations, some broad findings about the efficacy of psychological therapies for children (including behavioural and non-behavioural forms of treatment) began to emerge:

- In broad terms, those children who had some form of psychological therapy did better than those that did not.
- Younger children generally responded better to treatment than older children, although among the older group therapy was more likely to be successful when the child was suffering from anxiety and/or had referred themselves for treatment.
- Most change appeared to take place in the first six months of treatment, although for more severe difficulties longer and more intensive treatments appeared to be necessary.

While these findings are important, they leave many questions unanswered. By the early 1980s it was apparent that the question 'does psychotherapy work?' produced what had become known as the 'dodo bird verdict' (Lepper and Riding 2006), a reference to the Queen's declaration, in *Alice in Wonderland*, that 'all have won and all should have prizes'. The question 'does (child) psychotherapy work?' was probably too broad a question, and needed to be replaced by a more specific one: 'Which set of procedures is effective when applied to what kinds of patients with which set of problems and practiced by what sort of therapist?' (Barrett *et al.* 1978: 428). Or, in Fonagy *et al.*'s (2002) slightly pithier formulation, 'What works for whom?'

This specification of the research question has led child psychotherapy researchers in two principal directions. On the one hand, there has been an increase in research on psychodynamic child psychotherapy as a *specific* modality of treatment in relation to *specific* groups of children ('what works for whom?'). On the other hand, there has been an increased research interest in investigating the *processes* that take place in psychodynamic child psychotherapy that may lead to change, so that what goes on in treatment itself can be related to changes at outcome ('process-outcome' research).

There is not space here to review all the research that has taken place in the last twenty years in these two domains, which has been extensively reviewed by Kennedy (2004) and Kennedy and Midgley (2007). Instead, the following sections will give a brief overview of key findings and provide some flavour of the kind of work that has been done recently to address the questions of 'what works for whom?' and 'what are the processes that lead to change?' in the field of psychodynamic child psychotherapy.

What works for whom?

In a systematic review of the evidence base for psychoanalytic child psychotherapy carried out in 2004, Kennedy identified thirty-two distinct research studies that were of a sufficiently high quality to be considered appropriate for drawing conclusions about the efficacy of this form of treatment (including six randomised controlled trials). Kennedy noted that 'a vast majority of studies were undertaken in clinically referred samples rather than samples recruited for research', involving children with a range of diagnoses or problems and involving well-trained psychotherapists. This would indicate that the findings are likely to have relevance to the 'real world' setting.

The systematic review suggested that many of the children studied had high levels of clinical disturbance, and most of the studies made use of a broad range of outcome measures, including standardised psychiatric and psychological measures. Most studies were of children presenting with a range of difficulties, rather than one specific diagnostic group, although some studies also focused more specifically on particular diagnostic categories. Unusually, many of the studies (twenty) included a long-term follow-up, ranging from one and a half to forty years.

Some of the key findings are outlined below:

- Overall, beneficial effects were shown on a broad range of outcome measures, for children with a wide range of psychological disorders.
- Several studies indicated that improvements were sustained or even enhanced at long-term follow-up, suggesting the possibility of a 'sleeper effect' in psychoanalytic treatments (Trowell *et al.* 2002, 2007; Muratori *et al.* 2002, 2003).
- Follow-up into adulthood indicated the important long-term impact of psychoanalytic treatment in childhood, both in terms of objective measures and the former client's own perspective (Schachter 2004; Schachter and Target 2009; Midgley and Target 2005; Midgley *et al.* 2006)
- Some studies suggest that younger children are more likely to improve with treatment (Fonagy and Target 1994; Target and Fonagy 1994a, 1994b), and that work with parents or families alongside the individual treatment was an important component of the treatment (Szapocznik 1989).
- Evidence was also found to support the effectiveness of treatment with adolescents and young adults (Baruch 1995; Baruch *et al.* 1998; Sinha and Kapur 1999; Gerber 2004).
- Children with less severe levels of disturbance appear to respond equally well to less intensive (e.g. weekly) or short-term treatment as to more intensive (e.g. three to four times weekly) or longer-term treatment (Muratori *et al.* 2002, 2003; Smyrnios and Kirkby 1993; Fonagy and Target 1994).
- Children with more severe levels of disturbance, if they are to show improvement, appear to respond to more intensive treatment. Such improvement is especially noted at the point of long-term follow-up (Boston, Lush *et al.* 1998; Schachter and Target 2009; Heinicke and Ramsay-Klee 1986).

- Broadly speaking, children with emotional/internalising disorders appeared to respond to psychoanalytic psychotherapy better than children with disruptive/externalising disorders (Baruch *et al.* 1998; Fonagy and Target 1996; Muratori *et al.* 2002, 2003).
- Specific studies identified evidence for effectiveness with specific groups of children, including those suffering from depression (Target and Fonagy 1994b; Trowell *et al.* 2007; Horn *et al.* 2005), anxiety disorders (Target and Fonagy 1994a; Kronmüller *et al.* 2005), behaviour disorders (Kronmüller 2006; Winkelmann *et al.* 2005), personality disorder (Gerber 2004), specific learning difficulties (Heinicke and Ramsey-Klee 1986), pervasive developmental disorders (Alonim 2003; Reid *et al.* 2001), eating disorders (Robin *et al.* 1999; Vilvisk and Vagnum 1990), severely deprived children and children in foster care (Lush *et al.* 1998), sexually abused girls (Trowell *et al.* 2002) and children with poorly controlled diabetes (Moran *et al.* 1991).
- Some studies identified possible adverse effects of treatment, e.g. if inadequate treatment is provided for severe levels of disturbance (Target and Fonagy 2002) or, in one study, if individual therapy is offered without concurrent parent or family work (Szapokznik *et al.* 1989)

Although the development of an 'evidence base' for psychoanalytic child psychotherapy is still at an early stage, the above summary indicates that there is preliminary evidence for the beneficial effects of treatment, although the limitations of the research used to evaluate psychotherapy are substantial and questions still remain about how well such findings can be translated to the actual clinical setting.

Perhaps most importantly, even when outcome research suggests that a particular form of treatment does have an impact, it usually tells us very little about the reasons the treatment worked, i.e. what are the *mechanisms* whereby change is brought about. In a wide-ranging review, Kazdin (2000) noted that only 3 per cent of outcome studies incorporated any analysis of the actual process of treatment, yet as Shirk and Russell (1996) pointed out, 'we simply cannot turn to more or even better outcome research to identify the processes responsible for change':

> Instead we need to actually look at what is done in the therapy hour, and to connect significant therapeutic events in sessions, comprised of aspects of therapist-child interaction, to changes that may occur in pathogenic processes or structures that led to the child's referral.
>
> (ibid.: 89)

For this reason, many researchers are turning to the study of the psychotherapy *process* itself as a vital aspect of the child psychotherapy research agenda.

What are the processes that lead to change in child psychotherapy?

Process research – the empirical study of what actually takes place in a psychotherapy treatment – is the means by which we explore *why* and *how* change takes place as the consequence of a therapeutic intervention. Such research adds depth and understanding to the question of 'what works for whom?' (Fonagy *et al.* 2002) and has the potential to help identify the change mechanisms that form the basis for a successful clinical intervention. As such, this approach to research can help develop a more clinically-relevant research agenda and, according to a recent review, is 'probably the best short-term and long-term investment for improving clinical practice and patient care' (Kazdin and Nock 2003: 1117).

From a certain point of view, every clinical paper in the field of child psychotherapy could be described as a piece of research into therapeutic process and the nature of change (Midgley 2006a). Yet because of the range of theoretical models of therapeutic change found in the psycho-analytic literature – some compatible, others contradictory – Kazdin's words of caution, although addressed to all types of child psychotherapy research, are perhaps especially relevant to psychoanalytic child psycho-therapists:

> Conceptualizations often are at such a global level that they defy empirical evaluation . . . The safety of a technique is assured in the short run by hiding behind global interpretations and clinical experience. However, the techniques and their interpretations will wither with changing times and fads if not subjected to and bolstered by empirical findings.
>
> (Kazdin 2000: 217)

As Kazdin makes clear, such empirical study is not only of value to researchers examining the underlying mechanisms to explain the outcome of psychotherapy; it is also of value to clinicians who wish to systematically examine the nature of psychoanalytic work with children with the aim of clarifying and improving clinical practice.

The empirical study of the process of psychotherapy with adults has developed rapidly during the last twenty years, but progress in the systematic study of work with children has lagged behind. Llewelyn and Hardy (2001), in a helpful review of process research in *adult* psychotherapy, distinguish between three types of process research:

- studies which describe behaviours and processes occurring within therapy sessions (descriptive studies)
- studies which investigate the links between specific psychotherapy processes and treatment outcome (hypothesis testing)

- studies which examine specific psychotherapy processes and theories of change (theory development) (2001: 1).

Within the field of child psychotherapy, nearly all *clinical* case reports can be seen as contributing to 'theory development' (which is why psychoanalytic child psychotherapy is so theoretically rich), while most (but not all) *empirical* research studies carried out to date fall within the first category of 'exploratory studies' (making them more 'reliable', but often less theoretically interesting). This is to be expected in a fairly undeveloped area of empirical research, where the priority is on the development of measures and the meaningful description of the clinical process with children. After all, as Shirk and Russell point out, 'to understand *how* and *why* therapy works requires specification of *what* actually transpires in the therapy session' (1996: x). Nevertheless, it is important to keep in mind that such descriptive research is only a starting point, from which more sophisticated and clinically meaningful research can develop.

Descriptive studies of behaviours and processes within child psychotherapy

Shirk and Russell (1996) have helpfully reviewed the history of the development of measures in the wider field of child psychotherapy (both psychodynamic and behavioural). They note how early process research in the field of child psychotherapy was often done from the perspective of client-centred play therapy, and consequently focused on dimensions such as the level of therapist empathy, warmth and positive regard or the quality and type of children's play activity during therapy.

In more recent years, a psychodynamic perspective has led to some interesting work trying to categorise the quality of children's play in ways that go beyond themes and subject-matter (e.g. Marans *et al.* 1991). In a series of papers, Chazan and her colleagues (e.g. Kernberg, Chazan and Normandin 1998; Chazan 2002) have demonstrated the reliability and validity of a psychodynamically-informed measure of in-session play activity, the *Children's Play Therapy Instrument* (CPTI), and demonstrated its use in a number of different clinical contexts to reveal the formal structure and underlying meaning of play activity, as well as demonstrating the development of play-themes across the course of a particular therapy.

Alongside the more specific focus on play activity, researchers such as Alvarez and Lee (2004), Trowell *et al.* (2003), Harrison (2003) and Leudar *et al.* (2008) have attempted to provide a detailed, qualitative account of the process of psychoanalytic child psychotherapy, often at the level of detailed moment-by-moment interactions. Complementing such approaches, Philps (2009) has developed a form of 'systematic mapping' of the child psychotherapy process, which aims to capture the fine-grained transference and countertransference processes, as well as levels of interpretation, in a more nuanced way.

Philps' work responds to a pressing need for approaches that capture the complete process of a psychotherapeutic encounter in all its complexity, rather than focusing on the description of child and therapist behaviours in isolation from each other. While this has been done successfully at a qualitative level, researchers have also been keen to develop *quantitative* measures of the therapeutic process, which could be reliably coded and used to test specific hypotheses. A number of such measures have been developed for the broad range of child psychotherapies (e.g. Estrada and Russell 1999; Weersing *et al.* 2002; Schneider 2004), and initial studies have shown that these measures can discriminate successfully between psychodynamic and other forms of child therapy, such as cognitive behavioural therapy (CBT) (e.g. Schneider *et al.* 2009). Other measures (e.g. Fonagy *et al.* 1993; Gerber 2004) have been developed specifically to rate the process of *psychoanalytic* child psychotherapy, and offer a much more fine-grained account of the psychodynamic process. Inevitably, such fine-grained detail makes such measures more time-consuming to use, and less easy to rate reliably when used in a research context.

Hypothesis testing studies which investigate the links between specific psychotherapy processes and treatment outcome

While the mapping of the psychotherapeutic process can be seen as an aim in itself, in practice the development of reliable measures of what goes on in therapy has been driven by the wish to link aspects of that process to the outcome of treatment, in order to establish what aspects of treatment are most effective to promote change. This has led to what is called 'process-outcome' research.

In the field of *adult* psychotherapy, Lambert and Barley (2002) identified four primary aspects of the therapeutic process that have been reliably related to outcome, and assessed the relative impact of each of these factors, when all studies are combined together:

- 40 per cent – extra-therapeutic factors relating to the client (ego strength, willingness to engage in therapy, spontaneous remission)
- 30 per cent – relationship factors (e.g. level of therapeutic alliance, facilitative conditions, successful engagement)
- 15 per cent – expectancy (e.g. belief in treatment)
- 15 per cent – techniques (e.g. various aspects of how the therapist works, such as focus on interpretation) (from Lepper and Riding, 2006).

In the field of *child* psychotherapy, process-outcome measures assessing specific hypotheses about what aspects of therapy may lead to change are much rarer, especially when it comes to psychoanalytic approaches, and it would be premature to try and draw any broad conclusions. Nevertheless, specific studies identify some interesting findings, which deserve further exploration. For example, in a study of young adults with severe personality disorders in psychoanalytic psychotherapy (Gerber 2004), an analysis of the process measures from the first year of each treatment was carried out in order to explore links between process and outcome. The results of a factor analysis showed that higher scores in the first year on therapist dynamic technique, patient dynamic material and discussion of contract were predictive of positive outcome. Such studies deserve to be replicated, in order to establish the wider validity of their findings.

An extremely sophisticated approach to investigating the interaction between therapist and child was taken by Russell *et al.* (1996) using a confirmatory p-technique to examine therapist discourse in high-quality versus low-quality child psychotherapy sessions. They found that two factors – 'Responsive Informing' (i.e. responsively attending to the child in the present and using neutral description) and 'Initiatory Questioning' (i.e. acquiring novel information from the child about his or her recent past through questioning) – both characterised independently-rated high-quality sessions, with the former being most responsible for the distinction between 'good' and 'bad' sessions.

Some of the most persuasive research in the process-outcome field has examined single cases of child psychotherapy (e.g. Moran and Fonagy 1987). While the focus on a single case limits the degree to which the findings can be generalised, it allows for a much more in-depth exploration of the therapeutic process, thereby making the findings more clinically rich and meaningful. For example, a recent study of the long-term psychoanalytic treatment of a depressed child, analysed using the Child Psychotherapy Q-Set (Schneider 2004), was able to identify three key aspects of the therapeutic interaction that characterised the treatment, and tracked the shifts in the patterns of interaction across the course of treatment. Changes in the therapeutic process could be clearly related to overall changes in the child, as identified by independent measures of change (Duncan 2006; Schneider *et al.* 2009).

Studies such as the ones described above avoid some of the shortcomings of much of the process-outcome research that has been carried out in the field of psychotherapy generally, in which a whole range of process measures are computed with various measures of outcome in order to pick up any possible set of correlations, often in a very a-theoretical manner. Much of the process-outcome research also works with a false assumption that any given client or therapist behaviour 'is either "good" or "bad" without regard to the context in which it appears' (Rice and Greenberg 1984: 10), so that simply doing 'more' of a certain thing (e.g. making more transference interpretations) will lead to a better outcome. Such findings often tell us little about actual mechanisms of change because they rely merely on statistical correlations and do not emerge from the exploration of the psychotherapy process as it takes on meaning *specifically for a particular therapist–child dyad.*

For this reason, research in recent years has moved away from 'process-outcome' studies to a more theoretically-informed analysis of the therapeutic process, often focusing on the understanding of a small number of cases and explored in the context of a specific theoretical concept, as will be described in the following section.

Theory development – studies which examine specific psychotherapy processes and theories of change

Llewelyn and Hardy (2001) suggest that this third strand of process research, perhaps the most promising, is 'based on the belief that further progress [in studying the therapeutic process] will only be made if it is based more soundly on theory about how change is possible', taking into account the true complexity of the process and the way in which the meaning of behaviour is determined by its context. In the field of adult psychotherapy research, they argue that such studies, by adopting complex designs and abandoning the statistical correlation model, have illuminated our understanding of change processes, even if the findings are often limited in terms of their generalisability.

In the field of psychoanalytic child psychotherapy, few studies of this kind exist, but those that do show some promise. Carlberg (1997), for example, describes the importance of experiences of 'new intersubjectivity' in the process of therapeutic change, by identifying what can be considered key 'turning points' in the course of treatment. While these studies are based on therapist recall, the use of video-taped recordings of child psychotherapy sessions has also allowed micro-analysis of moment-by-moment interactions between child and therapist, such as the mutual regulation of affect-states (Harrison 2003), the therapist's use of 'affective scaffolding' to foster emotional emotional development (Kassett *et al.* 2004), or the strategies or 'devices' used by child psychotherapists by means of which the play activities of children are transformed, within a clinical setting, into emotionally meaningful communications which can be used in therapeutically relevant ways (Leudar *et al.* 2008).

It would be premature to attempt to synthesise the findings of these studies into an overall view of the key 'change processes' that characterise psychoanalytic child psychotherapy, and the empirical investigation of psychoanalytic hypotheses about the nature of therapeutic change is still in its infancy. However, the value of such work lies in the possibility of identifying theoretically-meaningful, empirically-based understanding of the process of child psychotherapy. This would make possible a more clinically relevant form of outcome research, in which statistical evidence for effectiveness could be coupled with increased *understanding* of why therapy works – and more importantly, sometimes does *not* work. Such research offers a potential bridge between researchers and clinicians, with potential uses in the training and supervision of therapists, with the ultimate aim of not only *evaluating* treatment, but also finding ways of *improving* clinical interventions.

Beyond process and outcome research: investigating the internal world of the child[3]

While investigations of the outcome of child psychotherapy, and into the kinds of processes that may lead to successful or unsuccessful outcome, have in certain respects dominated the agenda when it comes to research, there are many other areas where child psychotherapy research has begun to make a significant contribution. In particular, the long-standing interest of psychoanalytic psychotherapists in understanding the 'internal world' of the child has led to a number of interesting research developments.

In addition to the knowledge that has been built up through the cumulative experience and writings of numerous clinicians (as represented in the other chapters in this handbook), systematic research has also been carried out through various study groups and workshops, on topics such as children with visual impairment (Burlingham 1972) or children with autism (Reid *et al.* 2001). The advantages of the clinical workshop or study group as a form of research have been clearly outlined by Rustin (1984), and it has been one of the most productive methods of research within the field of child psychotherapy, leading to clearly-articulated models of psychoanalytic practice in specific fields. Such studies have been one of the principal ways in which new psychoanalytic concepts have emerged and are of clear clinical significance to others working in that field.

The limitation of such an approach, however, is the lack of systematic and explicit methods of data collection and data analysis, preventing others from independently evaluating the way in which the findings have emerged, thereby leaving such studies vulnerable to accusations of bias. For this reason, these studies have often had a significant impact on those already *within* the field of psychoanalytic child psychotherapy, but have had limited influence on those *outside* the field.

More systematic research, in which methods of data collection and analysis have been more explicitly delineated, while still retaining the basic procedures of psychoanalytic child psychotherapy, include Anderson's work on children exhibiting risk-taking and dangerous behaviour (2003), Reid's work on perinatal loss (2003) or Hindle's investigations of the experience of siblings in foster care (2000). All these studies have used the basic methods of psychoanalytic child psychotherapy – process recordings of unstructured clinical interviews – as the basis for their work, while introducing more systematic means of data analysis.

Some empirical researchers have attempted to focus on certain aspects of the child's inner world, as viewed from a psychoanalytic perspective. There have been studies of children's defence mechanisms (Laor *et al.* 2001; Cramer 2000); investigations of paranoid-schizoid and depressive functioning (Philps 2009); core conflictual relationship themes (Luborsky *et al.* 1995); and the quality of object relations (e.g. Tuber 2000; Kelly 2005).

Other studies have used 'mixed' methods, often combining a psychoanalytic and an attachment perspective. For example, recent work by Wright and colleagues looked at attachment in suicidal adolescents and explored the phenomenology of different presentations of suicidality from a psychodynamic as well as attachment theory perspective (Wright *et al.* 2005). This study found that high suicide risk adolescents tended to produce narratives which, in attachment terms, were characteristic of 'enmeshed/preoccupied' models of attachment. The study also found that characteristics of the young person's attachment pattern guided how they communicated their suicidality. The narratives of the preoccupied-insecure group were characterised by being trapped within a great sense of worry, having high degrees of incoherence and communicating anxiety to others. In contrast those classified as insecure/dismissing downplayed their suicidal feelings so that there was a risk that clinicians might underestimate the level of risk.

The impact of abuse on the development of the child's 'inner world': the Story Stems Assessment Battery

Wright *et al.*'s research is a good example of the integration of psychodynamic and attachment perspectives, which has also characterised much of the research looking at children in the care system and the impact of abuse on children's development. Some of the most interesting research of this kind has made use of the 'Story Stems Assessment Battery' (SSAP, Hodges *et al.* 2004), a series of thirteen stories told using a standard set of family dolls and animals in which an interviewer narrates briefly the beginning of the story and invites the child to 'show me and tell me what happens next'. The narratives are then systematically coded, with the stories being viewed not so much as an indicator of reality but rather of how 'the child reflects upon reality' (Hodges and Steele 2000) – in other words, the internal world of the child.

Informed by psychoanalytic ideas, as well as Bowlby's metaphor of 'internal working models' of attachment, the child psychotherapists who developed the SSAP, Miriam Steele and Jill Hodges, hypothesised that children's representations are built up over time in response to expectable interactions with others. They suggested that a narrative method would elicit 'generic representations of child-parent relationships, because these are, arguably, the most likely to affect later relationships' (Hodges and Steele 2000). Ratings on individual themes can be used for detailed clinical assessment and also to generate global constructs such as the nature of attachments, positive and negative representations of adults and children, defensive avoidance and disorganisation. The stems have been widely used in a clinical context, as a way of assessing the child's internal world, but they have also been used in the context of research with particular groups of children, especially those who have experienced abuse and maltreatment.

Understanding the ways that abuse can impact on children psychologically has been a crucial research question. Research suggests that children removed from families in which they have been abused and placed in foster or residential care demonstrated fewer themes of realistic or pleasurable domestic life in their narratives than children from a 'normal' control group. The abused group more often depicted themes such as a child being injured or dead; adults as unaware of children's needs or distress; lack of acknowledgement of distress; shifts in a character from being 'bad' to 'good' or vice versa.

The Thomas Coram Adoption Project (Hodges *et al.* 2003) went on to look at changes in these children's behaviour following adoptive placement. One year after adoption, changes in the SSAP could be identified in relation to narratives of parents helping children, although there was little change in terms of parents being represented as affectionate or aggressive. Some small changes were also noted in the child's self-representation and tendency towards 'magical/omnipotent responses' a year following adoption. Hodges and her colleagues' conclusion is that changes in the children's representations over time indicate 'not erosion but competition: not so much that earlier, negative internal working models fade away, but rather that alternative, competing ones get developed and may even become dominant' (Hodges and Steele 2000). The job of adopters could be seen as the 'active disconfirmation of existing negative models and building up of competing ones' (Hodges and Steele 2000).

Conclusion

Studies such as the Thomas Coram Adoption Project are a good example of the way in which child psychotherapy research can integrate methods – and ways of thinking –from different fields, while making an important contribution to the psychoanalytic understanding of the internal world. As such, it complements both more traditional forms of clinical investigation, and more formal research into the process and outcome of psychoanalytic child psychotherapy itself. It also bears testimony to the range of research activity within this field, and what it can offer as a method of exploration.

At its heart, the word 'research' simply implies a wish to investigate, to look again (re-search), to go beyond accepted viewpoints and to challenge the way we see things. As Dallos and Vetere (2005) have pointed out, this makes research a potentially subversive process – with a role to 'say unpalatable things, to surprise us' (p. 11). As such, it is highly compatible with the tradition of psychoanalysis itself, which has a long tradition of forcing us to 'look again' at those aspects of reality that may be hidden from conscious awareness and to confront us with unpalatable – yet important – truths. Research not only benefits those outside child psychotherapy, who may need empirical evidence for the claims made by the profession; it also benefits those within the profession, as it teaches us to question our own assumptions and has the potential to re-invigorate clinical practice. Ultimately, a thriving research culture within child psychotherapy is of vital importance both to those working in the field, and to those children and families who turn to child psychotherapists for help.

Notes

1 Some parts of this section of the chapter are based on the document, 'Process and Outcome Research in Child, Adolescent and Parent–Infant Psychotherapy: a Thematic Review' (Kennedy and Midgley 2007). Thanks to Dr Eilis Kennedy and the North Central London Strategic Health Authority (now NHS London) for permission to make use of this material.
2 These are studies in which large groups of children, often matched in terms of age, family background, nature of disturbance etc., are seen randomly for either psychotherapy or some form of 'control' situation (another form of treatment, or no treatment) and assessed using standardised measures, which are then analysed quantitatively to assess whether there are any statistically significant differences between the two groups.
3 Some parts of this section of the chapter are based on the document, 'Process and Outcome Research in Child, Adolescent and Parent–Infant Psychotherapy: a Thematic Review' (Kennedy and Midgley 2007). Thanks to Dr Eilis Kennedy and the North Central London Strategic Health Authority (now NHS London) for permission to make use of this material.

References

Alonim, H. (2004) 'The Mifne Method – ISRAEL: early intervention in the treatment of autism/PDD: a therapeutic programme for the nuclear family and their child', *Journal of Child and Adolescent Mental Health* 16: 39–43.

Alvarez, A. and Lee, A. (2004) 'Early forms of relatedness in autism: a longitudinal clinical and quantitative single-case study', *Clinical Child Psychology and Psychiatry* 9(4): 499–518.

Anderson, J. (2003) 'The mythic significance of risk-taking, dangerous behaviour', *Journal of Child Psychotherapy* 29(1): 75–91.

—— (2006) 'Well-suited partners: psychoanalytic research and grounded theory', *Journal of Child Psychotherapy* 32(3): 329–48.

Barrett, C., Hampe, I. and Miller, L. (1978) 'Research on child psychotherapy', in S. Garfield and A. Bergin (eds) *Handbook of Psychotherapy and Behaviour Change: An Empirical Analysis*, 2nd edn, New York: Wiley and Sons, pp. 411–35.

Baruch, G. (1995) 'Evaluating the outcome of a community-based psychoanalytic psychotherapy service for young people between 12–25 years old: work in progress', *Psychoanalytic Psychotherapy* 9(3): 243–67.

Baruch, G., Fearon, P. and Gerber, A. (1998) 'Evaluating the outcome of a community-based psychoanalytic psychotherapy service for young people: one year repeated follow up', in R. Davenhill and M. Patrick (eds) *Rethinking Clinical Audit*, London: Routledge, pp. 157–82.

Boëthius, S. and Berggren, G. (2000) *Forskning om Barn-och Ungdomspsykoterapi*, Stockholm: Ericastiftelsen.

Boston, M. (1989) 'In search of a methodology for evaluating psychoanalytic psychotherapy with children', *Journal of Child Psychotherapy* 15(1): 15–46.

Burlingham, D. (1972) 'Psychoanalytic studies of the sighted and the blind', New York: International Universities Press.

Carlberg, G. (1997) 'Laughter opens the door: turning points in child psycho-therapy', *Journal of Child Psychotherapy* 23(3): 331–49.

Casey, R. and Berman, J. (1985) 'The outcome of psychotherapy with children', *Psychological Bulletin* 98: 388–400.

Chazan, S. E. (2002) *Profiles of Play: Assessing Structure and Process in Play Therapy*, London: Jessica Kingsley.

Cramer, P. (2000) 'Changes in defence mechanisms during psychoanalysis and psychotherapy: a case study', in J. Cohen and B. Cohler (eds) *The Psychoanalytic Study of Lives Over Time*, San Diego: Academic Press, pp. 309–30.

Dallos, R. and Vetere, A. (2005) *Researching Psychotherapy and Counselling*, Maidenhead: Open University Press.

Desmarais, S. (2007) 'Hard science, thin air and unexpected guests: a pluralistic model of rationality, knowledge and conjecture in child psychotherapy research', *Journal of Child Psychotherapy* 33(3): 283–307.

Dreher, U. A. (2000) *Foundations for Conceptual Research in Psychoanalysis*, London: Karnac.

Duncan, A. (2006) *The developmental lines of child psychotherapy process*. Unpublished MSc dissertation. Anna Freud Centre/University College London.

Estrada, A. and Russell, R. (1999) 'The development of the child psychotherapy process scales (CPPS)', *Psychotherapy Research* 9(2): 154–66.

Eysenck, H. (1952) 'The effects of psychotherapy: an evaluation', *Journal of Consulting and Clinical Psychology* 60: 659–63.

Fonagy, P. (2003) 'The research agenda: the vital need for empirical research in child psychotherapy', *Journal of Child Psychotherapy* 29: 129–36.

Fonagy, P. and Target, M. (1994) 'The efficacy of psychoanalysis for children with disruptive disorders', *Journal of the American Academy of Child and Adolescent Psychiatry* 33(1): 45–55.

—— (1996) 'Predictors of outcome in child psychoanalysis: a retrospective study of 793 cases at the Anna Freud Centre', *Journal of the American Psychoanalytic Association* 44(1): 27–77.

Fonagy, P., Philips, B., Buchan, E., Target, M. and Weise, K. (1993) *The Anna Freud Centre session rating scale for children and adolescents*. Unpublished manuscript, London: Anna Freud Centre.

Fonagy, P., Target, M., Cottrell, D., Phillips, J. and Kurtz, Z. (2002) *What Works for Whom? A Critical Review of Treatments for Children and Adolescents*, New York: Guilford Publications.

Gerber, A. (2004) *Structural and symptomatic change in psychoanalysis and psychodynamic psychotherapy: a quantitative study of process, outcome and attachment*. Unpublished PhD thesis, University College London.

Harrison, A. (2003) 'Change in psychoanalysis: getting from A to B', *Journal of the American Psychoanalytic Association* 51(1): 221–56.

Heinicke, C. M. and Ramsay-Klee, D. M. (1986) 'Outcome of child psychotherapy as a function of frequency of session', *Journal of the American Academy of Child and Adolescent Psychiatry* 25(2): 247–53.

Hindle, D. (2000) 'Assessing children's perspectives on sibling placements in foster or adoptive homes', *Clinical Child Psychology and Psychiatry* 5(4): 613–26.

Hodges, J. (1999) 'Research in child and adolescent psychotherapy: an overview', in M. Lanyado and A. Horne (eds) *The Handbook of Child and Adolescent Psychotherapy. Psychoanalytic Approaches*, London: Routledge.

Hodges, J. and Steele, M. (2000) 'Effects of abuse on attachment representations: narrative assessments of abused children', *Journal of Child Psychotherapy* 26(3): 433–55.

Hodges, J., Steele, M., Hillman, S., Henderson, K. and Kaniuk, J. (2003) 'Changes in attachment representations over the first year of adoptive placement: narratives of maltreated children', *Clinical Child Psychology and Psychiatry* 8(3): 351–68.

Hodges, J., Hillman, S., Steele, M. and Henderson, K. (2004) *Story Stem Assessment Profile Rating Manual*, unpublished manuscript, London: Anna Freud Centre.

Horn, H., Geiser-Elze, A., Reck, C., Hartmann, M., Stefini, A., Victor, D., Winkelmann, K. and Kronmüller, K. T. (2005) 'Efficacy of short term psychotherapy for children and adolescents with depression', *Praxis der Kinderpsychologie und Kinderpsychiatrie* 54(7): 578–97.

Kam, S. and Midgley, N. (2006) 'Exploring "clinical judgement": how do child and adolescent mental health professionals decide whether a young person needs individual psychotherapy?', *Clinical Child Psychology and Psychiatry* 11(1): 27–44.

Kassett, J., Bonanno, G. and Notarius, C. (2004) 'Affective scaffolding: a process measure for psychotherapy with children', *Journal of Infant, Child and Adolescent Psychotherapy* 3(1): 92–119.

Kazdin, A. E. (2000) *Psychotherapy for Children and Adolescents. Directions for Research and Practice*, New York: Oxford University Press.

Kazdin, A. E. and Nock, M. K. (2003) 'Delineating mechanisms of change in child and adolescent therapy: methodological issues and research recommendations', *Journal of Child Psychology and Psychiatry* 44(8): 1116–29.

Kelly, F. (2005) 'The clinical application of the Social Cognition and Object Relations Scale (SCORS-R) with children and adolescents', in S. Smith and L. Handler (eds) *The Clinical Assessment of Children and Adolescents: A Practitioner's Handbook*, Mahwah, NJ: Lawrence Erlbaum Associates Inc.

Kennedy, E. (2004) *Child and Adolescent Psychotherapy: A Systematic Review of Psychoanalytic Approaches*, London: North Central London Strategic Health Authority.

Kennedy, E. and Midgley, N. (eds) (2007) *Process and Outcome Research in Child, Adolescent and Parent–Infant Psychotherapy: A Thematic Review*, London: NHS London.

Kernberg, P. F., Chazan, S. E. and Normandin, L. (1998) 'The children's play therapy instrument (CPTI): description, development, and reliability studies', *Journal of Psychotherapy Practice and Research* 7(3): 196–207.

Kronmüller, K. (2006) *Outcome of the Heidelberger Study – Research on working with children and adolescents in long-term psychoanalytic psychotherapy*, paper presented at the European Federation of Psychoanalytic Psychotherapy Conference, Berlin.

Kronmüller, K., Postelnicu, I., Hartmann, M., Stefini, A., Geiser-Elze, A., Gerhold, M., Hildegard, H. and Winkelmann, K. (2005) 'Efficacy of psychodynamic short term psychotherapy for children and adolescents with anxiety disorders', *Praxis der Kinderpsychologie und Kinderpsychiatrie* 54(7): 559–77.

Lambert, M. and Barley, D. (2002) 'Research summary on the therapeutic relationship and psychotherapy outcome', in J. Norcross (ed.) *Psychotherapy Relationships That Work*, New York: Oxford University Press.

Laor, N., Wolmer, L. and Cicchetti, D. (2001) 'The comprehensive assessment of defense style: Measuring defense mechanisms in children and adolescents', *Journal of Nervous and Mental Disease* 189(6): 360–8.

Lepper, G. and Riding, N. (2006) *Researching the Psychotherapy Process: A Practical Guide to Transcript-based Methods*, Basingstoke: Palgrave Macmillan.

Leudar, I., Sharrock, W., Truckle, S., Colombino, T., Hayes, J. and Booth, K. (2008) 'Conversation of emotions', in C. Antaki, I. Leudar, A. Perakyla and S. Vehvilanen (eds) *Conversation Analysis of Psychotherapy*, Cambridge: CUP.

Llewelyn, S. and Hardy, G. (2001) 'Process research in understanding and applying psychological therapies', *British Journal of Clinical Psychology* 40: 1–21.

Luborsky, L., Luborsky, E., Diguer, L., Schmidt, K., Dengler, D., Schaffler, P., Faude, J., Morris, M., Buchsbaum, H. and Emde, R. (1995) 'Extending the core relationship theme into early childhood', in G. Noam and K. Fischer (eds) *Development and Vulnerability in Close Relationships*, New Jersey: Lawrence Erlbaum Associates, pp. 287–308.

Lush, D., Boston, M., Morgan, J. and Kolvin, I. (1998) 'Psychoanalytic psychotherapy with disturbed adopted and foster children: a single case follow-up study', *Clinical Child Psychology and Psychiatry* 3(1): 51–69.

Marans, S., Mayes, L., Cicchetti, D., Dahl, K., Marans, W. and Cohen, D. (1991) 'The child psychoanalytic play interview', *Journal of the American Psychoanalytic Association* 39: 1015–36.

McLeod, J. (2001) *Qualitative Research in Counselling and Psychotherapy*, London: Sage.

Midgley, N. (2004) 'Sailing between Scylla and Charybdis: incorporating qualitative approaches into child psychotherapy research', *Journal of Child Psychotherapy* 30(1): 89–111.

—— (2006a) 'The "inseparable bond between cure and research": clinical case study as a method of psychoanalytic inquiry', *Journal of Child Psychotherapy* 32(2): 122–47.

—— (2006b) 'Psychoanalysis and qualitative psychology: complementary or contradictory paradigms?', *Qualitative Research in Psychology* 3(3): 213–32.

Midgley, N. and Target, M. (2005) 'Recollections of being in child psychoanalysis: a qualitative study of a long-term follow-up study', *Psychoanalytic Study of the Child* 60: 157–77.

Midgley, N., Target, M. and Smith, J. A. (2006) 'The outcome of child psychoanalysis from the patient's point of view: a qualitative analysis of a long-term follow-up study', *Psychology and Psychotherapy: Theory, Practice, Research* 79: 257–69.

Midgley, N., Anderson, J., Grainger, E., Nesic-Vuckovic, T. and Urwin, C. (eds) (2009) *Child Psychotherapy and Research: New Approaches, Emerging Findings*, London: Routledge.

Moran, G. and Fonagy, P. (1987) 'Psychoanalysis and diabetic control: a single-case study', *British Journal of Medical Psychology* 60: 357–72.

Moran, G. S., Fonagy, P., Kurtz, A., Bolton, A. M. and Brook, C. (1991) 'A controlled study of the psychoanalytic treatment of brittle diabetes', *Journal of the American Academy of Child and Adolescent Psychiatry* 30(6): 926–35.

Muratori, F., Picchi, L., Casella, C., Tancredi, R., Milone, A. and Patarnello, M. G. (2002) 'Efficacy of brief dynamic psychotherapy for children with emotional disorders', *Psychotherapy and Psychosomatics* 71(1): 28–38.

Muratori, F., Picchi, L., Bruni, G., Patarnello, M. and Romagnoli, G. (2003) 'A two-year follow-up of psychodynamic psychotherapy for internalizing disorders in children', *Journal of the American Academy of Child and Adolescent Psychiatry* 42(3): 331–9.

Philps, J. (2009) 'Mapping process in child psychotherapy – steps towards drafting a new method for psychoanalytic psychotherapy research', in N. Midgley, J. Anderson, E. Grainger, T. Nesic-Vuckovic and C. Urwin (eds) *Child Psychotherapy and Research: New Approaches, Emerging Findings*, London: Routledge.

Reid, M. (2003) 'Clinical research: the inner world of the mother and her new baby – born in the shadow of death', *Journal of Child Psychotherapy* 29: 207–26.

Reid, S., Alvarez, A. and Lee, A. (2001) 'The Tavistock autism workshop approach: assessment, treatment and research', in J. Richer and S. Coates (eds) *Autism – the Search for Coherence*, London: Jessica Kingsley, pp. 182–92.

Rhode, M. (2004) 'Infant observation as research: cross-disciplinary links', *Journal of Social Work Practice* 18(3): 283–98.

Rice, L. and Greenberg, L. (eds) (1984) *Patterns of Change. Intensive Analysis of Psychotherapy Process*, New York: Guilford Press.

Robin, A., Siegel, P., Moye, A., Gilroy, M., Dennis, A. B. and Sikand, A. (1999) 'A controlled comparison of family versus individual psychotherapy for adolescents with anorexia nervosa', *Journal of the American Academy of Child and Adolescent Psychiatry* 38(12): 1482–9.

Russell, R., Bryant, F. and Estrada, A. (1996) 'Confirmatory p-technique analyses of therapist discourse: high- versus low-quality child therapy sessions', *Journal of Consulting and Clinical Psychology* 64(6): 1366–76.

Rustin, M. E. (1984) 'The strengths of a practitioner's workshop as a new model in clinical research', in S. Miller and R. Szur (eds) *Extending Horizons*, London: Karnac, 1991, pp. 379–88.

Rustin, M. (2003) 'Research in the consulting room', *Journal of Child Psychotherapy* 29: 137–45.

Schachter, A. (2004) *The adult outcome of child psychoanalysis: A long-term follow-up study*. Unpublished PhD thesis, University College London.

Schachter, A. and Target, M. (2009) 'The history and current status of outcome research at the Anna Freud Centre', in N. Midgley, J. Anderson, E. Grainger, T. Nesic-Vuckovic and C. Urwin (eds) *Child Psychotherapy and Research: New Approaches, Emerging Findings*, London: Routledge.

Schneider, C. (2004a) 'The development of the child psychotherapy Q-set', *Dissertation Abstracts International: Section B: The Sciences & Engineering* 65(2-B): 1039.

Schneider, C., Pruetzel-Thomas, A. and Midgley, N. (2009) 'Concept and intuition in child psychotherapy research', in N. Midgley, J. Anderson, E. Grainger, T.

Nesic-Vuckovic and C. Urwin (eds) *Child Psychotherapy and Research: New Approaches, Emerging Findings*, London: Routledge.

Shirk, S. and Russell, R. (1996) *Change Processes in Child Psychotherapy. Revitalizing Treatment and Research*, New York: Guilford Press.

Sinha, U. K. and Kapur, M. (1999) 'Psychotherapy with emotionally disturbed adolescent boys: outcome and process study', *National Institute of Mental Health and Neuro Sciences Journal (NIMHANS)* 17(2): 113–30.

Sleed, M. and Bland, K. (2007) 'Parent-infant psychotherapy and research', in E. Kennedy and N. Midgley (eds) (2007) *Process and Outcome Research in Child, Adolescent and Parent–Infant Psychotherapy: A Thematic Review*, London: NHS London.

Smyrnios, K. X. and Kirby, R. J. (1993) 'Long term comparison of brief versus unlimited psychodynamic treatments with children and their parents', *Journal of Consulting and Clinical Psychology* 61(6): 1030–27.

Sternberg, J. (2005) *Infant Observation at the Heart of Training*, London: Karnac.

Szapocznik, J., Murray, E., Scopetta, M., Hervis, O., Rio, A., Cohen, R., Rivas-Vazquez, A., Posada, V. and Kurtines, W. (1989) 'Structural family versus psychodynamic child therapy for problematic Hispanic boys', *Journal of Consulting and Clinical Psychology* 57(5): 571–8.

Target, M. and Fonagy, P. (1994a) 'The efficacy of psycho-analysis for children with emotional disorders', *Journal of the American Academy of Child and Adolescent Psychiatry* 33(3): 361–71.

—— (1994b) 'The efficacy of psychoanalysis for children: prediction of outcome in a developmental context', *Journal of the American Academy of Child and Adolescent Psychiatry* 33(8): 1134–44.

—— (2002) 'Anna Freud Centre studies 3: the long-term follow-up of child analytic treatments (AFC3)', in P. Fonagy (ed.) *An Open Door Review of Outcome Studies in Psychoanalysis*, 2nd edn, London: International Psychoanalytic Association, pp. 141–6.

Trowell, J., Kolvin, I., Weeramanthri, T., Sadowski, H., Berelowitz, M., Glasser, D. and Leitch, I. (2002) 'Psychotherapy for sexually abused girls: psychopathological outcome findings and patterns of change', *British Journal of Psychiatry* 180: 234–47.

Trowell, J., Rhode, M., Miles, G. and Sherwood, I. (2003) 'Childhood depression: work in progress', *Journal of Child Psychotherapy* 29(2): 147–70.

Trowell, J., Joffe, I., Campbell, J., Clemente, C., Almqvist, F., Soininen, M., Koskenranta-Aalto, U., Weintraub, S., Kolaitis, G., Tomaras, V., Anastasopoulos, D., Grayson K., Barnes, J. and Tsiantis, J. (2007) 'Childhood depression: a place for psychotherapy. an outcome study comparing individual psychodynamic psychotherapy and family therapy', *European Child and Adolescent Psychiatry* 16(3): 157–67.

Tsiantis, J. and Trowell, J. (eds) (2009) *Assessing Change in Psychoanalytic Psychotherapy of Children and Adolescents: Today's Challenge*, London: Karnac.

Tuber, S. (2000) 'Projective testing as a post-hoc predictor of change in psychoanalysis: the case of Jim', in J. Cohen and B. Cohler (eds) *The Psychoanalytic Study of Lives Over Time*, San Diego: Academic Press, pp. 283–308.

Urwin, C. (2007) 'Revisiting "What works for whom": a qualitative method for evaluating clinical effectiveness in child psychotherapy', *Journal of Child Psychotherapy* 33(2): 134–60.

Vilvisk, S. O. and Vaglum, P. (1990) 'Teenage anorexia nervosa: a 1–9 year follow up after psychodynamic treatment', *Nordisk Psykiatrisk Tidsskrilt* 44: 249–55.

Weersing, V. R., Weisz, J. R. and Donenberg, G. R. (2002) 'Development of the Therapy Procedures Checklist: a therapist-report measure of technique use in child and adolescent treatment', *Journal of Clinical Child and Adolescent Psychology* 31(2): 168–80.

Weisz, J., Weiss, B., Alicke, M. and Klotz, M. (1987) 'Effectiveness of psychotherapy with children and adolescents: a meta-analysis for clinicians', *Journal of Consulting and Clinical Psychology* 55: 542–9.

Winkelmann, K., Stefini, A., Hartmann, M., Geiser-Elze, A., Kronmüller, A., Schenkenbach, C., Hildegard, H. and Kronmüller, K. T. (2005) 'Efficacy of psychodynamic short-term psychotherapy for children and adolescents with behaviour disorders', *Praxis der Kinderpsychologie und Kinderpsychiatrie* 54(7): 598–614.

Wright, J., Briggs, S. and Behringer, J. (2005) 'Attachment and the body in suicidal adolescents: a pilot study', *Clinical Child Psychology and Psychiatry* 10(4): 477–91.

Part II

Context

7 The child psychotherapist in the multi-disciplinary team

Gabrielle Crockatt

Introduction

Previous chapters have outlined basic psychoanalytic principles and some of the more recent theoretical developments relevant to child psychotherapy, including attachment theory, contributions from neuroscience and an overview of normal emotional development. These theoretical foundations have had a major impact on our thinking about the emotional development of children, and on the services that may need to be brought to bear when emotional difficulties emerge. They have led to concepts such as the need to think about 'the whole child' – physical and social, as well as psychological. This in turn has led to ideas about the 'multi-disciplinary team' of professionals that might be needed to assess and treat difficulties, and the 'multi-agency' systems that need to be developed if issues are to be addressed holistically.

This chapter will explore how the National Health Service (NHS), together with education, social care and voluntary agencies, has tried to develop relevant services – and how child psychotherapists have adapted their skills to work within this multi-disciplinary and multi-agency setting.

Together We Stand: towards a policy framework

The concept of the multi-disciplinary team (MDT) operating within a Child and Adolescent Mental Health Service (CAMHS) is one that has grown over time. The *Introduction* to this volume outlines the development of the Child Guidance movement in the 1920s, bringing together psychiatric social workers and specialists in Psychological Medicine to work with families. These were joined – especially in London – by graduates of the new Child Analyst/Psychotherapy trainings established after the Second World War and the new profession of Educational Psychology. London was one of many Local Education Authorities to develop a sophisticated network of child guidance units which had close relationships with mainstream and special schools. In the NHS, multi-professional Child Psychiatry Departments grew, hospital-based and led inevitably by consultant psychiatrists but including nurses, clinical psychologists and social workers in the team. These and other developments came about in a relatively organic way, often inspired by the enthusiasm of particular individuals, leading to an unevenness of provision throughout the UK. There was also much dispute as to whether CAMHS should be the responsibility of health, education, or (after 1970) social services.

In 1995 the NHS Advisory Service published a national review of CAMHS. Its report, *Together We Stand*, both described the patchwork that had developed and made recommendations for the establishment of services nationally. As the title of this document implies, the overarching thesis was that the most successful outcomes for children and their families came when services worked together to think about and address the needs of the whole child. This required teams of professionals who could offer different yet complementary perspectives in terms of assessment of need and psychopathology, and who could provide a variety of treatment options. It also required services that could be flexible in terms of working together with parents, and with other professionals concerned with children – schools and nurseries, social services departments, community and religious groups, and voluntary agencies.

Together We Stand also suggested that CAMHS should be tiered according to the complexity of the mental health condition to be addressed:

1   Tier 1 would comprise services likely to have an impact on the emotional well-being of children/young people, but where this is not the main focus of the service – for example, schools, GPs, social workers.
2   Tier 2 CAMHS would be services where a single mental health professional is able to address relatively simple conditions, and make a difference within a short space of time. Tier 2 would also represent an opportunity for access to Tier 3 for children whose condition turned out to be more complex.
3   Tier 3 was intended for more complex cases, where a team of professionals is likely to be required, with the expectation that they may need to work over time with a child/family, and in co-ordination with other services, in order to make a difference.
4   Tier 4 was for the small number of children and young people whose condition is so severe that inpatient services are required, and for those who demonstrate severe and often dangerous behaviours such as present to forensic services.

The philosophy behind the structure is focused throughout on multi-agency working: the 'multi-disciplinary team' as a team of child and family mental health specialists tends to operate at the higher tiers, 3 and 4. This system of 'tiers' has been adopted nationally and has proved helpful in organising thinking about services.

Further developments have taken place since *Together We Stand* to support this multi-disciplinary, multi-agency focus. The NHS Modernisation Board, established in 2000, comprised a partnership between management, patients, and frontline staff, to advise on the planning for the future. Advice from this body has led to some additional funding being allocated to CAMHS. A National Service Framework (NSF) for Children, Young People and Maternity Services was launched by the Department of Health in September 2004. This outlined a programme, designed to bring about sustained improvement in children's health and well-being, including the need to establish services for mothers with ante- and post-natal emotional difficulties, affirming the role of CAMHS at this stage of the life cycle. Local services are now required to demonstrate that they are able to provide a 'comprehensive CAMHS' in their area, and to identify any gaps in provision.

Children have been the focus of other important initiatives, notably the Children Act which put the onus on services to prioritise the needs of children, while working in partnership with their parents. The initiative 'Every Child Matters' (Department for Education and Skills 2004) grew out of the Children Act 2004, following the inquiry into the death of Victoria Climbié, carried out by Lord Laming and presented to Parliament in January 2003. It aims to improve the life of every child by focusing on five outcomes:

- *Being healthy*: enjoying good physical and mental health and living a healthy lifestyle.
- *Staying safe*: being protected from harm and neglect.
- *Enjoying and achieving*: getting the most out of life and developing the skills for adulthood.
- *Making a positive contribution*: being involved with the community and society and not engaging in antisocial or offending behaviour.
- *Economic well-being*: not being prevented by economic disadvantage from achieving one's full potential in life.

It is interesting that mental health is high on this list, and we can probably agree that good emotional health is an essential factor in most if not all of the five outcomes. Such a policy emphasises the fact that emotional issues cannot be separated from other aspects of life.

In line with the ambitions of 'Every Child Matters', the government has also recognised the particular importance of the early years. In addition to the inclusion of maternal mental health in the NSF, the Sure Start initiative, which has been established in the most deprived areas of the country, has aimed to improve opportunities for children aged under four and their parents.

The development of a Common Assessment Framework (CAF) for children's services is a recent government project designed to facilitate multi-agency working, beginning at the 'grass roots' level. It requires services to sign up to a system of assessment that can be recognised and accepted by all professionals working with children: it is hoped that this will prevent families having to 'tell their stories' to a succession of professionals. The CAF employs a system similar to the 'tiers' to indicate level of need and the type and level of service that is likely to be required to meet this need.

A national database for children, 'Contact Point', is also in the process of being established. There has been much controversy about it because of concerns about confidentiality, and details of the system and how it will operate remain to be worked out. Information about which services are working with a particular child will be held on the database and will be available to other professionals. No details of the actual work will be available, only the fact that a particular service is being provided to that child, and by whom. It is hoped that this will aid co-ordination of services, cut down on possible duplication, and enable the provision of co-ordinated packages of care.

In assembling a compelling evidence base for working together in CAMHS, Dr Zarrina Kurtz also drew attention to the multi-faceted nature of mental health difficulties and the services that are needed to address these (Kurtz *et al.* 1996). She placed particular emphasis on the positive therapeutic effect of, for example, being enabled to succeed in school. Her excellent short book *Treating Children Well* ends with the following statement:

> 'The evidence shows overwhelmingly that:
>
> • Multi-pronged approaches have the best chance of being effective;
> • A single service or a single source of knowledge can address only a part of the problem;
> • Small changes have a valuable additive effect;
> • The impact of one approach will be undermined if other services do not act in support.
>
> This highlights the value of multi-disciplinary working at grass roots level, and the involvement of whole communities.
>
> (Kurtz *et al.* 1996)

From its origins in the enthusiastic commitment of discrete individuals, child and adolescent mental health in the UK is beginning to become embedded in the thinking of policy makers in relation to the developmental needs of the growing child. Let us look now at the setting of the clinic team.

The multi-disciplinary team

The multi-disciplinary team is at the core of the Tier 3 service, and it would be useful to look at this concept in more detail, together with the place of the child psychotherapist in that team.

The exact composition of CAMHS teams may differ, partly according to availability of professional staff: child psychotherapists, for example, are members of a small profession, and may not be available in all parts of the country – although provision has grown markedly over the last 20 years. However, the hope is that the team will comprise professionals with expertise in medical/biological, social, and psychological aspects of functioning: and that they will be able to offer a range of interventions that will impact on these different areas and so on the whole. Treatment approaches will be based on a variety of theoretical premises, behavioural as well as psychodynamic approaches, and they will be offered to families, individuals, and groups as appropriate.

Some of the work of the team will be generic, and child psychotherapists will take a share of these tasks alongside other team members – for example, taking referrals, carrying out assessments, consultation, service development, audit.

The specific role of the child psychotherapists in the team can be defined in a number of ways, including the following:

- The primary task is the assessment and psychotherapeutic treatment of individual children. They may have additional roles in the team, but this is the basis of their training and experience, and their core professional role.
- The primary focus is the internal world of the child. They try to approach issues from the perspective of the child, to understand things through his/her eyes and through the internal sense the child has made of his/her experience. This may be particularly important in situations where children are not able to articulate what they are feeling, but are perhaps behaving in a particular way as an expression of distress, anxiety or confusion.
- Child psychotherapists embrace complexity. This may not always be popular when there is a hope that difficulties can be defined clearly and dealt with quickly: however, amidst the range of problems presenting at CAMHS, there are usually a number where it is helpful to have a team member who can take time to unravel puzzling and complex issues – including those that may be unconscious.
- Child psychotherapists are 'brought up' to be team members. D. W. Winnicott wrote that there is no baby without a mother (Winnicott 1957/64: 88). It is clear from psychoanalytic theory, and from the core training of a child psychotherapist, that in thinking about a child one must always think about upbringing, parents, and the wider family and context. As professionals who are trained to work with the child patient, this inevitably involves working closely with those professionals who are concerned with the wider world of the child. This includes being aware of unconscious processes in the parents, and at times in the professional network – not in order to interpret them, but to take account of them, help group understanding and work in the light of them.

A number of fantasies about child psychotherapists circulate in the NHS. These include that child psychotherapists live in a detached consulting-room-world of their own, and that they only see children for long and intensive individual psychoanalytic work. The fantasies may have some basis in earlier ways of working, but they also relate to some of the inherent paradoxes in working as a child psychotherapist. The confidential, internal-world, child-focused, individual psychotherapy does need to take place with the child in the consulting room, and be protected; but contact needs to be maintained with parents, schools, and other professionals working with the child.

In the past, the multi-disciplinary team would often facilitate this, in that a small team would be formed around each case with one worker for the parent and one for the child. Contact with the 'outside world' would mainly be taken care of by the professional working with the parents. There were some advantages to this, in that the child psychotherapist was then free to work within an atmosphere of 'psychoanalytic quiet' and concentrate on the relationship with the child in the room. However, colleagues working with parents sometimes felt treated as 'handmaidens of child psychother-apy', which did not foster good team relationships. In addition, it was often not the parent worker that schools, social services, or parents wanted to have discussions with, but the person with the direct experience of seeing the child. Child psychotherapists were in danger of seeming like mythical beasts who, together with the children they had captured, inhabited some secret and ideal world which bore very little relation to the 'ordinary difficulties' that were being experienced by key adults in the world outside the consulting room.

There are a number of advantages to having greater connection with others working with the child. These include being known by colleagues in other agencies and therefore being in a position to share perspectives on a child. The child psychotherapist may have a particular view on a child's experiences and emotions, which can helpfully be shared with a teacher, and which may illuminate some previously unexplained behaviour. Very often all professionals dealing with a child have similar difficult experi-ences, and can discuss these and empathise with one another, while also building up a more complete picture of the child's functioning. Meeting professionals from other agencies may also make it more possible to negotiate a clear package of care, in which work done in a clinic setting can be backed up by sympathetic help for the child in school.

It is helpful if the child in therapy is prepared for the therapist to have contact with parents or other professionals: there can then be some dis-cussion about those important aspects of the treatment that remain confi-dential, and also agreement about how to let the child know the outcome of such meetings. The child, indeed, may not primarily experience a ther-apist's having contact with others in the network as a loss of confidentiality. There may be positives for the child in feeling that there is a potentially protective connection between the therapist and other important figures in his world. Similarly, the sense that there is a working alliance between parent and therapist may feel reassuring.

What has interested me in terms of my own practice is the extent to which it is possible to go into a room with a child or young person and simply *be* with them. Sometimes the outside world of school or social services may intrude, but as often as not the power of the presence of the two people in the room is stronger than these outside influences.

Deborah

A brief example may help illustrate some of these points. Here a child psychotherapist is working in a Tier 3 multi-disciplinary context.

Deborah, aged seven, had come to the attention of the clinic because of her confrontational behaviour in school. As is usual in this particular clinic, Deborah and members of her immediate family were all included in the assessment. It quickly became clear that the relationship between her parents was also confrontational, and the marriage broke up soon after the first appointment. Family therapy was begun, but with a sense of the whole family being under immense strain. The school continued to complain that Deborah was rude and disobedient and that they might have no alternative but to exclude her.

The family therapist then suggested that a child psychotherapist could join her to meet Deborah and her mother, to explore whether individual psychotherapy for Deborah might help. As a result of that meeting, it was concluded that the mother was really struggling to bring up her three children as a single working parent, and that Deborah was demanding more from her than she felt she had the time or emotional energy to give. On the basis of this meeting, therefore, it was agreed that Deborah should be seen by the child psychotherapist for a psychotherapy assessment.

In the assessment sessions there emerged a little girl who was both very demanding and very needy. She rushed to use everything in the room, as though she was starving and wanted to make sure she would experience every single toy and piece of art material before she had to leave.

A meeting was called by the school before the assessment had been completed, and was attended by members of the education service and Deborah's mother and grandfather. Plans were put in place to provide additional support for Deborah in school but the bad feeling between the family and the head teacher was such that it seemed unlikely that these would be effective. The family decided that Deborah would not get a fair chance if she stayed in this school and found another school for her. Her mother also accepted the clinic's offer of parenting sessions with the family therapist, and occasional family sessions, alongside individual psychotherapy for Deborah. Her father no longer wished to be involved.

Deborah was seen in weekly psychotherapy for two years. It was most illuminating to see her family through her eyes. Each of her parents had children from different relationships, and she thought of all of these as her siblings. However, different brothers and sisters lived in different places and with different adults, and she saw more or less of them depending on current relationships between the adults. Moreover, she herself did not have a settled room, or even a bed, of her own, but often shared with her grandmother. Her main sense was one of utter confusion, and also anxiety that nothing was for her and that nothing could be counted on to be reliable. This feeling, of course, extended to her therapy, where each week it was difficult to end the session because of Deborah's anxiety that she might never get back to the clinic again.

Deborah's mother had very much wanted to bring Deborah to sessions, but this started out as chaotic: she worked nearby and would run from work to bring Deborah to the clinic and then to take her back to school – often arriving late, and both of them out of breath. She then had an operation on her feet, which meant that she was unable to bring Deborah at all. Luckily the clinic employs a driver who was able to step in. When he became ill, the school provided a learning mentor to bring her to her sessions. This was a very practical expression of multi-agency negotiation, achievable because of the close relationship that it had been possible to establish with the new school.

The school hosted regular termly meetings to review progress, including the learning mentor, Deborah's teacher, her mother, and the psychotherapist. In these meetings the group was able to move from identifying Deborah as 'rude and disobedient' to 'anxious, needy, and confused'. More importantly, both her new school and her psychotherapist identified the potential zest for life that lay behind her neediness, and so were able to find more positive words to describe her, such as 'lively' and 'enthusiastic'. Working on this premise, her teacher gave her responsibilities such as taking the register down to the office. This helped her to feel valued, but was also a task that was very regular and happened in the same way every day, and contributed to a sense of order and predictability.

Things began to change in Deborah's therapy when she had attended for over a year. She loved the sense that she could now say, 'Do you remember last year when . . .'. The biggest change in her material was that she began to be more able to settle down, and to take on large projects which might be started in one session and finished the next. Her therapist talked about the fact that she now did believe that she would come to the clinic again, and that not everything had to be savoured and finished then and there. She also began to trust that things could be kept safe and that she could be held in mind, from week to week – and she checked this out by making bigger and bigger lego models, which had to be carefully preserved. The climax of this came when she built a 'caravan', with a separate compartment for each member of the family so that everyone could have their own space, even as they travelled around. She had found a 'space' with her therapist where she could really stretch and become herself; and in her imagination she created a vehicle which could similarly accommodate all the children in her family.

By the time she completed her therapy, Deborah had moved from being seen as a disruptive pupil to one who was held up to others as an example of enthusiasm and commitment; she also represented her school at running. The work finished with a much happier child, parents, and school.

Deborah had a feedback and follow-up session with her therapist about 6 months after she finished therapy, when she told her that she had advised a girl in her class who was having problems to come to the clinic for 'anger management'.

The child psychotherapist at work

Another common fantasy about child psychotherapists is that they only do long-term and intensive individual work. In most NHS teams it *should* be possible for a child psychotherapist to do long-term intensive work, and to have this supported by the multi-disciplinary team. This is partly because there are some children who clearly need and benefit from more intensive work, where the nature of the 'stuckness' would indicate this approach. However, there is great pressure on NHS teams in terms of the numbers of children and families needing help, and child psychotherapists may also need to demonstrate that they are working in line with the priorities of the team by being able to balance their caseloads with a range of brief, non-intensive, flexible interventions. One way of putting this is that, along with other members of the team, child psychotherapists will offer the minimum treatment necessary to address the difficulties of the child – on the understanding that the minimum in terms of effectiveness will on occasion be long-term, intensive psychotherapy. This has been evidenced by retrospective research carried out at the Anna Freud Centre, which showed that for serious emotional difficulties intensive psychotherapy was more effective than once or twice weekly sessions – see Chapter 6.

Child psychotherapists apply psychoanalytic ideas in NHS settings in a range of ways. These include specialist assessments, joint working, group work, and brief counselling.

Specialist assessments

Teams may request a 'child psychotherapy assessment' for a number of purposes other than the usual 'assessment as to the suitability of psychotherapeutic treatment'. This will often be to contribute to the overall understanding of a case – to assist the multi-disciplinary team; as an aspect of an assessment for social services; or as an element of a court process. The aim is to shed light on particular behaviours, or on the extent of emotional damage that a child has sustained, through understanding and working with the internal world of the child.

Joint working

A child psychotherapist may join another team member, for example a family therapist, in working with a family. Sometimes it is hard for the child perspective to be highlighted in a family setting, and the role of the child psychotherapist may be to pay particular attention to the contributions of the child in the family meeting, and to ensure that this perspective is noticed and considered. This can be particularly useful when working with parents who suffer from major mental illness, whose difficulties may be quite overwhelming in a therapeutic setting as well as at home in the family.

Group work

A child psychotherapist may join a member of the multi-disciplinary team in running a children's group, either in the clinic or in another setting. The co-therapist may be someone who has particular training in group therapy, or a qualification in a creative therapy, which is complemented by the child psychotherapist's understanding of unconscious processes.

Brief counselling

Child psychotherapists have been instrumental in setting up brief therapy services, using a psychoanalytic focus. Examples of this are brief counselling services for adolescents, where there is an emphasis on working with the motivation of the young person to work on an issue identified by them, without having to go through an overly complex referral system. Similarly, services have been established for the families of under-fives, with the emphasis on intervention that can take place early – both in terms of the difficulty being caught at an early stage, and early in the child's life. This volume contains chapters on such brief work and parent–infant work.

The child psychotherapist in other settings

Child psychotherapists may be employed in particular settings where it is felt that their skills can make a useful contribution, or they may 'lend' some of their Tier 3 time to another agency through offering a direct service, through teaching, or through consultation.

Looked After Children (LAC)

A number of Looked After Children Teams have chosen to employ child psychotherapists because of the insights they can offer into the emotional and behavioural difficulties of children whose home lives have been seriously disrupted. Sometimes this therapist will be in a position to work therapeutically with looked after children or young people; sometimes she may be used more in a consultative capacity or to assist in decision-making. For further details of this work, the excellent book by Margaret Hunter (2001) is highly recommended.

Children's Centres/Sure Start

The establishment of Sure Start programmes and the development of Children's Centres have created new opportunities for CAMHS to offer accessible services to families with under-fives. This can involve early intervention with a toddler or young child but it is also a setting in which to reach mothers who may have been struggling with mental health issues associated with pregnancy and birth. Child psychotherapists have contributed to such services both directly and through offering consultation to front line staff such as midwives, health visitors and nursery workers.

Consultation

A range of colleagues from partner agencies may choose, for a number of reasons, to request consultation from a child psychotherapist. It could be in order to increase their therapeutic skills or to heighten understanding of a particular child and consequent group response. It could also be to forge a link with CAMHS so that cases needing a Tier 3 service can be referred confidently for further work. This development of local networks is important to ensure that children and families do not fall between services. Many voluntary agencies, and some professionals in education such as school counsellors, are effectively doing Tier 2 CAMHS work, and it helps them and their clients if this can be recognised and supported and if they can be included in local referral pathways.

Conclusion

There are times when working in the NHS can feel extremely tedious, and when 'working together' feels like a complicated dance in which each partner tries to retain the advantage. At times like this it is particularly important to try to retain a clear vision of what we are trying to achieve. If we take seriously the evidence put forward by Zarrina Kurtz, we should be paying much less attention to questions of 'Is this better than that?' or arguments that come down to 'Our service is more essential than your service.' The point is that children and families have complex needs, and require a range of services that have the capacity to work together.

It is a sad fact that most often when there is an inquiry into serious child abuse, or a child death, it is the network of services that has failed at some point. Professionals have not worked together, have not respected one another, and a child has fallen through the net. All the policy initiatives discussed above – *Together We Stand*, Every Child Matters, the Common Assessment Framework – represent government trying to develop systems whereby services can be enabled to work together.

It is sometimes said that 'joint commissioning' (where education, health, and social care share planning and budgetary responsibility for CAMHS) is the answer to the holes in the network. However, the outlook for the mental health of children and young people may not, in fact, be so good in an all-inclusive service. There is something about the differences between agencies that protects the different perspectives and allows us to define and address the complexities inherent in human beings. Equally, the differences between professions in the multi-disciplinary team can lead to professional rivalries and competitive behaviour, but they also lead to a richer and more effective means of addressing the needs of the 'whole child'.

Although multi-disciplinary and multi-agency working may at times be wearisome, the diversity and opportunity that it offers make it worth the exertion. Working together is, after all, not rocket science – if it were, we might have cracked it by now.

References

Department for Education and Skills (2004) *Every Child Matters: change for children*, London: DfES.
Department of Health (2004) *National Service Framework for Children, Young*

People and Maternity Services: the Mental Health and Psychological Well-Being of Children and Young People, London: DoH Publications.

Hunter, M. (2001) *Psychotherapy with Young People in Care: Lost and Found*, Hove: Brunner-Routledge.

Kurtz, Z., Thornes, R. and Wolkind, S. (1996) *Treating Children Well: a guide to using the evidence base in commissioning and managing services for the mental health of children and young people*, London: Mental Health Foundation.

Laming, W. H. (2003) *The Victoria Climbié Report*, London: Stationery Office.

NHS Health Advisory Service (1995) *Together We Stand: the commissioning, role and management of Child and Adolescent Mental Health Services*, London: HMSO.

Winnicott, D. W. (1957) 'Further thoughts on babies as persons', in D. W. Winnicott *The Child, the Family and the Outside World*, Harmondsworth: Penguin, 1964.

8 Race, culture and the therapeutic process

Iris Gibbs

In another paper (Gibbs 2009) I reflected on race and culture in the context of therapeutic consultation and assessment. This chapter looks more specifically at the impact of race and culture on the process of therapy. It takes for granted that the necessary attention is paid to the therapeutic setting – a clearly bounded space in time and space. Wilson (1991) defines this as the conditions of work that facilitate communication and enable both psychotherapist and patient to observe and think about what is happening between them. Horne (2004) includes in the conditions of work such things as a quiet therapy room that is welcoming to children and will also help with the establishment of a treatment/working alliance. Lanyado and Horne write in detail in Chapter 10 in this volume about the concepts that are central to the therapeutic relationships and process: transference and countertransference, interpretation, anxiety and defence, containment, internal and external worlds.

This chapter considers the above concepts from the point of view of race and culture. It raises such questions as to whether these preclude the development of an affective transference and the effect this may have on the outcome of therapy. It recognises that class and gender issues, as well as race and culture, can impact on the therapeutic process. Ryan (2006) has a helpful exploration of this subject in her study 'Class in You' and how it contributes to the structuring of the transference/countertransference relationship. For the minority therapist particularly, but not exclusively, the inclusion of class can bring additional concerns about one's character and competence and self-questioning about personal worth and acceptance (Sennett and Cobb 1972). This carries personal as well as professional and technical challenges. The challenges will vary depending on whether the therapist is working cross-culturally or in same race or cultural dyads. For therapists, whether white or minority, the implication is that we need greater vigilance in the work to guard against transference and countertransference collusions. Some case material from my practice will be considered, as will implications for outcomes in cross-cultural work. Finally, the issue of training is considered.

The therapeutic relationship and process

The constantly evolving relationship between therapist and patient lies at the heart of all psychoanalytic work and is the main vehicle for psychic change. For Bhugra and Bhui (2006) this relationship requires some nurturing even before the first interview and first session. Their view is that a potential patient has a potential therapist in mind before and after the first meeting, and racial and cultural stereotypes may come into play in the mind of therapist and patient. Skin colour also draws forth a rich variety of projections and stereotypes and can arouse anxiety about difference that is psychologically quite primitive, emerging out of our earliest efforts to define self.

Colour blind approach

If we accept the legitimacy of the above statement, it has implications for the way we work with race and culture in the room and the different emphasis placed on external and internal representations of race and culture. Liggan and Kay (2006) reflect on the subject of 'colour blindness' and highlight three core problems:

- It disregards the central importance that the black patient's blackness has for him/her.
- It ignores the impact of the therapist's whiteness on the patient. (Here I would prefer the expression 'the therapist's racial and cultural difference' as it also acknowledges situations where the therapist is from a minority culture.)
- It abstracts the black patient from the social realities of his/her experience: social realities of racism, colour prejudice and imbalance in power.

In acknowledging the black or minority patient's reality, the writers nevertheless warn against a psychodynamic formulation that adheres to an inflexible narrative or stereotyped attitude to race. This may result in such a model being seen as a template for constructing psychotherapeutic treatments for all black people. Therapists are similarly warned about seeing cultures as fixed entities and therefore unproblematic. The opposite extreme of dismissing culture as irrelevant poses another danger – a retreat into an autonomous internal world. Dalad (2002) views this presumption – that one can think, work and live outside social groupings – as equally erroneous. Such a view would conceptualise therapy as taking place (or that it ought to be taking place) at a level deep enough in the psyche to omit cultural configurations. The idea that analytic purity may be compromised in some way brings to mind similar arguments about developmental therapy being a watered down version of psychotherapy and therefore not appropriate for addressing intra-psychic conflicts.

Internal/external manifestations of race and culture

Hamer (2002) argues that race in the mind is determined by both internal and external factors and both are important in the analysis of racial material in the transference. He is critical of views that see race and culture as less important than other intra-psychic dynamics or content, or that conceptualise them primarily as resistance. In adopting such a position, we become less attentive as to how the discussion of other material helps us to avoid meaningful consideration of race. Similarly, racial material can also keep us from attending to uncomfortable feelings such as dependency and kinship. Rushing past or ignoring such potentially rich material, in Hamer's view, is both misguided and in its own way un-analytic. Ultimately, whether we emphasise racial material in terms of its racial meanings, cultural affiliations or intra-psychic meanings, each highlights to some extent 'who we are and how we got to be that way' (Hamer 2002).

External aspects: racism, colour prejudice, imbalance in power relationships

Who we are has much to do with how we perceive ourselves. Positive racial and ethnic identifications clearly have implications for self-esteem, identity formation, security and freedom. Holmes (2006) links race to conscious and unconscious processes that satisfy a fundamental need for historical continuity and sees race as a condensed way of representing a nest of emotional connections. However, people's perceptions and attitudes also have an impact, thus experiences of racism – personal and institutional – societal views of colour and difference, and where people are positioned on the ladder of power are all part of real, lived experiences. These external realities reinforce and shape us and cannot therefore be divorced from the thinking and practice of psychotherapy. Whether working cross-culturally or in same race and cultural dyads, therapists also have to acknowledge their own position in the system as well as their personal and professional conflicts. This is seen as a first condition for responsible, sensitive, practice (Holmes 2006). For this writer, it also has implications for how we function within the processes of the transference and countertransference. A therapist who is aware and has addressed his/her own issues, including racist thoughts, is through this better placed both to acknowledge the realities of the patient's external situation as well as to challenge and interpret intra-psychic conflict in the face of racial and cultural explanations.

Intra-psychic concerns

Andreou (1999) writes that when the reality of experiences such as racism and prejudice can be talked about in the consulting room, black young-sters, for example, become able to describe the impact that these can have on their states of mind. She quotes one youngster who said to his therapist, 'You have no idea what it feels like when you walk down the street and people assume you are going to mug them.' Similar feelings would also have been common among Muslims following the 2005 bombings in London. She highlights the importance of such experiences on the internal world of children and young people, which has to be part of any psycho-therapeutic relationship in which cultural issues are significant.

For Hamer (2002), discussions about external reality within the thera-peutic space give the opportunity to evaluate what is apparently inside and outside, how each influences the other and how the space between can be made vital for the purposes of newly adaptive functioning. This is viewed as particularly important where traumatic experiences such as racism obliterate the individual's ability to hold on to a transitional space and where the subjective cannot be experienced as such because external reality is so compelling.

The therapist, nevertheless, has to do this work without 'collusion with unduly paranoid perceptions of a hostile external world' (Akhtar 2006). She still needs to explore the internal and possibly exaggerated view and how these interact.

Disorders of ethnicity

Rendon (1993) draws attention to the fact that there are disorders of ethnicity just as there are with identity. For Liggan and Hay 'when an individual's ethnic/racial identifications are conflicted, the internal response is to mobilise defence mechanisms such as denial, projection and displace-ment to deal initially with the psychological dissonance and discomfort' (p. 104). Further, these defences could become maladaptive over time and impair the ability to resolve interracial conflict leaving people more vulner-able to traumatisation in future encounters with whites. This in turn can lead to 'a chronic state of over-reactivity to events; even benign situations may be experienced as threatening because of a perceived threat of discrimination' (Liggan and Kay 2006: 104).

Some defences associated with black and minority populations

Liggan and Hay list a number of psychological defences linked to black patients and which, in their opinion, stem from both external and internal sources. They write about internal parental models and rigid defences that develop in relation to 'intrusive mother/absent father' situations and lead to poor expectations of needs being met. Second, internal models of whites may be distorted by ascribed power and privilege; such models are rife for the projection of infantile fantasies. Lastly they point to an internal model of 'black' which can involve a central conflict between racial pride and an underlying image of self as inferior.

The authors are writing from the perspective of African-Americans and it is important to acknowledge that there are likely to be differences as well as similarities among European populations with different histories, rich inter-mixing of cultures and varying levels of assimilation to the host country's values and ideals. I would say the same is true among black and minority groups in America. The issue of absent fathers, particularly in black families, has however crossed continents and is taken up in media and government circles as an important factor in the proliferation of gang culture, gun and knife crime.

Stereotyping: its use and overuse

The above models carry their own danger of stereotyping, whether in America, Europe or elsewhere. As therapists we are cautioned about stereotypes. It is nevertheless important to acknowledge we all use them to some extent – to make sense of the world, to organise information, to make hypotheses. We may start from the premise that Asian families, for example, are all family orientated. It would, nevertheless, be a grave error to say all Asian families adhere to this pattern. This in itself could be perceived as racist as it overlooks such issues as class, education and the fact that, even within cultures, people behave differently. Such general-isations also overlook the experiential dimension and this is what we largely work with in psychotherapy.

Technical difficulties

The use of language and certain terms can lead to misunderstanding in terms of symptoms presented and the meanings attributed to them. Moodley (2006) writes that the emphasis on taking account of local meanings of illness patterns, together with a wide range of social culturally related behaviours, would be critical in the interpretations that a psychotherapist would make with ethnic patients. Difficulties with the subtleties and nuances of language may be as big a problem for the minority therapist as for the patient where neither is working in his/her mother tongue.

Akhtar (2006) looks specifically at difficulties relating to minority ther-apists, e.g. the pressure to collude can be strong where there are reality based identifications with the patient's problems. Important implications involve the maintenance of cultural neutrality, avoiding shared projections and nostalgic collusions in the work. The potential is also there for issues *not* to be explored and for aggression to be displaced onto whites and others. The writer stresses the importance of personal analysis in such situations as 'mourning', in terms of one's own minority status, may be necessary. Ticho (1971) writes that: 'An analyst living in his own country is less threatened by foreign values than an analyst working in a foreign country where he is deprived of the support of people who share his culture.'

We are also reminded that, though Freud could certainly be labelled an immigrant, there is little about such experiences in his writings. One analysis is that this group of European analysts were viewed predominantly as exiles rather than immigrants and were also able to assimilate rapidly at a professional level.

The psychoanalytic literature and views on race-based transference

It is Dalad's (2002) view that race is insufficiently explored in psycho-analytic literature. He looks in detail at the writings of four main theorists – Freud, Klein, Fairbairn and Winnicott – and considers how they help us to think about racism. Readers are directed to his book *Race, Colour and the Processes of Racialization* for extensive reading on the subject. For the purposes of this chapter, I turn to Kris and Kris (2006) who reflect on current psychoanalytic literature on race-based transference, which falls broadly into classical and Kleinian views. For these writers, the classical position, with its ideal of the blank screen therapist, may leave out the therapist's contribution to transference and may be too restricted to intra-psychic meanings. They see the Kleinian view as limited in its tendency to consider negative transference as defensive projections on the part of the patient – 'a defensive manoeuvre to dump unwanted mental contents onto the racial other' (Kris and Kris 2006: 87).

With this point of view, the problem of blaming the patient, of locating the problem in the patient, becomes more extreme: reliance on projective identification leads the therapist to assume that his/her negative reaction to the patient is caused by the patient's destructive impulses. The writers contrast this view with an 'inter-subjective based view, where race-related transference is seen as an instance of the person's ongoing organising activity and where the unique meaning of race for each patient is emphasised' (ibid.).

Working with race and cultural differences in therapy

As a child psychotherapist from a minority culture, I feel privileged to work with children and families from a range of cultural backgrounds. On the subject of difference, I agree with Tang and Gardner (1999) who propose that race and cultural differences can be of great potential value rather than a barrier to the therapy and can be useful windows into the unconscious. It is therefore not something to 'get past as quickly as possible to allow the real work of therapy to begin, neither should it be forced or brought up artificially'. It is best seen as fitting into a context in which there is some evidence – often in derivative material – that this is an area of curiosity, interest or conflict.

This section focuses on clinical material in my work with Rose, an 11-year-old white patient who was referred because of her persistent low mood and challenging behaviour at school. I also draw on material from recent teaching on the subject of race and culture with child psychotherapy trainees working across the cultural divide. Their work and also their comments about my work were insightful as well as challenging. Peer discussion about one's work is essential: it can throw new light on transference phenomena and therefore on countertransference responses.

Preliminaries

I started by meeting Rose's parents who are middle class professionals. Much of the early part of the consultation was taken up with discussing her early history and current functioning. The conclusion was that Rose clearly needed therapeutic help. However, before offering a space, I asked the parents how they thought Rose would feel about working with a black therapist. They were momentarily taken aback by the directness of my question but said they could not foresee a problem given the cultural mix of her school and the area they lived in. At one level, the question reflected my anxiety, or perhaps paranoid feelings, about being acceptable to these parents; however, I thought it an important question for them to consider and to discuss with their daughter. Second, by bringing the subject of race and difference into the room, I was both seeking the parents' permission to treat their daughter and to suggest that race, like any other subject, was open for discussion in the therapy.

Permission from parents for the work of psychotherapy is always welcomed by the therapist, irrespective of racial or cultural considerations. However, it can mean more for the minority therapist and white therapist working with minority patients. One trainee felt that she was working with her black patient in the context of extreme racial hostility from the black father who had been referred by social services. His attitude to the white therapist had serious implications for the child patient who was clearly in a dilemma about showing her positive feelings toward her therapist. Rose's parents have been supportive throughout her therapy and this has enabled her to struggle, in her own way, both to understand symptoms and to negotiate her own relationship with me.

Therapy with Rose

The first six months: transference and countertransference phenomena

The first few weeks were predominantly about engaging Rose and exploring her difficulties, particularly her battles with teachers. She felt they disrespected her and were the main cause of her low moods. The pressure in the room and therefore the transference was for a therapist/parent to join with her in condemning these authority figures and to collude with her behaviour and attitude towards them. Interestingly, my countertransference was taking me in the opposite direction. I felt an overwhelming urge to bring structure to Rose's life, in a way that allowed her to be less persecuted by limits and boundaries. Early interpretations addressed her wish to call all the shots yet her being aware at some level of the resulting chaos 'if everyone did their own thing'.

Over the following weeks I heard less about the teachers, but I was then put under constant pressure to divulge information about myself. This is not new for psychotherapists and I interpreted it in terms of Rose's curiosity about me. I did not particularly link it to race or difference at this stage. This came into the session gradually, mainly in a positive form. Rose began to bring material about minority people she had met, foods she had tasted. All the time she was scrutinising my reactions to get clues regarding my country of origin. Interpretations about similarities and differences came more naturally into the room but I did not pick up any discomfort or urgency in Rose around this subject. Nevertheless I was constantly on the look-out for such things as shifts in affect, tone of voice, use of phrases and racial categories, some of which might be fleeting, but having significance. This is no different from the ordinary conduct of psychotherapists, but may have a greater relevance in the context of race and cultural differences

Middle phase of therapy

Rose's sessions continued into the middle phase of therapy. The work in this middle phase often holds the key to change in the therapeutic process (Broughton 2005) as it incorporates self-reflection and negotiation of conflict. Rose attended well and seemed motivated to work on her issues. There were the usual moments of despair, and regression to complaints about teachers, but these were short-lived. I began to hear more about respect for one teacher who used humour to disarm her. Rose also became more able to locate the source of her distress – which lessened some projections onto teachers but introduced others. This coincided with the onset of puberty. Adults, male and female, were now viewed as sexual predators. This shift allowed us to look further at the whole issue of difference and in particular sexual stereotypes about black and minority people.

Emergence of the negative transference

Until this point the transference to me was relatively positive and the negative aspects were split off and projected elsewhere. It was now possible to interpret Rose's anxieties about safety and my real feelings and intentions toward her. The biggest conflict in the transference coincided with media reports of gun crime which involved black youngsters killing a white teenager. Rose did not bring this directly to her session. She seemed unusually quiet in the room and I sensed some emotional distancing from me. I commented on the silence and she said she was tired. I wondered about the tiredness, acknowledging that she had said nothing about her week, which was unlike her. My transference had returned to concerns about her safety which coincided with Rose talking about the killing. It was important for me to acknowledge Rose's real fears about her safety. In terms of the countertransference, I was also attuned to subtle changes in the patient to which I gave voice. It led to an outpouring of some real negative feelings against black boys who saw such attacks as gaining respect. She suddenly looked at me and said, 'I don't mean to be horrible.' I said I thought Rose was concerned that I would not understand her fears and might think her racist. She nodded but also seemed relieved that we could discuss this issue.

Racist defences and guilt

Morgan reminds us that 'when a black therapist is working with a white patient, racist defences for the patient will take subtle and secret forms. Because of the guilt attached to these responses, the patient will work hard to keep such feelings from surfacing in the room and is likely to quickly suppress them even as they surface in the mind' (Morgan 2008: 45). Morgan goes on to say that what the white therapist may be able to contribute to thinking about this matter – both theoretically and clinically – is personal experiences, both about the racist thought and the desire to get rid of it, and of the feelings of shame and guilt in our minds which keep us from acknowledging what arises in them.

In the case of Rose there would be many more occasions of external events triggering difficult internal feelings with racist overtones, but it was possible for these to be acknowledged, interpreted and contained within the therapeutic arena. The early positive transference enabled us to think about difficulties without destroying the therapeutic process. Rose's therapy ended with a significant reduction in her symptoms. The changes were confirmed both by parents and school and recent information suggests that Rose is maintaining this position.

Outcomes

It is equally important to keep in mind the impact of race upon outcome. Downing (2000) reminds us of potential barriers to effective outcomes for patients from black and other minorities, citing:

- conscious and unconscious racism that may produce feelings of superiority over an inferior race;

- the labelling of different lifestyles and coping skills as pathological;
- colour blindness that leads the therapist to deny that the black patient may differ from a white patient, thereby denying the impact of racism and closing off important issues for exploration.

Training issues

'It should not be up to the patient to instruct or enlighten us completely. This would be a gross perversion of the importance of learning from the patient. To rely on our patients of colour to educate we would risk exploitation.' David Downing goes on to highlight the need for education, research, and the experience of working with disadvantaged or minority groups in clinics and other settings if we are to alter perceptions of psychoanalysis. He continues:

> Given such circumstances, psychoanalysis can have a salutary effect on the sequelae of institutionalised racism as internalised and manifested at individual, familial and societal level. This in turn can inform social policy aimed at eradicating barriers and injustices faced by people of colour.
>
> (Downing 2000)

Until these issues are addressed and embraced by psychoanalysis, and there is serious exploration of how they impact on the human psyche in the consulting room, they will remain insufficiently investigated and mastered. The implications for training are evident: the challenge requires a response.

Conclusion

This chapter considers the therapeutic process from the point of view of race and culture and looks at some of the dilemmas in working both cross-culturally and in same-race relationships. It acknowledges that, though race is a social construct, it is often used as a means of organising our view of the world and others and where we are positioned in the power hierarchy. Class differences as well as gender will have an impact and both the external and internal reinforce and shape our perceptions. I take the view that intra-psychic meanings cannot be explored unless social reality is at least acknowledged. It is important that stereotypical views and inflexible attitudes do not lead to dangerous errors in service provision. These will ultimately deprive our minority patients of a service tailored to their needs and thus deprive them of a good outcome. It is also recognised that there are disorders of ethnicity that can colour our patients' view of the world and relationships. These have to be acknowledged and challenged. Finally, in relation to outcome, some writers see same race and cultural dyads as producing the best results while others such as Tang and Gardner (1999) believe that black and minority patients can receive effective therapy from any culturally orientated therapist if it involves the resolution of racial conflict. Similarly, when therapists, white or minority, are unable openly and critically to examine their own unconscious biases and perceptions, it can adversely affect and limit treatment and undermine our therapeutic efficacy.

I am aware that little attention has been paid in this chapter to the special circumstances of refugees and the necessity of integrating racial/cultural circumstances with their particular external life events. Sheila Melzak tackles some of this in Chapter 25, to which the reader is directed. Second, I have not dealt with the issue of children with mixed heritages and their conflicts around multiple identifications. This is perhaps the subject for a further paper.

References

Akhtar, S. (2006) 'Technical challenges faced by the immigrant psychoanalyst', *Psychoanalytic Quarterly* 75: 21–43.

Andreou, C. (1999) 'Some intercultural issues in the therapeutic process', in M. Lanyado and A. Horne (eds) *The Handbook of Child and Adolescent Psychotherapy: Psychoanalytic Approaches*, London and New York: Routledge.

Bhugra, D. and Bhui, K. (2006) 'Psychotherapy across the cultural divide', in R. Moodley and S. Palmer (eds) *Race, Culture and Psychotherapy: Critical Perspectives in Multicultural Practice*, New York: Routledge.

Broughton, C. (2005) 'Middle phase: elaboration and consolidation', in T. Baradon *et al.* (eds) *The Practice of Psychoanalytic Parent–Infant Psychotherapy*, London and New York: Routledge.

Dalad, F. (2002) *Race, Colour and the Processes of Racialization: New Perspectives from Group Analysis, Psychoanalysis and Sociology*, New York: Brunner-Routledge.

Downing, D. L. (2000) 'Controversies in psychoanalytic education: the issue of race and its relevance in psychoanalytic treatment', *Psychoanalytic Review* 87: 355–75.

Gibbs, I. (2009) 'Reflections on race and culture in therapeutic assessment and consultation', in A. Horne and M. Lanyado (eds) *Through Assessment to Consultation: Independent Psychoanalytic Approaches with Children and Adolescents*, London and New York: Routledge.

Hamer, F. M. (2002) 'Guards at the gate: race, resistance and psychic reality', *Journal of the American Psychoanalytic Association* 50: 1219–37.

Holmes, D. E. (2006) 'The wrecking effects of race and social class on self and success', *Psychoanalytic Quarterly* 75: 215–35.

Horne, A. (2004) 'The Independent position in psychoanalytic psychotherapy with children and adolescents: roots and implications', in M. Lanyado and A. Horne (eds) *A Question of Technique: Independent Psychoanalytic Approaches with Children and Adolescents*, London and New York: Routledge.

Kris, Y. and Kris, Y. I. (2006) 'Transference and race', in R. Moodley and S. Palmer (eds) *Race, Culture and Psychotherapy: Critical Perspectives in Multicultural Practice*, New York: Routledge.

Liggan, Y. and Kay, J. (2006) 'Race in the room; issues in the dynamic psycho-therapy of African-Americans', in R. Moodley and S. Palmer (eds) *Race, Culture and Psychotherapy: Critical Perspectives in Multicultural Practice*, New York: Routledge.

Morgan, H. (2008) 'Issues of "race" in psychoanalytic psychotherapy – whose problem is it anyway?', *British Journal of Psychotherapy* 24(1): 34–49.

Moodley, R. (2006) 'Cultural representations and interpretations of "subjective distress" in ethnic minority patients', in R. Moodley and S. Palmer (eds) *Race, Culture and Psychotherapy: Critical Perspectives in Multicultural Practice*, New York: Routledge.

Rendon, M. (1993) 'Race in the room: issues in the dynamic psychotherapy of African-Americans', in R. Moodley and S. Palmer (eds) *Race, Culture and Psychotherapy: Critical Perspectives in Multicultural Practice* New York: Routledge.

Ryan, J. (2006) '"Class is in you": an exploration of some social class issues in psychotherapeutic work', *British Journal of Psychotherapy* 23(1): 49–62.

Sennett, R. and Cobb, J. (1972) *The Hidden Injuries of Class*, New York: Norton, 1993.

Tang, N. M. and Gardner, J. (1999) 'Race, culture and psychotherapy: transference to minority therapists', *Psychoanalytic Quarterly* 68(1): 1–20.

Ticho, G. (1971) 'Technical challenges of the immigrant analyst', *Psychoanalytic Quarterly* 40: 9–21.

Wilson, P. (1991) 'Psychotherapy with adolescents', in J. Holmes (ed.) *Textbook of Psychotherapy in Psychiatric Practice*, New York: Churchill-Livingstone.

9 The international scene

Lydia Tischler and colleagues

Introduction

This chapter reflects the changes which have taken place on the international scene in the last 10 years with especially welcome developments in many countries in the former Russian bloc. The layout follows the previous edition in a division into separate continents; however, the countries in Europe are here listed alphabetically. In addition to those which have been revised – Australia, Canada, the Czech Republic, Denmark, Finland, Germany, Greece, Hungary, Italy, India, Israel, Norway, South Africa, Sweden, United States, Russia – there are new entries from a number of countries, mainly European, which were not included in the last edition. These include Flanders (the northern Flemish speaking part of Belgium), Bulgaria, the Baltic countries – the Estonian Republic (fortunate to be able to establish training with the financial support of an Estonian expatriate), Latvia, Lithuania – Luxembourg, Netherlands, Poland, Serbia (although Yugoslavia featured in the previous edition and that forms the basis for this account), Switzerland and New Zealand.

This chapter has many authors, who are acknowledged at the end of each entry. I have provided an introduction in which I have attempted to summarise the major changes which have taken place both in the development of trainings and mental health provision for children and adolescents. Where no update was available, it has not been possible to locate the author of the 1999 contribution and these appear sans scribe.

While a number of new trainings in child and adolescent psychotherapy have been and are being developed, they have to take into account the prevailing local conditions and culture. Thus the standard of training across the globe is variable. Many countries rely on trainers and teachers from other countries with no common language thus adding linguistic complications.

Europe

In Europe the EFPP (European Federation for Psychoanalytic Psychotherapy) has played an important role in encouraging and promoting trainings. Almost all national networks in Europe, including Israel, are represented in the Child and Adolescent (C&A) Section. The EFPP has been active in supporting the development of trainings in Bulgaria, Croatia, Serbia and Turkey. The C&A section has developed a European Certificate: a collaborative effort of the C&A section members. It sets out the minimum training standards which many countries, especially those with newly established trainings, aspire to follow. While pan-European certificates do not have official recognition in the European Union, the certificate is welcomed unofficially as a benchmark for trainings and has status in many European countries.

The development of child psychotherapy trainings has on the whole been very positive despite the fact that child psychotherapy is only recognised as a profession in a few countries in Europe – the Czech Republic, Germany, the Netherlands (where the title of psychotherapist is protected), Norway, Sweden and Finland.

In many countries where insurance companies pay therapy costs, the frequency and length of therapy is often time limited, as in Germany and Switzerland, and it is reported that short-term therapies are gaining preference in Switzerland and Sweden. Finland is the exception where child psychotherapy is now recognised as a treatment of choice – and the number of trained colleagues has doubled.

The world beyond Europe

In *Australia* there have been very welcome developments in training but these have still to be matched by the employment of child psychotherapists, which remains somewhat patchy. *Canada* has seen exciting new initiatives take place, including a school-based treatment for severely abused and neglected children developed in partnership with the Toronto school board. In *India* there has been a growth of training possibilities in the last decade with the qualification of child psychotherapists in 2004. Members from the Tavistock Clinic have been very active in promoting this. Currently, funded provision in the *USA* is minimal; however, recent (2008) legislation mandating parity for mental health services with medical services offers some hope of improvement in this situation. Finally, in *South Africa* the situation remains difficult though some advances have been made: a number of people have completed the Tavistock Observational Course.

REPORTS FROM THE FIELD

Africa

South Africa

Although currently there is no systematic training available for child and adolescent psychotherapists in South Africa, there are many clinical and educational psychologists as well as social workers who work in a psycho-analytically oriented way. The Parent and Child Counselling Centre, established as the Johannesburg Child Guidance Clinic in 1944, previously had a strong psychoanalytic tradition due to the influence of predominantly Tavistock-trained child psychotherapists, but this has been on the wane in recent years. The main centre for promoting child psychotherapy is now the Institute of Psychoanalytic Child Psychotherapy established in 1996 by Sheila Miller and Judy Davis, both ACP members. Several of the Tavistock Observation Course modules are now taught such as infant observation, clinical seminars, psychoanalytic theory and work with community projects – leading to Certificates or Diplomas in Therapeutic Communication with Children. Tutors from the Tavistock visit the seminars and projects twice yearly.

In Cape Town the visits by Henri Rey in the 1970s and 1980s were influential in spreading psychoanalytic thinking: the Cape Town Child Guidance Clinic and the Red Cross Child and Family Centre have been centres of excellence for many years. In 1995 pre-clinical components of the Tavistock Observation Course were set up by Judy Davis and Trevor Lubbe, who subsequently moved to Johannesburg. The infant observation component has proved to be extremely popular, with thirty-one people having completed a two-year infant observation, and a further twelve students are currently doing the course. Three other students have completed the Diploma and are now colleagues involved in course work.

Generally it is not easy for child and adolescent psychotherapists with overseas qualifications to obtain registration in South Africa unless they have a psychology background. However, in the light of the country's urgent need for clinical skills to address the needs of South Africa's children, this situation is under review.

Trevor Lubbe

America – North

Canada

The Toronto Child Psychoanalytic Program (TCPP) has been in operation for over thirty years, providing training in psychodynamic child and adolescent therapy. A new class commences every two years, with a maximum of twelve candidates.

The TCPP has traditionally offered a four-year training in psychoanalytic child therapy. However, a recent innovation, since 2005, has been the introduction of a choice of two or four years of study. The training includes a core curriculum of academic seminars, infant and toddler observations, ethics, and supervised clinical work.

In the first two years, leading to a certificate in child psychotherapy, instructors use a problem-based approach which is both innovative and comprehensive. The curriculum covers an integration of psychoanalytic theory with contemporary thinking in observational research and infant and child development. Candidates also learn about the common presenting problems in child psychotherapy, therapeutic technique, and the therapeutic relationship. The curriculum also includes the history of psychoanalytic ideas, the theoretical differences among the various schools and their respective views regarding transference, countertransference, interpretation, the representational world, and psychic structure.

The TCPP has graduated forty-nine candidates to date, with two more graduating in 2008.

A new initiative from the TCPP is the Child Psychotherapy Foundation of Canada, created in 1997 with a mandate to fund school-based treatment for abused and neglected children experiencing serious social, emotional, and learning difficulties. This is a population of children whose development has been severely compromised by longstanding abuse and neglect such that all aspects of their functioning and relationships are affected. They require individual attention – they are not able to benefit from group interventions. The treatment includes work with the child, teacher and caregiver to maximise results, and is not available through public programmes. An important element of its effectiveness is that it is school-based. The TCPP has a formal Partnership Agreement with the Toronto District School Board (TDSB) whereby therapists associated with the Child Psychotherapy Foundation are permitted to treat children in their schools. This partnership is noteworthy because without such an agreement, clinicians are not permitted to conduct treatment in schools within the TDSB. We are collaborating with Dr Faye Mishna, Director of Research, Faculty of Social Work, University of Toronto to evaluate the effectiveness of the treatment. Faye is a graduate of the Toronto Child Psychoanalytic Program and a member of the Board.

The Foundation solicits funds from corporations and banks and provides detailed reports every six months on the progress of each child. The candidates receive $50 per session for three weekly appointments – two for the child and one for the parent or teacher. Preliminary findings have been very positive. It was noted that, although our numbers were small, the in-depth findings are important and a longitudinal study might be feasible. Dr. Mishna presented the research at the Meeting of the Society for Psychotherapy Research in Barcelona in June 2008.

Rosalind Kindler, Director TCPP

United States

A great deal of child and adolescent psychotherapy is done in the United States, primarily through private clinics and individual practices. The United States has no federally- or state-funded psychoanalytic psychotherapy services for children and adolescents, although a very limited amount of support is available through Medicaid, which helps the poorest and most handicapped. Private insurance varies from state to state, but few policies support more than once-weekly work for two or three months. Recent (2008) legislation mandating parity with medical services for mental health services offers some hope of improvement in this situation.

Most psychoanalytic institutes affiliated with the American Psychoanalytic Association and the International Psycho-Analytic Association offer both child and adolescent psychoanalytic training, as well as child psychotherapy training. Many also include parent–infant psychotherapy training. Psychoanalysis and psychotherapy for children and young people is available through clinics associated with these training centres, often at low fees. There are also schools of professional psychotherapy in clinical psychology and social work which contain components related to the treatment of children and adolescents, although the psychodynamic character of such trainings has diminished.

A new development is the spread of psychoanalytic schools, many on the model of the Hanna Perkins Center in Ohio, based on Anna Freud's theories. Organised as the Alliance for Psychoanalytic Schools, the ten current members variously offer therapeutic services and clinical trainings in child and adolescent psychotherapy and psychoanalysis.

The international child analytic professional organisation, the Association for Child Psychoanalysis, headquartered in the United States, is a resource for information on local training institutions, clinical services, and professional matters.

Kerry Kelly-Novick

America – South

Argentina (no update)

Developments in the field over the past thirty-five years have been prolific, from the efforts of the first pioneers to promote the dissemination, teaching and practice of child psychotherapy and the organisation of the first course set up and taught by Arminda Aberastury in 1948 under the aegis of the Argentine Psychoanalytical Association. Since then until today, the APA and later the Buenos Aires Psychoanalytical Association have been involved in training, while there are in addition numerous independent associations which teach psychoanalytic theory according to different orientations such as the British, French and American schools. The first hospital service for psychoanalytic work with children in a Spanish-speaking country was created in Buenos Aires in 1934. The Psychiatry and Psychology Centre was part of the Paediatrics chair at the Hospital de Clinicas José de San Martin. Subsequently psychoanalysis was integrated into the understanding and treatment of children's disorders in many national and municipal hospitals. In the 1980s Kamala Di Tella, who had trained at the Tavistock Clinic, generated a space in the Hospital Italiano for the psychoanalytic treatment of children with autism. At the same time she started Infant Observation seminars and her work has been carried on by colleagues since her death. Recently there have been greater obstacles to the implementation of psychoanalytic theory and practice because of health policies which focus on seeing a larger number of patients in as short a time as possible.

Brazil (no update)

Child and adolescent psychotherapy has been established and developed in the main cities in Brazil such as Rio de Janeiro, Porto Alegre and Coritiba, with training centres established in São Paolo and Rio. Most notable of developments was the establishment in 1987 of the Centro de Estudos Psicanaliticos Mae-Bebe-Famila in São Paolo, which runs Tavistock–Martha Harris Courses in Infant Observation and in Child and Adolescent Psychotherapy. Recently the Latin-American Congress on Child and Adolescent Psychoanalysis was organised in Brazil, and there is a thriving and growing list of publications which reflect and extend the work in terms of thinking and practice.

Chile (no update)

Child psychotherapy training began unofficially in Chile in 1960, and has been going on since but without the recognition of a formal qualification, although it is recognised by the Institute of Psychoanalysis. After slow beginnings, psychotherapy has been available as a treatment mainly in the psychiatric clinic of the medical school at the University of Chile. While for a time there was a Mahlerian orientation, an influence which was introduced by those who had trained and worked in the United States, the orientation of the work is now largely Kleinian. Currently there is an initiative to reorganise the training and to establish it gradually in a more formal way; work with children has until now been undertaken principally by psychoanalysts.

Asia

India

The Psychoanalytic Therapy and Research Centre, Mumbai (PTRC) was established over thirty years ago and is run in conjunction with the Bombay Sub-Committee of the Indian Psychoanalytic Society – part of the IPA. An Observational Studies course was established in Mumbai in June 1996 and in June 1999 a Child Psychotherapy Clinical Training was instituted on the lines of the Tavistock Clinic Child Psychotherapy Training. Currently the PTRC offers three courses:

1 Psychoanalytical Observational Studies
2 Training in Psychoanalytic Psychotherapy with Children, Parents and Young People
3 Adult Psychoanalytic Training.

The faculty includes members from the Indian Psychoanalytic Society and from the Tavistock Centre. In April 2005, the PTRC moved to a new site housing the Centre office, the Library and the Horniman Circle Therapy Centre. The Horniman Circle Therapy Centre is the only clinic in Mumbai providing help with emotional difficulties through psychoanalytic psychotherapy with the aim of making psychotherapeutic help accessible to families of all incomes. Ms Banu Ismail is the Clinic Director. A PTRC newsletter is published bi-annually and distributed as widely as possible.

Between 2004 and 2007 six child psychotherapists and two adult psychoanalysts have been trained and they are currently working towards an increase in the quality and outreach of psychoanalytic training and services of the PTRC in Mumbai. The staff work mainly in schools, street children projects and in private practice. The links with the Tavistock – in teaching and reviewing – have continued and are a source of great richness.

In 2008, a workshop was established to focus on Infant Mental Health and plans are in progress to develop training in Infant Mental Health in 2009. Over the last ten years the Indo-Australian-Israeli conference has been held bi-annually, organised by Mr Sarosh Forbes together with Mrs Nuzhat Khan and Mrs Micky Bhatia. They have contributed greatly to the experience and training of the staff.

Although participants in the Mumbai Marathon have continued to support the centre since 2006, it was good to hear that the Lady Navajbai Tata Trust has awarded the PTRC a substantial grant for a range of applied psychoanalytic work with the following aims:

1 to provide therapeutic and supportive services to children, parents and teachers in schools, colleges and non-governmental organisations working with children;
2 for the wider dissemination of psychoanalytic ideas and understanding.

This will enable the members of the PTRC to hold conferences, offer lecture programmes and other outreach programmes for the next three years.

In 2008, the faculty organised a two-day seminar on 'Transference and Methodology' in Kolkatta, in collaboration with the Centre for Counselling Services and studies in Self-Development which is part of Jadhavpur University, Kolkatta. Study events have been organised with the Interned Foundation in Ahmedabad, Gujarat. In January 2008, the Lady Navajbai Tata Trust grant enabled the first PTRC-Tavistock Child Psychotherapy Conference to be held in Mumbai.

Aiveen Bharucha

Australasia

Australia

Child psychotherapy in Australia would probably trace its roots to 1936 when Ruth Drake, a nursery teacher and speech therapist, worked as a play therapist in the Psychiatric Clinic of the Royal Children's Hospital in Melbourne. She was subsequently appointed as the first child psychotherapist in the Department of Psychology at the hospital. Since then, developments in this vast country have continued to expand, and the originally 'English thinking' has now percolated down over two generations. This has resulted in innovations as Australian practitioners evolve from those original psychoanalytic models, responsive to the current need to be psychodynamically informed in a climate where the value of short-term early intervention is increasingly in the frame. Australia, equidistant between the United States and Great Britain, has benefited from a combination of thinking from both countries, and 'classic' psychoanalytic models have combined with theories of attachment and the rich thinking that emerged from that concept, through such pioneering work as that of Mary Main, Daniel Stern and Berry Brazelton. Notable developments include the setting up of the Child Psychoanalytic Foundation, where the Observation Studies course in Sydney was formally accredited by the Tavistock Clinic in 1997. This course was expanded to full child psychotherapy training. Also from 1998, the University of Melbourne has run a Masters course in Parent and Infant Mental Health; this will include a clinical training in infant–parent psychotherapy. A Graduate Diploma in Child Psychotherapy by Distance Education has also been offered by Monash University in Melbourne since 1998. This complements the Monash University four-year Master of Child Psychoanalytic Psychotherapy (MCPP), completion of which allows entry into the Victorian Child Psychotherapy Association (VCPA), the professional association for child psychotherapists in Victoria, which has been modelled along similar lines to the Association of Child Psychotherapists (ACP) in the United Kingdom. (As with the ACP, applicants who have completed an equivalent to the MCPP and meet the other entry requirements are eligible to apply for membership to the VCPA.) The training in Brisbane is developing, although as yet without university links.

Despite this, there is virtually no establishment of child psychotherapy posts within the public sector. In the State of Victoria, for instance (with about 4 million of Australia's total population of 18 million), there are only four full-time equivalent posts in the public sector, located at the Royal Children's Hospital, Melbourne. While the term 'child psychotherapist' is not a protected title, there have been recent moves towards setting up an Australian Confederation of Psychotherapists, and the VCPA would seek to be included. And there is keen interest in public meetings in which child psychotherapy topics are presented, or in conferences such as when the VCPA sponsors a speaker from overseas: When Dr Valerie Sinason was a visiting speaker for a psychotherapy conference in Melbourne recently, this was very warmly received by the wider public.

There is also an ICAP Institute which has been set up in Sydney.

Edited by Frances Salo

New Zealand

Child psychotherapy became established in the 1960s. The first formal training was offered at Otago University, in Dunedin, and later moved to Wellington, a more central venue. Some graduates of this course then joined the staff at Auckland University of Technology, where a former Graduate Diploma in Clinical Child Psychotherapy became the Masters in Health Science (Psychotherapy) in 1999.

The original classical psychodynamic and object relations focus of the course has never been lost sight of, and, as with Australia, the thinking in the profession is influenced from both Britain and the United States, with the work of John Bowlby, Donald Winnicott, Peter Fonagy, Daniel Stern and Mary Main and other attachment-based contemporary theorists as the basis. The course is currently under review but will continue to include a two-year infant observation and strong emphasis on child and adolescent developmental theory, infant mental health and childhood disorders.

Students learn to work with the child within the context of the family, and also within multidisciplinary systems, acknowledging the importance of socio-cultural ways of working with the child.

The New Zealand Association of Child Psychotherapy was formed in 1976 and was responsible for accrediting membership. In the 1990s it changed its name to the New Zealand Association of Child and Adolescent Psychotherapy to reflect more accurately the scope of the work of its members. Many adult and child psychotherapists have joined the recently inaugurated Infant Mental Health Association of Aotearoa New Zealand, which is now an affiliate of the World Association of Infant Mental Health. Regular branch meetings are held in several regions to work with issues in this increasingly important area.

Betty Robb

Europe

Bulgaria

Child and adolescent psychotherapy is a relatively new field in Bulgaria. At present there is no established network of state mental health services for children and adolescents and until now no formal training pro-grammes have been offered that meet the criteria of the EFPP. However, since the late 1990s various efforts have been made to introduce a

psychoanalytical approach to mental suffering in childhood and corresponding therapeutic interventions have been developed and offered by
several different professional societies – mostly non-governmental organisations active within the social service network, in a community context or
in private practice.

French psychoanalytic schools were amongst the first to introduce training programmes for Bulgarian mental health professionals working with
children. Two different analytical societies based on the theories of Jacques
Lacan (Espace Analytique and Champ Freudien) have developed training
programmes on their own, including seminars, public lectures, theoretical
readings (called *cartels*) and clinical supervisions, usually conducted by
visiting Lacanian analysts. As part of the training some of the local professionals have had clinical placements in child psychiatric hospitals in
France and Belgium and received supervision from analysts from the Ecole
de la Cause Freudienne and New Lacanian School. Strong institutional links
have been developed with the local network of specialised institutions for
children and adolescents at risk, especially focusing on infant-care and
developmental disorders.

Another organisation active in this field is the Animus Association
working with women and child victims of physical and sexual abuse. The
child psychotherapy department of the association was established in 2000
to offer psychoanalytically-oriented child psychotherapy, psychodynamic
counselling for parents, psychodynamic family therapy, etc. Most of the
child therapists in the centre are trained as clinical psychologists and are
receiving personal psychoanalytical psychotherapy or psychoanalysis as
well as regular individual supervision. Some are enrolled in psychoanalytical training at the Han Groen-Prakken Psychoanalytical Institute for
Eastern Europe, IPA. From 2001 all therapists from the centre take part in
clinical and theoretical seminars led by Dr Alberto Hahn from the Tavistock
Clinic, who also offers supervision. In 2007 a postgraduate course, Foundations of Psychoanalytical Practice with Adults and Children, was launched
jointly with the University of Sofia.

The first steps towards a child and adolescent psychotherapy training
were made in 2005 by the Palette Foundation in collaboration with the
EFPP, introducing regular theoretical and clinical seminars and supervisions
conducted by psychoanalytical psychotherapists and child psychoanalysts
such as Dr Anastasia Nakov from the FFPPEA (Fédération Française de
Psychothérapie Psychanalytique de l'Enfant et de l'Adolescent). In 2008 an
agreement was signed between the Palette Foundation and the FFPPEA
with a view to providing training in child and adolescent psychotherapy
according to the guidelines of the EFPP. As part of the prospective training,
training in psychoanalysis/psychotherapy will be provided to Bulgarian
trainees in the near future.

Malen Maleov

Czech Republic

During the period between the two world wars, child psychotherapy was virtually non-existent in Czechoslovakia. Some tentative beginnings were further interrupted by the post-war discouragement of existing initiatives so that, in effect, while adult psychoanalysis survived principally on an illegal basis, work with children disappeared completely. In 1971 the Children's Psychiatric Clinic in Prague was established under the leadership of Dr J. Spitz and a space for psychotherapeutic approaches was created, mainly with families, later developing into systemic family therapy training. It was not, however, until 1993 that the Society for Psychoanalytic Psychotherapy was founded, connected with the EFPP, and as part of this society a child psychotherapy section came into existence. In 2002, nine candidates completed the training initiated and led by colleagues from the British Association of Psychotherapists in Great Britain. All of the graduates are active in Prague, and employed in various mental health settings as well as in private practice. Two members have become training therapists and supervisors. The majority of the members regularly publish articles and give lectures, thus disseminating knowledge of psychoanalytic thinking about children and adolescents. A translation into Czech of the *Handbook* was published in 2005 and continues to arouse much interest.

Edited by Dr Martina Pilařova

(Editorial note by AH: Lydia Tischler's role in this continues to be celebrated in her mother country.)

Denmark

Interest in the practice of psychoanalytic child psychotherapy has grown during the past years, with practice mainly based in residential institutions, community services for children and their families, hospitals, and in private practice. The Danish Association for Psychoanalytic Child and Adolescent Psychotherapy was founded in 1992. In 1998 the Association started a training programme in accordance with the recommendations stated by the EFPP. The training programme is still dependent on subscription and funding, which limits the availability of the training. The first training candidate graduated in 2002. This training takes place in Copenhagen, and a shorter and less comprehensive training has been established in Aarhus. At the University of Aalborg steps have recently been taken to integrate psychoanalytic psychotherapy with children and adolescents as a possible choice in the curriculum for psychology students completing their MSc at the University Clinic. Following government legislation, authorisation to work as a clinical psychologist can be obtained after two years of supervised work following an MSc in Psychology. After further supervised work and theory courses, specialist degrees in psychotherapy and in child psychology can be issued by the Danish Psychological Association. The specialist degree in psychotherapy does not as yet distinguish between children and adults; however, this will change in the near future. The Centre of Infant Studies of the Institute of Clinical Psychology at the University of Copenhagen has a professional link with Harvard College in the United States, and it is also developing a similar link with the Tavistock Clinic in Great Britain. While there is not as yet a Danish academic journal specifically linked to work with children, such psychoanalytic work finds space for publication in the Scandinavian journal of psychology, *Nordisk Psykologi*, in the Scandinavian journal of psychotherapy, *Matrix*, and in the journal of the Danish Association of Psychologists, *Psykolog Nyt*.

Liselotte Grunbaum

Estonian Republic

Estonian child psychotherapy was re-established in 1995 when Nils Taube, an Estonian by birth, invited John Schemilt, Gillian Deane and George Crawford from the Scottish Institute of Human Relations to explore the possibility of developing therapeutic services for children in Estonia. Before and during the Soviet occupation treatment for children was available through family and cognitive-behavioural therapy. Some professionals were trained in the Erica method of sand-therapy from Sweden.

The first training in psychoanalytical child psychotherapy was established in 1997 under the auspices of the Scottish Institute of Human Relations (SIHR) with George Crawford as its director and with financial support from Nils Taube. The programme followed the 'Therapeutic skills for working with children and young people' programme. This consisted of infant and young child observation, discussion of cases, individual supervision, and theoretical seminars covering child and adolescent development and disturbances and an introduction to the main psychoanalytical concepts. Training events were held at weekends once a month. Reet Montonen was coordinator in Estonia and also its inspiration and its mainstay. Sadly she died in February 2008. The teachers who were mainly responsible for this training were George Crawford, Lydia Tischler and Marja Schulman, with a number of other visiting teachers from England. In 2004 eight trainees graduated from the Scottish Institute of Human Relations. They are the founding members of the Estonian Child Psychotherapy Association, which was established in 2003.

The project emerged and gained impetus from the initiative of Nils and Idonia Taube. In accordance with their wishes, members of the Estonian Child Psychotherapy Association established a school for training new child psychotherapists in Estonia: Anna School offered its first year of training in autumn 2008.

Dr Anna Kleimberg

Finland

Psychoanalytic child and adolescent psychotherapy trainings are quite well established and in recent years have spread to different parts of Finland. Since 1976 development has been rapid when the Finnish Psychoanalytical Association and the Therapeia Foundation formed the Finnish Association of Child and Adolescent Psychotherapy. The very first three-year training in child and adolescent psychotherapy started in 1978. The students were doctors, psychologists, social workers and psychiatric nurses. In 1987, when thirty-two students had qualified, the joint training by two different societies was stopped. Following this, two psychotherapeutic societies developed their own psychotherapy training programmes in Helsinki: in 1990 the Therapeia Foundation started a five-year course and in 1993 the Helsinki Psychotherapy Society started a three-year course. Both trainings still continue. The focus is on young and latency children and young adolescents up to fourteen years of age. The five-year programme aims to qualify child psychoanalytic psychotherapists for independent intensive psychotherapeutic work and teaching. Infant and young child observations on the Tavistock model, as well as supervised training cases and theoretical seminars, are included in the training requirements.

There are also a number of three- and five-year psychoanalytical child and adolescent psychotherapy training schemes outside Helsinki in Oulu, Turku, Kuopio, Mikkeli and Tampere, and in Vaasa and Helsinki in Swedish, and there are plans to include Rovaniemi in the Arctic Circle. These function independently of each other – some are organised by the University Extension Study Centres. In Helsinki, Turku and Oulu training institutes provide ongoing trainings while in other parts of the country the trainings are on a one-off basis and the teachers and supervisors, mainly child and adolescent psychoanalysts, travel there. The EFPP criteria are followed in all trainings. In Finland it is compulsory to become a registered psychotherapist after qualification.

The Finnish child psychotherapy trainings do not include adolescent psychotherapy. This is separate and only a few training institutes offer dual training. They are discrete professional categories with separate associations. The Adolescent Psychotherapy Foundation in Helsinki has provided a three- and five-year training since the 1980s – in Helsinki from 1980, followed by Oulu in northern Finland in 1994 with the help of Marianne Parsons and the Anna Freud Centre. The number of adolescent psychotherapists has grown rapidly.

The first European training in group psychotherapy for children was set up in Helsinki in 1994 by the Group Psychotherapy Association and the first four-year infant–parent psychotherapy trainings started in 2000 in Turku and Jyväskylä.

Today there are about 150 members in the Finnish Association of Child and Adolescent Psychotherapy. The Association arranges study weekends and training events and invites foreign guest speakers. Two textbooks – *Child and Adolescent Psychotherapy* and *Child Psychotherapy and its Relational Dimensions* – have recently been published in Finnish by two different societies and furthermore a twenty-year jubilee book on adolescent psychotherapy.

Many psychotherapists work not only in the public health sector but also in private practice. Private psychotherapy treatment for children and adolescents can be covered by the government or health district public money for up to three years twice weekly or even more intensively and long term in serious cases.

Big organisational changes are taking place in child psychiatric clinics and services at the moment in the Helsinki area. A new child psychotherapy centre with three functions – assessment, treatment and research – is planned for the Helsinki health district. Psychoanalytical child and adolescent psychotherapies have been accepted as important treatments of choice.

Marja Schulman

Flanders (north Belgium)

In Flanders, some forms of play therapy have been practised since about 1950. A milestone in the development of psychoanalytic practice was the foundation of an important residential setting for severely disturbed children using a child analytic frame of reference (e.g. Aichhorn, Redl and Wineman, and Anna Freud). Meanwhile, play-therapy was initiated in 1956 at the Department of Psychology of Leuven University: this gradually adopted a psychoanalytic orientation and built up a major amount of clinical and theoretical expertise. Some years later it developed into the current Centre for Child Psychotherapy and Developmentally Based Intervention (CCP-DI).

Since 1974, there has been a postgraduate training in psychoanalytic child psychotherapy at the CCP-DI, based on the Anna Freud Centre and UCL, the Tavistock Clinic, and Yale Child Study Centre. The training is associated with the child section of the Flemish Society for Psychoanalytic Therapy (VVPT), a member of the EFPP. In a joint venture between the CCP-DI and VVPT, many conferences, literature seminars and supervision groups are taking place and in several regions of Flanders trained child psychotherapists work in a diversity of settings. Furthermore, the CCP-DI is engaged in teaching psychodynamic developmental psychology and psychodynamic child psychotherapy to clinical psychology students at Leuven University. Gradually the CCCP-DI has become more oriented towards psychodynamic research and developed insights and principles about supportive-expressive psychodynamic child psychotherapy (in line with current mentalisation based therapy). Much work has been done on the integration of child psychotherapy with a psychodynamic oriented family approach and working with the parents. Several clinical monographs on child psychoanalytic work have been published (e.g. on children's drawings; supportive-expressive child psychotherapy; psychodynamic child assessment; adolescent therapy; early parent–infant relationship; play in psychoanalytic psychotherapy). Currently the CCP-DI's main interest concerns early parent–child relationships in Flemish and immigrant families, an interest supported by the regional government.

Christine Leroy

France

The Fédération Française de Psychothérapie Psychanalytique de l'Enfant et de l'Adolescent (French Federation for Psychoanalytic Psychotherapy with Children and Adolescents) was founded in 1997. Following the death of Claudine Geissmann in September 2007, Didier Houzel became its President. This Federation encompasses the following regional groups:

- ARPPEA (Association Régionale pour la Psychothérapie Psychanalytique de l'Enfant et de l'Adolescent) established in Caen (Normandy) in 1993;
- GAPP (Groupe Aquitain de Psychothérapie Psychanalytique) established in Bordeaux (Aquitaine) in 1995;
- AFPPEA (Association pour la Formation à la Psychothérapie Psychanalytique de l'Enfant et de l'Adolescent) established in Paris in 2000;
- Centre Martha Harris established in Larmor Plage (near Lorient, Britanny) in 1996 and co-opted into the Federation in 2003;
- RLFPPEA recently established in Lyon in January 2008;

There are also some isolated members in Nantes, Lille, Metz and Nevers.

Each group comprises between five and ten members and trains between ten and twenty students.

The courses consist of infant observation, weekly supervisions of child and adolescent psychotherapy, and seminars on theoretical and clinical topics. The Federation is affiliated to the EFPP.

For the time being this Federation is the only organisation offering training in child and adolescent psychoanalytic psychotherapy. The psychoanalytic societies belonging to the IPA do not train child psychoanalysts. A committee of the Société Psychanalytique de Paris (SPP) has existed for two years, its purpose to discuss problems of training in child psychoanalysis, but no conclusion has yet been reached.

Some institutions in Paris train their own psychotherapists.

Didier Houzel

Germany

The first association of German psychoanalytical child and adolescent psychotherapists was founded in 1953 (the Vereiningung Deutscher Psychagogen), and in the 1960s this association founded the Standing Conference of the dozen existing training institutes (now twenty-four institutes in 2008) in order to standardise and safeguard requirements for training. In 1975 the association was given its present name: Vereinigung Analytischer Kinder-und-Jugendlichen Psychotherapeutien (VAKJP), the association for analytical child and adolescent psychotherapists, and it has at present over 1,400 members. The association regards itself as a scientific and political association.

Since 1971 practitioners registered with the association have been recognised by health insurers and therapy is paid for according to health company guidelines: this as a rule may be up to 150 sessions for children and 180 for adolescents. In spite of its membership numbers, there is still a shortage of trained practitioners on the federal level. The training is costly and trainees tend to have to retain their previous work commitments, thus making the training itself longer in duration. As elsewhere, the training is open to teachers, social workers, psychologists and medical doctors between the ages of twenty-five and forty (generally) and it takes five years to complete. The training includes, alongside the usual components, specific psychiatric experience of one year with very disturbed children or adolescents.

The VAKJP publishes a journal which appears four times a year and a substantial newsletter three times yearly. The VAKJP organises two national conferences every year; one including a membership meeting. The VAKJP established a Science Board, which decides which studies for analytical child and adolescent psychotherapy should be promoted. Furthermore a group of specialists is working on professional guidelines for analytical child and adolescent psychotherapy. In the political field, members of the VAKJP are elected into national social, political and vocational law boards.

The VAKJP is represented by two delegates to the child and adolescent section of the EFPP and takes an active part in EFPP conferences. The VAKJP organised the 2006 EFPP conference 'Actual Parents – Inner Parents' in Berlin.

Kristine Gopel

Greece

A formal training in child psychotherapy developed from an in-service programme for staff in the Psychological Paediatrics Department of Aghia Sophia Children's Hospital in Athens. In the in-service programme, senior members of the British Association of Psychotherapists (BAP) were involved as visiting teachers. In October 1991 the Hellenic Association of Child and Adolescent Psychoanalytic Psychotherapy was officially inaugurated following the Tavistock training model and standards with an intake of up to eight students every other year. The Hellenic Association, part of the Psychoanalytic Psychotherapy Institute of Greece, is an active member of the EFPP with a constant presence in committees, publications, conferences and workshops. It organised the first conference of the Child Section in Athens in May 1994 and in 1998 inaugurated the biannual Summer Syros Workshop – three days in late May – a scientific exchange of limited EFPP membership on the Greek island of Syros. It hosted the first Infant Observation Workshop (Athens, December 2005), a special interest group which developed within the EFPP to promote infant observation.

The Hellenic Association has an active presence in the field of Greek mental health. Apart from offering a training of high standard with invited teachers (members of the Tavistock Clinic and psychoanalysts from many European countries), it undertakes a wide range of activities, including publication (a series on child and adolescent psychotherapy, translations of psychoanalytic literature, and a journal on the mental health and psychopathology of the child and adolescent); educational film productions; multinational research projects; organising public lectures, seminars, conferences and workshops.

The Greek government has not yet licensed the profession of Child Psychotherapist despite its wide recognition. There are, however, established Child Psychotherapy Units in the Child Psychiatry Department of Athens University Medical School, the Special Diagnostic and Psychotherapeutic Unit 'Spyros Doxiades', the Hostels and Day Care Units of the Hellenic Association for the Psychosocial Health of Children and Adolescents (HAPHCA), the Perivolaki Day Centre and Hostel for autistic children and a number of Child Guidance Clinics.

Effie Layiou Lignos

Hungary

In 1970, the mainly psychoanalytically oriented Child Psychotherapeutic Outpatient Clinic of Budapest set up theoretical seminars on child psychoanalysis for interested professionals. Two years later, seminars on technique became available for all child guidance clinics and in 1982 intensive short-term training began. In 1986 child psychotherapy became a part of the systematic psychotherapeutic training for psychiatrists and psychologists, and in 1990 the Ego Clinic, a private outpatient clinic for children and adolescents, became the training centre for child and adolescent psychotherapy. While it can be said that training in Hungary is largely concentrated in Budapest, there are private seminars on theory and technique led by trained psychoanalysts, and supervision is available outside Budapest. In 1992 'On One's Own Way' came into being, under the auspices of the Psychoanalytic Institute, as a centre for training and work with adolescents.

Hungarian child analysts have, since the 1970s, been in regular contact with both the Anna Freud Centre and the Tavistock Clinic, and there has developed a two-way link with, for instance, members of the Tavistock Young People's Counselling Service travelling to Hungary to exchange ideas with colleagues. Hungary has also been a regular participant from the inception of the EPF Standing Conference on Child and Adolescent Psychoanalysis. In 2001 the Hungarian psychoanalytical review was established under the title: *Adolescent and Child Psychotherapy*.

A special feature of child analysis in Hungary is the integration of Imre Hermann's theory of clinging, published in Budapest by Pantheon: Hermann, I. (1943) *Az Ember Ő'si Ösztönei* (The Ancient Instincts of Man).

(Editorial note: This sounds a very interesting theory and appears to anticipate Harlow's experiments with monkeys and to have similarities with Winnicott's theory of holding.)

Sára Klaniczay

Ireland (no update)

Since the 1980s, there has been a huge upsurge of interest in psychoanalytic psychotherapy with children and adolescents, and 1995 saw the publication of the first issue of the *Irish Journal of Child and Adolescent Psychotherapy*, currently published annually.

In the early 1980s concern was expressed about the relative neglect of intra-psychic processes in children, with an emphasis solely on family therapy and systems approaches. The Irish Forum for Child Psychotherapy (IFCAP) was established in 1986 and in 1990 the first diploma course began, subsequently converted into a master's degree in Child and Adolescent Psychoanalytic Psychotherapy. The course is now a part of the Faculty of Health Sciences at Trinity College Dublin. In response to a demand for wider discussion and dissemination of psychodynamic thinking, IFCAP has run a series of introductory courses for interested colleagues in related professions. It has also strenuously pursued a policy of promoting international links, and there is now a steady two-way flow of ideas, in terms of lectures and seminars, and strong links with the Anna Freud Centre and the Tavistock Clinic. IFCAP, in its role as part of the Irish Standing Conference on Psychoanalysis (founded in 1990), has been monitoring the issues of accreditation and harmonisation in Europe, as well as issues of registration and practice in Ireland itself. A voluntary register of psychoanalytic psychotherapists already exists, and a statutory register is in the offing. The most recent development was the setting up in 1996 of the

Irish Association of Infant Observation to monitor and promote the understanding and development of the work.

Israel

In the last ten years several psychotherapy courses varying in rigour have come into being. Most are parallel programmes for child or adult psychotherapy. Trainees choose one specific syllabus. In child psychotherapy this is at HELPABA (school for psychoanalytic psychotherapy) which is the only programme with a two-year infant observation requirement. A similar course exists in Haifa where it is the programme of choice for educational psychologists and social workers.

Tel Aviv University offers a few courses:

- a one-year group supervision of work with children;
- a two-year course of advanced studies in child psychoanalytic psychotherapy for more experienced therapists is planned for the next academic year;
- an external programme of child psychoanalytic theory for other professionals, e.g. doctors, movement therapists, nurses, teachers and other interested people.

Formal training in child psychoanalysis was launched at the Institute of Psychoanalysis in Jerusalem some six years ago, although child training cases have always been encouraged as part of analytic training.

There is an extensive network of services for children and adolescents. Public health services provide country-wide inpatient and outpatient services for children run either by the health insurance programmes or the Ministry of Health. Long-term psychotherapies unfortunately are being curtailed in favour of short-term 'quick fixes'. For those who can afford it there are many private clinics.

There are many kindergartens throughout the country for children with Asperger–PDD syndromes – a unique project, developed over the past twenty years. New programmes are being set up for children on this spectrum who need therapeutic intervention, like ALUT – a programme for the autistic child. Finally there are refuges for children in danger of sexual or physical abuse. Private organisations are now also offering services with therapeutic help for abused children and adolescents as well as child and adolescent abusers – this tends to be provided by social workers or clinical criminologists.

A more recent development has been the growth of clinics offering parent–infant therapy dealing with developmental and emotional disorders, eating problems, sleep difficulties. These clinics are all affiliated to the public health services.

Joel Miller

Italy

During the years of the fascist regime in Italy the practice of psychoanalysis was forbidden, but in the late 1940s the Centri Psico-Pedagogici (Psycho-Pedagogic Centres) were established with the aim of preventing anti-social tendencies in children and adolescents. There were 200 centres in all throughout Italy. It was not until the 1970s, however, that the emotional problems of childhood came to be seen not only to have organic origins, but very often to be rooted in family and society.

While continuous changes of government during the last thirty years have hindered the development of child and adolescent psychoanalytic psychotherapy in the public sector because of an absence of coherent policies for children, there have nevertheless been enormous developments in the field. The most severe consequence, however, of the lack of planning for children and adolescents in government policy has been that the role of child psychotherapists, for political and trades union reasons, has not been specifically included in the organisation of provision for child mental health. Notwithstanding, since the 1970s there has been a steady growth in opportunities for both preclinical and clinical training, hitherto predominantly on the Tavistock model, but with both Freudian and Jungian trainings about to be made available. The first Observation Course began in Rome in 1976, and the students from the first two courses, thanks to the pioneering help of a senior teacher at the Tavistock Clinic, set up a structure for clinical training. The training follows the Tavistock model originated by Martha Harris, and indeed was set up with her help and support. Subsequently the Observational Studies component has spread to other centres – in Trapani, Palermo, Bologna, Milan, Pisa, Florence, Naples, Pescara and Venice. These developments led to the foundation of the AIPPI and the association Centro di Studi Martha Harris, both in Rome, to offer a support structure for the training, now carried out in Rome, Florence, Milan, Naples, Palermo. Also in 1976 a training began at Rome University's Institute of Child Psychiatry: this is still operative, and regularly welcomes key international figures to give seminars and courses. Apart from this flourishing network, private associations in Rome, Turin and Monza-Milan have played an important role, promoted by university teachers in the departments of child neuro-psychiatry. In Turin observational courses and clinical training began in 1987 thanks to the help of senior teachers from the Tavistock Clinic and these are now carried out by the association ASARNIA-APPIA.

Together with the AIPPI and the Centro di Studi Martha Harris, these institutions are represented in the child and adolescent sections of the EFPP (European Federation of Psychoanalytic Psychotherapy) with about 300 qualified psychotherapists to date. While this represents a huge development, it is concentrated mainly in the north and the centre of the country, with the south of Italy and the main islands still having little or no provision.

Pia Massaglia

(Editorial note: one of the Independent trainings, of course, is the object relations one based in Rome where Vincenzo Bonaminio is Director. Apart from the internationally recognised journal Riccardo e il piggle *and joint editorship of the series* Psicoanalisi contemporanea: sviluppi e prospettive *making key texts accessible in Italian, Vincenzo was instigator and author of the translation into Italian of the first edition of this handbook.)*

Latvia

Psychoanalytic psychotherapy came into existence in 1991 when the Swedish family therapist Andrejs Ozolins first visited his country of birth and it has continued to develop. To begin with the main field of interest was adult psychotherapy. Help for children became possible when in 1994 Linda von Kyzerlink from the Frankfurt Family Therapy Institution introduced family therapy training in Latvia. In 2005 the Finish Association of Child and Adolescent Psychoanalytic Psychotherapy established a training programme in adolescent psychoanalytic psychotherapy in Latvia. Fifteen psychotherapists completed the basic training in 2008 and became adolescent psychotherapists. The Finnish association plans to continue the educational programme in future.

From 2006 two child psychoanalysts from Canada – Frieda Martin and Elizabeth Tuters – began work establishing an Infant Mental Health organisation, inviting all interested specialists to join. This might be considered a first step towards developing psychoanalytic help for children in the near future. Psychoanalysis proper for children does not exist at the moment in Latvia.

Anita Plume

Lithuania

Currently there are no dynamically oriented child and adolescent psychotherapists licensed in Lithuania. Some ten to fifteen years ago some members of the Lithuanian Psychoanalytic Society did work with children; however, when they began to train as psychoanalysts or psychoanalytic psychotherapists, they changed to working with adults.

There are some dynamically oriented psychologists and psychotherapists in work with children. In Vilnius there are two institutions where it is possible to get some professional help: the Vilnius Child Development Center and the Children's Support Center. Vilnius Child Development Center has inpatient, outpatient, and day care departments and they work and provide treatment for the most severely mentally and neurologically ill children. The Children's Support Center provides psychological guidance for children, adults and families to help them cope with psychological crises and overcome emotional disturbance; it provides psychological counselling to children and adults who have experienced abuse; it implements child abuse, suicide and substance abuse prevention programmes; and has developed the Big Brothers Big Sisters programme in Lithuania.

In 2005 the Lithuanian Psychoanalytic Society together with the Dutch Psychoanalytic Institute provided a two-year training programme – a basic course of psychoanalytic psychotherapy for child psychiatrists and neurologists over nine long weekends. The main idea was to introduce professionals working with children at the basic level to the main ideas of psychoanalytic thinking and methods. Eighteen professionals graduated from this course. Some of them later started to study psychodynamically oriented psychotherapy. Some of the child and adolescent psychiatrists who graduated from the programme are also working in small towns in Lithuania.

Jurate Uleviciene

Luxembourg

It is only recently that any real interest in child psychotherapy and psychoanalysis has come to the fore in Luxembourg. The first child psychiatrist, who was also a psychoanalyst, began practising here in 1989. In Luxembourg, there is no legislation regulating the training of psychotherapists or the practice of psychotherapy. Nevertheless, the various government departments that deal with children and adolescents realised that they had fallen behind in providing care facilities for the youngest members of the community and have since invested substantial funds in order to remedy that situation. There is now a hospital for children, a separate one for adolescents, day-care centres, hostel accommodation, etc. Educational psychology facilities have been developed and psychologists appointed. However, since there was an urgent staffing requirement for these facilities, the personnel often lack experience and adequate training.

In 1990 a Study and Clinical Research Group on Child and Adult Psychoanalysis (Groupe d'Étude et de Recherche Clinique en Psychanalyse d'Enfant et d'Adulte – GERCPEA) was set up. This Group is affiliated to the EFPP and to the European Association of Child and Adolescent Psychopathology (Association Européenne de Psychopathologie de l'Enfant et de l'Adolescent – AEPEA). The latter Association is well established in southern Europe and in French-speaking countries. The GERCPEA organises three scientific Symposia each year, in addition to four-year training courses under the title *The Psychotherapeutic Relationship and Clinical Interventions: the Psychoanalytic Approach*. Since the majority of the board of administrators of the GERCPEA are members of the Belgian Psychoanalytic Society, the conception and philosophy underlying these training courses are based not on the classical Eitingon model but on the one that the IPA recognises as the 'French' model.

Serge Frisch

The Netherlands

Psychoanalytic societies that are members of IPA/EPF have been in existence since 1917. In 1979 the Nederlandse Vereniging voor Psycho-analytische Psychotherapie (Dutch Society for Psychoanalytic Psychother-apy – NVPP) was founded. This society is represented by two delegates to the child and adolescent section of the EFPP. In recent years many contacts have been established on a personal as well as organisational level, espe-cially in scientific matters.

While until recently the societies had their own training programmes in child analysis or child and adolescent psychotherapy, a joint training pro-gramme has now been established covering the first two years of theoretical seminars for child and adult psychoanalysts as well as psychotherapists. Thereafter candidates have a choice of four options:

- *psychoanalysis* for adults and/or for children and adolescents,
- *psychotherapy* for adults and/or psychotherapy for children and adolescents.

In recent years between five and ten candidates have opted for the child and adolescent psychoanalytic training. Child observation is one of the important parts of the training.

In combination with several Belgian psychoanalytic societies, there is a journal *Tijdschrift voor Psychoanalyse*. Furthermore there is a national institute for psychoanalysis, the Nederlands Psychoanalytisch Instituut, with offices in Amsterdam and Utrecht. The institute is a centre for practice and has two clinics – for adults and for children and adolescents. It is a practice centre (psychoanalysis, psychotherapy, parent–infant treatment and group therapy), a centre for learning (short training courses) and a centre for scientific research. Policy initiatives are mentalisation-based therapy, new treatments for adolescents, parent–infant projects.

In addition there is a society for child and adolescent psychotherapy, Vereniging voor Kinder- en Jeugdpsychotherapie (VKJP), which unites psychotherapists of different types (psychodynamic, systemic and beha-vioural) working with children, adolescents and their parents. Although this society does not have its own training courses it publishes a journal *Tijdschrift voor Kinder- en Jeugdpsychotherapie*.

Perhaps it is important to mention that the profession 'psychotherapist' is legally protected with a special national register. As a psychotherapist one can be registered after a part-time course of six years. One needs to be registered as a psychotherapist before acceptance for a psychoanalytical training.

Jan Vandeputte

Norway

The history of psychoanalytic work with children in Norway began with the establishment of the Institute for Child and Adolescent Psychotherapy in 1952. The Institute (later to be renamed the Dr Waals Institute, after its founder) inaugurated a three-year psychoanalytic psychotherapy training with a particular emphasis not only on treatment but also on the multi-disciplinary framework which supports it. Subsequently this training and service has spread throughout the country, and there are now about sixty outpatient psychiatric clinics providing treatment to children and families. About 4 per cent of the population under 18 receives some service, and of this 9–10 per cent receive short- or long-term psychoanalytic psychother-apy. In addition there exists some private work. The goal is to increase the numbers of those in receipt of treatment, but this of course has budget and training implications.

Child psychotherapy training as such has not been formalised, and training within the National Health system varies in quality. For the last few years some geographical regions in Norway have offered a basic training in child and adolescent psychoanalytic psychotherapy, qualifying for a part of the EFPP training.

In 1991 the Norwegian Association of Psychoanalytic Psychotherapy was formed, and is now a member of the EFPP. The organisation has changed its name to the Norwegian Association of Psychoanalytic Psychotherapy with Children and Adolescents (NFPPBU), and now has 93 members. It is active with monthly meetings for members and an emphasis on stimulating post-graduate training. For several years an advanced training in child and adolescent psychotherapy has been on offer, qualifying for full EFPP recognition. NFPPBU also offers training in infant observation and parent–infant work and has also given an introductory course and clinical seminars in Kaunas and Vilnius in Lithuania on child and adolescent psychotherapy.

For many years senior practitioners, beginning with Martha Harris, have been visiting teachers, with infant observation seminars also running since that time. NFPPBU has arranged lectures and clinical seminars with Anne Alvarez for many years. There has also been a steady stream of Norwegian visitors to the Tavistock Clinic, and with international links increasingly being promoted. NFPPBU has delegates for the Child and Adolescent section of EFPP, and is currently working to establish international contacts.

Rune Johansen

Poland

Psychoanalytic psychotherapy with children and adolescents has devel-oped in Poland over the last twenty years. At first there were single psychotherapists working psychoanalytically in their hospitals. Later most of them also started training in adult psychoanalysis, as adult training was more available in Poland during the communist system and also after it ended. Until now in Poland psychotherapists who work with adults and those who work with children and adolescents have belonged to the same psychoanalytic associations. There were not separate sections and all members had the same theoretical training. Many psychotherapists work with both adults and children and adolescents. In the last few years a group for psychoanalytic psychotherapists who work mostly with children and adolescents was formed. They work in public sector hospitals or psychotherapeutic centres and also in private practice. Now we are on the way to establishing a formal child and adolescent section belonging to the EFPP. In Poland we have quite a few child and adolescent psychotherapists who have been trained to the standard or advanced level. However, there are some training requirements like infant observation which it has not been possible to realise in our country as yet.

Monica Jakubowicz

Russia

In the 1960s the first non-drug-related therapies were introduced in Russia, and the term 'psychotherapy' entered the professional language, although at that time psychotherapy was the prerogative of medical doctors only. As communication with the West opened up, so too did notions about treating children psychotherapeutically, but initially there was no specific training for the work which began at the Bechterev Institute in St Petersburg (formerly Leningrad) and the Serbsky Institute of Psychiatry in Moscow. In 1990 the course in child and adolescent psychotherapy was established in the Department of Psychotherapy of the Medical Academy for Postgraduate Studies in St Petersburg. The majority of students remain medical doctors, but there is an increasing intake of psychologists. As a consequence of opening up to Western influences, there was an undifferentiated explosion of ideas following previous deprivation, and this has yet to be rendered coherently. One of the most important events was the one-year course in psychoanalytic concepts taught by staff from the Anna Freud Centre (AFC). The twenty-five professionals who first took the course have carried on with the work and have established the St Petersburg Society of Child Analysis.

Psychoanalysis, long prohibited in Russia, was simply neglected during the time of perestroika. It was only in 1997 that the President's Decree was issued to support psychoanalytic work both morally and financially. Again, this opening up of a previously closed door brings its own difficulties in terms of a huge influx of ideas and initiatives, and time is needed to ground many differing approaches in appropriate structures for training and treatment. Such a new set of conflicts, as old structures change and anxieties are released, has aptly been described as 'post-totalitarian stress syndrome'.

New developments in services for the children in Russia include the Early Intervention Institute in St Petersburg which is trying to introduce non-medical ideas of dealing with the problems of infancy using the AFC model of mother–child interaction. Members of the St Petersburg society, having attended seminars at the AFC, run regular toddler groups based on the AFC model.

Some psychologists and MDs have completed their education through recognised IPA Societies (Finnish, German, Croatian, British, French etc.) and become direct IPA members. A psychoanalytic Study Group has been set up in Moscow. Some of the professionals (in Moscow as well as St Petersburg) have also additional training in psychoanalytic work with children. The recognised psychoanalytic groups provide training courses for newcomers from all over Russia (which include the trainee's own psychotherapy and observation seminars). Slowly and increasingly psychoanalytic psychotherapy is taking its place in the Russian reality and professional practice. In January 2008 the Society mounted a very successful international conference on the subject of 'Fear as an element in development'.

Nina Vasilyeva and Svetlana Chaeva

Serbia

The first initiative specifically for children was set up in Belgrade in the early 1950s in the Child Guidance Clinic for Children and Adolescents, where psychoanalytically oriented psychotherapy and psychoanalysis for children and adolescents was practised. The Clinic was set up by Vojin Matic in consultation with Serge Lebovici, Rene Diatkine and Donald Winnicott. It was the first multi-team clinic employing psychiatrists, psychologists, social workers and special teachers. It was also the first place at which after the 1939–45 war formal training in psychoanalysis was organised, including standard training analysis. The Child Guidance Clinic served as a model for similar institutions Europe-wide but was shut down after ten years for reasons which are still unclear today. The prevailing view is that it was to prevent the popularisation of psychoanalysis.

Almost fifty years later in Belgrade there is still no institution that can match it. Matic and his pupils educated a number of child psychoanalytic therapists. After the war in former Yugoslavia, the general level of child therapy in Serbia deteriorated. The situation with therapy for adolescents is somewhat better. At present there is only one IPA recognised child analyst in Belgrade. The Belgrade Psychoanalytic Society (IPA) in its curriculum has two seminars on development and is planning to introduce training in child analysis in autumn 2008 in cooperation with analysts from abroad. The Society has just finished a two-year introductory course for allied professions in child psychoanalytic psychotherapy – this will be continued next year. The Faculty of Medicine in Belgrade offers psychologists and psychiatrists a specialisation in work with children and adolescents. At the Institute for Mental Health in Belgrade there is a four-term child psychotherapy module. There is a sub-section of child and adolescent psychoanalytic psychotherapy within the society founded in Belgrade. It is hoped that the Serb Society will join the EFPP in the near future. Former Yugoslavia has been a member of the International Association for Child and Adolescent Psychiatry and Allied Professions with a member from Belgrade on its executive. Serbia rejoined the association a few years ago.

Tamara Šajner-Popvic

Sweden

In a climate where the mental health and welfare of children had already been on the agenda from the beginning of the twentieth century, the child guidance movement in Sweden began in 1933, following a previous initiative some ten years before. It was not, however, until the 1950s that specialists in child psychology and psychiatry were introduced, earlier work having largely focused on parents.

The Erica Foundation, an independent institution providing treatment, university level training and opportunities for research, was established in 1934, modelled on Margaret Lowenfeld's Institute of Child Psychology in London. Since then about 400 psychotherapists have been trained at the Foundation, where research and treatment are seen both as essential in terms of increasing knowledge and also in attracting government funding.

Since the start of the 1990s there have been other training programmes – one, for instance, at the University of Gothenburg. Most work is done in the public sector, but rapidly increasing demands for psychotherapeutic help in combination with insufficient government financial support have led to fewer opportunities for children to receive intensive treatment.

Siv Boalt Boethius

Switzerland

Switzerland has three linguistic regions – German, French and Italian – in which quite different situations concerning psychotherapeutic training prevail. The following text refers mainly to the German region.

Psychoanalytically oriented child and adolescent psychotherapy is in a rather difficult situation. On the one hand, there was until recently no specific psychoanalytic training for child and adolescent therapists. On the other hand, there is still no distinction made between adult and child therapists with respect to authorisations for private practice. As a consequence, many child psychotherapists in private practice have no specific training in psychotherapy for children and adolescents.

Training in psychoanalytically orientated child and adolescent psychotherapy is under threat, recruiting fewer candidates while other therapeutic methods, above all the cognitive-behavioural, which offer shorter and less expensive trainings, are growing. Only a few child guidance clinics and hospitals are psychoanalytically oriented. Moreover, the official requirements regarding therapeutic trainining for qualification in child and adolescent psychiatry are rather low.

Recently, some improvements have been made: different psychoanalytic institutes offer specific trainings or training modules for psychoanalytically oriented work with children. In collaboration with the EFPP (Swiss-German section) a training in psychoanalytically oriented work with children will soon be offered. The latter will meet the EFPP criteria, especially regarding infant observation and training analysis. Moreover, the Swiss Society for Child and Adolescent Psychiatry has recognised the importance of a solid training in psychotherapy and consequently raised the criteria for the therapeutic training of child and adolescent psychiatrists.

Gisela Zeller-Steinbrich

Part III

Diversity of treatments and settings

10 The therapeutic setting and process

Monica Lanyado and Ann Horne

The constantly evolving relationship between the therapist and patient lies at the heart of all psychoanalytic work and is the main vehicle for psychic change. In some respects this statement may seem surprising. The child comes to see the therapist with all manner of difficulties in his or her relationships with family and peers, and talks and plays around these themes, and yet in psychoanalytic work the most important insights which lead to deep change in the patient's relationships and internal world are gained from what is happening in the consulting room, in the 'here and now' of the meeting of two people, the therapist and the child.

Psychoanalytical psychotherapy does not involve specific treatment programmes for particular kinds of presenting problems as in, say, behavioural or cognitive therapy. It will be evident from many of the clinical examples in this book that the kinds of difficulties that lead to referral to child psychotherapists tend to be complex and long established – frequently with antecedents in the parents' own childhood. Often the multi-disciplinary clinic team will have offered other forms of treatment but have not been able to effect the deep-seated change that is needed or to sustain change over time.

What is it that makes a relationship therapeutic?

In normal caring relationships we listen to and share time with friends and family when life offers setbacks. This wish to help and protect those we care for when they are in physical or emotional pain is a capacity which some would argue is a basic human instinct, the counterpart of the instinctual need to form attachment relationships (Bowlby 1969, 1973, 1988). The good general practitioner will, as family doctor, offer to a distressed patient a listening relationship which may obviate the need to refer that patient for more specialised help.

The everyday caregiving components of ordinary relationships become highly refined and further concentrated within a specialised professional therapeutic relationship. Indeed, Winnicott draws attention to the parallels that exist between the way in which ordinary parents provide the facilitating environment within which their children can develop emotionally, and the therapeutic relationship which facilitates emotional growth in areas where development has become stuck (Winnicott 1965, 1971).

Yet the therapeutic relationship is also very different in important respects from relationships outside the therapy room. First, it is not a reciprocal relationship: in psychoanalytically informed treatment the therapist's personal and emotional life is not shared with the patient. The therapist makes every effort to be emotionally available and thoughtfully attentive to the patient, whilst retaining this privacy. Second, it is not a spontaneously available relationship: there are appointment times which are clearly boundaried in time by prior agreement between patient and therapist. Third, the location is a special room set aside for such work.

The therapy room and therapeutic setting

Child and adolescent psychotherapists work in many different settings – schools, child and adolescent mental health clinics, hospitals, residential units. They often have to share rooms with colleagues who work in very different ways, or they may see their patients in a room which is specifically put aside as a therapy room. Within the many external and practical constraints, there are some fundamentals that the therapist will strive for so that the therapeutic setting is as constant and reliable as possible for the child and adolescent patient.

There is a regularity of therapy room – the same room at the same time – and this is protected space, always booked for that time, defended against intrusion. In settings like schools, much explanation to colleagues goes on to ensure this fact. The child knows where he/she will be seen. As far as possible, the therapist will try to keep the contents of the room the same from one session to another. This applies to the furniture, as well as to the toys, which can be a mixture of communal toys – such as a doll's house with furniture, a sand pit with sand toys, lego, a train set – and the child's individual box of small toys which the therapist will have chosen with care at the start of treatment. These small toys are an aid to communication through play, and usually include small appropriately chosen families of dolls, wild and domesticated animals, cars, ambulances, police cars, fire engines, soldiers, paper and pencils, felt tip pens, scissors, sellotape, string. Such therapy equipment allows the expression of a range of feelings from rage to reparation. These toys are put away safely by the therapist at the end of the session and remain untouched until the child's next session. This concrete expression of the child having a private relationship with the therapist becomes very important to the child and the state of a child's individual toy box can be highly indicative of the child's frame of mind.

Each child's toy box gathers its own character and history in the course of the therapy: there can be times when there are many toys that the child has broken, and other times when the child is busy mending and glueing together broken bits, or making structures out of paper and sellotape. The drawings can be a crumpled mess, at times resembling the contents of a rubbish bin; at other times they may be carefully sorted and packed away. Unexpected or avoidable changes in the room, or toy box, can raise the child's anxieties about the therapist not being able to protect the therapeutic space sufficiently, and introduce unnecessary complications into the therapeutic process. The attention to these details of the therapeutic setting is not just the therapist being obsessional – it is fundamental to the therapeutic containment of the patient's anxieties.

Time keeping is another aspect of this therapeutic containing function. The therapist makes every effort to start and end the (usually) fifty-minute session on time. When a child has a regular therapy time, the therapist does not change the time or cancel a session without thinking long and hard about it. The commitment to the child takes priority, and children, young people and parents are similarly encouraged to give the therapy priority in the organisation of their lives. There are of course holiday breaks but wherever possible these are known well in advance and a calendar may be made on which the number of sessions before the break can be marked off, as can the number of weeks missed, and importantly the week that the child and therapist return to their work together. These practicalities are all indicative of how seriously the work with the child, and the child himself, is taken by the therapist. They are outward expressions of the therapist's efforts to be trustworthy, reliable and safe for the patient and contribute significantly to the real relationship between them.

Key concepts

Within this therapeutic setting, what is it that the psychoanalytic psychotherapist brings to the uniqueness of each therapeutic encounter? Experienced therapists develop their own style and 'way of being' with their patients – the result of training and clinical experience, as well as individual personality. As a result, each therapeutic encounter is the unique product of this very particular meeting of the mind and emotions of therapist and patient. The only equipment (apart from the toys) is the therapist's emotional attentiveness, receptivity and ability to maintain a space for thinking about what is being communicated by the patient and what is being experienced within the session. This is a specialised and highly honed way of listening which could be described as 'psychoanalytic listening', acutely informed by the key concepts described below.

Importantly, we recognise today that the therapist also brings the essence of who he or she is, what can be thought of as being the 'presence' of the therapist. This is something which cannot be left outside the door of the consulting room. It is this very particular use of self that plays a vital part in the therapeutic relationship as it unfolds (Lanyado 2004).

The basic assumption of all psychoanalytic work is the concept of the unconscious, 'that part of the mind which is inaccessible to the conscious mind but which affects behaviour and emotions' (Concise Oxford Dictionary). Indeed psychoanalysis is defined in the same dictionary as 'a therapeutic method of treating mental disorders by investigating the interaction of conscious and unconscious elements in the mind and bringing repressed fears and conflicts into the conscious mind'. Although separating out the components of the therapeutic relationship and process may seem a somewhat artificial device, it is important to be clear about them because they offer an interlinking framework for understanding in the therapist's mind. Particular concepts will have more significance in work with certain patients than with others.

The transference–countertransference relationship

The child's sense of who he is and how others will react to him is very much affected by expectations based on his past and present family relationships. It is the 'transferring' of these expectations onto the new relationship with the therapist which constitutes the transference–countertransference relationship (often abbreviated to the 'transference relationship'). In some ways the transference relationship becomes rather like a representative sample of the child's ways of relating to those who are important to him. As a result of this, specific anxieties and painful conflicts come alive and can be worked with, in the first instance, within the contained context of the transference relationship. The emotional changes resulting from the working through of these issues gradually become more generalised and a part of the child's repertoire in everyday relationships. The child's fantasies and imaginings about the therapist as a person are the medium through which past and present relationships are transferred into the therapeutic relationship. If, for example, the therapist gives personal information too readily, some of this transference may be forestalled and the scope for exploring the child's ideas, fantasies and expectations limited.

All patients can at times feel that their therapist is too impersonal, and may accuse the therapist of 'not caring' or 'only doing it for the money'; but if the therapist's way of being with the patient is one of compassionate attentive listening, these accusations can be understood as containing important information about the way in which the patient experiences many people – that is, as not really caring about them or being interested in them, or only being interested because this meets their own needs.

The countertransference is the therapist's response to the transferred aspects of the patient's ways of relating – that is, the feelings aroused in the therapist by this, as opposed to the therapist's own customary way of being. The particular qualities of the transference–countertransference relationship help the therapist to know more about the patient's fantasies, relationships, functioning and expectations in the past (as well as the present). There can also be aspects of countertransference that indicate unconscious personal difficulties and blind spots of the therapist – hence the need for a lengthy and in-depth personal psychoanalysis, central to the training, to enable the therapist to separate out what belongs to the patient's communication and what to the therapist. Such importance is placed on the need for the therapist to continue the process of self-exploration and understanding, so that the therapist's and the patient's issues don't become mixed up, that it is now mandatory for therapists to undertake continuous professional development (CPD) throughout their clinical working lives.

There are many different aspects to these transferred relationships. Possibly the most important distinctions are between the *positive* and *negative transference*. As these terms imply, the positive transference embodies those friendly, loving, trusting feelings which enable the patient to feel invested in the therapeutic process and come to his sessions, even when the sessions are painful and distressing. The negative transference contains feelings such as anger, hatred, rejection, envy and mistrust which may make the patient feel at times that he hates the therapist who is experienced as causing all the misery that he feels in his life.

The *infantile transference* is a way of describing those aspects of relationships that have remained active in the patient from infancy. The understanding of how these relationships, internalised during infancy, can still operate powerfully in the patient's everyday life is one of the most important aspects of the transference to be understood and interpreted before internal change can take place.

Many other aspects of ordinary developmental processes come alive within the therapeutic relationship, both as a part of the ongoing development of the child during treatment, and as a result of past developmental conflicts being expressed and hopefully resolved within the transference relationship. The leitmotif of facilitating normal emotional development resonates throughout the therapeutic process. Oedipal conflicts, to take one example, may be expressed through intense jealousy and sensitivity in the patient about the fantasised adult relationships of the therapist. The child may feel this particularly when there are holiday breaks in therapy, when the therapist may be imagined to be totally involved in a sexual and emotional relationship with a partner without a thought or care for the child patient. Sibling rivalry may similarly be expressed through painful feelings of jealousy and envy towards other patients or the fantasised children of the therapist. Similarly, a patchy pattern of attendance at therapy sessions, in which helpful and fruitful sessions are interspersed with sessions missed without explanation, may express the ordinary adolescent need to develop independence and separateness from parental figures, as well as the adolescent tendency to act rather than verbalise.

Acute awareness of what constitutes ordinary emotional development underpins the therapy. Indeed Hurry argues that psychoanalytic psychotherapy is in part 'developmental therapy': one of the important roles the therapist takes on for the child is that of being a 'developmental object', facilitating the return to ordinary developmental pathways (Hurry 1998).

It is important to bear in mind that, alongside the transference relationship, there will always be to some degree a 'real relationship' with the therapist. It is the gradual realisation in the patient, in his external reality, that past relationships are not always repeated in the present which is part of the untangling process. This fluctuates, depending on how ill the patient may be or how intense the transference relationship is at any particular time.

When working with children the real relationship is particularly apparent when, for example, one has to help a small child in going to the toilet or stop an angry older child from being physically violent. The therapist may also need to be actively involved in management issues that support the child's therapy – such as attending meetings or being available to the parents in a thoughtful way.

It must be emphasised that, whilst the relationship with the therapist is likely to become extremely important to the child for all the reasons described here, the relationship is not intended in any way to undervalue or become rivalrous with the child's relationships with his parents. The therapist is not trying to be a 'better parent' to the child than the parents themselves are, although at times parents who are feeling demoralised may express this view. These feelings need to be known about and recognised by the therapist, not only to disentangle possible misapprehensions, but also because they may indicate that the child is splitting his feelings into idealising the therapist whilst denigrating the parents – a form of primitive psychological defence which needs to be tackled and understood as relating to the child's difficulty in facing the fact that those closest to him can be both 'good' and 'bad', loved and hated at times. Working towards the developmental and therapeutic achievement of being able fully to express positive and negative feelings towards loved ones, and to make reparation when loved ones have been hurt by negative actions and feelings (known as the 'depressive position' in Kleinian thinking (Klein 1952) or the 'capacity for concern' by Winnicott (1963)) is a very important part of the process in a child's therapy.

Similar mechanisms of splitting and projection can operate within the staff group in multi-professional teams, making it very necessary at times to keep in mind the child's transference to the entire clinic. Thus all team members need to be aware of these processes at work – and at times the dangers of splitting (for example the 'good, kind receptionist' contrasted with the 'bad, uncaring therapist') that relate to the overwhelming feelings which the child unconsciously projects onto the clinic team, sometimes destructively and at other times in the hope of being understood. Recognition and discussion of the team conflicts thus engendered, which can be an externalisation of the child's internal conflicts, leads to further understanding that can aid the therapist in containing the child's anxieties and conflicts.

Anxieties and defences

Psychoanalytic therapy can be painful when distressing feelings come alive within the therapeutic relationship. Nevertheless, children come to value the personalised attention and thought that their therapy provides, even though entering this therapeutic space raises many anxieties and dis-comforts as well as many characteristic defences. The dynamic interplay and conflict between *anxieties* and *defences* needs to be experienced within the therapeutic relationship so that it can be witnessed and thought about first-hand by the therapist and patient as it occurs in the session, as well as explored in the patient's relationships in everyday life.

The problem of how to deal with anxiety – the fantasised or real threat of some form of loss, shame or otherwise deeply feared experience – is central to the concept of neurosis. This is a complex issue, and indeed Freud offered different formulations about anxieties and defences at different phases of his career (Freud 1894, 1917, 1926). The way in which clinicians think about and work with anxieties and defences depends considerably on their theoretical backgrounds and clinical experience. In classical Freudian theory anxieties and conflicts relating in the main to aggressive or sexual feelings can lead to the use of defences such as repression, regression, displacement, identifi-cation with the aggressor and idealisation (see Anna Freud 1936). From a Kleinian perspective, clinicians are more likely to think in terms of the defences of splitting and projective identification, particularly in the paranoid-schizoid position, and manic and omnipotent defences, together with reparation in the depressive position (see Klein 1952). The central human dilemma of how to express love and hate within close relationships is the essential source of conflict, with the inherent need to find ways of restraining destructive aggressive or sexual feelings at its core.

In addition, arising from the first days of life when the capacity to form relationships is rudimentary, there are the very primitive and early fears of abandonment, annihilation, disintegration and merging – all fears about the survival of the infant self. As will be apparent in the clinical examples in this handbook, in practice there is little evidence of theoretical demarcation lines and many child and adolescent psychotherapists use their knowledge of different theoretical perspectives to provide as broad an understanding as possible of the anxieties and defences that they encounter in their patients.

In ordinary life we all learn mechanisms of coping with anxiety (that is, defences) and these hopefully become more adaptive and flexible as we grow. Particularly for the infant and child, however, anxieties of a primitive and, at times, terrifying nature need the helpful presence of an attentive adult if they are not to become overwhelming. Night terrors are a prime example, known to most families with toddlers; separation anxiety in its various forms is another.

However, anxieties are also a very important part of life, giving realistic warnings when there is physical or emotional danger, as well as giving the kinds of false alarms which are so characteristic of anxiety driven by unconscious forces. In the latter case, which is typical of neurotic anxiety, the sufferer can be highly aware of the irrationality of the fears that he or she cannot consciously control, such as phobic anxiety of spiders, lifts or heights. The interaction between the way in which ordinary anxieties have been contained or exacerbated by parents and carers as a child grows up, as well as the presence or absence of real anxiety-provoking situations (severe childhood illness, physical or sexual abuse, or actual loss of an attachment figure) are likely to affect how anxious a person becomes in life and how he tries to cope with these anxieties. (For further introductory discussion of these concepts, see Brown and Pedder (1991) and Trowell (1995).)

Defences are developed and utilised by the ego (the functioning psychological self) to protect itself at times of anxiety. For example, one of the features of the primary-school-aged child is the development of appropriate defences which enable the Oedipal drama to be left behind and the acquisition of control and competence to proceed. Without defences, we are vulnerable in our interactions with others and may respond inappropriately or be hurt very readily (Freud 1936; Klein 1952).

At times of intense fear or anxiety, we all use the most effective defences available to us. A legacy of earlier and therefore primitive defences, however, leaves the child with a repertoire of defences that can become less effective or even destructive to other more developed parts of the personality and yet, because they have been so helpful in the past as a protection against anxiety, they may be held on to quite fiercely. This may be despite the fact that the child has other more sophisticated and less self-destructive means of protecting him or herself emotionally. While the transference relationship helps open new neural pathways and ways of experiencing the self, in times of acute trauma there may be a resorting to older, known ways.

When working with the defences in therapy there are two aims: to explore the defences that are neither age-appropriate nor helpful and to increase the range of appropriate defences available to the patient for coping with unbearable anxiety or emotional pain. In addition, anxiety in all its irrationality needs to be faced gradually, without raising further defences. This becomes possible through the medium of the therapeutic relationship: the infantile anxieties can be named and made sense of within an attentive, holding relationship. The processes of projection and introjection described later are crucial here.

It is a matter of experience and training whether the therapist decides to try to interpret the anxiety or the defence first; indeed this may vary within the same treatment depending on how integrated the patient is and how mature the ego is. Therapists can often find themselves both acknowledging to patients the existence of high levels of anxiety whilst recognising their need to maintain some levels of less appropriate defence as they do not yet feel safe enough to let these go. Particularly for very vulnerable patients, such as deprived and abused patients, defences always need to be treated with great respect as they may be the only way that the patient can hold him or herself together. If defences are tackled without this respect, breakdown, suicide and collapse may follow, or patients may feel unable to face continuing with therapy.

The process of waiting to see what deeply concerns the child can be puzzling to referring agencies who often ask, 'Have you tackled X with him?' By following the dynamic interchange between anxiety and defence within the child, psychotherapy can clear a way for later 'real world' exploration. But primitive anxieties and defences do not disappear in a brief few sessions – time and space are needed for the psychotherapeutic process to develop.

The interaction of the internal and external world

Why is it that a perception of other people as callous and uncaring can persist in the face of quite contradictory evidence? In psychoanalytic thought, this perplexing observation is understood in terms of differences between the individual's very personal experience of his *internal world*, and the *external world* of experiences which can be observed by other people. The dynamic interaction between these two worlds and areas of experience is pivotal in psychoanalytic theory and practice.

The internal world is made up of several components and could be described as the place where we live most intensely within ourselves, particularly when not communicating with others. It is a private world of thoughts, fantasies and feelings, many of which we would find it very difficult to articulate to ourselves, let alone to others – inchoate half-thoughts and fleeting fragments of feelings. It is a world where ordinary social values and relationships can be suspended, where it is possible in fantasy to love or hate whomever we want with impunity. It is also a world of many layers, some more subtle than others, in which conscious thoughts and fantasies mingle with the barely conscious, as in day dreams, and where unconscious thoughts and fantasies surface in dreams in ways which can surprise and at times shock and embarrass the dreamer.

The way in which the internal world and external world interact with and affect each other is the subject of much debate in terms of the 'balance of power' between them. Our external world is perceived through the eyes of the internal world filter, which in turn will have been affected by what has actually happened in our external world experience. The earlier in life that experiences have taken place, the more powerfully but often irrationally they seem to hold sway in the internal world.

To return to the patient who feels that the therapist and others in his life do not really care about him or only care as much as this suits their own needs: there may have been a time, possibly very early in that patient's life, when his mother really was emotionally unavailable to her baby and not responding well to his needs. This could have been for many reasons – maternal depression, marital tension, financial worries, bereavement. It may not have gone on for long or have been severe, but for a baby who perhaps found it particularly hard to cope with the feelings of frustration and anger, or even abandonment, arising from his mother's lack of her usual patience in trying to understand his communications, these feelings of persecution could remain long after the mother actually became emotionally available again. In other words, the baby might continue to perceive the mother as unavailable, or might have internalised the idea of an unavailable mother in his mind. He may actually have become harder to comfort as a result of this brief period of difficulty and not have been able to recover from the experience. Such a scenario can be further compounded by the mother's expectation of retribution from the infant for her emotional absence, which could be one response to her concerned guilt about her earlier unavailability. This can happen despite the reality that the 'good' mother had actually returned in the external world. The internal world and the external world can thus become very out of kilter (Klein 1952).

Some babies and young children do have an unfortunate number of negative and hostile experiences, in which case their internal worlds, if very persecuted, are in fact a fairly accurate representation of what they have experienced in the external world. Even in these instances, therapists are often amazed at the genuine fortitude, resilience and hope that some of these children demonstrate, suggesting that, despite awful life experiences, in their internal worlds they have managed to keep alive those few experiences that have been good, and internalise them into their constructs of 'self'. This raises the important question of the role of the child's constitution and its influence on emotional life. There is considerable debate about which factors can be considered constitutional; we would include individual differences in the capacity to tolerate frustration and express anger, to love and to hate, to feel guilty, to show gratitude (Klein 1957) and to be resilient in the face of hardship. This whole topic is very complex; we have simply tried to give a flavour of what is meant when we think about the interaction between the internal and external world and how this affects functioning and relationships.

The intermediate space and playing

During therapy, access to the patient's internal world is sought by the therapist through free association, dreams and, with children, through play. Freud's original dictum – when he abandoned hypnosis as a means of reaching into his patient's past – was that his patients should simply say whatever came into their thoughts when they lay on the couch, making every effort to overcome embarrassment or shame about what was in their minds. This non-directive method of working is vital for the painstaking exploratory nature of psychoanalytic work, which does not attempt to lead the patient in particular directions but chooses to follow the patient's conscious and unconscious thoughts and feelings. Imaginative play offers the same insights as Freudian free-association into the child's internal world.

However, many of the most deprived, abused and traumatised children seen by child psychotherapists have great difficulty playing in this free and imaginative way when they start therapy. This ordinary developmental process has been derailed as a result of early experiences and it is a sure sign that they are beginning to recover when they begin to play, however briefly, in a spontaneous way. This recovered developmental process will have been greatly aided by the therapist facilitating the creation of what Winnicott described as 'an intermediate space', or a 'transitional space', in which play can take place. He envisaged this space as the place between the internal and external world in which we 'live creatively' and which is paradoxically neither inside nor outside, but both (Winnicott 1965, 1971). The therapist, by being playfully present, enables this process to take place but does not direct the content of the play itself. This therapeutic stance and way-of-being with the child is an important part of what needs to be learnt at the start of the therapist's training.

Communication and interpretation

Communication between the therapist and patient is both verbal and non-verbal. The child patient talks and plays when with the therapist but may also be silent and resistant, communicating non-verbally a range of feelings by processes such as projection. In addition, many children, and particularly adolescents, will unconsciously stage situations in the therapy by acting out conflicts which they cannot put into words. For example, a child who cannot believe that the therapist is prepared to accept hostile, as well as more friendly, feelings without rejecting him may behave in a very challenging and difficult way in sessions, needing to experience that, however awfully he behaves, the therapist is still there to see him again at their next session.

The therapist is likely to respond to these various forms of communication in a variety of ways. Sometimes she may make a simple comment which clarifies the meaning of the child's play – this may be as straightforward as putting a name to a feeling. At other times she may be able to identify a common or recurring theme in the child's feelings or thoughts (as unconscious processes gradually come into relief in the child's conscious life) and comment on this to the child, watching to see how the child responds to this idea. In accordance with non-directive psychoanalytic technique, the emphasis is always on following the child's train of thought or feelings, not on introducing or suggesting issues that the therapist feels the child *should* be tackling, other than in very special circumstances.

The therapist starts with careful observation and reflection about the child on all levels, and, having commented on what has been observed, waits to see how the child responds in words, play or action. These comments should not be dogmatic, but offered more as something to think about that might be helpful or even interesting to the child. Developing a sense of curiosity and capacity for reflection in the child becomes an important part of the process, internalised through identification with the therapist. It is always important for the therapist to bear in mind how able the child is to listen to or understand what is being said. Naturally the language must be in tune with the child's ability to comprehend.

In addition, there can be many times in therapy when the therapist suddenly understands a particular dynamic within the child or in the child's relationships, but is aware that it is too soon to try to share this understanding because it may be too painful, or raise too many anxieties and defences. Such insights have to be very carefully put to the child, sometimes almost in stages over time. Meanwhile an important first stage in understanding and interpretation has been reached in the therapist's mind. This understanding may be offered at the time to the child, but it may equally well have to lodge in the therapist's mind for a considerable time without being shared with the patient – contained by the therapist for the patient until he is able to take in and digest the idea (Bion 1962). Once again the emphasis is on *how* to communicate in such a way that the communication can be received. It can be surprising to find that there are times when the understanding remains with the therapist and is never put into words, and yet there is a significant change in the child's relationships and level of disturbance (Lanyado and Horne 2006).

Interpretations made by the therapist, particularly interpretations about the transference relationship, can, if well timed, lead to real breakthroughs in therapy. However, interpretation is no longer seen as the only, or most important, way of bringing about significant change. Interpretation is the process of putting into words – making conscious and known to the patient – fantasies, aspects of relationships, anxieties, conflicts and defences, and insights into the way the patient's mind works, which previously could not be known because they were unacceptable, and thus had remained repressed in the unconscious mind. For Freud, this process of making the unconscious conscious was the main route to psychic change. Nowadays we are aware that there is often a lengthy build-up to such pivotal transference interpretations, of which there may be surprisingly few in many treatments.

This build-up includes what may be lengthy periods where the therapist contains painful feelings and thoughts projected into her by the patient, without understanding what they are about. Tolerating *not knowing* what is happening within the therapeutic relationship may be a very important experience which the patient needs the therapist to have, as this 'not knowing' and confusion may be the state of mind that the patient finds the most impossible to deal with. Premature attempts at knowing may detract from this. Thus, when insight finally comes to the therapist and it is possible to make an interpretation to the patient, the interpretation itself is the final product of what may be weeks or even months of verbal and non-verbal communication between patient and therapist. This is what gives it its power.

With adolescents in particular, but also with children where shame may be a factor, it can be helpful to take up the anxieties *in the displacement.* Adolescents may talk of 'a friend who . . .' and may need the vehicle of 'the friend' for several weeks before they can own the anxieties disclosed as their own. The younger child may focus on 'the angry crocodile' or the abusive doll and explore the emotions in the activities of the toys before rage can be personally owned. Although the process of therapy aims for the integration and personal ownership of feelings, such strategies are useful (Lanyado and Horne 2006). Equally, the therapist may differentiate the patient's infantile behaviour and feelings from his age-appropriate competencies. This can allow the patient to examine such feelings from a position which offers the possibility of control and lessens humiliation: 'that sounds like the two-year-old bit again' is more bearable and helps engage the patient's curiosity about himself. Again this can be particularly helpful when working with adolescents.

Finally, the therapist has to give thought to the timing of interventions. With verbal interpretation the child tends to let one know if this is right – although few will be like the eight-year-old who said to a psychiatric registrar of our acquaintance 'Gee, Doc – that's right!' hitting the heel of his hand to his forehead for dramatic effect. The lessening of anxiety in the room, a fleeting smile or a development in play are more usual cues. It is important for the therapist, however, to keep in mind the sometimes paradoxical impact on the child of being understood: Alvarez has commented thoughtfully on the child's need to adjust to and integrate the good experience, as well as to deal bravely with the terrifying or depriving one (Alvarez 1988). This is of particular importance when working with deprived children for whom the 'good experience', being understood, may in itself be overwhelming and need time to be internalised.

Containment and emotional holding

Interpretation and other forms of expressed understanding are sometimes not possible when a child is in a very anxious state – whether this is driven by actual external events or a general state of mind. The child may be so highly on the defensive that the therapist's words are drowned out by the noise the child makes or by general overactivity. Or the child may be so clearly distressed and barely holding himself together that words seem woefully inadequate – or the therapist cannot immediately find words to express the pain the child is communicating. At other times a child can express enormous anger (sometimes out of panic and fear) and become destructive of toys or furnishings in the room, or even attack the therapist. Adolescent patients can become deeply depressed and extremely fragile so that they feel quite unreachable.

When these kinds of feelings threaten to overwhelm, the therapist is likely in the first instance to try simply to 'contain' the feelings that are experienced as engulfing, before exploring ways of talking about what is being communicated. The distinguishing feature of containment as a process is that, at the same time as empathically responding to the patient in a non-judgemental and non-retaliatory way, the therapist is attempting to understand and reflect on the process of what is happening between them, by listening carefully to and accepting the patient's *projections* of intense feelings which often cannot be verbalised. This is more than an absorption of the patient's pain; it is an attempt by the therapist to use his or her mind to think about what feels almost unthinkable and to be in touch with feelings communicated by the patient that feel unbearable to the patient. This can help to bring these feelings and thoughts down to size, or at least make them gradually more tolerable. It is the way in which the therapist receives – that is, *introjects*, tolerates and survives, and tries to think about and understand these feelings – that is the key to containment. In time, the patient becomes able to own the feelings again when these have been received, modulated and, wherever possible, finally articulated by the therapist, when they can be fed back in manageable form.

This model of non-verbal communication derives from observation of and theories about communication during the earliest days of life. A mother has to be prepared to be emotionally available to her baby by attempting to understand what he needs, particularly when crying, by the same processes of projection, introjection and containment (Bion 1962; Winnicott 1960). These processes are at their most intense in mother–baby interaction and are studied in depth by all child psychotherapists in the two-year observation of a baby growing up in a family which forms a central part of training. As any parent will testify, the power of these non-verbal communications is astonishing. The baby's cries can mobilise great emotional and practical activity in parents until they feel they have understood and responded appropriately. The baby's smile can, in just as powerful a way, wipe away hours of tiredness, anxiety and frustration in parents, helping them to feel loved and loving, and 'good-enough' as parents.

The therapist also offers confidentiality and the possibility of talking about issues that cannot be talked about elsewhere for fear of shocking, distressing or angering the listener. This is one of the more obvious ways in which the therapeutic experience provides *containment* of the patient's anxieties. For children, in particular, fear of rejection and abandonment by those they most depend on and need is common, especially where aspects of the self that they feel to be ugly, shameful and unacceptable are concerned. This fear of rejection then comes into therapy where it can be noted and thought about, rather than feared. The therapist's continued commitment to being reliably available for the patient during his regular session times, and the ways in which this interweaves with the frustrations of the other times that the therapist cannot be available, help to provide both a growing sense of containment and a growing awareness that the patient is increasingly known and accepted as he truly is – beauty spots, warts and all.

Ending therapy

When patients and therapists have been involved in such intense therapeutic relationships, often for lengthy periods of time, the question of how and when to end the therapeutic process is complex and sensitive. Ideally, the consideration of a number of criteria would inform any decision on the therapist's part about the timing of the end of a child's therapy. Amongst these are: a lessening of anxiety and less of a need to resort to extreme and self-defeating defences; the establishment of a healing process with respect to traumatic experiences; the re-establishment of appropriate emotional development including more age-appropriate functioning; an improvement in the child's relationships with family and peers; an increased ability to play freely and creatively; a sense of self that allows feelings to be integrated and a future to be contemplated; and, underpinning all these achievements, an increased capacity to think about his or her feelings and the feelings of others. All of these criteria are comparative, not absolute, and highlight the need to think about the realistic aims of each patient's therapy.

Many forms and applications of psychoanalytic psychotherapy are offered to children, ranging from occasional consultations to intensive five-times-weekly psychotherapy. Some children with severe problems can be in therapy for a number of years. However, the norm within the public sector in the UK is likely to be once-weekly therapy for eighteen months to two years. Where the child is well supported by his parents and family or carers, and where they have also been able to engage in therapeutic work and to develop their understanding of and responses to their child during the time of his treatment, the therapist can feel reasonably confident that the child's healthy ongoing development is well-enough established and supported within the family for therapy to end – and indeed for the parents or the child to consult with the therapist if there are difficulties at later stages of development. A date for ending therapy can then be agreed by therapist, child and parents, ideally allowing enough time for the child to experience and explore his feelings of sadness and loss about therapy coming to an end.

Depending on the form of treatment, the date for ending could be many weeks or even months ahead. Again, taking the norm of once-weekly work in the public sector, a period of three to six months would allow for a thorough exploration of feelings about ending. These feelings of sadness and loss, as well as anger, abandonment and jealousy of new patients, can arouse further memories of past losses in the child's life. This can provide a renewed opportunity to explore past losses in the context of the anticipated loss of the therapist in the present. In addition, the planned ending of therapy offers the important experience of learning that loss and letting go can be valuable developmental experiences in their own right.

Unfortunately, there can also be times when children end therapy without the therapist feeling they are ready. This can be the result of practical issues in the child's life – difficulties in getting to therapy sessions because of the problems of trying to balance all the needs of the family members, or moving away from the area. Therapy can also end because funding has run out or there is disagreement between professionals about therapeutic priorities in a child's life. Although these practical issues are explored carefully at the start of treatment so that the limitations of what can be achieved are worked within, it is not always possible to anticipate the external changes which can affect a child's therapy. This can lead to what, from the therapist's and possibly the child's point of view, feels like a premature end of the therapeutic relationship.

In such circumstances, the sadness and anger of premature ending have to be faced in the final therapy sessions, and therapists will struggle to have as many sessions as possible in which to try to help the child to cope with the ending of a relationship they are not ready to let go, in as positive a way as they can. Often, in these circumstances, the therapist has a very difficult task in the countertransference, not only because of the feelings expressed by the child that the therapist is abandoning them – or indeed the defensive opposite of this, that the child doesn't care about therapy ending – but also in relation to the therapist's personal anger and dismay at decisions being made which she (the therapist) feels are not in the best interests of the child.

Disagreements about when to end treatment can also arise when there has been a clear symptomatic improvement in the child's problems – for example, soiling has stopped or nightmares have ceased – but the therapist is aware that the child still has many unresolved anxieties that are being held within, and worked on in the transference relationship. The 'flight into health' is a well-known psychiatric syndrome. The therapist's concern would be that, if the child stopped treatment at that time, the anxieties would become unmanageable again in the child's everyday life and, without treatment, the original symptoms would reoccur or new ones replace them. In other words, the process of recovery and growth started by the therapy would not yet be able to continue on its own when therapy ended.

This is one of the risks when treatment in the public sector is defined by budgets rather than the individual child's needs; in such instances, it is rather like trying to 'fit a quart into a pint pot' or only taking half the course of prescribed antibiotics. Consideration of the need to consolidate and 'work through' important psychic changes, so that they become a deeply established part of the patient's personality, affects the therapist's views about the timing of termination of therapy.

The ending of therapy is also a real separation and loss of the real relationship with the therapist. The way in which the child approaches this real loss is likely to emerge in many ways in the sessions leading up to a planned ending. Just as, throughout therapy, the child's ability to cope with breaks between sessions and holiday gaps in treatment can reflect the ways in which the child is internalising the therapeutic process, so the approach to the end of therapy gives an indication of how much of the therapeutic experience the child will carry within himself when he no longer comes for his therapy sessions. This partly relates to very clear memories of what has been said and shared between the child and therapist, but, more importantly, it relates to the change within the child's internal world that has taken place during the course of treatment. The child may simply express this in terms of feeling happier, more relaxed and 'different' or 'better' than when the treatment started.

There are varied views about what kind of contact is appropriate between therapist and child when regular therapy has ended treatment. Certainly some form of follow-up meeting is often offered a few months after ending treatment. Some patients and their families want to keep in touch, and others do not. It is important for children to feel that the therapist has not forgotten all about them, even if they choose not to come to a follow-up session because therapy already feels such a thing of the past. Some children or their parents keep in touch with the therapist for many years – possibly by an occasional letter or phone call. The very individual nature of each therapy and each ending, combined with the increasing need to provide research evaluation studies on psychoanalytic psychotherapy, has led to much more thought being given in the profession to the post-therapy relationship between therapist and child: what is helpful for the child needs to be balanced with what is helpful in research terms.

It is important to note that, whilst the last sessions of a child's therapy can be poignant for child and therapist, there is of course also a real achievement for the child in being ready to move on from therapy and start a new chapter in his or her life. It is a truism to say that, in order to move on and forward in life, it is necessary to let go of experiences and relationships that are no longer necessary. In many ways, at the end of therapy, when all has gone well, the child has outgrown the need for therapy at that stage of his life and is ready to move on. This is the very nature of emotional development. Like the Winnicottian transitional object (Winnicott 1971) the therapist may be remembered with fondness but becomes outgrown and is no longer needed. Although ending therapy is hard, the therapist must be seen in this context – as a very important figure in the child's life at the height of the therapeutic relationship, but inevitably to be left behind when his purpose has been served and therapy ends.

References

Alvarez, A. (1988) 'Beyond the unpleasure principle: some preconditions for thinking through play', *Journal of Child Psychotherapy* 14(2): 1–13.

Bion, W. (1962) *Learning from Experience*, London: Heinemann.

Bowlby, J. (1969) *Attachment and Loss, Vol. 1: Attachment*, London: Hogarth Press.

—— (1973) *Attachment and Loss, Vol. II: Separation, Anxiety and Anger*, London: Hogarth Press.

—— (1988) *A Secure Base: Clinical Applications of Attachment Theory*, London: Routledge.

Brown, D. and Pedder, J. (1991) 'Psychodynamic principles', in D. Brown and J. Pedder *Introduction to Psychotherapy*, 2nd edn, London: Routledge.

Freud, A. (1936) *The Ego and the Mechanisms of Defence*, revised edn, London: Hogarth Press, 1966.

Freud, S. (1894) *The Neuro-Psychoses of Defence (1): Complete Works of Sigmund Freud, SE* vol. 3, London: Hogarth Press/Institute of Psychoanalysis.

—— (1917) 'Mourning and Melancholia', in *SE*, Vol. 14.

—— (1926) *Inhibitions, Symptoms and Anxiety, SE*, Vol. 20.

Hurry, A. (ed.) (1998) *Psychoanalysis and Developmental Therapy*, London: Karnac.

Klein, M. (1952) 'Some theoretical conclusions regarding the emotional life of the infant', in J. Riviere (ed.) *Developments in Psychoanalysis*, London: Hogarth.

—— (1957) *Envy and Gratitude*, London: Tavistock.

Lanyado, M. (2004) *The Presence of the Therapist: Treating Childhood Trauma*, Hove and New York: Brunner-Routledge.

Lanyado, M. and Horne, A. (2006) *A Question of Technique: Independent Psychoanalytic Approaches with Children and Adolescents*, London and New York: Routledge.

Trowell, J. (1995) 'Key psychoanalytic concepts', in J. Trowell and M. Bower (eds) *The Emotional Needs of Children and their Families*, London: Routledge.

Winnicott, D. W. (1960) 'The theory of the parent-infant relationship', *International Journal of Psycho-Analysis* 41: 585–95.

—— (1963) 'The development of the capacity for concern', in D. W. Winnicott *The Maturational Processes and the Facilitating Environment*, London: Hogarth Press, 1965.

—— (1965) *The Maturational Processes and the Facilitating Environment*, London: Hogarth Press.

—— (1971) *Playing and Reality*, Harmondsworth: Penguin.

11 Individual psychoanalytic psychotherapy: assessment, intensive and non-intensive work

Viviane Green

Introduction

The core of psychoanalytic psychotherapy centres on the transference and countertransference relationship. This chapter will begin by attempting to capture and convey a qualitative feel of what is offered by this form of treatment. I hope to delineate something of the psychic, mental and affective processes involved in a therapeutic relationship: what sort of experiences does therapeutic contact offer a particular child and how, too, does a therapist reflect on his or her part in the therapeutic engagement in order to understand the child?

How though do child psychotherapists assess who needs what and on what basis are recommendations made? The second part of this chapter will offer a developmental framework and describe its theoretical underpinning as a systematic way of approaching assessments and making treatment recommendations. In broad brushstrokes a range of psychopathologies or developmental difficulties will be mentioned reflecting both the wide sweep of developmental possibilities themselves and the range of referrals to voluntary sector and NHS Child and Adolescent Mental Health Services (CAMHS). For the purposes of this chapter, and in line with the Association of Child Psychotherapists' definitions for training purposes in the profession's core skills, intensive work is a minimum frequency of three-times-weekly sessions. When indicated and in a limited number of settings, children can also be offered sessions on a four or five times a week basis. In demarcating a line between intensive and non-intensive work, I do not wish to suggest that there is necessarily a straightforward series of ensuing differences between the two, e.g. that there is a neat fit between quantity and quality or depth. Many children are able to make very good use of non-intensive psychotherapy – indeed, this is the principal approach offered by child psychotherapists working in the NHS today. For a number of children non-intensive work may well be the treatment of choice and greater frequency is not always more appropriate. Conversely, there are children for whom intensive work is both positively indicated and may also be considered the sine qua non in order for them to begin to engage in a therapeutic process. In such circumstances it will be considered the necessary level of contact required to mobilise processes of psychic change. Flexibility is often called for and treatment can begin non-intensively, and then step up to intensive and indeed, vice versa. This chapter will outline some of the diagnostic and technical issues in offering one or the other form of treatment.

Finally, the chapter will highlight the context for treatment and some further integral considerations.

The transference relationship

At the heart of psychoanalytic treatment is the belief that our psyches are formed by our conscious and unconscious life and that the meanings we ascribe to our experiences are constituted through this. How we develop is of course in great part experience dependent; shaped by the relationships and the attendant psychic possibilities that are both offered and withheld. The main people in our external reality do not translate into simple 'facsimile' internal copies. The internal version is also shaped by unconscious forces and fantasies. How we experience, regulate, 'organise', represent, live out and communicate our emotional lives is of primary interest to the child and adolescent psychoanalytic psychotherapist. In any form of psychotherapeutic treatment the therapist, drawing on both conscious and unconscious forces within the self, uses her sentient and reflective psychoanalytic self to attempt to understand and make sense of the child's emotional world. Through the therapeutic relationship the therapist will try to understand the child's central identifications, the internal figures who inhabit a child's emotional and mental life and, in conjunction with this, the ways in which the child feels and thinks about himself. Alongside this the therapist also tries to grasp and comprehend the ways in which the child seeks to protect himself against the pain, hurts, anxieties and confusions engendered by his inner life. Attention is also given to aspects of the child's experiences that are sources of pleasure, self-esteem and satisfaction, which promote resilience.

The medium through which all this is expressed in a clinical setting is the transference and the countertransference. The term transference refers to the way in which new and current relationships are coloured by past and ongoing experiences. The new person, in the form of the therapist, is related to in a way that conveys the child's internal sense of the important figures in his life. The child also conveys the ways in which he has incorporated and shaped a sense of himself through these relationships. In short, the therapist lends herself as a person on to whom the child's wishes, thoughts and fantasies can be transferred. It is an 'as if' phenomenon where the therapist can be responded to as if he or she were a mother, father, grandparent, sibling or other significant figure. The transference also encompasses elements of (often) unwanted aspects of the child's self that he wishes to psychically 'discard' by attributing them to the therapist. Very often, the transference is played out in displacement, i.e. with toys and/or enacted through a physical symptom, gesture or demeanour where the body 'talks'.

The corollary of the transference is the therapist's own countertransference, by which is meant particular aspects of the therapist's responses to the child. In keeping a vigilant analytical reflective watch on her reactions to the child, the therapist seeks to understand the many varied, subtle and sometimes not so subtle ways in which the child unconsciously evokes a response in his therapist. In brief the therapist's internal process might go something like this: she realises that in a given moment or interaction she is feeling one of any number of possible emotions, e.g. angry/sad/useless/ disconnected/confused/panicked/overwhelmed and unable to think. This is particularly evident when a therapist finds herself experiencing a reaction which she comes to recognise as not normally hers (role responsiveness) and that has arisen specifically in response to something that has happened within a session. This is eventually followed through by the therapist reflecting on the 'what', 'why' and 'how' of the child's communication.

> When eight-year-old Laura, a child with learning difficulties, issued a stream of incomprehensible maths questions to her therapist, the therapist became overwhelmed with a sense of frustration, shame and confusion as she remained unable to unravel what she was expected to do. Laura was conveying vividly her own daily experience of feeling horribly muddled and humiliated when she could not understand something. Another therapist was given a vivid account by Peter, a sixteen-year-old boy, of his various risk-taking activities. Peter was engaging in promiscuous, unprotected intercourse and took various drugs when he went clubbing. The therapist noted how she found herself feeling increasingly alarmed (and somewhat disapproving) whereas Peter was apparently unconcerned. The therapist concluded that, in order to remain free of any conflict and to sidetrack thinking about the implications of what he was doing to himself, he had psychically 'handed over' this part of his capacities to the therapist. She then had to take up the split off anxiety in the hope that he might 'reclaim' this into his own awareness.

The transference and countertransference often occurs at a visceral level where a feeling is unspoken but palpable. The therapist, picking up on this, gradually brings it into the realm of conscious and, ultimately, articulated thought.

This transference and countertransference occur in both non-intensive and intensive treatment and are the therapist's tools for increasing her understanding of the child's conscious and unconscious life. However, some would maintain that in many instances intensive treatment provides the optimal conditions for fostering the intensification and growth of the therapeutic relationship. For some children, intensive frequency secures the necessary conditions for the very establishment of a treatment relationship. Others might state that the capacity to work intensively in the transference and countertransference is related more to the capacities within a particular therapist and child dyad rather than frequency per se. Many child psychotherapists feel that non-intensive work requires a high level of concentrated psychic work to catch the 'moments' within a limited time. The precise course of any treatment differs widely according to each child and his particular unfolding 'story'.

Assessment for individual psychoanalytic psychotherapy

A developmental framework

The criteria indicating the need for therapeutic help will be based on an overview of the many different aspects of the child's overall functioning. Anna Freud offered a basis for considering these different dimensions in both her Developmental Lines (1965a) and Provisional Diagnostic Profile (1965b) which, in a modified, updated form, continues to influence and 'anchor' many clinicians undertaking assessments.

Children and adolescents referred (or who self-refer) for psychotherapeutic help have diverse developmental difficulties of varying degrees of severity and complexity. The underlying assumption is that the child's inner emotional landscape has been wrought from a dynamic interplay between forces from within and without and these forces are themselves subject to growth and change. Development is a complex weave and synthesis of many strands. The threads are woven together in a series of intricate interdependencies between maturational sequences, experiences afforded or withheld by the environment and developmental steps reflecting the growing internal psychodynamic organisation.

At the heart of a child's emotional development lies the relationship between the child and his primary caregivers. To a large extent this will be experience-dependent. Events in the child's life such as separation from parents or caregivers, divorce, loss, hospitalisations etc. exert an important impact. However, the picture is internally fleshed out in the more idiosyncratic ways a given child has attributed meanings to events, built up an affective sense of relationships with others and, in turn, a sense of himself. The particular manner in which the *self* and others are experienced will also be coloured by the child's level of development and his own psychic make-up.

The difficulties of any given child 'can only be evaluated against a concept of age-appropriate developmental status in many areas of psychological growth' (Edgcumbe 1995: 3). Many parents and professionals working with children or adolescents hold a working model of what age-appropriate means and will calibrate their responses and expectations accordingly. It is against this background sense of 'age-appropriateness' that we can see where a child's current and future emotional development is in jeopardy. Within this overall framework the child psychotherapist will try to gauge the child's level of development and nature of the difficulties along different dimensions.

How 'stuck' is the child?

An overarching consideration is whether, overall, the child's development is moving forwards, backwards, or is stuck. A developmental impasse, suggesting that the child will find it hard to move on to a further stage of development with marked repercussions for his future emotional relationships, is an indicator that help may be needed. For some children there may have been an early developmental curtailment of many capacities.

It is important to evaluate whether a difficulty is transient or more fixed with repercussions for future development. Sometimes, the move into a new developmental phase can in and of itself bring a period of strain for an otherwise well-functioning child. At other times, a child's development may seem to grind to a halt, or even regress, in the face of specific events such as divorce, hospitalisation, and the birth of a sibling. However, given the child's own resilience and previous experiences, with sensitive and appropriate parental handling these waters are navigable or require minimal intervention. If, however, alterations in parental handling and the child's own resources are insufficient to alleviate the child's distress then individual psychotherapeutic help may be recommended.

The nature of the child's relationships and sense of self

A crucial dimension in assessing emotional development is the nature and quality of the child's object world – i.e. how does the child relate to others and feel about him or herself?

The qualitative aspects of the child's primary relationships with the real parents or caregivers are critical to his growth. Any assessment needs to take into account the psychological milieu, i.e. the states of mind of members of the family, in particular the parents. Does the child feel safe and able to turn to his parent(s) or caregiver(s) for comfort? Are they themselves, usually because of their own difficulties and states of mind, more likely to generate ambivalence or even fear in the child, leaving the child without a safe haven? Where there is not enough safety for the child it can be part of the assessment process to work with the parents or caregivers and allied agencies to help provide a more containing environment.

The capacity to relate to others can be thought of as a progressive developmental line, moving from the child's initial necessary self-absorption growing gradually into an ever increasing capacity and wish to relate to others as people with their own and different feelings, wishes and thoughts. The outward expression of this is the difference between the two-year-old's impulsive grabbing of toys from another in pursuit of an interest to an eight-year-old child's wish to engage in friendships with other children built on an understanding that friendships entail reciprocity and that grabbing is unlikely to endear you to your playmates.

Treated as a psychological function, the capacity to make psychic room for others as separate people with their own motivations, thoughts and feelings is referred to in contemporary literature as children's capacity to hold a theory of mind about themselves and another.

Emotional understanding of oneself and others also brings about a capacity for concern for the other. Clearly this has profound roots in the manner in which the infant and child was held in mind and whether they themselves were recipients of parental empathy. Many of the difficulties referred for treatment lie in this domain.

The child's internal object world is inextricably linked to the manner in which he will negotiate the path towards separation and individuation. This refers to the incremental steps taken that lead from a state of total dependency on a caregiver to a gradual shaping of an internal feeling of separateness with a growing wish for increasing independence. Sometimes children want to rush precociously ahead before they are fully able to take care of themselves appropriately. In some cases a child might hanker for the state of early childhood and not want to move on. Acceleration, stasis or regression along this continuum can spell difficulties for both child and parents, impairing the capacity to take gradual steps towards carving out a sense of self as a different and separate person who can gradually move away psychically. This process is contingent upon the quality of the relationship with primary caregivers and their own unconscious conflicts.

For Simon, referred at the age of twelve years and six months, his difficulties in separating from his mother left him feeling very ashamed and distressed. If she went out he would feel unduly anxious and would need to cling to her. His difficulties had originally been fuelled from early on by his mother's impatient annoyance at his clinginess. Her impatience reflected an intergenerational difficulty in her own family of origin whose members had suffered severe losses. Simon's parents had altered their handling of him but his anxieties persisted. He made it abundantly clear that he felt internally restricted when he told the therapist: 'I mean I want to be able to leave my mother one day. It would look stupid to be still at home when I am thirty.' He then went on to reveal many fantasies about his fears which he recognised as irrational, confessing that every time his parents went out he was dogged by the thought that they would sneak away permanently. Simon was able to articulate his inner anxieties and to link them to his specific worries around separation which he recognised militated against his progressive wishes. He was offered intensive psychotherapy where the close regular contact rapidly enabled him to bring into treatment his fears around separation and loss evoked by the gaps between sessions, the weekend and holiday breaks in treatment.

The inevitable breaks in treatment, coupled with the frequency, regularity and consistency of the renewed contact with the therapist, facilitate the emergence of the child's feelings and fantasies.

Regulation and mastery of the self

In the course of early development children are gradually enabled to take steps towards regulating and mastering their inner impulses, wishes and feelings. In order to do so, they are dependent upon the continued presence of a consistent caring adult who 'scaffolds' the child's emerging capacities through their own capacity to 'manage' themselves and to attune to the child. The child's emotional life is engaged with and the parent 'weathers' the storms of different phases from the tantrums, love and hatred of the toddler years through to the courting, passions of the Oedipal child and beyond. The route to mastery can be impeded in different ways: the absence of a caring consistent caregiver, discontinuities in care and traumatic impingements or losses.

Davey was four and a half years old when he was referred for non-intensive psychotherapy. This was paralleled by regular work with his father who, following the death of his ex-wife in a car crash when Davey was four, remained Davey's principal caretaker. Mr S felt that his own conflicts around aggression (his father had been violent) did not allow him to manage Davey with firmness. When Davey, uncomprehendingly distraught at the loss of his mother, would rage at his father and lash out at other children in his nursery class, Mr S felt powerless to intervene firmly. In other respects Davey's development had progressed well. However, his attachments were marked by a prickly aggressiveness. Underneath this were his anxieties about feeling he was an unlovable, dirty, messy boy who had caused his mother to desert him by dying. The corollary was his anxiety about daring to allow himself to experience closeness to another who might also leave him.

The nature of defences and anxieties

The need to maintain a feeling of inner safety is an important part of our ordinary mental functioning and we keep anxiety at bay through the use of psychic defence mechanisms. Westen and Gabbard (2002) suggest that they can be thought of as unconscious implicit procedures to self-regulate a range of unpleasant or conflictual affects, particularly where there is a threat to self-esteem.

In the course of psychic development children build up ways of defending themselves against pain, worries and wishes they feel are unacceptable. The extent and range of the defences they employ is an important consideration in an assessment. Do they help keep anxiety at bay and if so at what cost? Does the use of, for example, an overly rigid obsessional defence restrict development and thinking? Broadly, children with 'internalising' difficulties – i.e. where they experience anxiety – fare better with psychoanalytic psychotherapy than children who have conduct disorders. The presence of anxiety helps them to form a treatment alliance. For some children with very rigid defences intensive help may be necessary to enable them begin to feel able to loosen up without the threat of being overwhelmed.

The ways in which the child regulates or fails to regulate his anxiety is a significant criterion for offering individual help and in deciding whether intensive or non-intensive help is the treatment of choice. Therapists need to be alert to children in non-intensive treatment who experience marked anxiety between sessions and they may need to be helped to 'seal up' at the end of sessions. A long gap between sessions may mean that the psychic work is three steps forward, two steps backwards. Intensive work can enable processes to be kept in a state of open fluidity with the anxiety contained by the frequency.

Jane was fourteen when she referred herself for help. She was able to articulate her fantasy that her mother would one day just wander off in the supermarket when they went shopping, and in so doing captured her emotional reality that her mother, who had episodes of mental illness, was not really able to keep her consistently in mind or indeed attend to her needs. Her own unconscious hostility and destructive wishes towards her mother were vividly captured in a dream she recalled. In that dream, a pane of glass had crashed down on her sleeping mother. Shortly after telling the therapist this dream, she distanced herself and became lost in her own thoughts. When the therapist asked what she was thinking about, she replied that she had been counting the numbers of squares on a picture in the room. Her obsessional type of defences, alongside a tendency to intellectualise, indicated the ways in which she protected herself from her frightening rage at her mother who, at the same time, she felt was vulnerable. Her defences were not overly rigid and she was able to make good use of non-intensive work.

There are also children who have a fragmented sense of themselves and others, and who may not even have begun to build up sufficient coping defences against their anxieties. Such children can be prey to overwhelming and disorganising anxiety and need the containment of knowing and feeling they will not be left too long in an unmanageable state.

We now know a lot more about the long-term sequaelae of developing within traumatising relationships and the effects this has on regulatory systems including anxiety. In short, there are a group of children whose 'systems' have been severely compromised. They do not experience a graded anxiety response but rapidly go into 'panic' mode and can dissociate or shut down. Often they have a history of emotional/sexual/physical abuse and this is frequently accompanied by numerous changes of caregivers. They comprise the complex cases with co-morbidity often referred to CAMHS. In some cases intensive treatment may be the least necessary to help build up a sufficient feeling of safety to help unfreeze their development. In other cases, the intimacy of intensive work may feel too intrusive or threatening in the beginning.

Ego development

The ego is the agency which enables the child to develop internal means of managing and regulating his internal world through the use of defence mechanisms. Other ego capacities include a range of cognitive abilities such as the ability to think, communicate verbally, reason.

Also falling under this heading is 'reality testing'. Gradually, the child needs to be able to orient himself towards an outer reality; gradually distinguishing what is occurring in his mind (the internal world of wishes and fantasies) from the external world.

Children with impeded ego functioning experience various types of difficulties that often manifest at school. During the primary and junior school years well-functioning children are developing peer group relationships and there is a rapid growth of their interests both in and outside school. This is in contrast to the child who has poor ego functioning.

The causes for ego impairment are manifold: environmental onslaughts, inadequacy in the provision of care, and/or reasons intrinsic to the vulnerable child. Often the roots will lie partly in the subtle dynamic interplay of the child's early emotional relationships which provide the matrix within which ego capacities can or cannot fully unfold. Where there are marked ego difficulties there will often be concomitant difficulties in the area of relationships. In addition to this, a child will also find defensive ways to adapt to the original difficulties in order to protect himself from further humiliation and exposure. The defensive adaptation may then compound the problem. Teachers are well acquainted with the class clown who plays up when he cannot do a piece of work or the child who omnipotently professes to know everything or conversely rubbishes everything, claiming it is not worth knowing. A feeling of damage, worthlessness, or a sense of confusion and disorientation may be the underlying experiential reality for the child.

John F was offered five-times-weekly intensive treatment at the age of seven years. The need for this was established on the grounds of his longstanding difficulties with his mother, which had resulted in impaired ego development. He was flooded with unmanageable levels of anxiety and terrifying fantasies against which he had not been able to erect sufficient defences. He was not free to use his mind to learn and in the context of the classroom was unable to concentrate or take in anything. John had developed within a not quite safe enough environment where he had been exposed to overstimulation. His wish for a continued early bodily intimacy with his mother was fuelled by her difficulties in setting appropriate relational boundaries. His mother was invested in maintaining his vivid fantasy life, unable to recognise that this frequently left him overwhelmed and over-excited. Intimacy was embroiled with mutual threats of attack and seduction. He had made little progress at school, finding it hard to manage his frustration or regulate his impulses. He was flooded with exciting and dangerous fantasies of destruction, which he expressed in his play with dolls. He attempted to draw the assessing therapist into a frightening and seductive relationship. He experienced her as a terrifying witch who needed to be simultaneously placated, seductively engaged and attacked. He expressed his chaotic inner feelings of helplessness and disintegration when he described the toy robot he had sent crashing to the ground as 'alive in his body but not in his spirit'.

Resilience

It is also helpful to look at the child's strengths. Are there important alternative figures in the child's life like a grandmother, teacher or aunt who can offer a close or caring relationship where maybe the parents are less able to? Does the child have some inner capacities to 'bounce back' from adverse experiences? Child therapists often experience, hear or read about accounts of children and adolescents who, against the odds, are nonetheless able to use their treatment to discover their inner lives and minds and are able to use their new found capacities. They reveal themselves in frequently very moving ways.

In summary, thinking about a child's development involves taking into account these many different aspects. A prime organiser for the child's overall way of being will depend on the qualitative nature of his internal object world. Integrally related are the ways in which he has been enabled to manage his developmental tasks within the overarching continuum of separation and individuation, his capacity to regulate and modulate his inner feelings and impulses and the growth of his ego capacities. The greater the number of realms in which a child has difficulties that affect his overall functioning, the greater the need for intensive work. Ultimately, it is hoped that such a relationship enables the child to tolerate rather than fend off the painful aspects of his world through the internalisation of a capacity for toleration, reflection and understanding of the self by means of a new self and object representation. This becomes part of the child's way of being and can continue after the treatment has ended.

Intensive treatment and non-intensive treatment

The research by Fonagy and Target (1996) confirms the common sense assumption that the age of entry into treatment, given the fluidity of the child's representational world, is a factor for good outcome. Hence treatment impact is greatest on very young children. Research also suggests that non-intensive treatment is preferable for adolescents. Broadly, children and adolescents with 'internalising' difficulties where there is sufficient anxiety to feed into a therapeutic alliance do better with psychoanalytic psychotherapy than conduct disordered children without anxiety. (For a more detailed discussion on what works for whom see Chapter 6 on research by Nick Midgley.)

Where there are a large number of domains in which the child is experiencing difficulties, the greater is the need for intensive treatment. Intensive treatments in CAMHS (often carried out by trainees) frequently involve highly complex cases with high levels of co-morbidity where other interventions have had limited success. The introduction of a new developmental figure, who through an intensive therapeutic relationship can help shape the course of the developmental stream, can offer the child a chance to move forward and to make better use of positive experiences offered by others outside the clinical setting.

The following case of Paul, a late adolescent, illustrates when there is an unequivocal need for intensive treatment due to acute longstanding difficulties.

Paul had severe restrictions in his capacity to relate, first evident in early childhood and continuing throughout his development. At each step of the way he found it hard to steer a course through age-appropriate development. Paul's difficulties in forming relationships with others had arisen despite adequate parenting. He had originally received and benefited from once-weekly psychotherapy. This had successfully allowed him to gain a degree of self-confidence. Nonetheless, the severity of his difficulties meant that, by late adolescence, both the NHS clinic Paul had attended and his parents continued to feel serious concern about his future. As a late adolescent his life had effectively ground to a halt. He was extremely withdrawn, suffered incapacitating self-consciousness and was addictively watching horror films on television, often until the early hours of the morning. He had no plans for the future. In the course of his therapy the door opened to reveal Paul to himself: that he had a whole range of feelings from which he had cut himself off. By the end of the first year of intensive psychotherapy Paul reported a number of changes. He had given up his addictive watching of television. His relationship with his family had improved and he had a job one afternoon a week, which involved working in pairs. He was considering starting a part-time training course, and overall he felt consistently better within himself and less socially isolated.

Children with severe or multiple difficulties such as borderline children, those with pervasive anxiety disorders, marked narcissistic disturbances or atypical development (as in the case illustration) need the depth afforded by intensive treatment.

Intensity of contact can also indicate where a child's history of inconsistent or discontinuous caregiving may leave him unable to engage safely or invest sufficiently in once a week contact in order to get to the point where separation from the therapist is meaningful. For some children, it is only where there is a great enough sense of trust and safety fostered by frequent contact that they can dare to begin to allow themselves to know what it is to miss someone, to rage against them for their absence and to experience that survival of self and other is possible. Conversely, for some children, in particular those with perverse aspects to their development, the very intensity of contact may initially be so threatening that it can militate against being able to form a treatment alliance.

From the therapist's point of view there are some distinct advantages in intensive work. The therapist can give herself full permission to relax into an unhurried pace, thus freeing her to be with the child in a frame of mind allowing free-floating attention. It allows a slow process of elaboration to take place. Where there is a stable holding environment for the child at home, the therapist can leave themes and anxieties looser without the need to 'parcel up' at the end of the session. Intensive work is, paradoxically, the necessary luxury of knowing that if at any given moment something is only barely expressed or manifested by the child, or only partially glimpsed or discerned by the therapist, then it is possible to wait until it re-emerges again in a more crystallised form in another session.

Many referrals are less clear-cut and include a group of children who would probably benefit from either mode. The assessment may involve asking what is the least intervention necessary to bring about change? The majority of individual psychotherapeutic work offered in the NHS is non-intensive and large numbers of children with less pervasive, longstanding or severe difficulties can be greatly helped. Thus the child who manages relatively well in most areas, who can enjoy aspects of his life but may have one or two more 'fragile' areas such as specific anxieties, may respond very well. The lesser frequency necessitates both addressing the underlying difficulties and at the same time helping to consolidate the creative and adaptive aspects of the child's functioning.

Adolescence presents particular considerations as difficulties can often present in risk taking and acting out behaviours so the assessment of the depth of underlying pathology requires great care. However, generally (other than in a limited number of cases where there is developmental breakdown in most areas) it goes against the progressive developmental grain of the adolescent process to offer them the 'dependency' inherent in intensive treatment. Non-intensive treatment is often the treatment of choice.

There are certain challenges with non-intensive work. It can be constrained by a sense of pressure and curtailment emanating from the feeling that unless very close, intense attention is paid then something might be lost irretrievably or for a long time to come. There is also the clinical question of whether certain material should not be taken up, given the long gap between sessions, particularly if the child may be left in a highly anxious state during the interval.

The context: further considerations

There are many issues involved in recommending and setting up both intensive and non-intensive psychotherapy. The importance of working with and involving the broader network when necessary, e.g. agencies such as Social Services, is of crucial importance not only to ensure the treatment is practically supported but that 'splitting' between the different professionals is limited. Often it is preceded by a preparatory period involving a therapist or a social worker working with the family to reach the point where the child's need for help can be fully acknowledged.

Stable arrangements need to be put into place to ensure that the child can be brought regularly by a parent, involved professional or escort. The investment of time and effort made needs to be weighed in relation to the impact this will have on the rest of the family's life. Interestingly, intensity of contact leads to a lower drop-out rate, suggesting that the enormous investment by all parties involved has a positive effect on treatment because the parents may be more motivated and willing to engage in the work.

A crucial and repeatedly stressed factor in a positive therapeutic outcome, irrespective of frequency, is the parallel work offered to parents. Once therapy is underway the therapist, or another professional, will work with the parents or caretaking adults to support the treatment. They, too, need a person with whom to weather the vicissitudes of change that will occur. Difficulties in a child often reflect intergenerational patterns of parenting and the parents also need help in reflecting on how their understanding and handling of the child promotes or holds up his forward moves. When the transference relationship unfolds and intensifies, the child may start to respond differently to his parents. A classic occurrence is when the transference becomes split. By this is meant the process whereby the child's positive feelings are concentrated on the idealised therapist and the parents receive the child's more negative feelings. At certain points in treatment parents can feel that their child is actually getting worse. Conversely, when the therapist is in the midst of the child's negative transference the child can be all sweetness and light at home: the parents may unwittingly collude with a changed child who refuses to go to therapy. The child can also prove resistant to attending sessions and need parental encouragement to express the resistance to the therapist. At points of apparent improvements at home, the parents may conclude that the change is permanently for the better. Understandably, this is particularly tempting if the child has relinquished a troublesome symptom such as bedwetting, nightmares or school refusal. Parents may need to come to terms with the uncomfortable reality that treatment should not end simply because there has been symptom relief or a period of improved relationships within the family. Both positive and negative feelings towards others need to be analysed within the therapeutic relationship until they can coexist in a more fully integrated way within the child. All this takes time. The length of treatment can vary enormously.

There is also the question of how to work in the termination phase of a treatment. In the course of therapy, hopefully, the child will have built up a capacity to integrate and hold on to the therapist as a new developmental object. Nonetheless, this period will herald strong feelings about separation, relinquishment and loss. Children may need a 'weaning period'. In intensive treatment this might be by reducing the frequency of sessions. Others may need the continuing intensity of contact to face and manage their acute feelings and fears.

From a Health Service perspective there is little doubt that need and demand outstrips provision. Clinicians working in child and family mental health teams are faced with the task of attempting to match resources to demand within a framework of operating constraints. There are inevitably occasions when, even if it is agreed that intensive or non-intensive help is the treatment of choice and the least help necessary, it cannot be offered or there is a long wait and other interventions are offered. However, some aspects have improved. Ten years ago this chapter in the first edition stated, 'Not only is child psychotherapy a relatively scarce resource, but the demographics of where it can be accessed point to real dearth in certain areas outside London. Where there is a concentration of NHS child psychotherapeutic resources, as in London, the mental health profile of the population means that need remains greater than the help available.' The majority of intensive work in the NHS is carried out by trainees and the presence of training schools in Birmingham, Leeds and Scotland has helped to redress the demographic imbalance. All child psychotherapists, although mainly practicing non-intensive and applied work, view their core intensive therapy skills as crucial to the quality of all their work. This is reflected in the ACP's continuing professional development requirements that encourage intensive case treatment at regular intervals.

Conclusion

The therapeutic relationship is one that is created and lived through by two people, the child or adolescent and the therapist. What comes to life through the transference and countertransference is a gradual process of unfolding and elaboration of the patient's unconscious life. Through the therapist's use of her sentient and reflective self, the child can begin to experience and explore himself and his thoughts and feelings about others in a new and different way.

The considerations that would lead to a recommendation of intensive or non-intensive contact are many and varied. In a sense it is, of course, a reification to separate out the various elements of the child's psychic organisation from the sum totality of how the child experiences himself and others. However, it can offer a useful way of conceptualising to a finer degree the nature of the child's difficulties. Of necessity, this chapter has expressed in broadbrush strokes ways of thinking about children; their development, their need for psychoanalytic psychotherapy and just some of the elements involved in both intensive and non-intensive treatment. Ultimately, each child's developmental story is a unique and complex mosaic. The therapeutic relationship is one within which the particular texture of the child's story, as it exists in his imagination, conscious and unconscious life, can begin to be lived out and expressed.

References

Edgcumbe, R. (1995) 'The history of Anna Freud's thinking on developmental influences', *Bulletin of the Anna Freud Centre* 18(1).

Fonagy, P. and Target, M. (1996) 'Predictors of outcome in child psychoanalysis: a retrospective study of 763 cases at the Anna Freud Centre', *Journal of the American Psychoanalytic Association* 44(1): 27–77.

Freud, A. (1965a) 'The concept of developmental lines', in A. Freud *Normality and Pathology in Childhood*, London: Hogarth Press.

—— (1965b) 'Assessment of pathology Part I – A metapsychological profile of the child', in A. Freud *Normality and Pathology in Childhood*, London: Hogarth Press.

—— (1972) 'A psychoanalytic view of developmental psychopathology', Chapter 4 in *The Writings of Anna Freud*, Vol. 8, London: Hogarth Press.

Westen, D. and Gabbard, O. G. (2002) 'Developments in cognitive neuroscience. I. Conflict, compromise and connectionism', *Journal of the American Psychoanalytic Association* 50(1): 53–98.

Further reading

Edgcumbe, R. (2000) *Anna Freud: A View of Development, Disturbance and Therapeutic Technique*, London: Routledge.

Fonagy, P., Gergely, G., Jurist, E. L. and Target, M. (2002) *Affect Regulation, Mentalisation, and the Development of the Self*, New York: Other Press.

Freud, A. (1972) 'A psychoanalytic view of developmental psychopathology', in *The Writings of Anna Freud*, Vol. 8, London: Hogarth Press, 1982.

Green, V. (2003) 'Introduction', in V. Green (ed.) *Emotional Development in Psychoanalysis, Attachment Theory and Neuroscience*, Hove: Brunner-Routledge.

Hurry, A. (ed.) (1998) *Psychoanalysis and Development Therapy*, London: Karnac.

Laufer, M. and Laufer, M. E. (1984) Adolescence and the final sexual organisation, in M. Laufer and M. E. Laufer *Adolescence and Developmental Breakdown: A Psychoanalytic View*, London: Karnac.

Sandler, J., Holder, A., Dare, C. and Dreher, A. U. (1997) *Freud's Models of the Mind: An Introduction*, London: Karnac.

The reader is also directed to accounts of clinical work in the *Journal of Child Psychotherapy* and *The Psychoanalytic Study of the Child*.

12 Brief psychotherapy and therapeutic consultations

How much therapy is 'good-enough'?

Monica Lanyado

The eminent psychoanalyst D. W. Winnicott coined the heartening phrase 'good-enough mothering' in an effort to provide a realistic perspective on what mothers can hope to provide for their children. He felt that mothers (and nowadays we would add fathers to this description) do not need to be perfect, indeed should not even try to be 'perfect'. But he did emphasise that they do need to be 'good-enough' if their child is to have a reasonable start in their emotional life. Good-enough parenting reflects the physical and emotional care given to the child, in thoughtful response to what the individual child needs. As individual needs differ so much, even from birth, what is good-enough mothering for one child may be inadequate for another. There is therefore no absolute pass or fail line when it comes to what constitutes a good-enough parent (Winnicott 1989).

A similar issue relates to the question of how much therapy is required for a child. This question arises at the very start of therapy when it is not clear what form of therapy to offer the child or how best to help the family as a whole, as well as when deciding at what point to end once-weekly or intensive psychotherapy. On first responding to a referral, there are many ways of setting up a treatment plan (Chapter 11). Will the child be unable to recover unless they have twice-, three-, four- or five-times weekly therapy for several years? Should the child be offered once-weekly sessions which are open-ended, and will continue for as long as the therapist and the child's family agree? Should the child be seen for a fixed number of consultations – maybe three or four times followed by a review of their progress? How should these sessions be spaced out – weekly, fortnightly, or pragmatically according to the therapist and family's availability? What kind of help needs to be offered to the parents, carers and school?

Within the public sector, quite apart from these important decisions about the best form of treatment for a particular child and their family, there is now often a clear directive from the managers of the treatment service that in order to cut down child mental health waiting lists and offer as broad a service to the community as possible, a limited number of consultations, often well under ten, should be the norm of any treatment plan. Open-ended, weekly or more intensive treatments may then only be offered to a small number of extremely carefully selected children, and there is likely to be a considerable waiting list for this kind of psycho-therapeutic treatment.

However, when thinking about consultation work, economic and prag-matic arguments can obscure the fact that for some children a fixed number of consultations, a clear focus for the work, or a clear date for ending the therapy, may be the best form of treatment plan for their problems at the time of referral (Lanyado 1996, 2006). This chapter will give some examples of this way of working and how consultation work is becoming an increasingly important part of the range of treatments offered by psycho-analytic psychotherapists.

Example 1

Joanne's parents contacted the clinic because she had recently been having powerful nightmares in which she became very angry, thrashing around in her sleep, fighting off her parents and not letting them comfort her. She was upset and disorientated by these dreams and she had also started to sleepwalk. During the day, she seemed well. Her parents felt that the sleep disturbance connected with a very unfortunate accident that Joanne had had three years before, when she was six years old, from which she had physically totally recovered.

Joanne had been playing in an ordinary way with another child who had pushed her over, but she had fallen awkwardly, causing a complicated fracture of her wrist, which over the course of the next eighteen months had required seven operations and in total twenty weeks in plaster. During this time, she had to be very careful about any energetic play (which singled her out from other children, particularly at school), because she was at risk from the rough and tumble of the playground. For many months she had a rigorous daily routine of physiotherapy which she carried out with little protest. She had coped very stoically and sensibly with this whole experience, as had the parents in their management of what became a very complicated and upsetting phase of their family life.

Having met her parents, we arranged that I would see Joanne for four consultations and then meet with her parents again to discuss how to proceed. It was clear from the outset, that I would see Joanne for as few consultations as possible, as she had had enough of being a patient and wanted to go back to being the same as other children. The parents' account of what had happened gave me good reason to believe that this was a family which had many strengths which would enable them to make good use of a few consultations.

In the first few consultations Joanne and I talked a lot about the accident and operations. This included Joanne showing me the small physical scars from her operations, and, unprompted, bringing to the consultations one of her plaster casts and some of the pins that had been in her wrists. It soon became apparent that rather than there being a profound sense of physical pain or fear surrounding these memories, there was a deep, unspoken sense of sadness and loss. I tried to talk to her about what these feelings might mean.

It gradually emerged that she had badly wanted her mother to be with her literally all the time when she was in hospital for operations, or in pain at home, but that her mother for a variety of reasons had been unable to do so. Her father had always been with her when her mother could not, but this was just not the same and Joanne was able to admit to feeling angry with her mother, as well as bereft and pining for her during these times. There were good and ordinary reasons why her mother could not be there all the time which Joanne fully understood, but this in turn led to intense feelings of guilt because nevertheless she still felt so angry with her mother.

Clinical experience suggests that in many cases of trauma such as Joanne's accident, the trauma victim on an unconscious level feels not only that her mother did not actively protect her from the dangers of the world when the trauma occurred, but that her mother actually stood by and passively allowed the traumatic event to take place (Laub and Auerhahn 1993). Joanne's parents, in a way which seemed to reflect the parental counterpart of this fantasy, irrationally blamed themselves for what had happened. Many parents of children who have been traumatised experience intense feelings of guilt about what happened to their child. Whilst this fantasy may well reflect ordinary but deeply unconscious aggressive feelings, it is also a powerful reflection of the biological caregiving role emphasised in attachment theory (Chapter 4) which in situations of trauma may be experienced as having failed to protect the child from danger.

Joanne agreed that I could talk to her parents about her feelings of anger and sadness, which I did when I met them (without Joanne present) to discuss how to proceed after her first four consultations. I met them on their own as I felt that they needed to explore their feelings, about how they had handled the accident and the acute phases of Joanne's hospitalisations and treatments, without her being present.

Joanne's mother was able to talk about her conflict and distress over how to balance the needs of her other two children and her invalid mother at the time of the accident and during all that followed. Both parents were relieved that Joanne was finally able to talk in her consultations about how hard it had been to share her mother with others when she had needed her so much. They reported that the nightmares and sleep disorder had stopped, but they did not want to end the consultations at this point as they could see that Joanne needed further help to consolidate this improvement and understand more about the feelings that lay behind her symptoms. We agreed that I would see Joanne weekly until the end of the school term – a further seven consultations, including one family consultation which Joanne's brother and sister would also attend.

Themes of rivalry and jealousy of my other patients started to emerge during the next few consultations and we were able to relate these to Joanne's growing awareness of her anger with her mother for sometimes choosing to look after her siblings or her grandmother instead of her. Joanne became irritated with me for seeing other patients when she was not there, and played the amateur sleuth noting when the small signals that she deliberately left in the therapy room to detect the presence of other patients, had been moved. She was annoyed that the planned family session was to include her brother and sister. This gave further opportunity to talk about the ways in which the attention her parents had needed to pay to her during all the problems with her wrist had affected the whole family – and how her brother and sister had felt fed up with all the attention Joanne was getting.

During the family consultation, which again deliberately focused on the impact of the accident on the family, I was able to talk about how it was still hard for Joanne fully to forgive her mother for the pain and distress that surrounded the accident and all that followed. Their relationship seemed to get caught on a rather difficult dynamic, in which Joanne seemed deliberately and successfully to be making her mother suffer and feel unduly guilty about this accident, as well as about many everyday issues. As we talked about this Joanne's mother was able to show how upset she felt knowing that Joanne was still distressed and angry such a long time after the accident and operations had taken place. Joanne was then able to go and sit next to her mother, cuddling up to her and sucking her thumb, and there was a sense of some rapprochement between them.

As Joanne was clearly getting quite involved in her relationship with me – seen in her possessiveness and rivalry with other patients – and I did not wish to encourage this in view of the limited number of consultations that we had left, it became particularly important to focus on what it meant to her to be ending her consultations with me in a few weeks' time. She knew that she did not want or really need to continue but found it hard to let go of me – rather similar to her difficulty in letting go of her anger with her mother. However, we could talk about this characteristic of her way of being – that she was someone who found it hard to let go of feelings.

This understanding helped her to move towards her last consultation at which we agreed to meet again in three months. At this follow-up meeting she remained generally less angry with her mother and siblings and was coping well with school and family life. On enquiry when writing this chapter for the original handbook, two years after the consultations took place, there had been no recurrence of the sleep problems and she was developing well. As there may be a concern that consultations do not have a lasting impact on emotional life, this kind of follow-up is helpful in demonstrating how effective this way of working can be.

One of the factors that helps consultation work to be brief is a clear focus for the treatment. In Joanne's case, the focus suggested by her parents' account of the problems – the accident and operations – made sense when I met with Joanne. There is often a fear that, in selecting a treatment focus, other important issues for the patient may be neglected. However, as work with Joanne illustrates, the chosen focus can have a 'tip of the iceberg' quality in that many other significant issues lie beneath the surface and can be associated with the chosen focus.

Balint *et al.* (1972) describe what they term 'Focal psychotherapy', with adult patients. They view this treatment as being a form of applied psychoanalysis and helpfully discuss the way in which a focus for brief work can be chosen and worked with. They emphasise that once chosen it is important to stick to this focus and not to be diverted on to other interesting paths of enquiry unless they look likely to supersede the existing focus by becoming a new focus. This idea of *applied* psychoanalysis remains central to psychoanalytically trained psychotherapists' approach to consultations and brief work. (For more clinical examples see Cleve 2008; Daws 1989; Edwards and Maltby 1998; Lanyado 1996, 2006; Onions 2009 and Chapter 14 of this book; Robson 2009; Winnicott 1971.)

From this example it can be seen that by exploring the focus of Joanne's accident and all that followed, themes of separation and loss, sibling rivalry, and angry feelings and fantasies about her parents leading to guilt and conflict could all be explored. These themes are ongoing life issues for everyone and would be very much a part of any open-ended therapy. In consultation work they are approached in a different way, the principles of which will be discussed later in this chapter. Many other themes which could have been taken up – such as Joanne's feelings of disfigurement because of scarring, or Oedipal feelings as expressed through her longing for her mother, and minimisation of her father's contribution to her care – were not taken up as they were not foremost in her conscious mind at the time of the treatment.

Joanne's relationship to me was not discussed other than very lightly – in the form of comments or observations about how she didn't like the fact that I saw other patients. If Joanne had been in open-ended therapy, I would have worked much more with her feelings towards me and they would have formed a core part of the transference relationship that needed to be interpreted over the course of the treatment.

Finally, a good deal of attention was given to how Joanne felt about coming to the end of her consultations and her clearly expressed wish to make me feel bad about not seeing her for longer. Simultaneously, she was also quite clear that she resented the time spent on her consultations and felt that she no longer needed to come! As already mentioned, this was very similar to the way in which she attempted to make her mother feel bad about the accident.

Who is most likely to benefit from therapeutic consultations?

The term 'therapeutic consultations' was coined by Winnicott (1971) to describe the kind of therapeutic work described in this chapter. It is a term I find helpful as it emphasises that the consultations are therapeutic in their own right, and not solely a precursor or assessment for more open-ended regular therapy. In the illuminating Introduction to *Therapeutic Consultations in Child Psychiatry* (1971) Winnicott describes this way of working as 'making sense of psychoanalysis in economic terms' and discusses what he means by this wise application of psychoanalytic skills. *Therapeutic Consultations* is full of clinical examples of Winnicott, as an enthusiast, doing this work and illustrates his use of the well-known 'squiggle' technique, as a means of encouraging therapeutic communication.

As he writes elsewhere, Winnicott sees his psychoanalytic work as having very wide and flexible applications:

> If our aim continues to be to verbalise the nascent conscious in terms of transference, then we are practising analysis: if not, then we are analysts practising something else that we deem to be appropriate to the occasion. And why not?
>
> (Winnicott 1962: 170)

For a fuller discussion of a range of therapeutic work where child and adolescent psychotherapists are 'practising something else appropriate for the occasion', see Horne and Lanyado (2009).

It is probably easier to say who is unlikely to get sufficient help from therapeutic consultations than to give a list of the types of problems that will respond well to this type of treatment. Broadly speaking, the earlier in life that relationship problems developed, or traumatic events took place prior to referral, the more intensive and long term treatment will need to be. For example, severely deprived children who are in care, autistic children, and abused children are very likely to need long-term relationships with their therapists if they are to establish or recover their mental health.

However, there are many children of all ages who come from essentially sound and loving homes, but where there are nevertheless relationship problems which the family is unable to resolve. This kind of work, *particularly when the referral can be responded to very soon after it arrives*, has all the characteristics of the old saying, 'a stitch in time saves nine'. Child and Adolescent Mental Health Services in the UK do their best to provide this kind of service alongside the many more severe and worrying cases that are referred to them. The wise and economic use of scarce psychotherapeutic time and services has to be apportioned between this type of clinical intervention, and the long-term in-depth psychotherapeutic work that is described elsewhere in this volume.

The dilemma of how to meet the psychotherapeutic needs of as wide a population of children and families as possible is acute and concerning for the profession as a whole. Some families who have the financial resources or have been able to secure funding for treatment may decide to approach child psychotherapists in private practice when they realise that they will need to wait too long, in their perception, for treatment. The Association of Child Psychotherapists runs a referral system to meet this need.

Joanne is a good example of how therapeutic consultations can be the appropriate and effective way to help such a child even when there are quite worrying symptoms. There were a number of factors which helped this treatment to work so well, such as the clear focus already mentioned and the fact that this was a well-motivated family who were open to change. The ripeness of a patient for therapy may well play an important part in whether consultations are effective or not. As already indicated, if therapeutic consultations can be offered reasonably promptly when help is sought, they may be more potent than a lengthier intervention offered to a family that has waited for nine months for consultations or for weekly psychotherapy. This is an important aspect of the 'demand feeding' aspect of consultation work and the flexibility of approach it implies (see example 2, Chapter 20).

It is important to remember that when a child is referred to a psychotherapist the family often do not have a clear picture in their mind about what form this help is likely to take. It may come as a surprise – at times a rather unwelcome surprise at that – for parents to hear that they will need to make a significant commitment to the child's treatment in terms of their own openness to change and willingness to engage in some therapeutic work (Chapter 13).

The frequency or regularity with which the child and parents will need to come for help is something the psychotherapist has to advise about, but it is important to bear in mind that many families who attend public sector clinics are unfamiliar with the idea of weekly or intensive long-term treatment. It may be that the kind of treatment model that many parents have in mind is more closely related to an out-patient medical model than open-ended weekly therapy sessions. The child and family may be surprised to be offered so many 'long' (forty-five minutes to one hour) consultations.

In other words, to return to the ideas at the start of this chapter, consultation work may very well feel as if it is 'good-enough' and sufficiently helpful from the child and family's perspective, providing a treatment programme to which they feel they can make a realistic commitment. If this is the case, the therapist's task is to be a catalyst for change in the family's emotional life, rather than the more constant companion for change that she becomes in weekly or intensive work.

In this time-pressured world, so-called 'brief' psychotherapy or therapeutic consultations offer a significant experience in time, of being attentively listened to and thoughtfully and compassionately responded to within a secure and confidential setting. The skill for psychotherapists is in judging how big the gaps between consultations can reasonably be and whether the work can realistically be time-limited. Consultation work builds on the strengths and coping mechanisms of the child and family, and their abilities to work through their problems with no more professional help than is required to help them move on from a 'stuck' period in their family life.

Consultations and brief interventions are particularly effective when working with under-fives. More and more child and adolescent psychotherapists are combining the depth of understanding and experience gained from their intensive and weekly work with a consultation model (Robson 2009; Onions Chapter 14 this volume and 2009). Cleve describes how time-limited consultations to a two and a half year old boy whose mother and baby brother died in a car accident helped what was a very worrying dissociated response to the trauma to change into a more 'normal' mourning process. The father was seen by a colleague for the same number of sessions – fifteen in all (Cleve 2008).

Therapeutic consultations with young people

Adolescence is a time in life when consultations may be much more acceptable than an open-ended long-term psychotherapy commitment. For many years, specialist adolescent services in schools, universities and the wider community have used this approach. The success of this way of working seems to relate to the ordinary age-appropriate need in adolescence to become independent and self-sufficient, which pulls in quite the opposite direction to the intimate emotions of the transference relationship that are stirred in regular open-ended therapy. Many teenagers are more prepared to enter into some thinking and feeling about their difficulties if they know that there is a clear point of separation decided at the outset that helps them not to feel trapped into a commitment which they feel unable and unwilling to make. The aim of these consultations in psychoanalytically oriented treatment centres is not to select patients for regular therapy, although this can be one of the outcomes, but to offer sufficient help for the youngster to feel somewhat clearer about the distress that bought about their referral (and this can be a self-referral in this age range) and to be more able to bear and understand his or her painful and confused feelings and thoughts (Bronstein and Flanders 1998). This can often help to free log jams in adolescent development and lead to a spurt of energy and growth that can be so typical of the peaks (and troughs) of the teenage years.

With this type of treatment structure, the adolescent can dip into and out of the consultations without feeling they have reneged on a therapeutic commitment when they feel well enough to manage without consultations for a while. He or she can also then feel more able to approach the service for further help when the need arises. This whole process feels much more in touch with adolescent process and is reminiscent of Ainsworth's concept of exploration from a secure base (Chapter 4). The adolescent seeking help may have a very shaky 'secure base' in their relationships with their parents, or may be unable to acknowledge or develop from this base. As a form of acceptable displacement so common in adolescence, where teachers and other adults are consciously much more acceptable figures for identification and open communication than parents are acknowledged to be, the clinic and therapist can come to represent the place to return to when in trouble. This can be so despite the conflict which may also be a crucial part of the therapeutic relationship. An open-door policy can help many a troubled youngster to find a way through the difficult transitional years of adolescence.

So far I have described those treatment situations in which consultation work is likely to be helpful. I would now like to look at a much more disturbed group of patients where consultations can also prove helpful, but for entirely different reasons.

Brief work with young offenders

Child and adolescent psychotherapists are all too familiar with the ways in which deprivation and abuse in childhood can lead to violence and anti-social behaviour in young people. The whole question of whether it is possible to rehabilitate young offenders so that they are not inevitably set on a life of crime and imprisonment is a matter of public debate. There is a conflict between those who are unrealistically naive about how difficult it can be to turn around a young person's life when they have started to offend, and those who feel that offering treatment, instead of punishment, to those who create such trouble in society is a waste of valuable resources and a foolishly soft and indulgent attitude. Consultation work can be valuable in differentiating those youngsters who are able to respond to longer-term therapy and who are capable of change, from those who cannot. This can be very helpful in the allocation of severely limited specialised treatment resources for young offenders.

A multidisciplinary hypothesis-generating research project into sexually abusive behaviour in young adolescent boys incorporated twelve consultations with a child and adolescent psychotherapist in which it was possible to explore the boys' emotional life. The consultations were an interesting mix of standardised questionnaires, a special adaptation of the adult attachment interview, and completely unstructured sessions. This work has been written about in more detail elsewhere (Hodges *et al.* 1994; Lanyado *et al.* 1995). I would like to focus here on the consultation work itself and the factors which helped us to enable some of the boys to accept more intensive treatment.

The boys had little motivation to seek help and were, in the main, reluctant to come for the research consultations at the start of contact. They were also a very unpromising group to work with psychotherapeutically because of the high level of acting out behaviour they indulged in (abuse and anti-social acts) – indicating a limited ability to think before they acted – and because of generally poor verbal skills, in addition to the ordinary difficulty of putting thoughts and feelings into words which is typical of early adolescence.

Despite these contra-indications, and although the consultations were there to explore their emotional lives for research purposes, some of the boys nevertheless found themselves getting drawn into the consultations and attracted by the attention to their feelings that was being offered. As psychotherapists we were not surprised to find this and gradually learnt to maximise the possibilities of developing this involvement in the boys. It was not that we thought it possible to adequately treat the boys in this context, but we did find that small but significant change could be bought about during the consultations. Sometimes a turning point could be reached in which utter hopelessness and unavailability for change could be alleviated enough for the youngster to see that there could be a different and more encouraging path ahead for them (Lanyado 1996).

Example 2

Billy came from a large family in which there was a long-established pattern of inter-generational sexual abuse. He and all his siblings had been sexually abused by their father who had eventually been imprisoned. Despite the abuse, and his anger with his father, he also missed him greatly and possibly this had increased the pressure towards him identifying with his father and taking his place as eldest male in the family by sexually abusing two of his younger siblings.

He was sixteen and living in a good and caring children's home when he came for his research consultations. Billy could not bear to think about what he had done to his siblings, particularly as he feared that they must now hate him as he had hated his father. He tended to blank off whenever his abusive behaviour was mentioned in the consultations, as if he hadn't heard the therapist and was miles away in his thoughts. This was partly a dissociated response to the trauma he had suffered from his father, as well as his horror about what he had in turn done to his siblings. When he could no longer blank off his feelings, he would go on mind-numbing drinking sprees, becoming violent to others and smashing up the children's home. By contrast, he was also able to express real affection and concern for his brothers and sisters, who were by now all in care because his mother had had a breakdown and could not look after them. He was also very remorseful about all the trouble he caused the children's home staff and this sometimes influenced his behaviour in a positive way.

As with other boys who found themselves increasingly involved with the consultations, the lessening of his sense of despair seemed to follow an experience during a consultation when I had felt acutely and painfully aware of what a terrible life he had lived and how much he was suffering underneath his nonchalant way of being with me. Other authors (Bergman and Jucovy 1982) have described this moment in their work when it feels as if an arrow has pierced their hearts and given them an intense awareness of the distress their patients are in. This is more than ordinary compassion or empathy and inevitably deeply moves the therapist, often staying within them for a long while – even years – after the session.

It is possible to have this experience in consultation work, as in weekly or intensive therapy, and when it happens it is a sign of a highly significant process taking place between therapist and patient. This process can be described as a kind of desperate non-verbal communication, an SOS message from deep within the patient, who just briefly believes that there is some point in sending out this message in a world that has, in the main, not heard his or her previous cries for help. Horne describes this process as being a 'brief communication from the edge'

(Horne 2006). It is probably only when the consultations have been established within boundaries that are very clear, safe and secure that youngsters such as Billy can dare to risk this type of communication. In this respect, consultation work can be very emotionally demanding for therapists as they must be highly attuned to the patient all the time, since the SOS can be weak and is not always easily recognised.

It is not that therapists do not try to be highly attuned to all their patients. However, with the time pressure implied by consultation work, there is more of a need for the therapist to use their countertransference response and informed intuition gathered from clinical experience, to be more ready to explore therapeutic hunches and to be generally 'less non-directive' than in weekly or intensive work. With experience this can make consultation work a very exciting and rewarding way of working, particularly when despair turns to the first glimmerings of hope, as it did for Billy.

Whereas he had previously tended to deny that there was any risk that he would ever sexually abuse again, he was able to face courageously the fact that, because he had no idea why he had abused his siblings, he also had no way of stopping himself doing this again. This is an odd kind of hope – but it became possible to think this way in the context of appreciating that the children's home and the research project were trying to understand him and his actions in all their complexity and felt that he was worth listening to and feeling for. The offer of helping him find regular open-ended psychotherapy did not therefore fall on entirely deaf ears and a closed heart. Following the research consultations he was able regularly to attend psychotherapy for a considerable period of time. Without the consultations and the turning point that took place in them, Billy would not have accepted any treatment and therefore had much less of a chance of changing his behaviour, and ultimately his future.

Whilst there were only a small number of boys within the research project who were able to respond in this way, with treatment resources as limited as they are, it was possible to have a conviction that these boys were worth struggling with in the difficult treatments that followed. (For a more detailed account of psychotherapists working in a forensic context, assessing risk for dangerous patients, see Horne (2009) and Parsons and Horne (2009).)

Beginning and endings

The importance of 'beginnings and endings' in therapy have long been recognised, and many have noted the way in which the first consultation with a patient contains, in a highly condensed form, so many of the major therapeutic themes which gradually unfold during subsequently lengthy treatments. Similarly, the way in which therapy ends is likely to involve many important emotional issues for the patient.

Beginnings and endings are highly emotionally charged and one could argue that brief psychotherapy deliberately draws on this, both in the care and attention that must be paid to separation issues in the last few sessions, and in being particularly alert and responsive to the anxieties present in the first session. As already mentioned, therapists experienced in brief work have learnt that careful exploration of their 'therapeutic hunches' can be particularly helpful when examining the clues about the child and family's internal worlds as seen at these crucial junctures in family life.

In attempting to give the flavour of consultation work with all its time pressures, opportunities, and intensities of contact, it is important to bear in mind how far child and adolescent psychotherapists have come in terms of working 'briefly' and extending the applications of their psychoanalytic training. Psychoanalysts writing about brief work with adults have a very different timescale to those described in this chapter (Malan 1976; Davanloo 1994; Molnos 1995). They are usually talking about thirty to forty sessions, which is a very far cry from the work I have just described. So how 'brief' is brief?

For many children, thirty or forty sessions is probably close to the median number of sessions in weekly therapy – about one year of once-weekly therapy including holidays. And a year is a long time in family life.

Child psychotherapists' abilities to respond to the time pressures of a busy clinic life indicate a confidence in being able to offer a variety of treatments which can be helpful to patients and their families, all of which are based on psychoanalytic principles and training and demonstrate, to paraphrase Winnicott, child psychotherapists 'practising something else that we deem to be appropriate to the occasion' (Winnicott 1962: 170).

References

Balint, M., Ornstein, P. H. and Balint, E. (1972) *Focal Psychotherapy: An Example of Applied Psychoanalysis*, London: Tavistock.

Bergman, M. S. and Jucovy, M. E. (eds) (1982) *Generations of the Holocaust*, New York: Basic Books.

Bronstein, C. and Flanders, S. (1998) 'The development of a therapeutic space in a first contact with adolescents', *Journal of Child Psychotherapy* 24(1): 5–35.

Cleve, E. (2008) *A Big One and a Little One is Gone. Crisis Therapy with a Two-year-old Boy*, London: Karnac.

Davenloo, H. (1994) *Basic Principles and Techniques in Short-term Dynamic Psychotherapy*, New Jersey/London: Jason Aronson.

Daws, D. (1989) *Through the Night: Helping Parents and Sleepless Infants*, London: Free Association Books.

Edwards, J. and Maltby, J. (1998) 'Holding the child in mind: work with parents and families in a consultation service', *Journal of Child Psychotherapy* 24(1): 109–33.

Hodges, J., Lanyado, M. and Andreou, C. (1994) 'Sexuality and violence: preliminary clinical hypotheses from psychotherapeutic assessments in a research programme on young sexual offenders', *Journal of Child Psychotherapy* 20(3): 283–308.

Horne, A. (2006) 'Brief communications from the edge: psychotherapy with challenging adolescents', in M. Lanyado and A. Horne (eds) *A Question of Technique. Independent Psychoanalytic Approaches with Children and Adolescents Series*, London and New York: Routledge.

—— (2009) 'From intimacy to acting out: assessment and consultation about a dangerous child', in A. Horne and M. Lanyado (eds) *Through Assessment to Consultation. Independent Psychoanalytic Approaches with Children and Adolescents Series*, London and New York: Routledge.

Horne, A. and Lanyado, M. (eds) (2009) *Through Assessment to Consultation. Independent Psychoanalytic Approaches with Children and Adolescents Series*, London and New York: Routledge.

Lanyado, M. (1996) 'Winnicott's children: the holding environment and therapeutic communication in brief and non-intensive work', *Journal of Child Psychotherapy* 22(3): 423–43.

—— (2006) ' "Doing something else": the value of therapeutic communication when offering consultations and brief psychotherapy', in M. Lanyado and A. Horne (eds) *A Question of Technique. Independent Psychoanalytic Approaches with Children and Adolescents Series*, London and New York: Routledge.

Lanyado, M., Hodges, J., Bentovim, A., Andreou, C. and Williams, B. (1995) 'Understanding boys who sexually abuse other children: a clinical illustration', *Psychoanalytic Psychotherapy* 9(3): 231–42.

Laub, D. and Auerhahn, N. (1993) 'Knowing and not knowing massive psychic trauma: forms of traumatic memory', *International Journal of Psycho-Analysis* 74(6): 287–302.

Malan, D. H. (1976) *A Study of Brief Psychotherapy*, London and New York: Tavistock, Plenum/Rosetta.

Molnos, A. (1995) *A Question of Time*, London: Karnac.

Onions, C. (2009) 'Infant mental health: a conversation with Dilys Daws', in A. Horne and M. Lanyado (eds) *Through Assessment to Consultation. Independent Psychoanalytic Approaches with Children and Adolescents Series*, London and New York: Routledge.

Parsons, M. and Horne, A. (2009) 'Anxiety, projection and the quest for magic fixes: when one is asked to assess risk', in A. Horne and M. Lanyado (eds) *Through Assessment to Consultation. Independent Psychoanalytic Approaches with Children and Adolescents Series*, London and New York: Routledge.

Robson, S. (2009) 'Consultation to an under 5's service', in A. Horne and M. Lanyado (eds) *Through Assessment to Consultation. Independent Psychoanalytic Approaches with Children and Adolescents Series*, London and New York: Routledge.

Winnicott D. W. (1962) 'The aims of psychoanalytic treatment', in D. W. Winnicott

The Maturational Processes and the Facilitating Environment, London: Hogarth Press.

—— (1971) *Therapeutic Consultations in Child Psychiatry*, London: Hogarth Press and Institute of Psycho-Analysis.

—— (1989) *The Family and Individual Development*, London/New York: Routledge.

13 Work with parents

Margaret Rustin

The context for thinking about the range of work done by child psycho-therapists with parents has changed greatly since the first edition of this handbook was published in 1999. This is particularly the case with respect to work done within NHS Child and Adolescent Mental Health Services and other publicly funded settings providing family support. The full impli-cations of the many changes in public policy and the changing shape of services continue to be worked out, but it is striking that public and governmental preoccupation with parenting is at a consistently high level. For example, commissioners of child and adolescent mental health services are expected to develop a 'parenting strategy' and to plan services accord-ingly. If we turn to the evidence provided by column inches in the press and the numbers of television programmes about parenting, we are confronted by a very high level of anxiety, a significant tendency to blame parents, and an emphasis on the need to educate and support parents in their responsibilities.

The challenge for child psychotherapists is to locate their practice within this active discourse on parenting. What is the particular contribution that we can make? What opportunities are there to influence thinking more broadly? What new services are likely to develop in the current conjunc-ture? What about the evidence base for traditional child psychotherapy approaches to work with parents? Most importantly, what are the growing points of clinical practice and the questions our psychoanalytic framework of understanding can enable us to explore?

It is worth bearing in mind that a significant proportion of child psycho-therapists undertake further training either as family, couple or individual adult psychotherapists. Perhaps one reason for this trend is the interest in work with parents and the conviction of its importance. Within the core initial training, there is a relatively small though significant requirement for such experience. In the clinical context, however, there is a continuing problem in finding colleagues from other disciplines willing to provide any long-term input for parents. This pattern is intensifying in the public sector with so much emphasis being placed on brief interventions. This has the laudable aim of ensuring that professional resources reach a much wider population and that waiting lists are reduced, but it has a problematic impact on the provision of child psychotherapy. One thing the evidence base (Kennedy 2003; Trowell *et al.* 2007) makes clear is that parallel work with parents is as important as we have always believed. This means that skilled practitioners are needed to undertake such work if child psychotherapy is to be effective. In some settings, family therapists, social workers, psychologists and other colleagues are willing to provide this, but it seems increasingly the case that this cannot be relied on, and that child psychotherapists may need to take on the role of parent worker more frequently. This can be a very potent and enjoyable co-operative effort, but it raises two obvious questions for the profession. The first is the issue of confidence and competence in parent work, and the second is that of the balance of different forms of clinical work – work with children and adolescents, work with parents, family work, short- and long-term work. If the demand for work with parents is growing, it has implications for the primary identity of child psychotherapists and for training.

The twenty-first-century parent is living in a world very different indeed from that of fifty years ago and the early days of child psychotherapy. The majority of mothers are at work through much of their children's childhood, the number of single parents has increased enormously, divorce and family break-up is much more common. Looking beyond the immediate family context, things are also much changed – the support of extended families is less available, due in part to geographical mobility, competitive and stressful aspects of the education system are writ large, and the impact of the visual and consumerist culture of television and computers is enormous. The multi-cultural and multi-ethnic neighbourhoods of our cities, the fearfulness with respect to children's safety in public spaces, the earlier incidence of puberty and changes in patterns of reproduction, including all the possibilities for assisted pregnancy, are other significant factors. The rate of social and technological change is awe inspiring, yet the human capacity for responding to change is a well-recognised area of psychological vulnerability, so it is by no means surprising that this is a period in which people struggle to make sense of what is happening. There is, perhaps, a degree of mis-attunement between the rate of technical change and the pace at which human beings can adapt their forms of life to the new conditions. The extent of uncertainty about what parents should be doing and the now widespread idea that they need to be taught how to be parents suggests both the destabilising effect of so much change on traditional identities, on a socially accepted notion of what it is to be a parent, and the fact that our society approaches its human problems in a technical spirit. Confused or failing parents are thought to require cognitive psychological techniques to fill the gap. The popularity of 'Super-Nanny' approaches is an aspect of this, as is the widespread enthusiasm for parenting classes.

This background is very important in understanding what parents are troubled by, what they expect, hope or fear from professionals, and similarly vital in thinking about what commissioners of services are looking for and what partnerships between health, social care and education services and voluntary agencies might work. Although this is a book for clinical practitioners, attention to the wider context seems to me to be essential if our clinical work is to be responsive to the inner world implications for our patients of ongoing social change. It also enables us to be in good dialogue with colleagues about what is helpful for parents in difficulties with each other and their children.

'Parenting strategy' is a phrase one comes across in many policy documents, including the recent report on the implementation of the National Service Framework (NSF) with respect to children's mental health (Shribman 2007). The interpretation given to the 'Every Child Matters' agenda is that all the agencies involved are to devise such a strategy, and one of the particular points made is the welcome emphasis on the needs of children whose parents have mental illness. But the predominant tone is to do with information and education for parents, through the provision of 'parent-management programmes' and training for foster and kinship carers, for example. The launch of the new National Academy for Parenting Practitioners in 2007 is a major plank in the British strategy. Advice lines for parents are another initiative, and seem to be quite well used. Here again the emphasis tends to be on providing information, but the listening skills of telephone counsellors also offer something more.

Partnership is the other concept espoused very broadly. This is a tricky idea in the clinical context. At one level, one can be sure that unless a partnership is achieved between the clinician and a child's parents, there is no basis for useful work – there has to be some trust, some agreement about what is wrong and what might be done about it. The old language of consent and therapeutic alliance is another way of describing this process. But as used currently, partnership can get to mean something rather different. The idea of parents choosing from a menu of what is available places the whole interchange at a consumerist and narrowly cognitive level and leaves to one side the meaning of the relationship that is being established as soon as a conversation about family difficulties is started. The unconscious is being ruled out as a significant factor once partnership is interpreted in a way which is designed to avoid recognising dependence on the therapist, and to assert equality, when the reality is that one person needs something that the other may be able to help them find. The 'partnership' discourse is related to the issue of rights, and the right of patients to be fully informed and to be given choices is sometimes interpreted in such a way as to reduce their right to be understood, looked after and given what is appropriate from the point of view of professional expertise. Interestingly, this confusion is quite similar to the problem of thinking about children's rights – parents can become so taken over by ideas of a child's right to have whatever they wish that they lose a sense of the authority and responsibility they have as adults to consider whether what the child would choose is good for him or not.

The concept of anxiety is what seems to be missing from much of the parenting discourse, and to be one without which the experience of parents cannot be properly described. Whether we are thinking of the parents of a distressed or ill baby, a defiant toddler, a bullied school-child, a depressed or acting-out or anorexic adolescent, what all are struggling with is their worry, panic or despair. There is a continuity between the absolutely unavoidable everyday anxieties of being a parent and the extreme ones which bring families to the attention of child psychotherapists. It is when the level of anxiety bursts through the parents' capacity to contain it that outside help is sought, but it is very helpful to keep in mind that it is ordinary and necessary for parents to be worried about their children. If we put it in the language of attachment, we might suggest that normal secure attachment is indeed the child's link to someone who is capable of being anxious about the child. Bion's understanding of the vital role of maternal reverie in the development of the capacity for thought gives a deeper account of the role which primary dependence plays in the development of a person. It is a mind which can register the child's anxiety which is the starting point of everything, and parents in trouble are very often in difficulties with respect to this function.

There are some other central psychoanalytic concepts which underpin child psychotherapists' styles of work with parents which can be usefully outlined at this point. Some of these concepts would be shared by therapists working in different conceptual frameworks, though perhaps differently understood when the unconscious dimension of mental life is taken into account.

The distinction between infantile and adult states of mind is a bedrock for thinking developmentally. It is all too easy to observe times when parental functioning, which requires adult capacities, is undermined because of overwhelming infantile feelings and phantasies. Finding a way to help parents to become aware of this process in themselves and thus able to protect themselves is probably our most cherished aim.

A second dimension is our characterisation of maternal and paternal aspects of personality and parental functioning. Very broadly this describes two necessary forms of parental behaviour – the receptive, nurturing and more relationally oriented maternal mode and the limit-setting, paternal mode with its greater focus on the outside world, the child's ambitions and curiosity and potential achievements. The balance of these within individuals and the way in which they are distributed in a parental couple is a fruitful vertex of development.

The third vital set of ideas is the Oedipus complex and its sequelae. The sexual tie between parents is an aspect of their relationship which is often difficult for their children but also difficult for professionals when their prime focus of attention is on the parent/child relationship. The couple element of the parental couple can sometimes be the key to the family difficulties, a point perhaps more often recognised when the couple relationship has broken down and the task of the separated pair is to find a way of continuing to function as parents. This may be rendered painfully problematic when feelings of sexual rejection and jealousy intrude, as they often do, when new partners enter the picture. The increasing numbers of reconstituted families with step parents, step and half siblings add an additional complexity.

Finally, the experience of shame among parents who need help with their children is a significant clinical problem – their sense of failure and incompetence, and their dread of being despised and humiliated by those felt to be more successful at being grown-up is a severe hindrance in parent work. Linked to this is unconscious envy, with its corrosive impact on relationships which stir up a sense of need.

The matter of confidentiality should be mentioned here as it impacts on relationships with parents as patients in very difficult ways. When there is already some involvement with the law or statutory bodies at the outset, taking the legal context – child protection issues, domestic violence, family court proceedings etc. – into account is built in. When, however, the origin of the referral lies elsewhere and the family expects total confidentiality, there can be great strain and anxiety on both sides if issues erupt or revelations get made which require a statutory response. The current expectation for more and more inter-agency co-work and for rather routine sharing of much information seems likely to throw up increasingly difficult decisions for professionals and to be a challenge to accepted practice.

Here is part of the overview of child psychotherapists' approaches to work with parents I wrote ten years ago, and some reflective comments. It was not a blueprint for a parenting service but rather a depiction of some kinds of work with parents which child psychotherapists are equipped to do.

Consultation with parents

The traditional role for the child psychotherapist limited contact with parents to meetings, held from time to time, to review a child's progress in therapy. Their purpose was to sustain a co-operative relationship between therapist and parents, to give the therapist a sense of the child's development in the family, at school and in the wider social world, and the parents an opportunity to enquire about the therapy and test out their confidence in the therapist's capacity to help their child. At their best, such meetings can offer a real chance to integrate diverse perspectives and to enrich the understanding of both parents and therapist, but they can also be difficult occasions in which divergences in aim between therapist and parent may erupt. Such reviews remain an important part of good practice.

Two examples will serve to illustrate these points.

Case example: Jacob

Jacob is a ten-year-old boy referred by divorced parents who remain very angry with each other, but who have managed to co-operate in supporting Jacob's therapy. He was referred for extremely aggressive and disruptive behaviour at school, which was threatening to lead to his exclusion, and for his difficult and unrewarding family relationships. His rigid defences made him rather inaccessible to help and his therapist found it hard to sustain hope in the face of a barrage of contempt from Jacob. Termly review meetings were held with each parent separately as neither felt able to sustain parental concern in company with the other. When the issue of choice of secondary school arose, parental conflict flared up, and there was potential for Jacob's much improved behaviour at school (his problems now being gathered, and more or less contained, in his relationship with his therapist) to be undermined. The review meetings could be used to support the more adult aspect of the parents' personalities and thus enable them to think about Jacob's needs at school rather than be drawn into another fight at his expense. The therapist's observations about Jacob's vulnerability to being upset by changes, his need for careful preparation and explanation, and his well-concealed panic about what secondary school would be like, helped them to hold back and work out their differences less flagrantly.

Comment

Trying to place work of this sort in the context of service development, one might want to draw attention to the importance of sustaining the involvement of father in families where parents have separated. In this particular family, Jacob's difficulties in managing his aggressive feelings and in differentiating between ordinary self-assertion, bullying, and risky or delinquent challenges to adult authority meant that his need for paternal attention, especially during the adolescent years, was likely to be intense.

It is interesting to note that developments in psychoanalytic theorising about fathers, male and female elements in the personality, and maternal and paternal aspects of parental functioning have been significant in recent years (Trowell and Etchegoyan 2001; Britton 1998). This may enable child psychotherapists to work more confidently with parental couples in conflict.

Case example: Elizabeth

Elizabeth is an adopted girl, aged nine, with a very sad and disrupted early life. She attends for intensive psychotherapy. Review meetings often provided rather crucial opportunities to test out realities. Elizabeth would often give a very convincing account to her therapist of external events which would interfere with her clinic appointments, leaving the therapist in doubt as to what was going to happen. Her parents, similarly, would hear disturbing stories about school and therapy whose reality they could not assess. Exploration suggested that Elizabeth was not telling lies in any ordinary sense, but rather conveying both just how hard it was for her to distinguish between reality and fantasy and how doubtful she was that adults could co-operate and stick to arrangements made for her benefit. In her first five years, she had little experience of consistent adult care and she continued to recreate opportunities to be let down, when her conviction that people did not really care would be confirmed. Helping Elizabeth's parents not to be pulled into rejecting behaviour was facilitated by the exploration of the details of her difficult behaviour. For example, Father complained of her tendency to scream right into his ear, but was helped to think about this symptom when we could identify the painful intensity and shock which she was forcing him to experience on her behalf. Perhaps this might be likened to the ordinary behaviour of a crying infant, but when the baby gets no response the screams stay lodged in the baby's head in an unbearable way. Seeing the baby within the nine-year-old helped Elizabeth's parents to find ways to cope with her.

Comment

Work with adopted and fostered children has become an increasingly large part of child psychotherapy practice as is described by Leslie Ironside (Chapter 22 in this book). The question of how to respond to the difficulties their parents face has led to many creative initiatives. Elizabeth's parents were seen regularly as a parental couple, in addition to the review meetings discussed, by a co-worker of the child's therapist. But the complex problems of parenting children who have usually had a traumatic start in life and whose capacity for basic trust is deeply compromised often require new forms of help. These can include groups of parents in similar circumstances, often combining some information giving and behavioural strategy emphasis with ongoing support; a telephone conversation service for emergency use (particularly relevant for foster carers whose lives are so frequently disrupted by emergency placements); and careful long-term work with adoptive parents or family therapy prior to any consideration of individual treatment for their troubled children. Adoptive parents are very vulnerable to feeling that their own capacities are being undervalued or that they are being blamed for difficulties the children brought with them from their earlier lives. Hence, sensitivity to these anxieties is needed and timing of interventions is a delicate matter.

Individual work

The supportive work with parents, very often provided in the past by psychiatric social workers, is now more frequently undertaken by child psychotherapists themselves. This may be alongside a child's therapy taken on by another therapist, or as an intervention in its own right, because the most helpful input is deemed to be work aimed at changing parental functioning. A considerable variety of approach is required in this work. The spectrum includes support for quite disturbed parents whose own mental state may impinge in damaging ways on their children, support for deprived and vulnerable parents (for example, bereaved families, mothers abandoned by their partners, refugee families), and work which attempts to explore ways in which parental functioning is disturbed by unconscious aspects of the parents' own way of seeing things (Bailey 2006). The balance of listening and receptiveness on the one hand, and insight-giving interventions on the other, will depend on what a particular parent seems likely to be most helped by. Some fragile parents may be able to take in very little reflective comment and have urgent need for a relationship within which they can express their confusion, depression, despair and self-doubt, and feel that they can be accepted as they are. Others, with some source of greater hopefulness within their personality, will respond to the opportunity to think in depth about their own contribution to their children's problems, and to consider their own family history as part of an attempt to understand the current family difficulties.

In working with parents, the therapist offers a model of how to respond to emotional distress which has some core elements. The first is attention to establishing and maintaining a reliable setting in which it is possible to talk about very upsetting things. As with a child's treatment, sessions for parents have regularity in time and space, and this helps to contain the infantile elements which are aroused. The second element is the co-creation of some shared language to describe painful emotional states. Finding words for anguish is a help in itself, because it provides the comfort of feeling understood and therefore not alone with one's pain. Many lonely or emotionally deprived parents discover resources for understanding their own children through the experience of feeling understood and acquiring ways of thinking about feelings which may be very new to them. Third is the valuing of boundaries and differentiation: the differences between parents and children, and between adult and more infantile aspects of the personality, can be clarified within a structured therapeutic setting. For example, an emotionally deprived parent can find it very difficult to distinguish between need and greed in herself and her child: if primary needs have never been met adequately, setting limits which are not arbitrary is almost impossible. Fourth is an adequately complex understanding of human emotion and intimate relationships. This involves exploration of the internal world and of the constraints and creative possibilities of external reality. To support the development of genuine parental functioning, attention has to be given not only to the individual but also to the marital relationship – where there is a partnership – to the role of work in the individual's identity, to the full range of family relationships across the generations, and to the community setting. Last, and most important, there is the focus on giving meaning to behaviour. The urge to blame and reject aspects of ourselves and others is most helpfully modified if our destructive impulses can be given meaning.

Case example: Mrs D

Mrs D was a divorced woman of fifty with two sons. The older, aged twenty-five, was on the edge of a third schizophrenic breakdown when Mrs D referred herself and her younger boy, Sam, aged thirteen for help. It quickly became clear that the help Sam wanted was that someone should take care of his troubled mother and relieve him of a very heavy burden of anxiety. Mrs D began once-weekly psychotherapy. Her concerns for her two sons were deeply interwoven with the overall pattern of her life. She had had two significant sexual relationships and each had produced a child, but neither father had a reliable relationship with his son or with her. Mrs D's struggle to find an identity of her own and emerge from compliance with what she felt had been an authoritarian and rather loveless family had contributed to her choice of partner, as each of them had represented a counter-cultural protest against the restrictions she so resented. Now she was struggling with two enormous anxieties: her schizophrenic son exploited her ruthlessly, stealing from her and taking a very unfair share of the emotional and physical space she tried to provide. How could she stand up to him? As she became more in touch with the anger she had never expressed to her own parents, whose work abroad had resulted in her being sent to a boarding school from age five, she developed a capacity to challenge him. Her second concern was her own health. She had had two life-threatening illnesses in the last five years and was anxious that her younger son might have to cope with her early death. Thinking about this meant facing all her own painful losses. The depression this precipitated took her deep into herself. Gradually Mrs D became more able to acknowledge and value her feelings, including those that made her feel guilty, and less prone to see them in others. Her creative capacities began to re-emerge.

Comment

A major current public health concern is the impact of parental mental illness on the development of children. This case highlights the reverse issue of how families cope with mental illness in children and young people. The individual work offered to Mrs D was once characterised by a child psychiatry colleague as 'family therapy done via individual psychotherapy', which makes a cogent point. The child psychotherapist's perspective is an inclusive one, because it acknowledges family dynamics – everyone in the family system is affected by everyone else. The choice of whom to help is usually a mixture of pragmatics (who is asking for it? – Mrs D was, her son was not, being understandably anxious not to seem psychologically ill, like his brother) and resources. The provision of psychotherapy for parents as an integral part of Child and Adolescent services seems to me a priority. Referral to adult services tends to lead to loss of the capacity to bear the child in mind and less attention to the ongoing projections into the children.

Case example: Mr J

Mr J was a father of two boys, the older of whom was autistic. He was troubled by his own deep passivity in the face of his son's regressed behaviour. He and his wife were initially seen jointly to talk about their children's difficulties: the younger son's omnipotent and manic behaviour seemed to complement his brother's autistic withdrawal from life, and the parents became aware that the division of labour between the boys and between the two of them was at the expense of all of them as individuals. Mr and Mrs J were offered individual help to understand this destructive process. As Mr J talked, he began to see that his two sons were confused in his mind with himself and his younger brother. This brother had had a heart condition from birth, and Mr J had given up much of his ordinary childhood desires to take care of him. This had evoked hatred of which he had been unaware, and when his brother died he had been left with a burden of guilt which lay heavily on his early adult years. His own child's autism and consequent need for special care had been experienced as just punishment. The younger son was left to express the ambition and longing for life and the anger which Mr J had had to disown.

Comment

Psychotherapeutic services for autistic children and their families are often very deeply appreciated by the small number who receive them, as discussed by Maria Rhode in Chapter 19 of this book. Concern about the poor quality of mental health provision for children with a learning disability (as noted in Standard 9 of the NSF) is leading to some real development, but there may be a tendency for relative neglect of parental need, especially if the children are offered therapy in school contexts. Mr J's preoccupation with intergenerational pressures may be especially relevant given the genetic element in childhood autism.

The possibility of preventative early intervention in this area is suggested by the pilot research in using a form of infant observation to support the mother–toddler relationship when autistic phenomena are emerging (Gretton 2006). The potential for the therapeutic use of observation in the home is one which combines provision for parent and child.

I now want to add a category of work not discussed ten years ago.

The couple as focus

A focus which can sometimes seem the obvious one, despite the referral being of a child, is that of difficulties in the couple relationship. This can be quite a challenge for child psychotherapists unless they have had additional training, but a psychoanalytic understanding of couple problems can be so fruitful that it is an area of work ripe for development, especially in the context of greater contemporary openness in acknowledging relationship difficulties. Relationship counselling often does not include much attention to the place of the children in the family dynamics, but the destructive impact of couple conflict, domestic violence and other less obvious signs of breakdown in family relationships is enormous.

Working with the couple is bound to involve marital and sexual aspects alongside the problematic identity as parents. Here is one example of couple work which includes the therapist's concerns about the child.[1]

Mr and Mrs A

This couple are 'semi-separated': the husband has moved next door to what had been intended as the family home when it was bought ten years ago. A large derelict Georgian house, bought with the aim of renovation, has remained untouched while they lived next door in a tiny flat. The wife complains that her husband has never really consulted her about the plans and he feels she dreams up impractical schemes which could never be carried out. As a result of this impasse, their belongings have never been unpacked and their flat is jam packed with crates and boxes. There is no room to move literally or metaphorically. They were in a stalemate. They were neither living in or out of the marriage. Mrs A poured out grievances and Mr A defended himself behind terse replies. He was very silent, ponderous, seemingly impenetrable, and Mrs A was either screaming with complaints about his inactivity or also silent, tight lipped and impenetrable. They both complained that they were not listened to but were completely unaware of their own deafness to each other. They have an eight-year-old daughter who moves between them. The daughter is a go-between in many senses; she seems to try to link them up. They compete for her attention and both want to claim her as their own.

The more lively, engaging aspects of themselves find expression in the relationship that they each have with their daughter. They both lighten up as they describe her as 'a live wire', and she is a source of great pride. Her liveliness, they insist, is an indication that she is fine. I realised my intense efforts to draw them out mirrored this. The couple told me that when she grew up their daughter said she wanted to be a gardener; her dream was to have a garden of her own so she could nurture plants and flowers. Because of my own experience of desperately trying to inject some life into this couple I suddenly could identify with the enormous burden for her parents' growth that this little girl was carrying. She had been triangulated into her parents' relationship to link them up and bring some life and growth into a family scene that was so arid.

If this couple can be helped to gain some understanding of the nature of their relationship, there is a possibility that their daughter might be released from the burden she is carrying and become once more an eight-year-old daughter whose parents can attend to her and not the other way round.

Group work

Some parents are more responsive to group therapy. The group offers the comfort that others, too, share a sense of failure, whether it be losing one's temper, failing to get a child to school on time or to bed at a reasonable hour, or trying to bear a child's failure at school, quarrelsomeness with siblings or antisocial behaviour. Group work seems to be helpful when there is a sense of social isolation, strong feelings of failure and an absence of supportive partners. The group culture, as long as the group does not contain deeply disturbed and destructive individuals, can create a place for each person's vulnerability and a sense of continuity over time as each member feels kept in mind by others. By and large, group work with parents builds on the constructive potential mobilised by the parental role and does not address so successfully negative factors, which are better tackled in the more protected space provided by individual work. This is because the members' identity as parents cannot be set on one side, as it might be in individual psychotherapy where their more infantile aspects can be contained. Parents do, however, challenge each other's evasions of responsibility, often with the help of humour.

Conclusion

Child psychotherapists bring some special capacities to work with parents. The place of infant observation and the broad study of child development in their training, together with their own analysis, put them in touch with the changing pressures on parents as their children grow and change, and the intensity with which parents' own infantile difficulties are stirred up by their children's emotional lives. This knowledge and sensitivity can be used well in responding to parental anxieties, but it can also be a source of trouble. A degree of competition, jealousy and envy is likely to be evoked by professionals who try to help when parents feel themselves to have failed. Tact, humility and a real belief in the shared nature of the task are essential. The direct use of transference and countertransference and interpretation are only appropriate when there has been explicit agreement that the parents wish to become patients in their own right. However, the understanding available through observation of the relationship made with the therapist can inform other kinds of conversation which have therapeutic potential. It is the capacity to empathise with both parental and child perspectives which is so valuable.

Note

1 I am grateful to Lynne Cudmore for this clinical example.

References

Bailey, T. (2006) 'There's no such thing as an adolescent', in M. Lanyado and A. Horne (eds) *A Question of Technique. Independent Psychoanalytic Approaches with Children and Adolescents*, Hove: Routledge.

Britton, R. (1998) *Belief and Imagination*, London: New Library of Psychoanalysis.

Gretton, A. (2006) 'An account of a year's work with a mother and her 18-month-old son at risk of autism', *International Journal of Infant Observation* 9(1): 21–34.

Kennedy, E. (2003) *Child and Adolescent Psychotherapy. A Systematic Review of Psychoanalytic Approaches*, London: North Central London Strategic Health Authority.

Shribman, S. (2007) *Children's Health, Our Future. A Review of Progress Against the National Service Framework for Children, Young People and Maternity Services 2004*, London: Department of Health.

Trowell, J. and Etchegoyen, A. (2001) *The Importance of Fathers: A Psychoanalytic Re-evaluation*, New Library of Psychoanalysis, London: Routledge.

Trowell, J., Jaffe, I., Campbell, J. *et al.* (2007) 'Childhood depression: a place for psychotherapy', *European Child and Adolescent Psychiatry* 16(3): 157–67.

Further reading

Klauber, T. (1998) 'The significance of trauma in work with the parents of severely disturbed children, and its implications for work with parents in general', *Journal of Child Psychotherapy* 24(1): 85–107.

Tsiantis, J. (ed.) (1999) *Working with Parents of Children and Adolescents who are in Psychoanalytic Psychotherapy*, EFPP Clinical Monograph, London: Karnac Books.

14 Parent–infant psychotherapy

Caryn Onions

'Do babies have problems?' is how Dilys Daws began her chapter in the previous edition of this book. She then added 'Well, yes babies *do* have problems, but even more, parents have problems about getting their relationship with their baby going'. Since Daws wrote this chapter in 1999 there has been a huge growth in interest in infant mental health both in the United Kingdom and internationally. Not only did Daws' book *Through the Night* (1989) offer many professionals a new way of looking at separation and sleep problems, but Daws herself has continued to campaign vigorously on behalf of the mental health of infants. She started the Association of Infant Mental Health (UK) and has supported health visitors and other professionals who work with parents and their infants. The campaigning has been effective as many government papers now refer specifically to the importance of supporting parent–infant relationships along with a growing understanding that intervening early can make a *real* difference.

So, ten years on where are we now? Douglas (2007) describes the 'current Zeitgeist in infant mental health [as a] move towards integration', and I think she is right. There has been a significant joining together of psychoanalytic theory, attachment theory, neuroscience and behavioural ideas, and the wealth of publications in this field shows it is an area of great interest and theoretical development, see: Balbernie (2001), Baradon *et al.* (2005), Douglas (2007), Gerhardt (2004), Tracey (2000).

A parent–infant psychotherapy project

OXPIP (the Oxford Parent–Infant Project), is the setting in which I see parents and infants. It is a charity which was founded in 1998. We have a base in Oxford and a number of 'satellites' in nearby rural towns. We see families with infants up to the age of two and take referrals from parents and professionals. There are many reasons why a parent brings their infant, and often the family will have already had some contact with their health visitor. It is not unusual to see women during pregnancy, or for referrals to be made following a particularly traumatic and difficult labour. Sometimes these women are diagnosed with post-natal depression when perhaps their symptoms are more related to the trauma of the delivery, which then interferes with their ability to get a good relationship going with their baby. We also see mothers who have concerns about sleeping, weaning and other separation difficulties (Daws 1989).

There is a steady increase in referrals of mothers not from the UK, suffering the effects of social isolation and being far from their families and country of birth. In the past ten years a very disturbing trend has been the increase in referrals where there has been parental substance misuse during pregnancy. Research into the effects of maternal alcohol and drug misuse clearly shows that this can have significant effects on early parent–infant relationships (Forrester and Harwin 2006), and long-term developmental problems for children.

In addition to seeing families we offer a range of other services including baby massage and baby chatting groups; work with Sure Start and Oxford Primary Child and Adolescent Mental Health Service, where we see families and consult to primary care workers; assessment and therapy for referrals from social workers which may involve court work; and a parent–infant training programme for Oxfordshire's Social and Healthcare staff.

The therapy rooms are comfortable with the adults sitting on floor cushions and a mat and toys for the infant. We meet at the same time every week. In some circumstances we see families at home or in hospital. Whilst my clinical approach to working with parents and their infants is based on psychoanalytic theory, my work is also influenced by attachment theory and research into infant development. My aim is to improve the relationship between the parent and infant, and as Daws said, 'to get the relationship going'. Helping benign relationships develop where parents are more able to see their infants in a realistic light allows the infant's development to progress. The way in which this is done depends on the reason for referral and broadly corresponds with Stern's (1995) 'port of entry' ideas. This means that to improve the relationship, work may need to focus either on parental issues or on the developmental needs of the infant.

I do not work to a set number of sessions. Some families come for a few weeks and manage to get things back on track, whereas others may come for much longer. Parents with past losses or traumas often find that having a baby stirs up unresolved issues and 'ghosts in the nursery' (Fraiberg *et al.* 1980).

One of the exciting clinical aspects of the process of parent–infant psychotherapy is the possibility of addressing a parent's psychological and emotional problems whilst also directly working at the level of the parent–infant relationship. It is as if you are looking at one relationship from within another, for example looking at a woman's relationship with her own mother or father 'from within' the relationship between her and her baby. In individual psychotherapy aspects of past relationships are transferred onto the relationship with the therapist, and in these cases this 'transference' is the psychotherapist's key therapeutic tool. In parent–infant work, whilst the therapist remains sensitive and alert to transference issues, it is how this is observed between the baby and mother, and then how it is carefully talked about, which largely becomes the focus of the work. Working out whom the baby represents for the parent is informed by my countertransference and it can take time to understand intergenerational patterns and then make links to present-day relationships.

A key factor in helping to bring about change is linked to whether the therapist manages to address a parent's sensitivity and hostility towards their baby. Increasing maternal sensitivity is known to have a positive effect on an infant's attachment status (Juffer *et al.* 2008). However, in my experience I think the work is most effective when a parent's hostility towards their baby can also be thought about. Babies who are frightened by maternal hostility are more likely to develop a disorganised attachment.

Different ways of working

Parent–infant psychotherapy is a specialist area and child psychotherapists are well equipped to do this work. Our particular contribution is the capacity of 'containment' (Bion 1962), which means the ability to receive strong powerful emotions, to think and reflect and then to respond.

The following sections describe detailed clinical examples of individual work, analytic group work and the therapeutic use of video. These are illustrations of the ways in which my practice has developed, building on previous experience before qualifying in child psychotherapy, through continuing professional development and further training, for example in group work and using video. Permission to use this material has been given, but it has additionally been deliberately disguised to protect the anonymity of families.

Individual work – Helen and Sam

Helen was referred by her health visitor when she was twenty weeks pregnant. She was a married, professional woman in her late thirties with two children aged five and three. Her thirteen-month-old daughter Ruby had died from a spontaneous brain haemorrhage six months earlier and Helen unexpectedly got pregnant six weeks later. She thought that the loss of Ruby had probably led her and her husband to think they might have difficulty having another baby, even though they had not had a problem conceiving in the past.

Helen was concerned about the reaction of family and friends, fearing they would say it was too soon. When I met her she did not look pregnant and until then had not wanted to think about it. She wondered if she wanted to replace Ruby but she hated the thought of that. One of her fears was that Ruby would be 'pushed out' by the new baby and that she would confuse them in her mind. She worried she might reject the new baby and be frightened of it, and possibly not even want to hold it or look after it.

Throughout the therapy I did not see her husband but Helen said he was surprised but pleased and excited about the pregnancy. I got the impression he was a calm and reassuring person. Scans indicated that she was carrying a big baby, and towards the end of the pregnancy she became extremely worried that something might go wrong and she would lose this baby as well. They also suggested that she was having a boy.

I visited Helen and her baby, Sam, at home for the first few weeks after he was born. Helen was anxious and agitated, very tearful, but able to look after Sam and be alone with him. For the first few months, feeds in the middle of the night were a regular time when she wept about Ruby, and together we wondered what that might be like for Sam. One idea we had was that she should tell Sam about Ruby and I helped her begin to put things into words.

It is important for parents to talk to their babies, especially when something significant has happened. Whilst Sam could not understand the actual words we were using he did have some understanding of the feelings being expressed, and so over time, by explaining her distress Helen was effectively reducing the likelihood of Sam experiencing a dissonance between what Helen was saying with words and what she was saying emotionally. Working out how to talk to Sam and how to be with him was hard for her at first, especially in front of other people as she worried that if she were playful and chatty with him that people might think she had forgotten Ruby.

As Sam grew, so did Helen's fears about him dying. She worried about leaving him on his own, and felt she had to respond to his every whimper. Helen feared that Ruby had suffered the night she died, and so bedtimes and putting Sam to sleep could be extremely painful and difficult; in fact all separations were difficult to manage. Helen also had a period of time when she worried about health-related issues with her other two children and had a series of dreams where children were accidentally killed. She worried about having children for tea in case she gave them food poisoning and was preoccupied with her ability to keep children alive and well. However, alongside her worries she was also pleased to see that Sam was developing a different personality to Ruby, it was as if she'd assumed he would be a clone of Ruby.

Sam's development brought mixed feelings. Helen worried that her grief would have a detrimental effect on Sam, so all developmental milestones were celebrated. However, every month that passed meant that she was a month further away from Ruby. She clearly expressed the difficulties of mourning a loss and celebrating a birth at the same time; anniversaries were agony for Helen. A particularly difficult time was when Sam reached the same age that Ruby was when she died. However, after this Helen started to think about the possibility of burying Ruby's ashes.

Helen had difficulty when Sam got upset or restless and her tendency was to immediately put him to the breast. She would also giggle sometimes when he got cross. We worked out that a part of Helen sometimes indulged Sam's tempers, especially when they were directed at her, as if she felt she needed to be punished for being a bad mother. Having the baby in the room and seeing these interactions is so helpful. I saw Helen and Sam weekly for eighteen months and then for the last six months we met less frequently.

The work was to help Helen mourn the loss of Ruby whilst at the same time come to terms with being pregnant and develop a new and separate relationship with Sam. Many authors have written about the impact of pregnancy on the mourning process (Etchegoyen 1997; Lewis and Casement 1986; Reid 2003), and as Helen shows us 'pregnancy deprives the mother of space and time for mourning' (Raphael-Leff 2000). Of course it might be that some parents become pregnant to avoid mourning the loss of a loved one. A key feature of this type of work is helping the parent to see the infant in its own right, and at the same time helping the infant not to be *shrouded* in the death of the sibling. At times Helen found it difficult to think about Sam in any other way than in relation to Ruby. She desperately wanted to hold onto the memory of Ruby but struggled to do this without the memory getting muddled up with Sam.

It is not unusual to get similar referrals where there has been a significant loss for the parents such as the death of a child, a parent, stillbirth or miscarriage and in all of these situations the loss can have a great impact, as it can for children and adults at all ages. In some situations the baby is a 'replacement child' where 'the child has been conceived with the conscious purpose on the part of one or both parents of replacing another child who had died a short time earlier' (Sabbadini 1993). In this case I did not think Sam was consciously conceived to replace Ruby, but her death unconsciously challenged Helen and her husband in terms of seeing themselves as a potent couple. In such cases, Reid (2007) prefers the term 'penumbra baby' to describe babies born following a loss, and I think this accurately describes Helen, she did not want to replace Ruby, she simply wanted to mother her, and so the mothering of Sam was in the shadow of Ruby's death.

Analytic group work

Parent–infant groups can be run in various ways depending on the needs of the parents. They could be time-limited closed groups, groups which focus on something specific, such as baby massage, or for a particular group of parents such as teenage or substance misusing parents. The group I am going to describe is based on group analytic principles (Foulkes 1948) and we were influenced and inspired by Paul and Thomson-Salo (1997). Briefly, by this I mean that issues relevant to individual parent–infant couples were also opened up to the whole group, and that the babies were seen as group members in their own right.

In this clinical example five mothers and their infants had been attending a slow-open, weekly parent–infant therapy group for four months. I co-ran the group with a colleague, with supervision from a group analyst.

> The mothers had been sharing similar feelings about how intense and passionate they could feel towards their babies and how this had taken them by surprise. Emily was standing, gently moving from side to side trying to help Edmond fall asleep whilst looking exhausted, and tearfully telling the group that she hardly has time to think about anything else but Edmond these days. She said she could not bear to put him down; she worried he would not feel loved by her. Faith made a joke about John (her baby) being her new partner now. Marie began to talk about her fears of weaning Chloe, 'I know it's silly but I'm scared that if I give her solids she'll die'. Marie was breastfeeding Chloe and would do so at any slight whimper. This meant that no one else could comfort or get close to Chloe. Marie was terrified that if Chloe were out of her arms then she would not survive.
>
> For a few weeks it had felt to my co-therapist and me as if Chloe was starving hungry and that Marie was not picking up her hunger cues (making sucking sounds and putting her fingers in her mouth). Chloe was pale and quite thin, rarely smiled and could be very restless and fractious. Emily and Faith had successfully introduced solids, and whilst they empathised with Marie's fear they kept reassuring her that it would

be OK. My co-therapist acknowledged Marie's dilemma that the fear of death is around both if she gives and does not give her solid food. Emily went on to tell the group that Edmond was in his own room now, but she felt mean and rejecting. Faith seemed to withdraw after about half an hour and although John was vocalising a lot, perhaps because of his mother's silence, he looked serious and unsmiling, possibly reflecting his mother's mood.

At the next session Faith said the week had been a 'disaster' and she talked about how hard she found it keeping up with the changes in John's development; feeling that she had just got something right and was in a good routine, but then having to change it all. John was definitely smiling more this week but Faith said 'you don't give your smiles to me anymore'.

Emily asked Marie about giving solids to Chloe and this was said in a jovial way, a bit like 'well, have you managed to give her anything to eat yet?' and Faith said 'what does she have to do to tell you she's hungry?' Marie replied as if with a real awareness of what she was saying, 'she'll have to get up and tell me herself'. We understood Marie to mean that Chloe would have to wait until she was old enough to walk to the larder, as Marie could not trust the safety of anything else except her own breast milk. We noticed that at this time Chloe was lying on her back with both arms out to the side as if shocked like a newborn, saying 'when are you going to feed me then mum?' Marie talked about Chloe getting very distressed at times, and after the group my co-therapist and I shared similar feelings of distress and anger with Marie. We had wanted to tell her that she had to feed her solids, just like her health visitor had done.

The following week we were very relieved to hear that Marie had started to introduce solids and we saw that Chloe was more content, and heard that she was sleeping a bit better at night. Faith began to share how she was becoming strongly attached to John, and she felt it acutely, as if his smiles to others were a rejection of her. She struggled with very powerful feelings of guilt for the ambivalence she'd felt during the concealed pregnancy.

Seeing mothers and babies in group therapy is therapeutically very powerful. Their relationship with their baby is there for all to see and so working in the 'here and now' becomes a potent tool for change. At this point (four months into the group), the mothers had 'bonded' well with each other, attendance was good and you could say they were 'securely attached' to the group. They could be very supportive to each other's dilemmas, but the support they got from the group was much more than a 'propping up'. For example, Faith felt safe enough to tell the others that she had kept the pregnancy a secret. In the early sessions she would make light of her feelings once saying 'I walked out of a shop on my own the other day as I forgot I had him', and this was in reply to Emily and Marie talking about how difficult they found it being apart from their babies. The group members were simultaneously grappling with feelings of intimacy and distance. However, over many months their ability to share in the group these opposite positions towards their babies, gradually helped them arrive at a more comfortable position, something less extreme.

Another feature of groups is that the members often say things which the conductors would find difficult. Group analyst Sabina Strich (2004 personal communication, following Foulkes) says 'trust the group' and in this example Faith and Emily were able to helpfully keep returning to Marie's fear of giving Chloe solids. Marie's health visitor, who had referred her, called us saying she was worried about the feeding, and obviously the other group members were concerned as well.

Given Marie's history we co-leaders might easily have been perceived as critical mothers, yet her 'group siblings' were able to help very effectively. This dynamic of mutual support moved around the group. Events like this contribute to the group's identity and increase the sense of the group being the place for therapeutic change. We know that in the early months parents have strong primitive anxieties about and towards their babies, and the group can be a safe yet powerful place in which to explore such feelings. Perhaps unsurprisingly, around the time of this example someone talked about babies being poisoned, and it was interesting how once voiced, this resonated with all of the mothers to some degree. The way in which the group process allows members to share dangerous and frightening thoughts is a major strength of analytic group therapy (see Chapter 15).

Where possible this type of intervention should be the preferred option for long-term parent–infant psychotherapy. Groups can be difficult to get started and they need the support and backing of the decision makers in an organisation, but once established a slow-open group where new members join along the way is a highly effective treatment.

Therapeutic use of video

It may seem unusual to think of a child psychotherapist using video during a clinical session. However, since the 1950s videotaping has been widely used in a variety of mental health settings (Zelenko and Benham 2000). In relation to parents and infants, researchers who were also established clinicians led the way in this new approach: Cramer and Stern (1988), Stern (1971) and Stein *et al.* (1994). Developing on from their beginnings there is now a wealth of literature describing different ways in which video can be used: Bakermans-Kranenburg *et al.* (2005), Beebe (2003), Crittenden (2001), Jones (2006) and Tucker (2006).

It can take a while to feel confident and comfortable using video but there are certain principles which I find helpful in establishing a way of incorporating video feedback into a session. First the parent has to give consent and in some situations a good therapeutic alliance may need to have been established before a parent feels comfortable with the process. However, it is not something which suits everyone. There needs to be discussion with the parent regarding their feelings about being recorded and an understanding that it is a 'joint venture' where together we are hoping to see something about their relationship with their baby. Using video fits in alongside a typical therapy session, and can be very useful for vulnerable and hard to reach parents who feel less comfortable talking about relationships. It is worth thinking about the toys which are used, as noisy rattles or the arches over baby gyms can obscure voices and faces. I always let parents know how long I will be filming and I keep quiet.

Depending on the situation and particularly with intrusive parents, I might suggest that the video will help us see things from the babies' point of view. This might mean that I introduce the parent to the idea of 'Watch Wait and Wonder' (Muir 1992), a technique where the parent is asked to let the infant take the lead and not to initiate or take over the play. On other occasions I simply ask parents to try to behave as naturally as possible.

Video feedback works best when the tape has been watched in advance and the therapist can identify certain key points of interest. When watching the video back on television it is helpful to see the parent's face (Helen Woolley 2005, personal communication) and I usually ask parents to say whatever comes to mind when watching. It might be that for a few weeks during therapy I video each session, but the frequency tends to change as we go along. I sometimes give parents still photographs or a DVD of certain significant clips of video.

I am going to briefly describe using video as part of ongoing therapeutic work with two mothers and their infants.

Nina and Archie

Nina was a mother who had experienced a very traumatic labour when giving birth to Archie. She had fourth degree tearing and needed surgery to repair damage to part of her bowel. She had been seriously depressed during her teens and suicidal and hospitalised once in her early twenties. She suffered from mild post-natal depression with her previous baby. Throughout her life she had been highly self-critical and following this harrowing delivery she could be very harsh and rejecting towards Archie. There were significant concerns about the quality of their relationship.

This is part of a feed that I filmed when Archie was seventeen months old and several months into therapy:

Archie takes a handful of rice and vegetables.
Nina: '*Yummy yummy you like that don't you?*'
Archie puts a handful in his mouth but keeping some in his hand holds his hand out towards Nina.
Nina momentarily frowns and says '*that was probably because you have a bit much*' (as if she thought he was giving her leftovers).
Archie again holds out his hand towards Nina.
Nina: '*Could you put it in your bowl?*'
Archie puts it in his mouth.
Archie puts food on a spoon and holds it towards Nina and the food tips off.
Nina: '*Oh don't worry have another go.*'
Archie takes a long drink and looks at me.
Nina: '*Good drinking.*'
Archie puts food on a spoon and puts it over the side of his bowl on the mat.
Nina: '*No, no . . . try again.*'
Archie holds the spoon towards dolly.
Nina: '*Dolly . . . dolly you want to give some to dolly? Mmm, mmm. Mmm* (Nina speaks for dolly). *Now some for Archie*' (touching his foot as if to emphasise he should have a spoonful).
Archie leans right over towards dolly with the spoon nearly making contact.
Nina: '*All for dolly? Mmm, mmm, mmm*' Nina puts dolly out of reach '*Dolly can have some later why don't you have some more?*' Nina takes a spoon to feed Archie.
Archie pushes her hand towards dolly, the food tips off the spoon.
Nina puts dolly behind her back '*Dolly's had enough now dolly's full.*'
Archie vocalises and I think I can make out a sound like he's saying '*Dolly*'.

As soon as we'd finished filming Nina was very excited and wanted to watch it again immediately. I wanted to hear more about her excitement first. She was thrilled that Archie had behaved so warmly towards the doll and felt it was real progress. Often his ambivalence meant that he could be harsh and rough towards toys, which concerned Nina, but today she saw a different side to him and it pleased her.

I decided at that point not to mention my thoughts about Archie's initial wish to feed her too. We watched the video and at the point where I thought Archie wanted to feed Nina, she spontaneously said that either Archie had tried to put too much into his mouth, or that she should have cut the food into smaller pieces, her default position being that someone had done something wrong. I then played back the beginning, and in the light of the doll play Nina saw the possibility that Archie had wanted to feed her as well. Using video was often a revelation to Nina. She saw that she and Archie did have fun and good times together and that he often smiled at her. She was very tearful when she really noticed for the first time his look of adoration.

Using video really helped Nina experience something far more benign and loving in their relationship. People sometimes think of a camera as an unforgiving persecutory third eye, so how can this help a parent whose superego is already extremely critical? Jones (2006: 110) cites Britton:

> The therapist can use watching the video with the parent to create a triangular space in which the therapist can enable the parent to observe him or herself in a relationship with their baby. This can lead to the parent being able to recognise that the baby has a point of view that is different from the parent's.
>
> (Britton 1989: 87, cited in Jones 2006: 110)

What Nina found helpful, was that in the context of our therapeutic relationship I was her 'developmental object therapist' (Hurry 1998), a supportive superego, this time with photographic evidence that her son might have wanted to feed her and do something kind and loving. Video repeatedly provided both Nina and Archie with a 'new object experience' (Baradon *et al.* 2005). We know the phrase 'the camera doesn't lie' and this was a particularly painful discovery for Nina, as she slowly came to realise that she repeatedly and negatively misattributed aspects of Archie's behaviour. She was unconsciously blaming him for the dreadful labour and delivery which they both endured, as well as for her earlier childhood family experiences.

Gemma and Thomas

Gemma had Thomas when she was seventeen. She had returned to college to take 'A' levels and Thomas was in nursery; however, the staff were worried about his repetitive play and Gemma's low mood. Thomas's favourite game was to repeatedly line up cars and he was content if left to do this, but would become distressed if asked to do anything else. When Gemma tried to play and join in with him he would go floppy, moan, and roll on the floor which meant that Gemma retreated feeling 'I can't do this'. This was the situation when we met, and Thomas was eighteen months old.

I had not been using video for very long, and suggested we give it a try and Gemma agreed. After the session I watched it through and it was painful to see how 'unconnected' they were physically and emotionally. The next week Gemma was in tears when we watched the tape; she said it was as if she saw for the first time properly that she was his mother. She said they'd had a good 'connection' when he was tiny, but that they'd lost it. I was anxious that they might not return and that the video had been too much, but the next week I was relieved to hear them chatting as they arrived. Over the next few months we regularly used video and Gemma really engaged with the process. One of the aspects she liked was that it took away the situation of me being the 'bossy therapist telling her what she was doing wrong' as she could watch the film alongside me and see and question things for herself. Thomas seemed to like it too.

As a young mother Gemma was grateful to have someone outside of the family with whom to share her worries, and after watching the first video she was immediately aware of how blank and expressionless her face could be. We were quickly then in the area of wondering what that might be like for Thomas.

Used with care, video can be like a 'third person container' (Schmidt-Neven 2004), perhaps reducing the sense of persecution a parent might have experienced in more traditional psychotherapy. This is why it is a good tool for child psychotherapists to use with hard to reach families and those who are in the Court arena. Having said that video is a powerful tool and it needs to be used carefully and sensitively; it should not be used to get a parent to 'see' something and one always needs to be mindful of identifying with a vulnerable infant and then the wish to punish the parent. Supervision from someone also experienced in using video is an advantage.

Some reflections

Parent–infant psychotherapy is a hugely rewarding and interesting area of work. In other areas of child psychotherapy we often come up against intergenerational patterns of dysfunction and so starting right at the beginning of life can give the child psychotherapist hope that they are effecting real long-term change.

Making good links with referrers is always important, as well as being able to see families quickly. Working in a small charity means that the financial situation can be uncertain and precarious, something akin to a new parent–infant relationship. This chapter has focused on the clinical applications of child psychotherapy with parents and infants rather than consultative aspects of the work.

Daws (2005) reflects on her thirty years of 'standing next to the weighing scales'. Not only has she observed and helped a great many families coming to that baby clinic but she has helped child psychotherapists and other professionals working in the field to help many more parents and infants.

References

Bakermans-Kranenburg, M. J., Van IJzendoorn, M. H. and Juffer, F. (2005) 'Discovering infant attachment and preventative interventions: A review and meta-analysis', *Infant Mental Health Journal* 26(3): 191–216.

Balbernie, R. (2001) 'Circuits and circumstances: the neurobiological consequences of early relationship experiences and how they shape later behaviour', *Journal of Child Psychotherapy* 27(3): 237–55.

Baradon, T., Broughton, C., Gibbs, I. *et al.* (2005) *The Practice of Psychoanalytic Parent–Infant Psychotherapy. Claiming the Baby*, London and New York: Routledge.

Beebe, B. (2003) 'Brief mother–infant treatment: psychoanalytically informed video feedback.' *Infant Mental Health Journal* 24(1): 24–52.

Bion, W. (1962) *Learning from Experience*, London: Heinemann.

Britton, R. (1989) 'The missing link: parental sexuality in the Oedipus Complex', in R. Britton, M. Feldman and E. O'Shaughnessy (eds) *The Oedipus Complex Today: Clinical Implications*, London: Karnac, pp. 83–101.

Crittenden, P. M. (2001) *CARE-INDEX Coding Manual 2001*, Miami, FL: Family Relations Institute.

Cramer, B. and Stern, D. (1988) 'Evaluation of changes in mother–infant brief psychotherapy: a single case study', *Infant Mental Health Journal* 9(1): 20–45.

Daws, D. (1989) *Through the Night*, Free Association Books: London.

—— (2005) 'A child psychotherapist in the baby clinic of a general practice: standing by the weighing scales thirty years on', in J. Launer, S. Blake and D. Daws (eds) *Reflecting on Reality. Psychotherapists at Work in Primary Care*, Tavistock Clinic Series. London: Karnac.

Douglas, H. (2007) *Containment and Reciprocity*, London and New York: Routledge.

Etchegoyen, A. (1997) 'Inhibition of mourning and the replacement child syndrome', in J. Raphael-Leff and R. Jozef Perelberg (eds) *Female Experience*. London and New York: Routledge.

Forrester, D. and Harwin, J. (2006) 'Parental substance misuse and child care social work: findings from the first stage of a study of 100 families', *Child and Family Social Work* 11: 325–35.

Foulkes, S. H. (1948) *Introduction to Group Analytic Psychotherapy*, London: Heinemann.

Fraiberg, S., Adelson, E. and Shapiro, V. (1980) 'Ghosts in the nursery: a psycho-analytic approach', in S. Fraiberg (ed.) *Clinical Studies in Infant Mental Health*, London: Tavistock. (Now in paperback as *Assessment and Therapy of Disturbances in Infancy*, 1989, Aronson: New York.)

Gerhardt, S. (2004) *Why Love Matters: How Affection Shapes a Baby's Brain*, Hove: Brunner-Routledge.

Hurry, A. (1998). *Psychoanalysis and Developmental Theory*, London: Karnac.

Jones, J. (2006) 'How video can bring to view pathological defensive processes and facilitate the creation of triangular space in perinatal parent-infant psychotherapy', *Journal of Infant Observation* 9(2): 109–23.

Juffer, F., Bakermans-Kranenburg, M. and van IJzendoorn, M. (2008) *Promoting Positive Parenting: An Attachment-Based Intervention*, Hove: Lawrence Erlbaum Associates.

Lewis, E. and Casement, P. (1986) 'The inhibition of mourning by pregnancy a case study', *Psychoanalytic Psychotherapy* 2(1): 45–52.

Muir, E. (1992) 'Watching, waiting and wondering: applying psychoanalytic principles to mother–infant intervention', *Infant Mental Health Journal* 13(4): 319–28.

Paul, C. and Thomson-Salo, F. (1997) 'Infant-led innovations in a mother-baby therapy group', *Journal of Psychotherapy*. 23(2): 219–44.

Raphael-Leff, J. (ed.) (2000) *'Spilt Milk': Perinatal Loss and Breakdown*, London: The Institute of Psychoanalysis.

Reid, M. (2003) 'Clinical research: the inner world of the mother and her new baby – born in the shadow of death', *Journal of Child Psychotherapy* 29(2): 207–26.

—— (2007) 'The loss of a baby and the birth of the next infant: the mother's experience', *Journal of Child Psychotherapy* 33(2): 181–201.

Sabbadini, A. (1993) 'The replacement child', *Contemporary Psychoanalysis* 24(4): 528–47.

Schmidt-Neven, R. (2004) Conference Review *AIMK(UK) Newsletter* 4:(2) 12–14.

Stein, A., Woolley, H., Cooper, S. and Fairburn, C. (1994) 'An observational study of mothers with eating disorders and their infants', *Journal of Child Psychology and Psychiatry*. 35: 733–48.

Stern, D. (1971) 'A micro-analysis of mother–infant interaction', *Journal of the American Academy of Child Psychiatry* 10: 501–7.

—— (1995) *The Motherhood Constellation*, New York: Basic Books.

Tracey, N. (2000) 'Thinking about and working with depressed mothers in the early life of their infant's life', *Journal of Child Psychotherapy* 26(2): 183–207.

Tucker, J. (2006) 'Using video to enhance the learning in a first attempt at "Watch Wait and Wonder"', *Infant Observation* 9(2): 125–38.

Zelenko, M. and Benham, A. (2000) 'Videotaping as a therapeutic tool in psychodynamic infant-parent therapy', *Infant Mental Health Journal* 21(3): 192–203.

Further reading and information

Dorman, H. and Dorman, C. (2002) *The Social Toddler*, Richmond, Surrey: CP Publishing.
Journal of Child Psychotherapy Volume 29 No 3 Special Edition: Under-Fives Work
Murray, L. and Andrews, L. (2000) *The Social Baby*, Richmond, Surrey: CP Publishing.

Oxpip (Oxford parent–infant project): www.oxpip.org.uk
Zero2three: www.zerotothree.org
The Association of Infant Mental Health (UK): www.aimh.org.uk
Alcohol Education and Research Council: www.aerc.org.uk

15 Group psychotherapy: the role of the therapist

John Woods and Katie Argent

Group therapy has been a neglected area of child and adolescent psycho-therapy. One important reason for this is the high degree of uncertainty in the role of the therapist. Much goes on for young people in groups, in the way of education and socialisation. Such groups are usually structured in terms of their activities, and have an appointed authority, teacher, youth leader or so on. Without such leadership and control the likelihood is that a given collection of young people will regress to a sort of anomie; the group tends to disintegrate, or may form a gang that finds an identity in antisocial behaviour, appointing its own leader who takes strength from opposition to adult authority. As therapists we do not usually welcome the role of manager or controller of behaviour. But non-directiveness may well be colluding with destructiveness. The group is a powerful force, for good or for ill, and it is often hard for psychodynamic work to find a place.

This problem could be seen as a microcosm of a more universal and profound conflict between the individual and the group. According to Bion (1961: 168) we are group animals 'at war with our own groupishness'. When asked to look at our relationship to that on which we depend, we become aware of a profound clash of interests. Every member of a group has ambivalence about the individual need to preserve an identity and the need for the security of belonging to a group. Thus it is that a group in action often appears to be in conflict with itself, whether about leadership, membership, or boundaries. Therapists who venture into this field are bound to feel at times in a maelstrom of powerful forces. There may be little opportunity for the 'quiet presence' of a therapist to cultivate a healing process (Lanyado 2004: 16). How can a noisy and impulsive group be a therapeutic space?

Which theoretical model?

Despite the history of having been somewhat marginalised, group work has received more attention in recent years – see for example in the UK, Reid (1999), Canham and Emanuel (2000), Canham (2002) and notably several contributions in a recent issue of the *Journal of Child Psychotherapy* (34(1)

April 2008). There is a thriving Group Workshop within the Tavistock Clinic's Child and Family Department. These bring psychoanalytic principles to group process, interpreting unconscious forces at work.

Work from the other side of the Atlantic has a somewhat different orientation, as can be seen for example from *The Journal for Specialists in Group Work* which devoted a special issue (see for example Gerrity and DeLucia-Waack 2007) to group work in schools. Here we find programmes of practical exercises for children to deal with social situations, based on models such as those established by Kehayan (1983), Riester and Kraft (1986), and Glassman and Kates (1990). These techniques, which could be called psycho-educational, for example anger management courses or bereavement counselling groups, have the advantage of providing a safe structure in the form of activities and exercises which are to an extent based on psychodynamic concepts. Such work can be 'manualised', measured in its effectiveness and so contribute more readily to evidence-based findings.

The psychoanalytic approach, by contrast, allows the group to interact spontaneously, and seeks to interpret meaning rather than direct activities – just as in one-to-one work the psychoanalytic therapist aims to follow the child's communications, not to impose values, but to reveal the inner workings of the child's mind so that interpretations can be made. This approach holds that directing activities and communications in a group according to preconceived plans may well obscure the genuine conflicts and difficulties of the child. One the other hand, an unstructured group provides considerably more opportunities for the child to enact conflicts than in individual therapy. It is much more difficult for the therapist to 'preside over the setting' as Meltzer put it (quoted by Lanyado 2004). We may find that too much freedom of expression becomes unproductive. Spontaneous expressions of the child's inner world can become impulsive reactions to provocation, whether real or imagined; children are not always kind to each other. The powerful projections of primitive states of mind that can occur are described by Canham (2002). In times of chaos it is certainly hard to maintain any sort of reverie or meditative state of mind (Lanyado 2004: 80). Earlier communications by Woods (1993, 1996) propose the need for structure and limits to contain freedom of expression, but clearly this is a difficult balance to achieve.

The role of the therapist

It is not surprising then that psychoanalytic psychotherapists experience confusion about their role in a group. In the Foulkesian tradition (which has admittedly been mostly concerned with adult groups) the therapist is known as group 'conductor' (Brown and Pedder 1979: 132). Like the conductor of an orchestra, he or she starts and finishes the whole, and is responsible for the concerted effort. Foulkes envisaged the conductor as less concerned with interpretation of meaning than with facilitating communication. He believed that there was an inherent therapeutic power in the group, which would overcome symptoms of disorder, seen as having a primarily social (or antisocial) meaning: 'The neurotic position is by its nature highly individualistic. It is group disruptive in essence, for it is genetically the result of an incompatibility between the individual and the original group, i.e. the family' (Foulkes 1964: 156). The conductor intrudes as little as possible, and only insofar as would enable participation, preventing anything that would deter good communication among group members. Interpretations by the conductor are less important in this model, just as the precise nature of transferences is less relevant than the relatedness of group members to each other. Reid puts it a different way when she says that 'becoming a group is the therapy'. Members might start out as self-centred individuals in discord with others, but move toward 'a recognition of the needs, wishes and feelings of others' (Reid 1999: 257).

Some group analysts speak about *modelling*, i.e. actively showing the group what is expected of them (Brown and Pedder 1979: 134). This can include a transference dimension. Evans (1998: chapter 9) for example demonstrates a creative use of transference interpretation, being 'real' in the here and now situation. When youngsters test limits and challenge authority, the therapist asks: are they perhaps really seeking acceptance by the group? This type of approach is certainly appropriate with adolescents, and when it comes to younger children it is also a matter of being genuine about what is going on, but in rather a different way. The adult represents (or should do) a safe and secure authority. A child from a dysfunctional family is accustomed to authority that struggles for control. A good group experience subtly loosens the tie with parents. In this process the child comes to perceive both adult and group in a different way from before; by feeling understood, he or she comes to accept authority out of choice, and is more able to relate to the group. Impulses are modified because of the inherent value in belonging, and a wish to keep a place in the group. The group in this way represents society as it exists outside the home. When an increased relatedness to the group is observed, it is a reflection of an internal change.

Getting the balance right

As well as taking adult responsibility for the safety of the setting, a group therapist needs to demonstrate genuine care and concern that each group member should feel heard and understood. A balance has to be achieved between management and interpretation, between authority and permissiveness. This cannot of course be done in a pre-packaged, false manner. The capacity to make a real response is one that is gradually developed, based on training and experience, as will be evident from the clinical illustration below. There needs to be a capacity to utilise conflicts within the group to therapeutic advantage. Children with behavioural problems often fear that their feelings and experiences are overwhelming, to themselves as much as to others. The group therapist has to integrate her own feelings and impulses, especially the tendency to use action to avoid intense emotional conflict (Lucas 1988).

Authenticity is an aim for any therapist, but in a group it is 'thinking under fire' (Bion 1982: 287). A nice example of this is presented by Maltby (2008: 89) who found herself 'set up' as some kind of counsellor who was supposed to stop unruly behaviour. Keeping her head and being able to understand the meaning of the hostile projections (which were to do with denial of certain losses) was based on a wealth of experience of working with groups of children.

Co-therapy

The opportunity to work directly with another therapist is one of the great benefits of group work. It provides an extra dimension to the thinking about each child and his needs. The therapeutic couple will inevitably be the object of projections, sometimes complex and hostile, especially from children who may never have experienced a co-operative parental couple. There is always the risk of the therapists being split, but working on the shared countertransference may be valuable and useful to the therapy (see the clinical illustration below, and also Westman (1996), Canham and Emanuel (2000), Sayder (2008)).

What the group therapist needs to know

The purpose of the group

Whereas adults, and teenagers to an extent, will share information about personal thoughts and feelings in a group, with children there needs to be a process of translation whereby behaviour and expressions of inner reality are made communicable to the rest of the group. The child shares difficult and perhaps unacceptable experiences or feelings with other group members who are perceived as having equal status and whose responses may well be more accepted than those of an adult. Group activity should be directed toward promoting interaction and the development of the child's awareness of his or her relatedness with the others. Communication, as in Foulkes's model, is fundamental. Boundaries naturally follow because bullying and hostility inevitably inhibit expression and so must be proscribed. Whereas some groups might cry out for complex and detailed rules it is usually more helpful for a group therapist to propose only one: *to do no harm*. Once there is safety to communication, then the psychodynamic work of understanding meaning can take place. It is interesting how, in the clinical example below, the group was able to elaborate on its own rule-making (the 'guidelines') as an expression of its increasing cohesiveness.

Outside forces seek to dictate the purpose of the group, usually to 'improve behaviour', and such expectations may be disappointed. Somehow the therapist has to engage with other professionals as a fellow worker seeking to understand the child, rather than being presented as some kind of expert who will (perhaps fail to) 'cure' the behavioural problem. It may well be that the group is most helpful in identifying the child who needs more special attention.

The therapist's understanding of the children

Developmental stages have to be taken into account; for example younger children cannot be expected to sit in a circle and discuss their problems. Nor might teenagers be expected to comply readily with a suggested game or shared activity. The therapist also has to have an idea which children are suitable for group therapy in general, and for his or her group in particular. There are some children who seem not to have the capacity to interact constructively with others, for example children who are murderous, psychotic or autistic. Some may not be able to use the group because of specific traumatic events or deprivations. Assessment is concerned as much with judgement about the group that is available, as about the child who is being assessed. Some groups may be able to tolerate the narcissistically damaged or withdrawn child. Doubts about suitability should be dealt with in preliminary work. An important part of preparation is the establishment of an agreed aim for the therapist (as below). If a therapeutic goal in respect of the child's relationship with other children cannot be defined and agreed upon with the child and the family, then it is likely that this child is not suitable for group therapy. Borderline cases may be helped by a short series of preparatory sessions with the group therapist.

The therapist's understanding of acting-out

Acting-out has a positive function, despite (and because of) its nuisance value. Winnicott (1956) viewed attacks on the environment (or object) as not merely an expression of destructiveness, but made in the unconscious hope of achieving a gratification that has before been denied. Unfortunately the adult who prevents 'bad' behaviour may also pre-empt the expression of difficult feelings. Children may well have had experiences of confusion, failure or despair, which have led them into disruptive or oppositional behaviour as they defend themselves with fantasies of being all powerful. The need to find a safe parental figure is likely to be unconscious, and denied. Troubling emotions, especially the suspicion that no such parent exists, have to be processed for the child in a way that facilitates a child's relinquishment of omnipotence. This has to be done gradually, by stages, and other group members may provide a transitional experience for the individual. As one child notably said, 'Hey, the group is more fun when there is no fighting!'

What to provide the group

Play, the spontaneous expression of the internal world through imagination and fantasy, is a normal method of therapeutic communication. The inability to play signifies emotional blocks or internal conflict. The group needs to learn to play together. But in contrast to one-to-one therapy, destructive elements can resonate among group members and build up momentum, so that the activities of the group may fail. Here the therapist has a responsibility not only to maintain the setting but to act as a kind of auxiliary ego (Freud 1982: 116), being at times more active and directive than in one-to-one work. Structured group activities are useful, according to the group's emotional needs of the moment: for example the therapist may judge that a shared activity is needed to bring the group together. Games involving actions or words lead on to more spontaneous communication. Rituals can become very important to the group life – for example, taking a few minutes at the end of a session for each child to comment briefly on what was enjoyable about the session, and what was not. In a well-functioning group where members feel secure, shared activities may be initiated by group members. As the group becomes more coherent, the therapist can be less directive.

Understanding the setting

The apparently simple requirement for the same room at the same time each week, free of interruptions, is essential to psychoanalytic work. This is just as necessary for group work, but will take time and effort to establish in settings other than a clinic. Partly this is due to uncertainty in professionals who may wonder what is going on. In a clinic it is easier for therapists to manage the therapeutic space. But other settings, for example a school, enable many children to benefit who would not otherwise be seen at all. Reliability of the physical space symbolises continuity for the child, and the safety from which to develop a new orientation in his or her relationship with others.

Therapeutic groups have an impact on the rest of the staff in any institution (Farrell 1984). Children's behaviour is not always completely contained, and there will be some sort of spill-over into other arenas of an institution. There may well be unrealistic fantasies about what is going on. Group therapists depend on colleagues for support in many ways, and will sometimes, as below, have to involve others. Therapists also need to represent their work in some form. Even those staff members who have nothing to do directly with a child therapy group have an important relationship to that group and its containment. When functioning well, a children's group can have a unifying and constructive influence on the whole staff in terms of self-esteem, and sense of purpose.

Clinical illustration

A psychotherapeutic children's group in a primary school

The school serves an area of long-term deprivation and disadvantage. Most of the children referred by the Special Educational Needs Co-ordinator (SENCo) came from families that had experienced traumatic upheaval and loss, including domestic violence. Some children had parents absent and/or with mental ill-health problems. Our referrals of children aged eight to eleven were not those who were at the extremes of conduct disorder or inhibition, but who nevertheless were in need of help.

Preparation took six months; the assessment process included agreements with parents and teachers setting out ideas about how a group might help, adapted from HETA, Hopes and Expectations for Treatment Agreement (Urwin 2007). For example: 'It is hard for Mark to express himself in a way that others can understand. He seems keen for us to know that it is difficult for him to put thoughts and feelings into words. We would hope to see him talking about things more.' There was ongoing contact with parents and with teachers.

My co-therapist and I (Katie Argent) are both women; my co-therapist is black, multi-lingual and her style of dress indicates that she is an observant Muslim; I am white, speak only English and my style of dress indicates that I am not religiously observant.

After a period of interruptions, absences and departures, the group expressed a strong wish for new members. The existing group was idealised, as were new members: the new group that would meet all our hopes and calm all our fears. However, the arrival of two new children precipitated explosive terror, fury and distress. My co-therapist and I found ourselves running after children up and down stairs on the way to, during and after sessions. I found myself almost bursting with vengeful anger when children repeatedly tried to abuse each other or the therapists, verbally or physically. It was not possible to think or talk about what was happening; my co-therapist and I had almost stopped trying to talk to each other in the session; we were intent on surviving by crowd control. We had fallen into isolated, blinkered, beleaguered positions: one of us feeling like retaliating with more anger, the other becoming immobilised. We agreed that the children needed ordinary, firm, clear limits around them in order to function as a group where some thinking could happen; trying to describe what was going on in terms of the worries, ambivalence, wishes and disappointment in the group was not helping, or certainly not helping enough. After a few weeks, with the help of supervision, we introduced more structure than before and this gradually helped the group to operate without violence. Aggression still simmered and sometimes boiled but on the whole we were more able to offer understanding about what was happening without amplifying the underlying fears and distress.

In the heat and upheaval of the changes in the group, my co-therapist and I had allowed ourselves not only to become split as a couple (Canham and Emanuel 2000) but also split off from helpful partnerships with the school and parents. It took some weeks and many uncomfortable conversations for us to realise that both the hatred *and* the sadness of the group must be taken into account. We discussed our difficulties with the SENCo and she agreed to join us for the beginning of a session and talk with the group about the ordinary rules of behaviour that apply everywhere in the school. We were also provided with a teaching assistant who could collect the children from the group at the end of the session and give them five minutes bridging time before going back into class.

In the weeks immediately prior to the following excerpt, my co-therapist and I had removed David on two occasions when he started hitting and verbally abusing other children, on the understanding that his place in the group was kept for him. In the earlier part of this session, David had arrived shouting about not wanting to come and protesting that the group was boring and useless. He sat far away from the others. His view was shared by Malik, while the two girls, Claire and Danielle, talked about liking the group but finding school boring, and the third boy, Kholil, said he used to think the group was boring but now that he did not have to miss football to come it was not so bad.

The main theme of David's complaint at this point seemed to be that in the group everybody had to draw and he didn't like drawing or felt he couldn't draw well. I wondered whether today David was expressing frustration on behalf of the whole group about a feeling that what the group offered, including what the therapists had to offer, was not the right thing or not enough. My co-therapist linked this to the limited number of sessions before the half-term break. Malik said that he was not coming back and that his parents were coming in to tell the SENCo that he wasn't going to be in the group any more. David said that his parents had a meeting with the SENCo today and he wasn't going to be in the group any more either. My co-therapist talked about the group remembering that we had discussed having meetings with the SENCo and their parents to think about how things are going. I added that some of the group wanted to make sure we knew about them not liking being in the group right now. David said he thought that the therapists would tell his parents that he was just having fun, which was not true. I suggested that the group was worried about what we might say; they were not sure that we would tell the truth and try to think about things properly in meetings with their parents. The group then became a little calmer and we continued with the 'angry mask' exercise we'd been doing the previous week.

My co-therapist suggested that the children might have questions for the angry masks, and that each child could answer pretending to be their mask character. David moved his chair nearer and did some black shading instead of a mask, which my co-therapist wondered about being to do with very angry feelings. Kholil found it hard initially to give his character a voice – he answered as a boy who had been asked to draw a mask of an angry face. But when he was asked by Claire why his character had such sharp teeth, after a moment's hesitation he said with conviction that it was to eat people. I talked about someone having such sharp feelings that they might want to eat people. Danielle's character was asked why it was so angry and she said it was because people were being rude and mean. The group agreed that if someone felt that people were being rude and mean to them it might make them very angry. Danielle told us that her character was a grumpy old giant who lived in a cave in the desert far away. We all talked about this being a picture of a rather lonely character, who perhaps does not believe that anyone else knows about grumpy feelings. It was quite hard to engage Malik. He got into arguments with the other children about what they were noticing or asking about his picture and my co-therapist and I intervened in the arguments several times to stop Malik from hitting out or the other children from trying to take his drawing away. However, when someone asked him what kind of a person his character was, he said that his character was dead. My co-therapist and I caught each other's eye and the children, who had anyway been finding it hard to wait and listen to each other, immediately started moving around the room. Claire and Danielle launched into raucous song. My co-therapist pointed out that no one else could speak or hear when they were that loud. I asked my co-therapist what she thought about the sudden noise and movement in the group and wondered about the impact of Malik's idea about his character being dead. My co-therapist said she thought this might have been something that worried the children. David had been getting increasingly disruptive, although he had managed to engage in a genuinely interested way earlier in the exercise. He now moved to the quiet corner from where he shouted things out abusively, aiming his remarks at Claire in particular (whose turn it now was).

Fears that there was not enough of what was wanted or needed in the group, including time and attention, dominated the group and became particularly pronounced as we approached holiday breaks. These children faced real emotional and material deficit in their lives, and being expected to share group resources felt intolerable, so they were quick to try and get out or do battle. However, supported by the school structure and links with school staff and parents, the therapists tried to address the group's worries, which enabled the children to feel a little less at risk of being blamed or got rid of and to come together as a group. Glimpses of painfully sharp feelings and loneliness that might lie behind the anger were afforded through the distance provided by character masks, which the children managed to keep thinking about until Malik's communication of stark despair. Malik seemed to express for the group a profound hopelessness, perhaps partly to do with fears about the power of destructive feelings, but also connected to a fear that at the heart of attempts to communicate with others or within oneself is a deadness. This difficulty in believing in the possibility of internal or external live company (Alvarez 1992) struck a raw group nerve. Impressively, even at this point in the session, David succeeded in getting himself to the quiet corner, rather than lashing out physically.

In subsequent sessions, the children talked about wanting respect and we wrote on a flipchart their descriptions of what respect would look like – listening, being sympathetic, being polite – which then became a set of guidelines that we referred to. This group needed the guidelines to be out in the open. David contributed 'being sympathetic' to these guidelines and, while often himself a key player in group mayhem, he sometimes took on the role of reminding the group of the guidelines they themselves had drawn up. He gradually stopped making himself the conduit for aggression or someone on the edge of exclusion. He grew a little more able to look at his own behaviour towards others and the way in which his claims of unfair treatment meant that he could miss out on being part of something he might enjoy.

After 18 months the group was facing its end. In one session at this time they talked about the different languages that each of them spoke. They took it in turns to tell words from their own languages. We commented on the fact that there were differences here that could be shared, like the thoughts that could be shared in the group, but, as had sometimes happened, differences could also be used to shut other people out. It seemed that by this point the children were able to deal with the ending not by treating the group as rubbish, but by helping each other to see the value in what each of them had brought to the group.

Conclusion

Group psychotherapy is not suitable for every child and more work needs to be done to establish which children are best helped in different modes of treatment. For children who are well selected a group experience is a powerful and effective method of producing observable, as well as internal change. It is a useful provision so that individual psychotherapy may then be reserved for those children who have a particular need for this. We have tried to show how the non-directive stance of the psychotherapist can be adapted to answer the need for the active presence of adult authority. This is because anxieties are amplified by the group and would otherwise overtake the group process. Although the transference relationship with the therapist may be less explicitly interpreted than in individual work, it is crucial to the treatment. By this means children form an attachment to the group, establish relationships with appropriate limits, and develop in their intrapsychic as well as interpersonal world.

Acknowledgement

Thanks to Fadumo Osman-Ahmed, the co-therapist of the children's group presented here.

References

Alvarez, A. (1992) *Live Company. Psychoanalytic Psychotherapy with Autistic, Borderline, Deprived and Abused Children*, London, Tavistock/Routledge.

Bion, W. R. (1961) *Experiences in Groups*, London: Tavistock.

—— (1982) *The Long Weekend 1897–1919; Part of a Life*, Abingdon: Fleetwood Press.

Brown, D. and Pedder, J. (1979) *Introduction to Psychotherapy*, London: Tavistock.

Canham, H. (2002) 'Group and gang states of mind', *Journal of Child Psychotherapy* 28(2): 113–27.

Canham, H. and Emanuel, L. (2000) 'Tied together feelings. Group psychotherapy with latency children: the process of forming a cohesive group', *Journal of Child Psychotherapy* 26(2): 281–302.

Evans, J. (1998) *Active Analytic Group Therapy for Adolescents*, London: Jessica Kingsley.

Farrell, M. (1984) 'Group work with children: The significance of setting a context', *Group Analysis* 17(2): 146–55.

Foulkes, S. H. (1964) *Therapeutic Group Analysis*, London: Allen & Unwin.

Freud, A. (1982) *Psychoanalytic Psychology of Normal Development*, London: Hogarth Press.

Gerrity D. A. and DeLucia-Waack, J. (2007) 'Effectiveness of groups in the schools', *The Journal for Specialists in Group Work* 32(1): 97–102.

Glassman, U. and Kates, L. (1990) *Group Work: A Humanistic Approach*, New York: Sane.

Kehayan, A. (1983) *Self Awareness Growth Experiences*, California: Winch.

Lanyado, M. (2004) *The Presence of the Therapist: Treating Childhood Trauma*, Hove and New York: Brunner-Routledge.

Lucas, T. (1988) 'Holding and holding on: using Winnicott's ideas in group psychotherapy with 12–13 year olds', *Group Analysis* 21(2): 135–50.

Maltby, J. (2008) 'Consultation in schools: helping staff and pupils with unresolved loss and mourning', *Journal of Child Psychotherapy* 34(1): 83–100.

Reid, S. (1999) 'The group as a healing whole: group psychotherapy with children and adolescents', in M. Lanyado and A. Horne (eds) *The Handbook of Child and Adolescent Psychotherapy: Psychoanalytic Approaches*, London: Routledge.

Riester, A. E. and Kraft, I. A. (eds) (1986) *Child Group Psychotherapy*, New York: International Universities Press.

Sayder, S. (2008) 'Joining up with "not us" staff to run adolescent groups in schools', *Journal of Child Psychotherapy* 34(1): 111–26.

Urwin, C. (2007) 'Revisiting "What Works for Whom?" A qualitative framework for evaluating effectiveness in child psychotherapy', *Journal of Child Psychotherapy* 33(2): 134–60.

Westman, A. (1996) 'Cotherapy and re-parenting in a group for disturbed children', *Group Analysis* 29(1): 55–68.

Winnicott, D. W. (1956) 'The anti-social tendency', in D. W. Winnicott *Collected Papers: Through Paediatrics to Psychoanalysis*, London: Hogarth Press, 1975.

Woods, J. (1993) 'Limits and structure in child group psychotherapy', *Journal of Child Psychotherapy* 19(1): 63–78.

—— (1996) 'Handling violence in child group therapy', *Group Analysis* 29(1): 81–98.

16 Working within schools and alternative educational settings

Claudia McLoughlin

An overview of the British education system

In the UK, a child's state education usually starts with nursery provision around three years of age, with children entering a more formal learning environment at reception stage, at age five. Children then attend primary school for six years until the age of eleven, at which stage they have to transfer to a larger secondary school for a further five years, taking them up to the age of sixteen years. There is a current debate in government whether to raise the compulsory school age to eighteen years. A broad-ranging National Curriculum is adhered to by all schools, with attainment in the key subjects of English, Maths and Science being measured at regular intervals. Some secondary schools teach mixed ability classes, others group pupils according to their academic attainment. At sixteen, adolescents either go into the sixth form or are encouraged to move on to further education colleges which cater for the full range of abilities and often offer vocational training courses alongside more academic subjects. From there, young people can enter university or the world of work. Average class sizes throughout the years tend to be around thirty children.

'Inclusion for all' – meaning an effort to keep all children in mainstream education – has been government policy for many years, and as a result only a small number of Special Schools have remained open to cater for the needs of those children unable to access mainstream education, either due to their learning, developmental or emotional and behavioural difficulties. Special Schools also follow the National Curriculum, albeit often modified to meet their pupils' specific needs, and administered in much smaller classes of around eight to ten children per teacher and teaching assistant. There are also a small number of day and residential schools for children with severe and multiple learning and developmental difficulties. In addition to state provision, there are private, fee-paying schools which some wealthier parents choose to send their children to, particularly at secondary level. These are often selective in terms of academic ability.

As an interim measure for those pupils who have either been excluded or are refusing to attend their mainstream schools because of emotional and behavioural difficulties, Pupil Referral Units have been established nation-wide. These are small, often chronically under-resourced local centres staffed by teachers and teaching assistants, with the stated aim of assessing these pupils' educational needs within two school terms and of facilitating their reintegration into mainstream education via a strict behavioural pro-gramme within that timeframe. In actual fact, though, this often proves to be an impossible task, as many of these children are conduct disordered and are unable to adjust to the behavioural boundaries required of them in secondary school in particular. As a result, some pupils remain in a Pupil Referral Unit for years, or move on from one to the next rather than ever re-entering mainstream education. The government is currently in the process of reviewing this part of state education provision in an attempt to develop a more effective form of provision for this very troubled minority of children and young people.

A brief history of child psychotherapy provision in educational settings

East London and Glasgow pioneered the provision of what used to be called 'Child Guidance Clinics' in the years after the First World War, in response to children having been traumatised by losses and separations during the war. These clinics were traditionally staffed by a psychiatrist, an educational psychologist and a social worker, in order to address all three aspects of the children's and their families' difficulties in a joined up team approach. The idea re-emerged after the Second World War, and the existing British psychoanalytic child psychotherapy trainings emerged from this context, as did what are now called CAMHS (Child and Adolescent Mental Health Services) as part of the NHS. It is sobering to reflect that following a long and chequered history of child and adolescent mental health provision over the last century, government policy is now returning to the same simple yet common sense concept of coherent, multi-agency service provision (cf. 'Every Child Matters' (DfES 2004), 'The National Service Framework' (DoH 2004)).

A currently quite controversial setting (because of their relatively high cost and present lack of measurable outcome of their effectiveness) where child psychotherapists have traditionally been and still are an integral part of the core staff group are therapeutic boarding schools or communities (e.g. Mulberry Bush School, Cotswold Community). A number of such residential schools were set up from the 1950s onwards in Britain, often run by charismatic and highly committed individuals drawing on the theories of Donald Winnicott in particular. They cater for emotionally highly disturbed children who have grown up in very abusive and neglectful families who were found to be unable to adequately cater for their emotional needs. Places at these schools are often jointly funded by Health, Social Services and Education, with child psychotherapists providing a mixture of staff support through supervision and case discussion groups, and individual psychotherapy onsite for the children. The philosophy behind the project of educating these very damaged children within a 'therapeutic milieu' where they could rebuild their trust in the possibility of benign relationships has been articulated most clearly by Barbara Dockar-Drysdale (1990). In a recent, education themed issue of the *Journal of Child Psychotherapy* (April 2008), Graham, and Midgley have described two very interesting early examples of experimental, therapeutic residential schools, for readers interested in further researching this area (Graham 2008; Midgley 2008).

In London during the days of the Inner London Education Authority (ILEA) providing a coherent and innovative service in all Inner London Boroughs, a full child mental health team consisting of a child psychiatrist, a child psychotherapist and what was then called a psychiatric social worker were part of the staff team of each special school 'for maladjusted children', as they were then known. Usually the child psychotherapist saw children for psychotherapy onsite in the school, with the psychiatric social worker meeting with the parent/s alongside this treatment, and the psychiatrist leading the mini-team. Detailed consultation to staff on therapeutic teaching methods and classroom management around particular children was also offered. Sadly this provision ceased with the dismantling of ILEA in 1990, and big spending cuts in this area of provision.

Outreach work into education since then has consisted mainly in isolated initiatives mostly in primary schools, Special Schools and Pupil Referral Units, of child psychotherapists providing regular consultation to the management and/or staff group about the children's emotional needs. These have sometimes been multidisciplinary too, with staff from local CAMHS commissioned by particular schools to provide this service. There have also been experiments with running small therapeutic groups in primary schools over the years, particularly by the Tavistock Clinic, as part of their pre-clinical training programme. Some child psychotherapists are employed by particular schools to provide a school-based psychotherapy service to individual pupils, and carry this work out as lone practitioners. They may also offer supervision and/or consultation to school counsellors and learning mentors as part of their role.

Only in the past five or six years have there been more comprehensive discussions in some places between what are now called CAMHS (Child and Adolescent Mental Health Services) and the Education Service, about the idea of Child Mental Health Outreach provision in mainstream schools. Historically, these discussions came out of longstanding frustrations on both sides about a perceived lack of communication and effective collaboration between the two agencies.

This chapter will mainly draw on the author's experience over the past five years in helping set up an innovative, multidisciplinary CAMHS Outreach Service in an Inner London Borough's nine secondary schools and three Pupil Referral Units (PRUs). The author will also make reference to other examples of child psychotherapists working in schools she has heard about through liaison with colleagues and through reading their papers. This is currently a recognised cutting edge area of service development within both CAMHS and Education, with the emphasis moving away from CAMHS offering expert consultation at one remove, to CAMHS and Education staff working in partnership in each school, jointly working out the most effective service model for their particular setting. All names and identifying details have been changed in the clinical examples contained in this chapter.

An evolving Inner London CAMHS in Education model, and the particular place of child and adolescent psychotherapy within it

The secondary school based service

After small, tentative beginnings as a pilot project within the clinic-based CAMHS, a separate, multidisciplinary Outreach Service now exists in the author's workplace in an Inner London Borough, with one child psychotherapist or clinical psychologist offering one day per week clinical time to each of the nine secondary schools there. Each school commits themselves to providing a reasonably private room suitable for therapeutic consultations with pupils and their families, and a link person who refers pupils to the clinician – this is usually the head of the school's Learning Support Centre which devises support programmes for those pupils finding it difficult to cope in lessons. In some schools, the clinician is able to take part in regular multi-agency meetings, where Heads of Year discuss pupils they are experiencing difficulties with. These meetings may also be attended by the Special Educational Needs Coordinator, the Educational Psychologist, Education Welfare Officer, School Counsellor, Careers Adviser, School Police Officer and School Social Worker. Meetings like these have proven to be very helpful for coordinated planning around the pupils' often multiple and complex needs which may well require a joint approach by more than one professional.

A school clinician's day is usually taken up with a mixture of meetings like the one described above, an informal drop-in time when education staff can access the clinician for advice on particular pupils' emotional and mental health issues, and appointments for specific, ongoing cases. Clinical work around referred pupils always begins with a family assessment of up to five sessions and is then followed where viable by specific interventions either with individual pupils, their parents or the family – whichever approach seems most helpful in any given case. The length of intervention can vary between short-, medium- or long-term, according to clinical need. Clinicians hold a case load of four or five cases on average, have individual waiting lists where necessary and are fairly autonomous in their decision making around their own cases. All school clinicians receive fortnightly supervision by the Service Coordinator. A Health Service file is kept for each case, with regular letters to the family's GP about the work carried out. Progress with each case is also regularly discussed with the referrer and other relevant school staff.

Clinical work is usually applied work rather than 'pure' psychotherapy, even when working longer term with individual pupils. The reasons for this are twofold: first, the rooms supplied by schools do not usually offer the necessary full confidentiality and reliability of a clinic-based room – teachers may inadvertently walk in, or the room may suddenly be needed at short notice for another purpose, e.g. end of year exams etc. Second and perhaps more importantly, sessions are 45 minutes long, like a lesson, and pupils are expected to return to their next lesson immediately following a therapeutic session. This means that the therapist has to pay particular attention to making this transition manageable for the young person. In addition, pupils often ask their therapists to help mediate school-based, conflicted or problematic situations with the relevant teachers. In that way, school-based therapists operate predominantly on the boundary between their patients' external and internal worlds, with the task of interpreting across that boundary both ways as and when needed. Here are some examples of the kind of work child psychotherapists have carried out in their respective schools.

Gradual engagement of a complex parent case

I was asked to see the mother of a student who had not been long at the school where I worked. Whilst the student herself was seeing the school counsellor for worries of her own, one of these worries was her mother who seemed to be very needy. The daughter was carrying the burden of this. Neither mother nor daughter seemed to be able to tolerate coming together at this point, and so I began an assessment of mother during which I discovered that she had deep-seated and longstanding mental health difficulties with their origin in an emotionally cold upbringing, compounded by parental alcohol abuse and domestic violence. She had run away from home as a student aged 17 and had begun a relationship with a fellow student from a different culture whom she had perceived as even needier than herself. These two 'babes in the wood' had married and had two daughters, whom she was deter-mined to bring up in quite a different way from herself. This perceived need to bring her children up with the warmth and affection she herself had been denied led to a symbiotic relationship with the youngest of her daughters (the needy baby whom mother felt herself unconsciously to be) whilst she perceived the elder daughter – who was seeing the school counsellor – as possessing many of the qualities of her father, from whom mother was now separated. The jealousy and competitiveness for mother's love was extreme between the two sisters.

As I explored some of these difficulties with mother, it was apparent that she was aware of her own mental health difficulties, and she decided that she wanted me to refer her for psychotherapy, which I did. I continued to work with her, however, on a weekly basis, on her relationship with her elder daughter. For a long while she was highly defensive, feeling she was the 'expert', whilst projecting her more needy and disturbed aspects into her daughter and into various men she became involved with. At these times I often felt I was on a knife's edge between alienating her by holding on to my views about what was needed for her daughter in terms of parenting and, if I did not assert my view, silently colluding with her view that her daughter, like her father in mother's view, suffered from a 'disorder' such as AD/HD or Asperger's syndrome, and therefore needed a diagnosis and 'psychiatric treatment'.

At a Christmas break when mother became acutely depressed and admitted that she was unable to think about her daughter's difficulties as she was overwhelmed by her own, I made referrals to the local Community Mental Health Team and to Social Services, as I feared she was becoming unable to manage basic parenting tasks without a lot of support. The crisis and the Christmas break were weathered, and mother gradually became able to tolerate a more realistic view of her daughter's needs as being different from her own. She began to see the need for boundaries between the generations and saw that she could, with support, provide a much needed firm paternal function as well as a nurturing maternal one. This was in contrast to the more sibling-like relationship, alternately loving and competitive, that had existed previously.

This change is not yet securely established and much more work is still needed. However, progress could be seen, as both mother and daughter are now better able to tolerate a coming together: they recently accepted the idea of a referral of the whole family into the local CAMHS clinic and are now regularly attending appointments there.

There is also scope for group interventions in school-based work – here is one example.

An 'anti-bullying group' experiment

Bullying was a major problem at the boys' school I worked in, and I was asked repeatedly for advice by education staff as to how to tackle bullying situations sensitively yet firmly. There was a recognition that it was often not a simple matter of victims and perpetrators, but that these roles could switch, e.g. with vulnerable pupils being bullied by older students and then passing the experience on to younger and even more vulnerable boys. Gradually the idea of a weekly, psychodynamic group emerged as worth trying with a small, mixed age group of boys who were at times victims, at others perpetrators of bullying.

It proved impossible at the time to find a suitable co-worker amongst the school staff, so I ran this group on my own for two school terms. It consisted of six boys between the ages of eleven and thirteen. We met once weekly, and a focus was provided in that the boys had been told by their teachers that this was 'the anti-bullying group'. I also quite soon introduced some structure in the form of providing a notebook for each boy to write and draw in, as it usually took them a long time at the beginning of each weekly meeting to relax enough to talk freely. I encouraged them to say whatever came to mind, not necessarily only things directly related to bullying. Topics raised included friendship, fear, power and status. The boys themselves suggested some role-play towards the end of the group, and we jointly devised a very interesting exercise in two groups of three, with boys alternating playing the roles of victims, perpetrators and bystanders of a typical bullying incident in the playground, and then reflecting on their emotional experiences in each of the roles. Three of the boys' behaviour in the playground changed quite dramatically for the better over the course of the group. One boy dropped out because he felt too persecuted and singled out. The other two reported some positive insights into their own and other boys' behaviour at the end of the group, and had formed a tentative friendship. Most of the boys wished that the group could continue, and expressed a hope that something similar would be offered to them again.

For readers interested in exploring this area further, the education themed issue of the *Journal of Child Psychotherapy* (April 2008), mentioned above, includes papers by Music and by Sayder (Music and Hall 2008; Sayder 2008) describing different methods of working therapeutically in schools, whilst papers by Maltby and by Jackson in the same journal discuss two models of consulting to school staff groups (Maltby 2008; Jackson 2008).

Work in Pupil Referral Units

The three PRUs the author's Service works in cater for an average of twenty-five pupils each, at any one time. Most pupils will have been permanently excluded from their mainstream schools for severe and persistent aggressive and disruptive behaviour which did not respond to the usual behaviour management methods employed by the school. Some will be prone to violence towards peers and/or adults, and either have or would warrant a psychiatric diagnosis of conduct disorder. A high proportion of pupils suffer from AD/HD type symptoms and may or may not have a formal diagnosis. Many come from emotionally deprived and dysfunctional family backgrounds, frequently with high levels of Social Services involvement.

The PRUs attempt to assess, teach and reintegrate these children through an intensive learning and behavioural programme administered in small classes of six to eight children, with a teacher and teaching assistant per class. Underfunding and the teaching staff's very low status have been chronic features of the Units. Both the staff and the pupils and their families tend to perceive them as a dumping ground for children who have been rejected by the mainstream education system. This in turn mirrors many of the families' social exclusion from mainstream society in terms of material prosperity and social acceptability.

The most crucial and difficult task for PRU-based clinicians has proven to be their ability to stay in the uncomfortable place at the boundary of their setting – i.e. not to join the staff team, yet not to be too remote from their concerns either. The fear of being rejected and excluded unless one colludes and complies with the status quo reverberates through all levels of relationships throughout the PRUs, and one has to be extremely resilient to withstand these powerful projections. Anton Obholzer's ideas (1994) have been very useful in helping us make sense of these dynamics. For that reason our Service has evolved the model of placing two clinicians (where possible from two different disciplines) in each PRU, so that they can establish a mini CAMHS team onsite and support and complement each other in their work. This also seemed a good starting point in view of the fact that these children and their families are notoriously difficult to engage therapeutically and to work with effectively.

Instead of operating a referral system, in the PRUs we have found through trial and error that the most effective way of working is to screen and if indicated assess each new pupil entering a PRU, as part of their induction process. Sometimes a child and family will already be involved in ongoing therapeutic work at the local CAMHS clinic-based service, in which case only liaison work will be needed. However, more often than not we find that these families either have never sought any professional help before, or have repeatedly dropped out of the clinic-based service through non-attendance. When managing to engage these families, we often hear a litany of their negative experiences with professionals, and a resulting lack of trust in their potential helpfulness. Clinicians have to work hard to overcome this formidable barrier, going out of their way to show that they are willing to start where the family are at. This may mean carrying out home visits initially, until a basic willingness to attend PRU-based appointments becomes established over time. Despite the challenges described, clinical work in PRUs can be extremely rewarding, particularly if a clinician does manage to engage and help a family against the odds. Geoffrey Baruch's work at the Brandon Centre inspired us with its innovative technical ideas of how to work with hard to engage young people in community settings, as well as its use of the Achenbach Child Behaviour Checklist as a clinically useful outcomes measure (Baruch 2001).

As in the school-based service, clinical work is generic and applied, although it may well include longer-term individual work with a child as well as parent or family work. Psychodynamic group-work has been tried, but the children found the lack of structure too challenging. Unfortunately, research (Rutter, 1985) has shown the propensity for groups of conduct-disordered children to form a delinquent gang, bringing the worst out in each other rather than helping each other change. This of course raises the more general question as to whether it can ever be effective to educate these children together in the small, intensive, group-based setting of a PRU. However, some touchingly positive interactions between pupils have been observed by teaching staff when the cohort of their pupils have included some more vulnerable and withdrawn children. Clinicians are currently exploring the option of offering a PRU-based parent group.

Here are some examples of the work of PRU-based child and adolescent psychotherapists:

Assessment and referral on

James was a fifteen-year-old boy who suffered from extreme temper outbursts that led to prolonged aggressive and disruptive behaviour. At times during these outbursts he seemed to be dissociated and he described not remembering the details of what had just happened. According to his mother he had had these difficulties since the family had suffered a serious car accident when he was two years old. James lived in a single parent household with his mother and several younger siblings. In the past there had been multiple referrals to Tier 3 CAMHS but the family had never managed to engage in a sustained way.

In my assessment it was clear that the need for containment for the family was paramount, as mother seemed extremely anxious and angry about her son's situation and was poised to battle with professionals because of a string of previous frustrations with the service she had received in the past. Further to this, the car crash seemed to activate an anxious state between mother and son which seemed to heighten as they talked about it. There was a clear wish in both mother and son for James' behaviour to be understood, and a feeling that this understanding was to be achieved by reflecting on the past. This was symbolically represented in the assessment material by James' association to the assessing clinician as a time travelling scientist or doctor figure, and also material from him about looking back down the road or having perspective.

James also brought material connected to being put in the proper place and also about families being held together within clear and containing boundaries. This was possibly connected to several unsettling factors in his life: his place in his mother's mind amongst his other siblings; his status as the problem child within the family; the uncertainty of father figures staying in the family; the instability of his school placements; and lastly his mother's tendency to be emotionally overwhelmed at times, and so becoming an uncontaining figure for the family.

The male assessing clinician also felt that James' interest in self-exploration, quite unusual in a child attending the PRU, was perhaps connected to his complex feelings around the absent and often unavailable father, particularly in the context of James' adolescent development. Primarily and most importantly for the assessment it seemed beyond doubt that James showed an extraordinary readiness to think about himself, and was highly motivated to change. On the basis of this assessment a referral for psychotherapy was made for James at the Tier 3 clinic, and at the time of writing this work is holding and proceeding well. Work with a psychologist around post-traumatic stress was also discussed with the family, but it was felt that this could be left as a future option, allowing for one clear intervention at a time.

A piece of short-term mother and child work

Tom (aged fourteen) had been at the PRU for more than a year before the PRU social worker and I finally succeeded in engaging the family in a coherent piece of short-term work of five fortnightly sessions with Tom and his mother together. Before this there had been many failed attempts at engaging Tom individually, his mother as a parent and the whole family together in the local clinic-based CAMHS service. The family pattern was to seek help in a crisis and then quickly withdraw. The five joint sessions took place in the summer term, when both Tom and his mother had become extremely anxious about his possible referral on to another PRU at the end of the academic year. Several attempts at mainstream reintegration had failed, mostly through Tom sabotaging himself just at the point where things looked very encouraging. My colleague and I decided that in the limited time available we would try to focus entirely on trying to make sense of this dynamic with mother and son, to which they readily agreed. It took a while for Tom to emerge from a sulky silence, but when he did, he showed a surprising capacity for insight. He realised with our help that he was frightened of losing the protective setting of his present PRU where he had felt helped and understood, and that this was compelling him to 'mess it up for myself' back in mainstream school. His mother was surprised by her son's articulate thoughtfulness, and also by how much he cared – both about school and about how his family perceived him, and the worry he was causing them. She had never seen this side of him before, and subsequently significantly softened in her own attitude towards him. Tom did eventually manage to secure a full-time place in a new mainstream school for the following term, with his learning mentor's help who reassured him that he would continue to receive support from him there over the first half-term, to help him settle in.

In addition to their clinical work with the children and their families, two child psychotherapists have recently started offering a fortnightly Tavistock Model Work Discussion Group to one of the PRU staff teams. The staff team meets fortnightly, with staff members taking turns in bringing either a written or verbal detailed interaction with a particular pupil or group of pupils. We use this presentation as a starting point for reflection on the dynamics involved in the situation, which may in turn lead to wider discussions of the emotional impact of the children's disturbance on staff members. After initial reluctance and some cynicism, this intervention has been well received by education staff, who in a recent review identified a number of specific positive gains they felt had resulted from the group:

- They felt grateful for a regular thinking and talking space without an agenda, where they could freely express their own often difficult and frustrated feelings around working with such troubled and challenging children day-in, day-out.

- They felt they could learn from each other and from the child psycho-therapists as to how to respond more effectively and sensitively to particular children.
- They felt that through 'having the child already in their minds' during the week following a work discussion, this then made their task of reviewing that same child's individual education and pastoral plan the following week much easier.

Clinicians are beginning to find that direct work with children and families and staff work discussion groups are a very potent and effective combination of interventions, through providing a measure of emotional containment to both staff and pupils. Work discussion groups also foster an atmosphere of all of us working alongside each other in genuine partner-ship, trying to help these hard to reach children and families.

Readers interested in finding out more about therapeutic work in PRUs should refer to Malberg who discusses the dynamics of exclusion versus inclusion in particular (Malberg 2008).

Conclusion

In this chapter the author has described a relatively new arena that child and adolescent psychotherapists are currently moving into – that of forming Child Mental Health Outreach 'mini clinics' onsite in schools and other educational settings. There are indications that this is an expanding field, with many schools and education services expressing an interest in commissioning this type of service from their local CAMHS clinics. Gabrielle Crockatt described child psychotherapists using a number of applied ways of working in multidisciplinary clinic teams, in Chapter 7. Our team has found that all of these methods can be adapted successfully for use in educational settings: specialist psychodynamic assessments, group-work, brief counselling and joint working with Education colleagues onsite.

In the author's view there are a number of unique qualities and skills child psychotherapists can bring to this work, to complement other thera-peutic disciplines:

- Child psychotherapists do not usually expect quick, visible changes and results and are able to bear the uncertainty of sometimes not knowing for quite some time whether or how they can help a par-ticular child or family. This can be helpful in withstanding rather than colluding with the pressure from schools and teachers to quickly 'fix' the problem child, which is of course impossible.
- Child psychotherapists are specifically trained to understand uncon-scious mental processes, and contain extreme and often irrational emotions as they arise in the clinical encounter. This skill is particularly useful when working in PRUs, to help understand and contain the

children's and families' as well as staff's feelings, and the complex dynamics that inevitably arise amongst and between pupils, parents and staff, due to the severity and often distressing nature of the children's needs, which are often linked to child protection concerns and inadequate parenting. Isca Salzberger-Wittenberg *et al.* (1983) and later Peter Wilson (2004) and Biddy Youell (2006) have eloquently described how dysfunctional attachment and relationship patterns in the family can be enacted and repeated in the education setting, and have suggested that a deep understanding and bringing into consciousness of these dynamics can have a beneficial impact on new relationships and situations the child enters into.

• Being trained in an unstructured, non-directive and open-ended therapeutic method can contribute to child psychotherapists using a flexible approach in their therapeutic encounters with a wide variety of children and families, and to be willing to be guided in their starting point and technique by what each particular child, parent or family can tolerate at that moment in time. This can be particularly helpful when trying to engage people who due to adverse life experiences find it difficult to ask for or accept therapeutic help.

Acknowledgement

I would like to thank Ruth Seglow and Mark Carter, my child psychotherapy colleagues in the CAMHS Education Service, for their contribution of case examples to bring this chapter alive. Many thanks also to Sue Coulson and Monica Lanyado for their helpful comments on earlier versions of this chapter.

References

Baruch, G. (ed.) (2001) *Community-Based Psychotherapy with Young People – Evidence and Innovation in Practice*, Hove: Brunner-Routledge.

Department for Education and Skills, DfES (2004) *Every Child Matters*, London: HMSO.

Department of Health, DoH (2004) *The National Service Framework for Children, Young People and Maternity Care*, London: HMSO.

Dockar-Drysdale, B. (1990) *The Provision of Primary Experience. Winnicottian Work with Children and Adolescents*, London: Free Association Books.

Graham, P. (2008) 'Susan Isaacs and the Malting House School', *Journal of Child Psychotherapy* 34(1): 5–22.

Jackson, E. (2008) 'The development of work discussion groups in educational settings', *Journal of Child Psychotherapy* 34(1): 62–82.

Malberg, N. (2008) 'Refusing to be excluded: finding ways of integrating psychotherapeutic modalities to the emerging needs of a pupil referral unit', *Journal of Child Psychotherapy* 34(1): 101–10.

Maltby, J. (2008) 'Consultation in schools: helping staff and pupils with unresolved loss and mourning', *Journal of Child Psychotherapy* 34(1): 83–100.

Midgley, N. (2008) 'The "Matchbox School" (1927–1932): Anna Freud and the idea of a "psychoanalytically informed education"', *Journal of Child Psychotherapy* 34(1): 23–42.

Music, G. with Hall, B. (2008) 'From scapegoating to thinking and finding a home: delivering therapeutic work in schools', *Journal of Child Psychotherapy* 34(1): 43–61.

Obholzer, Anton (ed.) (1994) *The Unconscious at Work*, London: Routledge.

Rutter, M. (1985) 'Psychosocial therapies in child psychiatry: issues and prospects', in M. Rutter and L. Hersov (eds) *Child and Adolescent Psychiatry: Modern Approaches*, 2nd edn, Oxford: Blackwell.

Salzberger-Wittenberg, I., Henry, G. and Osborne, E. (1983) *The Emotional Experience of Teaching and Learning*, London: Routledge and Kegan Paul.

Sayder, S. (2008) 'Joining up with "not us" staff to run adolescent groups in schools', *Journal of Child Psychotherapy* 34(1): 111–26.

Wilson, P. (2004) *Young Minds in Our Schools: A Guide for Teachers and Others Working in Schools*, London: Karnac.

Youell, B. (2006) *The Learning Environment*, London: Karnac.

17 The challenges of in-patient work in a therapeutic community

Denis Flynn

This chapter looks at how formal psychoanalytic psychotherapy, with its emphasis on the transference and the inner world, takes place within a therapeutic community at the Cassel Hospital and orientates itself to some of the realities of a specialist in-patient treatment setting. Here both adult and child psychotherapists and nurses work closely and intensively together. Although starting from different theoretical backgrounds and using different methods of intervention, the work of each discipline can inform and enrich the other. There is some sharing of information and of thinking so that, in terms of overall aim and purpose, there is a coming together to treat very difficult patients who may not be treatable elsewhere.

Despite the complexities of this setting, one can see that there are aspects of the overall work which are distinctively psychoanalytic. We can see that in the therapeutic community there are different issues from elsewhere for the child psychotherapist about the use of information and about the understanding of fantasy and reality. It is important for the child psychotherapist, as it is for other workers, to know and work with the patients' perception, adjustment to and conflict about the in-patient setting, and the affective impact of their experience, in particular, the psychodynamic processes operating amongst the patients and in the staff groups (Flynn 1998). The child psychotherapist needs to understand not just the disturbed child or adolescent as they are seen in the individual psychotherapy session, but to learn to deal with tensions about roles between workers and to tolerate severe infantile projections, often of hostility and despair, as they affect them personally. Such efforts by the staff to tolerate primitive psychological processes parallels the efforts of severely disturbed and traumatised patients to tolerate and to work through their problems.

History

The Cassel Hospital was founded after the First World War to treat patients who suffered conditions in civilian life which were similar to the 'shell-shock' which many soldiers had suffered in the war, but which were distinct from the most severe mental conditions, usually psychoses, that were treated in the old asylums, or psychiatric hospitals. Like other treatment institutions in Britain, such as the forerunners of today's Child Guidance Clinics, in the inter-war years the Cassel Hospital developed types of treatment influenced by developments in psychology and, in particular, in psychoanalysis. There is today a pervasive sense of continuity and history from this time, and indeed one of the units within the Cassel, the Families Unit, is still referred to colloquially as 'Ross', after the pioneering work of the consultant of one of the units in the 1930s. In 1948, when the Cassel Hospital had moved from Kent to its present site on Ham Common, in Richmond, Surrey, Dr Tom Main was appointed as Medical Director and, with Doreen Waddell, who was appointed matron – both of whom became psychoanalysts – there was a creative period of twenty-five years in which psychoanalytic psychotherapy was developed in an in-patient context, alongside psychosocial nursing in a therapeutic community.

Since this time there has been a continuous flow of ideas and personnel between the Cassel and the other major institutions involved in psycho-analytical training in Britain. Tom Main, like Wilfred Bion and a number of influential army psychiatrists, who were to become famous subsequently as psychoanalysts, group analysts and social researchers, had worked with soldiers with psychological problems which incapacitated them from active service – problems of morale and of rehabilitation into civilian society, back to work and family. One of the central ideas of this movement of thinking was that individuals, groups and organisations, if given the freedom and responsibility for organising and undertaking work in their own environment, would respond, have more human purpose and fulfilment, and individual problems, including formerly debilitating psychological problems, would be seen in a new light or indeed lose much of their debilitating effect. There are many telling continuities over this time: in how a type of hospital treatment, developed as a 'tool' to help 'shell-shocked' civilians with the devastation of their lives, that reflected the break-ups and devastation of war, is now used with our current problems of the devastating break-ups of family life and relationships, following serious problems of abuse and mental illness; in how rehabilitation of soldiers after war gives way now to rehabilitation of families after family breakdown; in how problems of morale facing the terrors of conflict in war gives way now to problems of morale amongst the staff and patients in a therapeutic community facing the pain, tensions and fears of those suffering severe borderline conditions which affect all aspects of daily functioning and routine.

The setting of in-patient work in a therapeutic community at the Cassel hospital

Treatment of the severely disturbed patient in an in-patient setting provides particular opportunities for supportive containment of the patient as well as particular dangers of severe regression and intensified disturbance. How in-patient treatment works, whether and why it works, depends on how different aspects of treatment are brought together. At the Cassel Hospital patients are offered psychoanalytic understanding and insight in individual and group psychotherapy, together with intensive psychosocial nursing in a therapeutic community context. But patients receive a range of other types of care. These include some tangible benefits, such as food, an overnight bed, spare time, opportunities for pleasures including recreational time and activities, and the company of other patients in a shared communal living and treatment space. There are indeed, then, other aspects of in-patient treatment apart from what is specifically psychoanalytic. Amongst the most important of these are: (a) real bodily care; (b) levels of protection, from total exposure to the reality pressures of outside life, and, within the hospital itself, from harmful and abusive attacks by others; (c) real sanctions to be invoked to prevent or reduce self-abusive attacks, and (d) supervision and appraisal of childcare issues and individual psychiatric mental state, as appropriate.

Usually psychoanalytic psychotherapy can only take place when the patient's ego is strong enough and the level of motivation sufficient for them to accept the limitations of the psychoanalytic setting, to attend the same place at agreed times, to accept rules of abstinence from actual libidinal relationships with the therapist and rules of restraint from aggressive attacks upon the therapist. For the borderline patient who has failed in treatment elsewhere, who may be caught in a chronic cycle of suicidal or self-abusive attacks, or for the abusing parent who primarily wants the child returned to them from foster care, or for the abused child who is showing disturbance when placed back with the family, such preconditions are rarely there from the outset.

The organisation of in-patient treatment

Psychoanalytic treatment is possible at the Cassel because the patient is held in treatment by the mutually co-operative effort of nurse and therapist, and by the sustained involvement of patients and staff together in a 'culture of enquiry' within the therapeutic community. There are many areas of shared aims and focus, particularly in concentrating attention on the capacity of the patient actively to address his or her problems around what Kennedy (1987) has called the 'work of the day', that is, the emotional issues which arise in the performance of the tasks of everyday life which give a structure to the patient managing the day.

Within the therapeutic community context of the hospital, patients have responsibility for their own treatment and parents have an actual and real responsibility for their children throughout the day and night (Flynn 1987, 1988). Nurses working alongside will help to make emotional sense of what the patients are doing, dealing not just with eruptions of disturbed

behaviour, but with the patients' capacities to take on specific responsibilities and tasks.

The day is organised so that there is only one meal, lunch, prepared by
hospital staff, which gives time for patients to have therapeutic meetings
with nurses, activities, and psychotherapy sessions. The other meals are
organised and prepared by patients. There is practical work to be done –
cleaning, cooking, ordering food and planning menus and managing the
therapeutic budgets. There are the ordinary tasks of the family with children, getting dressed, preparing for school in the Children's Centre, having
breakfast, and, after school, finding appropriate leisure activities, evening
meals, baths for children, settling down, managing the night-time. In unit or
'firm' meetings, practical and emotional issues are discussed.

There are three units: Family, Adolescent and Adult. These come together
in three-times-weekly community meetings to discuss the practical and
emotional issues affecting the whole community. Some patients become
'firm chair' or 'community chair', each for three months or so, and are actively
involved with, and have a special responsibility for, other patients and
patient–staff meetings during the day and especially in the evening. From 7
p.m. until 8 a.m. there is only one nurse and a night orderly in the hospital,
with duty team back-up, so patients effectively manage their emotional
issues together. It is the task of the 'firm chair' and 'community chair', and all
the patients, to hear concerns in the 'night meeting', to respond directly, aid
the nurse with crises and bring pressing and relevant issues into the more
formally structured day meetings. Staff review individuals' progress and the
community and firm process in daily staff meetings, and other formal
meetings, which involve nurses and psychotherapists together. In a weekly
'Strains' meeting, attended by all the clinical staff, the emotional impact of the
work on the staff is examined, including current pressures and strains
between staff. In effect this looks at the countertransference processes in the
staff working with these patients in a therapeutic community setting. I shall
mention nurse–therapist supervisions below.

The role of nurse and psychotherapist

There are essential differences between nursing and therapy and each brings
something quite distinct to treatment. Nurses use their own experience of
patients as a central guide to their understanding of them individually and
in community and institutional processes (Barnes 1976; Kennedy 1987;
Griffiths and Pringle 1997). Nurses help the patient to relate, to confront the
all-consuming aspects of personal conflict which take them away from a
focus or direction in life, and can reduce the ordinary to the superficial or the
irrelevant. As such it is essential to work with the underlying narcissistic base
of the patient's problems.

Nurse and therapist have separate tasks and separate roles. Yet each will
focus on the current processes of the patient's treatment over the last

twenty-four hours. The therapist primarily concentrates on an understanding of the patient as it becomes apparent in the individual transference. The nurse primarily seeks to elucidate the nature of the patients' capacities as manifested in their daily activities and relationships, guiding them with plans and stategies for moving forward, keeping in the forefront the emotional meaning, quality and impact of their behaviour and plans of action, using ordinary human reactions and responses. Each, nurse and therapist, will be aware of the work of the other. For the therapist, this provides valuable information to set alongside what is emerging in the individual transference, and may lead to an understanding of wider transferences, including split transferences, for example, to the nurse or to the hospital, or parts of it.

Patients form transferences to both nurse and therapist, and to other important figures and indeed to aspects of the hospital. Nurses also draw the transference around ordinary household issues to themselves, as they work alongside the patients in the kitchen, the pantry, the linen allocation or activities groups, and can more quickly than therapists become the focus of a community or institutional transference (Barnes 1967; Barnes *et al.* 1997; Griffiths and Pringle 1997; Flynn 1993). Some aspects of the transference may be apparent early on, but the patient's transference to therapist and to the hospital, including that of the child with his family, usually only becomes apparent as time goes on, and may come from therapy or nursing, or interestingly from both at once, after the importance of what each has been struggling with has been fully recognised (Flynn 1988).

In cases of primitive attacks and confusions, the staff themselves can begin to lose their own identity and capacity to work in their separate ways, and their effective functioning together may break down (Rosenfeld 1965). As Tom Main outlined in 'The ailment' (1957), the strain of working in what becomes a hostile environment can become manifest in a decline in the health and capacities of the staff. This can lead to failure in individual cases, effective splitting of the staff team and the possibility of retaliatory attacks by the staff upon the patients, or vice versa.

Such work, with its unremitting quality at times, does have its strain. Effective working together of therapist and nurse can, however, have a supportive and restorative effect for one another, and can produce more ongoing co-operative effort in the work. Work with the destructive, fragmented and depressed sides of the patients may move the patient out of a quagmire of regressions and regressive distortions, and may lead, with some relief, to a recurrent process where steps are taken towards something more lively and restored.

Nurse–therapist supervision

Both nurse and therapist then will have affective contact with the patient and what is most useful in nurse–therapist supervision is to understand how both nurse and therapist fulfil their separate roles and deal with conflicts that come to light. As Tischler (1987) writes, nurse–therapist supervision 'pays special attention to the feelings in the counter-transference which patients evoke in their treaters, and the effect these feelings have on their work'. There can be a 'proliferation of the transference to the institution, not only the transference of the patient, but also the counter-transference of the staff to patients and to each other'. Nurse–therapist supervisions are different and additional to other supervisions of clinical work. A senior therapist and a senior nurse meet with a primary team of workers with a family, including the nurse, the child psychotherapist and the adult psychotherapist. One or other of the workers will elect to speak first, talking of how they find working with the family, how they are working in their role and how they are communicating, or not, with the other workers. Each of the workers will follow, then the supervisors will pick out themes. It is important not to make it into a formal review and to keep it to a degree experiential, so that one may feel and see if there are processes of re-enactment at work in relation to each other or one or both of the supervisors; for example, does one of the workers feel squeezed out, dropped, neglected, and murderous towards the rival? This work requires a degree of freedom and trust of each other to be able to bring out in a group of workers countertransference feelings which may show up how adequately one is working in one's role with the family and how able one is to work with other professionals. Such supervisions augment, for many nurses and therapists, their own experience of personal psychoanalysis. In general, I believe the nurse–therapist supervision is experienced by staff as invaluable in developing working alliances when working with families which have intense disturbance and where there may be hidden severely destructive splitting processes.

Mother–infant sessions

Over the last fifteen years the Cassel Hospital Families Unit has developed a progamme for rehabilitating abused children, including very young children and small babies, with their families. When working with severe child abuse cases where there is a child under three years old involved, mother–infant sessions take place weekly and include a child psychotherapist and sometimes, too, a nurse. They are set up so that the mother can discuss with the child psychotherapist any issues of concern about the infant (Dowling 2006, 2009). The child psychotherapist can observe and work with the here and now of the mother–infant relationship, integrating outside observations from within the hospital or the foster home. When there is a father or stepfather involved, they sometimes also attend. Most of the infants are returning to their mothers after being in foster care. A few toys are provided and the mother is encouraged to bring some of the child's own toys. The sessions are usually very emotionally charged, and in most cases there are contentious legal issues about whether mother and infant should be together. Often, after abuse and neglect, and having lost and indeed missed out on emotional contact with the child, the mothers need to recognise and face up to aspects of their way of relating to the child which are hindering a deepening of their bond.

Mothers need to be able to accept responsibility for what happened, and, as treatment goes on, further blame, shame and painful awareness, so the sessions work against the danger of contact with the child being lost and weak links severed. This is especially so if the mother cannot accept responsibility. In effect, the mother does not bond again with the infant unless she can get beyond the abusive behaviour or her part in the abusive experience. If, as often happens, a defensive or protective shell is created around the mother–infant couple, the habitual responses of mother to child may be ignored, along with the infant's attempts at communication and his/ her changing developmental needs.

I have described in detail elsewhere some mother–infant work in two cases of successful rehabilitation (Flynn 1998).

Following the clandestine poisoning of two children, Mrs A used the mother–infant sessions, over a period of nearly two years, to get to know her next child Joan, aged eleven months on admission, as a real person. She needed also to use them to recognise she could unleash on a child her own disturbed feelings, and that she could be out of touch with her own dangerousness. An incident about giving the child an over-warm bath brought her hidden murderousness into view within the therapeutic community, and, on a smaller scale, in the mother–infant sessions other parallel examples of potentially dangerous behaviour could be faced. Important work too was done in the mother–infant sessions about intense fears over separateness of the mother from the child. Joan was encouraged to develop more as an individual, alongside parallel work in the nursing about developing Mrs A's social and group capacities with others, and, in her own psychotherapy, about the early breaks in her relationship with her parents as an infant, and the false solutions she adopted to cover over her hostile and embittered relationship with her mother.

In another example from mother–infant sessions, work was done with Susan, a mother who had been released from prison after serving a term for neglect, following the killing by her partner of their baby girl. Her older daughter, Ann, now aged three years, was being returned to her from foster care after eighteen months. In the work a new bond had to be formed between them, the positive wishes to be together nurtured, alongside other passive, muddled and negative wishes in both mother and child. The erratic and disturbed behaviour of the mother had to be relived to a degree in the therapeutic community before she could more fully accept the effect it was having and had had within her family. Overall it was Ann's tolerance of individual sessions and her wish to have her thoughts and feelings understood that showed her willingness to persevere through the painfulness of the process. Ann had to be able to know how it could have happened that her baby sister had been killed, in order to overcome her internal trauma, but importantly too, to know how thinking in her internal world could get killed off, and would need to be reformed and found. Susan had to face her own responsibility and some of her failings, and indeed she did do this and was capable of deep and genuine guilt and remorse, which she worked through in her individual psychotherapy. She also needed to be able to allow her child to express her feelings, including her anger with her mother and her acceptance of her stepfather's responsibility, indeed to allow herself to know what had happened. Sufficient support and tolerance were needed in the whole in-patient treatment team to survive negative attacks and to create the space for something new to grow between Ann and Susan.

'Tolerance or survival?' in the child during family rehabilitation

Within the hospital there are a number of elements of treatment for the family as a whole and for each member of it, but essentially relationships are tested not just with others in the therapeutic community but within the family itself, and, importantly, between parents and children. It is important to assess – not only in a narrower sense, in family meetings and mother–child work, but also in a wider sense, bringing together an understanding of all aspects of the work and centrally the intensive individual psychotherapy which the child has during treatment – the impact the treatment is having on the child. This is invaluable for assessing the overall impact of the therapeutic community work (Flynn 1988), and especially what the child can put up with or survive. I shall look at this theme in two cases which involve severe abuse. Children can survive abuse by learning to 'tolerate' too much, causing deep emotional scars. But unless they can tolerate the emergence in a painful way of central issues, attempts at rehabilitation may not survive. There are painful issues about when and what to tolerate or not to tolerate, and about whether this furthers or hinders the child's attempts to develop emotionally and survive psychically.

We know, after the work of Bowlby, that a child in a new foster or adoptive home, having left the family of origin following loss of parents or family breakdown, will face a major task of readjustment on return to the family, and that such experiences can be traumatic and disturbing. The task for an abused child coming back again into the family is that much more difficult, especially in coming to terms with how the abuse has severed family relationships, and when reliving aspects of the abuse. There are crucial questions we need to ask throughout this rehabilitative treatment: namely, is the child surviving emotionally, can the family now provide enough protection and security for the child, has the family survived?

Case example: Stefan

Stefan, aged four years, had suffered repeated physical and verbal abuse whilst in the care of his mother, a single parent who, isolated from her home environment, had had post-natal depression and then drug and alcohol problems. Through neglect Stefan had fallen out of a high window, but survived. In three-times-weekly psychotherapy, Stefan presented as a dull depressed child with a speech impediment, withdrawn sometimes, but with alternating wild out-of-control behaviour – hitting out, hurting himself and scratching me and him – and close clingy contact. In the therapeutic community, although now off unprescribed or hard drugs, his mother seemed locked in on herself as if she were drugged. She was sometimes warm and physically caring, but then hostile and lashing out as she felt he was punishing her. In a preliminary meeting with his mother present, he first drew on paper an outline of a crocodile, then played with fascination with a toy crocodile. When his mother handed it back, he flinched away with terror, as if it were a real crocodile that was going to bite him. I thought his experiences were so powerful that play could become concretely real so that his capacity for symbolic communication in play and speech became very tenuous.

In psychotherapy sessions Stefan occasionally shifted out of his depressive dullness and become a lively and expressive child. He was, however, often painfully confused, had a speech impediment, and one almost literally had to catch the words from his mouth to understand him. I was better able to do this when he began playing, which he could now do in an energetic and increasingly meaningful way.

In a session early on, an object was pulled out of the window of the dolls' house and fell. Then the biting crocodile pulled the tree-person out of the window. In another version it was pushed and then the building collapsed.

Stefan was pleased that I could make sense of his very bitty play. I indicated I knew he was talking about what happened when he fell. He felt guilt and bewilderment about this and the catastrophic destruction of his time with mother. This linked to earlier when his mother 'fell out of sight' during her depression. In sessions, if I was not fully attentive to him, he re-experienced this as another form of my 'falling out of sight'. Then his fear of catastrophic loss reappeared and with it all his difficulties. Usually he had a devilish streak, which was largely playful, but sometimes it gave way to frenetic repetitive activity. He then subsided into timidity and abject whinyness, which I found had a very wearing effect on me. Basically, however, he thrived on attention to his feelings.

After some months of treatment, Stefan's mother's behaviour became increasingly more disturbed (for reasons I shall not go into), and actively rejecting behaviour towards Stefan in the hospital was observed to increase. His behaviour now worsened. In one incident Stefan got up in the night and poured water over two other small boys. His mother was furious with him and poured a jug of water over him. She refused to change him or do anything, was quite out of control and abusive and threatening to staff. Typically she took a long time to come out of her rage. In brief, this is what happened in Stefan's psychotherapy session next day:

He and his mother had 'made up' and, as I approached the waiting area, he was asking his mother for a kiss and a cuddle in a whiny but playful voice. His mother did not look at me and insisted on carrying Stefan to the door of the room, supposing him not able to come. Inside the room, now his mother had left, he immediately complained there was no water in the bowl. He began impulsively hauling the water container off the shelf and knocking the side of it. I pointed out there was water in the bowl. He took it, put it on the table and began to put pieces from the teaset in it. He then jerked and tipped the bowl forward and poured some of it over his jeans and his shirt. He started whining that he was wet. This developed into a real cry and then sad sobbing. I said he had wet himself and felt I would leave him wet and unhappy, like his mummy had done in the bedroom last night. I said I knew about the incident last night. He said that he had wet the boys because they were 'too hot'. I said I thought he may feel the boys had his hot angry feelings inside them. Stefan did not reply but stood still crying saying he wanted his mum. I was undecided what to do, phone his mother or try to help him myself. I decided on the latter. I acknowledged he did want his mother really to do the drying for him, but for the moment I would see if I could dry him, so that he could continue to stay with me for the rest of the session. After I had dried him and begun to wipe up some of the mess, he became angry with me for doing this and threw over two small chairs in a rage. He cut his box with scissors and threw the toys all over the floor. He clutched his trousers and pulled on his penis, then used the pencil sharpener damagingly on some felt tips and crayons. He tipped the rest of his toys in the bin and then tipped this on the floor. I was left scrambling around, wondering if I could stop the devastation. Stefan clambered on to a small table and managed to fall, hurting himself and he began to cry again. I said again about how he was showing me how mixed up everything was, and how he felt I would leave him to fall and get hurt.

I had to choose in this session whether to help Stefan directly, call his mother to help him, or to continue deeper with interpreting his internal perceptions and conflicts in the transference and in relation to the current reality of life with his mother. My dilemma over this increased over the next weeks as the situation deteriorated further. Stefan then presented either as a very ideal child, quickly collapsing into acute disturbance, or as an openly depressed child, when he was passive and 'floppy', as if he had no effective skeleton. His relationship with his mother became increasingly impoverished, and he became more self-destructive, actually cutting and hurting himself – a disturbing thing to see in such a young child. Stefan was now showing that the continued efforts at rehabilitation were intolerable. Treatment was stopped at this point after nine months. I was left wondering whether in Stefan's interests we should have acted at an earlier point of the deterioration.

Since Stefan's treatment, we have begun to look for earlier signs of whether children find continued family rehabilitation tolerable or not. Careful monitoring is needed so that children do not become the victims of repeated abuse. When children find it intolerable, their psychic survival is threatened and there are open signs of deterioration. This can lead to further reactive disturbed behaviour from the parents towards them.

Case example: Stuart

Stuart, aged nine, suffered physical and sexual abuse (anal abuse) from his father. His mother was extremely deprived, had suffered continuous abuse and humiliation as a child, and came from an horrific, very large, incestuous family where each child barely found a way just to survive. Crucially, too, in the background, Stuart had a history of lack of maternal containment; his birth weight was just four pounds, he was in an incubator for several weeks, and he had a bad pneumonia during his first year.

When the psychotherapy setting was established, Stuart used it to express his vulnerability and his need to build up defences. He was sad and lonely, unsure about his mother and triggered easily into expressing violent feelings towards her. The experience of abuse had represented a physical and a mental threat and in particular was like being psychologically killed off. He tried to placate and fit in with what he thought I wanted of him, which was alarming, and expressed a deep mistrust of being himself. I felt it important to allow him to build up some of his own defences. He could use the sessions as he wanted, and only talk about the abuse if he wanted to.

Even when he knew this, his anxieties shown in his play were very much centred around anal abuse. He covered his toy box with plasticine and various types of covers so that it would be safe. Cups were thrown into a bowl of water to be tested to see if they were clean or dirty. I was tested by being given the dirty one and then observed with glee. The transference developed and he had a number of fantasies about secrets and showed fears that I would harm him. Confused sequences developed in which he would want to barter with me. I would be seen, in the play, to give him money, and he would do things for me. He did, however, genuinely want to develop a special affectionate relationship with me. I think he found my interpretations about his vulnerability relieving, but even 'being relieved' was a confusing experience, and he frequently had to rush to the toilet after points of anxiety or relief in our interchanges. Clearly he was suffering a number of types of zonal and functional confusions. He attempted to rework his experience and to gain some control over it. One frequent sequence of play was to make masks which he could use to see the top half of people but not their bottom half. Outside the sessions odd behaviour occurred too, for example, when he suddenly stuck a balloon into the nursing officer's face and nose. Going back to the record one discovers that he suffered from having his father's bottom stuck into his face.

From early on Stuart was preoccupied with why he, rather than his brother or sister, was being rehabilitated. He was lonely, guilty and confused about this, and behind it were the questions, why was he chosen for abuse, why was he now with mother, and was he special, or had he managed to push the others out? What now came more into focus was how he could identify with the sexual aggression he had suffered. He frequently poked sharp objects into the playroom wall and damaged it. He had misgivings about his sexual identity – was he a boy or a girl and how should he act to men and to women? At times he was very confiding in me in a genuine way, telling me all sorts of details about life with his mother and father. These periods were when he was settled. But at other times the effects of the abuse showed through in difficulties with other children and staff. Some of these involved reasonable sexual boundaries with other children, and some concerned his excitable and overactive behaviour.

As time went on it was apparent that it was increasingly difficult for Stuart to sustain progress. He became ill at points of stress, and his mother's alliance with me as his psychotherapist progressively lapsed – for example, in not telling me of fights he had had with his brother at the weekend, which at one point explained some of his depression. The accumulated impression was that he was not being thought about. As her alliance and capacity to care and nurture Stuart lapsed, it became impossible for him to talk about the abuse at all in the therapy. In other words he lost all sense of trust that I would be able to think about him. His mother at this point was finding it especially difficult to face the facts of her own abuse, and broke off treatment and her attempts at rehabilitation.

After a long period of time, clinical follow-ups and the ensuing court proceedings, Stuart's mother could accept his need for another family. The work for this had been done in the treatment. Crucially Stuart had learned to trust and understand more of his own needs, and he and mother could agree about her incapacity to meet them now. This recognition of reality allowed for a good placement in a family elsewhere to be made and for a number of years of intensive out-patient psychotherapy to be arranged for Stuart. Stuart's mother has independently made something of her life, and they are still in regular contact with each other.

Conclusion

During family rehabilitation the child's capacity to distinguish internal and external reality is affected. The terror inflicted on the child by abuse continues to affect them internally, through continued persecution and dread. Primitive feelings and emotions connected with the earliest emotional life are stirred, primitive confusion (Rosenfeld 1965), catastrophic anxiety (Bion 1970) and fear of annihilation (Winnicott 1956). Meltzer (1973) defines terror as 'paranoid anxiety whose essential quality, paralysis, leaves no avenue of action'. A dread develops because of a loss of protection against terror, and a tyrannical internal organisation may build up. This needs to be tackled therapeutically before progress can be made to understanding depressive and dependency needs. Because of this one needs both to understand the child's repetition of abusive contact and to confront the tyrannical and omnipotent element within the child which, in my experience, so frequently gives the therapeutic encounter with the severely abused child the quality of a battle. Only after addressing the underlying terror can progress towards rebuilding relationships be made. In family rehabilitation the parents need help to recognise the needs of the child and to understand how the child will react and behave with difficulties after the abuse. Importantly, they need to acknowledge responsibility for their part in causing the abuse, whether they are the actual perpetrator, or whether they have colluded in it. Intense work is necessary to build up trust. They have to recognise that they have duties and responsibilities as parents, including providing clear and safe boundaries for the child, which will determine whether the child finds the family safe enough.

The child psychotherapist has a central role in an in-patient therapeutic community setting to make and maintain contact with the deepest aspects of the child's feelings and emotional responses, to work with and help the child directly and to contribute to the thinking of the other staff. He or she will also face emotional pressure and conflict in the work as different levels of disturbance become manifest, either in a directly understandable form or as painful and irrational forms of enactment by the patients, or indeed amongst the staff struggling in the work. The tolerance of severe infantile projections of hostility and despair and the struggle to maintain co-operative work together, not just the technical changes of the in-patient setting, are what makes work towards successful rehabilitation of such families possible and, in the end, enables both the patients and the workers to survive and to continue to work in a psychoanalytic way.

References

Barnes, E. (ed.) (1967) *Psychosocial Nursing*, London: Tavistock Publications.

Barnes, E., Griffiths, P., Ord, J. and Wells, D. (eds) (1997) *Face to Face with Distress: The Professional Use of Self in Psychosocial Care*, Oxford: Butterworth-Heinemann.

Bion, W. R. (1970) *Attention and Interpretation*, London: Tavistock.

Dowling, D. (2006) 'The capacity to be alone. Rediscovering Winnicott and his contribution to parent-infant psychotherapy', in M. Lanyado and A. Horne (eds) *A Question of Technique. Independent Psychoanalytic Approaches with Children and Adolescents Series*, London and New York: Routledge.

—— (2009) 'Thinking aloud: A child psychotherapist assessing families for Court', in A. Horne and M. Lanyado (eds) *Through Assessment to Consultation. Independent Psychoanalytic Approaches with Children and Adolescents Series*, London and New York: Routledge.

Flynn, C. (1993) 'The patient's pantry: the nature of the nursing task', *Therapeutic Communities* 14(4): 227–36.

Flynn, D. (1987) 'The child's view of the hospital: an examination of the child's experience of an in-patient setting', in A. Heymans, R. Kennedy and L. Tischler (eds) *The Family as In-Patient*, London: Free Association Books.

—— (1988) 'The assessment and psychotherapy of a physically abused girl during in-patient family treatment', *Journal of Child Psychotherapy* 13(2): 61–78.

—— (1998) 'Psychoanalytic aspects of inpatient treatment', *Journal of Child Psychotherapy* 24(2): 283–306.

Griffiths, P. and Pringle, P. (eds) (1997) *Psychosocial Practice in a Residential Setting*, London: Karnac Books.

Kennedy, R. (1987) 'The work of the day: aspects of work with families at the Cassel Hospital', in A. Heymans, R. Kennedy and L. Tischler (eds) *The Family as In-Patient*, London: Free Association Books.

Main, T. (1957) 'The ailment', *British Journal of Medical Psychology* 30: 129–45 (reprinted in *The Ailment and other Psychoanalytic Essays* (1989), London: Free Association Books).

Meltzer, D. (1973) *Sexual States of Mind*, Strath Tay, Perthshire: Clunie Press.

Rosenfeld, H. A. (1965) *Psychotic States: A Psychological Approach*, London: Hogarth Press.

Tischler, L. (1987) 'Nurse-therapist supervision', in A. Heymans, R. Kennedy and L. Tischler (eds) *The Family as In-Patient*, London: Free Association Books.

Winnicott, D. W. (1956) 'Primary maternal preoccupation', in D. W. Winnicott (1975) *Through Paediatrics to Psycho-analysis*, London: Hogarth Press.

Further reading

Bandler, D. (1987) 'Working with other professionals in an inpatient setting', *Journal of Child Psychotherapy* 13(2): 81–90.

Coombe, P. (1995) 'The inpatient treatment of mother and child at the Cassel Hospital: a case of Munchhausen syndrome by proxy', *British Journal of Psychotherapy* 12: 195–207.

Flynn, C. (1993) 'The patient's pantry: the nature of the nursing task', *Therapeutic Communities* 14(4): 227–36.

Flynn, D. (1988) 'The assessment and psychotherapy of a physically abused girl during in-patient family treatment', *Journal of Child Psychotherapy* 13(2): 61–78.

—— (1998) 'Psychoanalytic aspects of inpatient treatment', *Journal of Child Psychotherapy* 24(2): 283–306.

Heymans, A., Kennedy, R. and Tischler, L. (eds) (1987) *The Family as In-Patient*, London: Free Association Books.

18 Consultation in residential care

Peter Wilson

There are good reasons for some children being in residential care. Despite prevailing concerns about costs, abuse and institutional dependency, it is nevertheless the case that many children need to be resident in establishments of one sort or another, at different times in their lives, in order to be adequately looked after, protected, educated and treated. Children who suffer chronic physical illness, children with severe learning disabilities, children whose behaviour is very irrational and bizarre or whose psychological illness is life-threatening, such as anorexia nervosa – all require continuous attention and treatment within a safe environment. Children with serious behavioural problems, sufficient to be a danger to themselves or to others, need to be securely held and helped within the physical constraints of a secure unit or youth treatment centre. Children with emotional and behavioural problems arising from abusive and traumatic family experiences require the sustained understanding and containment provided in special schools and therapeutic communities. Children whose lives have been disrupted by family tragedy, death, separation and loss may need to be accommodated by the local authority residential establishments, either temporarily whilst awaiting foster care placement or on a more long-term basis. And finally, children whose parents live abroad or who prefer their children to be educated in residential establishments require boarding school placements.

Given adequate and responsible residential provision, all of these children can benefit from a greater level of care, protection and commitment than they are likely to receive in their families and communities. This includes specialist assessment and treatment as well as the provision of structured therapeutic and educational milieux.

Whilst in residence the majority of children and young people suffer varying degrees of emotional distress and disturbance. Some manage well enough, though most would prefer to be at home and attend their local schools. Children who are physically ill or have severe physical, mental or sensory impairments contend with much pain and frustration and experience intense feelings of anger, fear and disappointment. Children in local authority children's homes, in secure units, youth treatment centres, therapeutic communities and special education establishments have significant emotional and behaviour problems. In the main, these derive from their inability to cope with either misfortune (e.g. family disruption following parental death) or maltreatment (e.g. neglectful or abusive experiences) earlier in their lives. They enter residential establishments feeling abandoned and ostracised (some, scapegoated by their families) and carry with them a great deal of anxiety and mistrust. Many cannot relax or settle to any task and feel inadequate and worthless because of their inability to learn or to achieve. In general, they have not received sufficient care or consistency in their lives – and in the residential setting they effectively demand that which they have lacked.

The impact of such distress in the residential establishments in which they live is considerable. Each establishment has its own resources and procedures to cope with the emotional demand; and in different ways, each is held together under the authority and expertise of a lead clinician (e.g. a consultant child psychiatrist or paediatrician), head teacher or director and bolstered by the operation of a multidisciplinary team. A great deal of burden, however, rests upon the residential care staff who are responsible for the day and night running of the establishment (Polsky 1962). It is they who provide the fabric of primary care – the feeding, establishing routines, maintaining order and discipline, getting children up in the morning, settling them at night – that constitutes the core of residential therapeutic activity. It is through their behaviour and response, in the close proximity of the living group, that children learn and develop. Much depends on their personal resourcefulness. In the midst of their everyday ordinary exchanges with children they deal with a wide variety of children's feelings, many of which are transferred on to them from past experiences. The residence becomes in effect an arena of transference re-enactment and residential care staff invariably find themselves all too easily perceived inappropriately, for example as depriving, abusive, neglectful or seductive (Ward *et al.* 2003). 'The essence of residential treatment is that each child projects its inner world against the macrocosm of the residence' (Ekstein *et al.* 1959).

In order to cope with these pressures, most establishments seek additional assistance to supplement and further support their mainstream provision. Child and adolescent mental health professionals are often recruited to provide specialist help both to children directly as well as to staff. Child psychotherapists have a particular contribution to make in this context by virtue of their psychoanalytic training and experience.

The contribution of the child psychotherapist

Child psychotherapists' knowledge of child development and psychopathology, and their understanding of the effects of unconscious processes on behaviour and attitude, are of considerable relevance to the central issues that arise in residential work with children. So, too, is their awareness of the influence of projective mechanisms and transference and counter-transference phenomena in human relationships. Their actual clinical practice, predominately based as it is on individual work in clinical settings in the community, is different from that of the residential care staff. Nevertheless, the application of their knowledge and understanding in the residential context is of considerable value. There are different forms that this can take:

(a) providing individual psychotherapy
(b) providing consultation to individual staff
(c) providing consultation to staff groups.

Providing individual psychotherapy

In view of the complexity of children's psychological difficulties, there is a clear argument for employing the specialist skills of child psychotherapists to provide individual psychotherapy in residential settings. For many children, such provision can be very helpful. However, in carrying this out, child psychotherapists need to be prepared to adapt their technique and understand their impact on the residential setting as a whole (Wilson 1986). Unlike in a clinical out-patient setting, child psychotherapists cannot practise with the same degree of privacy or confidentiality. Customary procedures of establishing the boundaries of an individual psychotherapeutic setting need to be modified. In a residential setting, individual psychotherapy is but one part of the overall therapeutic provision. There is a danger that its privacy can be seen as secretive, arousing suspicion and envy, and having a generally divisive effect on the coherence of the community. Children who are seen in individual psychotherapy are also affected; they are often confused and unsure about why they are being selected, whilst those children who are not clearly feel excluded. Furthermore, whilst confidentiality is important in individual psychotherapy, it is not something that can be fully upheld in a residential context. Staff need to know what is happening in individual therapy particularly when children become upset as a result of feelings aroused in sessions, leading possibly to agitated or disruptive behaviour or sometimes self-destructive activity (e.g. suicide attempts, self-harming, absconding). Progress, too, in individual psychotherapy can often be improved if the child psychotherapist is informed of significant events and experiences in the community.

Providing consultation to individual staff

In view of these difficulties and of the general scarce resource of child psychotherapists, it is often more productive that they act as consultants to staff. Residential care staff, in particular, require support to enable them to work effectively and to ensure that they do not become overwhelmed or demoralised by the emotional pressures placed on them. They need the opportunity to reflect on their work in order to understand better the interactions between the children and themselves.

It is important that in carrying out this work child psychotherapists, like all consultants, are clear about the meaning and purpose of consultation, as distinct from other associated activities such as supervision, training or psychotherapy. Caplan (1970) refers to consultation as work that is carried out when one professional (the consultee) involves another (the consultant) to help with a work problem. It is an activity that occurs between professionals as distinct from within a profession or between those who are trained and untrained. Central to the concept of consultation is the understanding that professional responsibility for the work remains with the consultee, as indeed the choice of whether or not to use or do anything that has been discussed in the consultation. This is clearly different from supervision in which the supervisor has managerial responsibility for the work and has the authority to require the supervisee to follow advice and direction.

There are many occasions in the life of a residential unit when staff are challenged and perplexed by the behaviour and attitude of children and confused and alarmed by their own reactions to them. It is not uncommon, for example, for a child to behave for several days in a co-operative and affectionate way only to change suddenly and relate to the residential care worker quite differently. The child may become sullen, withdrawn or tearful; he or she may become secretive, devious and undermining; or at other times obstinate, defiant and antagonistic. These changes and demands are commonplace in residential childcare and, for the most part, they can be adequately dealt with by the staff under effective supervision. However, it is often the case that, beyond this level of management, there arises a need for further thought. There may still be questions about why children are behaving in the way they are and uncertainty about how best to proceed. In this context, the function of consultation has its place.

> Fundamentally the question of consultation arises when someone or some group gets stuck or feels limited working within the mainstream of everyday business. A point is reached when there is a recognition that existing personal or established institutional resources are not enough – and additional assistance is required. It is here that consultation comes in . . .
>
> (Wilson 1991)

The purpose of consultation is to enable the residential staff to think more clearly about their own observations and experiences and to facilitate their greater understanding of the children and of the emotional impact of the children on themselves. Whilst staff may be aware of some of the reasons underlying children's behaviour, they may well miss out on others – not least because of their close involvement. They may see straight away, for example, that a child has become irritable or abusive following a distressing home visit; but they may not recognise the significance of the arrival of a new resident into the unit that exacerbates the child's fears of being excluded. In addition, they may not fully appreciate the extent of their own impatience or of how they themselves are getting drawn into a dismissive mode of response that repeats the child's experience of rejection. In consultation they have the opportunity to gain a wider perspective and catch hold of themselves and of the subtle yet powerful influence of the child's demands and provocations.

Consultations can take place both individually and in staff groups. In the following example, a child psychotherapist met with a residential staff worker in an adolescent unit on an individual basis. The achievement of this consultation was to make sense of a disturbing feeling in a staff member that was interfering with her capacity to respond appropriately to one of the girls in her unit.

> The problem that the staff member presented for consultation was her extreme anger with the girl. In particular, she could not tolerate the way the girl ignored her. The consultation initially focused on understanding the girl's behaviour in the light of her past experience with a domineering and violent mother. In large measure, this could be seen as her way of blotting out potential intrusion, at the same time attacking those who threatened her. With this in mind, the staff member understood her own anger as representing something of the girl's projected fury, as well as the mother's ambivalence. A further more personal dimension emerged in the course of the consultation. This related to the fact that both the staff member and the girl shared an experience in common, namely the death of a younger sister. The girl's apparent indifference to this and her tendency to mock the staff member's distress only added to the latter's anger and intolerance.

Providing consultation to staff groups

In a residential setting, staff tensions are inevitable; some may arise from organisational difficulties, others from external pressures, whilst a good deal arises from the emotional demands and expectations of the residential children and adolescents. It is crucial to the development of a coherent therapeutic environment that staff work well together and have the opportunity to discuss these tensions and share their common difficulties. Child psychotherapists, with experience and additional knowledge of organisational dynamics, may help facilitate staff groups to deal with organisational issues. For the most part, however, they are best suited to help staff groups explore the emotional tensions that arise from the residents in the course of their work.

In the following example, a staff group in a therapeutic community for adolescents met to review the progress of one of the residents. This was a sixteen-year-old boy who had become increasingly violent in recent weeks and whose future in the community was being questioned. The main part of the meeting was chaired by a senior staff member and a formal review was carried out of the boy's family circumstances and progress in the community. To further understanding of the boy's behaviour and address some of the key concerns amongst the staff, the final part of the meeting was taken up in considering the staff's reactions to the boy's behaviour. This part of the meeting was conducted by the child psychotherapist.

To facilitate discussion, the child psychotherapist invited staff members to express briefly in turn their feelings and reactions about the boy during the preceding six months. This was carried out with the clear understanding by management and all concerned that such views were necessarily personal and subjective and not intended to be in anyway prejudicial, but rather to broaden awareness of the boy's predicament.

Two major themes emerged. The first related to the nature of the boy's difficulties; the second to the impact of his behaviour on the staff group. It became clear that the boy aroused intense but varied feelings in different staff members. The men, in particular, were threatened by his violence: some wanted to retreat from him whilst others wanted to retaliate against him. The women staff felt less strongly, but were equally divided: some felt maternal and protective whilst others were frightened by him. The range and depth of feeling was disturbing yet revealing. In experiencing this together in an approved and structured meeting, the staff obtained a context in which to place their own individual reactions and, at the same time, gain a greater insight into the boy's emotional predicament. They could see, for example, the extent to which the accumulation of their feeling represented a group countertransference, reflecting in varying degrees the traumatic experience of this boy's past experience with a violent but often absent father and a mentally ill mother. The second theme related to a particular staff tension that arose from this situation. One of the staff members complained about the burden he felt he carried in confronting this boy's violent behaviour. He felt he was being left by other staff members to act as the 'hard man' in dealing with the violence; this distressed him, not least because of how it reminded him of his strained relationship with his own father.

This was a tense meeting in which a number of different issues were addressed – relating to the particular boy under review, divisions within the staff and the well-being of the community. After much discussion, it was agreed that every effort should be made to ensure that the boy was not excluded from the community. A number of important decisions were also made about staff cover to share more equitably the burden of the boy's violence.

A meeting such as this existed as part of a series that, over time, contributed to the greater understanding of the boy and of the staff group itself. The child psychotherapist had a key role to play, entrusted by the staff and sanctioned by the senior manager to facilitate and contain what was, in effect, a highly sensitive and crucial group learning experience.

Conclusion

In most residential establishments dealing with children and young people, there is a great deal of emotional turbulence amongst the children and amongst the staff. The effectiveness of such establishments depends on how well this is addressed. Establishments that employ well-trained staff who are properly managed can provide good quality care and therapy. Invariably, they value the additional input of specialists, including child and adolescent mental health professionals. Child psychotherapists have a particularly relevant contribution to make through providing individual psychotherapy and consultation to staff. Consultation is of particular importance since it can enable those who have fundamental responsibility for the residential care and therapy to be more effective (Wilson 2003, 2009; Horne and Lanyado 2009).

In providing consultation to staff, whether on an individual basis or in groups, it is crucial that child psychotherapists ensure that their work is understood and supported by the management of the residential units. In taking such a significant part in helping staff gain greater understanding of their work and considering various options about how best to proceed, child psychotherapists, as consultants, may well be mistaken for taking responsibility for the staff's problems. Equally, in engaging with the personal issues of the staff in carrying out their work, they may be misperceived as providing psychotherapy for residential staff. It is of key importance that child psychotherapists are clear in their own minds that they are neither managers nor psychotherapists in this context.

Given this clarity, the contribution of the child psychotherapist as consultant in a residential setting can be substantial. Their value resides in their objective and psychoanalytic perspective; and in their capacity to provide an experience in which staff feelings can be expressed and shared. The essence of consultation resides in its capacity to contain (Bion 1962) – to receive feelings and observations, to tolerate uncertainty, to allow for reflection and thought and, ultimately, to empower staff to move forward in their own way. In the two examples given, staff were helped to acknowledge the impact of the emotional pressures of children upon them and the extent to which these pressures impinged upon their own lives. Staff needed time to take stock of themselves in order to gain a greater measure of self-understanding and control and thereby to be more effective in withstanding the dictates of transference re-enactments inherent in residential experience.

References

Bion, W. R. (1962) *Learning from Experience*, London: Karnac Books.

Caplan, G. (1970) *Theory and Practice of Mental Health Consultation*, London: Tavistock Publications.

Ekstein, R., Mandelbaum, A. and Wallerstein, J. (1959) 'Counter transference in residential treatment of children', *The Psychoanalytic Study of the Child*, New York: New York University Press.

Horne, A. and Lanyado, M. (2009) *Through Assessment to Consultation. Independent Psychoanalytic Approaches with Children and Adolescents Series*, London and New York: Routledge.

Polsky, H. (1962) *Cottage Six: The Social System of Delinquent Boys in Residential Treatment*, New York: Russel Sage Foundation.

Ward, A., Kasinski, K., Pooley, J. and Worthington, A. (eds) (2003) *Therapeutic Communities for Children and Young People*, London and New York: Jessica Kingsley.

Wilson, P. (1986) 'Individual psychotherapy in an adolescent unit', in D. Steinberg (ed.) *The Adolescent Unit: Work and Teamwork in Adolescent Psychiatry*, Chichester: John Wiley.

—— (1991) 'Consultation to institutions: questions of role and orientation', in S. Ramsden (ed.) *Occasional Papers No. 6 Psychotherapy – Pure and Applied*, London: Association of Child Psychology and Psychiatry.

—— (2003) 'Consultation and supervision', in A. Ward, K. Kasinski, J. Pooley and A. Worthington (eds) *Therapeutic Communities for Children and Young People*, London and New York: Jessica Kingsley.

—— (2009) 'Beyond consultation', in. A. Horne and M. Lanyado (2009) *Through Assessment to Consultation. Independent Psychoanalytic Approaches with Children and Adolescents Series*, London and New York: Routledge.

Further reading

Caplan, G. (1970) *Theory and Practice of Mental Health Consultation*, London: Tavistock Publications.

Silveira, W. R. (ed.) (1991) *Consultation in Residential Care*, Aberdeen: University Press (reviewed by P. Wilson (1992) *Journal of Child Psychotherapy* 18(1)).

Steinberg, D. (ed.) (1986) *The Adolescent Unit: Work and Teamwork in Adolescent Psychiatry*, Chichester: John Wiley.

Part IV

Areas of special interest

19 Child psychotherapy with children on the autistic spectrum

Maria Rhode

Psychoanalytic work with children on the autistic spectrum has seen some of the most exciting advances in child psychotherapy that have taken place within the past thirty-odd years. When things go well, treatment can bring great benefit to the children and their families; it can also shed light on fundamental areas of human experience. In spite of this, it remains a controversial intervention. In many parts of the United Kingdom, children and families who might be helped are not referred for psychotherapy.

There are two main reasons for this. The first is historical: Bruno Bettelheim, in his book *The Empty Fortress* (1967), categorically blamed parents for their children's autism. He provided detailed histories of a few children whose parents had indeed expressed hostility; but he had not met them until they had been reduced to despair by years of feeling invalidated by their children's failure to respond and by the effect of their behaviour on family life (Klauber 1998). Hostility expressed at that point can indicate nothing about causation, even in these very few examples; but Bettelheim's reputation meant that his unwarranted conclusions were unjustifiably generalised beyond his small number of cases, so that, for many years, parents of children with autism were blamed by professionals. Most unfortunately, it has proved virtually impossible to correct the totally wrong belief that present-day psychoanalytic workers share Bettelheim's opinion, though Frances Tustin (1972, 1981a, 1986, 1990) led the way in describing her patients' parents as thoughtful, concerned people who inspired compassion and therapeutic ambition.

The second reason is that false and unhelpful dichotomies between emotion and cognition and between brain and mind linger on in the field of autism. This is in spite of contemporary work in neuroscience (e.g. Schore 1994) that has documented the effect of emotional experience (including psychotherapy) on brain structure and function. Many parents will be warned by other professionals that child psychotherapy is inappropriate because their child has a brain defect, and that the only right intervention is behavioural training and a good educational placement. However, most parents who do get referred welcome the opportunity to talk about their family's emotional experience. Child psychotherapy is particularly appropriate for those families whose parents are looking for meaning in their child's behaviour. It does not suit all children with autism and their families (or indeed all children with other kinds of problems). As discussed below, a thorough assessment is essential.

What is autism?

Infantile autism (Kanner's syndrome) was first described by Leo Kanner in 1943. He stressed the children's profound autistic aloneness – their failure to make eye contact or to relate to other human beings – as well as their cognitive deficits (such as the absence of symbolic play). Language was absent or rudimentary, and often featured echolalia or pronominal reversal (of 'I' and 'you'). Interestingly, when Kanner followed these children up many years later, it turned out that the degree of progress they had been able to achieve varied very widely, for no immediately obvious reason. This in itself points to the idea that most professionals now hold, namely, that the 'spectrum' consists of a range of subgroups (Wing and Gould 1979; Alvarez and Reid 1999). However, there is general agreement that children with autism are characterised by Wing's 'triad of impairments' – of social interaction, communication and imaginative activity – and that they most often develop rituals or stereotypies that seem to take the place of creative play.

Although Kanner at one point thought that the parents of children with autism were emotionally remote intellectuals, this has not been borne out by subsequent work. In his opinion, autism was an inborn characteristic of the individual child. Although a small number of his sample made a reasonable adjustment, autistic traits tend to be stable over time (Sigman 1999).

Independently of Kanner, the Viennese paediatrician Hans Asperger in 1944 described a group of children who resembled Kanner's cases in many ways, but whose language development was not impaired. Interest in this group has grown since Lorna Wing introduced Asperger's paper to the English-speaking professional community.

The diagnosis of autism and of Asperger's syndrome is behavioural and requires the child to show certain impairments, listed in DSM-IV and in ICD-10, before a certain age. Autism used to be thought of as a variant of childhood schizophrenia, but is now classed as a pervasive developmental disorder (Kolvin 1971). A number of scales have been developed as an aid to identifying autism, though these tend to lead to higher rates of diagnosis than do clinical interviews. For a fuller account of psychiatric approaches, see Simpson (2004, 2008).

Theories of autism

Most psychiatrists and psychologists subscribe to the idea that autism is caused by a defect in brain development. Rutter, for example, holds that 90 per cent of autism is attributable to genetics, although he stresses that interaction with environmental factors is crucially important. Interestingly, he has reported that a very small percentage of Romanian orphans who were later adopted in Britain developed a syndrome that was behaviourally indistinguishable from autism, and that this was not always reversed after adoption. However, boys and girls were equally represented in this group, whereas boys outnumber girls by a factor of 4 to 1 among naturally occurring cases of autism. This suggests that the underlying factors in the two groups were different although the behaviours were similar (Rutter *et al.* 1999).

A number of cognitivist theories of autism propose that the triad of impairments, including failures of emotional relatedness, stem from cognitive deficits caused by a brain defect. Perhaps the best known of these theories emphasises the failure of many children with autism to acquire a so-called 'theory of mind' (this is less true for Asperger's syndrome). Theory of mind describes a child's capacity to see things from someone else's perspective: to put themselves in their shoes. (Tustin (1986) proposed a psychoanalytic understanding of this phenomenon: namely, that it presupposes the capacity temporarily to assume another person's identity, and that children on the spectrum are insufficiently sure of their own identity to be able to identify with others in this way.) Hodges (2004) provides a helpful review of cognitive theories of autism and of those phenomena that each theory does or does not account for.

In contrast to cognitive theories, both Trevarthen and Hobson stress the primacy of emotional relatedness. Trevarthen's videos of face-to-face patterns of interaction between mothers and their babies document the musical rhythms of their 'protoconversations' out of which spoken communication develops (this links with Maiello's (2000) psychoanalytic work on the centrality of musical rhythms for children with autism). In Trevarthen's view, 'secondary intersubjectivity', in which child and adult share an experience of objects in the world, rests on the foundation of 'primary intersubjectivity', in which the parent and child directly share emotional states (Trevarthen 1980). Similarly, Hobson argues that cognitive development grows out of the sharing of emotional states between mother and infant. In *The Cradle of Thought* (Hobson 2002) he traces this process in detail as well as reviewing the implications for a general theory of development of his own experimental work on children with autism. For example, a child's developing relation to an object in the outside world depends crucially on his or her relationship both to the carer and to the carer's relationship to the object (the so-called 'relatedness triangle').

It is important for child psychotherapists working with children on the spectrum to be familiar with non-psychoanalytic theories. This is not only essential for communication with colleagues: it is also because findings from child development research genuinely enrich psychoanalytic theory and technique, as the work of Anne Alvarez (1992) abundantly illustrates. The study of autism, as Frances Tustin has said, has much to teach us about the bedrock of human experience, and insights from many disciplines need to be integrated if a fuller understanding is to be achieved.

Psychoanalytic approaches

The particular contribution of psychoanalytically-based work consists in its detailed attention to each individual child's emotional life. A child with autism is first and foremost a human being, not an instance of a syndrome; and, as such, has feelings and a unique personality. As Alvarez (1999) has pointed out, this personality will interact with the emotional and cognitive features that are characteristic of an autistic spectrum disorder. This is a useful way in which to explain to colleagues the contribution that psychotherapy can make: not as a corrective to 'bad' parenting, but as a way of addressing the emotional consequences of being on the spectrum, and in this way removing obstacles to the child's capacity to reach whatever his or her ceiling might be. Equally, psychoanalytic approaches provide a way of conceptualising a child's behaviour on a different level from the checklist of characteristics that informs diagnostic categories.

In 1930, Melanie Klein published a paper on the treatment of a mute child who made no eye contact, treated her as though she were a piece of furniture, and showed no signs of attachment to his parents or nanny. Although she wrote of him as a case of childhood schizophrenia, it is clear from her description that he was autistic. In her view, he had retreated from the world because of excessive fear of the consequences of his own aggressive impulses: she conceptualised his problem as a failure to develop rather than regression to an earlier fixation point. As she wrote, many of her early interpretations were based on her experience of other children, since 'Dick' did not at first relate to her. However, he responded to these interpretations, and a good outcome appears to have been achieved. One of the first signs of progress was that Dick began to show distress when he was separated from his carers, whereas previously he did not react to being left.

Frances Tustin's first paper on autism was published in 1966; many other papers and four books (Tustin 1972, 1981a, 1986, 1990) were to follow. Her work highlights the catastrophic bodily anxieties that children on the spectrum suffer, and their attempt to protect themselves from these and from the impingements of the 'not-me' environment by turning to sensations that they can generate by means of their own body, or with the aid of inanimate objects that are completely under their own control. For instance, many children with autism carry around a hard, so-called 'autistic object' that they value for the sensation of strength that it (or any other hard object) provides, rather than for the emotional meaning that other children invest in a special, irreplaceable cuddly toy. Therapy helps children to rely increasingly on human relationships, so that autistic objects are no longer needed to make them feel strong and self-sufficient.

Tustin found that her patients felt as though they had lost a part of their own body when they realised that they were physically separate from their mothers. This often centres around feeling that their mouth is broken or otherwise damaged. Her patient John, for example, showed her his amazement at realising that the 'red button' (his expression for the nipple) was part of the mother, not part of the baby's own mouth (Tustin 1972). When the 'red button' was absent, John felt that his mouth contained instead a 'black hole with a nasty prick'. Such a feeling of bodily damage is characteristic of what Tustin called an 'agony of consciousness', from which children with autism desperately try to shield themselves by blocking out awareness of their environment. This means that they remain psychologically 'unborn', since psychological birth – the awareness of being a separate person – can feel to them like a catastrophe (Tustin 1981b).

Tustin originally conceptualised autism as a regression to a stage of 'normal primary autism' in which the baby did not yet differentiate between himself or herself and the mother. This was also the position of Margaret Mahler in New York, who, together with Anni Bergman and Fred Pine, carried out pioneering work with autistic and psychotic children as well as on the stages by which 'normal' children attain emotional independence. However, the notion of a primary absence of differentiation did not hold up in the light of advances in child development research. From 1990 onwards, Tustin saw autism as a manifestation of skewed developmental processes rather than a regression to an earlier stage. This links with Trevarthen's model of development, according to which babies come into the world primed to relate to other human beings.

One of the areas Tustin's work opened up concerned the 'pockets' of autistic functioning that she felt could underlie other kinds of disturbance. For example, an anorexic patient thought of herself as a waterfall that could spill away and be 'gone', leaving nothing behind (Tustin 1986). This is the kind of extreme bodily anxiety that she observed in children with autism, and that Bick (1968, 1986) and Winnicott (1949) had described. Beginning with a paper by S. Klein (1980), the extreme anxieties and the self-protective strategies – such as encapsulation – that are characteristic of children with autism have also been described by psychoanalysts working with adults.

For many years, Donald Meltzer led a clinical research group of child psychotherapists and psychoanalysts working with children the severity of whose autism varied through a wide range. The clinical and theoretical papers that grew out of this are collected in *Explorations in Autism* (Meltzer *et al.* 1975). Some of the resulting concepts are widely used in work with children who are not on the spectrum – for example, the dimensionality of mental functioning, mental space, and adhesive identification (or, as Tustin preferred to say, 'adhesive equation'). Interestingly, the non-psychoanalytic intervention of sensory integration training, in which children on the spectrum are helped to focus on input from more than one sensory mode at a time, can be theorised psychoanalytically in terms of Meltzer's concept of 'dismantling': he proposed this term for a process by which children with autism allowed their mental apparatus to fall apart through becoming absorbed by sensory input from one channel only, which meant that they could not apprehend experience 'in the round'.

As already mentioned, Anne Alvarez' work with children on the spectrum integrates psychoanalytic theory with findings from child development research. This has had a major impact on psychoanalytic views of normal development, as well as on technical considerations in the treatment of many children who are not on the autistic spectrum, but whose capacity for symbolic function is impaired for whatever reason. Alvarez' contributions include a psychoanalytic approach to deficit that is founded on what she calls the 'two-person model'. This contrasts with the 'one-person model' of cognitivists, according to which a deficit is solely a function of the individual child. A two-person model, on the other hand, allows for the effect of the child's internal world: children often develop – or fail to develop – in line with what they perceive as their carers' expectations. Alvarez (1999) has traced the complicated interplay of deficit, defence, deviance and personality that can make it so challenging to frame interpretations in line with the fluctuating needs and capacities of a child with autism. Her concept of 'reclamation' – the active intervention of the therapist to call the child into contact – is an instance of the technical modifications that are often essential if the child psychotherapist is to get through to a child on the spectrum.

A particularly lively culture of psychoanalytic work on autism has developed in France. While Lacanian authors (Danon-Boileau, Joly, Laznik, Touati) have perhaps been particularly interested in language development, Haag, Houzel, Lechevalier and Golse have applied and extended the ideas of Tustin and Meltzer in original ways. Haag, for example, has integrated her long experience of working with children on the spectrum with findings from infant observation in formulating a developmental theory of the processes by means of which children acquire psychological ownership of their body (Haag 2000). This means that such seemingly diverse conditions as autism and dyspraxia can be understood in terms of the same psychoanalytic framework.

Recent years have seen the publication of a growing number of first-person accounts by children and adults with autism, which constitute a particularly valuable source of understanding. It is of interest that these often include descriptions of their bodies feeling scattered or unintegrated. 'Tito' Mukhopadhyay (2003) explains that spinning in circles helped him to feel that his body was gathered together; when his mother touched him, it provided awareness of that body part. (He also describes his inability to attend to input from more than one sensory channel at a time.) Equally, Gunilla Gerland (1996) recalls that, for a long time, parts of her body felt like 'terra incognita', and that the degree to which this was so depended on their distance from her head.

Case example

Daniel was a looked-after child who was referred for treatment at the age of nine because his teachers at a boarding school for children with moderate learning difficulties had recognised that he met all the criteria for autism on the *Is this autism?* checklist. He had been taken into care at the age of six, when he was found wandering the streets at night. His mother had herself been in care and had mental health problems. Although she loved her children and did her best to bring them up well, she was not always able to visit Daniel at pre-arranged times. Her own problems would have made it even harder for her to manage a child like Daniel, who reacted with terror and tantrums to any attempt to get him to conform. It is important to stress that her behaviour was not the 'cause' of Daniel's autism, and that none of his siblings was on the spectrum.

At the time of referral, Daniel was described as ineducable. Any attempt to get him to adapt to the routine of the school triggered a major tantrum, followed by a terrified collapse. As he got bigger, his tantrums became more destructive, so that the local authority officers were considering a fifty-two-week placement. However, Daniel inspired great affection in his teachers, and they pushed for a specialist assessment for him. Later, they supported his treatment wholeheartedly, even to the extent of bringing him a long way to the clinic, in their own time, if there was a hitch in the escorting arrangements.

Daniel inspired much affection in me as well: this may be understood as a sign that there was a part of his personality that was eager to establish contact and hopeful of a good outcome. At the beginning of each of his early sessions, he would repeat, with an expression of wonder, 'Green curtains! Three grey radiators!' However, his efforts to communicate and to build up a helpful relationship with me seemed to be undermined by a malign presence in the corner, into which he looked with a terrified, haunted expression as though he were hallucinating. At the end of an early session, he glanced into a dark bit of the corridor and said, 'Monster'. His rigidity and his need to be in complete control could be understood as strategies for keep the monster at bay.

Like many children with autism, even those who can speak, Daniel often communicated by means of veiled references to emotionally significant videos, nursery rhymes or advertising jingles. For example, at the beginning of his treatment, he would lie on the couch, sucking his thumb, pressing on one of his eyeballs, and muttering indistinctly. Out of the muttering there gradually emerged words that sounded like 'Cruella deVille'. I repeated, 'Cruella deVille', and said how important it was for him to be sure that I would not be a nasty lady who tried to kill puppies to make their skins into a coat for myself. In response, Daniel sang quite clearly, 'Cruella deVille, Cruella deVille', with one 'Daniella deVille' interspersed amid the 'Cruellas'. I took this to indicate that the 'monster' that Daniel was frightened of took the form of a cruel, murderous figure who wanted to tear off his skin. (Before the first holiday break in his treatment, he was to say, 'Poor mouth. Poor skin.') This is a terrifying fear of psychotic proportions, and the emergence of 'Daniella deVille' seems to imply that Daniel was confused about the extent of his own contribution to the frightening monster. The fear that being separate means having one's skin torn away is frequently encountered in the material of children on the spectrum; so is Cruella deVille, who is a very apt representation of the kind of nightmarish figure who might inflict this kind of torment.

Any deviation from the expected routine reduced Daniel to a state of terror. When his taxi was twenty minutes late, he arrived distraught, sobbing, shaking, and screaming 'I want a sweet', and he cowered away from me as though I had become the monster. His escort accompanied him to the therapy room, where the familiarity of the surroundings helped him to settle. It took half an hour of work before he suddenly looked at me and said, wonderingly, 'Mrs Rhode!' as though he were recognising me after waking up from a bad dream.

I would see Daniel as one of those children described by Tustin (1990) who use 'the straitjacket of autism' in order to master psychotic anxieties, including the fear of excessively bad figures who wanted to hurt him. His headmistress agreed that his rigidity became worse when he was frightened. A great deal of work had to be done on his unstable body image; on his fear of falling; on the anxiety that dangerous creatures might intrude into the room through the grouting between the sink tiles. These fears of being attacked, which were emotionally based, interacted with the visual and auditory hypersensitivity that is characteristic of children on the spectrum, so that Daniel's reaction to light and sound could be seen to vary depending on his state of mind.

At the beginning of his treatment, Daniel had no confidence in my capacity to cope with any anger from him without either becoming angry myself or collapsing. With the repeated experience that I returned undamaged from holidays, his confidence grew, and he began to express his feelings more directly through his play. Having his emotional preoccupations attended to in his sessions meant that his mind was less full of unrealistic terrors, so that he was freed to use it for other things. He rapidly learnt to read, and began to engage with schoolwork and to relate to other children.

When Daniel was thirteen, he began to use drawing as a means of communication. In his early pictures of water and sky it was hard to tell which was which. Soon, however, the outlines became more defined, he began to use perspective to indicate depth, and finally he used the drawings as a way of showing me what he had been doing in my absence.

Daniel was found a long-term placement with a foster-mother to whom he became very attached, and to whom he was able to say that he loved her. At the time of stopping treatment, after seven years of twice-weekly work, he was doing well at an excellent special school, and was integrating into mainstream for an afternoon each week. He enjoyed going to discos with his foster-sister.

Daniel was unusual in making this amount of progress in spite of not beginning treatment until the age of nine. His lengthy therapy was expensive, but less so than a fifty-two-week boarding placement would have been. On a personal level, his relationships with adults became a source of happiness for him and for them, and he could enjoy contact with his siblings and benefit by his schooling. He may in future be able to do paid work in an emotionally supportive setting. On balance, Daniel's improvement is gratifying and moving, but it highlights the need for treatment to begin much earlier where possible.

Assessment of children on the autistic spectrum

Daniel was offered therapy because he proved responsive to comments during assessment sessions, and because his school and carers were committed to supporting treatment. When families bring their children with autism for assessment, they often feel traumatised by the diagnosis of autism, by the years during which they have felt invalidated as parents by their child's failure to respond to them, and by the degree to which his or her vulnerability, tantrums, and rituals have made ordinary family life impossible (Klauber 1998). Not all children with autism respond to psychotherapy, and we do not yet know enough to be able to identify reliably those who will. A lengthy period of family work (Reid 1999; Rhode 2000) makes it possible to establish a partnership with the parents, to show them that their child's behaviour is more meaningful than they might have realised, to strengthen their confidence in their own capacity to understand and help their child, and to discover together with them whether thinking about their experience in this way is something that suits their family. The decision about proceeding to individual work can then be made collaboratively, based on whether or not improvement has already taken place. Where parents decide that they want individual psychotherapy for their child, this is accompanied by regular support for themselves.

Research

A single-case study based on detailed ratings of videotaped treatment sessions (Alvarez and Lee 2004) has demonstrated a significant increase in eye contact over the course of treatment. Preliminary results from a study of fifteen boys with autism under the age of five show a substantial reduction in the severity of autism as assessed by means of the Childhood Autism Rating Scale (CARS) at the end of a therapeutic assessment, though the untreated matched control group has yet to be recruited (Reid *et al.* 2001).

'Applied' interventions

Workers of all orientations agree that children on the spectrum need help as early as possible. Acquarone, who has developed an intensive intervention for all members of the family within the framework of the School of Infant Mental Health in London, has described her approach in a chapter in her edited book on *Signs of Autism in Infants: Recognition and Early Intervention* (Acquarone 2007). In France, Houzel (1999) has pioneered the use of therapeutic infant observation as an outreach intervention for babies and toddlers suffering from a range of severe problems, including babies at risk of autism. In Britain, this intervention is being used as part of a pilot research project (Rhode 2007; Gretton 2006), the very early results of which are encouraging.

Future directions

Many recent collections of clinical papers (Alvarez and Reid 1999; Barrows 2008; Mitrani and Mitrani 1997; Rhode and Klauber 2004; Rustin *et al.* 1997)) bear witness to the transformation that can be achieved through child psychotherapy with this group of children, as well as to the technical innovations that continue to be developed. There remains an urgent need for systematic studies, both to provide evidence of outcome and to place assessment on a firmer footing.

A psychodynamic approach can make an important contribution to a developing classification that extends beyond – and complements – behavioural description. Improvement following psychotherapy has often been dismissed as arising through faulty diagnosis, an issue that Urwin (2002) has recently addressed in considering 'when "autistic" is not necessarily "autism"'. Equally, it will be important to work out criteria for 'what suits whom', whether it be psychodynamic child psychotherapy; relatedness-based interventions such as RDI (Gutstein 2007); 'Floortime' (Greenspan *et al.* 1998); or, indeed, behavioural approaches, which fit well with the needs of some families.

Much remains to be explored in the field of autism, and child psychotherapy can make an important contribution. In the words of Lorna Wing (2003), 'Individuals with autistic disorders are endlessly fascinating. [Some] arouse feelings of wonder, astonishment and intellectual curiosity, which are among the many rewards experienced by those working in this field.'

References

Acquarone, S. (ed.) (2007) *Signs of Autism in Infants: Recognition and Early Intervention*, London: Karnac.

Alvarez, A. (1992) *Live Company*, London and New York: Routledge.

—— (1999) 'Disorder, deviance and personality: factors in the persistence and modifiability of autism', in A. Alvarez and S. Reid (eds) *Autism and Personality*, London and New York: Routledge.

Alvarez, A. and Lee, A. (2004) 'Early forms of relatedness in autism. A longitudinal clinical and quantitative single-case study', *Clinical Child Psychology and Psychiatry* 9: 499–518.

Alvarez, A. and Reid, S. (eds) (1999) *Autism and Personality*, London and New York: Routledge.

Asperger, H. (1944) 'Die "Autistischen Psychopathen" im Kindesalter', *Archiv für Psychiatrie und Nervenkrankheiten* 117: 76–136. (English translation by U. Frith: '"Autistic psychopathy" in childhood', in U. Frith (ed.) *Autism and Asperger Syndrome*, Cambridge: Cambridge University Press, 1991.)

Barrows, K. (ed.) (2008) *Autism in Childhood and Autistic Features in Adults: Psychoanalytic Perspectives*, London: Karnac.

Bettelheim, B. (1967) *The Empty Fortress: Infantile Autism and the Birth of the Self*, New York: Free Press.

Bick, E. (1968) 'The experience of the skin in early object relations', in A. Briggs (ed.) *Surviving Space: Papers on Infant Observation*, Tavistock Clinic Books Series, London: Karnac, 2002.

—— (1986) 'Further considerations on the function of the skin in early object relations', in A. Briggs (ed.) *Surviving Space: Papers on Infant Observation*, Tavistock Clinic Book Series, London: Karnac, 2002.

Gerland, G. (1996) *A Real Person: Life on the Outside*, translation J. Tate, London: Souvenir Press, 1997.

Greenspan, S., Wieder, S. and Simons, R. (1998) *The Child with Special Needs: Encouraging Intellectual and Emotional Growth*, Cambridge: Perseus Press.

Gretton, A. (2006) 'An account of a year's work with a mother and her 18-month-old son at risk of autism', *International Journal of Infant Observation* 9: 21–34.

Gutstein, S. E. (2007) *The Relationship Development Intervention*, Houston, TX: Connections Center Publications.

Haag, G. (2000) 'In the footsteps of Frances Tustin: further reflections on the construction of the body-ego', *International Journal of Infant Observation* 3: 7–22.

Hobson, R. P. (2002) *The Cradle of Thought*, Basingstoke: Macmillan.

Hodges, S. (2004) 'A psychological perspective on theories of Asperger's syndrome', in M. Rhode and T. Klauber (eds) *The Many Faces of Asperger's Syndrome*, Tavistock Clinic Book Series, London: Karnac.

Houzel, D. (1999) 'A therapeutic application of infant observation in child psychiatry', *International Journal of Infant Observation* 2: 42–53.

Kanner, L. (1943) 'Autistic disturbance of affective contact', *Nervous Child* 2: 217–50. (Reprinted in L. Kanner *Childhood Psychosis: Initial Studies and New Insights*. New York: Wiley, 1973.)

Klauber, T. (1998) 'The significance of trauma in work with the parents of severely disturbed children, and its implications for work with parents in general', *Journal of Child Psychotherapy* 24: 85–107.

Klein, M. (1930) 'The importance of symbol-formation in the development of the ego', in *The Writings of Melanie Klein, Vol. 1*, London: Hogarth, 1975.

Klein, S. (1980) 'Autistic phenomena in neurotic patients', *International Journal of Psycho-Analysis* 61: 395–402.

Kolvin, K. (1971) 'Studies in childhood psychosis. I. Diagnostic criteria classification', *British Journal of Psychiatry* 118: 381–4.

Mahler, M., Pine, F. and Bergman, A. (1975) *The Psychological Birth of the Human Infant*, New York: Basic Books.

Maiello, S. (2000) '"Song-and-dance" and its developments: the function of rhythm in the learning process of oral and visual language', in M. Cohen and A. Hahn (eds) *Exploring the Work of Donald Meltzer: A Festschrift*, London and New York: Karnac Books.

Meltzer, D., Bremner, J., Hoxter, S., Weddell, D. and Wittenberg, I. (1975) *Explorations in Autism*, Strath Tay: Clunie Press.

Mitrani, T. and Mitrani, J. L. (eds) (1997) *Encounters with Autistic States: A Memorial Tribute to Frances Tustin*, Northvale, NJ: Jason Aronson.

Mukhopadhyay, T. R. (2003) *The Mind Tree*, New York: Arcade Publishing.

Reid, S. (1999) 'The assessment of the child with autism: a family perspective', in A. Alvarez and S. Reid (eds) *Autism and Personality*, London and New York: Routledge.

Reid, S., Alvarez, A. and Lee, A. (2001) 'The Tavistock Autism Workshop approach', in J. Richer and S. Coates (eds) *Autism: The Search for Coherence*, London: Jessica Kingsley.

Rhode, M. (2000) 'Assessing children with communication disorders', in M. Rustin and E. Quagliata (eds) *Assessment in Child Psychotherapy*, Tavistock Clinic Book Series, London: Karnac.

—— (2007) 'Helping toddlers to communicate: infant observation as an early intervention', in S. Acquarone (ed.) *Signs of Autism in Infants: Detection and Early Intervention*, London: Karnac.

Rhode, M. and Klauber, T. (eds) (2004) *The Many Faces of Asperger's Syndrome*, Tavistock Clinic Book Series, London: Karnac.

Rustin, M., Rhode, M., Dubinsky, A. and Dubinsky, H. (eds) (1997) *Psychotic States in Children*, Tavistock Clinic Book Series, London: Duckworth.

Rutter, M., Andersen-Wood, L., Beckett, C., Bredenkamp, D., Castle, J., Groothues, C., Kreppner, J., Keaveney, L., Lord, C., O'Connor, T. G. and the English and

Romanian Adoptees (ERA) Study Team (1999) 'Quasi-autistic patterns following severe early global privation', *Journal of Child Psychology and Psychiatry* 40: 537–49.

Schore, A. N. (1994) *Affect Regulation and the Origin of the Self*, Hillsdale, NJ: Erlbaum.

Sigman, M. (1999) 'Change and continuity in the development of children with autism.' *The Signal* [Newsletter of the World Association for Infant Mental Health] 7: 1–14.

Simpson, D. (2004) 'Asperger's syndrome and autism: distinct syndromes with important similarities', in M. Rhode and T. Klauber (eds) *The Many Faces of Asperger's Syndrome*, Tavistock Clinic Book Series, London: Karnac.

—— (2008) 'A psychiatric approach to autism and its relationship to a psychoanalytic perspective', in K. Barrows (ed.) *Autism in Childhood and Autistic Features in Adults: Psychoanalytic Perspectives*, London: Karnac.

Trevarthen, C. (1980) 'The foundations of intersubjectivity: the development of interpersonal and cooperative understanding in infants', in D. Olson (ed.) *The Social Foundations of Language and Thought*, New York: Norton.

Tustin, F. (1972) *Autism and Childhood Psychosis*, London: Hogarth.

—— (1980) 'Autistic objects', in F. Tustin (1981) *Autistic States in Children*, London and New York: Routledge.

—— (1981a) *Autistic States in Children*, London and New York: Routledge (2nd Revised Edition, 1992).

—— (1981b) 'Psychological birth and psychological catastrophe', in F. Tustin *Autistic States in Children*, London and New York: Routledge.

—— (1986) *Autistic Barriers in Neurotic Patients*, London: Karnac.

—— (1990) *The Protective Shell in Children and Adults*, London: Karnac.

Urwin, C. (2002) 'A psychoanalytic approach to language delay: when "autistic" isn't necessarily autism', *Journal of Child Psychotherapy* 28: 73–93.

Wing, L. (2003) 'Foreword', in T. R. Mukhopadhyay *The Mind Tree*, London: National Autistic Society.

Wing, L. and Gould, J. (1979) 'Severe impairments of social interaction and associated abnormalities in children: epidemiology and classification', *Journal of Autism and Developmental Disorders* 9: 11–29.

Winnicott, D. W. (1949) 'Birth memories, birth trauma and anxiety', in D. W. Winnicott *Through Paediatrics to Psycho-Analysis*, London: Hogarth, 1958.

20 Psychotherapy with severely traumatised children and adolescents

Far beyond words

Monica Lanyado

Trauma. The word is used in such sweeping ways and can encompass so many different kinds of experiences – all of differing severities and durations: what kind of experience really warrants this word? The list is grim and includes: rejection, divorce, serious illness, accident, abandonment, sexual abuse, physical abuse, separation, bereavement, wartime experience, torture, witnessing or experiencing violent attack, seeking political asylum, moving home, emotional cruelty, poverty.

This book is full of clinical examples of children, families and parents, who have suffered these experiences and whose emotional life and behaviour bears the scars of what has happened to them. In listening to and being deeply receptive to their patient's suffering, therapists come to know in an intimate way, about the worst side of human experience and what one human being can inflict on another, as well as the sheer randomness of the way life dishes up distressing and at times terrible experiences to us all. The helplessness of children in these awful situations can be particularly painful to hear. So much so that we probably all in some measure find ourselves defending against knowing the fullness of such distress. It feels too much to bear. Unthinkable. Intolerable.

Even reading about what has happened to these children can be very distressing. Perhaps this chapter and those others which deal directly with different forms of trauma such as sexual abuse and abusing, and child victims of torture and political violence, should come with a 'health warning' as they are inevitably shocking and very hard to think about.

What is the difference between an individual's 'ordinary' pain in response to these (sadly) everyday events in many parts of the world, and becoming traumatised by the same events? Why are some people unable to move on with their lives after these kinds of experiences, whilst others, who seemingly have suffered even more, appear to be able to make a go of it? Clearly there are enormous individual differences involved and it is not the event itself, however horrific or long-lasting it may be, that defines whether the sufferer finds a good-enough way of carrying on with life. It is not that the person who seems to be able to manage is not also deeply affected and distressed by what has happened

– not at all. But somehow he has managed to find a way of living with it. The traumatised person has not.

These are complicated questions involving many variables, which lead to one of the key issues at the heart of what psychoanalytic treatment is all about – the interaction of external events and the internal world of the person to whom they are happening. The prevailing state of the individual's emotional well-being at the time of the trauma, together with the availability of loving emotional support following the trauma, plays a very significant part in shaping how severely the trauma affects the rest of a person's life.

In some instances, the full implications of trauma may not be perceived until the child becomes an adolescent or even an adult. It can be bewildering when traumatic experience resurfaces, having been thought to be long 'forgotten' or dealt with. Often it is not clear what has triggered the re-evoking, or even first clear memories, of past traumas. In other cases, possibly particularly with sexual abuse, there are some clearly vulnerable life stages such as the first adolescent sexual relationship, childbirth – or simply seeing a baby's genitals when changing the nappy. In situations such as these, parents who have been traumatised before their child was born can be greatly affected in their ability to care for their children. This is one of the mechanisms for the inter-generational transmission of traumatic experience.

Often, when treating traumatised children, there is a powerful experience of several generations being present in the room, with the child who is being offered treatment potentially breaking the cycle of traumatisation which has been transmitted through the generations. This is particularly evident when there have been generations of physical and/or incestuous sexual abuse, and where there is a history of religious or political persecution.

Example 1

A mother, who was severely sexually abused by her mother as a child, could barely tolerate changing her baby's nappy. Despite the seriousness of the trauma, she had managed to make something of her life, probably by using a form of useful 'splitting' within her mind which kept her well away from memories and feelings about what had happened to her. She had a good job and had married. She was a good-enough and conscientious mother in many respects, wanting to overcome her unhappy childhood experiences and to give her daughter a happier childhood than she had had, but when it came to potty training she became excessively punitive, at times screaming at her daughter and hitting her when she could not use the potty. The mother did not understand this, but could not stop herself, although she felt very guilty about her behaviour.

Unfortunately the daughter remained incontinent well into adolescence, became very disturbed and had a deeply troubled relationship with her parents. However, this mother was able to seek help. It was only well into the daughter's intensive treatment that the mother was able to talk to her daughter's therapist about her own childhood sexual trauma. This information helped the whole clinical picture to make sense, and the daughter started to be freed from her mother's projections and was able to begin to make a recovery, whilst the mother was offered more intensive help with the repercussions of the sexual abuse that had happened so many years before.

'Second generation traumatisation', as it is known, may lie behind a number of otherwise incomprehensible emotional disturbances in children. The children do not know the nature of the traumatic memories they evoke in their parents, but may nevertheless be aware of their parent's fragility through glimpses of traumatic or incomprehensible fragments of behaviour in their everyday interactions. It is as if they are living under the shadow of the trauma with no way of knowing that life could be otherwise. The children may be aware of 'no go' areas in otherwise communicative parents' emotional lives. Therapists are often aware of a 'missing link' that would help them to make sense of a confusing clinical picture. This has been written about with regard to traumatic experience in general, as well as specifically in accounts of second generation Holocaust survivors (Bergman and Jucovy 1982).

The novelist David Grossman gives a particularly vivid description of this phenomenon in his book *See Under: Love* in which a little boy tries to make sense of the many things he knows (without having ever been told) not to talk about or ask questions about, to his parents or their friends. It gradually becomes clear to the reader that the adults are all Holocaust survivors, but the child has no conception of this, only the fear that it will cause a catastrophe if he dares to try to find out more (Grossman 1990).

And indeed, many parents who have survived terrible experiences in wartime or in their childhood or contemporary lives, make a clear conscious decision never to talk about it to anyone, particularly their children. This is the best way they can find of living with these experiences. Other people take the opposite view, feeling that traumatic experiences must be talked about as a kind of exorcism of the evil that has been planted within them, as well as a warning to others, particularly those they love most, about the dangers in the world. Still others, although they wish they could put the traumatic experiences and memories out of their minds, are unable to do so, suffering from traumatic nightmares and flashbacks, and flooding many of the people in their everyday lives with their traumatic experiences.

In trying to describe the complexity of the concept of 'trauma', Laplanche and Pontalis helpfully suggest that:

> . . . in adopting the term [trauma], psycho-analysis carries the three ideas implicit in it over to the psychical level: the idea of violent shock, the idea of a wound and the idea of consequences affecting the whole organisation.
>
> (Lapanche and Pontalis 1988: 466)

These three ideas, of shock, wound and consequences leave the question of how the duration and intensity of each of these elements contributes to traumatisation unanswered. The idea of the individual's mind and emotional life becoming flooded and overwhelmed is central to identifying whether traumatisation is playing a key role in a child's emotional disturbance or not. Another difficulty is that people can seemingly 'get by' for many years following traumatic experiences, but with a change in life events, such as puberty, becoming a parent or facing the death of an elderly parent, old wounds that have been dormant are re-awakened. The triggers for this kind of re-awakening could also be quite obscure. But the immediacy of the impact of feeling overwhelmed is undeniable. Post-traumatic stress disorder, of the kind noted during the First World War in 'shell shock', is the most vivid example of this kind of traumatisation. Severe and repeated traumas of the kind described in this book can't ever be thought of as having gone away completely, and it is because of this that treatment may be episodic.

Example 2

Nancy's family home, from which they ran a small business, was broken into by armed robbers when she was two and half years old. They had been tied up and threatened at gunpoint until her father opened a small safe. Nancy had been less tightly bound and had managed to raise the alarm after the robbers left. In the days that followed, Nancy kept going into prolonged periods of screaming which no-one knew how to help her with. The parents were also traumatised and found their daughter's distress and fear unbearable. This was an ordinary family in traumatic circumstances. The father sought help for Nancy and his whole family, and fortunately I was able to see them together as a family very soon after the robbery for two lengthy consultations. They were all still very frightened, but the consultations seemed to help and were followed by a few consultations with Nancy on her own. The parents then felt that they were able to manage their own anxiety as well as Nancy's much better, and wanted to 'get back to normal'.

Ten months later the father contacted me again, saying that Nancy had been fine for a number of months and they had all started to feel safer but suddenly, she was having awful nightmares again, like she had when the robbery had first taken place. She woke, got out of bed as if to go to her parents' bed, but then became rooted to the spot and just screamed and screamed, unable to move. They had to go to her to release her from this frozen position, but the screaming continued. Nancy came to see me and I was able to make the connection between her nightmare about ghosts and monsters, and her helplessness when she was tied up and unable to move, during the robbery. When I had seen her initially, she had been particularly distressed by seeing her father helplessly tied up and unable to rescue her. This added to her panic at the time and re-emerged in her nightmares. The fact that her parents could now move and come to her when she was locked in her nightmare helped her to put the trauma back into the past. Making this link was sufficient, in this healthy family, for Nancy to settle down again and resume her ordinary development, although we now decided to meet every few months so that the memory, however awful, of what had happened, remained acknowledged and conscious rather than getting lost in the unconscious in a potentially unhelpful way.

Eighteen months after the robbery father rang me, clearly in a very distressed state himself. Having been a 'tower of strength' to his family throughout this time, he had suddenly gone to pieces. He could become so terrified in the street, particularly if he saw a man who looked vaguely like one of the robbers, that he started to shake violently, became unable to speak and felt absolutely terrified. He could not carry on with his work and needed to be referred for specialist post-traumatic stress disorder counselling which helped him to get over the worst of the symptoms, but left him a very different and more anxious person than he had been before the robbery.

Maybe a key indicator in this complicated clinical picture is whether authentic emotional growth and development have been possible in reasonable measure after extremely distressing experiences, or not. When the individual has become stuck in life in a way which hinders the experience of current good-enough relationships and experiences, traumatic experience may be at the root of the problem. This is because one of the most recognisable features of traumatisation is that the same fundamental fear or experience arises again and again – in an undigested, repeated and unprocessed form. It is as if the moment of abandonment by a loved one, or the moment of helpless terror at the time of abuse, is happening right now, in the present. Nothing has changed despite the actual external event having happened years before. In this aspect time has stood still.

Hard-fought-for recovery is on its way when time starts to move on again and the traumatic events are felt to lie clearly in the past. It is a sign of great progress when the sufferer can genuinely begin to feel 'that was then, this is now' – and recognise that his life has truly changed for the better in some very important ways. (For a vivid account of this process where the therapist and patient battle with the 'unlaid ghost' of a two-year-old child witnessing the murder by her parents of her baby brother, see Marsoni 2006.)

The rapid expansion of neurophysiological research on the impact of trauma on brain development and consequent hormonal regulation of the whole body puts the treatment of emotional trauma into a physical/bodily as well as a psychical developmental frame. We now know that from birth, and possibly before, the baby's body and brain development are powerfully affected by actual experiences and relationships, good and bad (see Music (Chapter 5) and Midgley (Chapter 6)). Psychoanalytic treatment and theory has always placed great importance on the impact of relational and external trauma on the development of the individual's internal world. The advances in this important area of research have ensured that the separation of body and mind that has existed in the past when thinking about trauma has come to an end. We have to think holistically.

In particular, this research is of great significance because it shows that the physical consequences of relational and external trauma are that they stop or inhibit vital brain development, particularly during the first two years of life. Important neural pathways between the 'reptilian, ancient' limbic system and the advanced thinking cortex may not have been sufficiently formed to enable children severely traumatised during the first two years of life in particular, to be able to use the cortex to think about their impulsive behaviour before acting on what the limbic system dictates (see Music, Chapter 5). Early childhood trauma which is unregulated by parental care also impacts, through hormonal disregulation, on the bodily expression of fear, rage and violence. Gerhardt describes this process very clearly in terms of the stress hormone, cortisol, not only flooding the traumatised person's body leading to fight/flight hyper-reactivity, but also corroding the brain itself (Gerhardt 2004). This research has clear treatment implications.

Example 3

A nine-year old boy who had been severely traumatised by his birth family for the first five years of his life before being fostered long-term in a stable family had great difficulty in playing and thinking. In his three times weekly therapy, he got caught in highly repetitive and boring play for weeks on end, so much so that there was a growing feeling that he might be on the autistic spectrum. Slowly, through the playful presence of his therapist, who did not in any way direct his play but was simply playfully alert and available to the patient, small variations started to appear in his play, although it still remained largely stuck in stories about children's cartoon characters.

Gradually, the play started to gather some meaning, but when the therapist tried to say something very simple about this to the child, the child hated this attempt to think about what he was doing, and shouted at the therapist: 'Come on, let's just play!' This went on for some while, but the therapist did his best to persevere with the thinking and sharing this in a timely way with the boy, until eventually the boy started to become curious and interested in the things his therapist was saying – and less frightened by this alarming business of 'thinking'. This reduction of the patient's fear of words was a reflection of work that had been going on in the transference–countertransference relationship. It was possibly also a recognition by the child that 'thinking' was not only all right, it also helped him.

This process progressed to the therapist not only being able to think alongside the play and say to the child 'I want to have a think about this' with the child tolerating it, but to the child eventually being able to declare, loudly and often, to his therapist and his foster parent 'I like thinking!' Quite an achievement.

We can now understand that this kind of progression, which is evident in many clinical accounts of psychotherapy with severely deprived and traumatised children, is the result of the therapeutic relationship enabling new neural pathways between the reactive limbic system and the cortex to be established. It is a lengthy and uphill struggle, but it is nevertheless possible.

One of the theoretical foundations which I find helpful when thinking about the treatment of trauma is the work of Winnicott. Based on his direct observation as a paediatrician of many ordinary babies and children, as well as his psychoanalytic practice with children and adults, he conceptualised natural developmental processes as being disrupted, derailed, or in extremis, shut down, as a result of what he called 'impingements' from the external world on the baby/child's ongoing sense-of-being (Winnicott 1963). When there is ordinary 'good-enough' care of children, parents constantly strive to look after and protect the child in such a way that he or she is not overwhelmed by experiences which cannot as yet be managed. At the same time good-enough parents need to encourage age-appropriate independence in the world by providing a 'facilitating' emotional environment within which the natural potential of the individual child can mature. These ideas can be linked with Bowlby's thinking about the protective role of attachment figures (Hopkins and Phillips, Chapter 4).

The other concept that is very helpful when working with people who have been traumatised, and whose communications about what they have experienced have moved 'far beyond words', is that of the projection of intolerable, unspeakable and unthinkable feelings into another person who is prepared to receive and listen to them (Horne, Chapter 3; Lanyado and Horne, Chapter 10). These projections are received by the other person's whole body and mind, often much more powerfully physically than emotionally, to start with. The other person, who may or may not be a psychotherapist, then tries to process and make some sense of what has been projected into him or her, and try to judge how much of this can be talked about and shared with the traumatised person. These psychic processes have their origins in the earliest forms of ordinary non-verbal communication between parents and baby. Bion has written extensively about this process, both as an ordinary process and as a part of the therapeutic process (Bion 1962).

Example 4

A nine-year-old girl who had been severely incestuously abused by female members of her family within a paedophile ring was, not surprisingly, for a long while unable to communicate in words, her experience to her therapist. However, the shocking nature of what had happened to her was often projected into her therapist, who was repeatedly given a brief but awful emotional experience of the abuse, which was gradually processed in the countertransference relationship.

On one occasion, smiling slyly, the child asked the therapist to close her eyes saying 'You have to trust me'. The therapist felt she needed to go along with this briefly even though she was well aware of risks involved. The child put a paper towel in water and then swiped it all over the therapist's face, pushing it this way and that as you would to clean a baby's bottom, except that this was done roughly and sadistically, with the child saying 'we have to clean you all up . . .'. The therapist was shocked, and felt as if at that moment she knew what it had been like for her patient to be abused by her mother, when she was still a baby.

Opening her eyes and stopping the behaviour, the therapist said to the girl that she (the girl) wanted her (the therapist) to know what it had felt like to be a little baby, trusting someone and then feeling they hurt you and did things you didn't like and that were very frightening. The repetition of many such experiences of being understood in this way gradually helped the girl to make some recovery from her terrible trauma.

The difference between the ways in which close family and friends try to listen to and help their loved ones and the ways in which a psychotherapist tries to do the same thing lies in the specialised training, and in particular the training analysis, which fortifies the therapist to be able to bear to listen fully to, and try to endure the awfulness and to think about what is being communicated. There is a limit to what most people can stand to know about the distress of their loved ones before it becomes too unbearable for them as well. This non-verbal process of communication is very powerfully present in the transference–countertransference relationship when working with traumatised patients as many detailed clinical accounts illustrate (Emanuel 2004; Grunbaum 1997; Hindle 1996; Hopkins 1986; Jackson 2004; Lanyado 2004, 2006; Marsoni 2006; Mendelsohn 1997). The therapist's capacity to experience, observe, think about and 'contain' these communications, which can then be identified with and 'introjected' by the patient, is central to the therapeutic process with traumatised patients (Bion 1962).

Seen in these terms, it is possible to conceptualise the path to recovery as being through re-connecting to the developmental pathways that have been ruptured by the trauma. In ordinary parlance, people talk about trying to 'get back to normal life' or to 'get on with life'. It is usually only when this has been tried, over time, in multiple ways by parents, foster carers, adoptive parents and concerned professionals, that the help of child and adolescent mental health services, and a child psychotherapist in particular, will be sought. In terms of Laplanche and Pontalis' conceptualisation, the therapist is dealing with the consequences of the trauma so that the internal world of the survivor starts to grow and mature again and innate personal strengths start to re-surface. The shock and wound may scab over and scar, but they will always be vulnerable areas within the inner world of the survivor; vulnerable to being re-awakened. If this re-awakening takes place within a strengthened personality structure and mind, its impact will be more like a controlled explosion which, although destructive is still contained, than a terrorist attack. Hurry describes this as the therapist functioning at times as a 'developmental object' for the patient (Hurry 1998).

Far beyond words

Each referral of a child for therapy is accompanied by an adult's account of the child's history and current life experience. The fact that external events which could have been traumatising for a child can be substantiated by 'witnesses' locates the treatment of traumatisation in children in a different place from the psychoanalytic treatment of adults. External reality is bound to play a much bigger part in the treatment of a child than in the treatment of an adult where other important people in the patient's life are unlikely to be in contact with the adult's therapist, and the internal world is likely to take on a more powerful role in the internal–external world dialogue.

One of the most difficult technical issues when working with traumatised patients is how to judge when to put a non-verbal communication into words and when to simply stay quiet. This connects to another difficult and central issue, regarding how emotionally close the patient can bear to let the therapist be – and indeed how close the therapist can bear to be – to the traumatised patient. Traumatised patients often feel aware of how people back off from them, in a kind of horror of knowing what has happened to them. This can lead to a sense of isolation, or for some patients a feeling of further rejection and abandonment. The trauma survivor can feel in some strange way, emotionally untouchable, leading to an irrational feeling of shame about what has happened to him or her. The traumatic experiences can also create an enormous chasm between the survivor of trauma and those who have not been traumatised, in which there is a longing for loving intimacy and a tremendous fear of it. This is particularly true for 'looked after children' (see Chapters 21 and 22).

Example 5

It is unlikely that Lesley would have needed the help of the child and adolescent mental health services had she not experienced a terrible trauma when she was nine years old. She came from a secure and stable family, with extended family close by, had a good circle of friends and was doing well at school. But then she was attacked and raped and everyone in her small community knew what had happened to her. After a few weeks of her family trying to cope with this awful event – which was eventually followed by the successful trial and conviction of her attacker – the family doctor referred the whole family for help. She came for twice weekly therapy for some years and her parents were seen once weekly by one of my colleagues. The most striking feature of her therapy was how inadequate words were in helping her to recover. We spent many months, in the middle period of her therapy, with barely anything being said between us. However, she became deeply absorbed in delicate drawings, and cuttings and stickings. I realised that, whenever I spoke, I seemed to be interrupting an important, wordless, therapeutic process in which the healing of a 'basic fault' (like a geological fault line) was taking place (Balint 1968).

The quietness was suffused with emotion and distress and also partly related to her fear that if she started to talk about what had happened to her, she would start screaming and never be able to stop. It was significant that she had been gagged at the time of the rape. She never told me any of the details of what had happened to her, but through the process of projecting her wordless terror, shame and sadness into me, I felt that I received fifty-minute doses of what she had been through and continued to go through, and this seemed to help.

It became apparent to me that more than anything, she was benefitting from my 'quiet presence' in the room. Winnicott writes about this important developmental process, when a young child is starting to play and explore the world and is only able to do this because of being 'alone' but 'in the presence' of another person (Winnicott 1958). My experience in the room with Lesley was well described by this evocative phrase, which to me means being highly alert and 'present' in the room using as much of my 'Self' as possible to be available in what could almost be thought of as a contemplative or meditative state of mind (Lanyado 2009).

The work with her parents was also tremendously important as they were at a loss over how to cope with their own distress as well as their daughter's terror at being out of their sight, and her dreadful nightmares.

Other child psychotherapists have noted how repeatedly and multiply traumatised children – often children who are being fostered or adopted, or who live in children's homes – cannot bear the words of the therapist, and will run out of the room, cover their ears and scream at the therapist to shut up. This hyper-reactive behaviour is accompanied by violent and threatening behaviour towards the therapist as well as an ambivalent longing to be close to and cared for by the therapist. These are children who are physiologically caught in fight/flight behaviour for quite a lengthy period at the start of therapy. They often experience the therapist's words as traumatic triggers and actually attack the therapist or run. It may take several years of therapy, during which such projection is the main form of communication, before gradually first play and then words become the main forms of communication (Emanuel 2004; Jackson 2004). The therapist's wise use of his or her countertransference experience is the main way of working with the onslaught of these children who need both to get under the therapist's skin, and to be survived by the therapist. Clinical supervision of these very difficult cases by an experienced colleague may become essential if the clinician is to be enabled to survive in as healthy a way as possible.

Play is a vital means of communication in the process from wordless projection to beginning to have an internal and external narrative for the traumatic life events. However, initially, the most severely traumatised children are much too reactive to be able to play in any way that might help them or the therapeutic process. Often the developmental process of playing itself has been disrupted by the very poor and neglected starts they have had in their lives. One of the most helpful things that the therapist can facilitate, is enabling such a child to start playing. The emphasis here is on facilitating, not leading, play. However, this is greatly helped by a willingness on the part of the therapist to be 'playfully present' for the child as in example 3 above. (For a fuller discussion of the importance of playing in the therapeutic process with traumatised children, see Lanyado 2006 and 2008.)

Survival mechanisms

There are two particularly important, but extreme defence mechanisms which can help the individual to survive his ordeal: dissociation, and identification with the aggressor. However, on both a conscious and an unconscious level, there is a strong tendency for these survival mechanisms to continue long past their usefulness and become means of denying psychic reality in ways which threaten mental health and bring new problems in their wake. One of the aims of therapy in these situations is to enable the patients to modify these extreme defences so that a bearable but not overwhelming amount of distress can be tolerated. The extremity of the defence which is needed when the individual is initially overwhelmed by fear is not needed when the external threat has passed. Other more moderate defences will suffice and take less toll on the mental well-being of the survivor.

Example 6

Cleve describes her work with a two-year-old child who had been in a car accident in which his mother and baby brother were killed. The father was offered treatment by a colleague alongside the boy's therapy (Cleve 2008). Several months after the accident, the little boy had still not acknowledged that his mother and brother were 'gone'. He had a fixed but vacant smile on his face and had shown no distress. He was in a dissociated state of mind which his therapy helped him to find words for, when he was finally able to say to his therapist 'A big one and a little one is gone'.

'Identification with the aggressor' is a very worrying defence because it perpetuates the aggressor's violence and turns the victim into the perpetrator of trauma (A. Freud 1936). It gives mastery over weakness, humiliation and shame and is often amplified by the aggressor's insistence at the time of traumatisation that the victim likes what is happening, or that the prisoner (for example) deserves the torture he or she is suffering. This is a very destructive mechanism over time and may lead to the kind of thinking that believes that 'it happened to me and it didn't do me any real harm, so I can do it to . . .' or in adulthood to sadism or psychopathy . This is a denial of an intolerable psychic reality.

The mother in my first example, who had been sexually abused by her mother as a child, had the determination *not* to do the same thing to her child. However, despite her achievement of not sexually abusing her child, the unconscious pressure of the power to repeat traumatic experiences still came through in her physical abuse of her child. But she was able to recognise that her daughter needed help and this ultimately started to break the inter-generational cycle of abuse. However, for some children, it is only by removing them from their abusive families that this mechanism can be addressed.

Example 7

A nine-year old boy was adopted when he was six, because of the violent and neglectful behaviour of his parents. He was referred for psychotherapy because of his sadistic and aggressive behaviour towards his adoptive mother and soon started to behave in this manner with his therapist. He would menacingly and convincingly strut about the room, threatening to and at times attacking his therapist, who often had to stop his sessions early because of this. He was verbally extremely abusive and shouted his hatred and denigration at his therapist. He would wreck the room deliberately and do all he could to humiliate her (as he saw it) in front of her colleagues and other patients. In supervision, a powerful image started to emerge of this boy being in identification with his extremely violent and abusive gangster 'father', who came and went as he pleased in the family home, sadistically and deliberately leaving pain and destruction in his wake.

In the therapy room, this boy was extremely frightening to be with because the identification was so total. It really felt to the therapist that she was at the mercy of a psychopathic adult gangster who would stop at nothing. As this was gradually understood in supervision, the projection of the boy's terror into the therapist gained some meaning and she was able to be in touch with the reality of this nine-year old boy's terrors from the past and to remember that he was a child, she was an adult, in a clinic with other staff at hand to help her. Her perseverance, and continued ability and determination to carry on working with this boy, gradually enabled him to see that he was not omnipotently able to destroy everything around him. The fact that his therapist did not retaliate to his sadistic behaviour, but tried to understand its roots, was also a revelation to him and gradually enabled him to show his intense feelings of helplessness and vulnerability, although initially he needed to do this in ways she could hear but not see. This happened in a session in which he allowed himself to sob loudly and genuinely about a feared loss – but from behind a closed door.

How does the therapist cope?

The clinical examples illustrate the complexity of the issues that traumatised patients bring to psychotherapeutic treatment and it is this complexity that indicates that psychotherapy rather than cognitive behavioural therapy or EMDR (eye movement desensitisation and reprocessing) is indicated. Patients such as this inevitably raise the important question of how the therapist copes with such an onslaught. We are not superhuman and of course session after session like this is bound to affect the therapist on a personal level, despite all the professionalism and training. Supervision, by an experienced colleague, of such cases may become essential when destructive behaviour is at its height, so that the therapist is enabled to think about what is happening and not become as flooded by it as the traumatised patient has been, and indeed often still is.

In addition, therapists may at times in their careers decide to have further therapy not only for personal reasons but also for professional ones so that they can process the feelings that such patients arouse in them. It also becomes very important for the therapist to live as wise a work/ private life balance as possible so that 'burn-out' from too many cases like this does not set in. This means making sure that there is enough relaxing and enjoyable leisure time in their lives and that there is sufficient emotional space for their loved ones. These are restorative factors which facilitate the mental well-being of the therapist and need to be taken very seriously if the therapist's life is not to suffer as a result of his or her demanding profession.

This chapter therefore ends with a 'health warning'. There can be whole days in which the child and adolescent psychotherapist is receiving deeply disturbing projections and other forms of communication about the worst aspects of life. What makes it worthwhile is the realisation that, without being unrealistically full of therapeutic zeal, it is possible, if at times very difficult, to do something to help these children to live happier and more normal lives than might otherwise be the case.

References

Balint, M. (1968) *The Basic Fault*, London: Tavistock.

Bergman, M. S. and Jucovy M. E. (1982) *Generations of the Holocaust*, New York: Basic Books.

Bion, W. R. (1962) *Learning from Experience*, London: Karnac.

Cleve, E. (2008) *A Big One and a Little One is Gone. Crisis Therapy with a Two Year Old Boy*, London: Karnac.

Emanuel, R. (2004) 'Thalamic fear', *Journal of Child Psychotherapy* 30(1): 71–87.

Freud, A. (1936) *The Ego and Mechanisms of Defence*, revised edn, London: Hogarth Press, 1965.

Gerhardt, S. (2004) *Why Love Matters. How Affection Shapes a Baby's Brain*, London and New York: Routledge.

Grossman, D. (1990) *See Under: Love*, London: Jonathan Cape.

Grunbaum, L. (1997) 'Psychotherapy with children in refugee families who have survived torture: containment and understanding of repetitive behaviour and play', *Journal of Child Psychotherapy* 23(3): 437–52.

Hindle, D. (1996) 'Doubly bereaved', *Journal of Child Psychotherapy* 22(2): 261–78.

Hopkins, J. (1986) 'Solving the mystery of monsters: steps towards the recovery from trauma', *Journal of Child Psychotherapy* 12(1): 61–71.

Hurry, A. (1998) *Psychoanalysis and Developmental Therapy*, London: Karnac.

Jackson, E. (2004) 'Trauma revisited: a five year old's journey from experiences, to thoughts, to words, towards hope', *Journal of Child Psychotherapy* 30(1): 53–70.

Lanyado, M. (2004) *The Presence of the Therapist. Treating Childhood Trauma*, Hove: Brunner-Routledge.

—— (2006) 'The playful presence of the therapist: "anti-doting" defences in the therapy of a late adopted adolescent patient', in M. Lanyado and A. Horne (eds) *A Question of Technique: Independent Psychoanalytic Approaches with Children and Adolescents*, London and New York: Routledge.

—— (2008) 'Playing out, not acting out: the development of the capacity to play in the therapy of children who are "in transition" from fostering to adoption', in D. Hindle and G. Shulman (eds) *The Emotional Experience of Adoption. A Psychoanalytic Perspective*, London and New York: Routledge.

—— (2009) '"Dwelling in the present moment" . . . an exploration of the resonances between transitional experiences and meditational states', *Psychoanalytic Perspectives* 5(2): 69–85.

Laplanche, J. and Pontalis, J.-B. (1988) *The Language of Psychoanalysis*, London: Karnac/Institute of Psycho-Analysis.

Marsoni, A. (2006) 'Battling with the unlaid ghost': psychotherapy with a child traumatised in infancy', *Journal of Child Psychotherapy* 32(3): 312–28.

Mendelsohn, A. (1997) 'Pervasive traumatic loss from AIDS in the life of a four year old African boy', *Journal of Child Psychotherapy* 23(3): 399–415.

Winnicott, D. W. (1958) 'The capacity to be alone', in D. W. Winnicott *The Maturational Processes and the Facilitating Environment*, London: Hogarth Press, 1965.

—— (1963) 'From dependence towards independence in the development of the individual'. in D. W. Winnicott *The Maturational Processes and the Facilitating Environment*, London: Hogarth Press, 1965.

Further theoretical reading

Freud, S. (1914) 'Remembering, repeating and working through', *Standard Edition*, Vol. 7, London: Hogarth Press.

Khan, M. M. R. (1963) 'The concept of cumulative trauma', in M. M. R. Khan *The Privacy of the Self*, New York: International Universities Press, 1974.

21 Child psychotherapy for children looked after by local authorities

Margaret Hunter-Smallbone

In the past ten years there have been renewed government efforts to change the life trajectory of children whose birth families fail them. This has been welcome, focusing our attention on changing for the better the cycle of deprivation we recognise passes so easily from one generation to another. For the first time we have public records of the numbers of children accommodated and we have at last, systems in place that monitor and report these children's progress. There are aims and targets for these children's health, social and academic welfare against which statutory agencies are measured. We know that our experience of the mental fragility and social exclusion of these children is substantiated by statistics – making unavoidably clear the depressing roll call of suffering and mental health disorders found in this population.

The Office for National Statistics (ONS) survey of 1999 told us that mental health disorders are occurring at the rate of one in every ten children between the ages of five and fifteen in England and Wales. Risk factors for disorder were increased by parental poor health, unemployment, poor housing and low income. It was little wonder therefore that families that had many of these risk factors, as well as having neglected, abused or rejected their children, would leave those children a legacy of low resilience to mental disorder. Nevertheless the ONS 2003 survey, *'The Mental Health of Young People Looked After by Local Authorities in England'* provided evidence that shocked.

Among young people 5–17 years old in care, 45 per cent were assessed as having a mental disorder, defined as 'a clinically recognisable set of symptoms or behaviour associated in most cases with considerable distress and substantial interference with personal functioning'.

Comparing children aged 5–10 residing in their own families, 3 per cent suffered from an emotional disorder, whereas for those in care 11 per cent suffered an emotional disorder. For emotional disorders in the older age range of 11–15, 6 per cent of young people in general contrasted with 12 per cent of young people looked after. Emotional disorders included anxiety, phobias, panic attacks, post-traumatic stress, obsessions, compulsions and depression.

Comparisons continued to show the burden carried by accommodated young people: 36 per cent of 5–10-year-olds in care and 40 per cent of 11–15-year-olds in care had conduct disorders compared with 5 per cent and 6 per cent respectively of those in private households. Conduct disorders were defined by aggressive disruptive behaviour, bullying, stealing and cruelty to animals.

For those young people living in residential care or at home with care orders, more than two-thirds were assessed as having mental disorders, 68 per cent. This residential population were four times as likely to have depression as those in foster care – 9 per cent and 8 per cent compared with 2 per cent – whilst those in foster care were already depressed at double the rate of other non-care children.

These figures convey the scale of the task in caring for the mental health of accommodated children.

If we look at the work of Child and Adolescent Mental Health Teams in England currently, these accommodated children are the ones forming a large and long-term section of child psychotherapists' caseloads. Their foster parents also need a great deal of help (see Chapter 22). The skill of attuning to these multiply hurt and insecurely attached children is one well suited to the training of child psychotherapists. These are complex cases where loss, trauma and abuse provoke a variety of symptoms and a heavy burden that affects many aspects of these children's lives. Against the trend for short-term focused interventions, the experience of dedicated mental health interventions for children in public care indicated the necessity of longer-term work that took account of the need to build trust, and ongoing support to secure good therapeutic outcomes with this population. Kurtz and James (2002) reported the high level of demand on these services:

> The core work of the majority of projects was planned to be assessment and short-term intervention. However many projects identified unexpectedly high levels of mental health need. It was clear that it takes time. The capacity to keep in touch with young people over the long term proved key.

However, research reports and statistical surveys alone fail to illuminate the nature of the problems hindering children in public care. What are they depressed about? Why do they drop out of education and work? What would help them access and use new chances? Some of the answers were rightly sought in external barriers and blocks to services for this population. Changing schools frequently can mean for example that an educational psychology assessment never gets completed or that every time a child moves address they start again on a Child and Adolescent Mental Health waiting list. New initiatives like 'Care Matters' (DfES 2007) sought to remove these barriers.

Even with extra provision targeting children looked after, the system continues to throw up unexpected barriers. A recent example known to me was of a young woman in a foster home out of area where the Children Looked After local mental health service was not funded to see out of area children, the local CAMHS said she did not reach criteria for urgency but must wait three months, and she was left in the no-man's-land of 'the responsible commissioner' who should, since 2007, have made provision for her (DfES 2007). Such provision takes time and planning whilst the placement was an emergency quick fix decision and inevitably there were delays.

Yet all barriers to good outcomes for this population are not only external ones. These are young people who are mistrustful, often angry and despairing and these emotional states mean that they can be hard to help and self-destructive. Gianna Henry, in a seminal paper that threw light on these psychological barriers, pointed out to us that such children are 'doubly deprived' (Henry 1974).

I will give an example of a boy I shall call Stanley.

Stanley

He enters my consulting room with his foster father looking around it carefully and hardly at me at all. Stanley is a slight eleven-year-old who has the appearance of a nine-year-old, a fragile quiet air, an innocent face. He is polite and answers my questions minimally. Foster dad says nice things about him and I explain my role to assess his need and wish for individual therapy. We have a stuttering three-way conversation where he opts out if not directly addressed. He lapses into a resigned silence as foster dad and I cover his brief history in care and the court case that will determine his future home. I ask him if we can let the carer go downstairs so I can get to know him a little.

He agrees very quickly and no sooner are we alone than he pulls a toy under the table and sits cross-legged on the floor to assemble it; it is a chute-system for marbles to run along. Having effectively distanced himself from me, I pull back my chair from the table and watch him. He assembles the toy intelligently, does not ask for my help or assistance although I can see from what he is doing that he is not familiar with the way it works. I describe what he is doing and give a suggestion or two which he quickly grasps.

Without warning or words he pulls the pieces apart, returning them neatly and swiftly to the box. He crosses to the sand tray behind me and I turn to see him making a small figure crawl through the sand. He takes a bird of prey from a selection of animals and has it swoop onto the man/boy figure and devour him. He moves to the dolls house . . . the whole 30 minutes is conducted in silence. Despite my gentle descriptions and questions he does not answer.

The experience of being with this boy was one of witnessing despair. He was compliant but removed, solitary in my room. It was hard to identify him with his history of proving unmanageable in three successive foster homes since being accommodated five months earlier. A flat resigned quietness seemed to communicate a burden he carried with him. He seemed to have little energy for engagement or protest.

In the final moments of our time together I asked him if he had three wishes – what would he wish for? 'To live with my dad. To see my mum. To have my brother live with me.'

In the silence that followed I found myself angry that such simple desires were every child's birthright, things to be taken for granted by most children. Instead for him and sixty thousand other accommodated young people they were as unlikely to be granted as extravagant wishes for riches.

The core of psychotherapy with children looked after is the work of mourning. These are young people who have had grave losses. As we know from Freud's 'Mourning and melancholia' (1917) and Melanie Klein's 'A contribution to the psycho-genesis of manic depressive states' (1935), the psychic process involved in the loss of a loved person is not simple grief for absence. It involves feelings of anger and aggression at being abandoned; it involves guilt and the implicit thought 'did I drive them away?' It involves ideas of punishment of the self for transgressions and feelings of hostility toward the loved one; it involves feelings of rage, helplessness and fear of reprisals, plunging the mourner into the passion and dependency of infancy.

In mourning experienced by children in care, the loved missed parent may not be dead and therefore may repeatedly re-connect then re-abandon the child. The relationship with the lost parent is already likely to be characterised by ambivalence and insecure attachment; the child likely to be deeply troubled that they are not loveable or good enough to merit parental concern. Most children in care will sacrifice their own self-worth in an effort to protect and keep ties with a loved parent. At least consciously such children blame themselves and say that the parent did their best. Only in their behaviour does a different narrative prevail; their attacks on authority and property indicate distrust and revenge as motives whilst the child disowns these difficult acted-out feelings.

The core belief of unworthiness in the heart of many abandoned children means that they are disadvantaged in their ability to regulate emotions, to endure in challenging tasks, to persevere with hope and to expect fulfilment and success (Fonagy *et al.* 1992). Instead they struggle without adult help, draw punishment to themselves, cannot easily cope with challenges or failure: they display the short fuse of uncontained emotions. Some children like Stanley cannot bear success at all and hurriedly tear up schoolwork that has gained praise. Many lose or damage their possessions with wearying regularity. Their actions say 'I cannot and must not try to succeed; I must crush hope before it gets a hold on me and upsets the balance of my world. I live with despair in the certain knowledge that I cannot fall further, knowing I never was good enough and my parents never have to have me back'. To be with Stanley is to be instructed in the ways of endurance.

To build a therapeutic relationship with a child as cautious as Stanley inevitably takes time. When children are in transition, moving from one placement to another, psychotherapists have to be particularly aware of not adding themselves to the list of 'abandoning adults'. (For greater exploration of working with children in transition, see Hunter-Smallbone 2007.) The usual course of therapy shows how slowly and grudgingly the child allows the therapist to become trustworthy. In this work, reliability, calm positive regard and the ability to follow and reflect the child's state of mind are prerequisites to thoughtful engagement. The young person we have before us is often deeply cynical, deeply wary of the therapist's intentions. And yet these youngsters are not usually hard to engage: quite the reverse; they hunger for the therapist's attention (see Hunter 1993). What children of trauma and neglect show is their need for relationship and their utter confusion as to what to do with it; their anger and humiliation at the attraction of the interested other and their approach–avoidance emotions with what they are offered.

Another young person, Rosie, presented different complex difficulties.

Rosie

A child in a long-term foster home, eleven-year-old Rosie was referred for continual stealing and lying. She was a clever girl and had just qualified for a much sought-after local school. The concerns were that she was alienating her classmates by her behaviour and exasperating her teachers by denying her actions. Her theft was usually rifling other girls' packed lunches and she could consume large quantities of sweets and chocolate.

Rosie had been very badly traumatised, neglected and abused in her mother's care: she had been starved and regularly beaten. Her younger brother was preferred to Rosie and she had the constant experience of being neglected whilst he was fed and better cared for.

Rosie was emotionally abused by her mother but came into care at seven only when her mother's partner was suspected of sexually abusing her. In a foster home, Rosie told her carers of her treatment in her family and later was one of those few children who refuse to see their birth mother. 'She never loved me' said Rosie with bleak accuracy. 'I am glad I do not have to see her any more.'

Gradually, Rosie became attached to her second foster carer who told her early on that she could stay for life if she wanted to. Rosie's gratitude to her foster mother was keenly felt but it played a part in her refusal to own her difficult behaviour. She found it hard to believe she could be forgiven; she found it impossible to control a part of herself that believed she was still hungry and needed to steal from the other children in order to survive.

I have treated other children who suffered an infancy of starvation and life-threatening neglect. In my experience, they continue to be plagued with sensations of hunger, felt somatically, not psychologically. This drove an obsessive need to steal. For Rosie the pattern of behaviour did seem to be obsessive because she did not consciously want to steal and she described to me the grip these thoughts had on her and the tension she felt until she complied, shaking uncontrollably. But we talked about this much later, years on, when we were finally allies in understanding and helping her.

At the outset, when she was eleven, Rosie's sessions began with an instant transference of her *idée fixe*. She believed that I had delicious food locked in my desk or stowed in the staffroom that we passed on the way to my room. She felt passionately that I was starving her, that I would treat other children better and that I kept all the good things for myself.

In trying to reflect on her grievances, I was handicapped by her collapses into tears and victimhood, and a torrent of words that poured out of her: 'Shut up and don't try to get round me! I bet you have just finished a big mug of hot chocolate and I have to come here all the way from school, missing my tea, missing TV and not allowed to get on with my life; you are so selfish and if you would just give me some, that's all I am asking for, and I can see your face and that expression proves it . . .'

These tirades made me feel quite mad at times, but gave me room to contemplate what it was like to be so beset by starvation. Like Music's references to brain states, there was little point in interpreting these fits of hunger with too complex interpretations and I arranged for her foster carer to provide her with a tea-time snack that she could have just before or during therapy, which was at 4 o'clock (Chapter 5). Of course this did not obviate the need to talk about and understand her hunger, a subject that was to re-emerge at frequent intervals in her years of therapy. The mood of her first year of therapy was that of unbearable touchiness and complaint. At any moment in the session she would take offence at whatever I had or had not said and collapse into a fury of complaint, each accusation enlarging on the one preceding so that it was almost laughable and difficult to respond seriously. I began to think about being on the receiving end of a paranoid, perhaps personality disordered mother. In these tirades, Rosie would become excessively histrionic, begging me to respond and then working herself into a fury of indignation at whatever response I gave.

The concept of negative transference was my rock in this storm. I thought with wonder how she had managed to conceal this madness from her foster mother, and gradually I could see with what relief she flung these emotions into my consulting room each week.

There was a decisive turning point in her second year of therapy.

One day in the second year, she excused herself to the toilet. Concerned by the noises I heard, when she came out, I looked and found she had smeared cleaning products all over the toilet, walls and floor. She was hysterical when I caught her and hopped from foot to foot, white-faced as I discovered the mess. Calming her as best I could, I cleaned up. Sobbing in my room, she seemed finally to believe I forgave her and she often referred later to the fact that no-one was told about this incident, that I did not get her into trouble.

In this sort of incident one behaves instinctively and there was something about my clearing up for her that moved us further than any words could have done: she finally had some belief that I would not abandon her to her angry mess.

It was in the sessions following this that Rosie built a house, entirely of paper. In the house a paper girl, Amelia, lived. Amelia was angry, critical, demanding and totally ungrateful for anything Rosie or I did for her. Of course it was Rosie who made the paper furniture, the delicate chairs and table and bed. But it was I who put the house into the cupboard each week, and Amelia complained of the cold, the dark and the neglect in between sessions. Before the long summer holiday break, Rosie made Amelia 'five million chips and two thousand hamburgers'. When we returned in September, Rosie looked at me, shaking her head: 'She has been starving. She ate all the food on the first day!'

With Amelia in the role of the hungry child, Rosie and I could have conversations about how she felt without being overwhelmed by this infantile perspective. Gradually, Rosie and I became a therapeutic duo, a parental couple. Later, the need for Amelia waned and we could have very frank discussions about Rosie's compulsion to steal and her use of lies.

In this interesting and challenging work I was struck by the power of our unconscious meeting; of the constant sub-text to our engagement. I seemed to know how to relate to Rosie with instinctive confidence. She seemed to communicate to me, even in the throes of furious complaint; there was another level at which we related, where gratitude and trust were just out of reach but nevertheless operated in her turning up early for sessions, staying to the time limit and accepting her occasional sighting of me with other children with surprising generosity.

Rosie broke through her defensive barrage of negative complaint to become a young woman capable of self-reflection with a quirky but strengthening ability to befriend others. At moments of stress her critical verbosity reappeared and she told me toward the end of her treatment that she never lost the feeling of starvation when upset. In her good-natured way she maintained that she knew her hunger was a hole in her feelings rather than in her stomach, but it was not so bad to have a weakness for which a chocolate bar could be an instant comfort.

In thinking of work with teenagers in care, the work seems to entail a great amount of team effort and supporting each other in the network to keep the young person on track.

Zoë

Zoë was a fifteen-year-old girl who had been accommodated in foster homes since she was seven. In her early years she cut a tragic figure, afraid of her older sister and competing with twin younger brothers for her single mother's attention. Mother's increasing alcoholism and relationships with sexually predatory and aggressive men resulted in all but the eldest girl coming into care. The two-year-old boys were placed for adoption. That left Zoë feeling abandoned and the only one placed in foster care. Zoë's behaviour showed how extreme was her anger at her experiences in life. She rapidly went through eight foster homes over two years. She grew into a tough, difficult to please girl who used sly aggression toward more vulnerable children and played adults off against each other in pursuit of material things. She could dominate an unsuspecting foster carer, locking one out of her own house several times and timing her temper tantrums for maximum effect to coincide with foster family outings. She spoiled a foster family's grandchild's christening but complained vehemently to her social worker when she was subsequently not taken to their relative's wedding. She bullied other children into compliance and spread a rumour about a teacher who disciplined her that he was involved with child pornography. At eleven years of age Zoë was almost unfosterable.

Individual psychotherapy with Zoë began at this late juncture, and when she had been accommodated by a specialist fostering agency. Her foster carers had access to regular support, to 24-hour assistance on request, to regular respite weekends. Her individual psychotherapy continued over four years and several placements.

For a young person so adept at wrecking relationships I counted it an achievement simply to have Zoë turning up each week. We were quiet and thoughtful together. I gently reflected on her various rages with adults. I wondered aloud what it would mean for her to let go of her satisfaction at destruction. For her it often meant powerlessness, depression, humiliation: the core of her refusal to grieve and her deter-mination to have sadistic revenge instead was laid bare. Was there no way to feel her own agency except through hurting others? She thought not. In Zoë's world there were bullies and victims and she shuttled between the two roles; victimised by her birth family, determined to victimise in her turn.

In her relationship to me I was aware of the difficulty of holding my position, neither bullying her nor allowing her to bully me. Following the sudden reappearance of her birth mother at thirteen and mother's disappearance six months later, Zoë turned her considerable anger to her foster carers and repeatedly asked to be moved. Gradually, she gave up on schoolwork, social activities and any semblance of co-operation with her foster family.

After four years she was moved to other carers. Zoë's attitude to me publicly became contemptuous, telling her Child in Care Review that I was useless, boring and she had never liked me. Still she attended. Her newly appointed social worker took her remarks at face value and suggested she transfer to another therapist. She began to see a school counsellor the day before she saw me 'to compare whether she was better'.

I had only to reflect on my own anger, frustration and sense of injustice in all of this, to be aware of how neatly my countertransference mirrored Zoë's feelings. I persevered, interpreting her wish to project feelings of helplessness and abandonment onto me. I recalled how painful it had felt that her sister had stayed at home with mother: she was showing me what it felt like to be scapegoated whilst another is preferred.

Had I been seeing Zoë in a less containing setting, therapy would probably have foundered on this rock of revenge where the end of therapy could be used as an acting out of the scenario of the rejecting mother: Zoë now in the lead role. But the work was undertaken in a fostering programme where even moves between carers meant school and therapy could be sustained. When her attendance at sessions became spasmodic, I sent her cards simply acknowledging her absence and hoping to see her next time. When I considered closing her appointments her new foster carers changed my mind. They told me that she had kept every card I ever sent her, going back four years.

School counselling was disrupted when Zoë was finally permanently excluded. Despite an icy beginning at sessions, usually with mobile phone interruptions, Zoë would now ask to play hide and seek. In a room of tiny dimensions and at fifteen years of age, she returned to the first attachment game of infancy. She heard me look for her. I think she needed to hear me search for her, showing her difficulty trusting that with me, out of sight was not out of mind. Like the posted cards that she secretly treasured, Zoë needed concrete evidence that relationships could endure over absence: if I could find her physically, perhaps she could believe I would find her emotionally.

At this point Zoë began to reconnect with her older sister and, through her, to other relatives in her birth family. In these difficult re-attachments, Zoë at last brought her worries and problems openly to therapy. An attachment to me had finally been acknowledged, and we could co-operate in sharing her difficult life.

A further corner was turned when her local authority, mindful of government targets, set in place a private coaching system whilst she diffidently attended college. Nine months later she had achieved the equivalent of four GCSEs. This educational success had a lasting positive effect on Zoë. She framed her certificates and told me that at last she felt as good as others in her class. It was not a belief she could always hold onto, but it showed the despair underneath her destructiveness and the importance to her of continuing investment and acknowledgement from society. Educational attainment in the hard currency of certificates can endure as evidence of self-worth to a young person with damaged self-belief. This is also what statistics show us for children looked after: that educational attainment will play a crucial role in their future life. What the statistics do not illuminate is the amount of struggle, investment and support that goes into these achievements. Zoë again changed foster placement and opted for a residential setting.

We were able to work together during her time of transition, finally at a decreased rate of sessions. When she moved to live in assisted accommodation near her relatives, we ended well and years later she visited me from time to time, to tell me of her achievements and to share a mutual respect which had somehow come to be taken for granted.

The trajectory of development for children who have grown up with unreliable attachments can require a longer time-frame and greater stores of endurance and hope from the adults involved in their care. At last government is coming to terms with the fact that support cannot all be ended at eighteen and the law now gives a framework for support into their twenties. The young people we see in the care system have difficult business to transact in their teenage years: they have to recover from past abuse; they must find a way to individuate, to become separate, functioning individuals ready to take their place as adults in society. But they do so with a burden of broken attachments, mistrust and rage at the adults who dropped them.

Their internal model of the adults they will become is often poor, their parents' failings mixing uneasily with their ideas about themselves. In psychotherapy there is an opportunity to test assumptions, to ask questions, to reflect, to rage without repercussions, to grieve. Most importantly, psychotherapy allows a new attachment of a different kind. The relationship between the young person and the therapist may be seen as happening in a setting of deprivation (Bion, 1971): the therapist does not feed or parent or practically provide for the young person. But analytic psychotherapy can also be characterised as an event offered in a setting stripped of inessentials, an experience where the relationship between the two people present is what is primary. In this sense, it is not deprivation which echoes from the consulting room of young people in care but the human capacity to continue meeting, relating and reflecting ourselves in each other.

References

Bion, W. R. (1971) 'Container and contained', in W. R. Bion *Attention and Inter-pretation*, London: Tavistock.
Department for Education and Skills (2007) *Care Matters: Time for Change*, Cm 7137, London: DfES.
Fonagy, P., Steele, M., Steele, H., Higgitt, A. and Target, M. (1992) 'The theory and practice of resilience', *Journal of Child Psychology and Psychiatry* 37(2): 231–57.
Freud, S. (1917) 'Mourning and melancholia', in *Standard Edition* 14: 237–60.
Henry, G. (1974) 'Doubly deprived', *Journal of Child Psychotherapy* 3(4): 15–28.
Hunter, M. (1993) 'The emotional needs of children in care: An overview of 30 cases', *Association of Child Psychology and Psychiatry Review* 15(5): 214–18.
Hunter-Smallbone, M. (2007) 'Making sense of transition', in B. Luckock and M. Lefevre (eds) *Direct Work: Social Work with Children and Young People in Care*, London: British Association for Adoption and Fostering.
Klein, M. (1935) 'A contribution to the psycho-genesis of manic-depressive states', in M. Klein *Love, Guilt and Reparation and Other Works*, London: Hogarth Press, 1975.
Kurtz, Z. and James, C. (2002) *What's New: Learning from the CAMHS Innovation Projects*, London: Department of Health.
Office for National Statistics (1999) *The Mental Health of Children and Adolescents in Great Britain*, London: HMSO.
—— (2003) *The Mental Health of Young People Looked After by Local Authorities in England*, London: HMSO.

22 Working with foster carers

Leslie Ironside

> The greatest need of a child is to obtain conclusive assurance (a) that he is genuinely loved as a person by his parents, and (b) that his parents genuinely accept his love . . . frustration of this desire to be loved as a person and to have his love accepted is the greatest trauma that a child can experience.
>
> (Fairbairn 1952: 39–40)

Introduction

Mrs Smith, a very experienced and well-respected foster carer, was referred to me as she had thrown a plate of hot food at her fifteen-year-old foster child and this led to the end of a long-term placement. This was not a simple one-off incident and as her story unfolded it became clear it was the painful culmination of many years of living in a stressful situation. Emotions had been running high for a considerable time and 'like those little wooden birds that sit on a pole, we fill up . . . until *donk*, we tilt into the drink' (Enright 2008: 173).

The task of fostering can be very rewarding but, as indicated in this vignette, it can also be very stressful and challenging. A child's sense of self generally develops within the context of their birth family. In the context of fostering, a child has separated from the birth family, usually as the result of harmful parental care. The self then develops in a different context, a context of 'loss combined with fresh opportunities for loving and being loved, healing and growth' (Schofield 2008: 43). The states of loss and mourning are, however, complex and may, besides sadness, involve feelings of aggression at being abandoned and implicit aspects of guilt of the form of 'did I drive them away?' (see Chapter 21).

The shared task, for both child psychotherapists in sessions with foster children and for foster carers looking after these children, is that of the maintenance of a reflective capacity, often in the face of states of extreme despair and feelings of rejection. This level of 'emotional exposure' can be difficult enough for a child psychotherapist to bear for the limited time they may see a child each week (see Chapter 21) but may be impossible to bear for a foster carer who is carrying responsibility for a child twenty-four hours a day.

In this chapter I will describe some of the challenges that often face foster carers and discuss how a child psychotherapist is well trained to work with them and to help them to think about and manage the some-times extreme emotional states and problematic behaviour of the children in their care. I will then describe the importance of the maintenance of a reflective state of mind and, drawing upon my work with Mrs Smith, I will illustrate the complexity of this work. Finally, I will briefly outline a suggested training model for carers that draws upon principles from psychoanalytic thinking and infant observation and aims to aid the main-tenance and development of a reflective space in the minds of the carers.

The challenge of foster care

Effective parenting is founded on the capacity to establish and sustain a reflective state of mind (Fonagy *et al.* 1992, 2004). Bion's understanding of the vital role of maternal reverie in the development of the capacity for thought also gives a deeper account of the role which primary dependence plays in the development of a person. The parental mind needs to be a mind that can register a child's emotions and anxiety (see Chapter 13).

It is important to note, however, that it is also, so often, this very experience that has been missing in the formative years of the foster child in their family of origin and often the child then seems caught in re-creating the unresolved, traumatic and traumatising attachment style arising from this earlier experience. Ironically this can lead to conflict in a foster family as the developmentally crucial, and ordinarily thoughtful, approach to parenting can be felt by the child to be quite alien (see Ironside 2004). The maintenance and development of this reflective capacity, however, remains as important in fostering as it is in general parenting.

The task of a foster carer can then be strenuous and challenging. The children and young people will by definition have experienced things having gone very wrong in their lives and in one way or another they will have experienced a breakdown in the basic need for the continuing and conclusive assurance of the cycle of love between children and their parents (Fairbairn 1952). Regardless of the difficult behaviour so often associated with looked after children, simply to be emotionally in touch with such traumatised minds is likely to be psychologically testing. Indeed, one of the hard questions carers have to ask themselves is whether or not they, and their family, can bear this emotional charge. If the answer is no, thought needs to be applied to a planned ending of a placement or, as with Mrs Smith, the carer's ability may become overstretched. This can be a very traumatising experience for all concerned.

The task for carers is to maintain a reflective capacity and to be able to be close enough to the child to experience the often traumatic, emotional nature of such a relationship, to bear witness to, and to contain the child's states of despair, and yet be distant enough not to be overwhelmed by it. This is not an easy undertaking as there can be something inherently disturbing about such a contact. It can at times even seem as though the difficult states of mind that the children find themselves in can become quite 'contagious' as emotions are evoked in the foster carers through the child's projection of intolerable feelings. The foster carer can then become filled with the very feelings that the child cannot deal with and the psychological boundary between the carer and the child may be breached in an overwhelming fashion (Ironside 2004). Foster carers may then find themselves in states of mind that feel quite alien to themselves (Ironside 2004, 2008). This may lead to acting out behaviour and foster carers seeking ways of avoiding the emotional impact of the experience. Understanding the pressures involved in such intricate relationships is extremely important and this is where the training and experience of a child psychotherapist may be of immense value to foster carers.

The training of a child psychotherapist

Child psychotherapists have had the privilege of undergoing their own intensive analysis and are trained in analysing and thinking about emotionally stressful situations, to experiencing emotionally charged relationships and to endeavouring to maintain a thoughtful capacity in the face of pressure such as that experienced by Mrs Smith. They are trained not to react on impulse, though they may with more problematic patients, and foster children so often fall into this category, feel like acting out in some way. The training of a child psychotherapist is then suited to the 'careful weaving together of such children's shattered emotional lives' (Hunter-Smallbone Chapter 21) and, besides endeavouring to manage the often problematic behaviour displayed by foster children, the child psychotherapist is also well trained to bear witness to, emotionally contain and reflect upon, the child's 'despair' and the extreme unresolved states of mourning often experienced by foster children.

How to be of help?

The work with foster carers is about helping them manage, think about and also weave together the shattered lives of the children in their care. A state of *harmony*, however, conjured up by the idea of a joining between a child in need of being looked after and an adult wishing to do this, is by no means something that can be taken for granted. It is, rather, something that in all likelihood will need to be created and re-created. A compassionate approach, where the foster carer is able to reflect upon and sustain the impact of the child's state of mind, may not always be possible (Ironside 2004, 2008). As with Mrs Smith, a carer may act out and seek ways of avoiding emotional contact and this can disrupt this all important capacity to contain and reflect upon a child's presentation (Ironside 2008). A great deal of thought then, needs to be applied to the training and support of foster carers in order to help them to contain and best manage the sometimes severely traumatised children in their care.

Work with foster carers, whether carried out by a child psychotherapist or other professional, belongs within the wider category of working with parents and is often a necessity in achieving a successful outcome for a foster child. Work with foster carers can also take on various forms. It may be work 'beside' work with a child who is in therapy, either with the same therapist or with a colleague, it may be work with the carer(s) and the child, it may be family work or it may be work independently with the foster carers individually, as a couple, or in a group.

Therapeutic approach

Each situation has to be seen as unique and it is important to view the fostering experience as being rather like that of the foster child and foster family belonging to a different tribe, with many similarities, but also profound differences, from the tribe of people living in some form of an intact family.

The therapeutic approach with foster carers has much in common to work with birth parents (see Chapter 13) but it is also work that is unique and different, and, indeed, one of the main points of discussion with foster carers is often that of the difficulty of differentiating what is 'ordinary' from what is 'extra-ordinary' in both the behaviour of foster children and the emotional response that can be stirred up in carers through the experience. How, for instance, do you differentiate between a greedy child and a needy child within the fostering situation? This can be a difficult enough task for any parent but can be much more extreme and complex in the fostering situation when there is often such a pull towards 'compensating' a child for the hardships they have had to endure. Need and greed, however, require a different parental approach but they can be difficult to differentiate and may co-exist. In the extreme this can then leave the carer feeling, as Mrs Smith alluded to in one of her sessions, like 'driving with the brakes on, you sometimes can't do both things at once, and, you end up going up in steam'.

At the point of referral, matters are often felt to be very stressful and feelings of failure and shame are often high in the ascendancy. The therapist then has to try to contain and think about very problematic situations and provide carers with the experience of a space where the often very destructive forces that may abound within the fostering experience may be thought about. The hope behind this work is that this will be useful in terms of helping foster carers themselves to better contain and understand the children in their care (Ironside 2004, 2008), or, if this is not possible, to work towards a planned ending of a placement.

The sessions themselves are often complex and, indeed, it is important to maintain a sense of complexity and to think about things from a variety of different angles. It is also crucially important to be aware of the feelings of carers and work towards a non-judgemental approach within good enough bounds of care. In common with work with parents the balance of listening and receptiveness and insight-giving interventions will depend on what a particular carer finds most effective. 'Some fragile parents (*carers*) may be able to take in very little reflective comment and have urgent need for a relationship within which they can express their confusion, depression, despair and self-doubt, and feel that they can be accepted as they are. Others, with some source of greater hopefulness within their personality, will respond to the opportunity to think in-depth about their own contribution to their children's problems, and to consider their own family history as part of an attempt to understand the current family difficulties more fully' (Rustin Chapter 13, my italic word).

When working with parents or foster carers the therapist offers a model of how to respond to emotional distress which has some core elements. These are:

- establishing a reliable setting in which it is possible to talk about upsetting things;
- creating a shared language to describe painful emotional states;
- valuing boundaries and differentiation, particularly between the adult and infantile parts of the self;
- maintaining an adequately complex understanding of human emotions and relationships;
- focusing on giving meaning to behaviour.

And in talking about the children in their care there are further interlinking elements that need to be kept in mind.

First, it is important to think about behaviour management and to help carers to find their way of managing issues around discipline and consequences of behaviour. This can be very complex when faced with some omnipotent and apparently fearless children.

Second it is important to think about reciprocity, how do they all 'fit' together, what is it like to 'be' with the child, how do the different attachment styles and personalities fit? How does each person spark the other off? What does the current situation feel like?

And third, it is important to think about the role of reflection and containment, the 'taking a step back to see where we are going' aspect of the relationship. Here the therapist tries to address issues such as:

- How to maintain a balance between the above two points and explore the tensions between the behaviour management, limit setting, paternal role and the receptive nurturing and more relationally orientated, maternal role (see Chapter 13).

- How to maintain the balance between being close enough to the child to experience the emotional charge and yet distant enough not to be overwhelmed by it.
- How to think about the child's projections and how to recognise when the carer is also projecting into the child.
- How to recognise and maintain a balance between what might be termed the age appropriate and the infantile parts of the mind in both the foster children and the foster parents.

Learning from experience

This work is then multifaceted and each story is different but in order to illustrate some of these themes I would like to now turn to Mrs Smith's story.

Mrs Smith was a long-term carer with many years of experience and Stephen, the foster child, had been living with the family for many years. The family consisted of mother, father and two children, a daughter a year younger than Stephen and a son, two years older and about to leave home for university. It seems that Stephen's behaviour had always been difficult but he had managed to maintain mainstream school until recently and the family had a great deal of support. Mrs Smith was also a devoted and experienced foster mother with a very solid reputation. She was involved in the training of other carers and was held in high esteem. Much of the care fell on her shoulders, her husband being supportive but working full time, with a stressful, management career.

Stephen, it transpired, was seen to have been falling into a deeper and deeper pit as he struggled to cope with school, with turning sixteen, with ideas of leaving home and with access issues to his birth family. He harboured great hopes of returning to live with them though their circumstances were far from ideal. On the day Mrs Smith threw the plate of food she had been under a lot of stress but the last straw was yet another refusal by Stephen to eat the food she had prepared for him, even though it was something he had earlier requested for dinner. Now how can we begin to think about this material?

My starting point was that of recognising, together with Mrs Smith, the complexity of the situation and the dominant feeling of shame that was palpably in the air at the first meeting. Mrs Smith felt she would be harshly judged and harshly judged herself. As we began to talk we could begin to think about how she was only human, a person who had been subject to verbal abuse, threatening behaviour and rejection, and as such it was little surprise that she had had enough and exploded. Yes, we might not endorse the throwing of the plate but we could well understand why things may have reached that point.

In addition here was a mother/adolescent son relationship with all its tensions. At this point she had felt completely exasperated as a 'mother' badly treated by a 'son' who yet again rejected the food he both requested and was offered. But this was on the back of years of caring for a person who was so problematic in his behaviour and the experience had, as she described it, left her feeling as though she had gone up in steam. Prior to the incident she had often felt she both never wanted to see Stephen again, feeling so abused by him, but so feared for his future and felt so responsible for him that she felt she could not contemplate letting him go.

And, we discussed how here also was a traumatised young man, facing the enormous challenges of his age and finding the tasks overwhelming and seemingly making sure Mrs Smith also found the task overwhelming. Mrs Smith had, it seemed, for years been the recipient of massive projections of feelings that could not be verbalised (Ironside 2004) and now could not be contained by herself, Stephen's main attachment figure.

As we explored these issues further a developmental perspective also rose into the ascendancy in terms of a young man and his mother (foster), in a process of separating, conjured up by his approaching sixteenth birthday, though he had been told he could stay in the family till eighteen. Primitive fears of abandonment seemed to dominate but an infantile backlash that, at times, led to extreme splitting processes, had also to be reckoned with. This took the form of a preoccupation of going back to live with mother (birth) in an idealised, 'unreachable, yet putting everything else into the rubbish bin' style of thinking. Mrs Smith reflected on how, looking back, she feels she might have found it hard to be ordinarily firm with him because of her fear of 'losing him to his birth mother.' And within the family dynamics the burden of discipline issues had also fallen firmly on her shoulders.

Oedipal issues were also not far from the surface, but within the complexity of the fostering relationship, 'this son is not my son and yet we are together as mother and son'. And Mrs Smith also bravely acknowledged, 'and yes, I suppose I did find him attractive'. There had not, to the best of my knowledge, been any overt physically inappropriate behaviour but I think it is fair to say there was some sexual tension between Stephen and Mrs Smith.

Mrs Smith also went on to describe her own complex developmental position. She was on the cusp of enormous change. Her children were on the edge of leaving home, what was her role to be? The family had long felt that things were too difficult to manage with Stephen but, in contrast to the other family members, she had felt she just had to 'hold on to him' for his sake. She had been consumed with the feeling that if she did not provide him with a home he would have 'nothing, just bounce from one carer to another. He had always been difficult but now with his age no one would want him.' (And this alongside her fears of 'losing' him to his birth mother.) Her understandable fears for him were then also leaving her in a very isolated position with regard to her own family and were confused with her changing relationship with her own children. As our sessions developed, and Mrs Smith grew increasingly able to think about things in further depth, we were able to gradually name this and explore how the relationship had also given her a sense of still having a vital role to play, giving her life meaning and therefore being something she needed to cling onto in the face of the loss of such a role within her family and with her own children.

She was also able to describe how she felt that the sexual relationship with her husband was under threat as she felt she was no longer attractive to him. The couple element of the parental couple then seemed to be a vital element within this family difficulty. Mrs Smith seemed to be struggling with problematic and painful feelings of sexual rejection from her husband, and, at a particularly sensitive stage of her life in that she felt she was approaching the menopause. These complex issues did not belong to the relationship with Stephen but seemed confused with it.

Mrs Smith had also described how she had been at an extreme edge through a lack self-confidence that had begun to deeply affect all aspects of her life. She described how she had felt barely able to do things even as mundane as the household shopping.

Here then we see something of the complexity of this work. On the one hand, the feelings of being overwhelmed, the lack of attractiveness, sexually and physically, the feelings of loss of competence and rejection could all be thought about in terms of Stephen and the projection of feelings that needed to be understood and contained. Stephen could not verbalise to his foster mother, who was his closest confidant, the extent and level of his feelings but he could make her feel these things. He was a young man trying to negotiate a painfully difficult time in his life, with many echoes of past experiences, feeling like he was failing and pushing his foster mother to reject him, and possibly endeavouring to satisfy the inner script 'I drove them away'.

But, alongside this, here was a woman at a very particular stage of her life, here was a couple at a particular stage of their lives and here was a family at a particular stage of its life, with all the challenges, tasks and risks of this developmental stage. The coming together of these various ingredients made for an explosive cocktail that led to this dramatic ending of the placement. If any of the ingredients had been slightly different matters might not have taken this turn.

I continued to work with Mrs Smith but also saw Mr and Mrs Smith as a couple and, later, met with them and their two children to reflect on the experience they had all shared. Stephen went on to live in supportive lodgings and continued to have contact with the Smith family. It did not prove possible to meet with Stephen. However, his absence now endeared him more to the family as whole, and they, as opposed to Mrs Smith alone, stabilised into a position of being deeply concerned and committed to his future development and continued to be able to see him on an occasional but very meaningful fashion. As a family they also felt it was perhaps not right to foster for a while but all remained committed to the idea for the future, with thoughts of perhaps short-term rather than a long-term placement – at least initially.

Training for carers

This is the complexity of work with foster parents and indicates the need for a flexible and inclusive approach. It is from work such as this that I developed a training for foster parents which draws upon principles from psychoanalytic thinking and infant observation (Miller *et al.* 1989), also an essential part of the training for a child psychotherapist.

When doing an infant observation a student observes an infant in his/her home for an hour a week, writes this up as a process recording and presents this to a group of fellow students with an experienced facilitator. Drawing upon this model, for the training for foster carers, the participants are expected to attend a fortnightly group and are asked to observe and complete a weekly process recording of a half hour interaction with a foster child to present to the group. The carers are also encouraged to note their own thoughts and feelings during the observational time. The foster carers are expected to maintain this weekly observation at a consistent time and for the eight-session duration of the course. Each session lasts two hours and the training aims to aid the maintenance and development of a reflective space in the minds of the carers in a proactive rather than reactive fashion.

The group is open to six individual carers and/or couples. Apart from the first introductory meeting and the last concluding meeting, a different child, along with the most recent observation of that child, is presented at each session. The experience then acts as a developmental training in observational skills, as well as a consultation space to think about each child with myself and, of utmost importance, as part of a group with other carers. The group participants benefit enormously from the experience of being part of a group consisting of other members of their 'tribe' and this enhances the feeling of being able to bring to the group the more problematic and painful observations and experiences that are generally difficult to discuss.

The feedback from the experience has been positive. Foster carers have felt that it did enhance their ability to understand and to 'live with these children' and help them to develop. They felt that it particularly enabled them to 'take a step back' and observe both what was going on for the child and how it was impacting upon them as carers.

Conclusion

To be a good enough foster carer is very demanding and it is a role that demands a great deal of support and respect. An essential aspect of defining what is meant by a good enough placement has to do with the all important but mercurial quality of maintaining a reflective and in consequence respectful view of the child. To be a good enough child psychotherapist is also extremely demanding and the equally demanding training a child psychotherapist undergoes, with its focus on the development of observational skills, reflective practice and personal analysis, bodes well for equipping a child psychotherapist to both work with foster children directly but also to work with foster carers in enabling them to understand, contain and best manage the children in their care.

References

Enright, A. (2008) *The Gathering*, London: Vintage Books.

Fairbairn, W. R. D. (1952) *Psychoanalytic Studies of the Personality*, New York: Brunner-Routledge

Fonagy, P., Steele, M., Steele, H., Higgitt, A. and Target, M. (1992) 'The Emanuel Miller Memorial Lecture 1992. The theory and practice of resilience', *Journal of Child Psychology and Psychiatry* 35(2): 231–57.

Fonagy, P., Gergely, G., Jurist, E. and Target, M. (2004) *Affect Regulation, Mentalization, and the Development of the Self*, London: Karnac Books.

Ironside, L. (2004) 'Living a provisional existence: thinking about foster carers and the emotional containment of children placed in their care', *Adoption and Fostering* 28(4): 39–48.

—— (2008) 'Difficulties with reflective thinking in direct work with children in care: the role of supervision and consultation', in B. Luckock and M. Lefevre (eds)

Direct Work: Social Work with Children and Young People in Care, London: British Association for Adoption and Fostering.

Miller, L., Rustin, M. E., Rustin, M. J. and Shuttleworth, J. (1989) *Closely Observed Infants*, London: Duckworth Books.

Schofield, G. P. (2008) 'Providing a secure base – an attachment perspective', in B. Luckock and M. Lefevre (eds) *Direct Work: Social Work with Children and Young People in Care*, London: British Association for Adoption and Fostering.

23 Sexual abuse and sexual abusing in childhood and adolescence

Ann Horne

Prologue

Wayne was four years old when his new 'stepfather' first abused him sexually. His natural father had left six months previously, following a relationship with Wayne's mother characterised by absence, frequent drunkenness and unpredictable violence. Wayne's mother also had a serious drinking problem and said she was unaware that her new partner had a previous conviction for the sexual abuse of an infant. The nursery reported their concerns to Social Services when Wayne became preoccupied with the genitals of other children whom he would invite into the toilet with him. His attempts to remove another child's trousers led to complaints to his mother but no apparent action other than her rage with Wayne. The realisation of his mother's partner's conviction, together with her reluctance to give up the relationship, led to Wayne's being removed into care. He was placed with temporary foster parents in a family where he was the youngest, and then with another family when the first found his sexually inviting behaviour towards the foster father too provocative and his attempts to insert objects in his anus too disgusting. Disclosure interviews were indecisive; there were no corroborating witnesses; no prosecution followed. No referral was made to any service for therapeutic work.

Wayne returned to his mother at the age of six when she separated from this partner. His behaviour became strange: at home he would defecate in corners of his room and hide soiled underpants in corners or amongst clean garments. At school he spoke little and had no resources for engaging with other children. He could be goaded into silly and often dangerous behaviour. He stood on his desk and removed his clothes; he hid in the teacher's cupboard. Frequently he ran out of the class and the school worried about their capacity to keep him safe. An ongoing curiosity about younger children was equally worrying: his peers dealt with it by calling him 'Jayne' or 'pervert'; his teachers were more wary, monitoring his opportunities for being with smaller children. His mother found him unmanageable at home – angry with her, oppositional and often running away. Her complaints led to a referral at age eight to child guidance where sterling efforts were made to engage the family, but his mother's unreliability meant that no solid work could be undertaken. By now, many agencies were involved and concerned. A new partner arrived; a new baby was born. The social work network hoped that a 'father' would help. Mother turned up at Social Services when Wayne was ten: she wanted rid of him before he broke up her current relationship. She saw him as malicious, deliberately trying to destroy her and 'evil'.

Wayne went to stay with a foster family who found him 'unlikeable'. A change of placement was made to an experienced family where Wayne settled, although he was still exhibiting severe learning and behavioural difficulties in school. The illness of the foster mother's mother led to the former's frequent absence and distraction and Wayne, now aged twelve, was moved again. This placement broke down after three months. After much co-ordinated work with the foster family and Social Services, Wayne was sent to a residential home from which he attended a weekly boarding school. Contact with the family was disorganised with Wayne frequently running from school to home and from home to school. A preoccupation with women's soiled underwear was hard for the school to handle. Wayne at thirteen was accused of 'interfering sexually' with his four-year-old sister and a neighbour's three-year-old boy on a home visit. At this point he was finally referred to a specialist clinic in London for assessment, advice and treatment.

Introduction

There may be those who object to one chapter covering the work of the child psychotherapist with sexually abused and abusing children and young people. The one group, after all, is victimised by the other. Several therapists have told me of how they feel unable to work with young abusers and link this to the intensity of feeling experienced in their work with abused children: anxiety that this outrage might spill over, be uncontainable in work with the latter group seems common. There is also an interesting but intellectually flawed position which sees work in this area as of necessity polarised – either one helps the victims or one is, by treating the abuser, somehow condoning the acts committed. It becomes an almost impossible task to try to integrate the developmental trauma that is a feature of both groups into one's internal picture and to hold in mind the abuser as both offender and victim.

It may be that part of the process at work is the impact of the act of abusing on the mind of the therapist – with *both* groups of young people. Both touch the therapist's 'perverse core' (Chasseguet-Smirgel 1985). Our basic tenets of morality are challenged in a most disturbing way (Freud 1913). Both, equally, engage the network surrounding the child/adolescent in what can too often become an exercise in non-communication, contradiction and split functioning – sometimes it feels like a war zone. It is vital, therefore, to give thought to the re-enactment of abuse and the mirroring of the internal world of victim and offender (Davies 1996) which occur all too easily amongst those involved in this work. Central to this process is making space for thought: the process of memory, recollection and thinking is attacked so easily in child and network, and in the often disbelieving outside world. It is, after all, only twenty years ago that Butler-Sloss strove to convince the public of the presence of sexual abuse in Cleveland (Butler-Sloss 1988).

Prevalence and definition

From the research surveyed by Kolvin and Trowell (1996), key areas in the definition of sexual abuse are:

(a) direct acts – molestation, penetration and force all appear on a spectrum of greater or lesser psychological damage
(b) indirect acts – e.g. enforced watching of pornography; genital exposure
(c) exploitation – the balance of power between abused and abuser is an important factor.

Each of these factors needs to be weighed when thinking of the impact of abuse on children.

Prevalence is an inexact science, not least because of differences in definition. Apart from clear-cut incidents, there are times when clinical judgement may indicate abuse but evidence and witnesses be lacking. Under-reporting is also likely to be a feature. Estimates, such as that by Smith and Bentovim (1994), that 15–30 per cent of women are likely to have experienced some form of undesired sexual contact during childhood, may therefore be cautious. The rate for men seems to be a little less than half of that for women:

about 20,000 to 40,000 16 year old boys will have experienced sexual
abuse involving bodily contact at some time.

(Flood 1994)

It is even more difficult to ascertain the prevalence of organised abuse, in
part because there is resistance to taking on board further depths to the
human psyche and to hearing the unbearable. That it exists is not in doubt
and, as Trowell notes, increased recognition will follow increasing awareness (Trowell 1994). The detailed clinical reports given by Sinason demonstrate the different depth of fear and the desperate psychological measures
required of children subjected to such abuse (Sinason 1994).

Recovered memory and false allegations

The issues surrounding 'false memory syndrome' and recovered memories
tend to be less problematic in child psychotherapy than in work with
adults. Any abuse tends to be more available – further detail may be
recovered but rarely abuse which comes as any surprise to those working
with the child. Children are usually referred for therapy following disclosure or where some investigation has been pursued in relation to
sexualised or otherwise worrying behaviour. It was Wayne's misfortune, in
the introductory vignette, that, following the initial Social Services intervention, no referral was made to Child Mental Health services.

It can, however, happen that a child in therapy makes allegations of abuse.
Mostly, children's allegations are true: indeed, concern tends to be over the
non-reporting of abuse rather than about the 2 per cent of allegations which
turn out to be false. In a review of the literature on false allegations, Adshead
(1994) gives a helpful context when she states:

> children very rarely make up malicious false allegations of their own
> accord: in 98 per cent of allegations, children are *not* deliberately
> setting out to make trouble for adults. . . . False allegations appear to be
> much more likely when adults initiate them (such as in custody
> disputes), and these appear to be the majority of allegations.
>
> (Adshead 1994: 59)

Indeed, Goodwin found that false retractions (where a child withdraws a
claim of abuse yet that abuse is later found to be corroborated) were as
common (Goodwin *et al.* 1978).

Displaced allegations are not unknown in this work, where the child,
usually when he feels safe in his situation (perhaps in a good foster home),
accuses a safe adult of acts which another adult figure committed. Allegations are also made against therapists. Ironside (1995) provides a painful,
important and thoughtful comment on the meaning of the 'disclosure'
when false allegations are made by a child about his therapist. The

experience of early trauma and the defences marshalled against this are noted as influences in the child's concrete thinking and re-enactment, and helpful comment is given on the varied responses triggered in the network in three case examples. The capacity to continue to think becomes vital as therapy is disrupted and therapist attacked by an unthinking system. Regaining a position in which thought becomes available once more is vital in such a scenario.

Thinking developmentally about the impact of abuse

When one considers theories of normal development in children, it is possible to see many points at which an experience of trauma can leave the child ill-equipped to grow emotionally and meet the world with confident curiosity. It is important to keep in mind the resources – inner, psychological and external – available to the child in coping with experiences which are overwhelming to the immature sense of self, and to reflect on the strategies to which the child must have recourse in order to survive. A sense of developmental insult is the strongest legacy of the sexual abuse of children.

We know that the consequences of sexual abuse are more traumatic when the abuse has involved body contact:

> Abuse involving penetration, abuse which is perpetrated by a father/ step father or other trusted adult, or abuse which involves violence or force, are all likely to be particularly damaging. Repeated abuse which endures over a long period is also associated with a more serious impact.
>
> (Flood 1994)

It is clear from our knowledge of normal emotional development that the body not only is the first 'self' or 'ego' for the child, but also that its changes have constantly to be incorporated into the changing sense of identity finally established by late adolescence. Keeping in mind the importance of early, in-tune relationships for the healthy psychological development of the child, and our knowledge of the drive for engagement and attachment present in the infant, the impact of abuse on what should be positive and essential aspects of the child's experience cannot be underestimated. It therefore follows that:

> an act of child abuse bisects the line of normal development and disrupts the natural timing of the biological clock and turns the oedipus complex upside down. Incestuous wishes are gratified with parents, siblings or adolescents or adults who are perceived as sibling or parental substitutes.
>
> (Campbell 1994)

Although a clear distinction is made in psychoanalytic theory between perpetrators of incest and of paedophilia, it is important to keep in mind that, for the child, the incestuous relationship may be one involving the principal caring person in that child's life, the only person to whom the child feels special, and so add to the difficulty in recognising right and wrong and in talking about it. Indeed, it can in many ways be easier to deal with abuse by an outsider whom one can hate, than by a loved person where love and hate are then difficult to integrate.

To this one would add that we are only beginning to understand the impact of abuse when the child is a pre-verbal infant: Graham Music (Chapter 5 in this volume) explores the effect on the capacities of the developing brain of cortisol release and of the 'activation of the para-sympathetic nervous system', to which the reader is directed. Khan's concept of cumulative trauma would also have a role – that the child traumatised early will lack defences against later impingements which will be experienced as traumatic (Khan 1963). The importance of an adult who believes the child's disclosure and takes immediate action to ensure the child's protection is a known protective factor in relation to recovery from the trauma and the capacity to resume a developmental path. For the pre-verbal child, beginning to gain a sense of body ego, which becomes cor-rupted, and with no recourse to language, the situation is critical unless an attuned adult can make sense of other cues about distress. Equally, the role of mothers in abuse is only beginning to be explored (Welldon 1988). Smith and Bentovim (1994) propose that as much as 5–15 per cent of child sexual abuse is at the hands of women; Sinason (1996) provides a vivid comment on what the child experiences as abusive in her descriptions of pubertal and pre-pubertal boys who are made to share a bed with their mothers.

If the abuse happens within the family, the capacity to make and use attachments and object relationships is severely damaged, and the sense of normality is turned upside down. Adults blame children for their seduction; children are made responsible for the adults; boundaries between parents and children become totally muddled; ideas of 'loving' and 'caring' are confused. The capacity, then, for any Oedipal resolution and for making use of other adults and identifications is limited. Equally, the ego ideal, devel-oping in toddlerhood, is corrupted and the protective function of shame damaged (Campbell 1994). The sense of control, fairness and conscience that should develop in latency is inhibited and often a cruel and punitive con-science, driven to seek punishment, results. It becomes impossible to dis-tinguish rules and to take in from peers and other adults. Indeed, learning is disrupted (Sinason 1991): how can one 'take in' in a meaningful way or even use any orifices for hearing, seeing, talking when all are rendered unsafe.

The integration, in adolescence, of this traumatised body–self into the adolescent identity may become a matter of impossible conflict. Within the development of girls there comes recognition of the permeability of the body, preparation for intercourse and pregnancy. Attacks on this body (self-mutilation, eating disorders) and the body products (babies/children) are one response to overwhelming, indigestible memories of sexual trauma (Welldon 1988). For boys, the boundariedness of the body has been violated, leaving a fear of feminisation, or homosexual fears (which may be dealt with by violence) at a time when fluidity of sexual feeling and object choices is a normal, expected possibility. Equally, the role of the penis at adolescence can become a matter of conflict – how can it be used in a potent, creative and penetrative way that does not become destructive or abusive?

The defences available to the child to deal with abuse will depend on the maturity of the child at the time of the abuse, as well as on the capacity of the adults to hear and act on any disclosure. Where there has not been suitable intervention at the time, this may result in the child growing older but resorting to a repertoire of very primitive defence mechanisms, normally found in much younger children. Issues about the body will be re-enacted through the body: the young child may repeat his sexual anxiety by trying to interest other children in his body and explore theirs – as Wayne did in the prologue to this chapter. The older child may put himself in dangerous situations with no internalised sense of self-preservation. In adolescence, the young person may turn to abusing others or seek a repeat of the original abuse by prostitution: the sisteen-year-old rent boy feels in control of the older men whom he seduces, but is, in fact, repeating his abuse with a veneer of being in control. The fourteen-year-old girl who has turned to prostitution and to encouraging others in this is both assuming a false control over her compulsion to repeat and creating other victims as safe locations for her sense of powerlessness.

The choices in such an extreme are to identify with the aggressor and become an abuser, repeating the cycle and making someone else into a victim; to externalise the abuse; or to adopt a victim role as a way of feeling that at least this choice is under one's control. The final choice is suicide. For many children, a 'splitting' process takes place as they try to deny what has happened: the memory of the abuse sinks to the bottom of the preconscious memory to enable the child to continue to function. This, however, leaks gradually into the conscious mind (Trowell 1992). One young man, abused at boarding school, described it as 'having a fire in my head. I close a door on it and it's OK for a while. Then it burns through again and I close another door – but it doesn't go away.' This 'splitting-off' process is an attempt to deal with the experience of powerlessness and humiliation only too common in victims of abuse: sexual abuse by an adult or parent-substitute is, after all, also abuse of a relationship of power and responsibility. Such denial is often used in the service of retaining some sense of being parentable. All children have to deal with the conviction that their parents have failed them – at the least, by not protecting them. For some, an identity as 'disgusting' and 'bad' is preferable to the dramatic loss and abandonment to be faced in acknowledging the failure in parenting.

It is the memory of humiliation and powerlessness that is unbearable and needs to be evacuated or located elsewhere. One can see, in many adolescent abusers, the flashback memories of their own abuse being turned into the fantasy of abusing a weaker, more vulnerable victim as a way of getting back in control. The leap from memory/fantasy to action, denying any space for thought, results in acting with the body in a repetition of the abuse.

The clinical task in individual psychotherapy with sexually abused children

Preliminary issues for the therapist

The therapist working with the sexually abused child has first to face personal issues: in a sense, the fact of the abuse cannot be mended. We work often in NHS teams where 'treatment' and 'cure' are concepts used daily. Yet trauma cannot be undone; the now sexualised child cannot turn back from adult awareness and the experience of being a child has been corrupted. The challenge to omnipotence in the clinical team is great and may be one of the reasons why the work is so stressful.

> Bridie, a thoughtful fourteen-year-old, had been abused while at primary school over a number of years by her babysitter, a boy of sixteen. Thinking about ending her weekly therapy (appropriately) she said, 'It's like taking a walk through the forest. The hunters have laid traps for the wild animals – dug holes and covered them over, so that you can't see them on the pathway. I can't fill in the traps but I have learned to walk round them and not fall into them.'

The therapist is also faced with internal conflict over the need, therapeutically, to hear the child's story and give it full acknowledgement, while struggling with a wish not to do so. Such stories are disturbing, not simply in content but also in the realisation that we are all, as human beings, capable of perverse and unimaginable acts. It is imperative, in work with sexually abused children, to have a venue for sharing feelings aroused in the work – somewhere to take them where space is given for thought. Without this, there is not only a danger of the re-enactment of sadistic and abusive elements in the therapy – a process unconsciously sought by the child – but of exhaustion and burn-out in the therapist who, like the child, becomes overwhelmed and rendered impotent by the abusive experience.

The most immediate expectation of the abused child is that the adult – any adult – will wish to repeat the abuse. This has to be allowed into the transference relationship where the therapist must be available to be perceived as a potentially abusive adult (Sinason 1991). It challenges our professional identity as belonging to the 'good guys', those who listen and help mend, but such work cannot achieve anything unless the potential to abuse is addressed in the transference.

When beginning work with a sexually abused child, the clinician should give thought to issues of confidentiality. It is usual to explain this to children in terms of privacy, and to talk of breaching it only when issues of safety are paramount. For the abused child, this can become very confused with the enforced secrecy that is inevitably part of sexual abuse. The abuse of power in the sexually abusive relationship will have involved secrecy and threats of what would follow any disclosure – usually threats of loss of parents and parental affection. It is useful, therefore, in preliminary meetings with child and carers to go over the ground carefully together in relation to what is confidential, and it will be necessary from time to time to ascertain together what can be told to the outside world.

Finally, there are often severe issues for the clinic team. Sexually abused children have a capacity for acting-out that can take in the whole clinic setting. The need to evacuate memories and anxieties may, from time to time, be dealt with by running from the room, screaming and attempts at seduction of therapist and clinic staff (as a way of taking control). This can be terrifying and humiliating for the therapist, and enraging for both therapist and team as children appear to try to break all the careful treatment boundaries. Five major issues must be addressed within teams, in the interest of the progress of therapy:

(a) There must be an agreed understanding of the processes at work – that the child has recourse to the body, in a primitive way, as a way of avoiding thought and memory. The therapist and team, therefore, need to be able to think in the face of the child's overwhelming anxiety.

(b) The breaking of boundaries is a repeat of the perversion of boundaries between adults and children that has already taken place. It is helpful if the team has a strategy, supportive of the therapist, for children who insistently challenge the boundaries – e.g. comments about return to the room; not engaging in prolonged conversation with an out-of-session child. These should be clear and sustained approaches.

(c) The team needs to hold together and be aware of the danger of splits and recriminations that would repeat the unheld and scapegoated early experience of the child. It is too easy in clinics for comments to be made about each other's clinical practice and competence when what is needed is thought and mutual support. It is easy for the anger felt by all at the predicament of the child and the relentlessness of the challenging work to be acted out amongst team members. Some understanding of the countertransference of the whole clinic – receptionists and cleaners included – helps enormously in containing this and enabling the team to function together.

(d) It is essential that a team member be appointed to liaise, meet and think with the external network – a case manager. This will involve work with the parents/carers (vital) but also with the social workers, court guardians, teachers and other professionals involved in the care of the child; it will also entail attendance at planning and review meetings. The aim is to free the therapist to be simply that – the child's therapist. This will be attacked and it takes great resistance on the part of teams to keep the lines of communication open but the boundaries firm and clear.

(e) Finally, all team members, including child psychotherapists, need a thorough knowledge of their employing Trust's Child Protection Procedures and of the recommendations of their local Area Child Protection Committee. This should be an automatic part of the induction of any new staff member.

Key themes in the process of therapy

The early process with abused children often involves great care in building basic trust. The presence of an attentive, non-abusing adult in an intimate relationship like therapy is, to the child, extremely risky. Expecting the therapist, in the transference, to be another abusing adult, yet hoping that it might not be so, the child experiences swings of hope, sudden trusting intimacy and equally sudden re-enactment of terror and the invitation to abuse. The process of coming to therapy itself can be interpreted as merely a repetition of abuse as the child struggles with ambivalence.

> Wayne took care to keep his therapist at a distance. Card games allowed him to show her that he felt he was 'tricky', untrustworthy, but a small sense of hope emerged when he carefully showed her how the tricks were done – a glimpse of the wish to be understood. He dismissed any sign of his competence, rubbished himself and her, struggled to draw and tore up his work. He wondered if she could look at horror videos – bear his internal world. Recounting one gruesome story, he suddenly saw a connection to his own experience and dashed to the far end of the room, shaking. Calm interpretation of his suddenly expecting the therapist to be like the video mother (attacking and annihilating) allowed him to return to his seat, but he remained fearful and dashed out at the end of the session.

Technical aspects remain vital with such young people. The defences that they have organised must be respected. They can be noted, verbalised and slowly explored but it will take time before sufficient ego solidity is gained to allow real questioning.

> For the first few months Wayne found the process of attending for fifty-minute sessions desperately persecutory. Arriving felt like being locked away by his father, when anything could happen; leaving – no matter how carefully the therapist tried to prepare and warn him – was a repetition of abandonment. After much thought, his therapist gave him control of the last ten minutes of the session: he could choose at what point he left within this ten-minute space, although the therapist would always remain in the room for his full time and he would wait in the waiting room with his escort until she emerged to say good-bye. He rarely used this control, although he occasionally drew attention to the fact that it was now 'me to choose' time. Much later in his therapy he reflected on this and on the impotence he had felt as a child. He could now recognise states of anxiety and think rather than act.

Such strategies, while they collude briefly with the defence, give space for thinking seriously about the necessity for that defence. Space for thought takes time to achieve, as does any capacity for reflection. It is, after all, an Oedipal achievement to be able to take up a position of observing oneself and reflecting on that (Britton 1989) and Oedipal resolutions are few in seriously abused children. The process between therapist and child, whereby the therapist seeks space for reflection, takes time to internalise and recognise as safe. Even when much has been achieved, there will be regression at times of high anxiety to action rather than thought.

Attending to one's countertransference comes as a matter of course in child and adolescent work. However, the depths of feeling aroused in working with abused children, the rage and sadism unconsciously pro-voked and the profound and paralysing helplessness felt in the counter-transference, make this more essential than ever. For therapists in this work it is vital to have individual or group supervision, or a regular clini-cal workshop to which one can take the experiences (Morice 1995; Trowell 1997).

When therapy is well-established, when more mature ego functioning has been achieved and a greater sense of integration is present – and this could take months or even years to achieve – it is possible to arrive at three important themes:

(a) *Damage*: 'Who am I and who can I possibly be sexually?' is an issue for all abused children. Fear of pregnancy, of menstruation and of internal damage (possibly exacerbated by paediatric internal examination for police purposes) arises frequently in work with girls. Such concerns, while taken up in relation to their internal meaning, may also require external advice and intervention that can be secured, with permission, via the case manager. In boys, fear of feminisation and passivity must be addressed to enable fluidity of sexuality in adolescence. For both, there is otherwise a danger of foreclosing on any prospect of adolescent and adult sexuality.

(b) *The sense that the mother wished this to happen.* All children – even these for whom the circumstances of the abuse meant that parental failure to protect was understandable – have to deal with the sense that their mothers wished the abuse to happen and colluded with it (Trowell 1992). This internal, early-Oedipal revengeful object comes into the transference for attention in the context of the Oedipal wishes of the child. Working through is essential not only for Oedipal resolution but also in preparation for adolescent and adult sexual roles.

(c) *The child's view of his own role and responsibility* – the sense children feel of having been the seducer in an Oedipal drama replayed. This can be exacerbated by the child's awareness of betrayal by his own physiological reactions – the body is, after all, programmed to respond to sexual invitation (Sinason 1996). The child may also, as the only possible position available, have adopted a pose of enjoying or seeking the abuse as a defence against humiliation and impotence. Or the child's wishes for a loving relationship (frequently present in sibling incest) have been granted. It takes a lot of time to reach the loss of intimacy, of feeling special to the abusive attachment figure. All of this must be analysed before work can be completed.

Court

It is often very difficult to explain to colleagues why one is reluctant to provide court reports for children in therapy. The intimacy and confidentiality of the relationship, the delicacy of the transference – everything can end up frustratingly being construed as 'preciousness' on the part of the therapist. Yet – as will be evident in the section 'Thoughts on networks' (below) – such external intrusions arrive frequently, often as a result of requests for Access Orders and Residence Orders that the court must hear. It is possible to negotiate a position, with the child, of providing information via the case manager that allows another professional – either case manager, expert witness or guardian – to present a child-centred case to the court. Greater sophistication and understanding of children's needs amongst judges and barristers has helped in this process. Nowadays, this should be achievable. Nevertheless, it occasionally becomes necessary to appear in court. There can be a danger that the therapy begins to focus on the therapist's need to explain to the child, or even that the therapist's anxiety about court appearance interferes with the therapy, and helpful supervision is a great aid here. With the child, there will inevitably be a regression to former anxieties in the transference relationship. The idea of adults working together and planning together may, on the other hand, offer a practical interpretation to the child that Oedipal boundaries can be held and can work.

It must be noted that this is, of course, different from the request to appear as an expert witness where experience and proficiency have been gained by a number of child psychotherapists. It is, in that context, an arena where our voices should be heard. Two recent publications are recommended: Thorpe and Trowell (2007) and Dowling (2009).

Forgetting and returning: an experience of normality

With the child, one seeks a 'good-enough' resolution that enables the abuse to be confronted and articulated, responsibility located, the internal sense the child makes of him or herself to be less persecutory and the defences to be more appropriate, allowing development to continue more on track. Indeed, for many sexually abused children and young people, there is a need thereafter to have an experience of forgetting (Alvarez 1989; Lanyado 1991) and a sense of returned normality. The door should be left open, however, for a return for therapeutic input: when the next developmental challenge comes along (e.g. a first boyfriend, a first equal sexual relationship, the birth of a child), the abused young person often needs to touch base again to rethink 'Who am I now?' and to accommodate the memory of the abuse into his or her evolving identity.

Working with adolescents who sexually abuse children

Assessment

It has long perturbed those working in the area of child sexual abuse that research consistently shows us that 50 per cent of abusers have themselves been abused. What, then, about the 50 per cent who say they were not abused? Are they simply unable to recall their own abuse? The discoveries by the research team at Great Ormond Street Children's Hospital, London, develop our understanding further (Hodges *et al.* 1994; Lanyado *et al.* 1995). It has become clear from this work that trauma, especially violence, is a key factor in the early lives of young abusers. The experience of continuing and often unpredictable violence, with concomitant feelings of rage and helplessness and with no attendant adult to make sense of or make safe the situation, is frequent in the histories of adolescents who abuse other children:

It took Wayne ten months to talk of his terror at his father's drunken violence. His distress at remembering was evident, and he could say how afraid he was that talking of it would make him remember more. He was locked in a cupboard under the stairs while his father beat and raped his mother. He soiled himself in his fear and was beaten on his release. He wanted to murder his father. Patchy memories grew as he gained a sense that he had deserved better. He recalled his parents drinking together and his uncertainty as to whether this would end in laughter or violence: both were possible and he could not predict which would occur by the end of an afternoon's drinking. His ambivalence towards the unprotecting, weak and yet colluding mother was unbearable. The smell of alcohol, he said, made him physically terrified. He had hit his first foster father when he came to tuck him in bed with beer on his breath. It took him a long time to recall that his sexually inviting behaviour towards this man had been his only strategy to preclude the violence that he was certain would come from him. He struggled in therapy with the knowledge that his therapist would not violate him and the uncertainty that she might change, or that he himself might be violent to her. His notion of adult sexuality was bound up with fantasies of violence. He presented fantasies of revenge for small slights, threatening and trying to shock the therapist, and drew cartoons of blood, bodies, graves and sadistic violence. His key worker was essential at this time in escorting him safely and in containing his terrifying anxieties on the way to therapy.

This experience of impotent helplessness in the face of unpredictable violence may emerge in the assessment of young abusers; it may, however, take some time to reach and marks an important point in therapy when it occurs.

It is also important at the initial stage to gain a differential diagnosis of the young person and his acts. Campbell (1994) includes in this the victim's story: the victim's feelings provide an important indicator both of the degree of the young abuser's dangerousness and of the unmanageable feelings that he is trying to decant outside him. Wayne's sister expressed unease at his attentions but also conveyed a sense of puzzlement and playfulness at her brother's actions. It was his invitation to her to touch his genitals that led to her certainty of inappropriateness and disclosure to her mother. Ali, a sixteen-year-old Kurdish refugee, who had experienced horrendous ethnic violence in his homeland and who was regularly physically abused by his father at home, approached the women he assaulted diffidently but left them with feelings of terror and intrusion.

Within the young person's recounting of his actions, it is helpful to get a sense of where responsibility for the offence is located – is this a young person with a clear idea of responsibility or is the child-victim blamed for being seductive, seeking a sexual relationship? The rationalisations used in this description are helpful in assessing where, developmentally, the abusing adolescent places himself. Primitive defences of denial or projection indicate concerns about the survival of a basic sense of self. Guilt and fear often feature in an assessment; shame may only emerge (indeed, only be possible) after months of therapy. Fantasies should be explored, if at all possible, and their relation to ideas of sexuality, violence and being violated. Fantasy often begins as a reaction to flashbacks and the beginnings of fantasising with its quality of rehearsal is important, as is the impact of masturbation and how the fantasy then changes. Beliefs about children can also be reached, giving clues about the young person's own experience, but also indicating whether sexually abusive acts are indicative of part-object rather than whole-object relationships, and whether they contain information about power and compliance.

> Wayne's abuse of his sister happened when he was left babysitting for her and the neighbour's three-year-old son who was sleeping over with them. He described his enormous loneliness and worry at his mother and stepfather being out for the evening, and had terrifying flashbacks of waiting for his drunken parents to return and being locked away from them in a state of fear. His relief when the children crept downstairs to join him was great. When they began somersaulting in their nightwear, he became – unaccountably to him – angry at their freedom and also sexually aroused. He touched his sister's exposed body and genitals, and those of the neighbour's child, and invited both children to look at his. At this point his sister said, 'Dirty!' and he angrily put them to bed, shut them in their room and could not understand why he wept as he masturbated alone downstairs.

A good psychosocial history is essential, preferably one covering at least three generations of the family: identifications, vulnerabilities, family myths, scripts and stories. Much serious abuse is transgenerational. That said, the frequent breakdown in attachments in the histories of such young people means that it may take an enormous effort to get a relatively clear picture of the early years in particular. Masses of paperwork may well make its way to the clinic; the therapist often has to piece together a story that has never been seen as a whole or as a developmental, sequential history before. For these adolescents, continuity of experience may not have been available –

the pressure in them and in the network has been *not* to connect, that it is dangerous to bring things together.

Wayne's mother's drinking and her inability to protect him were not unconnected to her own abuse by her stepfather. Never close to her mother, she told no one but ran away from home several times in her early teens. Towards the end of her clinic sessions, she wondered if her mother had hated her or if she, too, had been abused and could not bear to remember. Wayne's father, she recalled, had been 'knocked about all the time by his Dad'. She considered therapy for herself, but, as yet, has not taken up the offer.

Finally, the assessment should cover the adolescent's capacity for engagement in therapy. This involves considering whether thinking can be tolerated and links may be made; whether a capacity for basic trust can be developed; whether the abusing is defensive against psychotic breakdown; whether there is more than simple denial of responsibility and harm; and – most importantly – whether the network will hold this young person while he represents a risk to society. Taking the support structures into consideration is vital: is a therapeutic residential setting necessary? Will the foster parents cope and support therapy? Can care staff in a children's home be consistent and understanding enough to deal with a person who is both victim and risk? Planning supportive intervention with the network and clarifying what is basically necessary if therapy is to proceed as a treatment of choice are an essential part of the assessment.

This is obviously work that cannot be done quickly. Several sessions will be necessary to build up a picture of the adolescent's functioning and psychological position. The Great Ormond Street team interspersed open-ended psychotherapy sessions with semi-structured interviews and standard questionnaires over twelve sessions (Hodges *et al.* 1994; Lanyado *et al.* 1995); the Portman Clinic in London, where work with such young people has been going on since 1933, offers up to six assessment sessions. There is containment in knowing that one is taken seriously, particularly when the adolescent has a sense of fear about his own potential for hurt and for retribution. There is also terror of abandonment – described poignantly by Lanyado in her case study (Lanyado *et al.* 1995) and evident in Wayne's description of what happened when he abused his sister – which also should be addressed.

Issues in the therapy

The externalisation of humiliation and powerlessness on to the victim for observation and, if more fixed, for enjoyment is repeated in the transference relationship in the therapy. There is a fine line between exploring this, being felt to collude and in being an abuser. Lanyado provides a vivid case example of this process (Lanyado *et al.* 1995: 235). In the transference, one can gain a sense of whether this is a process of externalisation or whether projection, with a sense of an object, is involved, and how near this has grown to sadism.

For all workers with abusing young people, the need to reach the victim behind the aggressor is prime (Lanyado *et al.* 1995; Woods 1997). This is one reason why a psychoanalytic approach may ultimately offer long-term benefit, if appropriate. Cognitive methods do not always approach this, and too confrontative a style, one which does not hold 'abused' in mind, has been known to end in the suicide of the young person. Where there is a mature ego and stronger sense of self, cognitive approaches offer possibilities. With young people like Wayne, however, where there are atolls of functioning in a sea of anxiety and dysfunctionality, much ego structuring has to occur first.

Woods describes three key factors that he has noted in working with adolescent abusers: the sexualisation of the therapeutic relationship, the re-enactment of trauma and anxieties and acting-out around boundaries (Woods 1997). While these may well be experienced in work with the abused but non-abusing child, his comments on the need to mobilise the network are very apt and reflect experience with Wayne:

> Wayne found that his sister's presence on home visits both made him feel guilty and tantalised him. He was able to say that he did not feel she was safe with him. After much discussion, he agreed to the therapist's talking to the case manager who would alert and help the network. The next home visit was put on hold while plans were made to ensure contact was supervised. Wayne expressed fury with the therapist at his next session – which he had been reluctant to attend – then suddenly reflected on his own position, when little, and his rage and sadness that 'no one did anything'.

Guilt is often accessible with abusing adolescents, as is a sense of imminent retribution that parallels their earlier abuse, but it takes time to reach a sense of shame. This can emerge when being heard as a victim is certain for the young person, and when he can then begin to address what he has done. This is a risk time for depression – as is the growing admission of early abused impotence – and needs a holding structure. There is also a risk of harm when the young person begins to trust attachments as he may well lack appropriate defences:

In the waiting room before therapy, Wayne began to engage in conversation with an older male patient. His need for a benign father was recognised by his escort who brought it to the therapist's attention delicately in front of Wayne, allowing scope to address both the wish and the need to protect himself.

In creating a space for thought, inserted between fantasy and the immediate rush to activity, the therapist makes use of technical strategies normally helpful in work with adolescents where preventing humiliation has to be kept in mind: taking up anxieties in the displacement, splitting the age-appropriate concern and capacities from the infantile worries.

Wayne began to talk of a school friend who was uncertain whether his girlfriend liked him or not. For several weeks ideas about sexuality and the risks of denigration, engulfment and loss of individuality were explored in the displacement of 'the friend'. More recently he has begun to talk of a girl whom he likes, and to draw Valentine cards for her, opening the way to integrating his concern for his friend with his own anxieties.

Thought also involves the capacity to integrate, to connect things together and bear their being together.

Thoughts on networks

Throughout this chapter, networks have been mentioned. Constant attention has to be paid to developments within the network surrounding abused and abusing children and young people. In part, this is to ensure that all workers have access to support, the work being stressful. Partly, however, it is because things frequently go strangely wrong. Decision-making suddenly becomes difficult; placements break down through lack of input to foster parents and children are further abandoned; mothers who have been sentenced for their part in abuse suddenly become possible carers for their children again with no intervention or assessment; social workers go silent and the therapist hears from the child that he or she is being moved again; good social workers are removed suddenly from the case with no warning to the child; therapy becomes perceived as a process which is not effective speedily enough, or which keeps the child a victim, and review meetings suggest it should stop forthwith; the therapist is decried for not being able to state categorically that an adolescent is no longer a risk. Every therapist, social worker and foster parent can probably add to the list. As if in an *Alice in Wonderland* world, one moves around the triangle of victim–rescuer–abuser, taking up each position in turn (Jezzard 1992, personal communication). What, therefore, gets into the system?

Three factors may help in thinking about this. First, Kolvin and Trowell (1996) point to a mirroring process that takes place in networks around abuse: different agencies or different professionals will find themselves adopting the position of different family members and identifying with them. Such identifications are helpful in bringing transference feelings into the discussion, but only when it is clear that it *is* transference that is being experienced. Otherwise they can militate against any sense of an integrated position – particularly regarding being clear about the risk presented by the young patient and the structures necessary to help. Thus with abusing adolescents there can be a split between those who see the young person only as a victim and those who see a dangerous perpetrator. It is essential that both views are held at the one time, and that these should be held in common by all the workers involved, or different parts of the structure will pull against each other. This trend can often be seen in professionals' meetings in relation to abused children. The danger occurs when one partial perspective prevails, to the detriment of the child.

Second, one can also see the process as being a reflection of the dys-functional family system itself – the system being more than the sum of its parts. The secrecy, denial, abuse, collusion and misapplication of power are then unconsciously replicated in the support system which, like the family, may also experience difficulty in seeing the situation, hearing the evidence and acting in the child's interests.

Finally, in all such work there is a propensity for those engaged in the network to re-enact the internal world of the child (Davies 1996). The defences and projections used by the child will find themselves, again unconsciously, lodged in the network where, unless the process becomes conscious, they will be harmful. Amongst these there will inevitably be the child's expectation of abuse. There can also, however, be deep empathy for the child's wish to be parented, to have parents who can parent, and often an ill-placed desire to return home a child who is ready to be victimised once more by a family that is not yet ready or able to be different. If the therapist is to be able to work, a colleague who has a clear understanding of such dynamics and processes is an essential partner in the process.

Epilogue

After twenty-two months of therapy Wayne is able to connect fantasies of harming smaller children to times when he feels small, despairing and victimised. His stronger ego can recognise this and preclude his acting on it. While understanding his mother's position more – he has had several helpful joint meetings with her at the clinic – he does not wish to live at home although he is a welcome weekend visitor. He is planning a college course on building and working with computers – a new preoccupation with a different kind of 'insides', which makes him smile. He has found a capacity for work and concentration in school that he enjoys and can accept his teachers' praise. Suicidal thoughts have gone, although his sense of shame remains and he is overwhelmed by his sister's continuing affection for him. Relationships with girls remain an area for work, encompassing adolescent sexuality and his sexual future. Although he knows that he is now in control of the degree of risk he might present, he is aware of work remaining to be done and will continue in therapy for some time.

References

Adshead, G. (1994) 'Looking for clues: a review of the literature on false allegations of sexual abuse in childhood', in V. Sinason (ed.) *Treating Survivors of Satanist Abuse*, London: Routledge.

Alvarez, A. (1989) 'Child sexual abuse: the need to remember and the need to forget', *The Consequences of Child Sexual Abuse*, Occasional Papers No. 3, London: Association for Child Psychology and Psychiatry and Allied Disciplines.

Britton, R. (1989) 'The missing link: parental sexuality in the Oedipus complex', in R. Britton, M. Fieldman and E. O'Shaughnessy (eds) *The Oedipus Complex Today: Clinical Implications*, London: Karnac.

Butler-Sloss, E. (1988) *Report of the Inquiry into Child Abuse in Cleveland 1987*, London: HMSO.

Campbell, D. (1994) 'Breaching the shame shield: thoughts on the assessment of adolescent child sexual abusers', *Journal of Child Psychotherapy* 20(3): 309–26.

Chasseguet-Smirgel, J. (1985) 'Perversion and the universal law', in *Creativity and Perversion*, London: Free Association Books.

Davies, R. (1996) 'The inter-disciplinary network and the internal world of the offender', in C. Cordess and M. Cox (eds) *Forensic Psychotherapy: Crime, Psychodynamics and the Offender Patient. Vol II: Mainly Practice*, London: Jessica Kingsley.

Dowling, D. (2009) 'Thinking aloud: a child psychotherapist assessing families for court', in A. Horne and M. Lanyado (eds) *Through Assessment to Consultation: Independent Psychoanalytic Approaches with Children and Families*, London: Routledge.

Flood, S. (1994) 'The effects of child sexual abuse', *Young Minds Newsletter*, Issue 18, June 1994.

Freud, S. (1913) 'Totem and taboo', *SE* 13, London: Hogarth Press.

Goodwin, J., Shad, D. and Rada, R. (1978) 'Incest hoax: false accusations, false denials', *Bulletin of the American Academy of Psychiatry and Law* 6: 269–76.

Hodges, J., Lanyado, M. and Andreou, C. (1994) 'Sexuality and violence: preliminary research hypotheses from psychotherapeutic assessments in a research programme on young offenders', *Journal of Child Psychotherapy* 20(3): 283–308.

Ironside, L. (1995) 'Beyond the boundaries: a patient, a therapist and an allegation of sexual abuse', *Journal of Child Psychotherapy* 21(2): 183–205.

Khan, M. M. R. (1963) 'The concept of cumulative trauma', *Psychoanalytic Study of the Child* 18: 286–306.

Kolvin, I. and Trowell, J. (1996) 'Child sexual abuse', in I. Rosen (ed.) *Sexual Deviation*, 3rd edn, Oxford: Oxford University Press.

Lanyado, M. (1991) 'Putting theory into practice: struggling with perversion and chaos in the analytic process', *Journal of Child Psychotherapy* 17(1): 25–40.

Lanyado, M., Hodges, J., Bentovim, A. *et al.* (1995) 'Understanding boys who sexually abuse other children: a clinical illustration', *Psychoanalytic Psychotherapy* 9(3): 231–42.

Morice, M. (1995) 'A community group for abused children', in J. Trowell and M. Bower (eds) *The Emotional Needs of Young Children and their Families*, London: Routledge.

Sinason, V. (1991) 'Interpretations that feel horrible to make and a theoretical unicorn', *Journal of Child Psychotherapy* 17(1): 11–24.

—— (ed.) (1994) *Treating Survivors of Satanist Abuse*, London: Routledge.

—— (1996) 'From abused to abusing', in C. Cordess and M. Cox (eds) *Forensic Psychotherapy: Crime, Psychodynamics and the Offender Patient. Vol. II: Mainly Practice*, London: Jessica Kingsley.

Smith, M. and Bentovim, A. (1994) 'Sexual abuse', in M. Rutter, E. Taylor and L. Hersov (eds) *Child Psychiatry: Modern Approaches*, London: Blackwell.

Thorpe, C. and Trowell, J. (eds) (2007) *Re-rooted Lives: Inter-disciplinary Work within the Family Justice System*, London: Jordan Publishing.

Trowell, J. (1992) 'Child sexual abuse', talk given to British Association of Psychotherapists.

—— (1994) 'Ritual organised abuse: management issues', in V. Sinason (ed.) *Treating Survivors of Satanist Abuse*, London: Routledge.

—— (1997) 'Child sexual abuse', in Hon. Mr Justice Wall (ed.) *Rooted Sorrows: Psychoanalytic Perspectives on Child Protection, Assessment, Therapy and Treatment*, Bristol: Family Law.

Welldon, E. (1988) *Mother, Madonna, Whore: The Idealisation and Denigration of Motherhood*, London: Free Association Books.

Woods, J. (1997) 'Breaking the cycle of abuse and abusing: individual psychotherapy for juvenile sex offenders', *Clinical Child Psychology and Psychiatry* 2(3): 379–92.

Further reading

Association for Child Psychiatry and Psychology (1989) *The Consequences of Child Sexual Abuse*, Occasional Papers No. 3, London: ACPP.

Kolvin, I. and Trowell, J. (1996) 'Child sexual abuse', in I. Rosen (ed.) *Sexual Deviation*, 3rd edn, Oxford: Oxford University Press.

Lanyado, M., Hodges, J., Bentovim, A. *et al.* (1995) 'Understanding boys who sexually abuse other children: a clinical illustration', *Psychoanalytic Psychother-apy* 9(3): 231–42.

Sandler, J. and Fonagy, P. (1997) *Recovered Memories of Abuse: True or False?*, Psychoanalytic Monograph No. 2, Monograph Series of the Psychoanalysis Unit of University College, London and Anna Freud Centre, London: Karnac.

Woods, J. (2003) *Boys Who Have Abused: Psychoanalytic Psychotherapy with Victim/Perpetrators of Child Sexual Abuse*, London: Jessica Kingsley.

24 The roots of violence: theory and implications for technique with children and adolescents

Marianne Parsons

Is there a difference between aggression and violence? Why does someone act violently? Are there developmental factors that set a young person on the road to violence? Are there danger signs or triggers that we can be alert to? How can we work with youngsters who are violent? These are some of the questions addressed in this chapter, which considers violence perpetrated by an individual, rather than in groups or gangs. (For a psychoanalytic account of adolescent group violence see Hyatt Williams 1997.)

Is there a difference between aggression and violence?

Basically, yes! Aggression is a natural part of life and a major source of energy. It is vital for progressive development but without appropriate control and management, it can get out of hand and lead to violence. Without aggression we would not be able to assert or protect ourselves or others, learn or work effectively, separate or develop autonomy (Winnicott 1963). Like sexuality, aggression can be used constructively and progressively, or destructively and regressively. Its appropriateness in any specific situation depends on the manner of its expression and the developmental level of the individual. In situations of very real danger, violent aggression to protect the self or others may be entirely appropriate. On the other hand, such behaviours as sadism, contemptuous denigration, bullying and wanton destructiveness are largely regressive and arise from pathology not health.

The main difference between aggression and violence is that violence involves a *physical* attack on the body of another person when this is not an age-appropriate act. The toddler who physically attacks someone is being aggressive, not violent, because it is developmentally expectable for toddlers to express their anger and frustration in bodily ways; and the teenager who attacks another with verbal abuse is also being aggressive not violent, but if that adolescent were to resort to physical attack then that would constitute an act of violence.

Why does someone act violently?

Violence is the most primitive and physical response to a *perceived* threat to the integrity of the psychological self. Although an act of violence may be unacceptable, it may also be understandable if we can see how and why the individual felt provoked. During psychotherapy when we look into the internal world of the violent patient, we begin to understand that all kinds of overtures that to us would seem harmless or even friendly are deadly provocations for the patient. For example, an old woman who befriends a disturbed young person, invites him into her house and feeds him, but then is not available to him in the middle of the night when he is wandering the streets alone and depressed, may be perceived by the young person as someone who deliberately wants to tantalise him and then abandon him.

Violence can be understood as an attempted solution to the overwhelming *unprocessed trauma of helplessness in the absence of a protective other.* The feeling of being completely helpless and alone without protection brings about terror of annihilation. If there is no protective *internal* function in the ego that facilitates the regulation of fear and anxiety, violence is used as the only means of defence. Someone who has been able to internalise a protective function will have developed a permeable psychological membrane which allows for some flexible give and take in relation to helplessness, frustration and aggression. He will be able to tolerate some frustration and criticism, and will also be able to make use of his natural aggressiveness appropriately to assert and protect himself. Someone prone to violence lacks this adequately flexible internal protective membrane. Failures in his earliest nurturing mean he has developed instead a rigid protective barrier, like an impenetrable fortress. He may feel omnipotent and invincible, but in fact he is extremely vulnerable to the frustrations and anxieties of daily life. Being so rigidly fortified, he is constantly on guard but actually unprepared for danger. He cannot register anxiety as a danger signal that would help him to make use of appropriate defences to deal with his helplessness, anger and frustration, and any threat which penetrates his rigid barrier will feel traumatic and trigger the most primitive defences of flight or fight.

This formulation draws on the distinction between 'self-preservative' as opposed to 'sado-masochistic' violence (Glasser 1998). Someone who uses *self-preservative violence* feels his psychic survival is in mortal danger and he has to destroy the source of the danger to save himself. The aim of self-preservative violence is to destroy the one who threatens psychic annihilation of the self. *Sado-masochistic violence* is very different. It involves no wish to get rid of or kill the other person – instead there is a desperate *need* to *engage* the other in a very particular kind of relationship built on control and sadistic interaction.

The concept of the 'core complex' (Figure 24.1) developed by Mervin Glasser (Glasser 1996), Chair of the Portman Clinic for many years, concerns very primitive anxieties experienced by both violent and perverse patients.

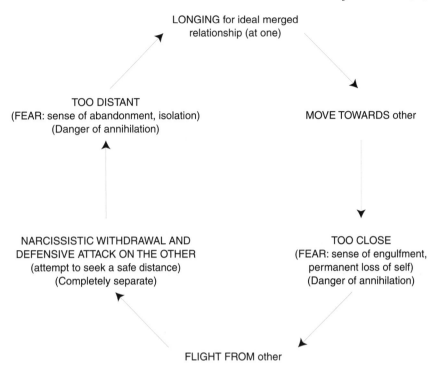

LONGING for ideal merged
relationship (at one)

TOO DISTANT
(FEAR: sense of abandonment, isolation)
(Danger of annihilation)

MOVE TOWARDS other

NARCISSISTIC WITHDRAWAL AND
DEFENSIVE ATTACK ON THE OTHER
(attempt to seek a safe distance)
(Completely separate)

TOO CLOSE
(FEAR: sense of engulfment,
permanent loss of self)
(Danger of annihilation)

FLIGHT FROM other

Figure 24.1 The 'vicious circle' of the core complex (based on Glasser 1979).

The individual struggles to deal with the contrasting anxieties of being intruded upon, engulfed, overwhelmed and taken over by another on the one hand; and of being abandoned, completely lost and alone on the other. Both of these anxieties involve the same underlying primitive terror of annihilation – annihilation because of being taken over by another and therefore losing one's self, or annihilation because of being abandoned and therefore feeling lost and disintegrated. The individual becomes caught in a vicious circle, revisiting these two extremes. When anxious about engulfment by another, he tries to protect himself by distancing himself emotionally; but then he experiences the opposite anxiety of being abandoned and alone, so he moves towards the other again. He is in an impossible situation and desperately needs to find a position of safety – not too close (to avoid feeling engulfed) and not too distant (to avoid feeling abandoned). Sado-masochism (either as a style of relating or as a full perversion or as a violent response) is the desperate but false solution that some people use to defend against core complex anxieties. By keeping a grip on the object at arm's length, the sado-masochist tries to keep the other within his control and at a safe distance. In the Portman Clinic Violence Research Project, under the leadership of Mervin Glasser, we noticed that all the violent men in the research study attempted to protect themselves by habitual sado-masochistic modes of relating. When this defence broke down, their core complex anxieties surfaced and they again experienced the other as completely engulfing or abandoning. Self-preservative violence then erupted to destroy the person who had become the source of the ultimate danger – annihilation of the psychic self.

Developmental factors that set a young person on the road to violence

Early environmental failures and the way they are carried in the child's internal world can lead an individual to become violent. In order to understand what can go wrong, we need to consider the usual paths of development of aggression, defence and mastery, the self, ways of relating and the superego (see Colarusso 1992; Edgcumbe 1976; Freud 1949, 1972; Parsons 2006; Stern 1985; Tyson and Tyson 1990). In this section I will refer to some aspects of development that are relevant to the notion of the construction of a rigidly fixed internal barrier and to the development of habitual sado-masochistic modes of relating.

Winnicott's view was that aggression arises from environmental impingements, especially traumatic early relational experiences, as well as instinctual forces (Winnicott 1950-5). Heimann and Valenstein concur:

> Our psychoanalytic experience tells us that certain patients who show particular problems with aggression have had to suppress or otherwise defend themselves in infancy and childhood from environmental influences that were not conducive to the progression of their developmental needs for the normal expression of aggression.
>
> (Heimann and Valenstein 1972: 34)

The power of love to bind hatred is crucial. People showing uncontrollable, apparently senseless destructiveness tend to be those who were not enabled in childhood to develop a secure attachment in which they felt loved and contained, such as institutionalised children with multiple caretakers, traumatised children and those who have suffered severe physical pain, neglect or over-stimulation, and children for whom fear has been a daily currency. Anna Freud noted that the pathological factor in such cases was not the aggressive tendencies themselves, but the deficiencies in emotional development which leave aggression unbound by love:

> The pathological factor is found in the realm of erotic, emotional development which has been held up through adverse external or internal conditions, such as absence of love objects, lack of emotional response from the adult environment, breaking of emotional ties as soon as they are formed, deficiency of emotional development for

innate reasons. Owing to the defects on the emotional side, the aggressive urges are not brought into fusion and thereby bound and partially neutralised, but remain free and seek expression in life in the form of pure, unadulterated, independent destructiveness . . . The appropriate therapy has to be directed to the neglected, defective side i.e. the emotional libidinal development.

(Freud 1949: 41-2)

The earliest form of mental aggressiveness concerns the baby's need to get rid of intolerable feelings (Edgcumbe 1976) in order to achieve a sense of internal balance, safety and well-being. When a tiny baby feels hungry or frightened he has no resources for making himself feel better and has to rely on his caregivers. If his needs are not adequately met, his distress, helplessness and frustration will become overwhelming. He will yell and cry, kick and flail his arms. This is the earliest kind of response to an overwhelming experience – a *bodily* one. The most important thing from the point of view of development is the mother's response to the baby. Good-enough mothering will give the baby sufficiently often an experience of not yelling and flailing into a vacuum, but of having been able to get a protective response that relieves his distress. This is more than the meeting of a need; it is the *meeting up* with an empathic and receptive other. It lays the foundations for the capacity to tolerate vulnerability because helplessness is associated with a protective other.

If the mother is able to act adequately as a protective shield (Freud 1920; Khan 1963) against both internal and external dangers, keeping her baby safe until he gradually develops the resources to do this for himself, he will develop a sense of basic safety and trust, and will form a secure attachment to her. He will begin to internalise her ways of looking after him and will gradually be able to tolerate small amounts of anxiety and frustration as he learns that she *will* do something to make him feel better. The mother's empathy with the baby and her active attunement to his physical and emotional needs help him not only to feel loved, but also to develop a capacity to be attuned to his own internal states. Over time he will begin to recognise and tolerate his needs and to differentiate between shades of feeling, so that not every internal state has the same urgency. A space opens up for thought and reflection. In order to become receptive to his internal states and to tolerate feeling needy, the child needs a good-enough experience of dependence on a reliably protective mother. The prolonged absence of the mother's protective function leaves the baby with unmanageable amounts of anxiety (Fraiberg 1982) and unable to develop internal adaptive resources. He will develop a false or precocious independence – something often seen in violent individuals, who tend to act out their frustration and anxiety, unable to use their minds for self-reflection or containment of feelings. He will develop an insecure or disorganised attachment and have no reliable sense of being loveable. Thus, lack of the mother's protective function leads to the child having to resort to constructing a rigid internal barrier instead of a more flexible protective psychic membrane.

As the baby gets older and begins to develop a sense of self-agency (Stern 1985), the good-enough mother intuitively recognises that he can tolerate more frustration as he begins to internalise her protective function. She gradually gives him more space to learn how to manage his own feelings and experiences without immediately managing them for him. Repeated experiences of small amounts of manageable frustration in the context of empathic mothering help the baby to learn that he can survive feelings of helplessness without being overwhelmed, and promote the development of healthy aggression.

As the child becomes more mobile, he can begin to move physically away from his mother. Increasingly, the mother has to say 'no' to protect him from dangers of which he is not yet aware or to protect herself and others from his behaviour. The toddler has to face the reality that he is not all-powerful and cannot have everything he wants. This painful blow to his previously omnipotent sense of himself arouses enormous frustration and often results in the temper tantrums typical of the so-called 'terrible twos'. The way the parents relate to their frustrated angry toddler is crucial – the question is how to contain the child's frustration calmly and control his aggression without increasing his fear and without abusing the child's sense of an active self. The toddler in a tantrum can feel overwhelmed and out of control, and he needs the continuous presence of the adult to help him regain an internal balance. Being angrily controlled or left alone in an aggressive and out-of-control state leaves the child with unmanageable panic and does not help him to learn ways of containing his frustration and aggression. The parents' ability to treat the child with respect and enable him to feel a 'somebody' (Furman 1992), whilst at the same time setting limits to his behaviour, offers the child a model for internalisation. This helps him to develop self-respect and to accept limits, which in turn lay the foundation for being able to respect others who will not always do what he wants. In the absence of a good-enough experience of 'no', future limits are experienced as the mere exercise of power, which the child deals with by alternating between compliance and defiance – a dynamic characteristic of violent patients.

During healthy toddlerhood the child asserts more independence by actively doing more things for himself and wanting to do them his way, but he also wants to please his mother because his sense of well-being is dependent on her love for him. Here he faces a major conflict of ambivalence. He loves his mother when she comforts him and provides for his needs, but hates her when she does not gratify him. In the state of hatred, his sense of loving and being loved disappear. Good-enough mothering gradually helps the child to recognise that the hated and loved mother are the same person, and that the mother who may sometimes be angry with him also still loves him. As he integrates his loving views of the mother with the angry and hostile ones, he also develops a sense of trust that his affectionate relationship with his mother will survive even when he is angry with her or she is angry with him, and when he is separated from her. In the absence of such integration, omnipotent and magical ways of thinking will persist unmodified, the power of love to tame destructiveness will be diminished, and the child's belief in the enormity of his aggression will be unchecked.

Imagine the common sight of a mother struggling with a screaming, demanding child in the supermarket. If the mother does not attend to him but lets him go on screaming, the child will feel more and more left alone with his unmanageable feelings. If she cannot think about his state and try to help him manage, she may hit him or give him a sweet to shut him up. By acting on the basis of her own needs her child will not be able to integrate and master his omnipotence as well as his helplessness. Being given the sweet is gratifying, but it is a hollow gift because the child is being given something only to be kept quiet, instead of containment and help to manage his frustration. If the mother hits the child, he feels punished; but he also gets some contact with the mother, though of a negatively exciting kind. These kinds of interactions, if repeated often, set up a pattern for future relationships where *aggression is sexualised*. This sado-masochistic mode of relating, with its mixture of punishment, humiliation, control and excited contact with the other, can become a fixed part of the child's personality. Instead of having a view of relating that is based on negotiation and give and take, the child learns that there are two opposing sides – the attacker and the attacked, the controller and the controlled – and his sense of identity will inevitably include both these opposing sides. In order to escape from the position of being attacked, humiliated and controlled, he may identify with the aggressor and take on the attacking role.

The parents' capacities to recognise, tolerate and manage their own frustration and aggression help the child to develop an understanding of his aggressive feelings and a capacity to process and manage them. They give the child repeated opportunities to see that aggression may be contained, expressed in an assertive but not damaging way or channelled into other activities. They show him that using language is usually more appropriate than the physical expression of aggression, and they open up the possibility for reparation and forgiveness. Their tolerance of their own aggression will allow them to perceive their child's aggression as that of a child, enabling them to respond appropriately as adults instead of reacting on the basis of their own childlike needs and impulses. All this promotes the child's mastery of his feelings and anxieties, which increases his self-esteem and well-being – in other words healthy narcissism.

Some parental attitudes and behaviours promote violence in children. The most obvious example is violence towards the child or a violent relationship between the parents. The most straightforward route to forming a violent temperament is through identification with a violent parent, but it is not the only one. A parent may not be physically violent towards the child but may act on unconscious hatred in less obvious ways, for example leaving the child unprotected from physical danger because of unconscious death wishes towards him. At the other extreme there are parents who are too fearful or guilty about their own aggressive feelings. This leads to a failure of authority and consequent lack of safety for the child. Some parents use the child inappropriately as a partner. This prolongs the child's sense of being special, and interferes with his relinquishment of omnipotence and with his capacity to separate effectively. A child needs to be allowed to experience and then be helped gradually to give up age-appropriate omnipotence and grandiosity in toddlerhood, in order to learn to tolerate frustration and set his own limits on his behaviour and become a person capable of sharing and relating to others with concern and respect.

The basis of the child's superego is formed in identification with the parents' styles of relating, with their standards and values and with how he is treated by them. One aspect of the superego decides what is and is not acceptable (thus providing standards for behaviour), another specifies the conditions in which the person feels loved and appreciated (thus offering means of regulating self-esteem). It is a fallacy to think that violent children and adolescents do not have a superego. What we discover in therapy is that their superego is particularly harsh and primitive and offers little forgiveness, flexibility or self-worth. In effect it creates an internal source of danger that is so punitive that it can only be dealt with by fight or flight; that is, by defying or avoiding its persecuting voice. The benefit of a healthy superego is that it makes less rigid and unforgiving demands on the self and other, but at the same time it ensures effective and appropriate control and offers satisfactions and self-esteem when conflicts can be mastered.

Several varieties of pathological development of the superego and its relationship to the self are common in violent patients. To defend against feelings of being helpless and vulnerable, the child may form an ideal picture of himself as invincible, such as the 'tough guy; or the 'dictator'. As well as providing an idealised self to live up to, this is also a tyrannical model of both internal and external control. Another pathological path in superego development involves compliance: fearing his own or his parents' uncontrollable aggression, the child avoids all conflictual situations, especially competition, and becomes compliant. He gains self-esteem from living up to his ideal of himself as 'good' and by perceiving others as aggressive. Such a child does not learn to differentiate between shades of angry feelings (ranging from mild irritation to murderous rage), nor does he find ways of asserting himself appropriately. When faced with an extreme situation, his defensive compliance may break down, causing him to erupt with violent fury.

Danger signs and triggers

We need to remember that it is fear and anxiety that lead to the pathological use of aggression and violence. Understanding what has gone wrong developmentally for a youngster who acts violently can alert us to the danger signs and triggers to his violence. Anything that touches his vulnerability may be experienced by him as an attack on his rigid internal barrier and cause him to react violently. Such vulnerability includes anything that could arouse a sense of helplessness, humiliation or fear of annihilation in relation to core complex terrors, including feeling controlled, cornered, trapped, smothered, intruded upon, criticised, bullied, rejected, being treated dismissively or ignored, neglected, abandoned, feeling teased, mocked, shown up and exposed to shame, feeling small and silly.

How can we work with youngsters who are violent?

If we can understand how healthy aggression can go wrong – the developmental factors that lead to a young person becoming prone to violence – and if we can be alert to the danger situations and triggers, we are then in a better position to think how to work with violent youngsters. The psychotherapist has the difficult task of combining two contradictory perspectives. She needs to offer the patient safety but she also needs to understand that her efforts to reach him will inevitably represent a danger situation for him because of his core complex terror of intimacy. She has to think about and process what is happening in the room in the way the child cannot, recognising his bodily enactments as concrete expressions of his emotional states. By empathising with and naming his feelings tactfully and without being intrusive, she acts like a protective shield. He may gradually be able to begin to internalise this protective function in a way that was not possible in his early development. As violent-prone people are extremely sensitive to core complex terrors and to feeling humiliated, we have to be more than usually careful about what and how much to say and how we say it. Saying too much will be experienced as intrusive, being silent will feel dismissive and abandoning, and anything we say may be experienced as threatening or punitive.

The following clinical examples highlight some of the difficulties of working with violent children and adolescents and give a feeling of what the experience is like for both the therapist and the patient.

Charles

At the age of six Charles was referred for five times weekly analysis because of violent outbursts, an inability to relate to peers, and alarming swings between infantile behaviour and pseudo-mature language. In his first session he began by behaving like a toddler. He crawled on the floor, threw the toys over his shoulder aimlessly and named the toys in a babyish voice: 'car', 'horse'. When I said that I knew he was very unhappy sometimes and that I was there to help him understand his worries so that he could be happier, Charles said in quite a different voice, 'Well, shall I tell you about my worries then? I don't like school, I have a devil inside me, and I get cross with my mummy.'

Such direct communications were extremely rare, and were followed by infantile and aggressive behaviour. He suffered from extreme fears of abandonment and perceived himself as a 'devil' hated by his parents. This was repeated in the relationship with me – he seemed determined to prove that I hated him and wanted to get rid of him, like his mother who had unconscious death wishes towards him. I remember seeing him leave the clinic one day with his mother, little sister and the nanny. The nanny and little sister walked out together first, followed by the mother and then Charles separately. Charles climbed onto the high wall beside the steps outside the clinic. There was a long drop from this wall onto the stone floor of the basement underneath. The mother turned round and saw Charles climb onto the high wall, then turned her back on him and walked on. She did not do what most mothers would do – ask him to be careful, go back to him and hold his hand to prevent him from falling or help him to climb off the wall. I was terrified that Charles would fall and hurt himself, but she seemed completely unconcerned about his safety.

Charles' physical attacks on me were very violent. At times he behaved like a wild animal: he would spit and bite, hit and kick, throw toys at me, and lunge at me by using every bit of his body as a weapon. At first these attacks seemed unprovoked and unpredictable, but I began to understand that *I* was the source of danger for him, representing in the transference the dangerous mother of his internal world. I felt shaken, helpless, and overwhelmed. I had to set limits for my own safety and to safeguard my capacity to continue working with him; I was also convinced that allowing him to hurt me would confirm his view of himself as unstoppably evil. Setting limits was more a case of trying to dodge missiles and trying to think quickly about what he might do next. When I could not escape the physical assaults I had to restrain him physically – I have only needed to do this with two children in twenty-five years of working as a child psychotherapist. What was so hard about this was that I was in an aroused state which involved a wish to be sadistic towards him. I had to watch this very carefully. When I had to hold him for my own safety, I tried to talk calmly to him, saying that I knew this was awful for him and that he felt controlled and trapped, but that I needed to keep us both safe. I said that I knew he would be scared of me and might not want to come to the next session, and that he would be frightened that I would stop liking him.

It was wholly inadequate to understand these physical attacks as expressions of rage. Rather, they were driven by his panic – enactments of his internal chaos and of feeling hated by and terrified of his mother. Being unable to process his emotional experiences in symbolic form through play or words, he could only act. There was, however, a very primitive attempt to hold himself together by perceiving himself as a devil – in identification with his perception of his mother. Because he also saw me as the dangerous and murderous mother in his internal world, he became phobic of me and would either resist coming to the room or run out of the building where I had to try to keep him safe from running in front of cars in the street. Or if he came to the room he would try to defecate there. When I took him to the toilet he would smear his faeces, then collapse in distress and ask me to clean him up. This demonstrates his terrible problem: he desperately needed the protective intervention of the very person who terrified him.

At first I tried to help him organise his chaos by talking about his fears and phantasies. With most children this would bring relief, containment and a sense of being understood, but with Charles it had the opposite effect – it increased his anxiety and made his emotional experiences even more concrete. As his anxiety increased, so did his bodily enactments. I had to show that I could survive his attacks and not reject him, and I frequently talked about my need to keep us both safe until he could manage this for himself. I had to find a therapy 'language' to communicate with Charles in a way that made words meaningful yet safe. I began to speak of his enactments as 'body talk' and to talk about his 'spilly feelings', but only at times when he was more calm and not when he was actually 'spilling' out his chaos. As his experiences were sufficiently contained, understood and described in a way that he could hear, there was a shift towards symbolic communication. For the first time he began to play and his violence diminished.

He became obsessed with building gold mines, nuclear power stations and dams, which expressed his concerns about murderously anal explosions and dangerous substances leaking out and destroying everything. One day he built a dam and spoke with increasing anxiety about the dam breaking and destroying the nearby town. I realised that a dangerous 'spilly' situation was approaching, but I did not interpret this directly because I knew that Charles would experience my words concretely as if I was telling him that he definitely *was* going to be 'spilly'. Instead, I addressed the approach of spilling out his chaos in displacement through the play. I said that I thought he was frightened of the town getting destroyed because the water could not be contained, and that he wanted to keep it safe. I suggested that we could make special openings in the wall of the dam to let out small amounts of water at manageable intervals so that there would not be a huge sudden flood. Charles was immediately relieved and kissed me! I then said that I understood how frightened he was that his feelings would spill out, like the water in the dam, and that I was going to try to help him find ways of managing his 'spilly' feelings so that they would not flood him.

Initially everything spilled out of Charles – the contents of his body (urine, faeces, spit), and his feelings and aggression. He did not have any sense of safety and containment, which I had to try to provide. However, the aim was not just to keep him safe but to enable him to internalise a protective function. It was essential to help him to develop some symbolic capacity to play and use words meaningfully. These capacities gradually helped him to begin to deal with small amounts of feeling in a similar way to the openings in the dam that let out small amounts of water to prevent flooding.

Much later, when his good progress caused his parents to want to end his analysis suddenly, Charles reverted to concrete enactments. He had now become attached to me and therefore frightened of losing me, and he responded to his fear in a concrete self-destructive way by trying to climb on the banisters outside the therapy room (at the top of the building). This self-endangering behaviour increased towards the end of each session. Words again proved useless, and to prevent him from falling downstairs, I had to restrain him physically. But as this became an excited sado-masochistic battle for him, I decided instead to stand in front of the therapy room door to prevent him from dashing towards the stairs. Charles then erupted into a huge tantrum, throwing himself around the room and screaming, but he did not attack me. I tried to stay calm, telling him it was very important that he did not get hurt. I said I knew that he got 'wobbly' (chaotic) at the end of the session because he was worried that I wanted to say goodbye, and perhaps he needed to know that I wanted to see him tomorrow. (This was a transference reference to his fear that his mother hated him and wanted him to die.)

Finally the orgy of extreme emotions subsided and Charles fell to the floor in a heap, clinging to my ankles and crying over and over again in a loving voice, 'My Marianne, my Marianne'. He was then able to leave the session calmly, and did not attempt to throw himself downstairs again.

Although Charles was physically aggressive towards me, it was possible to tolerate his aggression sufficiently to be attuned to his internal state of panic and chaos, underlying which was terror of anni- hilation. So, what looks like a child attacking his therapist is understood as a child who is terrified that the therapist wants to kill him. I had to act to keep us both safe, and I had to contain my own sadism and try to empathise with his terror of me as murderously dangerous.

This case illustrates how feelings of humiliation and helplessness trigger violence. In the absence of symbolisation, humiliation and helplessness are not emotional experiences but body-feelings of internal contents spilling out. It also illustrates the desperate attempt to defend against the ultimate danger – annihilation – with self-preservative violence. Work with a child as young as Charles provides an opportunity to understand the absolute life and death nature of the anxieties which trigger violence. It is often much harder to understand what is going on when we work with a violent adolescent as the underlying helplessness is less clear. The next clinical example demonstrates this.

Tom

Seventeen-year-old Tom had no compunctions about his violence – he gloried in it and his whole sense of identity was shaped by violence. He was referred for once weekly psychotherapy after attempting to rape a young woman who looked like the girl who had dumped him for another boy. He had planned to lie in wait for a suitable girl and rape her at knife-point. He got as far as holding the knife to her throat, but was unable to carry out the rape and demanded money from her instead. Unsatisfied, he returned to the same place the next day determined to carry out his plan fully this time, but the police had been alerted to the previous incident and lay in wait to arrest him.

As a child, Tom was treated both dismissively and violently by both parents and would run to his grandparents' house to escape being beaten. In therapy he denied any hatred towards his parents, and shrugged his shoulders as if his history had no effect on him. Later, it became clear that he had a strong sense of grievance that his younger brother had received the attention and care Tom had been denied. Tom was bullied at primary school, but now loved getting into fights. He planned to join the violent wing of a neo-Nazi organisation and had fiercely racist opinions. He terrorised Asian boys whom he described as 'keeping themselves to themselves, taking our jobs, always getting their way, and having their own shops'. He felt morally justified in attacking them because he thought they were looked after and given everything they wanted. His earliest experiences of feeling unacknowledged and unprotected by his parents, especially mother, were carried as an unprocessed trauma that could only be enacted.

He had no wish to give up his violence towards boys, but was anxious about his fantasies of violently raping a woman, fearing that he would enact them again and get punished. He hoped that therapy would somehow get rid of the rape fantasies. It gradually became clear that his sexual fantasies were linked to feelings of murderous rage towards his mother whom he experienced as humiliating and utterly rejecting. The rape fantasies stopped when he had his first sexual relationship soon after therapy started. Significantly, this relationship was with an older woman who was in a position of authority over him – in fact, one of his school teachers.

The experience of being in the room with Tom was very different from being with Charles. With Charles everything was chaotic, but with Tom I felt a constant, heavy emptiness that was very hard to bear. The sessions felt lifeless and as though they would never end, but something boiled dangerously underneath the surface. It felt like being at the edge of a volcano, where the bleak grey ash might make one forget the raging power that could erupt at any moment.

Tom's fear of trusting me made it very hard for him to engage in the therapeutic process. He was polite but mostly silent. Unlike most adolescents who are silent in therapy and tend to avoid eye contact, Tom stared at me in a challenging and expectant way that was extremely uncomfortable. I felt both shut out by him in the silence, but also intruded on because of his penetrating gaze. Tom found the silences very awkward too and wanted me to ask him questions; but when I did, he experienced me as forcefully intrusive. This was a very powerful dynamic. As I thought about it, I began to understand how he was trying to defend himself against very terrifying core complex anxieties of abandonment and engulfment. He identified with the aggressor (his neglectful, abandoning but also intrusive mother, and his violent and uncaring father), and in the sessions he made me feel both abandoned and engulfed. One can also see the link here with his fantasy of invading a woman forcefully by raping her. I told Tom that I had a dilemma to think about with him – that my words as well as my silence made him feel awful, and he seemed to feel very unsafe and uncomfortable in the room with me.

As I tried to explore his discomfort with me, it emerged that he found all verbal communication difficult. He felt he had nothing interesting to say and that nobody noticed him. I said that this must make him feel terribly lonely and it might be very hard for him to feel he was a 'somebody' worthy of notice. Perhaps it was as if he felt invisible? He agreed and said that the only thing that would always make people pay attention to him was when he talked about his racist political opinions. It did not matter whether the person agreed or disagreed, all that mattered was to get an intense reaction. I linked this urgent need to get through to people with his helpless isolation of never having felt noticed in a good way by his parents, especially his mother. I wondered if the only way he felt he could make an impact on someone was by force – by his forceful political views or physical violence. This seemed to reach him, and he responded thoughtfully by saying for the first time that he felt helpless and vulnerable sometimes.

Tom had organised himself around a complete denial of any regressive wishes for nurturing, although he did let me see very brief glimpses of his extreme neediness. He presented himself as an immaculately besuited adult with none of the typically adolescent anxieties about growing up. The capacity to acknowledge regressive wishes implies healthy narcissism and an internalised image of a protective other who can be relied on. Without these, Tom could only deal with his regressive wishes by denying them and externalising them onto the ethnic minorities whom he then murderously attacked for being like greedy children who got everything they wanted.

Tom had built a pseudo-identity for himself as the 'tough guy' to protect him from feeling vulnerable. This fortified his rigid internal barrier as a substitute for the missing protective function, dramatically illustrated when he spoke of having no fear of physical danger.

With violent and negating parents and no age-appropriate allowance for omnipotence in early childhood, the smallest humiliation was experienced by Tom as the most terrible trauma. Underneath the presentation of himself as an all-powerful young man, there was a frightened and humiliated child whose only way of protecting himself from an over-whelming sensitivity to feeling a rejected nobody was to act violently. Coldly calculated violence shaped Tom's identity so that he could try to avoid dealing with his terrifying core complex anxieties and therefore would not experience the ultimate threats to his psychic survival.

David

The final example illustrates the importance of thinking about technique when working with violent adolescents. David was a traumatised and narcissistically vulnerable adolescent who defensively needed to protect himself from acknowledging that he was in need of help. His dread of regression and intimacy was especially intense, and his story illustrates Winnicott's thesis that 'at the root of the antisocial tendency there is always deprivation' (Winnicott 1961).

David, aged fourteen, was referred because of violent and sexualised behaviour. He aggressively grabbed at girls' bodies and said he wanted to be a rapist when he grew up. He bullied boys at school and was rude, physically aggressive and out of control. His background of extreme neglect and violence included not having enough to eat and a home like a slum with rats and rubbish everywhere and no usable toilet or bath. David sometimes witnessed his father hitting his mother when she was having an epileptic fit, and the dad was also violent to his four sons, especially to David. He watched pornographic videos with David and it is likely that David also witnessed parental sex. All the children were taken into care. The parents then separated and sought no contact with the children. David's three younger brothers were all adopted but David refused, still hoping to return to his mother one day even though she had shown absolutely no interest in him. After several failed placements because of very disturbed behaviour, David eventually settled with a foster family whose children were in their early twenties.

In our first meeting David made it clear that he didn't want therapy and that the long journey to the clinic was boring and too tiring. He said he'd been told off for what he'd done and it was all in the past. I said many people felt like he did about therapy because they weren't sure what it was about and thought it was a sort of punishment; but therapy was really to help people understand themselves, begin to sort things out and hopefully like themselves better so that their life in the future could be happier.

David remained hunched up in his chair looking very bored, so I suggested quite light-heartedly that maybe he thought I was talking a load of rubbish. He looked a bit surprised and said hesitantly, as if he wanted to be polite but also honest, that perhaps I was right!

He said he was quite happy now that he'd got a job on a farm after school and at weekends. As he was still trying to convey that he needed no help, I had to find a way to help him with his defences against shame and the fear of facing his difficulties. I showed great interest in his job and asked him to tell me about it. As if relieved that he could talk about things that he knew about and could do well, he started to speak very enthusiastically about the cows on the farm and how he milked and cared for them. I said that I could see that he was very attached to the animals and had a lot of skill in the way he treated them. He began to relax and seem less wary of me.

The way he then described how you should approach a strange, frightened animal indicated movingly how I should relate to him. He said, 'You should never make a big fuss or a lot of noise around an animal if it doesn't know you, but you should approach it very slowly and gently and let it get to know you gradually until it feels safe. It might be scared at first but then it will become very attached to you.' I asked a lot about the animals and how he managed them, and he grinned with pleasure when I admired his enthusiasm and proficiency. He was surprised when the session had to end.

In the ensuing once weekly sessions, David talked more about the farm animals and about his skill in driving and mending the tractors. This conveyed his capacity for tenderness and reparation as well as pride in his phallic skills. Therapy helped him to begin to value himself more as someone who wasn't only just 'trouble', and to risk being curious about himself and his difficulties. He began to take more responsibility for his feelings and actions and the bullying and sexual-ised behaviour stopped. By the end of therapy, when he started at agricultural college, he seemed to have begun to face the major devel-opmental tasks of adolescence. He had a more solid view of himself, a positive attitude towards his future, and a better capacity to stand up for himself without being exploited or resorting to physical aggression. He thought more about himself and his impact on others, he had found a girlfriend, and he had finally been able to give up his vain hope that his mother would come lovingly to claim him.

Conclusion

Work with David shows the importance of not being exclusively pre-occupied with aggression when working with violent youngsters and the need to acknowledge the health and strengths of patients in order to help them develop a sense of themselves as a 'somebody' who is worthwhile and not only an unwanted dangerous nuisance to be criticised and condemned. Otherwise, the patient will continue to relate to the therapist as his externalised persecutory superego to be defied or avoided, and he won't be able to develop benign superego aspects or moderated self- and objects-representations that could facilitate the binding of aggression by libido.

The clinical examples show the importance of establishing a safe setting in the mind of the patient as well as the therapist, so that the therapeutic work can proceed. This is no easy task. From the youngster's point of view, the therapist is someone to be feared because she represents for him the original unprotective parent as well as an externalisation of his own primitive superego. The therapist needs to be extremely careful not to make the situation worse for the patient by seeming in any way dismissive, intrusive, humiliating or punitive, and she also has to deal with the impact on her of the youngster's very primitive anxieties that will inevitably trigger her own. The dangers are that she may either defend against her own anxieties by denying that she is with a patient who might attack her, or she may be so afraid of being attacked that she cannot be receptive to the patient's needs. It is vital to remember that the patient will not be able to tolerate being at the receiving end of the very defences he relies upon: for example, if the therapist fails to be receptive to the patient, she will be experienced as building an impenetrable barrier against him. This is a major provocation to the patient and could unleash his violence or cause him to walk out of therapy.

Violence needs to be understood as an attempted solution to overwhelming trauma that the individual has not been able to process, and this trauma has been defined as helplessness in the absence of a protective other. This does not imply condoning violence and only treating the violent patient as a victim. On the contrary, the violent individual is both a perpetrator (because of his violent behaviour and in his defensively powerful ideal self-image), and also a victim (having been failed at a point of maximum helplessness, lacking an internalised protective membrane and in relation to his primitive punitive superego). He enacts all this, causing harm to others and inviting punishment unconsciously from the law. The psychotherapist's task is to resist collusion either with the values of his ideal self (violence) or the demands of his harsh superego (sadistic punishment); rather, it is to try to understand the patient's predicament, something he cannot do himself. To this end, it can be helpful to think about the concept of the rigid internal barrier as a desperate attempt to fortify the self against overwhelming dangers. This understanding helps in trying to make emotional contact with patients who find it extremely difficult to communicate effectively with others or even with themselves without resorting to violence.

Acknowledgements

I am grateful to Sira Dermen, my co-author in the first edition of the handbook, for the thinking we did together; and I wish to pay tribute to the memory of Mervin Glasser for his leadership of the Portman Clinic Violence Workshop and inspiring teaching.

References

Colarusso, C. A. (1992) *Child and Adult Development: A Psychoanalytic Introduction for Clinicians*, New York and London: Plenum Press.

Edgcumbe, R. (1976) 'The development of aggressiveness in children', *Nursing Times* April (RCN Supplement): vii–xv,

Fraiberg, S. (1982) 'Pathological defences in infancy', *Psychoanalytic Quarterly* 51: 612–41.

Freud, A. (1949) 'Aggression in relation to emotional development: normal and pathological', *Psychoanalytic Study of the Child*, Vol. 3/4, New York: International Universities Press.

—— (1972) 'Comments on aggression', in *Psychoanalytic Psychology of Normal Development*, London: Hogarth Press, 1982.

Freud, S. (1920) 'Beyond the pleasure principle' *SE* 18: 27–31.

Furman, E. (1992) *Toddlers and their Mothers*, Madison, CT: International Universities Press.

Glasser, M. (1979) 'Some aspects of the role of aggression in the perversions', in I. Rosen (ed.) *Sexual Deviation*, 2nd edn, Oxford: Oxford University Press, pp. 278–305.

—— (1996) 'Aggression and sadism in the perversions', in I. Rosen (ed.) *Sexual Deviation*, 3rd edn, Oxford: Oxford University Press.

—— (1998) 'On violence: a preliminary communication', *International Journal of Psychoanalysis* 79(5): 887–902.

Heimann, P. and Valenstein, A. (1972) 'The psychoanalytical concept of aggression: an integrated summary', *International Journal of Psycho-Analysis* 53: 31–5.

Hyatt Williams, A. (1997) 'Violence in adolescence', in V. Varma (ed.) *Violence in Children and Adolescents*, London: Jessica Kingsley.

Khan, M. (1963) 'The concept of cumulative trauma', *Psychoanalytic Study of the Child*, Vol. 18, New York: International Universities Press.

Parsons, M. (2006) 'From biting teeth to biting wit: the normative development of aggression', in C. Harding (ed.) *Aggression and Destructiveness: Psychoanalytic Perspectives*, London: Routledge. (Also in D. Morgan and S. Ruszczynski (eds) *Lectures on Violence, Perversion and Delinquency: The Portman Papers*, London: Karnac, 2007.)

Stern, D. N. (1985) *The Interpersonal World of the Human Infant*, New York: Basic Books.

Tyson, P. and Tyson, R. L. (1990) *Pychoanalytic Theories of Development*, New Haven, CT: Yale University Press.

Winnicott, D. W. (1950–5) 'Aggression in relation to emotional development', in D. W. Winnicott *Collected Papers: Through Paediatrics to Psychoanalysis*, London: Tavistock, 1958.

—— (1961) 'Adolescence: struggling through the doldrums', in *The Family and Individual Development*, London: Tavistock, 1965.

—— (1963) 'From dependence towards independence in the development of the individual', in D. W. Winnicott *The Maturational Processes and the Facilitating Environment*, London: Hogarth Press, 1982.

Further reading

Campbell, D. (1996) 'From practice to psychodynamic theories of delinquency in adolescence', in C. Cordess and M. Cox (eds) *Forensic Psychotherapy: Crime, Psychodynamics and the Offender Patient. Vol. l. Mainly Theory*, London: Jessica Kingsley.

Chiland, C. and Young, G. (1994) *Children and Violence*, New Jersey: Jason Aronson.

Varma, V. (1997) *Violence in Children and Adolescents*, London: Jessica Kingsley.

Winnicott, D. W. (1947) 'Hate in the countertransference', in D. W. Winnicott *Through Paediatrics to Psycho-Analysis*, London: Hogarth Press, 1978.

—— (1962) 'Integration in child development', in D. W. Winnicott *The Maturational Processes and the Facilitating Environment*, London: Hogarth Press, 1982.

—— (1969) 'The use of an object and relating through identifications', in D. W. Winnicott *Playing and Reality*, Harmondsworth: Penguin Books.

25 Psychotherapeutic work with children and adolescents seeking refuge from political violence

Sheila Melzak

Refugee and asylum-seeking children

This chapter explores the external and internal situations of asylum-seeking children and adolescents. Abusive external events in the life of a refugee child, both during times of community conflict, and in exile in Europe, are clearly internalised and impact on subsequent development. A holistic focus is required, on rehabilitation, social integration, care, asylum, education, practical support, health and therapeutic needs. Refugee children usually come from 'good enough' (Winnicott 1960) functional families and clearly experience abuses and their consequences in later phases. Abuses are usually perpetrated by authority figures from outside their families, and often only later result in the symptoms of the complex post-traumatic state, separation and disrupted attachments. Thus treatment should focus as much on developing resilience as on understanding vulnerabilities. Young people often need time and help in sharing their stories, which initially emerge as a series of fragments that may be unspeakable and shared non-verbally. Gradually, they become able to articulate these experiences. This process, where a young person shares aspects of his story with the psychotherapist who bears witness to a variety of experiences, is itself therapeutic, providing antidotes to unbearable emotional pain. The psychotherapist must build a relationship of trust (a therapeutic alliance) with each young person and hold their experiences for an extended period, gradually returning aspects of experience to the young person in bearable chunks. Slowly the young person becomes able to take responsibility and ownership of their experiences.

The legal context and practice

Although Britain and other European countries have signed the *UN Convention on the Rights of the Child* (1991) and the *UN Declaration on the Rights of Refugees* (1951), it would seem that, for governments, using immigration law to maintain national boundaries takes priority over human rights. In 2007, 26 million people were forcibly displaced in their home countries and 11.4 million sought asylum (most in the developing world) (UNHCR 2008).

Such forced migration results in divided families and communities, and separated and unaccompanied children and adolescents, all of whom must struggle with the emotional impact of their experiences of death, violence, persecution, confusion, secrecy, separation, loss, change and exile. Such emotional struggles, which might ideally be worked through in an atmosphere of genuine safety and asylum, are, in fact – given our current asylum processes – experienced in a context of further uncertainty and insecurity. This makes the necessary internal, emotional work difficult and often impossible, with serious implications for the well-being of asylum-seeking children and adolescents.

An important aspect of our work concerns writing reports for the Asylum Adjudicators who consider young refugees' asylum claims. This is part of the process of bearing witness and acknowledging with the child the impact of violence and loss he has experienced, and the detail of these experiences both for the child and for their community. Working with the child to prepare such reports sometimes begins the process of 'working through' (Freud 1914) past experiences by slowly verbalising feelings. Thus even extreme and terrifying feelings and memories become available for review and transformation.

Human rights context

The people whose stories feature in this chapter have all experienced human rights abuses as defined by international law. The existence of Human Rights Instruments raises many questions about rights, justice and injustice with populations who have experienced abuse and scapegoating. I assume that at the heart of every individual survivor of community violence there is a conflict which could be expressed as 'Am I entitled to life?' or 'Am I expendable?'

One frame of reference is insufficient to think appropriately about therapeutic interventions. A multi-dimensional approach is necessary, embracing psychoanalytic, systemic, structural, historical, phenomenological, social, political and philosophical perspectives, and reflection about inequalities of rights and power. We must enter the academic and community debates about the universality of human rights in relation to children's development. We must also consider issues of truth, responsibility, impunity, compensation, reconciliation, justice and non-violent conflict resolution.

I work as a community child and adolescent psychotherapist in a human rights context, as an independent clinician and consultant to a London-based charity that works with survivors of cruelty and organised violence. This includes assessment and treatment of children, adolescents, young adults, parents and families, and research. I have worked with this population for almost twenty years and currently work individually and in groups with forty-six young people who mostly arrived in Britain as unaccompanied minors. The work also involves training, supervision and consultation with teachers, social and health workers, lawyers and advisers from various statutory and voluntary organisations, and workers from the refugee communities. This is essentially *applied* child psychoanalytic/ developmental work, in which the theory and principles involved in understanding child development from a psychoanalytic perspective and in working psychotherapeutically with children are applied to the needs of children in different contexts within the community.

Implications of work in a human rights context

If we assume that the child's developing mind is modulated by both the internal and the external world, it is important to understand how children during different phases of development make sense of their experiences, and the specific impact on the developing mind of extreme external events. This is no easy process. Faced with the most destructive human acts and their consequences, it is natural to turn away, to close our eyes and to cover our ears, as Louis Blom-Cooper (1985) described in his introduction to the Beckford report. This tendency not only makes working together difficult but also inhibits open and reflective thinking. Additionally, the presence of refugees and asylum seekers in a community seems to highlight pre-existing difficulties between agencies in that community. A group of professionals recently told me that allocation of resources to meet the needs of refugees, deprived working class British people of mental health services. Children from different cultures are an easily identifiable group who can be scapegoated as the cause of social problems that in fact they only highlight.

The psychological consequences of impunity

Community leaders, healers and clinicians with long experience in work with survivors of human rights violations highlight the importance of acknowledging the psychological consequences of impunity, i.e. that such crimes are often not acknowledged by the perpetrators, who additionally escape punishment (Rojas 1996). This lack of acknowledgement can reinforce victims' tendency to deny and avoid acknowledging their own experiences, making them feel empty, ashamed, guilty, confused, invisible, inaudible and expendable. Part of the psychotherapist's work therefore involves 'bearing witness' (Blackwell 1997) to these abuses and to their consequences by acknowledging and 'holding' (Winnicott 1960) the extreme, complicated and painful emotions. Clearly, painful memories and feelings are hard to acknowledge. Survivors try to wall off memories, to protect others who, in turn, try to protect the survivor. This can result in profound family secrets that transmit the consequences of human rights abuses to the next generation.

Themes from the external world

The external world of children and adolescents seeking asylum in Britain (with or without parents) can be sketched via a few concepts, each of which characterises a complex network of events that can potentially cause significant stress in the child's development.

Repression and war

Asylum-seeking children come to Europe to seek safety from countries at war, where children may become victims of soldiers' actions, or made to be perpetrators by forced recruitment to government and rebel armies, or from repressive societies where any dissident voice or assumed dissident voice is dealt with by violence, including imprisonment and torture. Various techniques are specifically designed to terrify and divide the population so that constructive collective opposition is impossible. The target of this kind of psychological warfare is the civilian population – usually women and children (Summerfield 1993; Van-Beuren 1994). Social values are attacked, with frequent violence and murder on the streets alongside societal disintegration. Many are murdered, or arrested and imprisoned without trial. Others are forced into exile, separated from family, community and culture. Every situation is different, and this work requires us to inform ourselves about these specifics.

We also must ask how the young person left his country: with a benign or malevolent agent? Were they trafficked? Repression is not confined to the Third World but also occurs in Europe, where refugees seek safety but where they are marginalised, have few rights and usually cannot re-establish their former social positions. They often experience both institutional and individual prejudice, and xenophobia.

Violence

Refugee and asylum-seeking children will all have experienced violence, whether physical violence personally, violent war situations, or being forced to watch their parents being arrested, tortured or beaten. Others will have heard about violence to their community. Children and adolescents may have had experiences as victims, perpetrators, collaborators, bystanders and rescuers during situations of community violence All will have experienced psychological violence due to the loss of familiar adults, siblings and friends, and most will have been excluded from the decision-making process by which they have come to seek asylum in Europe. This is almost invariably an adult decision, whether children and adolescents arrive with parents or adult substitute carers, or unaccompanied. A crucial mediating factor in the lives of refugee children is whether or not they have access to adults who themselves are able to develop an explanation that integrates many layers of meaning and whether they have the psychological space and encouragement to develop their own narrative in relation to their internal representations of violence.

Scapegoating

Many people seek asylum after being blamed for problems in their communities. A significant proportion of young refugees experience further scapegoating and prejudice in exile, as well as racism, xenophobia and bullying in school. A favourite form of abuse in London schools is 'mothercussing' (where adolescents attempt to humiliate their peers by calling their mothers prostitutes). This has particular effects on refugee children raised in communities with very traditional values, whose mothers have been raped or murdered. Physical fights often ensue. The victims are often blamed, especially when they don't have the language (technical or emotional) to describe their own experiences.

In our psychotherapeutic group for adolescent boys, the majority had lost at least one parent through organised violence. They regularly raised the issue of racist and xenophobic abuse at school and how best to manage their anger whilst keeping to the school rules. Loyalty, protectiveness and respect towards parents, both dead and alive, are fundamental to the identity of children raised in traditional cultures.

In addition to the importance of individual and group therapy, there is a need for work with schools on policy, practice and curriculum issues (Rutter 1996). This includes oral history, the development of awareness of others and of feelings, including extreme and difficult emotions connected with violence and loss, and work on difference, prejudice, racism and conflict (Kriedler 1984; Bolloton and Spafford 1996).

External and internal aspects of separation and loss

In the National Health Service, preoccupations with short-term treatments for symptoms of trauma overshadow the traumatic impact of the loss of key attachment figures on developing young people. In psychotherapeutic work with young refugees, loss and mourning are often neglected in the context of trauma-centred treatments. The mourning of loss after violent events leads to huge changes in the mourner's relationship with himself and the world and with community violence. Young people discover aspects of relationships of which they were previously unaware. Working with refugee children I am both moved and impressed by frequent expression of pacifist views, and by how few young survivors want revenge on the perpetrators of extreme violence against their families. For all young refugees leaving home, extended family, climate and a familiar cultural world inevitably brings about separation and loss. The issue is not whether or not separation and loss have occurred, but whether mourning is possible and the implications of this. Relevant questions are:

(a) Has a mourning process begun?
(b) If so, has it become arrested or frozen in some way?
(c) Is it ever possible to mourn massive and traumatic losses completely?
(d) What are the developmental costs of incomplete mourning?
(e) What strategies do children and adolescents use to avoid experiencing emotional pain and other associated extreme emotions?
(f) Is it possible to remain in a state of continuous and unresolved mourning?
(g) How are unresolved mourning issues expressed, e.g. mentally, somatically?

People travelling into exile do not know whether they will ever return home. The longer that asylum seekers remain in exile, the more they and their home society are likely to change, and the wider becomes the difference between their remembered communities and their current situations in exile. In this context, mourning can be protracted and unresolved. Moreover, family members separated by wars and corrupt regimes often lose touch. Because people disappear, without any way of knowing if they are alive or dead, there can be no funeral or mourning rituals.

Many children and adolescents arrive in Britain alone (3000 in 2007). These unaccompanied children and adolescents have been sent to Europe for their protection, much in the same way that European children were evacuated before and brought after the Second World War. Some may know that their parents have disappeared, been imprisoned or died. Others know nothing about why they had to leave and experience exile as a rejection.

Frequently parents are lost and no substitute parental care is arranged, suddenly forcing young people to care for themselves and sometimes for relatives. In these confusing circumstances, some will lose their sense of identity. Some try to cope with these feelings by clinging to their cultural identity in its most traditional form. Others become very westernised and rapidly abandon their traditions. Surprisingly few break down completely, though they cope at considerable cost. They have all, to a greater or lesser extent, lost their childhood and experience the fundamental loss of a sense that adults can keep them safe. Each young person's individual situation merits reflection as each will have had a different experience of violence and persecution, and each will experience different consequences.

Mourning, for an adult, is a both difficult and unexpected process of grief, discovery and transformation. For children without a firm sense of self, not only is mourning difficult at the time of the loss, but these losses are revisited and create further difficulties, during each subsequent phase of development.

Through the mourning process, an adolescent refugee comes to build an integrated adult identity out of the childhood/young adolescent world view of the absent adults and peers known during previous developmental years. For those unaccompanied by parents or parental substitutes, the task of identification is confusing, e.g. do you identify with your memories of parents and elders from whom you have been separated for many years? Young refugees have the developmental task of taking responsibility for their actions and thoughts and finding ways to bear emotional pain at the reality of losses either alone or with the help of relative strangers. Processing work continues directly and indirectly (via stories, art, drama and music, Schwartz and Melzak 2005) in individual sessions and in groups. Individual work explores memories, feelings and conflicts. Adolescent refugees often ask why the world is like this and what they might they do about it as adults.

Most young people who arrive in Britain as unaccompanied minors have no parental care. This leads to particular vulnerabilities. Also, some asylum-seeking children who are physically accompanied by parents or substitute parents may be 'psychologically unaccompanied', having lost parental care because parents who functioned well at home may have changed profoundly due to torture, loss and the stresses of exile. They are also vulnerable, and often unable to comprehend the changes that led to violence and eventual exile, so they cannot explain them to their children. Many are angry not only with their home country, but also with the country of exile for their loss of position and status and their inability to find adequate housing and work. The children must deal with anxiety about changes in their parents and with their feelings of grief, fear and rage that a reliable containing parent is no longer present. Parents may be unaware of or bewildered by changes in their children.

Ongoing uncertainties make mourning complicated for refugees. Losses may be denied for many years, with both parents and children clinging to a fragile hope that they are temporary. The asylum-determination process is very long, and families often must wait many years for a decision. Even if family members are known to be alive, temporary status prevents family reunification. This period of uncertainty is too long for a child's mind to understand and hold. Family splits can arise when the children live in the present by adapting to the country of exile's values, but the adults are locked in the past and adhere to strict interpretations of their original culture's belief system as a form of coping with enormous losses.

In some families the impact of pervasive losses is defended against in various ways which affect the child's development, and delicate long-term therapeutic work is required to facilitate individual and family mourning, and to enable children and adolescents who have lost their sense of self to regain and reclaim a sense of identity and self-respect by accessing their histories (see case studies in this chapter).

Separate work with children and with parents is often necessary, as family members characteristically try to protect each other from the 'truth' of their own mixed feelings. Children will especially protect parents whose level of emotional investment in their children has changed. Individuals often feel that verbalising their feelings will cause unbearable pain that could potentially incapacitate both themselves and other family members, frequently leading to illness (psychosomatic complaints). Our therapeutic task is to 'hold' these difficult feelings, to acknowledge their roots, and eventually to enable them to be bearable. Our work is not to help people to forget, but to enable them to move beyond the past, so that they can live in the present and think about the future.

Some parents become emotionally unavailable or unconsciously expect their children to assume the role of lost loved ones. This style of parenting, arising from parental difficulties in mourning, may create a lack of sense of self or a false self in children (Winnicott 1960).

A child in a family: the challenge of finding your own voice

Lamine and Kaima, aged seven and three, were the younger two children of an African family, with two parents and one older sister, Ayesha, aged nine. When rebel soldiers came to their village, they lost their father and the rest of the family were abducted. In order to protect her children their mother was forced, against her will and her morality, to live as the partner of one of the rebel leaders. All family members were helpless bystanders to the rebels' grotesque acts of violence including shootings, burning of homes, rapes, amputations of limbs and heads and the common practice, in these contexts, of gambling on the gender of unborn babies and the subsequent murder of the pregnant mother and the cutting open of her womb. They were forced to be reluctant perpetrators of violence. After some time, Ayesha was kidnapped by another rebel group. The family was held by rebels for more than two years and then, by a series of chance connections, was enabled to travel to Britain to seek asylum. A further series of chance events led Ayesha to find her family and decide to live with them again. Ayesha was initially uncommunicative in family sessions. In her weekly psychotherapy she made pictures about her community at war. Her story emerged over years. Lamine was unusually quiet when we first met. We felt that he had spent much time trying to be invisible and inaudible, although he obviously listened in family sessions. Kaima in contrast talked a lot and could not sit still.

All these children depended on their mother and were deeply attached. She tried to give them affection and material care and to hold her family together. They ate, talked and prayed together at home and at the mosque. Sometimes the mother was overwhelmed with helpless grief. At other times she thought that the only solution to her difficulties was escape and her suicide. She shared her feelings with her children.

We began a process of both individual and family therapeutic work: each family member used individual sessions, working verbally and non-verbally through art, to explore terrifying and difficult fragments of experience. Family sessions have continued over years. Initially while talking about their worries about their mother, her tears, and her talking about her wish to die as her life was too difficult, the boys made repeated pictures of rebel soldiers holding guns. All seemed relieved to share their worries with adults who wanted and were able to listen. During one early session when child psychotherapist and family therapist asked about the soldiers with the guns in the pictures, and if the soldiers had showed them how to use the guns, Kaima began to scream and cry in terror and ran to his mother. His screams lasted several minutes.

At that time his mother hugged him, and his siblings were silent. In the context of this meeting no one in the room could find words for what Kaima was thinking about, what he had done and what exactly he had seen. Everyone in the family was enthusiastic about coming regularly to explore these issues but it became clear that talking was very hard.

Over the next three years we talked with different individuals and groups within the family as well as the whole family together. It was very difficult to enable them to speak to each other about shared memories and symptoms. Though the details of these symptoms were different all mourned the loss of their community, of their father (husband); all suffered intrusive thoughts and all had nightmares related to the loss of childhood innocence. The family could not talk with each other about these overwhelming events both because they did not want to upset each other but also because each conversation returned them mentally to the war and to their sense of helplessness and fear of annihilation. At another level they felt anxious, ashamed and guilty about what they had done, observed and suffered, and about their own survival.

After three years of monthly sessions, Lamine and Kaima started to talk in front of the family about their thoughts, feelings and memories. It emerged that they were both angry and frightened at the sense of unsafety they felt both in the community and at home as asylum seekers. This sense of unsafety echoed their feelings during the war. Both had been stopped in the street outside their London school by gangs with knives. Kaima could not mentally bear anxiety or protect himself.

A key theme was that of dreams and nightmares. All family members felt alone with their repeated dreams which contained fragments of their most extreme experiences of helplessness, near death experiences and shock at the grotesque violence they had observed. We encouraged the now adolescent members of this family to talk to each other whenever they had bad dreams and to listen to each other. For Lamine this brought huge relief. He could talk with us and with his sister. He could remember consciously what had happened. In contrast Kaima had no memories of the events that had taken place. He experienced his dreams as reality and that he was regularly thrown back into the civil war and a situation where he was not safe, would imminently lose his mother and soon be killed. His siblings and his mother needed to explain to him events that had occurred in his history that he was unable to remember.

Interpretive disentangling only became possible after a long period of building a therapeutic alliance, reflecting back comments, naming feelings and reconnecting them to the experiences from which they originated. Kaima and his sister had internalised the authoritarian force of the rebels that they should be obedient and the fear that if they refused they would be killed. They found saying 'no' difficult and when they did say 'no' they felt guilty, ashamed and anxious about imminent disaster.

For Kaima and Ayesha the magical thinking of their earliest years persisted. Both believed they were bad and that everything that went wrong for them, including their bad dreams, was a punishment for their past actions and associations. In school Kaima became involved in fights and was often suspended for a day or two. He was flooded with anxiety and could not reflect. Ayesha made several suicide attempts.

We discussed dreams at length. They were unsure whether dreams foretold the future, or if they were a punishment for past misdemeanours. We put forward the view that dreams were a very helpful natural resource to work out problems while we sleep. Sometimes dreams were only about real events and at other times they mixed real events and imagined stories (fantasies). The key was to find out which problems the dream was struggling with. Each family member engaged with great enthusiasm and involvement in the discussions, though sessions were slow to start.

Another theme was the exploration of the roots of the aggression between Lamine and Kaima. Lamine agreed that his anger expressed physically against his brother was much greater than the anger he felt towards his brother. In one family session he told the family that whenever he felt not respected and not listened to he had a flashback memory of a day during the war when he saw the mother of one of his friends begging the rebels for her life. He told us: 'They just did not listen to her and killed her.'

Lamine's expressed thoughtfulness about roots of his enraged feelings and actions enabled each member of the family to talk about their sense that others saw them as having no worth and feeling often not respected and listened to both in the family and in the community.

Parents in general may lose their authority if they cannot support the family at the former living standard. Much child-centred work and support may be needed to re-establish parental authority when parents are used to different models of childcare and discipline from those in Britain. Refugee parents may become afraid to set firm limits on their children (who often have special problems with respecting authority after life in a repressive society) because they fear that children will be taken into care by the authorities if they use traditional physical punishments.

Our work could not have taken place before the mother in this family trusted that we recognised the difficulties of her parenting task and that we were not going to criticise her. We felt that her task was huge and that she needed all the help that we could find, psychotherapeutic and therapeutic and supportive. Kaima and Ayesha are amongst the relatively small proportion of refugee children for whom the psychoanalytic psychotherapeutic techniques of clarification, validation and confrontation are insufficient to facilitate forward development, and for whom interpretation of unconscious conflict is necessary.

Change in a developmental context

People thrive on secure attachments. However well prepared we are, change is always connected to losses which can be painful and need time for adjustment, but unplanned change brings separation, loss and shock for which there has been no opportunity for preparation. When assessing an asylum-seeking child, it helps to think about the number of changes he has undergone since leaving his home country and to discuss his feelings about these changes with him. Whether the child's strategies for coping with change are good-enough depends both on his internal resilience and on the capacity of the people in his external world to promote that resilience, to help him to reflect on the changes and their consequences and to find ways to make connections between old and new situations and ways of coping.

One significant change after several overwhelming experiences is the emergence of developmental difficulties. These are experienced as shameful and often integrated into the self-concept and the identity. Young people with recently acquired developmental gains may find themselves not simply having lost these gains but with additional frightening difficulties. Adolescents may feel embarrassed that they have lost bladder control at night or that they cannot concentrate in school. Children may experience frightening dreams and nightmares. Adolescents who are trying to be independent find it particularly difficult to bear regressive symptoms, such as intrusive thoughts and encopresis; and symptoms of trauma and bereavement can make children and adolescents feel that they are losing control and going mad. They may find themselves unrecognisable and much more angry and sad and frightened and confused than previously.

Generally, refugee children and adolescents show uneven emotional development which is likely to have become stuck in many ways at the developmental age when they experienced community violence. Though they may seem sometimes to assume adult roles and to care for family members, arrests and regressions in development emerge clearly when they begin to engage in new relationships. These developmental changes need exploration during psychotherapy sessions where the psychotherapist will see that relating to the young person at his developmental age initiates the slow unravelling of developmental difficulties.

Formal legal transitions concerning support and educational rights in the UK at sixteen, eighteen and twenty-one highlight these developmental issues. Owing to the developmental unevenness resulting from trauma, it is often inappropriate to place these young people in adult single person accommodation, while also requiring compliance with complex Immigration regulations, when they have severe psychological symptoms which drastically impair their ability to function.

Culture

Cultural identity is complicated. Individuals may feel connections to a variety of cultures and also criticise and disown certain aspects of their own culture. Working with refugee children means forming relationships with children who have some differences and some similarities between their world view and that of the therapist. It is important that the differences are acknowledged and respected. As child psychotherapists, we need to inform ourselves about the culture and belief systems of young refugees. This includes special exploration of culturally familiar ways of dealing with stress and problems, in order to discuss these during psychotherapy sessions.

Resilience and protective factors

In trying to help traumatised children, it is important to know what factors can foster the development of resilience (Emanuel 1996). There seem to be six important features:

1   *Belonging*: Having an involved parent, parental substitute, befriender, advocate.
2   *Thinking*: Being enabled to reflect on one's experiences, past and present, both the 'difficult to understand' and the truly overwhelming experiences.
3   *Active problem-solving*: After prolonged experiences of helplessness and powerlessness, being enabled to make real choices that affect the present and the future and to think about past events where almost no active involvement was possible.
4   *Ability to utilise natural healing processes*: Including play, dreams, community processes and rituals in order to make sense of and work through complicated feelings connected with extreme events.

5 *Ability to utilise community healing processes*: Sharing, remembering and being sustained by family and community stories, legends and values that connect with altruism, empathy, hope and commitment.
6 *Ability to access your own sense of growth and creativity* which may have become constricted and limited after prolonged time spent in a frightening environment.

Child psychotherapists spend too little time discussing survival and resilience. The processes described above can help us to explore and uncover the child's roots and familiar culturally appropriate coping strategies, and develop links to the refugee community and to the community of exile and their capacity for survival as individuals and as parts of a community.

The internal world and the therapeutic process: validation, acknowledgement, clarification and interpretation

Psychotherapeutic work after prolonged experiences of violence and many losses aims to enable young people to bear their complex painful experiences. These experiences will never be totally repressed and will painfully enter the pre-conscious and conscious mind at irregular intervals. Anna Freud's ideas on ego development and on ego support are relevant here (Edgecumbe 2000). One aspect of the psychotherapist's role is to enable children and adolescents to reflect on their internal world and to remind them that their thoughts and their sense of self are separate. It is not a straightforward task for a young person to focus on fragments of traumatic memory as they may experience these thoughts not as memories but as present events. Those young people who wish to explore their experiences need the support and trusted relationship with the psychotherapist to reflect on events that may seem senseless. Some survivors of violence wish, when they arrive in exile, to live in the present and stop themselves from thinking about the past. Sometimes this impairs their functioning and after some years they may be flooded with thoughts about past events.

Psychotherapeutic work aims to focus on thoughts, feelings and relationships and to explore aspects of these memories that are lost, forgotten, or split off. The split off aspects may be unexpected feelings. The young person often shifts from private fragments of thought, connected with shame and guilt and fear, and grief about the human condition as well as their personal losses, thoughts that may be almost unthinkable, to sharing them with the psychotherapist. This enables them to take ownership of the experience and for many to normalise experiences by sharing them. This phase of the therapeutic process is rather like the Buddhist ways of reflection where the task of meditation is to focus on thoughts in a mindful way, from a distance, and to become neither too attached to thoughts, nor let them escape nor be denied without some careful scrutiny. In the language of Anna Freud this aspect of the therapeutic work develops the observing ego. The therapeutic work is also about exploring past and present relationships as well as mourning and grief in relation to the self and others. Many young refugees clearly value a prolonged transitional time during which they can explore these difficult issues with and in relation to their psychotherapist. These young people choose to explore difficult experiences related to extreme emotional pain, shame and guilt and helplessness and the wish to die. They feel it is helpful initially to discuss and experience these complicated feelings in individual sessions with one psychotherapist and later in group sessions with other young refugees as phases towards their integration and rehabilitation into the community of exile.

I am especially interested in how unspeakable stories and implicit beliefs come to be either censored or told and see a progression between four levels of acknowledgement:

(a) fragments of stories that remain in the unconscious, emerging in daydreams, intrusive thoughts and dreams;
(b) stories that we can think about consciously but cannot share with others;
(c) stories that we might become able to share with one other person;
(d) stories that we might share with a group of others.

Through the process of sharing with others via the transitional phase of sharing with a psychotherapist, exiled young people who initially feel hopeless about their capacities for survival explore the strengths and coping strategies of their pre-war life. They need to be reminded of these internalised resources, and must also explore what they have learned through their experiences of war, i.e. the paradox of their knowledge that life is fragile and precarious, that losses take a long time to mourn, that violent wars in general cause more problems than they solve. Young people who have experienced violence acquire this knowledge much earlier than usual. They eventually find hope and involvement with their present life when they can recall the good in the past and find pleasure in the present. These are sources of resilience. They can only be accessed as resources when the roots of guilt and shame about contamination, perpetration and survival have been worked on. The act of eventually sharing with others in the social world is very important (Haigh 2005).

Trauma

Trauma results from overwhelming experiences of feeling helpless, powerless and hopeless, and being unable to make sense of the world. Refugee and asylum-seeking children are likely to have experienced overwhelming events. Even in these circumstances most children are able to use the protective, mediating factors in their environment to develop resilience; but for some, the capacity to learn and socialise is seriously limited. Many writers refer to the phenomenon of 'retraumatisation' where survivors cannot think about present difficulties without the symptoms of the original traumatic events emerging. Others use Krystal's term 'psychic numbing' to refer to the absence of feeling after some traumatic events.

In therapeutic work with these children, the most useful models refer to the disintegrating and disconnecting effects of trauma and to the therapist's role in enabling integration and synthesis of past and present. Some children may remember difficult experiences but lose connection with the accompanying emotions, like Ahmed, who laughed loudly whilst telling me about his cousin being shot and killed next to him. Psychotherapeutic work involves the reconnection of memories with the original painful and difficult affects. Recovery from the consequences of trauma can occur within the context of a safe, healing relationship (Herman 1992) where remembrance and mourning can take place. Only then will some integration of the trauma and an awareness of the commonality of the experience of human rights abuses be possible.

Emanuel suggests that in working with traumatised children:

> the psychotherapist's primary function . . . is to help them to make sense of their emotional experience. This involves initially receiving and containing the emotions surrounding it by attending to the fragments presented and to the emotions evoked by them in the therapist . . . The child has to learn to label or name the elements of his emotional experience before thought about the relationships between the elements is possible.
>
> (Emanuel 1996)

He refers to Greenacre, and to Hopkins who notes the importance of helping people 'not only to accept the reality of traumatic events and the feelings which they engendered, but to become able to grieve about the damage done to them and to express appropriate anger about this' (Hopkins 1986). This requires an extremely painful mourning process about what has been lost as well as what can never be regained. In fact, no traumatic event can be wholly assimilated and vulnerability will always remain (Greenacre 1953).

The potential for retraumatisation is high. It is not uncommon for adolescents who report being imprisoned and tortured in their own countries to be disbelieved when they apply for asylum in Britain. In fact 5 per cent of unaccompanied young people who entered Britain in 1996 were detained in prison (Smith 1998). There is a similar potential for retraumatisation in many schools where there is no attempt to be democratic and which are rife with bullying, racism and xenophobia.

Secrecy and the relationship between private and public space

Secrecy is a helpful concept when considering young refugees' experiences and needs. Many must keep a series of political, familial and personal secrets in order to survive physically and psychologically. Once they arrive into exile and safety, some children, especially those who arrive unaccompanied, cannot decide whom to trust. Using emotional energy in keeping various secrets (e.g. through fear of rejection or of putting the lives of family members at risk) restricts the energy available for thinking, mourning, adjustment to a changed personal and social situation and for general development. Children may protect vulnerable parents upon whom they depend by keeping secret the fact that the parent cries constantly, is violent or is absent (physically or emotionally). Similarly, children may conceal their assumption of adult responsibilities at home – cooking, cleaning and caring for siblings and parents.

Personal secrets include feelings of guilt, shame and anxiety about past or present actions and thoughts, as well as carrying the burden of remembering what human rights abuses have been perpetrated against your people. These secrets may be held in the conscious or unconscious mind, or find expression somatically via bodily pain. Children are most at risk in families where parents cannot discuss either the past or the present problems of their children. Children, in an act of loyalty, protect parents and deny themselves (Melzak 1992).

Moral and ethical dilemmas

Any psychotherapeutic work with this population must give enough attention to the moral and ethical concerns of young refugees who are preoccupied with the society where they were born, the society where they live now and the ways in which they have seen humans treat each other in the task of conflict resolution, often through corruption and violent abuses of power.

The issue of cultural transition

Psychotherapeutic work with this population also must make a space for the concerns of the young people with cultural issues, cultural change and transformation and finding ways to empower young people who become afraid in exile to use aspects of their culturally familiar ways of coping. These themes need to be explored. While young children seem to adapt easily and be able to both learn the new culture and maintain a split between the new and the old culture, those who arrive in exile during adolescence need time to reflect on how they might develop a firm adult identity that can hold aspects of their childhood culture and the culture of exile in a comfortable way.

Memory – forgetting and remembering

A main task of young survivors of human rights violations is to acknowledge the reality of their memories of abusive events. The feelings linked with these memories are sometimes extremely painful and humiliating for an adolescent to bear, especially in situations where close family members were, in their presence, hurt or killed or arrested and subsequently disappeared. The child may feel a profound sense of his own failure, involving denial of his actual helplessness in the face of organised violence. Another central therapeutic task is to think with the child, at his own level of understanding, about the specific effects and meaning of these traumatic events for him during the particular phase of his development when they occurred.

By listening carefully to the accounts of survivors' experiences in concentration camps during the Second World War, Langer was able to describe in detail the problems of remembering and forgetting (Langer 1991). To save their own lives, survivors were forced to participate against their will in actions that surprised and horrified them at the time, let alone later when living in a society not at war. He describes the changes in their language and affect to a more concrete, emotionally disorganised idiom when they talked about their Holocaust experiences. They spoke of the past as if they were in the present. Sometimes, children find this 'reliving' unbearable and will bring into play all kinds of defensive strategies so as not to remember the feelings connected with overwhelming memories, or the memories connected with strong feelings.

This begs the question of whether child survivors of human rights abuses must acknowledge their experiences (verbally or non-verbally) in order to move forward in a good-enough way. My answer to this question has psychosocial, child-focused and psychotherapeutic dimensions. There are significant numbers of asylum-seeking children whose capacity to learn and socialise is profoundly restricted both by their past experience of violence and also by their present social position in exile. Such children certainly need attention, and some need psychotherapy, but their social environment also needs attention. All children need the opportunity to enhance their self-esteem and their capacities to reflect, acknowledge difference and resolve conflict if they are to be able, via the school curriculum, to think about their own history and the histories of their classmates, including those involving abuses of power, exploitation, war and violence.

Children who have a basic resilience rooted within their family history, and who have adult care and support, are able to address these traumatic issues. For other children, key aspects of their experience become repressed – a process which is reinforced by an environment that does not want to listen. Such children are likely to demonstrate their difficulties in partial remembering and partial forgetting via learning, emotional, social and behavioural difficulties and via internal conflicts, like Kaima and

Ayesha. The difference in capacity to cope lies not in the degree of violence experienced but in the presence or absence of mediating and protective factors that can enable children to reflect – to remember, to acknowledge and perhaps to repress. Some of these issues about persisting and newly developed resilience and vulnerabilities are illustrated in the case examples in this chapter.

Ismael

Weekly psychotherapy with Ismael highlights his needs for treatment, and for an older adult in his life who can help him reflect on decisions about his present life and understand the decisions he had to make in the past from both within and outside his moral frame of reference. Ismael, a former unaccompanied minor and child soldier, comes on time to every session and brings conflicts and anxieties and unbearable and sometimes unspeakable pain connected directly to both personal losses and his horror at the violence to which he was exposed. I have known Ismael for about three years.

Ismael was born in an African country into a privileged family where his father was connected with the government. He was the eldest son and especially close to his mother. He went to an academically oriented school and recalls trips to other countries in Africa with school and family, where he saw aspects of nature that gave him huge pleasure and a sense of wonder about the world.

The thread of continuity of this secure life was broken when he was fourteen. His father was often away from home on missions. On one visit to join his father for a weekend, trouble began in his country. They observed soldiers on the streets, and guns being used. Their father told them that there was a conflict in the government. When they returned home their father was arrested. The remaining family members heard later that he had been killed.

After a few days soldiers came and knocked on the door. Ismael's mother called out that she was coming to open the door and in the intervening seconds she told her children to hide under the stairs. They sat squashed together in the small dark space and heard the soldiers come in and go upstairs to the main room, above the cupboard. They heard shouting, sounds of struggle and then blood leaked through the ceiling of the cupboard. When the noise stopped and they heard the soldiers leave, Ismael and his siblings came out. He took the others downstairs and went alone to find his mother's beheaded body and amputated limbs strewn around the room.

Ismael took his distressed siblings to the nearby home of an uncle. They stayed there for a few days after which Ismael never again saw them. He went out to try to find food and was kidnapped by a rebel group engaged in a violent conflict with the government forces. He was forced to join them, trained and given his own clean syringe and a daily supply of cocaine.

Ismael had no experiences during his years with the rebel army that gave him pleasure in violence. He had some experiences that made him strongly anti- war.

He recalls now while he lives alone in London the strong bonds with his comrades and how they cared for each other and he misses the emotional intimacy and interdependence they shared. He has a particular memory of his closest friend standing in the same trench:

> We stood in a row in the trench and I knew all the young soldiers but my good friend was placed three or four men down the row. When the bullets began to fly, my friend called out to me that I should keep my head down. After a few moments my friend stood up and called out, 'Are you all right Ismael?' You see, Sheila, his concern for me was greater than his concern for himself. A bullet hit his head and I could see he was very injured. There was a lot of blood. He managed to walk towards me and I saw that half his head was blown off. He looked at me, put his arms around my neck and died in my arms. His last words to me were, 'You are OK, you listened, I see you are OK.'

As he told this story tears dropped from Ismael's eyes and he began to sob when he finished.

Other strong memories are connected to the terrible sadness he felt and feels about the loss of human life in war, especially as it impacts on the connections between parents and children, close attachments that had been severed for Ismael and which were a predictable and unacknowledged aspect of violent conflicts. In one of his weekly sessions he talked about his sadness at the ways in which civilians are caught up in wars. He was in a rebel army, forced to shoot at the enemy lines, and recalled that during a lull in the fighting he saw across the lines a child had been shot:

> Sheila, I saw the father run from the building opposite the rebel lines and I went towards the man. He picked up his son and told me that this was his one son, his favourite child. He was very agitated and upset and told me that I must help him to find a hospital. I was fourteen at this time. It was clear to me that the boy was dead but the father insisted

that his injuries could be healed. In the few minutes before the fighting began again I tried to tell the man very carefully that I thought that the boy was not alive. The man insisted that I had to help his son to reach the hospital; he had to make his son better. I had to return to my position and later saw the man shoot himself. I guess when he realised that his son was dead he did not want to live any more.

Ismael told this story repeating over and over his feelings of sadness then and now about these events. He sometimes re-experiences them as flashbacks that are so real that he feels that these remembered events are happening in the present time.

Ismael eventually was brought to Britain after he was injured in gunfire near the end of the war. A comrade carried him until they found NGO workers who took him for treatment to another African country where he remained in hospital for some months until he was well enough to travel into exile.

Able to talk about his own strengths and his vulnerabilities, Ismael can be proud of his own mind:

> I feel so grateful that I have a good mind. This got us out of trouble several times. Sometimes I disagreed with the stupid commanders and did something different from what they told us to do, when I believed that we would all be killed.

While he values his capacity to solve difficulties he is aware that it is the same mind that feels pain that is often at a level that is often unbearable. He often says: 'It is so very hard to lose your loved ones before you become an adult.'

For his first years in Britain Ismael had to work against his forced addiction to cocaine. He suffers for several days at a time from flashbacks of past events, especially the killing of his mother, the death of his friends and the civilian casualties of war.

Ismael acknowledges that there is now a separation in his mind between the pessimistic and sometimes suicidal side of himself and the more hopeful aspects. Now living alone in Britain, Ismael knows what he has lost and sometimes he is not certain that he can bear this reality. He plans one day to go back to one or other African country and contribute to its development. Though he feels safe in Britain, Ismael has no illusions that the corruption that he observed and experienced in his home country is absent from British society.

Comment

We might ask what is the impact on a child or young adolescent of experiencing adults in their communities attempting to solve conflicts relating to inequalities of power, through the use of brutal violence. I assume that in order to move forward developmentally after such experiences, young people need to be able to mourn what they have lost and to work to integrate their good and their difficult experiences of life.

Ismael is aware that as a young adolescent in his home country he had a strong sense of identity. After a series of overwhelming experiences he has noticed parts of himself that he cannot manage or like very much or integrate into his sense of himself. He uses his psychotherapy sessions to explore these parts of himself and the process enables him to accept and to integrate these unfamiliar and alien aspects of himself. He is troubled most by what he calls the 'ill' aspects of his identity and the parts that he sees to be pessimistic and helpless and the parts that feel sad and hopeless. He is able to appreciate his mind and in particular his abilities to critically analyse situations and social and political contexts. One of our key aims is to enable him to integrate these different aspects of himself.

In sessions we talk about the way in which we all have different parts of our identities, and explore together those parts of his self that he has much difficulty in accessing when he is frightened and low. Ismael has huge strengths and with some encouragement he can access these in a way that he is unable to when he is alone. This kind of therapeutic conversation reminds him that he is able to enjoy life and relationships. Ismael also attends a psychotherapy group for young people of a similar age with similar experiences to his own. Here, when he feels well enough to attend the group, he's able to share in the present concerns of the group and share his own feelings about his past and present life. He is kind and sensitive to the others and feels both contained by the group and involved with his peers, even though he finds listening to their accounts difficult. He especially likes our talking about African politics, themes of cultural identity, working with African traditional stories.

Ismael is able to acknowledge and explore his experiences as a victim and a perpetrator of violence, unlike some former child soldiers who cannot acknowledge actions and behaviours that they have been forced to carry out.

Ismael is very keen to have psychotherapy and to address his own memories in order to find ways better to bear these memories and to find antidotes to his own sense of profound emotional pain. The psychotherapy sessions are clearly a form of mourning and meditation for him. He feels that he wants to share his experiences with his psychotherapist who can bear witness to his pain and help him simply to feel better. We work not towards forgetting, but towards finding ways to rebuild the boundaries between the past and the present and between internal and external experience that often collapse after sequential traumatisation.

When referred, Ismael was tormented by dreams that he called flashbacks and intrusive thoughts. We began a long piece of work in which he talked each week about what was on his mind in an effort to separate interwoven and confusing thoughts and images, some of which were memories, some memories elaborated by fantasies, and others dream stories where he could find no links with his own experiences. The memories and fantasies and thoughts had been incorporated into his sense of self. They made him not simply sad and frightened but also strongly dislike himself. In our work we allot a portion of time in each session to examine together the nightmares/flashbacks which sometimes disable him for two or three days and stop him from going outside because he fears having an accident as he cannot focus his mind. He finds helpful the process of calling these thoughts 'memories'. He must be reminded that certain events did occur, and that his sad and frightened feelings underline his humanity and his compassion. We need to return frequently to the feelings of guilt and shame, linked with his helplessness to save his family and friends and to keep his family together. He easily forgets that he was a young adolescent surrounded by many adult men with weapons and needs reminding of this. He must be reminded that his feelings of guilt and shame and his ruminating self-doubt and self-criticism are paradoxical in the context of his reality. This work of exploring in some detail Ismael's memories and dreams provides a bereavement process that is too difficult for him to carry out on his own.

The therapeutic task was initially to gain his solid sense of trust by listening in such a way to his fragmented narrative, that he had faith that his therapist was able to listen in an ongoing way to the reality of his experiences and for a while help him to bear the weight of his pain at his relationship with this sequence of overwhelming events and help him to change his relationship with these events.

We intend that this psychotherapy will continue for as long as is necessary and helpful and certainly while his difficulties are exacerbated by his worries about his asylum status. From my perspective, we are working towards Ismael developing his own spontaneous narrative that includes the destructive and traumatising and the nourishing and creative aspects of his life. In this sense he works towards recovery. What is important for him, he says, is that he feels that the sessions help him feel better because he feels understood and relieved, that his terrible weight of memories is shared, so that he can think with the depth and detail he needs about what he has lost that is not replaceable and about what he does have.

Working together: conclusions

Child psychotherapeutic work with child and adolescent survivors of political violence must be informed by detailed knowledge about the past external world of these children and about the social position and practical situation of families and unaccompanied children and adolescents seeking asylum in Britain, given the current asylum laws in Europe and their restrictive and xenophobic interpretation.

It is helpful to apply child psychoanalytic ideas in training and supporting adults who work with and care for young refugees – teachers, social workers, lawyers, health workers and members of the refugee communities. With the ongoing support of a child psychotherapist's focus on the developmental needs of children, the adults in contact with refugee children can increase their understanding of the child's experience of trauma, loss and change and promote the factors that facilitate the development of resilience.

Children who need only involvement, acknowledgement, clarification, explanation and clear authority do not need direct help from child-centred mental health workers; but the significant adults in their lives may need some help in assessing and disentangling the child's experience from their own response to these experiences, and time to assess what the child's special needs might be in school and at home. Consultation with a child psychotherapist, in this context, can give time and space to clarify the special needs of asylum-seeking children. A child psychotherapist might run a regular consultation group for adults who work with refugee children and adolescents, providing the opportunity to discuss the children's needs and to address the institutional problems and personal feelings raised, and present opportunities to address these.

Those children for whom unconscious feelings, conflicts and confusions profoundly interfere with their development will need direct child psychotherapeutic intervention. This may be brief but is more likely to be long term (especially for unaccompanied minors), which conflicts with currently popular clinical models. Involvement with the mental health needs of refugee children makes us all 'political' in terms of thinking about children's rights and human rights, as well as the abuses of these rights. It involves daily contact with vulnerable children and young people who are marginalised in this country and who do not receive their basic right to parental care and education. Awareness of the dire situation of such vulnerable children, coupled with the knowledge gleaned in long child psychotherapy trainings, will hopefully galvanise our profession to campaign to improve the situation of children whose basic needs for development (as set out by the United Nations in its *Convention on the Rights of the Child* (1991)) are not met, and to think together with others about how these needs might best be met in our community. Key for child psychotherapists is Article 39 of the Convention which relates to the need for treatment and thus to direct and applied psychotherapeutic work.

As child psychotherapists we might wish to think about our obligations as set out in the *UN Convention on the Rights of the Child* (Article 39). This article states:

> States Parties shall take all appropriate measures to promote physical and psychological recovery and social reintegration of the child victim of any form of neglect, exploitation or abuse; torture or any other form

of cruel and degrading treatment and punishment; or armed conflicts. Such recovery and reintegration shall take place in an environment which fosters the health, self-respect and dignity of the child.

References

Blackwell, R. D. (1997) 'Holding, containing and bearing witness: the problem of helpfulness in encounters with torture survivors', *Journal of Social Work Practice* 11(2): 81–9.

Blom-Cooper, L. (1985) *A Child in Trust: The Report of the Panel of Inquiry into the Circumstances Surrounding the Death of Jasmine Beckford*, London: London Borough of Brent.

Bolloton, W. and Spafford, T. (1996) *Teaching Refugee Children: A Guide to Resources*, London: Newton English Language Service.

Edgecumbe R. (2000) *Anna Freud: A View of Development, Disturbance and Therapeutic Techniques*, London and Philadelphia: Routledge.

Emanuel, R. (1996) 'Psychotherapy with children traumatised in infancy', *Journal of Child Psychotherapy* 22(2): 214–39.

Freud, S. (1914) 'Remembering, repeating and working through', *SE* 12, London: Hogarth Press.

Greenacre, P. (1953) *Trauma, Growth and Personality*, London: Hogarth Press.

Haigh, R. (2005) 'The quintessence of a therapeutic environment: five principles of a therapeutic group', in P. Campling and R. Haigh (eds) *Therapeutic Communities Past, Present and Future*, London and New York: Jessica Kingsley.

Herman, J. L. (1992) *Trauma and Recovery*, New York: Basic Books.

Hopkins, J. (1986) 'Solving the mystery of monsters: steps towards the recovery from trauma', *Journal of Child Psychotherapy* 12(1): 61–71.

Kriedler, W. J. (1984) *Creative Conflict Resolution*, Glenview, IL: Scott Foresman.

Krystal, H. (1978) 'Trauma and addects', *Psychoanalytic Study of the Child* 33(8): 81–116.

Langer, L. L. (1991) *Holocaust Testimonies: The Ruins of Memory*, New Haven, CT: Yale University Press.

Melzak, S. (1992) 'Secrecy, privacy, survival, repressive regimes and growing up', *Bulletin of the Anna Freud Centre* 15: 205.

Rojas, B. P. (1996) 'Breaking the human link: the medico-psychiatric view of impunity', in C. Harper (ed.) *Impunity: An Ethical Perspective*, London: World Council of Churches Publications.

Rutter, J. (1996) *Refugees in the Classroom*, Stoke on Trent: Trentham Books.

Schwartz, S. and Melzak, S. (2005) 'Using story telling in psychotherapeutic group work with refugees', *Group Analysis* 38(2): 293–306.

Smith, T. (1998) *Children Behind Bars*, London: British Refugee Council.

Summerfield, D. (1993) *Addressing the Human Response to War and Atrocity: Major Themes for Health Workers*, London: Medical Foundation for Victims of Torture.

United Nations (1951) *United Nations Convention Relating to the Status of Refugees*, UN Treaty Series 189: 137.

—— (1991) *United Nations Convention on the Rights of the Child*, London: Children's Rights Development Unit.

UNHCR (2008) United Nations High Commission for Refugees (United Nations Refugee Agency) Press Release 17 June, available on internet as PDF.

Van Beuren, G. (1994) 'The international protection of children in armed conflicts', *International and Comparative Law Quarterly* 43: 809–26.

Winnicott, D. W. (1960) 'Ego distortion in terms of true and false self', in D. W. Winnicott *The Maturational Processes and the Facilitating Environment*, London: Hogarth Press, 1965.

26 Delinquency

Peter Wilson

Introduction

Delinquency is a term that has different meanings and usages. Most commonly, a juvenile delinquent is defined as someone who has transgressed the law: 'a young person who has been prosecuted and found guilty of an offence that would be classified as a crime if committed by an adult' (Graham 1991). This definition has the virtue of precision. Its limitation, however, is that it does not take into account the full extent of behaviour or attitude. In psychodynamic terms, delinquency carries a much broader meaning: it relates to a more fundamental concern about responsibility and honesty, both in relation to oneself and to others. The essence of delinquency lies in its failure of duty to meet both the legal and moral requirements of the prevailing social order. The word itself draws its source from the Latin *linquere* – to leave, forsake or abandon. The delinquent is unable or unwilling to do that which is owed to the group, community or society. Delinquency is thus not an activity confined to a criminal minority, but refers to a tendency that is integral to the development of all social relationships.

There can be few children for example who do not break rules, who do not tell an untruth, who do not take what is not theirs, who do not defy those around them. All children, from time to time, do what they are not supposed to; they try the forbidden and test the limits. In the interests of their growth and curiosity they break new ground, often ruthlessly and regardless of constraints and consequences. There is in the very process of becoming social an anti-social necessity. Delinquency in this sense is part of being a child and adolescent.

The nature of delinquency and child and adolescent development

Delinquency expresses itself in three major ways: through stealing, deception and physical or verbal violence. All constitute an attack on or an abandonment of the other; all, as it were, 'leave' the other. The spectrum of delinquent activity is wide. Stealing covers many activities: 'borrowing', shoplifting, taking and driving away, robbery and burglary. Deception includes a broad repertoire of lies from the periodic white lie to systematic deviousness, duplicity and fraud. Violence consists of fighting, bullying, intimidating, physical and sexual abuse, assault, torture or murder. Many of these activities are not criminal (and thus not delinquent in the legal sense); they are, however, in one way or another, dishonest and offensive (and thus delinquent in the psychodynamic sense). The degree to which these activities become problematic is in part determined by the requirements of the law, but also by the sanctions and prohibitions of the social group – whether this be the family, the peer group, the community or society at large. Some groups turn a blind eye to certain forms of theft; others collude with different kinds of deception or condone various forms of violence. Delinquency is thus relative to the tolerance of the group.

To a large extent, delinquency, as a failure in social adaption, is a mental health issue. Mental health refers essentially to the capacity to function effectively and creatively in the social group. It consists of the ability to initiate and sustain mutually satisfying relationships. Crucial to children's development is their ability and readiness to develop sufficient self-control and conscience to guide their behaviour within the rules of the group. Mental health problems and more severe mental disorders and illnesses reflect, in varying degrees, impairments of these abilities. Delinquency is one particular form of such impairment. Some delinquents behave in a disruptive and aggressive way which is excessive and impervious to modification by the normal range of social sanctions; their behaviour gives rise to disapproval and is associated with significant suffering and disturbance in personal functioning. In psychiatric terms, these young people are classified as having a conduct disorder; an indication of the extent and problematic nature of their delinquency.

The conditions that are likely to determine the development of mental health or of delinquency are now well documented in the literature on risk and protective factors (Farrington 1996, 1997; Utting *et al.* 1993; Wadsworth 1979). These can be grouped broadly into those pertaining to the inborn characteristics and personal resources of children, and those relating to familial and societal circumstances. In the first group, a number of genetic and early physical pre- and perinatal factors (e.g. physical abnormalities, premature birth) can be identified that produce vulnerabilities in infants. Inherent temperamental differences are of key importance pointing to whether or not children are overly sensitive, cranky or regressive/progressive in their basic tendencies. The personal resources of children – intelligence, ego resilience, social skills development – determine whether they are able to comprehend and adapt to what is happening in their lives and thus gain a sense of self-efficacy and control over events.

Familial and societal factors cover a broad range of circumstances. Major risk factors in the family include parental psychopathology and criminality,

discordant family relationships and divorce, inconsistent parental supervision, harsh and erratic punishment, physical abuse and neglect, and lack
of emotional warmth. Set against these are a range of protective factors,
most notably the establishment of secure infant attachment and bonding,
the provision of authoritative and consistent parenting, a basic belief in the
family in the value of education and residential stability. The degree to
which mothers can cope with adversity is critical; this in turn is dependent
on the stability of their marriages or partnerships and the presence of
significant care networks in their families or neighbourhoods.

Psychoanalytic thinking (e.g. Bion 1962; Bowlby 1951; Freud 1965;
Winnicott 1960b) emphasises the significance of infant and early childhood
experience and attachment. The role of the family in ensuring sufficient
emotional containment of children is crucial to the provision of a sense of
inner safety and coherence. This lays the foundation of basic trust and
positive expectancy. Children feel essentially nourished, understood and
affirmed; they are enabled to think and to learn, with a readiness to enter
into relationships and to accept the constraints necessary for socialisation.
Later experiences of feeling held and valued within a reliable family
environment that establishes clear expectations and boundaries are
necessary for the development of self-control and the establishment of
ideals and of a moral sense. Children's capacity to benefit from school and
community opportunities is greatly influenced by these primary family
experiences. In contrast, where such favourable conditions do not prevail,
children are less likely to be equipped to process adequately and make
sense of their experience. The impact of maltreatment – whether it be
physical, sexual or emotional neglect or abuse – is essentially traumatic,
overwhelming children with sensations, tensions and feelings they cannot
assimilate and exposing them to primitive anxieties over which they cannot
achieve mastery – fears of annihilation, loss of control, disapproval and
rejection. Children feel betrayed by parental failure to safeguard their safety
and integrity. In response, they become resentful and on guard, without
faith in those around them and disinclined to comply with their social
requirements.

Delinquency represents an attempt to defend against these anxieties and
give expression to this resentment. Delinquents find ways of ridding themselves of tension, through various projective mechanisms, and rendering
others prey to the very feelings of anger, fear and confusion that they
themselves find so intolerable. Campbell (1996) emphasises that 'it is the
reliance upon action to project painful thoughts and feelings outside of
himself and into the environment that is a fundamental characteristic of the
delinquent's psychological defences'. He also draws attention to the delinquent's tendency to master traumatic experiences through sexual fantasy.
This contains elements of excitement and risk (Stoller 1975) that both serve
a defensive purpose and give expression to sadistic and revengeful wishes.
Galway (1991) refers to deficiencies in the internal capacity to contain

anxiety, and in more disturbed young people, a lack of an 'internal container altogether'; they are unable to make use of fantasy or the development of the capacity to think in order to process experience. As a result their behaviour is more determined by the impulse to act and by a need to seek containment externally through provocation and manipulation.

It is clear that mental health or delinquent outcome is dependent on the interplay of multiple factors within the child, family and environment, and in relation to the severity of the child's circumstances. The extent to which children are resilient, and thus able to rise above negative circumstances or manage to mitigate the effect of these circumstances, is a major variable. Horowitz (1987), for example, refers to the complex interrelationship between children's inherent vulnerability and the 'facilitativeness' of their environment: resilient children in adverse environments may make remarkable progress whilst vulnerable children in more facilitating ones may not.

Adolescence and the circumstances that surround it have a further determining effect on the development of delinquency. The peak age for all offending in England and Wales is eighteen for males and fifteen for females (Home Office 1995). There are numerous environmental risk factors that can lead to delinquent activity, including disadvantaged neighbourhoods, community disorganisation and neglect and availability of drugs. Poverty, poor schooling and unemployment also play their part. Young people's internal experience of adolescence, however, is of key significance in determining how able they are to cope with these adversities. Ordinarily, adolescence is an exciting, if at times alarming, time of growth and discovery. For those adolescents, however, whose early experiences have been unfavourable, the process of adolescence can be very unsettling. They are less able to negotiate adequately the developmental tasks of adjusting to the impact of puberty and negotiating separation and individuation (Laufer and Laufer 1984; Wilson 1991); their adolescent state does not excite them; they are fearful of their physical growth and sexuality and of taking responsibility by themselves for their actions. A great deal of delinquent behaviour in adolescence can be seen as a breakdown in the capacity to deal with these anxieties and to fill a developmental void (Greenberg 1975) inherent in the process of the separation. Some adolescents become extremely overwhelmed and disorganised, breaking down severely in suicidal and psychotic type behaviour. Others are more able to 'manage', drawing on the adolescent tendency to find expression through 'a language of action' (Osorio 1977) and veering towards a delinquent outcome.

According to the severity of negative childhood experiences and adolescent turbulence, the degree of delinquency becomes more marked and problematic. Most young people whose delinquent behaviour is persistent and extreme experience the world as fundamentally uncaring, withholding and untrustworthy. They harbour within them a sense of injustice and outrage and an abiding resentment that leads to a contempt and disregard for others. The delinquent act is intended to attack and confound those perceived to be responsible for their difficulties. In effect it carries its own sense of justice – the delinquent feels emboldened to take what he perceives to be his, and to deceive and violate those whom he believes have betrayed and abused him. There is in all of this an exhilarating and powerful mixture of despair and hope – the delinquent determined both to 'leave' the ungiving or hostile other and yet engage and register protest. Winnicott (1965) emphasised the essential purpose of the delinquent act as a positive, self-affirming protest. He viewed 'the anti-social tendency' as a consequence of and response to 'environmental failure'; it represents a testing of the environment and a way of 'staking a claim' on what has hitherto been withheld. He expressed his position most clearly in the following passage:

> First I must try to define the word psychopathy. I am using the term here (and I believe I am justified in doing so) to describe an adult condition which is an uncured delinquency. A delinquent is an uncured anti-social boy or girl. An antisocial boy or girl is a deprived child. A deprived child is one who had something good-enough, and then no longer had this, whatever it was, and there was sufficient growth and organisation of the individual *at the time of the deprivation* for the deprivation to be perceived as traumatic. In other words, in the psychopath and the delinquent and the antisocial child there is logic in the implied attitude 'the environment owes me something'.
>
> (Winnicott 1965)

Child psychotherapy and delinquency

Child psychotherapists face major problems in working with delinquents. Many of the factors that give rise to delinquency fall beyond the reach of psychotherapy: little can be done through psychotherapy to change inherent personal characteristics or environmental factors. In relation to inner experience, many delinquents are unable or unwilling to acknowledge their suffering or learn through self-exploration in a therapeutic relationship. They are mistrustful and defiant and unable to hold in mind ideas and thoughts without defensive recourse to action. In adolescence, their need to preserve privacy and defend against dependency additionally works against therapeutic enquiry. In view of these difficulties, the issue of motivation is complicated. Some delinquents for example feel little remorse or concern about their behaviour and thus see no reason to change. As Eissler (1958) puts it,

> the technical difficulty in treating a delinquent arises from his total lack of desire to change. His symptoms are painful not to him but to others in his environment. He has no need or motive to reveal to his analyst

what is going on in him. Further more, he sees the analyst as representative of that society against which his aggressions are directed and therefore meets him with distrust and fear.

On the other hand, beneath their antagonism or indifference, many delinquents feel anxious, confused and ashamed of their destructiveness. They are sometimes painfully conscious of their failings in their social, family and vocational lives, and yet they feel helpless in their predicament and unable to stop or comprehend their delinquency. Such acknowledgement of vulnerability is a potential source of motivation; it is, however, difficult for them to bear and invariably defended against through attacking those who offer care and interest.

Child psychotherapists need to take into account these various factors that complicate motivation for change and improvement. They need also to be realistic about the extent of their contribution, set alongside other initiatives in the field, tackling the problem of delinquency (Sheldrick 1985). These include vocational and educational training, diversionary programmes in the Youth Justice System (Jones 1987; NACRO 1988) and a range of psychosocial treatments, such as problem-solving skills training, parent management training, family therapy. Many of these have a behavioural and cognitive focus and have been positively evaluated (Kazdin 1997). Psychodynamic child psychotherapy has been less well evaluated and needs more outcome research, despite methodological problems, to counter criticism (see, for example, Rutter 1985).

Despite these difficulties, however, child psychotherapy can be of considerable value to many delinquents in helping them to acknowledge and understand better their internal experience and thus gain a greater sense of self-control. In many respects, the practice of child psychotherapy with delinquents is no different from that with more neurotic or psychotic young people. Basic to the process is the establishment of a secure setting in which sufficient stability is ensured to enable young people to feel safe enough to explore and discuss their difficulties. The endeavour is to create an experience for them in which they can learn about themselves through the therapeutic relationship and from observations, clarifications and interpretations (Wilson and Hersov 1985). The fundamental purpose is to improve their understanding of the anxieties that interfere with their development and contribute to their delinquency.

The establishment of these basic conditions is especially important in working with delinquent young people whose need for clear boundaries, reliability and predictability is central. Beyond this, however, there are three issues that need to be addressed in particular in order to deal with the mistrust and hostility of delinquents and their equivocal motivation to change. The first concerns the establishment of *a working alliance*, the second, *the management of transference*, and third, the *adaptation in approach* to different types of delinquency.

Establishment of a working alliance

Without the establishment of a working alliance (Meeks 1971) there can be no prospect of collaborative or explorative work. In view of the many resistances inherent in delinquency, it is incumbent on child psychotherapists to reach out – to convey in some way an appreciation of the delinquent's behaviour and underlying difficulties and to engender a sense of direction and hope in the possibility of change. This requires their willingness to take a more proactive and supportive approach than is customary. Some writers (Miller 1983), drawing on the work of Aichhorn (1965), suggest that psychotherapists adopt a relatively forceful, almost omnipotent position, in order to capture the imagination of otherwise indifferent and hostile delinquents who nevertheless seek leadership and guidance. Whilst this approach may be effective in certain circumstances with some adolescents, it carries with it considerable dangers, not least in compromising the stability of the therapeutic setting and building unnecessary expectations and inevitable disappointments. What is paramount, however, particularly in the early stages of therapy, is to find ways of engaging delinquents' curiosity about themselves and their circumstances.

The maintenance of a working alliance is of central importance throughout the course of therapy. It is dependent on mutual trust and as such is vulnerable to pressures within the therapeutic relationship. Delinquents may attack the alliance in many ways and child psychotherapists may overly protect it at the cost of therapeutic progress. It is not uncommon during psychotherapy, for example, for young people to continue their delinquent and criminal activities both within and outside the therapy. They may conceal what they are doing or seek to manipulate child psychotherapists to accept and condone their delinquent behaviour. Child psychotherapists need to hold a difficult tension between alliance and non-compliance with these delinquents' manoeuvres; this corresponds with the delinquent's ambivalence about being caught and found out. Much depends on child psychotherapists' insight into their own relation to delinquency and to authority; it is through this that they can best hold the balance within themselves between moral censure of, and indulgent collusion with, delinquents' activities.

The management of the transference

Whereas transference (Freud 1914) is always a powerful phenomenon in therapy, its impact in the psychotherapy of delinquents is especially forceful. In the transference, young people re-enact childhood experiences intensified in their revival in adolescence. They convey through their behaviour that which is familiar to them. They bring into the therapeutic relationship aspects of how they themselves felt in the past and of how they perceived others who were involved with them. A teenage girl, for example, who has endured sexual abuse by her father as a child is likely to feel, in the reliving in the transference, her own childhood sensations of terror and excitement as well as the fears of a domineering and invasive father. In psychotherapy, she may find herself, in the growing dependency of the therapeutic relationship, having similar sensations as well as anticipating abuse from the psychotherapist. She may retreat from the therapy, or, alternatively, re-immerse herself in the entanglement of her past in the therapeutic relationship. She may find ways to seduce or provoke the therapist into bullying her – both to repeat the past experience and to master anxiety, through turning a passive experience into its active counterpart. She may reverse the past experience and attempt to dominate the psychotherapist, rendering him or her both harmless and as abused as she had felt. It is likely, too, that she may act out outside the therapy through violent behaviour, prostitution or theft in order to relieve this intolerable tension and to be apprehended and punished.

The value of such transference experience is that it opens up possibilities for the understanding and working through of central anxieties that underlie the delinquency. The above picture, however, gives some indication of the volatile and potentially disruptive nature of this experience. Unless the transference can be properly managed, it can become anti-therapeutic. Much depends on child psychotherapists' capacities to withstand the impact of these powerful and conflicting feelings and to provide some degree of containment so that they can be perceived and understood. The key therapeutic task is to resist the young person's implicit invitation to repeat the past – for example, for the psychotherapist to behave like a dominant or abusive father, or to become overwhelmed by feelings of helplessness. The child psychotherapists' ability to find ways of responding that are different from what the young people expect and which do not meet the dictates of the transference is essential. Ultimately, it is through the child psychotherapists' behaviour that they convey their understanding of the meaning of the young person's delinquency and provide the safety and boundary that the delinquent needs. Such behaviour, sustained by the child psychotherapists' own insights, constitutes interpretation and serves as a stimulus and basis for further verbal forms of communication and understanding.

Adaptation in approach

There are many individual differences between delinquents, and psychotherapeutic work clearly needs to be adapted to address these differences, taking into account historical and personal circumstances and based on careful assessment and diagnosis. Various attempts at classification have been made of delinquent and criminal people (e.g. Galway 1991; Winnicott 1960a); for the most part these have attempted to identify the degree of persistence and extremity of the offending behaviour and the neurotic or psychotic basis underlying the delinquent personality. For purposes of clarification, delinquent young people can be broadly divided into three main groups: those that are impulsive, explosive and/or compulsive. These categories are not intended as diagnostic categories, but rather as guides to consider the predominant elements of the delinquent behaviour in question and to make the most appropriate response. None, of course, is intended to be seen as exclusive of the others.

The impulsive delinquent

Impulsive delinquents are young people who are largely dominated by the sheer pressure of their wishes and desires. Their behaviour is demanding, insistent, grabbing in nature. They take things on impulse and steal without apparent remorse or concern. They lie frequently and are often aggressive, bullying if they can get away with it, and at times violent if cornered or threatened. There is a sense in which their delinquency is 'mindless' – defensive, reactive, without thought or regard for others and with little comprehension of the consequences of their actions.

Delinquency of this kind has many causes. In some young people, there may be genetic factors, as in hyperkinetic syndrome, as a result of which they have inherent difficulty in focusing their attention or controlling their impulsive behaviour. In others, early abusive or neglectful childhood experiences may have left them with inner feelings of chaos and terror and with limited resources to manage their anxiety. Anna Freud's (1965) developmental perspective on the nature of lying and stealing is of particular relevance. Some of these young people, because of their immaturity, are less able to distinguish between inner and outer reality or between ideas of what is 'mine' and 'not mine'. In terms of their functioning they are more likely to react to intolerable realities through regression to infantile forms of behaviour and wishful thinking.

The therapeutic response to these delinquents needs to address their basic difficulties in controlling their impulses and tolerating frustration as well as the underlying anxieties that propel them into such trouble. Systematic behavioural and cognitive approaches are useful in enabling them to develop problem-solving skills, build social competencies and clarify their thinking in relation to the consequences of their actions. These approaches can be carried out either individually or in groups, in different settings in school, special educational establishments or in the community in various diversionary schemes. The involvement of the family in supporting these therapeutic interventions through family therapy or parent management training is important. Child psychotherapists have a significant contribution to make in working to understand the anxieties of these young people, particularly those who have some rudimentary capacity for self-reflection and a wish to change. Despite the apparent randomness and remorselessness of their behaviour, many feel fundamentally very frightened and confused and desperate that they cannot control themselves or indeed what happens to them. Child psychotherapists may have to adapt to their needs, through being relatively more structured, focused and supportive in their approach. In view of the need of these young people to feel held within a consistent and comprehensive system of care, it is important that child psychotherapists do not work in isolation but maintain regular liaison with other practitioners involved with the young person – for example, teachers, social workers, youth workers.

The explosive delinquent

By contrast, explosive delinquents function at a higher level of organisation; their personalities are more structured, less buffeted by impulse and more coherent in relation to others. For most of the time they appear to behave normally and get along well enough with others. The problematic area of their delinquency resides in their periodic outbursts of violence and revengeful preoccupations; the latter can lead to acts of theft, deception and intimidation with no apparent regard for their victims. At the core of this kind of delinquency is often a major narcissistic disturbance, in which the young people are highly sensitive to perceived rejection or humiliation.

The causes of such disturbance are complex, but are frequently associated with what Greenberg (1975) has described as a 'symbiotically warped' mother–infant relationship. In this, vulnerable young people have experienced, as children, an accumulation of narcissistic injuries in response to their mother's extreme ambivalence: that is, they have been subjected both to the mother's often engulfing and sexualised over-involvement and yet sudden and unpredictable withdrawals of affection, indifference and hostility. This perplexing intimacy can have a highly disturbing effect leaving them feeling as children and as adolescents helpless, valueless and confused. There is engendered from such experience a deep sense of hurt and anger that constitutes what Kohut (1972) refers to as 'narcissistic rage'. This vulnerability is intolerable and is for the most part defended against through compensatory grandiose or idealising fantasies. When these are challenged, whether through direct criticism or rebuke, or through actual or perceived betrayal (e.g. in an idealised relationship), the rage may erupt and find expression in acts of violence.

The extent of the denial in this kind of delinquency is extensive, often fortified by a sense of righteous justification that allows for no recognition of wrongdoing. The violent outbursts are troubling, but experienced as episodic and 'forgettable'. Cognitive and behavioural therapeutic approaches that have a useful structuring and guiding effect for impulsive delinquents are largely irrelevant for these delinquents. Anger management techniques may be helpful, but they do not meet the depth of the underlying disturbance. Long-term psychodynamic therapy can, in some cases, be effective in reducing the extremity of behaviour and preoccupation. This psychotherapy needs to be based on an understanding of narcissistic psychopathology and to proceed on the basis of building an essentially supportive and affirming relationship. Once this is established, there exists the opportunity of re-experiencing and working through elements of the early narcissistic hurt and rage in the transference, and thus of greater integration and control. The work of Kohut (1972) in treating narcissistic personality disorders through mirror transferences is of particular relevance.

The compulsive delinquent

Compulsive delinquents are those whose behaviour is repetitive and chronically destructive both to themselves and to others. It is behaviour that combines both impulsive and explosive elements but is relatively more controlled and sustained. Behind this behaviour is an attitude of contempt that derives from a basic fear of dependency and dread of humiliation. These delinquents are often clever, streetwise, well resourced in terms of social skills and competence; they are adept at controlling others through seduction and manipulation and are callous and sadistic in their attacks on others. Their overriding purpose is to get what they want as quickly and immediately as possible, regardless of the rules or sensibilities of others. To this end, they are able and willing to defy and undermine others through concealment and duplicity.

At the source of this kind of delinquency is again a fundamental narcissistic disturbance drawn from comparable early infantile circumstances as described in relation to the explosive delinquent. There is additionally a complex overlay of more neurotic conflicts that give rise to a sense of guilt which, though denied, has a powerful unconscious influence on behaviour. It is this factor, together with a fear of omnipotence (a sense of limitlessness, of there being no bounds to what they might get away with), that gives rise to the self-destructive and compulsive nature of their delinquency. This takes the form not only of theft, deception or fraud, but also of activities that are self-punishing – for example the burglar who repeatedly breaks into houses until he is caught; the boy who takes and drives away cars until eventually he crashes.

Delinquency of this kind is perhaps the most difficult to deal with in psychotherapy; it is habitual, a way of life that for many may be 'successful' enough. Nevertheless despite this, many such young people experience a pervasive sense of unease that can lead to a desire for change. They are frightened of their destructiveness, of their potential loss of control, of their sense of being bad and unwanted. Many express a strong need for a relationship and to be understood.

In the following example, an account is given of the psychotherapy of a young person whose delinquency contained impulsive and explosive elements but whose life was built upon deception and compulsive delinquent activity. The fundamental task of the psychotherapist was to establish and maintain a working alliance that could allow for moments of experience that were genuine and non-delinquent and that could be used for exploration and gradual integration.

Case illustration: Paul

Paul was a fifteen-year-old boy, tall, well built and always dressed stylishly. He was referred for psychotherapy by his mother who had decided she could no longer tolerate his behaviour. The school had complained to her for some time about his stealing from other pupils, his tendency to bully and sexually pester girls. In recent months he had got into trouble with the police. He had been questioned about a number of car thefts in the neighbourhood; matters had come to a head recently when he had been caught driving a stolen car. His mother felt she could never trust him.

Paul lived alone with his mother. Paul's father had left the family home when he was aged six. There had been numerous violent marital arguments when Paul was a small child and he had at times been victim of his father's violence. His relationship with his mother had been very close and it was clear that in many ways she was very proud of him. However, she had also been preoccupied with her own design business and had had several relationships with other men. This, Paul had resented; he had, for example, stolen money from the wallets of his mother's boyfriends. His father had remained a constant presence in his life, though always elusive and unpredictable. Paul remained loyal to him and looked up to him, although he never could be sure where his father was or what he did. 'He comes and goes in big cars and flash suits.'

Paul was seen in once-weekly psychotherapy for just over a year. His attendance was erratic although this improved towards the end. The therapy terminated because of his family moving to another area; this was premature and progress was by no means complete. Enough was accomplished, however, to help him understand his delinquent behaviour better and to begin to try to change his ways.

Paul made it clear from the outset that he was happy to come to therapy. He said that he knew he needed to sort himself out. His mother worried too much but he could well understand her feelings. He loved his mother and he did not want to upset her. He also wanted to do well and 'go into the design business' with her. He intended to go to college and get down to studying. He understood that I knew the extent of his mother's concern and of his delinquency and police involvement. He acknowledged that he was 'in a bit of trouble' but he was quick to point out that he had learnt his lesson and was about to change.

In all of this, his tone was assured, grown-up, conciliatory. He smiled a lot and it seemed that his overall purpose was to disarm and circumvent me as much as he could. To some extent, the early sessions moved along well enough as he began to talk about his feelings towards his parents, his memories of having felt frightened and confused as a child and his wish to know more about his father. He talked, too, at the beginning about his interest in cars and achievements in computer design. There remained, however, a lack of depth or connectedness. Despite his apparent sincerity, I felt as if he were play-acting, almost in mockery of the therapy. His attitude was flippant, he turned up late for sessions with poor excuses, he hinted at various criminal activities – but never explicit, always keeping me guessing. At one level, it seemed clear that he was attending therapy to be 'good' and to get out of trouble with the police. The degree of control and manipulation, however, in the way in which he maintained distance in the therapeutic relationship, indicated a more profound level of fear of dependency in the transference. His mockery seemed an effective way of rendering me powerless, feeling as foolish and duped as he did.

Throughout, Paul's delinquency was a feature of the therapy. This was something I needed constantly to keep in mind whilst always remaining open to his underlying vulnerability and possible search for help. It was an achievement in itself that Paul attended therapy, albeit at times irregularly, and that he opened up the opportunity to talk about aspects of his life. Nevertheless, there was much in what he said that was false and in denial of his difficulties. This became particularly noticeable when he talked about his relationship with girls. On the one hand, he said he had a steady girlfriend whom he would never leave; on the other hand, he talked of other girls whom he had 'had' – seemingly oblivious of his effects on them or indeed on his girlfriend.

A turning point occurred in psychotherapy towards the end of the third month. Its impetus was a telephone call from Paul's mother informing me that he had been arrested with someone else for a burglary in a large house in the neighbourhood. Paul attended his subsequent session in his usual breezy manner without making any reference to this information. Eventually I informed Paul of what I knew. Paul's initial reaction was to smile, shrug it off; it wasn't really him who was involved, it was his friend. His mother, he said, fretted too much; she wasn't well. I stayed silent for a while and then said simply, 'I am listening; but I am wondering why I don't feel convinced about what you're saying.' Paul smiled again and picked up a pen on the desk. He mimed at smoking it like a cigarette and asked uncertainly what I was getting at. I repeated what I had said and added I thought that Paul was kidding himself as well as his mother and me about what he was up to. Paul was at first quiet, but then, suddenly and violently, threw the pen across the room and got up to walk towards the door. He swore at me, accusing me of being a flash Harry, a twisting bastard, a bully who 'couldn't give a toss'. As he opened the door I simply but firmly said, 'Stay – don't leave this'. Paul hung about but eventually walked over to the pen, picked it up, put it back in its proper place and slumped back into his chair. Suddenly he cried – at first in anger at me for not caring, and then at the police and at his mother for messing him about and his father for never being around. He sat in his chair for several minutes and said nothing. He then looked directly at me and said 'I am well and truly messed up, I hate it, I don't know what to do'.

This was an extraordinary moment in therapy, quite uncharacteristic. It touched on something genuine in Paul that for the most part he sought to conceal. There were other comparable experiences later in the therapy, but this first moment served as a central reference point – to understand the desolation and vulnerability that underlay his delinquency. Following this, he became more open to exploration of his feelings, not least his sense of betrayal by his mother and father. He was able to gain some understanding of his excitement in invading the privacy of the house that he had burgled; it had belonged to a woman who was a friend of his mother. He also acknowledged that he had been relieved to be caught. He felt bad and he deserved it. Throughout he conveyed a sense of yearning for a relationship – wanting in the moment of burglary to be close to and inside his mother – and in his taking and driving away cars, seeking to be alongside his father. The reality of his impending court experience and sentencing together with his experience of therapy had a moderating effect on his delinquency.

Summary

This chapter has drawn upon a broad definition of delinquency, encompassing a wide range of activities, some of which are criminal, all of which are designed to attack and confound other people. Delinquency represents an inability or unwillingness to relate to others with respect and honesty. Although integral to development and to mental health, it becomes problematic according to its persistence and extremity and to the extent that it disturbs the social group. Numerous risk and protective factors exist to determine a delinquent outcome. Psychodynamic thinking emphasises the importance of early childhood experience, in particular the traumatic impact of childhood maltreatment. Delinquent behaviour is understood in relation to the failure of the environment to provide sufficient care and emotional containment for children to develop the capacity to process and master anxiety. It is seen as a necessary expression, defensive against anxiety and purposeful in evoking a compensatory response from the environment.

In the face of considerable complexity and perplexity, child psychotherapists are faced with considerable therapeutic difficulties, not least delinquents' antagonism, mistrust and equivocal motivation to change. Their responsibility is to find ways of engaging with young people to enable them to overcome their resistances to change and to make sense of the inner experience. This requires a capacity to develop an effective working alliance with young people, to manage the therapeutic potential of the transference and to adapt therapeutic approaches to meet the needs of the different kinds of delinquents. Child psychotherapists need to appreciate the depth of narcissistic disturbance that resides at the centre of much delinquent behaviour and to ensure a secure therapeutic setting in which delinquents can feel contained and facilitated to think. The main struggle in the psychotherapy of adolescents is about trust – to acknowledge and explore what is genuine and authentic. It is that which child psychotherapists search for and delinquents avoid, but need to find.

References

Aichhorn, A. (1965) *Delinquency and Child Guidance: Selected Papers*, New York: International Universities Press.

Bion, W. R. (1962) *Learning from Experience*, London: Heinemann.

Bowlby, J. (1951) *Maternal Care and Mental Health*, Geneva: World Health Organization.

Campbell, D. (1996) 'From practice to psychodynamic theories of delinquency in adolescence', in C. Cordess and M. Cox (eds) *Forensic Psychotherapy: Crime, Psychodynamics and the Offender Patient*, Vol. II, London: Jessica Kingsley.

Eissler, K. R. (1958) 'Notes on problems of technique in the psychoanalytic treatment of adolescents: with some remarks on perversions', *Psychoanalytic Study of the Child* 13, New York: International Universities Press.

Farrington, D. (1996) *Understanding and Preventing Youth Crime*, Joseph Rowntree Foundation/York: York Publishing Services.

—— (1997) 'A critical analysis of research and the development of antisocial behaviour from birth to adulthood', in D. M. Stoff, J. Breiling and J. D. Maser (eds) *Handbook of Antisocial Behaviour*, New York: Wiley.

Freud, A. (1965) *Normality and Pathology in Childhood*, New York: International Universities Press.

Freud, S. (1914) 'Remembering, repeating and working through', *Standard Edition*, Vol. 12, London: Hogarth.

Galway, P. (1991) 'Social maladjustment', in J. Holmes (ed.) *Textbook of Psychotherapy in Psychiatric Practice*, London: Churchill Livingstone.

Graham, P. (1991) *Child Psychiatry: A Developmental Approach*, 2nd edn, London: Oxford University Press.

Greenberg, H. (1975) 'The widening gyre: transformation of the omnipotent quest during adolescence', *International Review of Psychoanalysis* 2: 231–44.

Home Office (1995) *Aspects of Crime: Young Offenders 1993 Statistics* 1, London: Division of Home Office Research and Statistics Dept.

Horowitz, F. D. (1987) *Exploring Developmental Theories: Toward a Structural/Behavioural Model of Development*, Hillside, NJ: Erlbaum.

Jones, D. W. (1987) 'Recent developments in work with young offenders', in J. Coleman (ed.) *Working with Troubled Adolescents*, London: Academic Press.

Kazdin, A. E. (1997) 'Practitioner Review: psychosocial treatment of conduct disorder in children', *Journal of Child Psychology and Psychiatry* 38(2): 161–78.

Kohut, H. (1972) 'Thoughts on narcissism and narcissistic rage', *Psychoanalytic Study of the Child* 27, New York: International Universities Press.

Laufer, M. and Laufer, M. E. (1984) *Adolescence and Developmental Breakdown*, New Haven, CT: Yale University Press.

Meeks, J. E. (1971) *The Fragile Alliance: An Orientation to the Outpatient Psychotherapy of the Adolescent*, Baltimore: Williams and Wilkins.

Miller, D. (1983) *The Age Between: Adolescence and Therapy*, London: Jason Aronson.

NACRO (1988) *Diverting Juveniles from Custody*, London: NACRO.

Osorio, L. C. (1977) 'The psychoanalysis of communication in adolescents', in S. C. Feinstein and P. L. Giovacchini (eds) *Development and Clinical Studies*, Vol. 5, New York: Jason Aronson.

Rutter, M. (1985) 'Psychosocial therapies in child psychiatry: issues and prospects', in M. Rutter and L. Hersov (eds) *Child and Adolescent Psychiatry: Modern Approaches*, 2nd edn, Oxford: Blackwell.

Sheldrick, C. (1985) 'Treatment of delinquents', in M. Rutter and L. Hersov (eds) *Child and Adolescent Psychiatry: Modern Approaches*, 2nd edn, Oxford: Blackwell.

Stoller, R. (1975) *Perversion: The Erotic Form of Hatred*, New York: Pantheon Books.

Utting, D., Bright, J. and Henricson, C. (1993) *Crime and the Family: Improving Child Rearing and Preventing Delinquency*, London: Family Policy Studies.

Wadsworth, M. (1979) *The Roots of Delinquency*, London: Martin Robertson.

Wilson, P. (1991) 'Psychotherapy with adolescents', in J. Holmes (ed.) *Textbook of Psychotherapy in Psychiatric Practice*, London: Churchill Livingstone.

Wilson, P. and Hersov, L. (1985) 'Individual and group psychotherapy', in M. Rutter and L. Hersov (eds) *Child and Adolescent Psychiatry: Modern Approaches*, 2nd edn, London: Blackwell.

Winnicott, D. W. (1960a) 'Classification: is there a psychoanalytic contribution to psychiatric classification (1959–64)', in D. W. Winnicott *The Maturational Processes and the Facilitating Environment*, London: Hogarth.

—— (1960b) 'The theory of the parent-infant relationship', in D. W. Winnicott (1965) *The Maturational Processes and the Facilitating Environment*, London: Hogarth.

—— (1965) *The Maturational Processes and the Facilitating Environment*, London: Hogarth.

Further reading

Cordess, C. and Cox, M. (eds) (1996) *Forensic Psychotherapy: Crime, Psychodynamics and the Offender Patient*, London: Jessica Kingsley, Vol. I, Chapters 2, 7, 8, 10; Vol. II, Chapters 7, 17, 18, 20, 23.

Holmes, J. (1991) *Textbook of Psychotherapy in Psychiatric Practice*, London: Churchill Livingstone, Chapters 14, 15, 19.

Freud, A. (1965) *Normality and Pathology in Childhood: Assessments of Development*, New York: International Universities Press, Chapters 4 and 5.

27 Working with people with eating disorders

'What if I die without knowing why?'

Roberta Mondadori

Introduction

what if i die?
before i've made up my mind
whether or not i want
to live?
(and now i lay me down to sleep
pray my heart is not too weak
to let me live just one more day
in case my hatred blows away)[1]

This very poignant poem was written by a fifteen-year-old anorexic girl, Emma, who does not refer to herself with a capital 'I' in her diary. The painful account of Emma's illness and slow recovery was written and published by her loving godmother (Lee 2004). Emma finds herself in the grip of an internal conflict, a battle between life and death, for no apparent motive. Why do Emma and so many other girls, belonging to different countries, backgrounds, social and religious cultures, let themselves fall into a pit from which some of them will never climb out? Why do they refuse help, in spite of their deep unhappiness?

Anorexia, with its counterpart, bulimia, has become one of the most widespread mental illnesses, and the number of people suffering from these disorders is still increasing.

This chapter will try to supply some indications of what seems to lie at the root of such illness, following a Kleinian perspective. My clinical experience is based on my work in an Adolescent Service in the Community (CAMHS) as well as in private practice. Valuable insights have also been provided by members of the Eating Disorder MA Courses at the Tavistock (London) and in Bologna (Italy), who work in different settings and have different professional roles.

What anorexia and bulimia are

Anorexia and bulimia are complex syndromes, and represent a wide range of psychopathologies. The conflict at the root of their symptoms, as described in DSM-IV (American Psychiatric Association 1995), is a morbid fear of fatness. The difference is that anorexics achieve their goal, while bulimics do not and are often looked down on in hospitals by the 'real' anorexics.

Both anorexia and bulimia can be life-threatening disorders: it has been suggested that up to 10 per cent of anorexics die from their illness and bulimics occasionally do (American Psychiatric Association 1995). This means that more people die from eating disorders than die each year from any other mental illness. Anorexics with bulimia and bulimics show more frequent use of alcohol and drugs, as well as episodes of self-harming by cutting. Eating disorders are often associated with other psychiatric disturbances, such as depression, anxiety, and obsessive compulsive behaviours.

Eating disorders are largely prevalent in affluent Western countries but immigrants to these countries are also particularly vulnerable; the illness may be precipitated by problems of transition, dislocation and cultural changes (Treasure *et al.* 2003). The percentage of male cases appears to be smaller in anorexia (8 per cent) than in bulimia (roughly 15 per cent) (Treasure *et al.* 2003).

Having an eating disorder can become a way of life: the syndrome is used in order to hide other problems and the body becomes the vehicle where conflicts and emotions are handled. Constant thinking about food and calories, dieting, restriction to only certain food, exercising, become the focus of anorexics' and bulimics' lives. In the less severe cases an ordinary life continues, but minds are still preoccupied with food and fear of fat.

Linking feeding difficulties in children with eating disorders in adolescents

The usual explanation that anorexics give for their starvation is terror of fatness. Most of them believe they are fat, in spite of their emaciated state; others, possibly more insightful or with a less severe pathology, recognise that this is not the case. They would say, 'I know I am not fat, but I don't know why I have stopped eating' or, 'I say I am afraid of being fat because it is what people expect to hear.' These statements can, however, be denied a moment later, which implies that an exploration of other meanings and a need for help is too terrifying.

The link between feeding difficulties in children and eating disorders later on in life, which has been made by some clinicians, provides fruitful ground for future research.

The following is an account of an infant observation conducted following the discipline initiated by Esther Bick in 1940, where a newborn baby is regularly observed by a student for one or two years. This method has increased understanding of the emotional states of infants, providing valuable insights into the early mother–baby relationship and consequently the feeding relationship.

Tina

Tina is the first child of a young couple: father is English and mother is from Eastern Europe. At birth Tina was delivered later than expected by an emergency caesarean section. Mother returned home feeling exhausted; her state was exacerbated by two bouts of mastitis during Tina's fourth and fifth weeks of age. Since the mastitis affected only one breast at a time, mother was able to continue the breastfeeding, even if it was painful.

Both mother and baby enjoyed the breastfeeding, with loving and happy interactions between them. However, when Tina was seven weeks old, mother had a third bout of mastitis and could not continue the breastfeeding. She looked sad and upset, and was lonely because her parents, who had come to stay with their daughter for the baby's birth, had returned to their home country. Father worked long hours and was often away. The observer noted that there was now a sense of distance between mother and baby, which was graphically expressed by the introduction of the dummy and by mother's worry that she had suddenly forgotten the nursery rhymes she used to sing to Tina in her own language.

Although the transition from the breast to the bottle seemed smooth, something of the liveliness in the nursing couple's relationship had disappeared. The home atmosphere was quiet and lifeless. Mother often complained about Tina's restlessness and aggressiveness at feeding times; her words, however, were in sharp contrast to the observer's perception of Tina as a relaxed and contented baby, both during and after feeds. It seemed that the weaning process had been accepted better by the baby than by the mother. The real feeding difficulties began when solid foods were introduced, around Tina's fifth month: Tina's attitude to food and to her mother now had a marked and even hostile manner. She was suspicious of any new item, though she did in the end accept them, but avoided any eye contact. She also wanted to hold on to spoons or little food containers, often repeatedly throwing these on the floor and demanding them back in a very controlling way. She would adamantly refuse to continue to eat if there was any interruption such as a telephone call or the observer's voice, in contrast with her usually friendly mood. Mother passively accepted her child's hostility and control without trying to understand this change, or to make feeding times more enjoyable.

At times there were improvements, but on the whole the situation remained the same until the end of the observation. Tina, at two years of age, was certainly a happy, resourceful and bright little girl, able to engage actively with her parents and with the observer. However, her hostile and controlling attitude around food issues had not changed much.

This is not one of those cases where a baby fails to thrive or where developmental difficulties take place, but it provides a clear example of how something can easily go wrong between the nursing couple. Tina's and mother's love and affection for each other could not counteract the ambivalence which found an expression in the feeding encounter. Tina was able to accept gracefully the loss of the breast, therefore helping her mother in her seemingly both depressed and guilty states for not receiving enough support and for not being able to continue the breastfeeding. However, when Tina had to start eating solid food she exhibited great suspicion about what she was given and resentment towards her mother.

There is no evidence that Tina will develop an eating disorder as a girl, and her sunny, inquisitive and resilient temperament are good indicators to the contrary. The majority of children who present some sort of feeding difficulties at some stage – the percentage of males and females is equal – will not develop eating disorders later on. However, clinical experience shows that people who develop eating disorders experienced less or more serious difficulties as babies. Tina did not refuse to eat, but the problems in the feeding relationship were expressed as suspicion of new food, together with her avoidance of acknowledging where the nourishment came from; in her lack of enjoyment of the food coming from her mother and in her refusal to eat whenever the unconscious phantasy of oneness was disrupted as shown in her intolerance of any external interference. These are characteristics of eating disordered patients. The latter attitude is particularly reminiscent of the anorexic's refusal to eat if the person who supervises their meals, usually the mother, is distracted, even if only for one moment.

There are several factors which might have contributed to Tina's ambivalence towards her mother and which only found expression in the food area: one is mother's mastitis, which made the breastfeeding painful. Tina might have perceived mother's pain and discomfort which negatively coloured her phantasies while at the breast, and later on were shown both in her avoiding and aggressive attitude around food. Another important element is mother's sense of displacement and isolation, strengthened by the lack of a husband who could support his wife as well as provide some space between the nursing couple. Was mother's distress and perhaps anger about her own predicament projected into her baby? Was Tina's ambivalent acceptance of the food provided by mother a reaction for being at the receiving end of unwanted projections? While each of these features displayed by Tina would not in themselves be particularly worrying, what makes this picture more concerning are their relentlessness and continuation. The tension and the anxieties which pervaded the feeding perceived by the observer reveal how much the giving and the receiving was without pleasure: mother was not sure that what she offered could be accepted and enjoyed.

It is very significant that Williams (2004) has given the subtitle *The Generosity of Acceptance* to the two volumes she co-edited about eating disorders (Williams *et al.* 2004), pointing out the difficulty that these patients have in accepting from another person. This includes becoming dependent and therefore facing the risk of rejection, thus showing that they have not been able to build up a secure internal object.

Psychoanalytic views and the process of building a good internal object

It was Melanie Klein's theory of object relations which was of great importance in thinking about development of eating disorders. If the baby–mother relationship is the first and the most important in the building of the child's internal world, it follows that a good or ambivalent relationship to the breast will inevitably colour all the subsequent relationships.

Klein wrote of the importance of the process of building a good object inside ourselves, which comes from repeated good experiences of taking in something which comes from the outside: especially from mother's milk and love. When an identification with a secure object is established the ego is strengthened and is able to preserve its identity (Klein, 1957). If this does not happen, introjection of a good object is then impaired. In her work about manic defences (1935), Klein makes a very important link between feeding difficulties in very young children and their fear of introjecting dangerous objects and stresses the role of aggression in infantile development.

Anna Freud (1946) suggests that children's conflicting behaviour towards food originates 'from conflicting emotions towards the mother, which are transferred to the food, the symbol for the mother'.

Briggs (1988), in stressing the analogy between bodily process – the feeding – and emotional and mental processes, suggests that when the maternal containment of the baby's anxieties is inadequate, the development of particular feeding difficulties might take place. We can then observe a failure in the 'container-contained' relationship, described by Bion (1962), which jeopardises the child's process of internalisation.

Williams (1997) suggests that with some patients, and among them the severely anorexic, it is possible to think that not only the infant's own anxieties have been uncontained by the mother and instead returned back in an undigested form (Bion's 'nameless dread', 1962) but some of the mother's own anxieties may have been projected into the infant. Thus there is a reversal of the container–contained relationship: the baby, instead of being contained, is at the receiving end of the mother's projections. The child might try to defend himself from such projections, which he does not have the means of digesting, by developing disturbed patterns of taking in nourishment. Williams suggests that these patients have developed a 'no-entry system' of defences. In these cases the development of the process of mentally and emotionally taking in from the mother is impaired. There is no secure internalisation of a good object, which is a prerequisite for the development of the child's healthy dependence on the mother and the consequent capacity later on to separate from her, gradually acquiring a sense of separateness and its own identity.

Anorexia: a protective shield or a lethal addiction?

It is around puberty when the child feels the push to separate from his family, both internally and externally, that the first signs of some disturbance in development appear. Very often anorexics are described as having been obedient, adequate, complacent little girls. This picture changes dramatically around puberty and adolescence. Instead of healthy, even if at times violent attempts to turn away and find their own ways of thinking and behaving, in other words to build their own identities, as displayed by their peers, the anorexic girls try to achieve the same goals by resorting to desperate manoeuvres in the area of food.

The very ambivalent and conflicting feelings towards food – mother's milk – experienced in the early mother–baby relationship, feelings which might have remained dormant during latency, are now violently re-experienced. The adolescent girl, whose body is becoming similar to her mother's, is afraid of not being able to differentiate from her, of concretely becoming her mother, thus losing herself; she re-experiences the wish for and the fear of a fusion with her mother, as many authors have emphasised (Bruch 1974; Boris 1984; Sprince 1984; Hughes *et al.* 1985; Birksted-Breen 1989; Lawrence 2002). Anorexia represents the girl's desperate attempt to have her own body, separated from her own mother's body; it also gives her the possibility to remain mother's little girl for ever. By refusing to move towards adulthood, she avoids all the challenges of growing up, of making choices, for which she does not feel sufficiently equipped, particularly becoming part of the sexual couple. The anorexic sees herself as having succeeded in acquiring her own body and her own identity: she is now 'the anorexic girl'. However, she soon discovers that this state, where the passing of time and the difference between sexes are denied, is at once both idealised and terrifying. The anorexic solution has become a lethal trap, in which she feels totally stuck. Consciously or unconsciously anorexics know that what they have acquired is a temporary solution, a poor and false substitute for something fundamental which is lacking in themselves. They are faced with an impossible dilemma, since seeking help means running the risk of being stripped of their defences, the anorexic state, and having to face their deep underlying anxieties. It is then not surprising that eating disordered patients are so reluctant to accept treatment.

Sarah[2]

Sarah was seventeen when she was referred to a CAMHS Adolescent Service after her admission to the local hospital because of anorexia. Her eating problems dated back to her primary school, but this was the first time that her weight had dropped dramatically, to seven stone. Sarah knew she needed help as she was also afraid of her suicidal impulses and agreed to start twice-weekly therapy on the ward, and then to continue in the local Adolescent Service.

A thin but not emaciated, and attractive girl, Sarah is an only child. Her parents recently separated after years of unhappy marriage. This seemed the precipitating factor for her weight drop, but Sarah denied any possible link and was pleased for her mother, since she hated her father and believed that the separation should have taken place much earlier.

Another puzzling, but not unusual feature in anorexics, was her not knowing the reason why she had stopping eating: she saw herself as too fat but at the same time she knew she wasn't.

Sarah's attitude to the therapy was also quizzical: she was extremely suspicious of what I would give her, refusing any exploration of her own feelings and emotions. I was very often left feeling confused and lost, inadequate and rejected: I was made to feel that I had nothing helpful to give her. Nevertheless she complained that two sessions a week were not sufficient.

The extent of how her anorexic relationship to food was mirrored in her relationships became clear when, after her weight improved, plans were made for her to leave the hospital. During her first weekend at home she went to a party where she fell unconscious and was brought back to hospital in an ambulance.

I quote from a session which followed.

> 'Sarah flatly described that she had been reluctant to go to the party because she felt fat and ugly. Then at the party a girl had complained to her that she had been dumped by her boyfriend. Sarah had felt guilty for not wanting to be involved with her friend's problem. She had become panicky, couldn't breathe and had fallen unconscious. She added lightly, however, that she was looking forward to leaving the hospital soon, but was not sure about continuing her sessions, as "all her badness had now come out". Feeling extremely worried about Sarah's denial of the severity of her state, I commented on her apparent lack of concern about finding herself without the safety net of the hospital and of the therapeutic support. At this point Sarah began to cough so violently that I was afraid she was going to throw up. Only when I suggested that my words had been perceived as if I was forcing her to swallow something disgusting, something which, far from being helpful, was felt as very intrusive, did her cough diminish and she relaxed.'

In the session Sarah had projected her anxieties into me. I had to experience, as I did, her feeling of rejection and her fear for her own survival. Not surprisingly, my attempt to show her that her perception of reality had no basis had been seen as a return of her own projections, moreover they were increased by my own worries. My words were thus equated with disgusting and lethal food.

It seems that the girl at the party who had been abandoned by her boyfriend mirrored in Sarah's eyes her terror of being 'dumped' by the hospital environment, a terror which she had completely denied. She felt so invaded by panic that she had become unconscious.

This understanding on my part led me to hold on to Sarah's projections without trying to push her towards both an exploration of herself and of the transference relationship which was premature.

Very gradually feeling more contained and less challenged, Sarah began to accept my help; consequently her anorexic symptoms improved. However, at the same time her suicidal impulses became stronger, and she bitterly complained that I had taken away her anorexia, which was her protective shield, whose aim was to keep fears and psychic pain at bay. Containing her fears without being myself overwhelmed by anxieties about Sarah's survival became the essential centre of our work.

It was only much later on in the therapy that Sarah had the courage to begin to try to explore her internal world, which was full of cold, unreliable and violent figures, of which the most powerful was a cruel parental couple from which she felt totally rejected. This had very little to do with her real parents, who were described to me as an ordinary couple. At the same time Sarah's guilt for having succeeded in destroying, in her mind, her parents' marriage in order to have her mother all to herself, was so unbearable that it could only be denied and led her to attack herself.

When her persecutory feelings lessened, and her internal objects became more benign, Sarah was able to resume her life, finish her A Levels successfully and start a job. It was before the summer break in the third year of her therapy that Sarah suddenly decided to follow her boyfriend on a round-the-world trip, which was going to start the following Christmas. However, when we met after the holiday, Sarah told me that the departure date had been brought forward to the end of October. We thus had only very limited time to work through the end.

I now quote from a session around this time.

'Sarah said she had fainted a few days before, for no apparent reason, since she was now eating regularly. She was furious because two valuable bags had disappeared from the shop where she worked. A woman had then brought them back, asking for a refund. Sarah had refused because she knew that the woman had stolen the bags, but her boss, who was both lazy and a coward, had "lacked the guts" to confront the woman and had given her the refund. I said that apparently she felt that I, too, was very lazy since I had left her over the summer to do all the work by herself; moreover she felt that I was not able to confront her theft of two valuable months therapy before the previous planned date. Sarah looked sheepish and stressed apologetically that it had been her boyfriend's idea to bring forward their trip. On the other hand, she was fed up with all this endless thinking and talking during the sessions. I said that the moment she became aware of depriving herself of my help she also refused to recognise its value and did not want to resume thinking together.

Towards the end of the session Sarah looked around and said movingly that she would miss our room, the pictures on the wall and the trees outside. It had been a long journey from her admission to hospital and the beginning of her therapy.'

It is interesting to note that as in the session quoted before, Sarah again reacts by fainting when she is confronted with something unpalatable: in this case the stealing of what she had come to consider as very valuable, her therapeutic time. The summer break certainly reactivated her anxieties: the realisation of our separateness with subsequent feeling of rejection; her intolerance of having to share her therapist with others; and finally her fear of intimacy which is both desirable and terrifying. However, now Sarah is more aware of the meaning of her acting out and expects me to confront her destructiveness and is able to take in my 'food' instead of spitting it out.

She regretted her decision to leave but did not change her mind, which indicates how powerful the conflict of her childhood, the wish to be completely fused with a mother figure and the terror of being trapped, still was. This time, however, she found a much healthier solution, taking the risk of a move into adulthood. In our last sessions her sadness and gratitude for the help received confirmed that she was experiencing more depressive feelings, far away from the persecutory feelings which had led her to the start of her anorexia and of her suicidal ideations. She also kept in touch with me, through a series of thoughtful postcards from different countries, which were aimed both to keep herself in my mind and also to reassure me that she was all right.

We know very little about Sarah's early relationship with her mother, but her difficulties around food as a child seem to indicate a failure in the nursing couple, therefore a failure in the 'container–contained' relationship (Bion 1962). Williams's (1997) already-mentioned description of the consequences if there is a reversal of such a relationship seems present in Sarah's pathology. Her refusal of help, her lack of a sense of herself, and the massive use of projecting outside what was unbearable to her indicate that she might have been herself an infant who had been the receptacle of mother's anxieties.

Another feature of Sarah's internal world is the presence of an 'abnormal' form of the superego, which Bion (1962) has called the 'ego-destructive superego'. Instead of a 'normal' superego, the anorexics have internalised a very harsh superego which tries to convince the ego to turn away from life and destroy itself (O'Shaughnessy 1999).

Rosenfeld (1971) also describes a terrifying presence that acts as an internal 'gang' which offers a protection from psychic pain to its members, but requires total obedience. The increase of Sarah's suicidal thoughts during her therapy when she abandons 'the protective shield' of anorexia shows that she believed she should punish herself for having defied this inimical presence by allying herself to the therapy.

Which treatment?

Anorexics often do not perceive anorexia as a problem; on the contrary they are afraid of being without the therapeutic function of the symptom, therefore they are reluctant to form and maintain a therapeutic relationship. Several psychodynamic authors, among others Bruch (1974) and Selvini-Palazzoli (1978), have come to the conclusion that psychoanalysis is not the treatment for anorexia, since the anorexic is impervious to interpretation. Knowledge and food go together; they are both persecutory and create precisely what the anorexic rejects, a sense of being full, saturated, while the therapist becomes the mother of her early experience who stuffs her.

Although this view is certainly true, as so many clinicians have painfully experienced themselves, the meaning of the anorexic symptom is so buried in the unconscious that psychoanalytic psychotherapy and psychoanalysis are the best therapeutic approaches, provided that these potential obstacles are borne in mind (Boris 1984).

Communication and understanding can sometimes only take place through the use of countertransference and projective identification (see Chapter 10). Containing the patient's projections, tolerating one's own feelings of rejection, frustration, anger and in the most severe cases anxieties about the patient's survival, form in clinical experience the only equipment, even for long periods of time.

Exploring, linking and interpreting, if premature, are not accepted, as I have described in my vignette about Sarah; the anorexic is immediately faced with the unbearable image of two people coming together, a parental couple (Britton 1989) from which she feels excluded.

There is no space for a father in the mother–anorexic daughter relationship. The father is not necessarily absent; what is missing is the parental function. The anorexic's description of her father as passive, distant, not at ease with his adolescent daughter; or as violent, abusive, 'disgusting', might at times appear similar with reality – increasingly cases of abusive fathers or male figures have been reported. However, very often this picture is far from being a realistic one, and needs to be challenged: the lack of the paternal function is much more caused by the omnipotent phantasy shared by the mother and daughter couple that theirs is the only couple. It is only when a space for a third object is created that anorexia, which has replaced the space, is no longer needed.

Some authors (Selvini-Palazzoli 1978; Minuchin *et al.* 1978) have stressed the importance of family therapy for eating disordered patients, as they believe that the dysfunctional family is a major cause for one of the members' illness. Other clinicians consider family therapy with adolescent anorexics a helpful starting point, but that it is necessary later on to offer the anorexic individual treatment, in order to get at the root of the symptom. It is a general view that when the preferred treatment is individual therapy, the anorexic's parents too are offered help (see Chapter 13): parents are often at a loss and overwhelmed by feelings of guilt, rage, impotence and despair, and need support in order to bear their own emotions and to understand the nature of their child's illness.

A common view among clinicians from different perspectives is the vital need for *early* intervention in order to prevent the illness from becoming chronic and thus much more difficult to treat.

Concluding remarks

Finally, the characteristic features of eating disordered patients can be found in other patients who have not developed such a disorder. We know that the enmeshment in the mother–daughter relationship, the lack of a paternal function, the destructiveness of the superego, the difficulty of acknowledging one's needs and a consequent reluctance to accept help, and the fear of dependency are present in different measure in many narcissistic personalities. However, what is unique in anorexics and bulimics is the degree of their destructiveness, their attraction to death. This, accompanied by their delusional determination to fend off views different from theirs, makes the task of treating these patients particularly challenging and disheartening. However, to return to Emma, whose poem is quoted at the beginning, these are people who suffer deeply 'without knowing why' and need all the help we can provide.

Notes

1 'What if I die' by Emma from *To Die For: A Young Woman's Battle with Anorexia* by Carol Lee, is reprinted by permission of The Random House Group Ltd.
2 This material in a different form first appeared in *Exploring Eating Disorders in Adolescents* edited by G. Williams *et al.* (2004).

References

American Psychiatric Association (1995) *Diagnostic and Statistical Manual of Mental Disorders (DSM-IV)*, Washington DC: American Psychiatric Association.
Bion, W. (1962) *Learning from Experience*, London: Heinemann.
Birksted-Breen, D. (1989) 'Working with an anorexic patient', *International Journal of Psychoanalysis* 77: 29–40.
Boris, H. (1984) 'The problem of anorexia nervosa', *International Journal of Psychoanalysis* 65: 315–22.
Briggs, S. (1988) 'The contribution of infant observation to an understanding of feeding difficulties in infancy', *International Journal of Infant Observation* 1: 44–59.

Britton, R. (1989) *The Missing Link in The Oedipus Complex Today*, London: Karnac, pp. 83–101.

Bruch, H. (1974) *Eating Disorders: Obesity, Anorexia Nervosa and the Person Within*, London: Routledge.

Freud, A. (1946) 'The psychoanalytic study of infantile feeding disturbances', in *The Psychoanalytic Study of the Child*, Vol. II, London: Hogarth Press, pp. 119–132.

Hughes, A., Furgiele, P. and Bianco, M. (1985) 'Aspects of anorexia nervosa in the therapy of two adolescents', *Journal of Child Psychotherapy* 11(1): 17–32.

Klein, M. (1935) 'A contribution to the psychogenesis of manic-depressive states', in *The Writings of Melanie Klein*, Vol. 1, *Love, Guilt and Reparation and Other Works*, London: Hogarth Press (1975), pp. 262–89.

—— (1957) 'Envy and gratitude', in *The Writings of Melanie Klein*, Vol. 3, *Envy and Gratitude and Other Works*, London: Hogarth Press (1975), pp. 176–235.

Lawrence, M. (2002) 'Body, mother, mind, anorexia, femininity and the intrusive object', *International Journal of Psychoanalysis* 83(4): 837–50.

Lee, C. (2004) *To Die For*, London: Century.

Minuchin, S., Rosman, B. and Barker, L. (1978) *Psychosomatic Families: Anorexia Nervosa in Context*, New York: Harvard University Press.

O'Shaughnessy, E. (1999) 'Relating to the superego', *International Journal of Psychoanalysis* 80: 861–70.

Rosenfeld, H. (1971) 'A clinical approach to the psychoanalytic theory of the life and death instincts: an investigation into the aggressive aspects of narcissism', *International Journal of Psychoanalysis* 52: 169–78.

Selvini-Palazzoli, M. (1978) *Self-starvation: From the Individual to Family Therapy in the Treatment of Anorexia Nervosa*, New York: Jason Aronson.

Sprince, M. (1984) 'Early psychic disturbances in anorexic and bulimic patients as reflected in the psychoanalytic process', *Journal of Child Psychotherapy* 10(2): 199–205.

Treasure, J., Schmidt, U. and van Furth, E. (2003) *Handbook of Eating Disorders*, Chichester: Wiley.

Williams, G. (1997) *The 'No Entry' System of Defences in Internal Landscapes and Foreign Bodies: Eating Disorders and Other Pathologies*, London: Duckworth, pp. 115–22.

Williams, G., Williams, P., Desmarais, J., Ravenscroft, K. (eds) (2003) *Exploring Feeding Difficulties in Children (Vol. I), Exploring Eating Disorders in Adolescents (Vol. II), The Generosity of Acceptance*, London: Karnac.

Further reading

Caparrotta, L. and Ghaffari, K. (2006) 'A historical overview of the psychodynamic contributions to the understanding of eating disorders', *Psychoanalytic Psychotherapy* 20(3): 175–96.

Lask, B. and Bryant-Waugh, R. (eds) (2007) *Eating Disorders in Childhood and Adolescence*, Hove: Routledge.

Lawrence, M. (2008) *The Anorexic Mind*, London: Karnac.

Psychoanalytic Psychotherapy (2004) Special edition on eating disorders, 18(4).

28 Gender identity dysphoria

Barbara Gaffney and Paulina Reyes

Introduction

Charlie was sixteen when she was referred for psychotherapy because of extreme distress about being a girl. She would cry inconsolably at the time of her monthly periods and it would take her some days to overcome her feelings of horror at her body's reasserted femaleness, so at odds with her own sense of male identity. She had felt she was a boy since she could remember and when she first heard about the existence of 'sex-change operations' she clung to that as the only solution to her predicament. Her conflict had come to a head during the pubertal changes accompanying adolescence. With the onset of the menarche she had started having suicidal feelings which caused extreme concern in her parents and was affecting her otherwise good school life. By the time the therapist met Charlie, she was extremely distrustful of anyone who tried to explore her feelings of identity and her conceptions of femaleness and maleness, and their meanings for her. From this description of Charlie's feelings we get a vivid illustration of gender identity dysphoria.

In Charlie and other children and teenagers like her, we encounter one of the most basic and painful of possible alienations, that of psyche and body, where the body is felt to be so alien to one's sense of self that it cannot act as the physical container for the psyche. They find themselves in a radical dissociation that does not allow them to develop in a more or less seamless interaction with the self and with the social environment. Rather, the body is felt to be constantly negating the child's sense of who he or she is and the later arrival of pubertal bodily changes are experienced as an attack on the very core of the sense of identity.

Developments in the understanding of sex and gender

The nineteenth century saw growing interest in sexual behaviour; atypical sexual behaviour in particular became an object of study in the medical literature. Freud's ideas revolutionised even further the understanding of human sexuality, particularly with the publication of *The Interpretation Of Dreams* (1900) and *Three Essays on Sexuality* (1905) where he put forward the idea that sexuality was not only determined by inheritance, bio-chemistry and organic factors, but also by life's experiences from infancy onward. Freud juxtaposed with this his important insight about the bisexual nature of human sexuality: that men and women are bisexual at the interface of their biological and psychological strata. This conceptualisation also emphasised that all sexual behaviour forms part of a continuum stemming from an ever-present neonatal bisexual potential.

The appearance of the diagnostic category of 'transsexualism' was not the result of a theoretical breakthrough. Rather it appeared as the result of the development of surgical treatment in the 1950s for what was thought at the time to be an extreme form of transvestism. The term 'gender dysphoria', in turn, emerged from a consensus a decade later about the diagnosis of transsexualism, and it was often used to indicate the extreme affects, in particular depressed affects, experienced by transsexuals, who were found to be much more distressed than transvestites by the incon-gruity between their gender identity and their biological sex.

The relative independence of gender and sex

In the 1950s, John Money conducted studies that led his team to differ-entiate between a set of feelings, assertions and behaviours which define maleness and femaleness, which they called 'gender role', as distinct from the biological characteristics which define a person's sex. Money (1955a) did extensive work to prove his thesis that sex and gender are not necessarily directly interrelated. Later (1955b) he defined the term 'gender role' as a set of feelings, assertions and behaviours that identify a person as being a boy or a girl.

The concept of gender identity

After many years of research Money concluded that 'gender identity' and 'gender roles' were even more complex than he had anticipated and that 'gender dysphoria' related to complex and multiple physiological and psychological causes, by which he meant that children with 'gender identity development disorder' were a very distinct group who were very entrenched in their identification with the opposite sex (Money 1994).

A study group on identity at the University of California in the mid-1960s was the first to use the term 'gender identity'. Robert Stoller (physician and psychoanalyst) defined it as:

a complex system of beliefs about oneself: a sense of one's masculinity and femininity. It implies nothing about the origins of that sense (e.g.

whether the person is biologically male or female). It has, then, psychological connotations only: one's subjective state.

(Stoller 1968)

Additionally, Stoller designated as 'core gender identity' the child's aware-ness of being either a boy or a girl, which develops during the first year of life. In his view this 'core gender identity' is the product of the interaction of three variables: the infant–parent relationship, the child's perception of its external genitalia, and the biological force that springs from the biological variables of sex.

It is important to exclude from this debate 'sexual orientation', which refers to erotic object choice: a person may know that he/she is a man or woman but choose a same-sex or opposite-sex sexual partner. Stoller differentiated between transvestite and transsexual boys, defining the first group as being fetishistic – sexually aroused when wearing women's clothes, they first go through a phase of clear-cut masculinity. Transsexual-ism, on the contrary, starts early, even appearing by the end the first year and 'it more completely possesses the boy's gender'.

Theories of cause and incidence of gender identity disorder

Stoller indicated that he could find no evidence that there was any genetic, constitutional or biochemical abnormality in most transsexuals. In 1976 he linked gender identity disorder with a mother–infant symbiosis wherein the father was either psychologically or physically absent. For girls, he sug-gested a depressed mother during the first months of life and again an absent or unsupportive father. Depicting the cases of three young boys whom he saw at the ages of between four and five because they insisted that they were girls and had feminine gestures, he described the mothers as 'neuter' in their appearance and demeanour. They had been boyish young women, and all were unhappy with their marriages. The fathers were busy with their own lives and not attentive to the children, so the boys lacked male role models.

The idea that socialisation can produce a permanent gender identity was challenged in 1979 by J. Imperato-McGinley *et al.* who reported the case of thirty-three children born in a village in the Dominican Republic with a rare hormonal disorder. At birth most had been labelled girls and lived as girls until puberty, when their bodies manifested and functioned according to their biological maleness. After this momentous change they all managed to change to a masculine identity.

Richard Green undertook a longitudinal study of a population of children who appeared to be at risk of a transsexual adult life (Green 1987; Green *et al.* 1987). He reported a fifteen-year follow-up of a sample of fifty 'feminine boys' who exhibited a high degree of cross-gender behaviour. These boys were matched with a control group of fifty boys of comparable age, ethnicity and parental education. The major finding of the study to date is that 'feminine boys' are more likely than most boys to mature into homosexual or bisexual men. Only one boy in the study had a transsexual outcome. These findings certainly suggest that not every feminine boy grows up to cross-dress, but they do not tell us much about the genesis of transsexualism. Green carefully tested Stoller's assertions that mothers who spent too much time holding their boys may have made them feminine, but Green's data did not support this hypothesis. He was able to show that feminine boys spent less time with their fathers, but it is not clear whether this was a cause or a consequence of their feminine behaviour.

The incidence of childhood cross-gender identification has not yet been definitely established. Zucker *et al.* (1985) and Green (1968) both state that cross-gender behaviours are uncommon among the general population of boys and there is too little epidemiological research regarding girls to be able to make a statement.

Coates and Spector Person (1985) have shown that children with gender identity disorders also present with separation anxiety, depression and emotional and behavioural difficulties. In a number of children referred to the Gender Identity Unit at the Tavistock Clinic, learning difficulties and school refusal are also evident. In a small percentage of cases, child sexual abuse has been associated with a gender disorder. Suicidal attempts in adolescents are frequent; indeed, this can be how they come to professional attention.

One can therefore say that no single cause has been identified for the development of atypical gender identity. A number of authors (see Money 1994 and Coates 1990) agree that many biological and socio-psychological factors need to be present at the same time and work together during a critical period to produce a real gender identity disorder. There have been studies of hereditary and genetic factors which could play a part in influencing gender-specific behaviour; however, these factors by themselves are not considered to produce gender identity disorder (Michael and Zumpe 1996). According to Brain:

> An individual's core-gender identity and sexual orientation evolve as a consequence of many complex factors on the background of genetic predisposition and humoral conditioning. Further reproducible data from ongoing research is clearly needed before we can attempt to understand fully this fascinating conundrum.
>
> (Brain 1998: 78)

As the causes of gender identity disorder (GID) are unclear and multifactorial, the primary therapeutic aim should not be to alter the child's gender identity disorder as such but to try to facilitate the child's development by addressing any associated emotional, behavioural and relationship difficulties.

Psychoanalytical views of GID

From the psychoanalytical literature there seemed to be at first two distinct views about the causality of GID. Some writers linked it to a pre-Oedipal wish to merge with the mother, so there would be no conflict for the boy between the desire for the mother and the fear of retaliation from the father. In the view of these authors psychotherapy or psychoanalysis would not be able to effect change because psychoanalytical treatment is based on the resolution of unconscious conflict. The main representative of this non-conflictual view is Stoller (1975), who thinks that a behavioural approach should be the treatment choice.

Other writers link GID to early object loss, abandonment and/or abuse, whereby the symptoms would be a compromise solution due to intra-psychic conflict and then the gender identity disorder would be a defence against anxiety. These authors think that if those conflictual issues are addressed in the therapy the child may be able to find more benign defences and overcome the cross-gender identification. Two representatives of these views are reviewed below.

Bleiberg *et al.* (1986) link gender identity disorder, in a particular sub-group of boys, to early maternal object loss, and they found that therapeutic work which centres on issues of separation, loss, abandonment and concerns about trust in parenting and caring figures brings positive change in gender identity.

Coates *et al.* (1991) describe familial influences on GID in boys – mother/son dyad, father/son relationship and marital and family dynamics – concluding that the cross-gender fantasy allows the child to manage traumatic levels of anxiety. They consider it a rare disorder that appears before the pre-Oedipal phase due to an interaction of biological, developmental and psychological factors. Temperament, family traits and state, and severe stress lead into a common pathway in which massive anxiety occurs in the child during a developmentally sensitive and vulnerable period. They have found that early therapeutic intervention, before the boy reaches the age of five, plus work with the family, can reverse the boy's cross-gender identification.

Treatment

The Gender Identity Development Clinic

Working as child and adolescent psychotherapists in the Gender Identity Development Clinic, we have had a unique opportunity to see many teenagers and children with difficulties in gender development, and subsequently to explore and begin to understand with them the many interacting influences in the development of a sense of self. The service was started in 1989 by Domenico Di Ceglie, child psychiatrist, as a response to the increase in the number of young people self-harming due to gender issues. Since then it has grown and evolved into a specialist, national, multidisciplinary service based in London at the Tavistock and Portman NHS Trust.

A range of children and adolescents are seen. These include those who have expressed gender dysphoria; children whose parents are concerned by their cross-dressing and enduring gender dissonant behaviour (Green 1987; Zucker *et al.* 1985); teenagers who may cross-dress either wishing to be of the opposite sex (transsexual) or wishing for comfort or sexual arousal (transvestic fetishistic) (Bradley 1998). The service has been involved with the Royal College of Psychiatrists in the establishment of national guidelines as to the treatment, hormonal and surgical, of gender identity disorder.

In recent times there has been a sudden increase of interest and availability of information, at times helpful, at times voyeuristic, about the plight of children with gender difficulties and their families. On the internet one finds information about research and treatments, or chat groups and blogs, from the serious and considered to the bogus and exploitative. Against this background, the clinic endeavours to provide information about the needs of children with gender difficulties. The clinic also keeps informal links with an independent self-help parent group called Mermaids.

Children in a family where a parent has undergone sex reassignment surgery may be seen (Green 1978), and children born with inter-sex disorders. The different needs of these children and their families are only briefly referred to in this chapter.

Technique and treatment is adapted because of the limitations of geographical distance and the resources of the family and child. A variety of work is undertaken: assessment of the child with a diagnostic formulation and treatment recommendation, with referral back to local resources; supervision or network meetings with professionals doing direct work at a local level; and treatment at the clinic.

Treatment includes family work, individual work, network meetings, liaison with school and other agencies so as to provide a facilitating environment for the child and so as not deprive him or her of ordinary developmental influences. This is all in conjunction with the availability of a medical assessment by a paediatric endocrinologist which in adolescence could include a recommendation of hormone treatment and advice about adult surgical procedures. The weekly team meeting has a co-ordinating and containing function which is especially important in work where intense feelings are provoked in therapist and network.

The work of the child psychotherapist

The clinic exists within a given historical and social context at a time when there are changing understandings of gender and sexuality from moral, social, political and medical perspectives. This evokes internal passion and conflict. Questions about gender, identity, masculinity/femininity provoke the nature–nurture debate (Golombok and Fivush 1994). The development of surgical techniques and hormonal knowledge has given rise to the possibility of improved if imperfect sex reassignment interventions. There is a growing social awareness of transsexualism, linked both to intolerance of difference and an increasing social acceptance of diverse life styles. This social context impinges in many ways on the treatment of children and adolescents seen at the clinic; such young people undoubtedly suffer, provoking the question of which is primary and which secondary to the disorder (Coates and Spector Person 1985).

> The mother of a teenager who referred herself attended at her daughter's request. She painfully castigated the therapist for perverting her child and encouraging disabling surgery, eventually weeping with sorrow when the therapist spoke of her mourning of the feared loss of her daughter. The teenager, Orla, verbally attacked the therapist for not providing immediate relief through hormone treatment and surgery, whilst being critical that the therapist might try to make her change her mind. The therapist continued to try to establish a possibility of thinking about this fear of being unheard, deprived or overwhelmed.

The clinic psychotherapists have adapted and applied their skills in direct individual work and in family work in a variety of ways, always questioning what is possible. For young people who feel conflicted with their own bodies the realities of biological gender particularly confront them soon after starting school and again in adolescence, provoking increased and intense distress.

Families arrive with varied expectations despite being prepared by referrers and receiving an information sheet. Assessments engender anxiety, and tensions may arise when exploring possibilities and how to manage change. Engagement is an important first step along with the need for careful diagnostic history taking. A developmental history is essential with particular reference to separation anxiety and the clinical presentation of the following:

- statements about perception of themselves as boys or girls
- cross-dressing
- persistent preference for toys stereotypically used by the other sex
- interest in cosmetics and jewellery for boys; refusal to wear skirts for girls
- preference for female roles for boys and male roles for girls in play acting

- preference for peers of the other sex
- female mannerisms in boys and vice versa
- avoidance of rough and tumble play for boys.

In adolescents one would also explore frequent passing as the other sex and the desire to live and be treated as the other sex. Engagement can entail voicing the child's gender dysphoria for the first time in a family.

> William, an eight-year-old, gradually moved from talking about not liking school to talk of bullying and name calling to revealing to his parents his secret feminine fantasy life. In contrast Olwyn, also eight, came to the clinic brittle but overt in her silence, refusing to go to school unless accepted in male clothing, and the family complained of the school's resistance to her male dress. From this the therapist attempted to engender some curiosity and exploration, wondering if the family's support reflected a premature foreclosure. Some parents question if they should allow their child to cross-dress, so risking ridicule and social isolation and a damaging developmental path, or fight their child's wish and feel distant.

The approach of the team is that while treatment and amelioration of behavioural and emotional problems can be addressed, atypical gender identity may remain unchanged – indeed it may be a solution to a greater problem and the aetiology may remain uncertain (Money, 1994). Fostering a facilitating environment for each child is a principal aim.

For adolescents who refer themselves to the clinic, the referral may be a wish for support for a decision that they feel they have made by approaching the clinic, or a wish to understand unbearable inner terror. They can be very sensitive to how the therapist views them: are they seen as ill, mad or suffering from a biological mistake from birth? Adolescents can be both hopeful at finding a place where they feel recognised and not alone, but they bring a terror of feeling mad – mentally ill – or of losing control; there is a terror of a loss of self (Hurry 1990). In the brief work and intermittent attendance of many of the adolescents, the therapists find themselves addressing powerful issues about hope and despair, suicide or the possibility of a future. The therapist is touched to the core in her *own* bodily awareness. What therapy is possible: a struggle to engage, to maintain something of a possibility of thought; to collude or to support someone at a critical time especially in adolescence?

David came to the clinic relieved that after two suicide attempts he had finally told a local therapist of his wishes for sex reassignment. He now saw a future for himself as a transsexual. However, James came questioning that he might be mad for thinking this and if so he should end his life. He requested further appointments to consider this dilemma: what was the best decision for him? He then requested support whilst living in an ambiguous gender role awaiting medical rectification of a biological mistake from birth. He dropped out of school and wanted to start college in female role. If gender identity is felt to be a psychological solution to the bigger threat to psychic integrity then the psychotherapist can best proceed with great caution and work with what is possible for that individual (Limentani 1977). James could not entertain the thought of sexual contact with a male until after surgery, adamantly stating that he was not gay and furthermore would despise this. In the past he had felt in love with a boy but saw himself as a female in relation to him.

David had few friendships and remained very close to his mother whom he felt would oppose his sex reassignment. He had arrived at the clinic to explore his distress and gender dysphoria. He hated his genitalia, shaved his legs and face vigorously, and had long hair. He saw men as aggressive and difficult to understand. What seemed important for David was that these concerns could be talked about for the first time to his great relief. Through therapy there has been a lessening of his brittle stereotyped identifications as reflected in his move away from pursuing a transsexual outcome to taking time to think about himself in occasional therapy. He made a career change, starting a drama course so as to discover varying possible identifications and enact feared emotions (Waddell 1992).

Fiona, an older adolescent, came to the clinic after finding she could not sustain living a dual gender, known differently to different people. After she and the therapist had survived several difficult sessions, she began to bring drawings done during her earlier adolescence containing some of her terror of disintegration, a ravaging aggression and a central enduring integrating but also watchful, angry and persecuting eye. She requested once weekly therapy, unsure of how she would proceed whilst waiting to see the paediatric endocrinologist and seeking somewhere to live in a male role.

It is in the work with younger children that there is likely to be more fluidity, less rigidity and the possibility of more profound change. Susan Coates and colleagues in New York do not accept children for treatment beyond the age of five as from their long-standing research they see treatment beyond this age as ineffective. This is at odds with the research finding that very few children who cross-dress become transsexual, and contact with mental health professionals seems a significant influence (Money and Russo 1988). Both girls and boys with gender identity disorder are seen at the clinic but very few under five have been referred.

The children can be distant, self-sufficient and mistrustful, tending to keep their inner lives hidden and not immediately accessible to individual psychotherapy.

William, aged eight, presented with a long-standing well-established gender identity disorder which had become a cause for concern when he began to refuse to go to school. His headteacher spoke of William being bullied and teased by name-calling such as 'poof'. Initially the family was reluctant to speak of William's gender disorder behaviour, perhaps seeing him as troublesome. They attended family sessions over a couple of years. His father often worked away. His early care had been shared between mother and paternal grandmother after mother returned to work when he was five months old. His mother felt that he was a sensitive, difficult to please baby with many reports of separation anxiety. As he grew older he seemed to prefer his grandparents' care. After grandmother's sudden death when he was five, William had been unable to tolerate her loss but concretely identified with her, repeating in detail her ways of cooking and cleaning and criticising his mother. William revealed the comfort and early tactile gratification of touching the silky female clothes he chose to wear. He talked with embarrass-ment and pleasure. His absorption with external appearances sug-gested an identification with what he felt to be a vain preoccupied mother (Henry 1974). It is also interesting to look at the developmental stages of a child's concept of gender; when young children are asked how they can tell the difference between boys and girls they identify clothes and hair as the means for categorisation. Only later are genitals viewed as the essential component of categorisation (Fagot 1985).

In family sessions, using a genogram initially, these painful feelings were gradually approached by William and his mother. William revealed his fantasies of being and wishing to become a girl; he began to mourn the loss of his grandmother; and his father became engaged with his son in a more lively manner, both on advice from the therapists and after his own and his son's fear of their explosive rage was explored. As William became increasingly able to trust the therapists he asked to be

seen once on his own when he recounted an incident before his grandmother's death where he had been naughty towards his grandmother.
His parents did not know of it – William felt fearful of rejection, guilty and
responsible for her death. His fear of his loss of self-control, the imagined
power of rage and a dread of abandonment underlay many other
difficulties and could then be approached. He longed to be accepted by
other boys but could see no way in – to engage in football might mean no
one would pass the ball to him but to seek or ask for the ball seemed to
be an act of aggression. William gradually let go of his feminine identification and could countenance age-appropriate activities away from his
family. He successfully negotiated a move to a new school.

Through this work both therapists, male and female, attempted to hold in
mind various possibilities so as to enable the child and family to tolerate
uncertainty with the area of gender identity development. The imagined
disastrous outcomes which William's defensive feminine identification
attempted to avoid were spoken about with the gradual establishment of a
secure base in therapy. William's atypical behaviour, wishes and fantasies
which incurred social difficulties for him, and which he felt would possibly
mean rejection and ridicule, was something enduring. For William it was a
way of holding on to something which had meaning in the development of
his sense of self, for his own intrinsic integrity (Wilson 1998). William, with
the support of his family and therapy, seemed to have discovered other
possibilities.

There are fewer comments in the literature on work with girls so we
would like to make some observations from our perspective as female
psychotherapists. As the baby begins to develop a sense of self, for the baby
girl her sense of gender identity is the same as that of her mother, the first
object of love, from whom she has to separate and individuate. The gender
of a baby girl is the same, not 'the other', 'it' (Chodorow 1978; Benjamin
1990). For girls and boys there is a different pathway to an independent
identity and to a choice of sexual partner. Perhaps gender dysphoria in girls
reflects an anxiety about the mother's/female's integrity? The masculine
identification could reflect both a move to find a pathway to the mother in
identification with the father but also a protection of the mother.

Orla in adolescence referred herself to the clinic giving a thoughtful
written account of various familial and psychological factors shaping her
sense of being a male trapped in a female body. At interview she came
with photographs showing her in male clothes with short hair, aged two,

in a family where for generations the women had long hair. Her family reported her as a young tomboy, which to Orla implied a biological origin to her discomfort. She also described how she perceived the qualities of females. Her petite mother had been mistreated by her unpredictable husband. Orla's older brother had been favoured and also was violent and frightening to her as long as she could recall: he was later diagnosed as mentally ill. Orla had not been protected by her mother who was also physically ill at times. She became increasingly protective of her and indeed her mother relied greatly upon her. It was only in respect of her gender that Orla was anything but ideal in her mother's eyes.

She despised her female body for it represented weakness and vulnerability. She found her breasts intolerable, binding them out of sight. She longed to be tall, male and potent. As she spoke of her turmoil the therapist felt increasingly aware of her own delicate, feminine body and dress. Every so often Orla would stop to apologise, saying it was nothing personal, as if attempting to undo a feared attack upon the therapist whom she felt could not withstand it.

Orla's longing for a biological explanation for her gender dysphoria was reflected in her bringing photographs and family recollections from when she was under two years old. She could find no psychological solution to her dilemma in being either a feminist or a lesbian; she despised femininity and loathed her female body. The reality of her body was recognised and investigations were offered by the paediatrician. Orla was intensely distressed and close to despair following the biological investigations which showed nothing unusual and confirmed her as female. She continued to see her therapist and did not act upon suicidal thoughts. Orla had been in danger of excluding herself from home and from further education for fear of disapproval and rejection (as well as her envy of the apparent secure identity of others). Colleagues from the team met with her mother and the educational network. Orla started at a new college and requested a referral to a service nearer to home for more frequent psychotherapy. This work extended over some time and involved much active reaching out by the therapist with phone calls and letters.

Some reflections

Though there is consensus around certain important issues like the absence of biological explanations and its probable relational nature, its early determination and onset in the pre-genital phase, these do not guarantee diagnostic stability or outcome as Horne remarks (1999). She emphasises our need as therapists to keep a very open mind to counter the rigid modality of thinking we can find in gender dysphoric children and in the reactions they induce in their social context, including of course the therapeutic context. The experience of working with children and adolescents in the clinic can be intense and distressing with a strong countertransference to process: the horror of the sense of dislocation within and without, the shock of descriptions of attacks upon the body, the overwhelming anxiety which engenders fear about survival from one session to the next, the struggle to find a way in. These reflect some of the experiences that we have come to hear of as the daily life of such children and adolescents. Reflecting on our work, it became apparent that we adapt and modify psychoanalytic psychotherapy – we feel ourselves to be 'a bit of this and a bit of that', leading us to question our experience and whether we are proper psychotherapists. This dilemma and question, which confronts one's professional identity, could be understood as a reflection of the internal world of the children and adolescents we have seen at the clinic.

References

Benjamin, J. (1990) *The Bonds of Love*, London: Virago.

Bleiberg, E., Jackson, L. and Ross, L. (1986) 'Gender identity disorder and object loss', *Journal of the American Academy of Child Psychiatry* 25(1): 58–67.

Bradley, S. J. (1998) 'Some developmental trajectories of gender identity disorder in children', in D. Di Ceglie (ed.) *A Stranger in My Own Body: Atypical Gender Identity Development and Mental Health*, London: Karnac Books.

Brain, C. (1998) 'Biological contributions to atypical gender identity development', in D. Di Ceglie (ed.) *A Stranger in My Own Body: Atypical Gender Identity Development and Mental Health*, London: Karnac Books.

Chodorow, N. J. (1978) *The Reproduction of Mothering: Psychoanalysis and the Socialisation of Gender*, Berkeley, CA: University of California Press.

Coates, S. (1990) 'Ontogenesis of boyhood gender identity disorder', *Journal of the American Academy of Psychoanalysis* 18(3): 414–38.

Coates, S. and Spector Person, E. (1985) 'Extreme boyhood femininity: isolated behaviour or pervasive disorder?', *Journal of the American Academy of Child Psychiatry* 24: 702–9.

Coates, S., Friedman, R. and Wolfe, S. (1991) 'The etiology of boyhood gender identity disorder: a model for integrating temperament, development and psychodynamics', *Psychoanalytic Dialogues* 1(4): 481–523.

Fagot, B. (1985) 'Changes in thinking about early sex role development', *Developmental Review* 5: 83–9.

Freud, S. (1900) 'The interpretation of dreams', *SE*, Vols 4 and 5, London: Hogarth Press.

—— (1905) 'Three essays on sexuality', *SE* Vol. 7, London: Hogarth Press.

Golombok, S. and Fivush, R. (1994) *Gender Development*, London: Cambridge University Press.

Green, R. (1968) 'Childhood cross gender identification', *Journal of Nervous and Mental Disease* 147: 500–9.

—— (1978) 'Sexual identity of thirty-seven children raised by homosexual or transsexual parents', *American Journal of Psychiatry* 135: 692–7.

—— (1987) *The 'Sissy Boy Syndrome' and the Development of Homosexuality*, New Haven, CT: Yale University Press.

Green, R., Roberts, C. W., Williams, K., Goodman, M. and Mixon, A. (1987) 'Specific cross gender behaviour in boyhood and later homosexual orientation', *British Journal of Psychiatry* 51: 84–8.

Henry, G. (1974) 'Doubly deprived', *Journal of Child Psychotherapy* 3(4): 15–28.

Horne, A. (1999) 'Thinking about gender in theory and practice with children and adolescents', *Journal of the British Association of Psychotherapists* 37: 35–49.

Hurry, A. (1990) 'Bisexual conflict and paedophilic fantasies in the analysis of a late adolescent', *Journal of Child Psychotherapy* 16(1): 5–28.

Imperato-McGinley, J., Peterson, R. E., Gautier, T. and Sturla, E. (1979) 'Androgens and the evolution of male-gender identity among male pseudohermaphrodites with 5-alpha reductase deficiency', *New England Journal of Medicine* 300: 1233–7.

Limentani, A. (1977) 'The differential diagnosis of homosexuality', *British Journal of Medical Psychology* 50: 209–16.

Michael, R. P. and Zumpe. D. (1996) 'Biological factors in the organization and expression of sexual behaviour', in I. Rosen (ed.) *Sexual Deviation*, 3rd edn, Oxford: Oxford University Press.

Money, J. (1955a) 'Hermaphrotidism, gender and precocity in hyperadrenocorticism: psychologic findings', *Bulletin of Johns Hopkins Hospital* 96: 253–64.

—— (1955b) 'An examination of some basic sexual concepts: the evidence of human hermaphroditism', *Bulletin of Johns Hopkins Hospital* 97: 301–19.

—— (1994) 'The concept of gender identity disorder in childhood and adolescence after 39 years', *Journal of Sex and Marital Therapy* 20(3): 163–77.

Money, J. and Russo, A. (1988) 'Homosexual outcome of discordant gender identity/role in childhood: longitudinal follow-up', *Journal of Paediatric Psychology* 4: 29–41.

Stoller, R. (1968) 'Male, childhood transsexualism', *Journal of the American Academy of Child Psychiatry* 7: 193–201.

—— (1975) *Sex and Gender Vol. I, Splitting: A Case of Female Masculinity*, London: Hogarth Press.

—— (1976) *Sex and Gender Vol. II, The Transsexual Experiment*, London: Hogarth Press.

—— (1996) 'Gender disorders', in I. Rosen (ed.) *Sexual Deviation*, 3rd edn, Oxford: Oxford University Press.

Waddell, M. (1992) 'From resemblance to identity: a psychoanalytic perspective on gender identity', *Proceedings of the Conference on Gender Identity and Development in Childhood and Adolescence*, London: Conference Unit, St George's Hospital Medical School.

Wilson, P. (1998) 'Development and mental health', in D. Di Ceglie (ed.) *A Stranger in My Own Body: Atypical Gender Identity Development and Mental Health*, London: Karnac.

Zucker, K. J., Bradley, S. J., Doering, R. W. and Lozinski, J. A. (1985) 'Sex typed behaviour in cross-gender identified children: stability and change after one-year follow-up', *Journal of the American Academy of Child Psychiatry* 24: 710–19.

Further reading

Di Ceglie, D. (ed.) (1998) *A Stranger in My Own Body: Atypical Gender Identity Development and Mental Health*, London: Karnac.

Hurry, A. (1990) 'Bisexual conflict and paedophilic fantasies in the analysis of a late adolescent', *Journal of Child Psychotherapy* 16(1): 5–28.

Loeb, L. (1996) 'Childhood gender identity disorder', in I. Rosen (ed.) *Sexual Deviation*, 3rd edn, Oxford: Oxford University Press.

Index